THE FIGURE

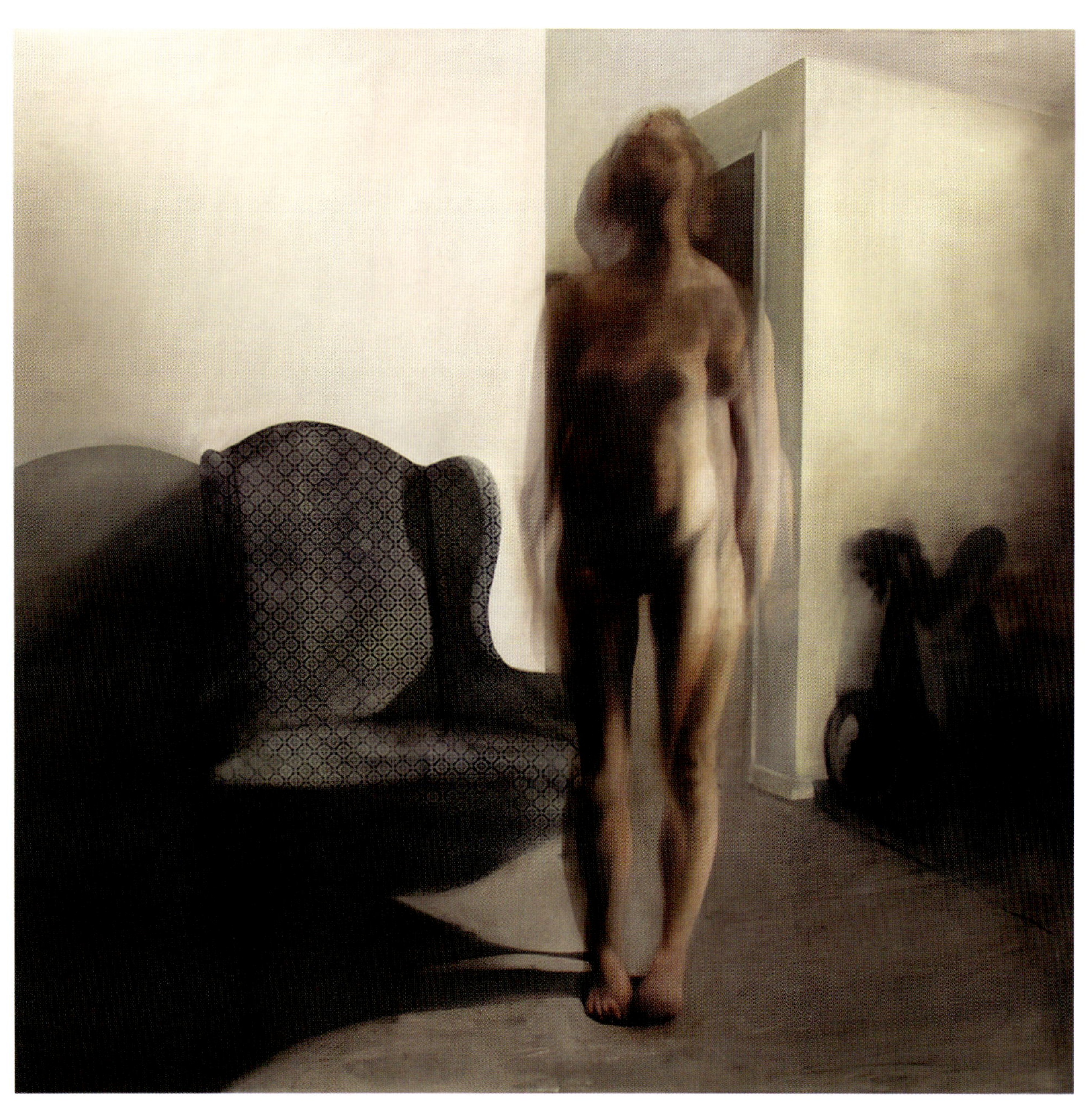

THE FIGURE

PAINTING, DRAWING, AND SCULPTURE

CONTEMPORARY PERSPECTIVES

EDITED BY

MARGARET McCANN

NEW YORK ACADEMY OF ART

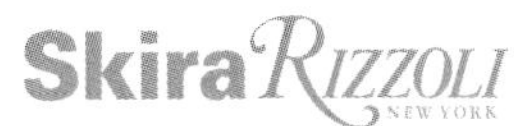

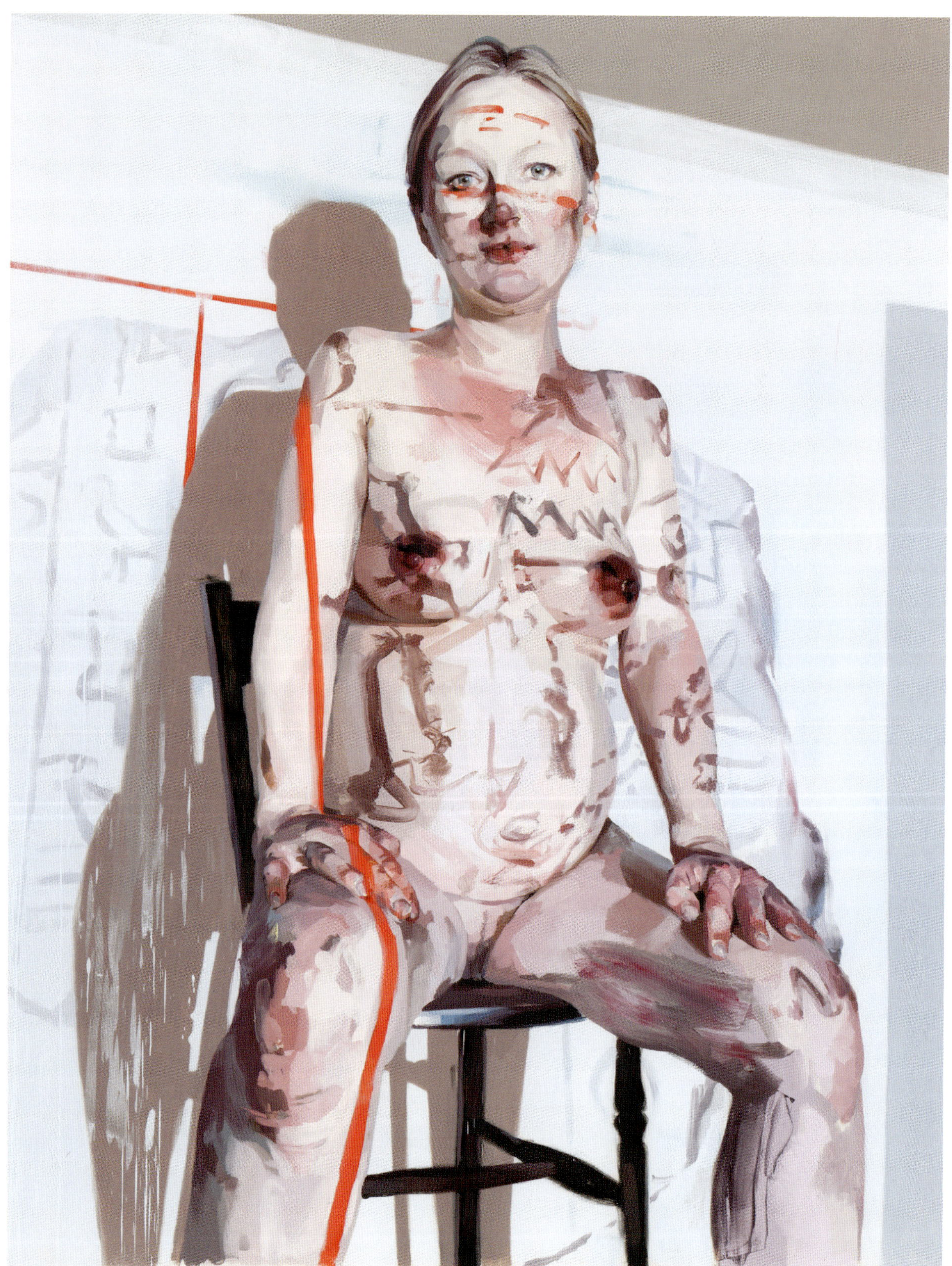

Jenny Saville
Isis, 2011
Oil on canvas
99 x 74 inches

(page 2)
Robert Fundis
Presence, 2012
Oil, spray paint
on canvas
71 x 71 inches

CONTENTS

7 Bob Colacello Andy and the Academy: A Perfect Match
9 David Kratz Preface
11 Margaret McCann Introduction

PART I PAST MOMENTUM

17 Judy Fox The Once and Future Sculpted Figure
ARTIST METHODOLOGIES Harvey Citron and Judy Fox

27 Thomas Germano A Brief History of Traditional Painting Pedagogy
ARTIST METHODOLOGIES Andrew Raftery and Frederick Mershimer

36 Lisa Bartolozzi A Brief History of Traditional Painting Techniques: Fresco, Tempera, and Oil Painting
ARTIST METHODOLOGIES Steven Assael and Wade Schuman

51 Robert Simon Outsourcing Technique: Mimesis, Method, and Metaphor in Figure Sculpture
ARTIST METHODOLOGY Randolphlee McIver

60 Vincent Desiderio Toward an Allegorization of Method
ARTIST METHODOLOGY Edward Schmidt

PART II PRESENT REFLECTIONS

79 Alexi Worth The Invention of Clumsiness: Photography and Modernism
ARTIST METHODOLOGIES Edgar Jerins and Alyssa Monks

92 Margaret McCann Refiguring History Painting: Representation Meets Modern Techniques
ARTIST METHODOLOGIES Steve Mumford, Michael Ananian, Margaret McCann, and Alex Kanevsky

115 Donald Kuspit Freud and the Eternal Feminine in Modernist Painting
ARTIST METHODOLOGY F. Scott Hess

126 Kurt Kauper Representational Art and Kitsch
ARTIST METHODOLOGIES Peter Drake and Dik Liu

143 Robert Taplin Twentieth-Century Figurative Sculpture
ARTIST METHODOLOGIES Bruce Gagnier and Michael Ferris Jr.

150 Irving Sandler Representing Avant-Garde Representation: From Painterly Figuration to Matter-of-Fact Realism 1950–70
ARTIST METHODOLOGIES Andrew Lenaghan, Scott Noel, and Richard Phillips

165 David Ebony Monsters Rule: The Grotesque in Contemporary Painting and Sculpture
ARTIST METHODOLOGY Trenton Doyle Hancock

173 Julie Heffernan Looking Back at the Male Gaze
ARTIST METHODOLOGIES Anne Harris and Hilary Harkness

PART III FUTURE CONTINUUM

187 Laurie Hogin The Echo in the Picture: The Social Potential of Representational Painting
ARTIST METHODOLOGY Natalie Frank

200 Mark Mennin Scale, Materials, and Self-Perception in Contemporary Figurative Sculpture
ARTIST METHODOLOGIES Mark Mennin and Rona Pondick

209 Jean-Pierre Roy Painting and Digital Technology: From Film to Photoshop
ARTIST METHODOLOGIES Judith Schaechter and Jerry Kearns

216 John Jacobsmeyer Pictorial Space Enters Virtual Reality: From Perspective to 3-D Modeling
ARTIST METHODOLOGY John Wellington

225 Nicola Verlato Perspective, Representation, and Democracy
ARTIST METHODOLOGY Nicola Verlato

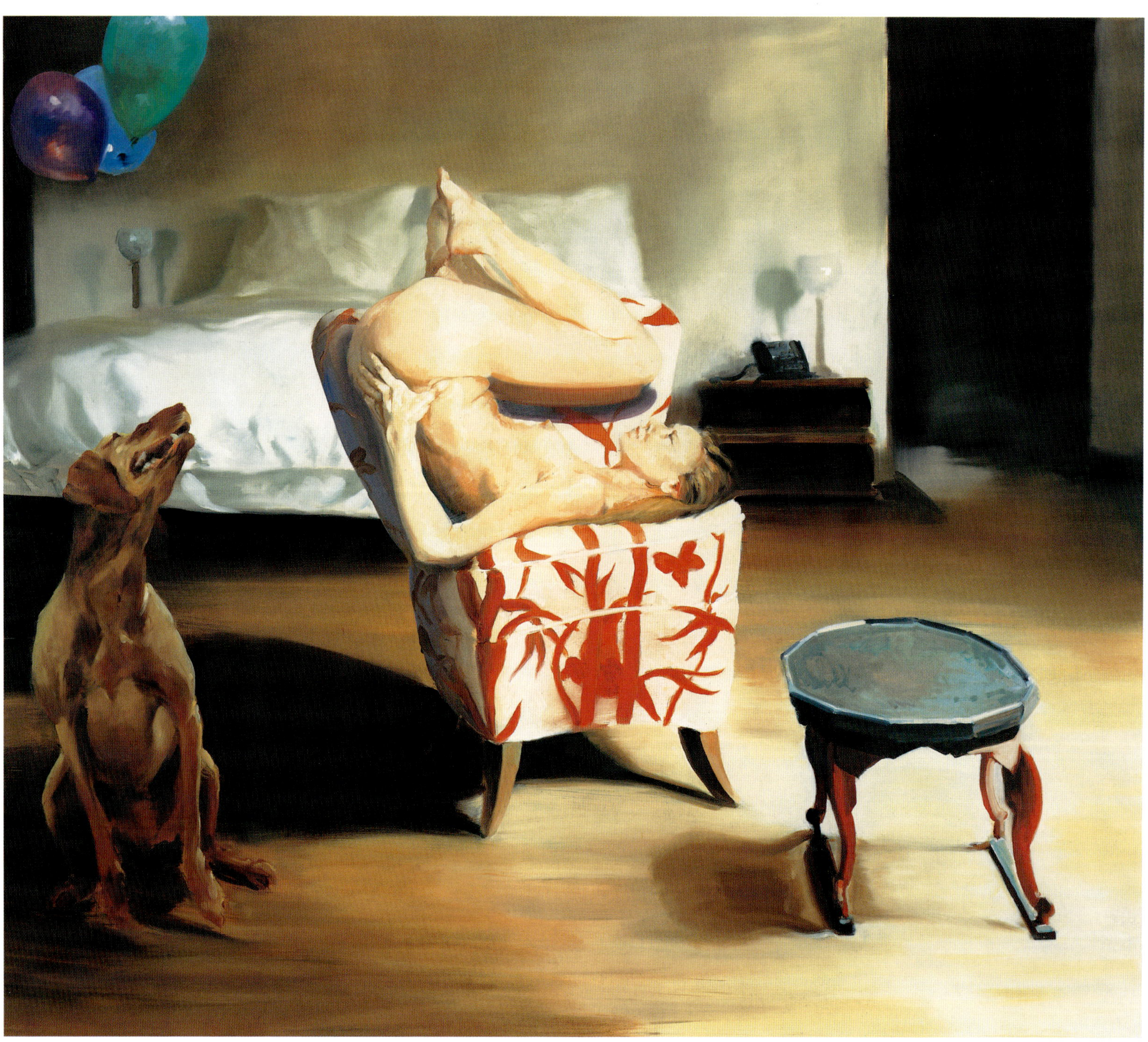

ANDY AND THE ACADEMY: A PERFECT MATCH

BOB COLACELLO

IF ANDY WARHOL BELIEVED IN ANYTHING, other than his own success and a superstitious form of Catholicism, he believed in Art—the power of art to illuminate, shock, confound, comfort, uplift, and transcend. And he had very high standards grounded in the long, rigorous, and full art education he received during his formative years in Pittsburgh. In fifth grade, when he was ten years old, his elementary school art teacher recommended him for special Saturday classes at the Carnegie Museum of Art. In the mornings he studied art history; in the afternoons he learned the basics of drawing, painting, and printmaking. This was his first exposure to the visual treasures of the world's great civilizations, from antiquities to Modernist works, and he continued to attend these classes until he graduated from high school. In 1945, he enrolled at the Carnegie Institute of Technology (now Carnegie Mellon University) in the Department of Painting and Design, where students were expected to master the traditional academic practices of anatomy, perspective, and drawing from life. By his senior year, Andy was ready to declare his creative independence by submitting a self-portrait titled "The Broad Gave Me My Face, But I Can Pick My Own Nose" to the annual exhibition of the Associated Artists of Pittsburgh, which declined to show it.

Andy Warhol knew as much about color theory as Matisse, could draw as fluidly as Cocteau, and understood compositional structure as well as Picasso. But what does the Pope of Pop have to do with the New York Academy of Art? In fact, he was involved with the school from its inception in the early 1980s. Like its rather unlikely trio of founders—plastics tycoon Stuart Pivar, firefighter Dennis Smith, and philanthropist Russell Wilkinson—he strongly believed in the necessity of a classical art education, though it was seen as hopelessly archaic by the then dominant Conceptual Art establishment, and generally unavailable at the country's top art schools. Andy loved everything new, but he lived with lots of things that were old, including American primitive portraits, Navajo blankets, and Art Deco cookie jars. And even while he was making experimental videos with Blondie and The Cars, he was buying up works of art by the likes of Bouguereau on his almost daily shopping sprees with Stuart Pivar, himself an insatiable collector. Most significantly, he befriended and encouraged a group of young painters, including Julian Schnabel, Francesco Clemente, Jean-Michel Basquiat, Keith Haring, Kenny Scharf, and George Condo, who were reinventing figurative art in bold and unexpected ways.

I was working for Andy at the time, as editor of *Interview*, and recall how enthusiastic he was about the fledgling Academy. As Russell Wilkinson told me recently, "Andy came to every little event we did and was very supportive financially." Moreover, after Andy's death in 1987, the executor of his estate, Fred Hughes, authorized a substantial grant to help the school buy its present home in Tribeca, knowing that's what Andy would have wanted to be done.

Both Andy and Fred would be amazed and thrilled to see how the Academy has grown and flourished in that building. As a member of the President's Advisory Board, I feel privileged to follow in their footsteps in supporting the school and its mission. As I said in accepting an honorary doctorate at the school's 2013 Tribeca Ball, "How can you break the rules if you don't know the rules?" I personally believe this principle applies to every field of creative endeavor. And that is what the New York Academy of Art stands for: learning the rules, so you can bend, twist, and reinvent them; using the past to take your art into the future; and transforming the great traditions into something never seen before.

(opposite)
Eric Fischl
The Bed, the Chair, Waiting, 2000
Oil on linen
72 x 80 inches

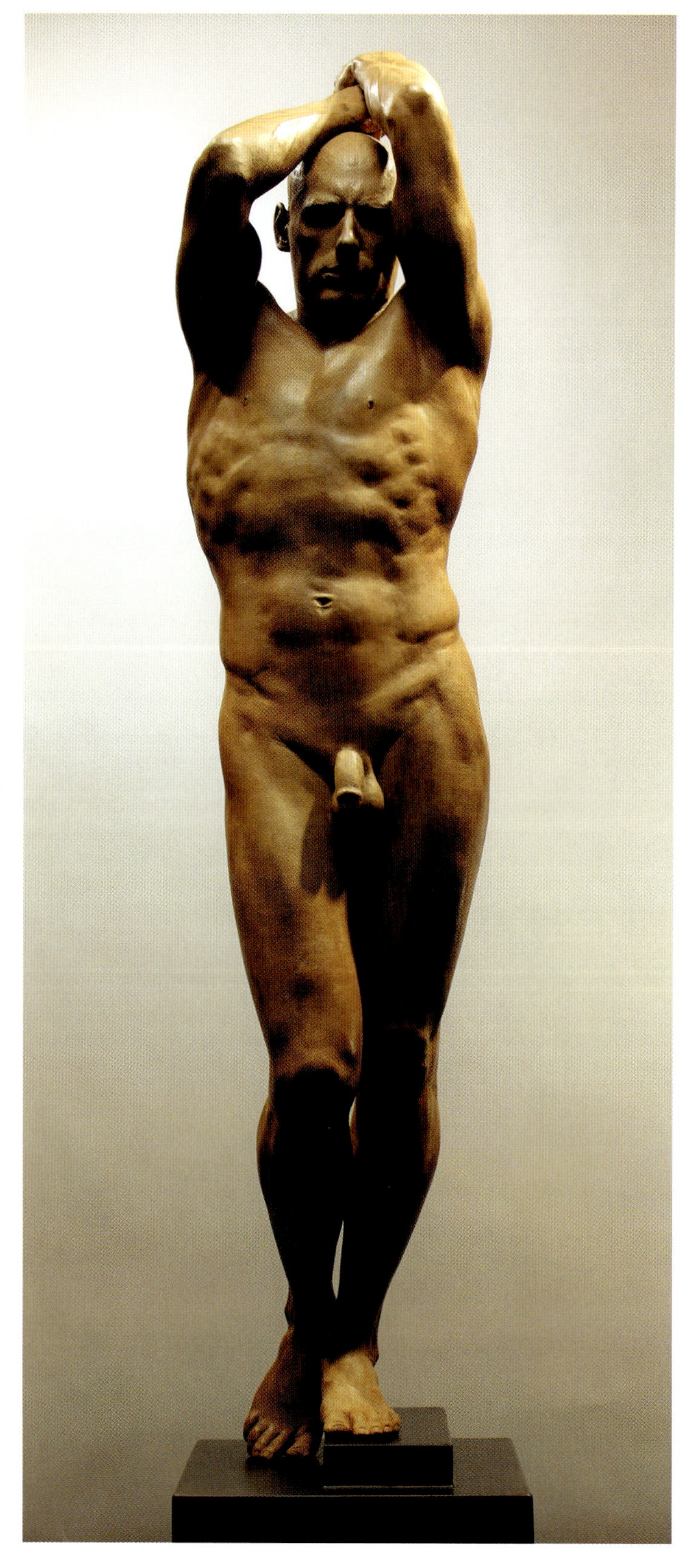

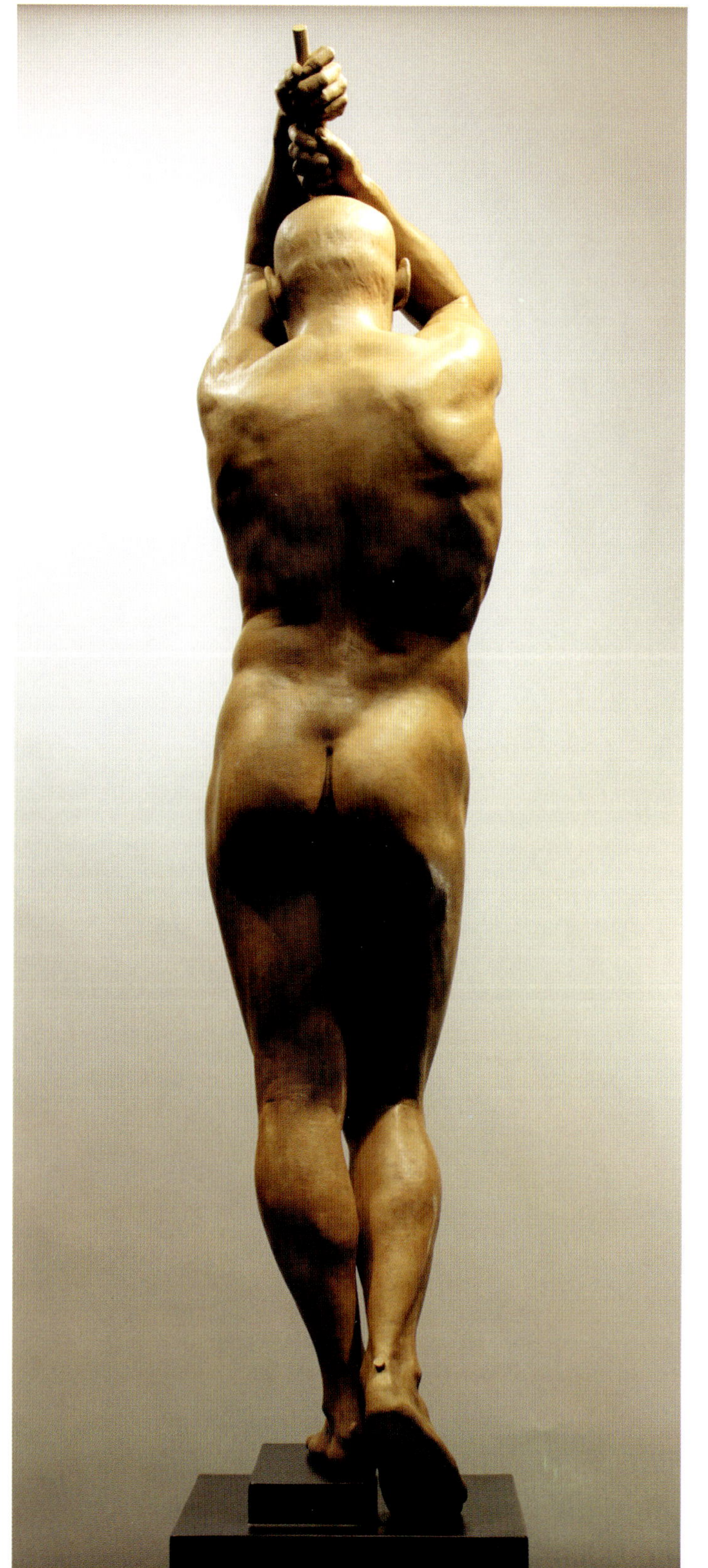

PREFACE

DAVID KRATZ

PRESIDENT, NEW YORK ACADEMY OF ART

FIGURATIVE ART IS STILL ONE OF THE MOST controversial subjects in today's art world. Depending on your point of view, it's either an academic backwater or a lively contemporary dialogue. At the New York Academy of Art, we turn on that axis.

The school was started in the early 1980s, as part of an attempt to ensure that the time-honored skills and techniques of traditional art making — no longer in favor at many graduate art schools around the country — would continue to be taught. At the time, de-skilling was the rage, Conceptual and Minimalist art reigned supreme, replacing, as the next new thing, abstraction, which had nearly vanquished figurative art. There were practically no schools a young artist could attend that would encourage the study of drawing, painting, or sculpting of the figure. There were very few galleries that were showing it, and in museums you could hardly find it in galleries not devoted to the art of prior centuries. However, the group of artists that formed the New York Academy understood the importance of this training.

The school started in a church rectory on Lafayette Street in New York City. At that point it was almost an atelier. Classes were free, there was no curriculum, no degree, and no guarantee of a forum for recognition. There was, however, a belief that rigorously trained, highly informed artists would be best able to attain their creative goals. There was a faith that the study of the art that preceded us was necessary in order to participate in the dialogue of today. That as a foundation, almost anything an artist needed to learn in order to have the visual vocabulary to express him- or herself freely and articulately could be learned through the study of the figure. That anatomy, structural drawing, perspective, rendering, composition and design, and an understanding of historical technique would give artists a complete set of tools to work with as they sought to say something new, different, and fresh.

Roberta Smith, the legendary *New York Times* art critic, in a 2007 review of a Mark Greenwold show, referred to "the tense interplay of tradition, innovation and *personal necessity* [emphasis my own] that fuels most art." Nowhere is this observation more true than in the world of figurative art. It is so laden with history, so rich with masterpieces, so compelling in narratives, that to embark on it today, one would be a fool not to be cognizant of the minefields awaiting the unsuspecting artist trying to chart a fresh, new course.

That's what makes this book so captivating. Through the work of the community of artists and writers surrounding the New York Academy of Art, it surveys some of today's most compelling figurative art and makes a convincing argument for its relevance. It examines not only the "why" but the "how" through the writing of some of its most brilliant practitioners. It's exactly that combination of traditional skills and contemporary discourse that makes the school and its community so unique in the art world today.

(opposite)
Brian Booth Craig
Suicide Machine,
2012
Bronze
67 x 20 x 10 inches

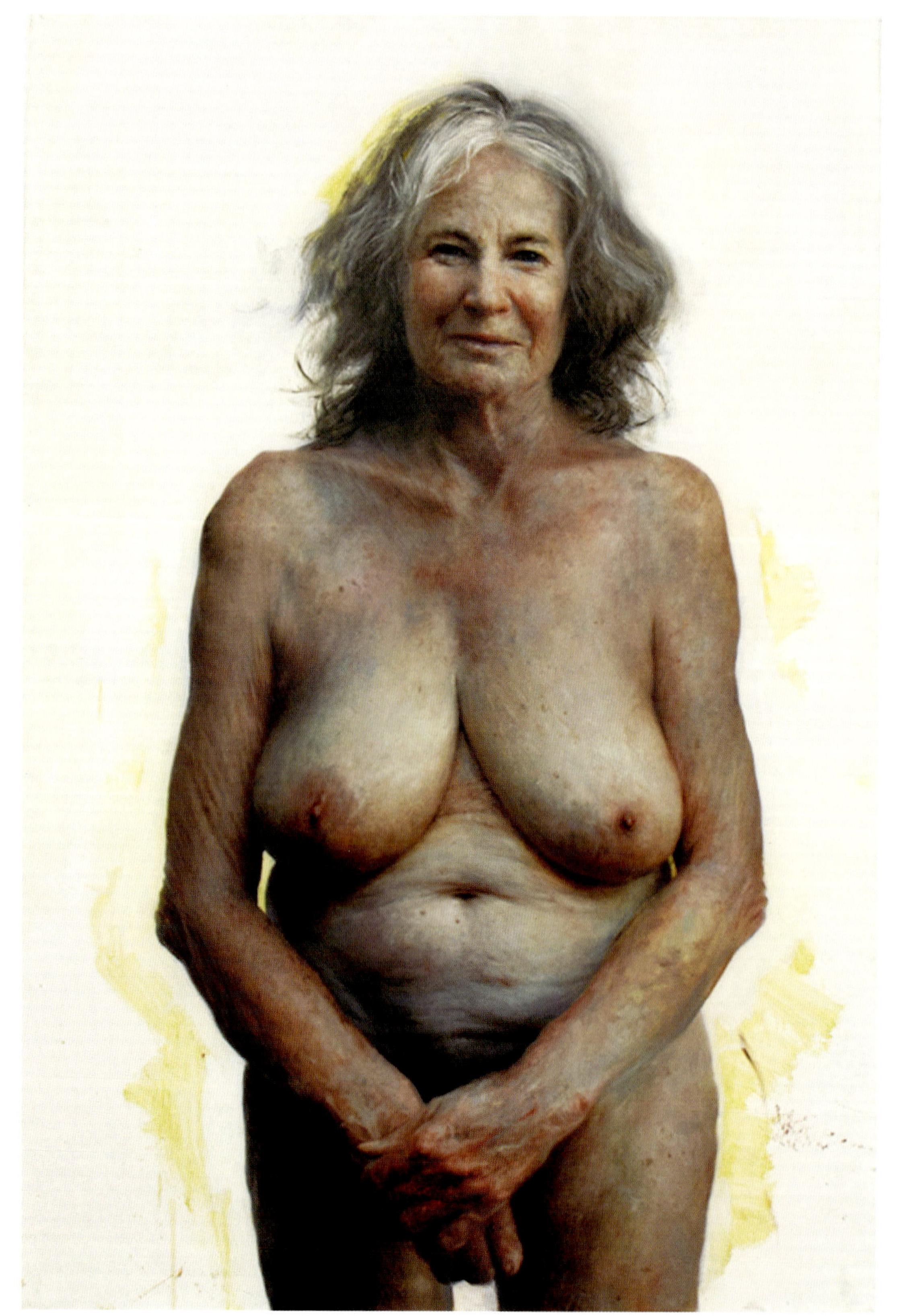

INTRODUCTION
MARGARET McCANN

THIS BOOK MAPS OUT VARIOUS CONCERNS of practitioners and admirers of figurative art. Essays are by established artists, historians, and critics, and by teaching artists accustomed to describing art historical and theoretical contexts to students. Texts, along with artwork of New York Academy of Art alumni, faculty, and visiting artists whose practice or pedagogy is relevant to the school, occupy a three-part historical continuum encompassing changing values and techniques: from pre-Modernist methods still engaging contemporary artists, through avant-garde technological and cultural issues including photography, psychology, fascism, and feminism, to the impact of the Internet and computer capabilities, such as Photoshop and Maya, on figure-based art. These margins are permeable: as described in artist methodologies, both traditional and advanced techniques can be applied in assorted styles, options that reflect the diversity of the Postmodern and "Meta-modern" art world.

The art world has changed greatly in the last few decades, as the world has. The Cold War's official end in 1992, echoed in China's economic opening up, allowed painters trained in figure-friendly Socialist Realism, like Komar and Melamid and Neo Rauch, to revive mimesis. As the American anti-aesthetic devaluation of skill waned, Neo-Expressionism, New Image, Bad Painting, Appropriation, and other movements also rendered the art world safe for figuration again. The establishment of the public World Wide Web in 1991 synergized global economic interdependence and created a timeless and multilingual cyberspace, a forum that gives images an edge over words. This profound twenty-first-century shift makes the camera and the computer mandatory for artists to contend in the marketplace.

Crucial to a discussion of artist techniques, therefore, is how the handcrafted and mechanical intersect, following the important questions raised in David Hockney's *Secret Knowledge: Rediscovering the Lost Techniques of the Old Masters* (2001) over the role of optical devices in heightened realism, from the Renaissance on. Yet while Caravaggio or Ingres may have used a camera obscura or lucida splendidly, others did so with mediocre results. While it can take just one tool or pioneer to create a prototype or author a trend, a nexus of cultural factors, from enlightened patronage or market demand to invigorated learning centers and compelling techniques, is more causal. The verisimilitude of Greek sculpture and its imitators, the spatial gymnastics of Rubens, or the compositional ingenuity of Velázquez's *Las Meninas* (1656), which elliptically orchestrates self and royal portraiture to place the viewer in an imperial (and amusingly parental) position, exceed any immediate technological advantage. This book fleshes out contexts for other skills and conceptual qualities—many that can be learned—that go into making art "fine."

When art history was a burgeoning field, and the point of view of what we call "the Western canon" was forming, connoisseurs wandered European picture galleries and churches, making critical discriminations about art worth studying and collecting. Partly because museums generally house exemplary pieces, the concept of the masterpiece can seem narrow and oppressive, especially as the art world accommodates multi-culturalism. Yet transformative ideas like perspective's rationalization of deep space, or the Greek notion that change—technical progress rather than iconic timelessness in representation—was a good thing, and that portraying divinity in highly realized human form was appropriate, have established powerful trajectories. Virtuosic figuration has lately reemerged as a worthy pursuit, with exemplars like Lucian Freud's intensely perceived and vividly imperfect beings, or John Currin's obliquely reverent, superbly sarcastic ones. How Western cultures might otherwise have envisioned heroic human perfection without its archetype is interesting to ponder; nonetheless "The Nude"

(opposite)
Aleah Chapin
Auntie, 2011
Oil on canvas
58 x 38 inches

(opposite)
Kristy Gordon
Passing Through II, 2012
Oil on canvas
96 x 54 inches

as an ideal form[1] has persisted in academies, been emulated and rebelled against, and at last circles the globe.

No discussion of Western art's figurative fluctuations is complete without conceding the devastation that painting's imitative exceptionalism suffered from the Industrial Revolution's mechanical reproductivity, investigated in Aaron Scharf's *Art and Photography* (1968). The alarm that portrait and history painters must have felt in the nineteenth century echoes to a lesser degree in the digital revolution's shuttering of countless darkrooms; a similar conversion probably awaits sculpture with advances in computer modeling. The decline in official American portraiture of the twentieth century—versus the presiding portrayals of Gilbert Stuart and Mount Rushmore, for example—reflects the successes of photography, of visual advances beyond representation, and of the rejection of neoclassical illusions of grandeur. Hence, ironically, for a new monument to an icon of freedom, Martin Luther King Jr., a Chinese artist (who had sculpted Mao) was chosen for his requisite large-scale, representational skills. Fortunately, learning to draw, paint, and sculpt from the figure is no longer seen as a proclivity toward fascism, or as creative weakness, in the West. Pluralistic approaches, less ideologically than personally driven, are thriving, enhanced by a cyber-blurring of political boundaries.

Visual art's power draws on that of discrete visualizations, utilized as mnemonic devices since antiquity in imagined architectural schemes, medieval abstract diagrams, and biblical depictions. Striking images assist recollection, any "table of contents" a likely vestige of the art of memory. Photographs have since directly held remembered experience, now supplemented by an abundance of digital information. Perhaps simulation is attaining a new reality. But art can withstand this visual pandemonium, for we tend to bring to its appraisal not a casual but our finest selves—most discerning, sensitive, and creative. Thereafter, the memory of that heightened, hopeful state of mind also returns to the image, encouraging further review.

Beyond the pleasure of our best projections, current scientific revelation supports the figurative revival's endurance. Alberti would no doubt be delighted to see his fifteenth-century assertion that scenes "move spectators when [people] in the picture outwardly demonstrate their own feeling"[2] vindicated by research regarding mirror neurons. The power of aesthetic reverie joins that of empathic imitation when, in rendering or observing a figure, we intuitively grasp its full range of motives—physical, psychological, and instinctual. We can anticipate neuroscience's future illuminations further unveiling the moving drive of figurative art.

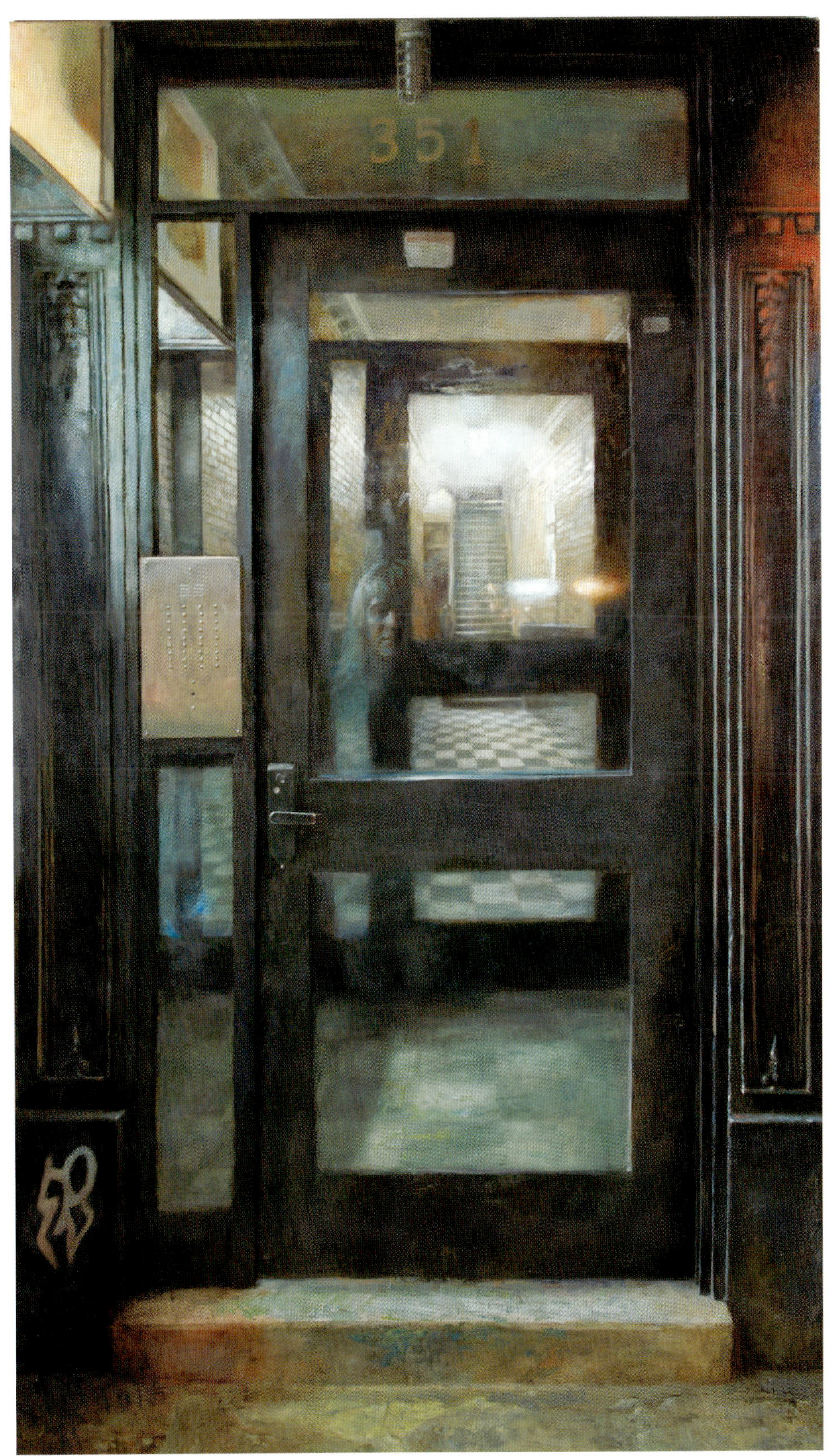
351

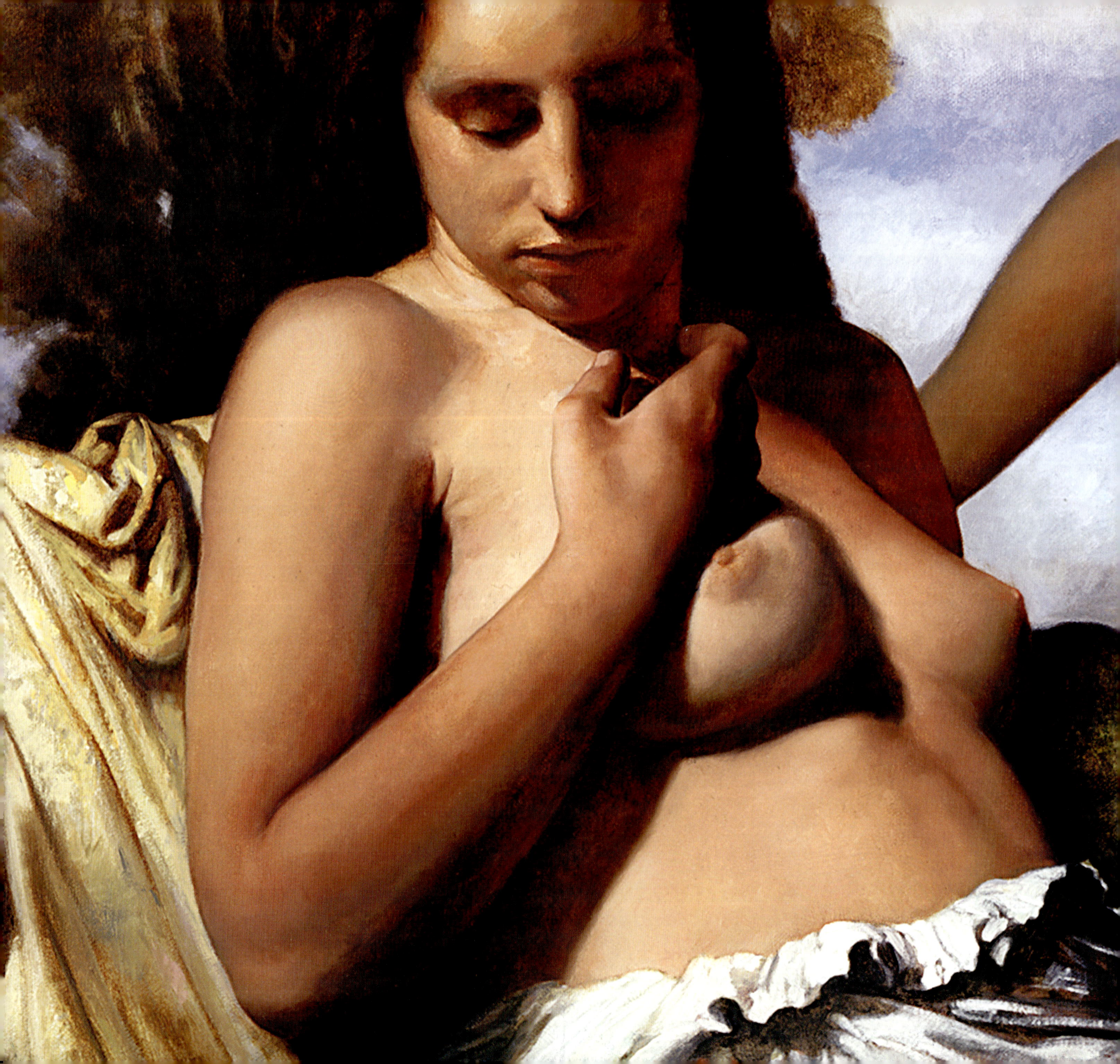

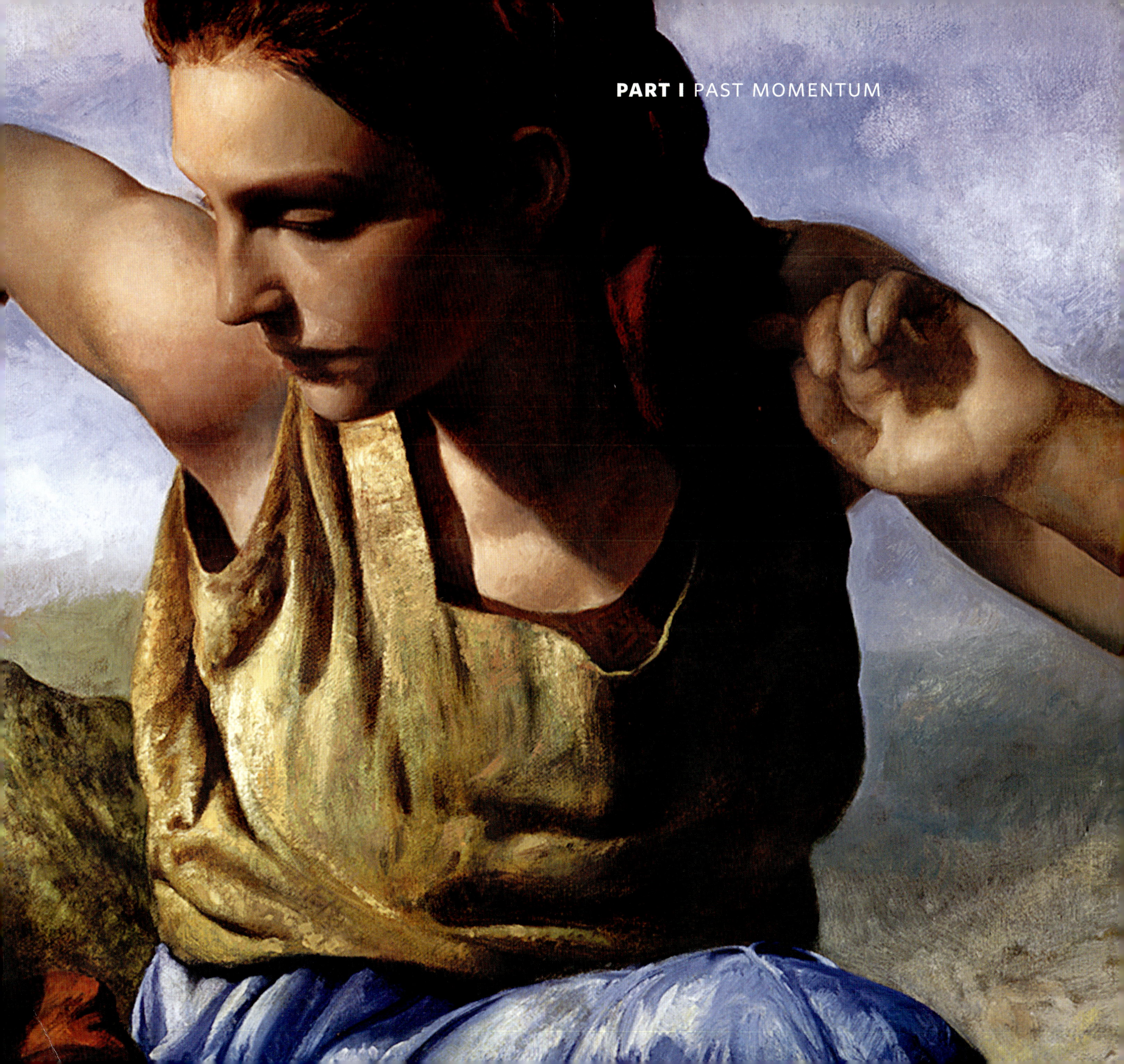

PART I PAST MOMENTUM

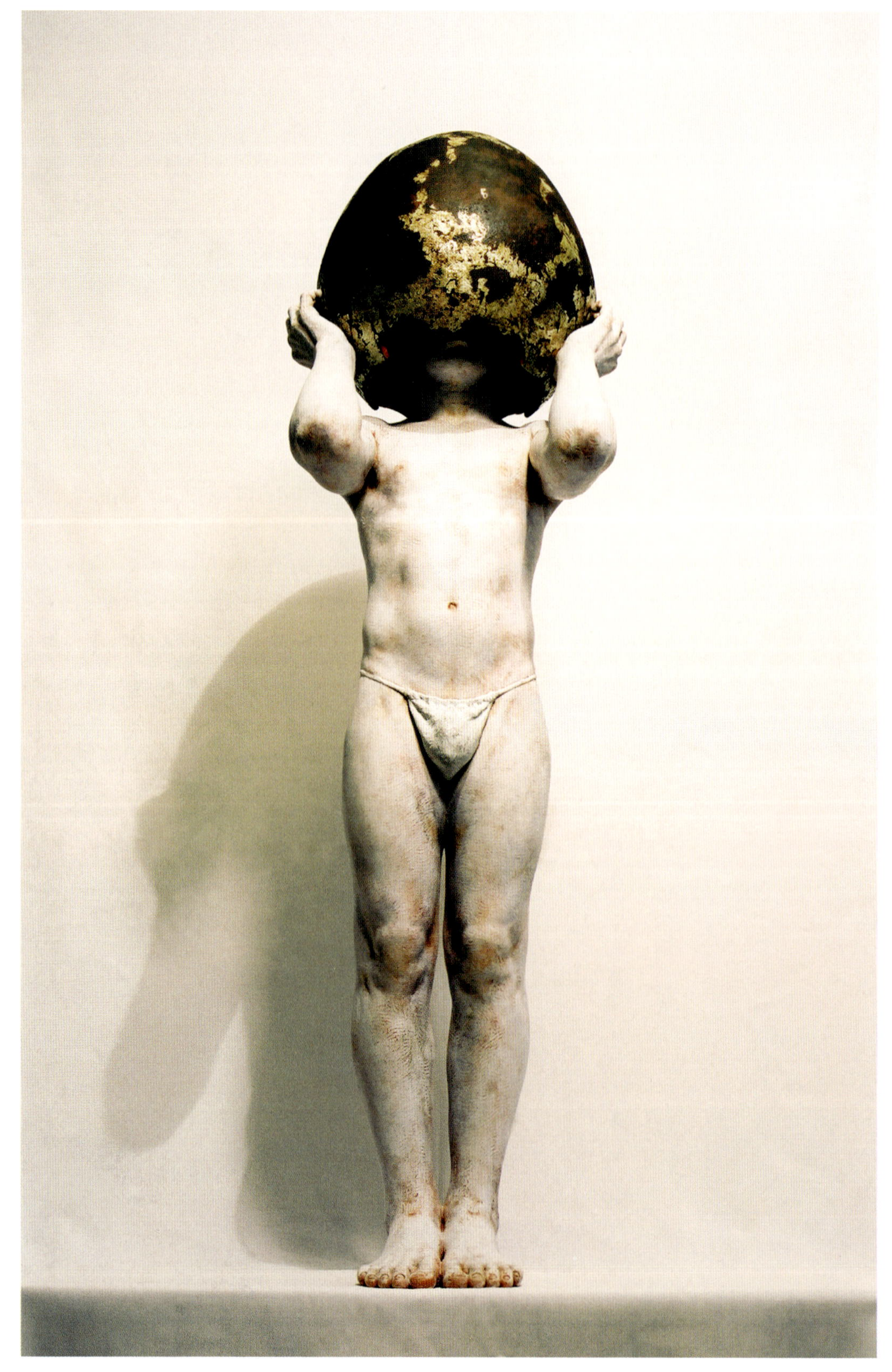

THE ONCE AND FUTURE SCULPTED FIGURE

JUDY FOX

FIGURATIVE SCULPTURE HAS A SPECIAL ROLE within the freedom, range, and disorder of contemporary art. Part of an age-old tradition, it avails itself of an evolved formal language that excels at conveying subtle and profound insight into the human condition. An artist's execution must add impact to a work or it isn't worth the trouble; a likeness can be knocked out by computers and craftsmen. Concept and execution must intertwine in order to reach beyond what fabrication can do to compete with the great achievements of the past.

There was a time when all sculpture was figurative. Statues presented iconic characters, exemplary types that embodied the traditional values of each society. Style changed gradually, along with changing attitudes. Contemporary art, however, has no unified traditions. It reflects the mercurial complexity of cosmopolitan life, where cultures cross and conflict and social hierarchy has dissolved. The articulated figure must find a place in the mind-expanding contemporary environment. All of history and culture provide a vast palette of styles and subjects to inspire and inform visual commentary on human experience.

A figurative sculptor is obliged to both address tradition and update it, as great artists have done in the past. At the beginning of the twentieth century, Modernists did just that. They freed "The Nude" from the stale conventions of anatomy and proportion followed by the European Academy, and used its form like a language. The universal grammar of form entails subdivision into volumes that interact in variable ways, and different kinds of lines and curves that connect contours and unify a composition. Exposure to foreign traditions that interpreted the body with abstract clarity catalyzed this new approach. Tribal African figurines segment the body, with sharp rhythmic lines concisely codifying gesture; Indian figures animate round shapes with springy, fanciful curves; Japanese tomb guardians pack the abdomen with bulging balls of muscle. A reading of these styles suggests very different venerations: the power of spirits, sensuality, ferocity.

With volutionary individuality, Modernists abandoned the stylistic consensus that had characterized Western, Eastern, and tribal art alike. They remixed formal elements to create intensely personal icons, commensurate with the advent of psychotherapy. Lachaise's inflated maternal sex bombs, Maillol's placid columnar mannequins, Lehmbruck's transcendent giants communicated a personal sensibility through style as well as physical proportion. Pressured, stretched, or relaxed, the visual rhythms of contour acted like a musical score, guiding the emotional impact of a psychologically loaded image.

But formalist figuration would self-destruct. Rodin's turbulent surfaces damaged underlying structure, conveying melodrama, even violence. Picasso's sophisticated formal play, contradicting volume with line ornament, used composition to question its own principles. Giacometti's pointillist texture dissolved the boundary between form and perception. As experimental abstraction dominated, "The Nude" was seen as conventional and boring, yet another reference to the classical ideal of seeking balance and proportion within universal types. The blank face, meant to signify classical universality, now read as mindless. The sanitized nude could not address pressing issues in society; as in relationships, a good body was not enough. Body casting aside, figuration fizzled by the 1970s. Robert Graham was the only modeler admitted into the art world at the time. His miniature naked ballerinas were diagrammed, genitals uncensored, with an eye for detail both heartless and worshipful. My own observed work of the 1980s inhabited an empty field. Looking back to Gothic carving, I reintroduced the painted surface and explored issues of conflicted identity and role.

(opposite)
Chie Shimizu
Untitled, 2006
Plaster, resin,
mixed media
36 x 12 x 12 inches

Despite iconoclastic movements like Dada, Pop, Postmodernism, and anti-aestheticism, the human image has come back, for it is still a potent metaphor for the human condition. Nudity fraught with moral peril is no longer a bore. It is meaningful form, abstract or representational, that needs resuscitation. The modern discovery of abstraction was profound, but it is time to revisit the past with a contemporary eye and see what was missed. It is well worth an overview of the history of sculpture, to demonstrate the reading of form with an eye toward understanding how it interacts with content. The masters show best how to enrich content through the deliberated execution of a work of art.

Typically described in a neat progression, the Western canon starts with the first empires. The rigid geometry of Egyptian style conveys cultural conformity to an eternal cosmic structure. Greek statuary gradually sheds that dominant influence. A lyrical movement of aliveness takes over, until Hellenism whirls with agitation. Atop the peak of the classical arc stands the Praxiteles nude, in contrapposto. Celebrated for perfected proportions, it was rendered with a balance of segmentation and flow, geometry and anatomy. It became a benchmark for all Western figuration. Classical proportion was not simply a look. It symbolized a specific belief: the interpenetration of human and divine. Classical nudity, characteristic of only gods and athletes, recalls a connection between the divine and the animal. To mimic pagan idealism now is nostalgia, but it lords over figurative art like a patriarch.

One thousand years later the arc of the ancient Greek aesthetic was echoed in Europe. From early Christian crudeness emerged the stately arches of High Gothic. Finally, lyricism maxed out in Baroque spirals, eventually bursting with a spray of nineteenth-century French frou-frou. The apex of the arc this time was the Renaissance, which once again established a standard to which subsequent work pays tribute. Michelangelo's nudes exemplify the fully developed Western sculptural language: a combination of reference, character, anatomical animation, and formal composition. His *Pietà*, with Christ lying across Mary's lap, refers to a familiar scene from the crucifixion, brought to life by Mary's timeless beauty and Christ's natural fleshiness. The anatomy is both representational and abstract, adhering to a hierarchy of volume that corresponds to a descending dominance of skeleton, muscles, and fat. The rigid core sections—skull, ribs, pelvis—remain inviolate. Their mechanics deform musculature, unaffected by fat and skin. Superficial ornament might compress fat and push muscle but does not penetrate bone. This hierarchy empowers the form such that evocation and metaphor merge. The tectonic plates of Christ's stomach press and churn in an enactment of strife. Michelangelo's dramatic hyping of the pagan Greek balance of segmentation and lyricism serves a philosophical transformation of idealism itself. Divine nudity merges with mortal humiliation, and indicates Christ's recent degradation. Mary's attire identifies her as a modest commoner, while facets of drapery offset the body of her child. The new ideal both acknowledged mortal suffering and escaped it. Christian perfection inhabited a Neoplatonic realm that advertised heavenly transcendence. Today, attempts at reproducing such a High Renaissance style without its underlying philosophical convictions are bound to read as nostalgia or kitsch.

The complexity and control of anatomy and composition peaked with Bernini. In stark psychic contrast to Michelangelo, his sensuality was external and interactive. In *The Rape of Persephone*, thigh muscles are pressed aside by the grip upon the hipbone, soft fat puffs around plunging fingers. In the swirling composition of *Apollo and Daphne*, a similar subtlety of anatomical layering is topped off by spectacular ornamental details of clothing and foliage. Bernini contained it all within controlled compositions of outlines that shift with each viewpoint, so that you feel the trembling flesh in your own hands. Utilizing all aspects of structure and reference, the young master turns familiar narratives into passionate fugues about the elusive capture of intimate beauty.

Bernini's unequaled understanding of the behavior of flesh in its various consistencies was clearly indebted to intense observation. The discipline of the measuring eye brings subtlety and surprise to what might otherwise become predictable constructions. Even stylized African, Indian, and Japanese figures show delightful astuteness in their portrayal of local body types. At Naumburg Cathedral, generic royal robes sheathe expressive portraits. In the Renaissance, a marvelous integration of subtle observation, anatomical sensitivity, and rhythmic contour imparted a magical feeling of natural beauty to portraiture. The classical figure revised repeatedly until codified in nineteenth-century academicism, so that style and proportion no longer varied in pursuit of meaning. Conventionalized figures, used as allegorical performers like "Justice" or as war heroes, all have the same legs. Beautiful rendering by facile sculptors abounded as decoration.

Beauty, however, is not the whole truth. Historically, realism tends to prevail during periods of disenchantment. Late Roman statuary moved away from the classical ideal, reveling in common circumstance, fashion, and imperfection. Medieval art, with its aversion to pride and vanity, developed a representationalism bordering on caricature. When observation is divorced from curvilinear resolution, grace is lost. But this loss is not necessarily without purpose, even if unconscious. Ugliness, decay, and damage are part of life, and are evoked abstractly when details violate structure. An awkward body conveys disapproval of physicality, while painful details reveal a penitent's fascination with the flesh. Medieval depictions of naked figures, usually in hell, are awkward and scrawny, their skeletons protruding graphically. Sharp incising of muscular definition and external features undermines the hierarchy of form, destroying the solidity and flow of the composition. A medieval pietà with an emaciated Christ—his torso a cage of ribs, body a stiff rack of bones—dramatizes Christ's distress and rigor mortis better than Michelangelo's languid savior.

It makes sense, then, that figuration by respected contemporary artists often revels in a lack of articulated rendering. The rejection of skill can be seen as a rejection of euphemism, an embrace of candor and honesty. When Kiki Smith rescued the human image from obsolescence in the 1980s, she presented the body awkwardly, or involved raw body casts in

(opposite)
Leonid Lerman
Drawing, Figure Study, 1975
Sanguine chalk on paper
34 x 24 inches

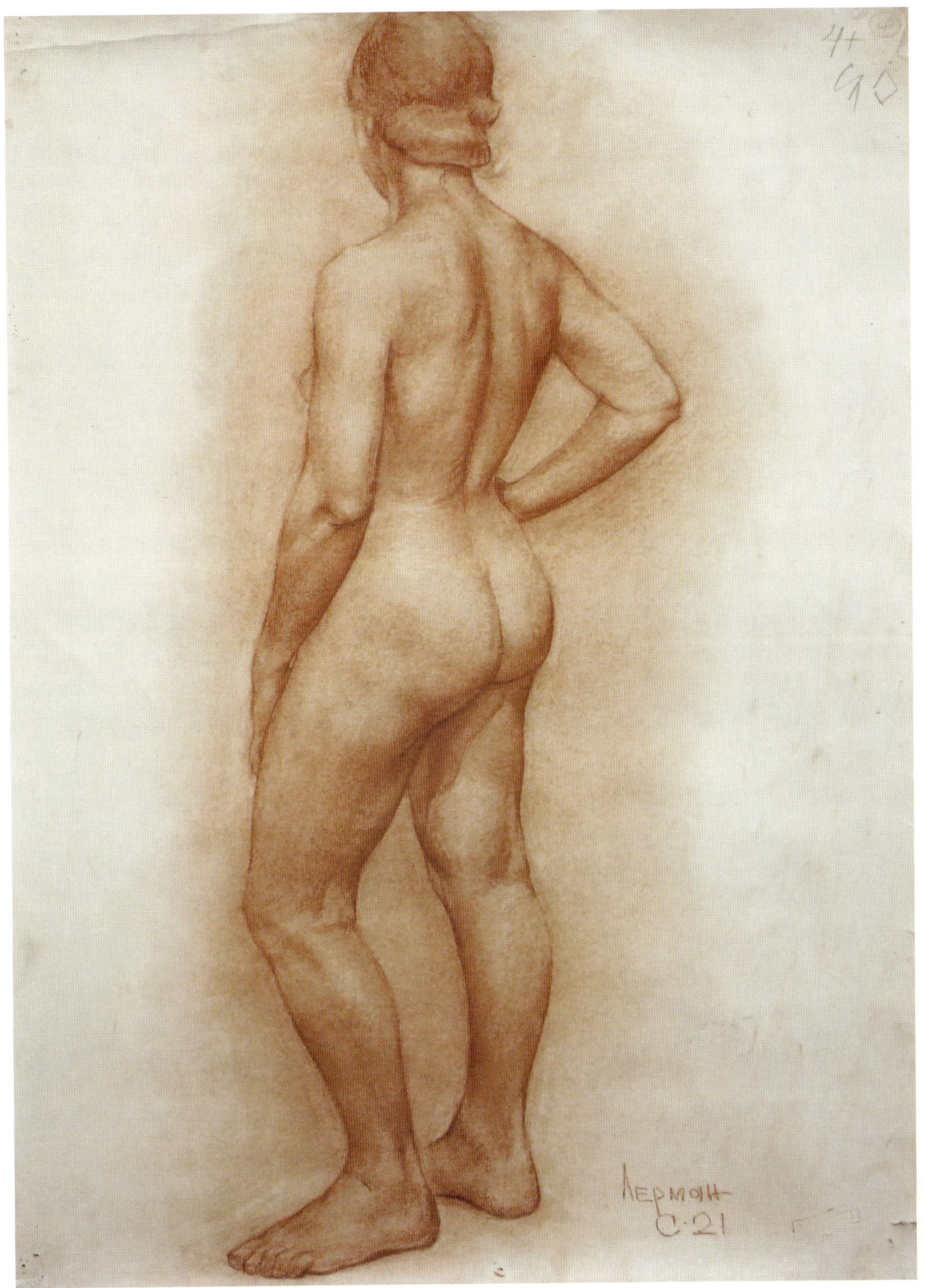
Лерман
С·21

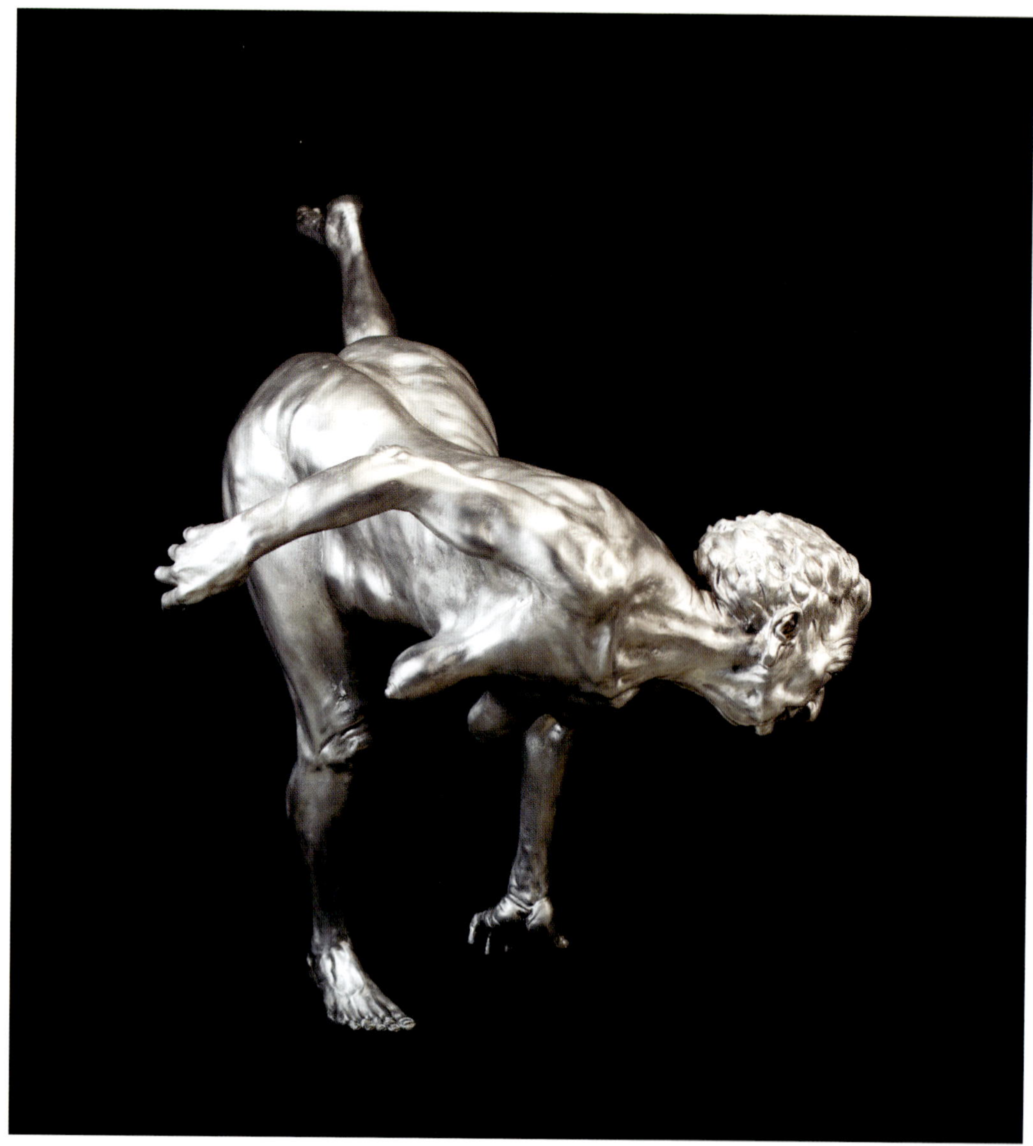

Peter Simon Mühlhäußer
Phoenix, 2007
Aluminum
60 x 36 x 60 inches

(opposite)
John O'Reilly
Bitch, 2011
Resin and porcelain
21.75 x 24 x 32.5 inches

dramatic installation. Like a medieval artist, she used crude articulation to poignant effect.

Figuration is not about to dominate sculpture as it did long ago. The messy spread of contemporary art reflects a teeming, commercial, confusing world. A rebellious and destructive vigor has challenged every orthodoxy and destroyed every limitation of the definition of art. Still, the intense connection people feel with their own form is a powerful tool for the artist. Judiciously employed, the elaborate language of the Western tradition is intriguingly well equipped to articulate the complexity and contradiction of contemporary life. Its marketing of values through transcendent mythification, heroic narrative, honored hierarchy, or moral rebuke is ripe for reassessment and reconfiguration. All of history and culture awaits critical appreciation.

So how does an artist begin to consider options? Know what you want to say. Be ambitious, then work with your limitations. If you want to tackle the figurative tradition, educate yourself. Reflect upon social change. Consider old ideas, and then reform them. Look at all kinds of great work, and be inspired to take command of your sense of form and say something interesting with it.

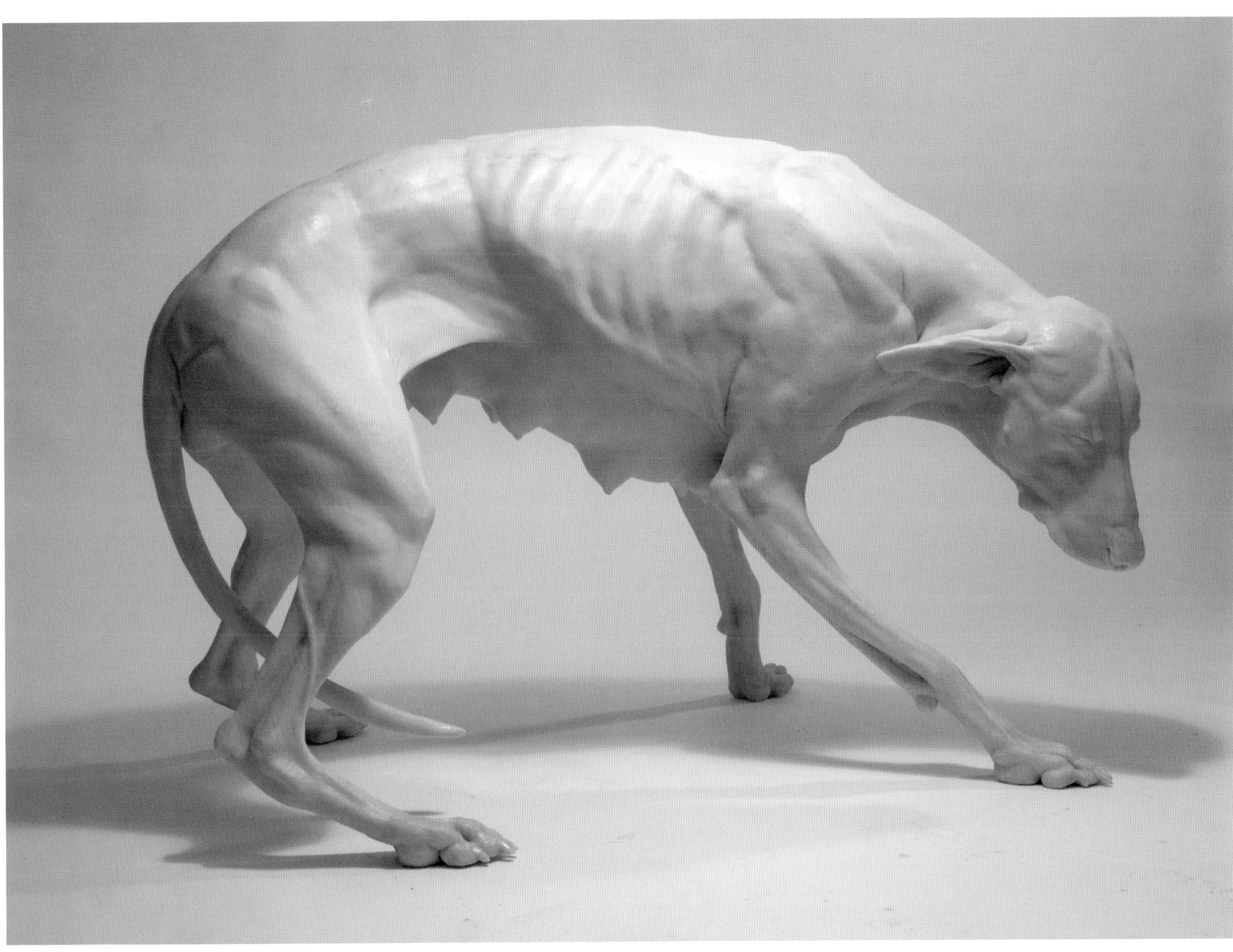

HARVEY CITRON

Minimalism dominated sculpture in the United States in the 1960s and '70s. Representational painting was asserting itself alongside abstract painting—Pop art made painting objects okay again—but figurative sculpture had not broken through in the same way. Some painters working from perception, like Alice Neel, Al Leslie, Gabriel Laderman, Philip Pearlstein, and Louis Finkelstein, attended meetings at the Alliance of Figurative Artists to discuss art—it was very rowdy and contentious. There were only a few sculptors there, so there was more of a sense of a shared mission among painters, but sometimes the conversation would drift to European statuary I admired, like Donatello, Michelangelo, Bernini, and Canova. My interest in how the human condition was expressed in sculpture from the Greco-Roman and French-Italian fifteenth- to nineteenth-century periods, especially involving the applied study of anatomy and *écorché*, I believe made me something of an outsider. I wanted to understand past sculptors' working procedures and was fascinated by their form development, subject matter/content, and iconography.

At Pratt, Walter Erlebacher introduced me to a sculptural convention derived from anatomical structure and to Robert Beverly Hale's book *Anatomy Lessons from the Great Masters*. I had an idealized notion of becoming an artist after my father took me to see John Huston's film *Moulin Rouge* when I was young. Later I went to Italy and studied at the Accademia di Belle Arti in Rome, with Pericle Fazzini. The year 1968 was one of great political unrest and an earthquake in Sicily, and Italy's capital was in turmoil. The school was closed down; I had to avoid authorities and radical personalities when attempting to enter the studio to keep a large sculpture in a workable state. My thesis project, based on the figure Haman from the Sistine ceiling, involved *écorché* through finished surface form, and an iconographic analysis. The years spent as a student in Rome were those I value most.

When I returned to the United States, I earned a living as a commercial sculptor producing sculptural illustrations for *Esquire* magazine, three-dimensional representations for two-dimensional images—for example, medical models for advertising agencies, where my understanding of anatomy was useful. I also worked with *The Muppets* television show producing clay prototypes and in the film industry—on *Altered States*, with FX (special effects) master Dick Smith, and other films with Carl Fullerton. I greatly admire and enjoyed working with such highly gifted, professional, skilled, and ingenious people, directed by a head artist, within their methodical apprentice system. Skills were prioritized and specifically directed to a clearly defined objective. This training influenced my own practice and teaching method.

I find anatomically driven sculpture a long developmental process. I've done some carving but I'm an additive sculptor, a traditional modeler. Water-based clay has greater fluidity and surface qualities than oil-based clay, and initially requires more skill to handle. The resulting airborne dust has become a problem; therefore for larger work I use a high-grade soft plasteline. Oil-based clay doesn't dry out and doesn't need to be completely covered at the end of every working session, so you can see the whole sculpture during interim periods, for continuous review. I prefer an architectonic sculptural form convention with narrative content drawn at times from literary subject matter. Narratives involving two figures have been a running theme, partly for the formal challenge. Multiple views and spatially dynamic sculptural conventions I admire in some Mannerist and Baroque sculpture have influenced me.

I consider ideas with drawings, and then further develop these into maquettes from imagination, for the underlying structure of the work. I use several small maquettes representing the essential compositional idea but never replicate them explicitly in the larger sculpture, because the change in scale inevitably necessitates spatial reconsideration of the composition. My sculpture incorporates some Baroque strategies; I also have been influenced by the work of Clodion, Rude, Carpeaux, Barye, and Rodin. When I have enough information to construct an armature, I model the full-scale sculpture directly from drawings, or from earlier work modeled from life or imagination, and/or the live model, always using my sense of form and knowledge of anatomy.

Figurative sculpture should have a sense of incipient movement, apparent through modeling or carving technique and skill. Since internal form is static in a still photograph, I find it useless as a working tool. Photographs can serve as reference for identifying features, but not the subtlety of slight variation of structural change over and across the surface form of the model's body as it fatigues, constantly shifts weight, and slightly moves. If the model isn't available to provide information and I run into a problem, I may photograph aspects of sculptures at the Metropolitan Museum of Art to refer to for specific formal strategies and solutions. I feel extensive empirical and kinesthetic knowledge is required to use photography correctly.

When the sculpture is finished, I hire an assistant to help cast the clay model as a waste mold in white Hydrocal (plaster) and with Hydrocal FGR fiberglass internal backup. A large waste mold may contain fifty pieces, and I often work four to six months on the cast. I prefer no patina; polychrome sculpture, too, at times, often camouflages poor form development. Ideally I'd cast my sculptures in bronze, because its fluid surface highlights subtleties of perceptual modeling, but the form should be first resolved in non-reflective white. It's amazing what three-dimensional copying can do, though it can't articulate surface tension. Technology will probably advance to do that, too, but presently it's fortunate there has been a resurgence in direct perceptually modeled figurative sculpture.

Art history greatly interests me, but I've never cared for art theory, deconstruction, or irony. I'm not interested in mimetic sculpture of individuals, either—the current interest in hyperrealism reminds me of taxidermy. At present the criteria for being a visual artist seem too equivocal. The surrounding contemporary context doesn't concern me much. If mid-fifteenth-century literary antiquarians and subsequent Renaissance artists looked back fifteen hundred years to their perceived heritage to be inspired, I have no problem looking back further than the conventions of literary criticism and Postmodern doctrine of the past forty years.

(opposite)
Harvey Citron
Sisyphus, 2009
Hydrocal FGR over fiberglass
40 x 46 x 33 inches

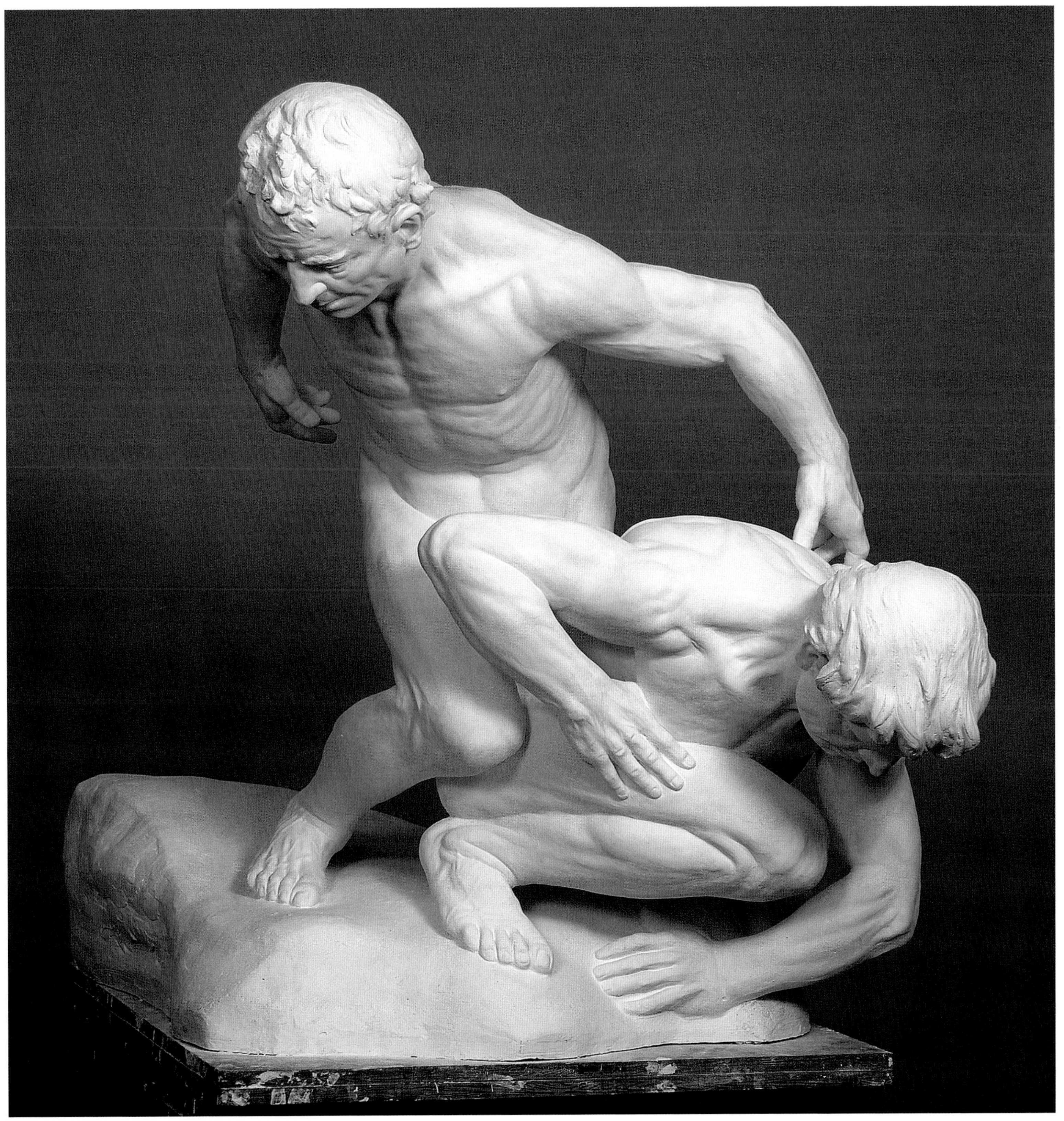

JUDY FOX

My life-size children and adults of various ethnicities, as well as my surrealist creatures, combine a Modernist's love of abstract form with High Gothic idiosyncrasy and color. Works are built and carved in clay, fired, and finally painted with casein. This use of ancient traditional media reflects the participation of the past in the impact of my work now.

I had to rethink the figurative legacy critically in order to engage it with contemporary attitudes. When I was an undergraduate at Yale, contemporary sculpture classes dismissed figuration as a tired convention: academicism was hackneyed, Modernism had become abstract, and Realism was achieved with body casting. My first mentor was Erwin Hauer, a Modernist who loved precise observation and twisting planes, but I knew I would have to reach beyond his approach to figure modeling in order to disprove its obsolescence.

In graduate school I studied art history as part of training in art conservation at New York University. I fell in love with older statuary traditions, each with a distinctive style that reflected the values of its particular culture. Looked at from a contemporary point of view, their iconic subjects, whether heroes or enemies or gods, promoted interpretations of role, identity, and personality that to me invited reexamination. Who is a leader, a mother, a warrior, a beauty? Eventually, I applied the Modernist convention of nudity to the statuary tradition, stripping the hero and exposing him or her to the harsh contemporary eye.

I begin a figure by reflecting upon a typical image from art or history that might have an interesting reading from a contemporary point of view. Then I photograph a model of the same ancestry, from many angles. From those photographs I model and carve the clay sculpture, putting a closely observed portrait into an art pose. I integrate the parts through an understanding of anatomy and the geometry of gesture. Identity is channeled through the subjects but also projected onto them. The resulting characters are at once individual and stereotyped, natural and contrived, vulnerable and grandiose. Interpretation of gesture becomes uncertain, as when cultures cross.

My form is highly worked so that its abstract qualities convey an attitude. I meticulously render physical idiosyncrasies, but also control all outlines so there is a harmonic undulation to the surface. It's not realism or idealization, but a beauty interwoven with flaws. To me it manifests a striving and perfectionism that easily downshifts to inadequacy, appropriate to a culture of plastic surgery. So the style is an important iteration of the challenged mythification that my subject matter embodies.

Recently I've also been making surreal "creatures" that explore deeper, archetypal aspects of human nature. Fanciful anatomy might combine clothing, body parts, and viscera. I play with double entendre, using shapes reminiscent of other things. I might take a crude or frightening reference and render it in a beautiful way, so that it is simultaneously attractive and repulsive. This gets deep into fear of primitive nature, and mortality.

My technique starts out like making a pinch pot. While the clay stiffens I shape it with general tools—hitting inside and out with a flat stick and shaving with a large-toothed loop tool. When it's leather hard, I carve with ever smaller serrated tools, finishing details with a fine rasp. For larger pieces I work from the bottom up, hugging a removable armature at the base, letting the clay firm up as I climb at a rate of several inches per day. The clay is kept leather hard by spraying and plastic, so that I can carve the surface for months, adding new wet clay where needed and carving that. A larger piece will crack above the base when it reaches a certain height. At that point I finish the lowest portion, fire it, and put it back on the armature before replacing the next section and continuing to build up. All along, I break off parts to get at unreachable spots. For example, I'll cut off an upper lip to carve teeth, then put it back, or cut the forearm to get at the palm. A life-size adult will be built up in a month, but I'll work on finishing for eight more months. The carving is finished when curves and observation are all reconciled.

After sections are all fired, I glue them together and fill the gaps with plaster, carving it to blend with the clay. The surface is painted in casein medium, which is water- and protein-based. The paint sets overnight, so it can be layered. I use many layers translucently to get skin tones, pull out the high points, and simulate light effects. The painted surface looks not so much real as like the surface of a painting.

I feel that the strength of the experience I give to the viewer is a direct result of my skill as a craftsperson. My figures look intensely like "art," and at the same time look intensely like live individuals. So people want to both inspect them and approach them aesthetically with the complex feelings they would have toward an exposed person on display. My work offers no moral guidance to viewers who react in their own particular way to stereotyping or contrivance, body parts or sensuality. It exposes people to themselves.

(opposite)
Judy Fox
Mermaid, 2011
Terra cotta and casein
64 x 26 x 13 inches

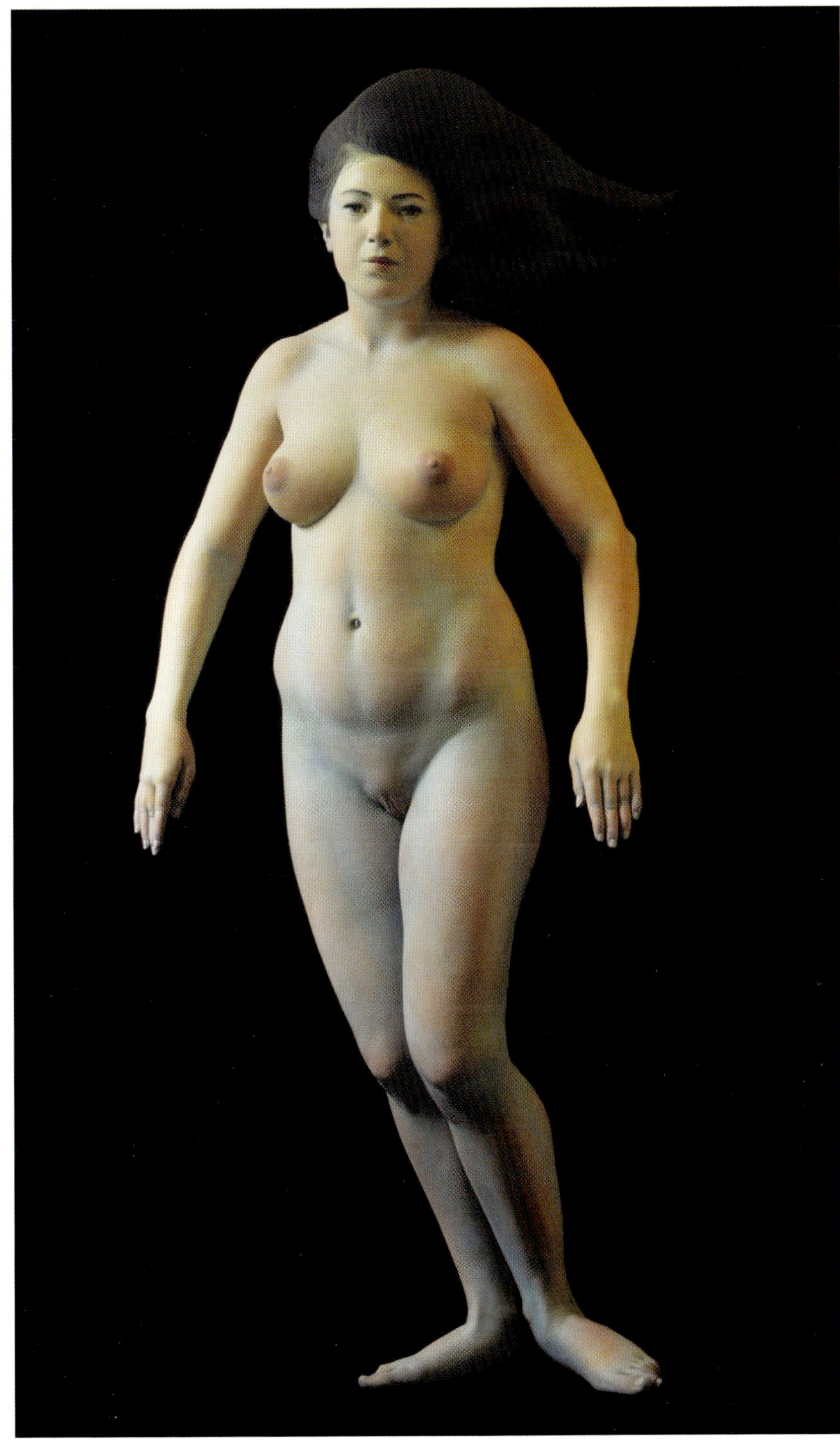

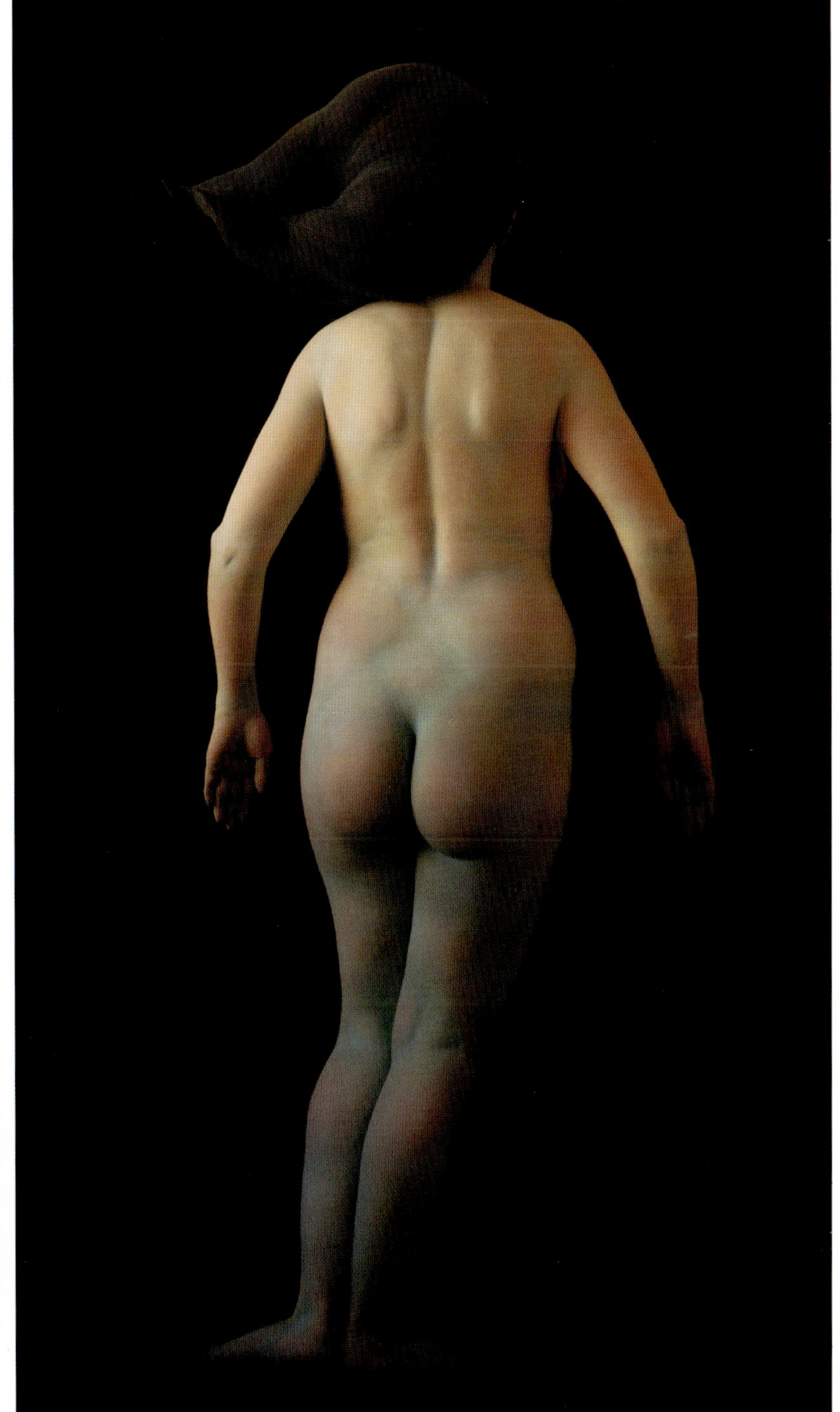

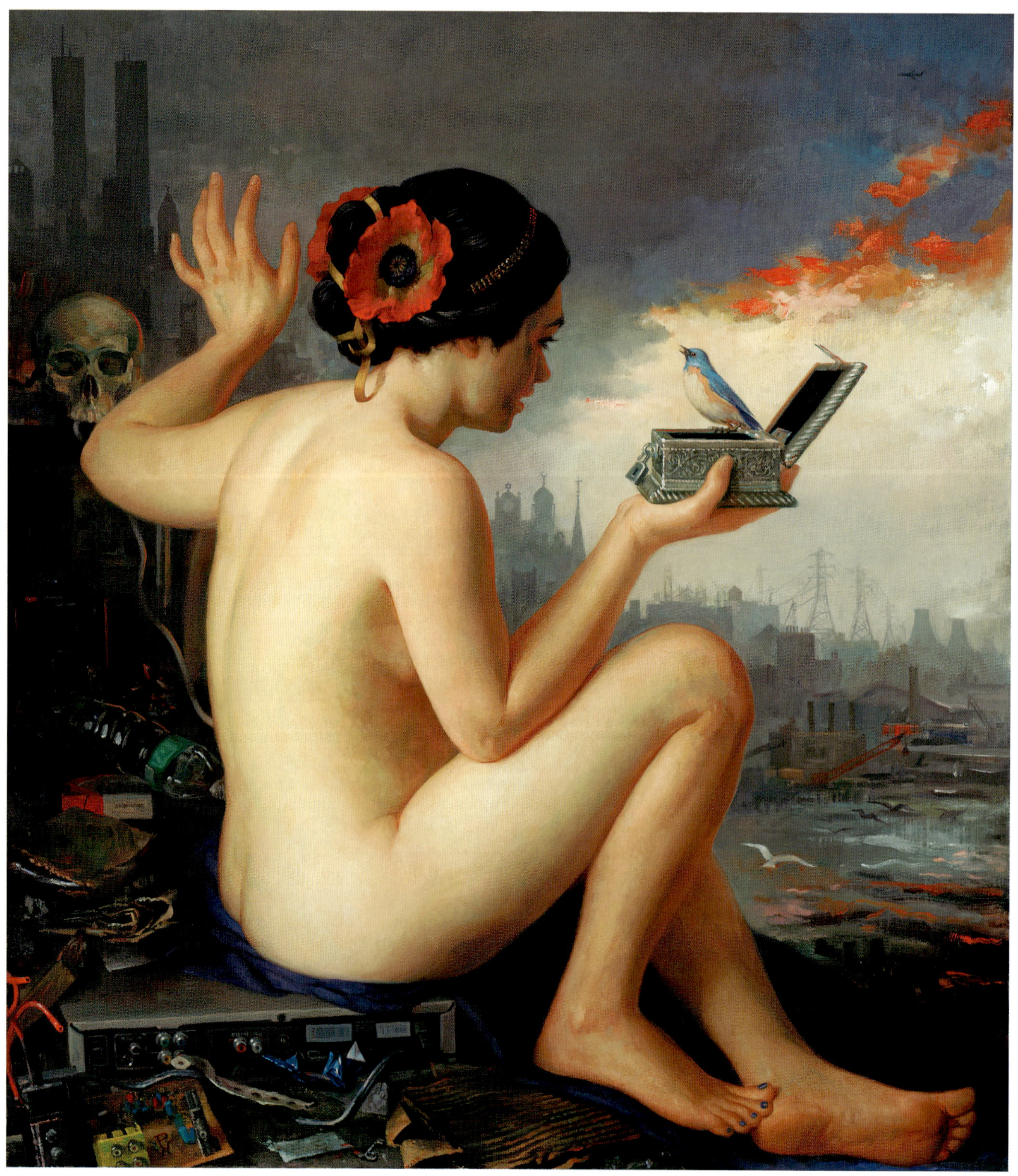

A BRIEF HISTORY OF TRADITIONAL PAINTING PEDAGOGY

THOMAS GERMANO

RAPHAEL'S *The School Of Athens* (1510) DEPICTS one of the four Renaissance branches of knowledge, art and philosophy. It relates the artist's time to the teachings of the masters. Egyptian, Greek, Roman, and Renaissance representations of human proportion were based on a grid. The Greco-Roman classical canon followed the principles of the first-century Roman architect Vitruvius's geometry, proportion, and naturalism regarding the human body. Math was necessary to creating the well-constructed pictorial stage of Raphael's acclaimed Vatican fresco, which also highlights knowledge of classical anatomy. The system of perspective Raphael used was developed by Filippo Brunelleschi in early fifteenth-century Florence and codified in *On Painting*, by Leon Batista Alberti. This treatise, which also covered other aspects of figuration like proportion, might be seen as the Renaissance "visual philosophy." Perspective circulated throughout Italy, including the court of Urbino, where Raphael's father learned it and passed it on to his son.[1] Unlike the eye-balling technique used by Flemish masters that approximated believable space, perspective required the artist to apply mathematical tenets; the optical difference between them is a visual intuitive experience versus a scientific method.

In addition to technical virtuosity, *The School of Athens's* iconography celebrates teaching. Reflecting the Renaissance reawakening after the millennial dormancy following the fall of Rome, Raphael depicted ancient teachers of art, philosophy, science, astronomy, mathematics, and design. Euclid, Pythagoras, Plato, Aristotle, Diogenes, Socrates, and Ptolemy appear in the guise of Raphael's notable contemporaries: the architect Bramante as Euclid plotting a compass over a chalkboard while enlightening, confounding, and mesmerizing his students; Leonardo as Plato in the act of debating his student Aristotle; Raphael and Il Sodoma listening to the astronomer-priest Zoroastro. Heraclitus, disguised as Raphael's rival Michelangelo, is the lone self-consumed exception, brooding over a drawing problem. The medieval focus on Aristotelian qualities was succeeded by a focus on Platonic quantities, which would support the mathematical basis of perspective and, later, the scientific method. Marsilio Ficino, founder of the fifteenth-century Platonic Academy of Florence, provided a contemporary translation and re-contextualization of ancient writings influencing Renaissance Neoplatonism. *The School of Athens* is about, and would itself become for the artists who for centuries studied it, a critical passing of knowledge through the centuries.

Little ancient painting has survived, and less is known about art instruction in ancient times. Accomplished artists like the fifth-century BCE Phidias of Athens probably oversaw and trained assistants to carry out his vision for the Acropolis and the Temple of Zeus. Classical Greek bronzes, faithfully copied in marble by Roman artists, are known principally through their Roman imitations. The Italian Renaissance imitation of ancient statues' graceful idealism (albeit without their high color) applied similar rigorous anatomical knowledge.

Before the Renaissance rediscovery of the visual remains of Greek pedagogical canons, and the establishment of Renaissance academies that imitated ancient ones, knowledge in the Middle Ages was conveyed generationally. Evolving medieval technology and craft were shared through guilds (prototypes of modern-era workers' unions), and the master-apprenticeship model. Visual artists guilds were traditionally called the Guild of Saint Luke, named after the disciple believed to have painted the first portrait of Mary and Jesus. Saint Luke guilds covered sacred visual arts and medicine because visual artists purchased some supplies at apothecaries (later called pharmacies or chemists), where doctors also obtained medicinal plants and remedies.

(opposite)
Patricia Watwood
Pandora, 2011
Oil on canvas
32 x 26 inches

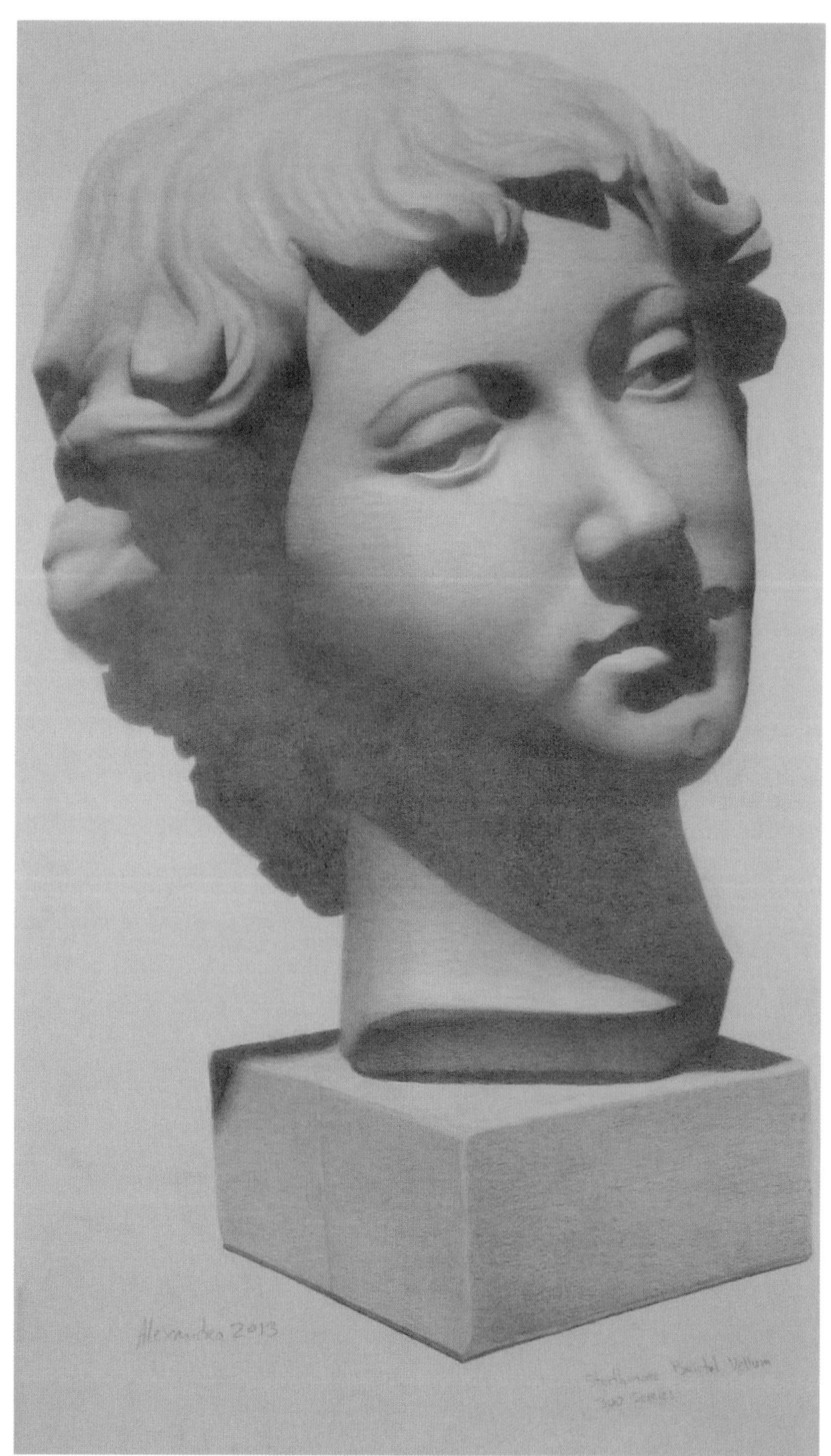

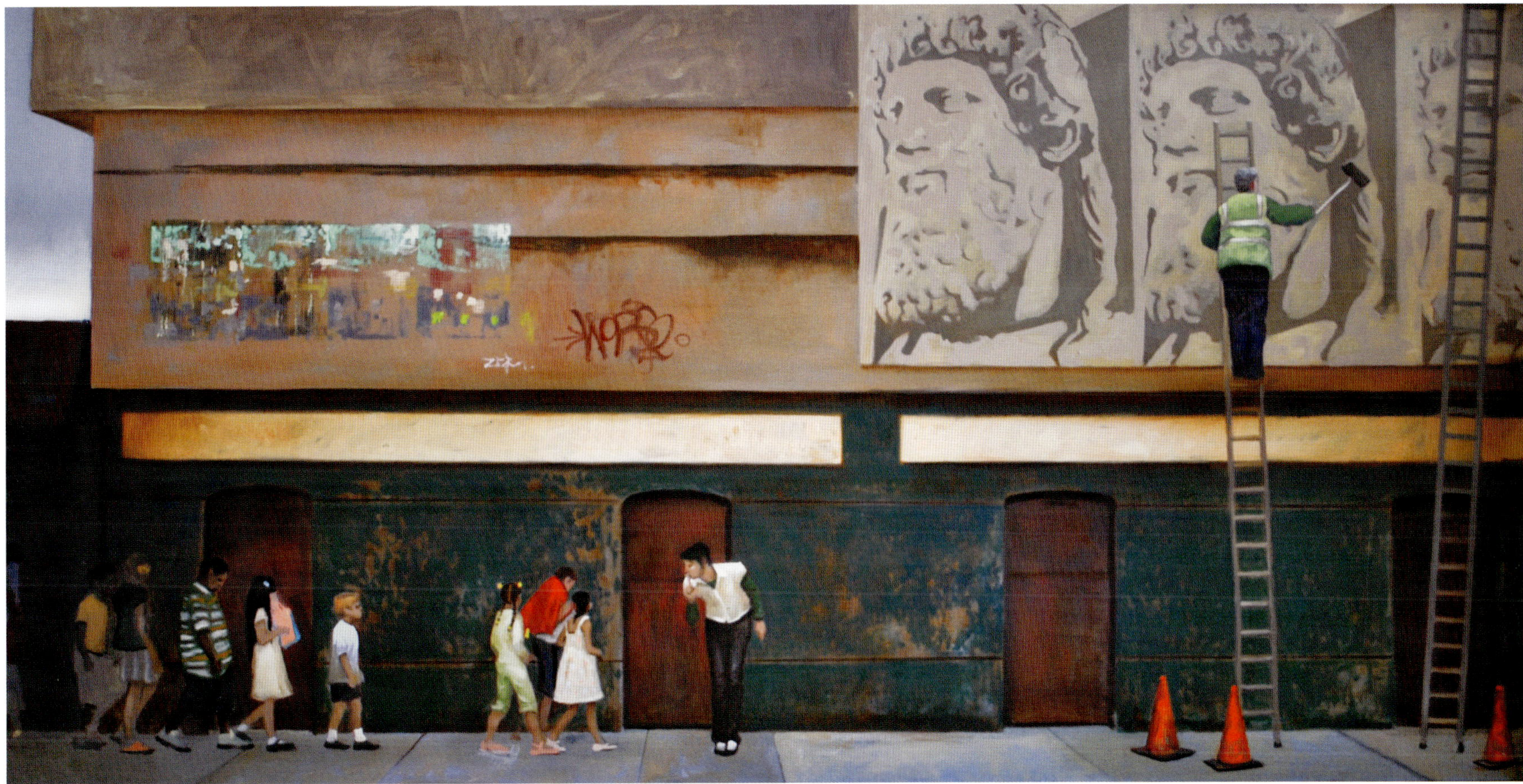

Giorgio Vasari's *Lives* of 1550 relays a story of Cimabue's noticing the powers of observation[2] of his young apprentice Giotto, who eventually surpassed his teacher's late-medieval, proto-Renaissance, Italo-Byzantine style. Byzantine art relied on a canon that viewed the human form as sinful in its articulated and hence sensual, erotic form, and the Italo-Byzantine style intentionally flattened the figure for potent abstraction. Volumetric form was absent but linear properties were decoratively fluid. In the Middle Ages, imitative perfection was a transgression; Celtic manuscript painters even left complex interlacing animal designs unfinished as a sign of Christian humility.[3] Giotto's interest in direct observation set the Renaissance return to the classical figure in motion. Renaissance artists reinvented the classical visual language, replacing pagan subjects with Christian ones, combining the linear emphasis carried over from medieval decorative tendencies with volumetric drawing, as in the works of Giotto, Masaccio, Filippo Lippi, and Sandro Botticelli. While the art of Leonardo defies this stylistic trajectory, linearity appears in Michelangelo's painting combined with an emphasis on plasticity that greatly inspired the expressive distortions of the human form in Mannerist painters like Vasari, Jacopo da Pontormo, Il Bronzino, Parmigianino, and Rosso Fiorentino.

In Raphael's time, talented youth would have entered an apprenticeship by the age of twelve, spending years drawing plaster casts and imitating techniques of the master. Renaissance workshops, a model later echoed in the atelier system of Paris, France, Spain, England, and elsewhere, were individualistic, despite the commonalities of the religious subject matter commissioned by their patrons, the Catholic church and the nobility. Pietro Perugino and Leonardo, for example, both studied with Andrea del Verrocchio but developed into very different artists. Highly original artists like Leonardo, Michelangelo, and Caravaggio set trends that inspired a great number of imitators. Through the early modern period, schools or academies gradually replaced medieval visual artists guilds across Europe. The first Accademia di Belle Arti was established in Florence in 1563, followed by one three years later in Rome. Academies emphasized studying ancient (and, later, Renaissance) masters, and the practice of accurate drawings from antique sculpture, life drawing, anatomy, classical history, ancient literature,

Steve Forster
New Republic, 2012
Oil on canvas
26 x 54 inches

(opposite)
Alexandro Berrios
Boy in Round, 2013
Graphite on paper
16 x 9 inches

and chemistry. Eventually the fine arts would be taught in public academies established throughout Europe and beyond.

Leonardo's center stage appearance in *The School of Athens* reflects the profound contributions to painting and scientific knowledge he made in his epoch. His stylistic idioms, particularly the use of light and shadow, chiaroscuro, to establish form, his *sfumato*'s representation of light and air, and his careful studies of nature in an empirical manner, appeared in Leonardo's students and in Venetian painting following Leonardo's sojourn there circa 1500. Painterly and atmospheric approaches to pictorial environments appear in the work of Giorgione, Titian, and Giovanni Bellini. Leonardo's legacy continued in the sixteenth-century artists Tintoretto, Paolo Veronese, and El Greco, and again in the seventeenth-century Baroque era's emphasis on impasto, atmosphere, and dramatic tonality. Before Leonardo's impact, Venetian art had been dominated by the workshop of Jacopo Bellini, who passed the Florentine traditions from his teacher, Gentile da Fabriano, to his sons, Giovanni and Gentile. The Bellini workshop included Jacopo's son-in-law Andrea Mantegna, and combined the influences of Florentine, Byzantine, International Gothic, and the palette of the region's historic colored-glass artistry. The church and nobility competed for the most accomplished painters, like Piero della Francesca, Botticelli, and Leonardo, and later Diego Velázquez and Francisco de Goya in Spain, to serve at court and fulfill commissions.

With masterpieces like the Sistine Chapel and *The School of Athens*, the High Renaissance saw a shift of importance from Florence to Rome, which became dominant by the seventeenth century. The Spanish painter Jusepe de Ribera entered the Accademia di San Luca in 1613 in Rome, adopting a Caravaggesque chiaroscuro style before relocating to Naples three years later, where Caravaggio had recently worked. Many northern artists like Dürer traveled and worked in Italy, studying its masterpieces and recording their journeys.[7] Many Flemish artists had no interaction with Italy, yet developed a non-classical yet highly refined, detail-oriented late-Gothic realism. In Holland, artists studied under a single master, and the middle class patronage system supported Dutch artists throughout the seventeenth-century "Golden Age." Rembrandt van Rijn had at least fifty students, and instructed his pupils not just in figure drawing but in dramatic storytelling using theatrical staging of historic, biblical, and mythological stories. Like Phidias and Raphael, Peter Paul Rubens ran a large workshop to assist him with numerous commissions. His protégé, Anthony Van Dyck, worked in England for King Charles I, and his work became the basis for the style adopted by the Royal Academy, founded 150 years later. French Baroque painters Nicholas Poussin and Charles Le Brun spent significant time in Rome, and were later instrumental in the formation of the French Academy.

The French Academy became the role model for the creation of a national art by developing modern nations. It was established under Louis XIV as the Académie Royale de Peinture et de Sculpture in 1648, then was stripped of royal prestige after the French Revolution of 1789; renamed under Napoleon the *Institut de France* in 1803, it later became the Académie des Beaux-Arts. Before the French Revolution, the influential neoclassical painter Jacques-Louis David and other members of the Academy were granted studio space and lodgings in the Louvre, later opened to the public in the nineteenth century. Through the French Academy and its Salon exhibitions, which established artists in society, Enlightenment France concerned itself with the promotion and self-critique of French culture. David, who had studied Roman antiquity and Italian masters like Raphael in the French Academy in Rome (founded 1666), had forty to fifty student apprentices, some of whom helped him complete his largest commissions. Large commissions gradually involved fewer religious and more secular subjects, and more individualistic approaches. Ingres's outspoken advocacy for the neoclassical style contrasted with the Romantic inclinations of Eugène Delacroix and Théodore Géricault, and later Realist factions like Gustave Courbet and Édouard Manet, who altered the course of cultural production toward images of modernity rather than classical history.

Roughly one hundred European art academies following the French model were opened by 1790—Berlin in 1696, Madrid in 1744, Milan in 1776, St. Petersburg in 1775. The aesthetic values of French art, principally neoclassicism, spread through Europe; The Royal Academy in London opened in 1768, where William Blake, Turner, and John Constable studied. Its president, Sir Joshua Reynolds, attracted colonial America's finest painters, including Benjamin West and John Singleton Copley. Later, due in part to the wars of Independence and of 1812, American artists developed a closer alliance with the German Academy rather than the British; more than four hundred American artists studied at the Munich Academy, founded in 1808, while Hudson River School painters Albert Bierstadt and Sanford Gifford studied at the Düsseldorf Academy.

American artists who studied in Europe promoted academies in the new world, and taught at or presided over these new academies. Thomas Eakins studied in the French Academy in Jean-Léon Gérôme's atelier, before becoming the director of the Pennsylvania Academy of the Fine Arts, established in 1810. Eakins combined the classical tradition with an interest in motion photography.[8] Eakins's art was championed by Robert Henri, the influence behind the Ashcan School and teacher of George Bellows and Edward Hopper at the New York School of Art (an offshoot of the Art Students League, which opened in 1875). Henri advocated adopting subject matter from modern urban life. Hopper later refused an elected membership to the National Academy of Design in 1932, as the institution's influence was waning. The twentieth-century art world increasingly ignored or attacked the classical model and atelier system of the academy; in America, artistic training was generally absorbed into private and public higher education with new Modernist role models. Yet with the twenty-first-century revival of figurative and representational painting, the perennial lesson of *The School of Athens*, that ancient pedagogical foundations and traditions of painting remain relevant and vital, is reaffirmed.

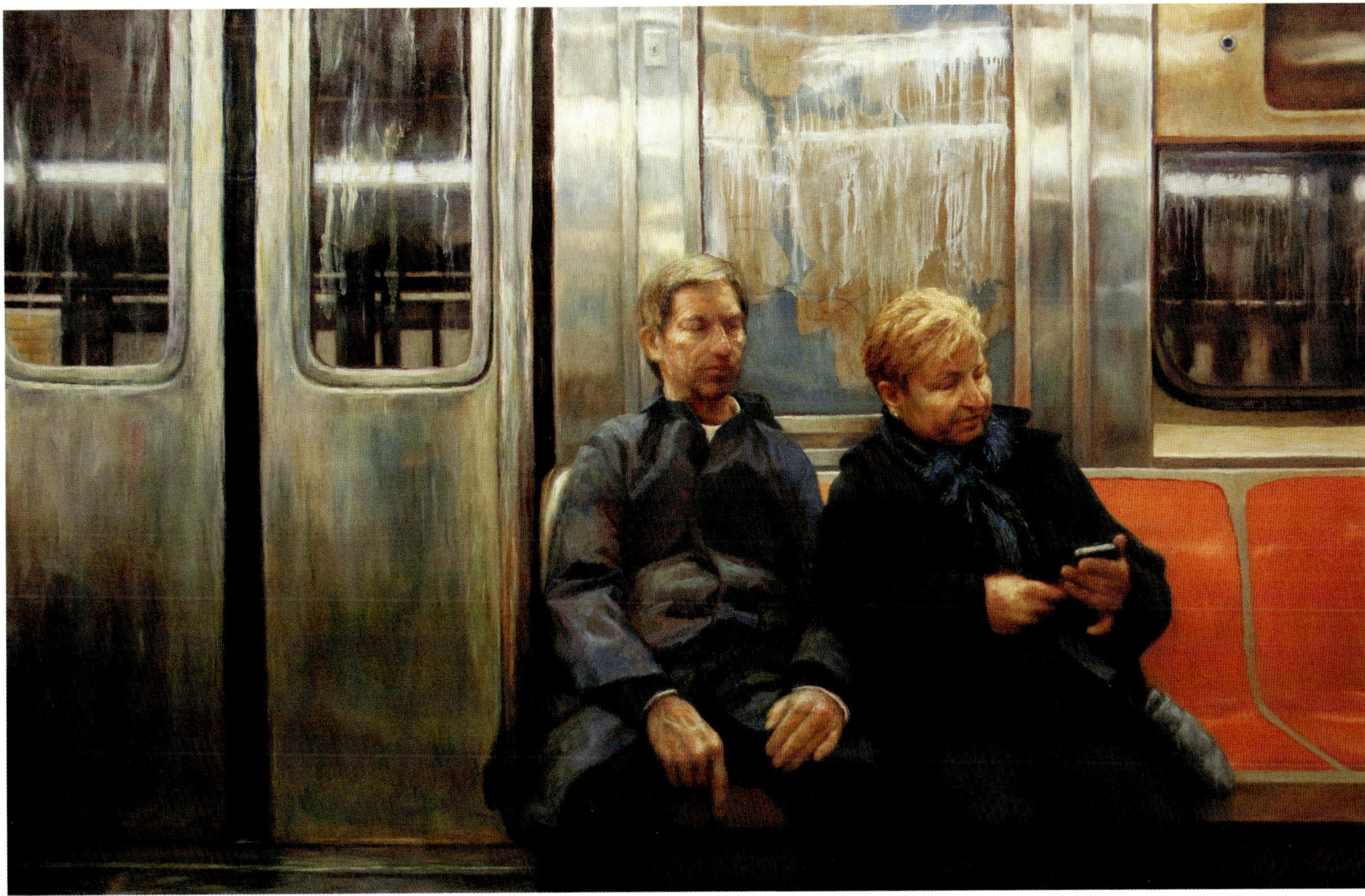

Adam Carnes
M Train, 2012
Oil on canvas
47 x 71 inches

ANDREW RAFTERY

Very few rooms in the world are all of one date. Every room that each of us occupies does not represent the crystallization of a single moment in time. There tends to be overlapping usage and overlapping styles. Even in a new building, presumably of one date, it does not take long before light fittings of another date go in, then different textiles cover the seats, and something will change here and there; within a year or two of human usage the time dimension of such a room will be expanded. This is the way we experience culture—in terms of temporal overlapping and complexity.
—Lawrence Alloway, 1974

The genesis of *Open House: Five Engraved Scenes* started when my mother moved to Providence, Rhode Island, in 1996 and spent a year looking for a house. Some may find endless outings with realtors and Sundays spent at open houses a waste of time, but I relished the opportunity to observe human habitats with impunity. Real estate transactions are fraught with emotional tensions. Every house, a potential home for the prospective buyer, is usually filled with the personal effects of the current owners. In Providence almost every home has been used before and contains some remnants of each occupant. This intersection of the domestic sphere and commerce combined with intense personal interactions and layers of history made real estate an irresistible subject for me. I often did furtive sketches while dodging watchful realtors, firming up the drawings from memory in the car.

After many reconnaissance missions I came up with a premise: five engravings, each depicting one moment of time in an open house. Interactions among people would be incidental to the main theme: the character of the temporarily absent house owners, as understood through what can be observed about the way they live. My first step was the construction of a two-inch-to-one-foot scale model for both stories of the house. Wax figures were made for each of the characters. The nature of the finished engravings would be determined by the initial experience of the subject in three dimensions. Although I had made use

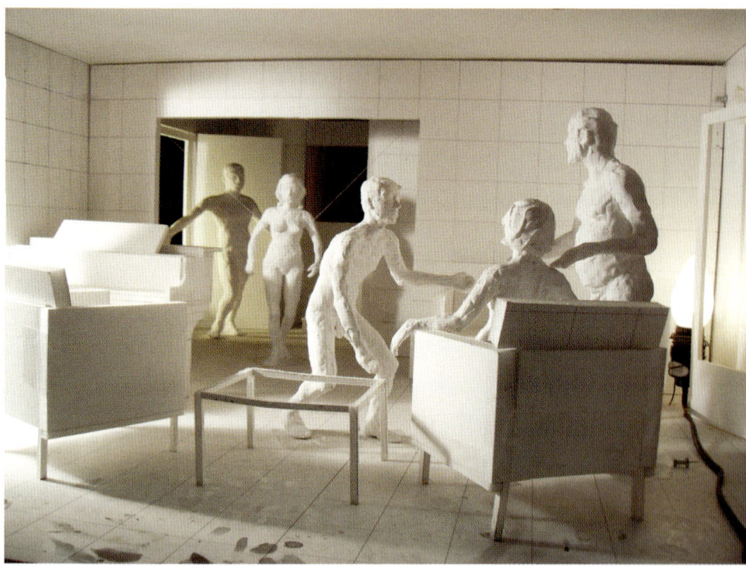

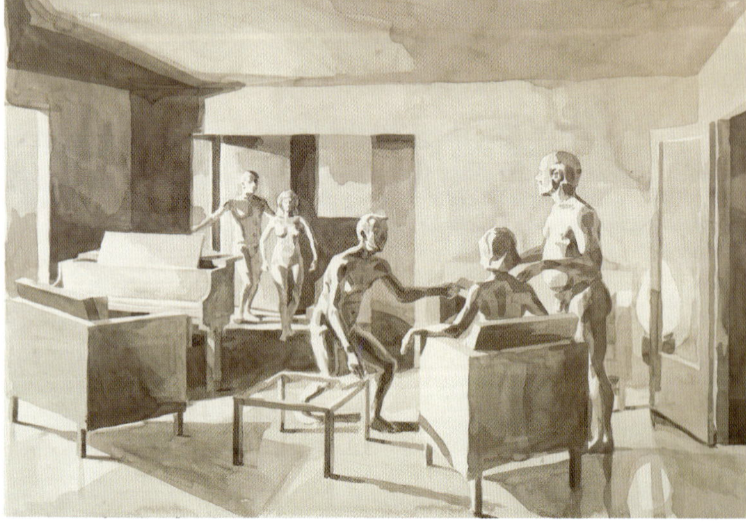

(top)
Andrew Raftery
Open House Model (Maquette), 2006
Foam core and wax
18 x 36 x 48 inches

(bottom)
Andrew Raftery
Scene One Study, 2006
Ink wash, graphite on paper
15.75 x 23 inches

(opposite)
Andrew Raftery
Open House: Scene One, 2008
Engraving
15.75 x 22.75 inches (image)

of models (maquettes) before, this was the first time they preceded any compositional drawings.

I drew these maquettes extensively, making several studies in wash, perspective drawings in line, and studies of the nude figures. The maquettes offer multiple views of the interior, allowing the figures to be moved around the space as my point of view subtly shifted. My aim was to distill the complexity of the scenes in a way that would allow them to be comprehended in a single glance. The definitive wash drawing of the maquettes with the nude wax figures, on my engraving table throughout the laborious execution of the plates, reminded me to make the details take their proper place in relation to the whole.

With the composition established, I began to consider the particulars of setting and character that would determine my narrative. I drew interiors of my friends' homes in Cranston, Rhode Island. A nice manager at Design Within Reach let me draw her wares for several days. I did Internet research on many products that appear in the various rooms and purchased most of the clothes and all of the shoes seen in the finished work. Most essentially, I studied every person I saw, looking for the perfect outfits, faces, body types, and gestures that would serve to flesh out the characters developing in my studio.

A final line drawing on clear acetate of the figures and setting was created to transfer the image to the copper plate. The master outline-transparency was used to expose a photosensitive lithography plate, printed in pale gray on hot-pressed watercolor paper. The printed outline formed the basis of a definitive tonal study, encompassing all the details while retaining the essential structure of the drawing from the maquette. To understand the individual bodies in anticipation of casting the cloth, I drew the wax figures again as if they were living persons. More studies focused on understanding the lighting, and the clothing in relation to actual garments purchased.

Elaborate preliminary work allows me to focus on the invention required on the copper plate, as the burin carves each line. The linear syntax of my engravings is based on a close study (many sessions in the print study room at the Museum of Fine Arts in Boston) of the work of seventeenth-century French engraver Claude Mellan, who perfected a method of describing form solely through parallel swelling lines, without crosshatching. I purchased several prints by the master and worked on the plates nearby. The direct presence of these great engravings challenged and energized me. I wanted to see how far I could push the engraved line, and with each plate the lines became bigger and farther apart. The abstract qualities of my linear system were emphasized on close viewing, while the image resolved optically into representational clarity at a considerable distance.

My understanding of my subject grew throughout the six-year process. I often thought of a phrase, the "inevitable eclecticism of our world today," used by Leslie Cheek in 1963 regarding John Koch's work. My eclecticism embodies more than is implied by a home with too much Design Within Reach furniture, Sub-Zero appliances, and 1980s decorative arts, all layered onto a finely crafted building from the teens of the twentieth century. It speaks to current definitions of home, family, and standards of interpersonal interaction. This eclecticism is as much about the characters and the way they negotiate the contemporary world as it is about material surfaces.

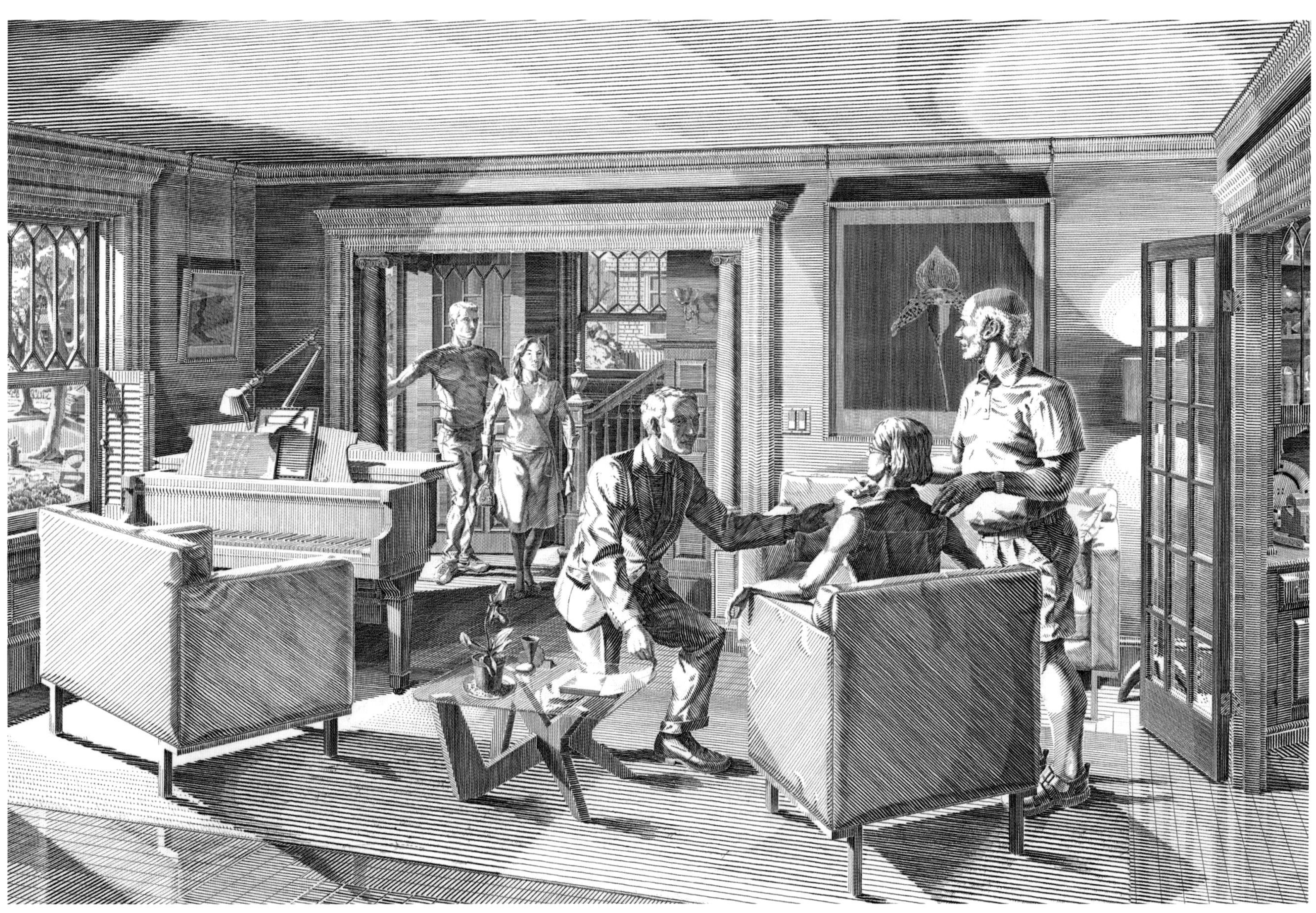

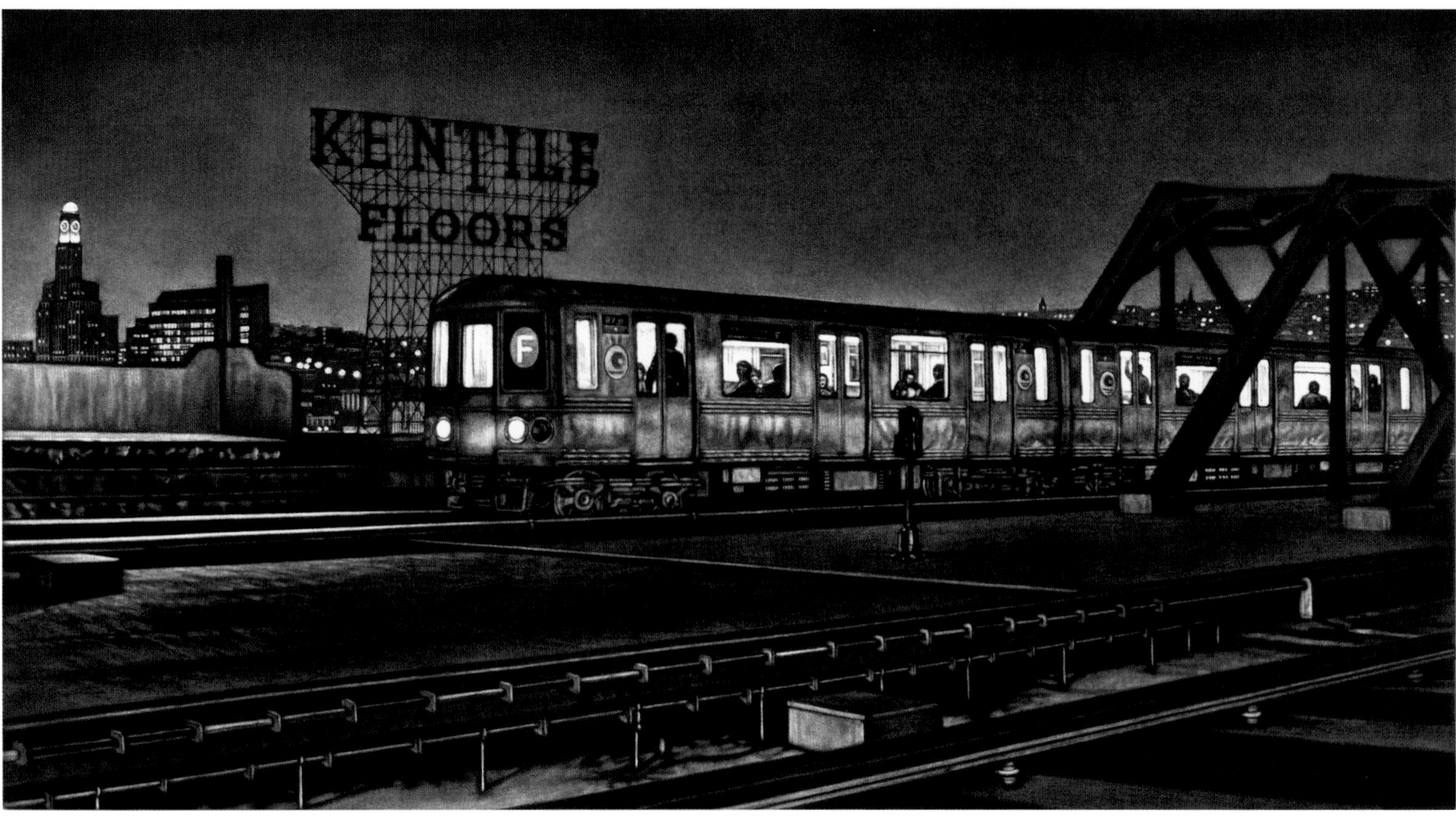

FREDERICK MERSHIMER

My subject matter explores the mystery of New York City at night, a magical place of escape and reinvention, but I also relate to its shadows. When I moved to New York City in the 1980s my mother had just died, and the AIDS epidemic was just beginning. I try to say something about the city's imposing environment, adventure and risk, and its darker undertones which mezzotint's "noir" character captures so well. Light and shadow can be subtly expressive; danger lurks in the sunshine, and in the darkness there is hope. I was initially drawn to the slow, direct, and laborious mezzotint process because it echoed the way I approached drawing, which I'd studied along with painting at Carnegie Mellon University. My artistic influences include an idiosyncratic group of artists who have deeply personal visions—Rockwell Kent, Elie Nadelman, Ferdinand Hodler, and Édouard Vuillard—as well as comic books and old movies.

Mezzotint engraving is a relatively obscure form of printmaking that creates dramatic chiaroscuro, with white highlights emerging out of rich velvety dark tones. Italian for "halftone," mezzotint was a seventeenth-century improvement on engraving's tonal crosshatched lines because it can produce an even gradation of tones. Known as the "black manner," its unique process entails working from black to white. An initial "roughing up" of the copper plate with a rocker tool forms a textured field that prints as flat black. Lighter gray passages and white highlights are created by slowly erasing the texture with a burnisher. Mezzotint's challenging nature makes it less popular than other kinds of printmaking. It takes weeks to ground a plate with a rocker; the expression "off your rocker" dates from child labor of Victorian London's publishing industry, when children became human metronomes, rocking the plates until the tedium drove them to act out.

Copper is a difficult material to change, so I do a lot of preparatory drawings before I touch the plate. They start with a light hand and very hard lead, slowly laying very light silvery tones on the paper, gradually working with a heavier hand and softer pencils to evolve darker tones. The burnishing tool works like a pencil in reverse; the harder I bear down in mezzotint, the lighter the tones become. Working on a plate is also like relief sculpture in that developing the image means shaving away part of the plate. A finished plate is like the surface of a coin with the white areas being the lowest point. Since mezzotint is a subtractive process, I err on the side of making the plate print darker, since I can always lighten the image by reducing the textured ground. Printing a mezzotint is difficult since the white highlights are the lowest point in the plate, which tend to pool with ink. Care must be taken when printing because the copper burrs can wear down if the plate is proofed (printed) too often before being steel faced for editioning. Working in this painstaking medium finds its rewards in the rich blacks and sensual tones that cannot be equaled in any other type of intaglio process.

My work is full of details that I see as puzzle pieces to arrange and orchestrate: information can be removed, perspective altered, and lighting, shadows, and details manipulated to choreograph, distill, and conjure a sense of place. Originally I was a purist and worked strictly from drawings on location, but now I take photographs for reference material. On-site drawing is impractical due to inadequate lighting at night, unsafe locations, and inclement weather. Photos let me capture more information, but I am careful not to let their details control my vision. The figures in my work were initially monumental statues, such as the ones on Grand Central Terminal, but eventually actual-size humans appeared. They create a sense of scale for the architecture, add a narrative element, and capture the energy and experience of New York as a beehive.

My ability to edit and construct an image was greatly facilitated when friends dragged me into the computer age. Previously I had used tracing paper (because the image prints in reverse) to collage elements, taking figures from one drawing and positioning them into another setting, but drawings and reference materials are manipulated more easily with Photoshop. I also discovered that the "level" feature in Photoshop can make virtual proofs, saving the fragile plate from extra printing. Though the digital proof is not exact, it gives me a sense of what to expect, and when I do pull a proof I can digitally lighten passages to preview how they'll appear. If I am unsure whether to lighten the foreground or the background, I can see both options before touching the plate.

Making art has always been a way for me to communicate and find order in the world. I let a central theme or mood lead my process, and occasionally it comes together exactly as I planned. More often the piece has a life of its own, and I have to be open to going on a journey to see how to resolve it. When I pull a print, I have a three-day rule: no changes until I have lived with it. I like to leave the proof near my bed so it will be the first thing I see. In that foggy moment of morning, I can have a clear vision of what is working and what is not. Once I know the composition is balanced in every way, the work is done.

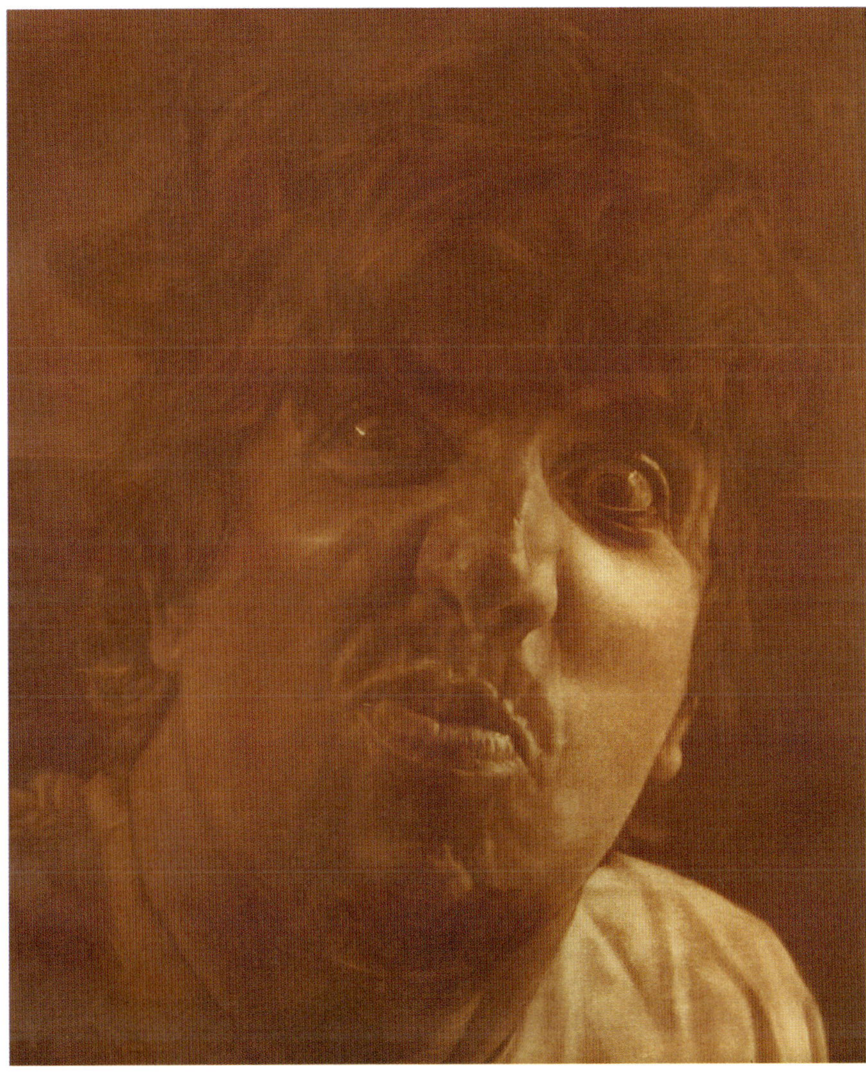

Nate Gaefcke
Rubbernecking, 2012
Mezzotint
17 x 15 inches

(opposite)
Frederick Mershimer
Manhattan Bound,
2006
Mezzotint
6.5 x 11.75 inches

A BRIEF HISTORY OF TRADITIONAL PAINTING TECHNIQUES: FRESCO, TEMPERA, AND OIL PAINTING

LISA BARTOLOZZI

IN THE WORLD OF PAINTING TODAY, one can rapidly alter images through digital media, spread biological organisms that will grow across a canvas, or fill a painted surface with a thousand handprints. One can also explore the rich history of painting techniques. New technical books join the numerous treatises written, and anecdotes recorded, about materials and the many ways artists have used them. At times incomplete, purposely cryptic, obsolete, or written by well-intentioned but misinformed observers, historical terms and phrases have meanings that may alter over time and through translation. But whether applied to a surface in a cave, a palace ceiling, or the white walls of a gallery installation, traditional Western painting methods can be broken into categories (and sometimes combinations) of water- or oil-based, and of direct, indirect, or mixed technique.

Today, painting can be a very spontaneous process, but concept and image traditionally required material preparation, design planning, and research. As described by Italian Renaissance writers like Cennino Cennini (1370–1440) and Giorgio Vasari (1511–1574), research sketches (*schizzi;* also *pensieri,* "thoughts") in metal point, charcoal, graphite, or ink were formalized into a composition, or design (*disegno*). Drawings "heightened with white" with darker marks for shade and white for highlights functioned as presentation drawings for a patron's approval. Leonardo da Vinci (1452–1519) was one of the first to use sticks of charcoal, whose deep range of value and blending nature create soft tonal transitions, as in his his graceful *sfumato* ("smokiness").

Italian Renaissance *alla prima* ("at the first") exemplifies a usually one-session direct painting. Today the term indicates general spontaneity, but traditionally any painting's design, drawing, surface, ground, and palette were prepared before brush dipped into paint. Mixing pigments on the palette and applying paint with the appropriate tool, the artist worked wet paint onto the ground, and "wet-into-wet" paint. Indirect painting instead involves a layering technique where the final color is a product of multiple paint layers that create a range of complex color effects. Underlayers may include the ground treatment, "underdrawing" (monochrome underpainting), "dead coloring" (first painting), local coloring, form building (second painting), with the "final" painting consisting of accents, touch-ups, and glazing. The layering of multiple colors, as body colors (opaque), translucent veils or as glazes (transparent layers), can create degrees of enhancing or muting a final new color. Each layer can be visually apparent or a presence only felt with the eye.

Prior to the invention of the oil painting method, European paintings were mostly water based. The fresco technique of brushing limewater pastes made of mineral pigments onto a freshly laid layer of white lime plaster thrived from antiquity through eighteenth-century Europe. Fresco is durable; the sophisticated palette of Hellenistic and Pompeian wall frescoes are still evident. Cennini's *Il libro dell' Arte*[1] explained the rigorous training Italian Renaissance *buon fresco* required, as demonstrated by his teacher Giotto di Bondone (1267–1337), and its preparation and method. The design's outline was transferred to the wall through a "squaring up" method based on a proportional grid, or using a to-scale *cartone* ("cartoon," large paper) drawing. "Pounce bags" held colored powders that sifted through pierced holes along the drawing's contours, tracing the design. A stone or plaster wall would be prepared with a rough coat of lime and sand, the design painted onto this dried layer, *arriccio,* in red earth pigment. Sections of wet plaster, *intonaco,* were painted while wet. Artists might use a cartoon transfer as a guide, incising the outlines into the wet layer with a stylus. Pastes of mineral pigments were mixed in limewater, the paint's "vehicle," with the knowledge that they would appear differently in value after dry, chemically bonded to the plaster wall. Precision was essential because it was difficult to correct

(opposite)
Lisa Bartolozzi
Caught, 2005
Oil on panel
14.5 x 17 inches

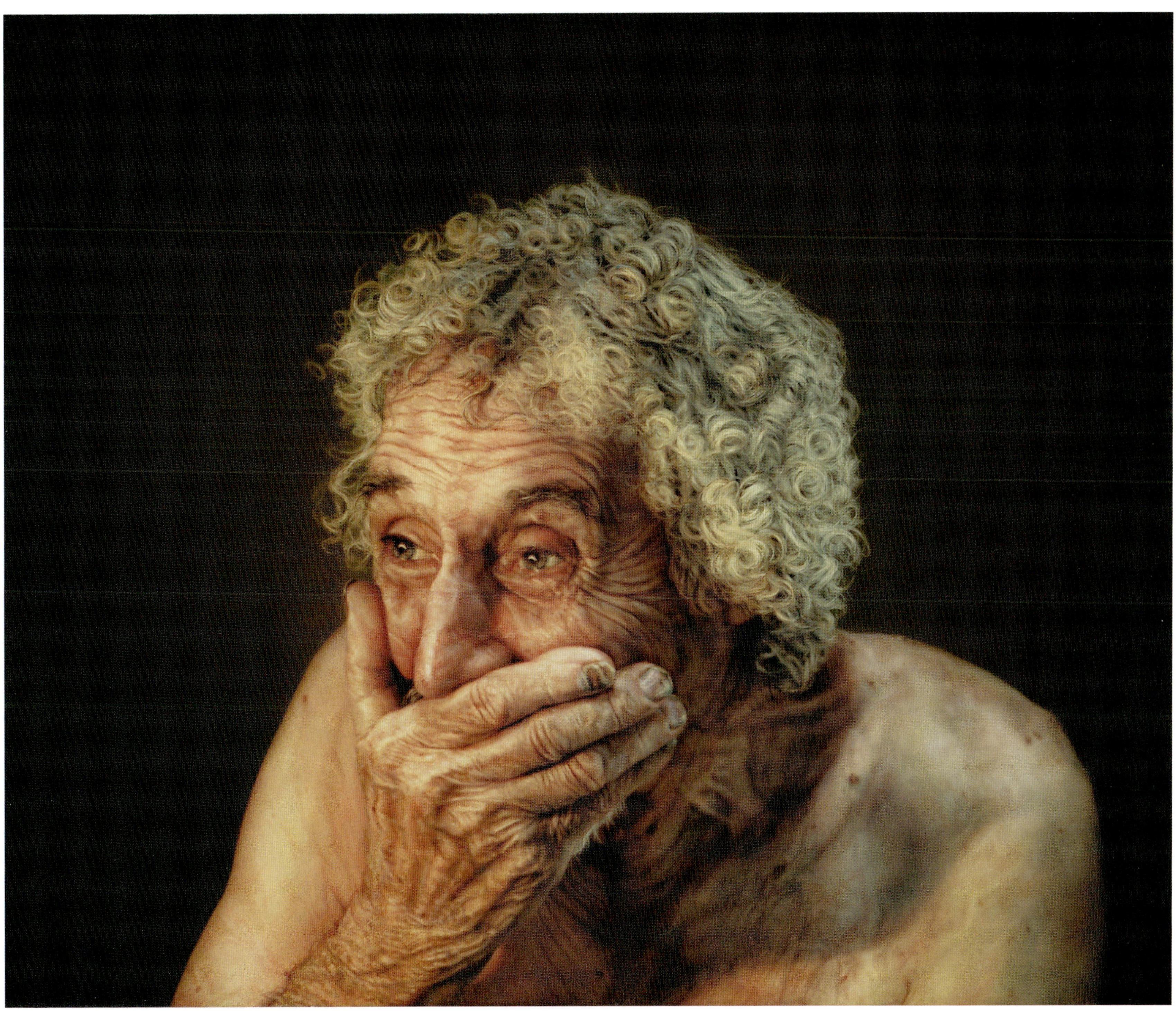

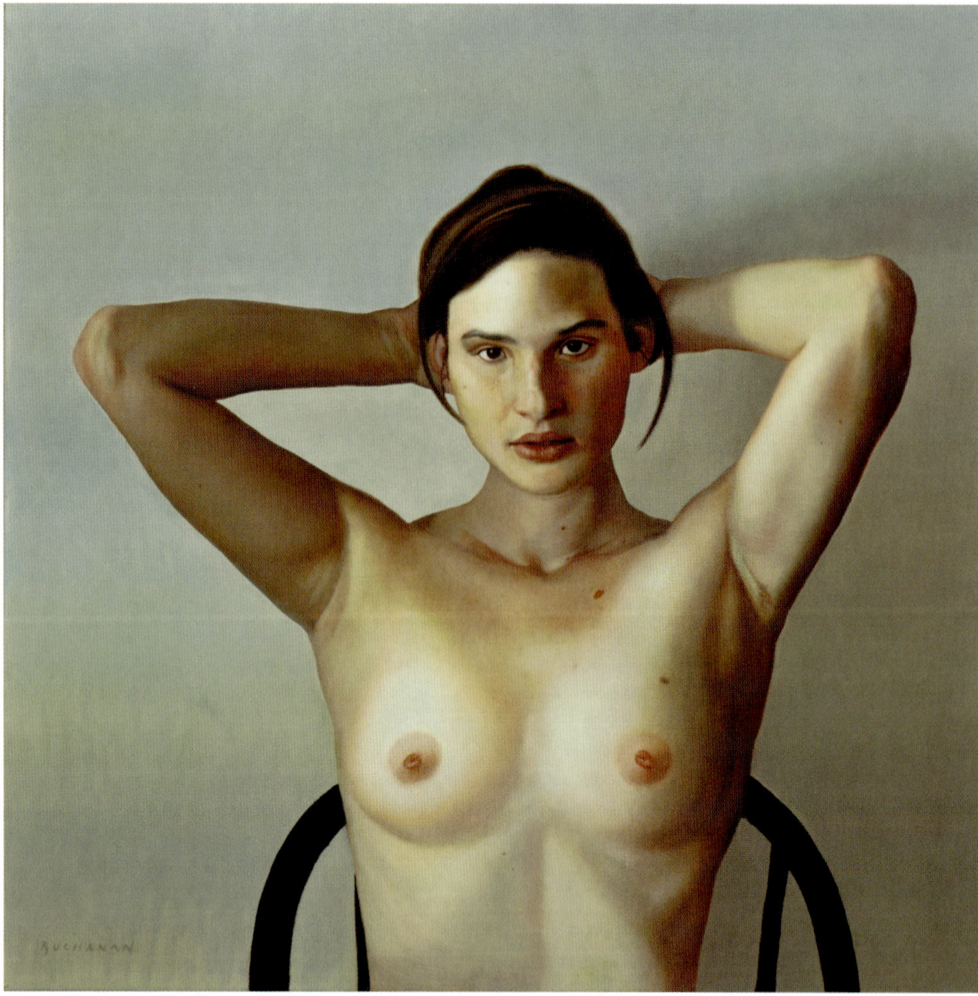

Noah Buchanan
Summer, 2012
Oil on linen
23 x 23 inches

(opposite)
Melanie Vote
In Tub, 2006
Oil on panel
50 x 35 inches

mistakes without having to remove the embedded day's work and start all over again.

The virtuosic fresco technique of Michelangelo Buonarotti (1475–1564) is evident in the clarity of form and the purity of color in the Sistine Chapel. The damage to Leonardo's *Last Supper*, on the other hand, was due to his unconventional approach with *fresco secco* ("dry"), a technique used to overpaint, correct, or retouch a dried fresco or embellish with gold leaf and gilding. *Fresco secco* and another method popular in the mid-sixteenth century, *mezzo* ("half") *fresco*,[2] were susceptible to peeling and flaking. Leonardo also used various types of experimental "binders" (the fluid that holds the pigment) on the dried *intonaco*. The enduring frescoes of the Renaissance assisted in the rediscovery of sound methods, as seen in mural works of the Nazarene painters of the nineteenth century, and American and Mexican artists in the twentieth century.

Throughout the Middle Ages and High Renaissance, the practice of decorating large wooden storage trunks, *cassones*, with scenic paintings established methods for the preparation of supports that would be adapted to easel ("off the wall") painting. A wood surface was first "sized" with animal skin glue or gelatin, then layers of a warmed liquid made with glue, white pigment, and *gesso* (gypsum) were applied to protect the wood from the paint and the painting from the wood. Gesso comprised differing grades of natural chalk (calcium carbonate) from deposits of limestone or dolomite. The white surface was polished to a smooth sheen with a stone or animal tooth. Wooden supports were used for large multipaneled paintings (polyptychs, "many folds," triptychs, "three folds," etc.) that fitted into ornamental frames, and for more portable *ancona* panels. Planks of wood were joined and fastened with a glue of lime and cheese, their backs "cradled" to prevent warping or splitting, wood battens laid across the grain in a flexible

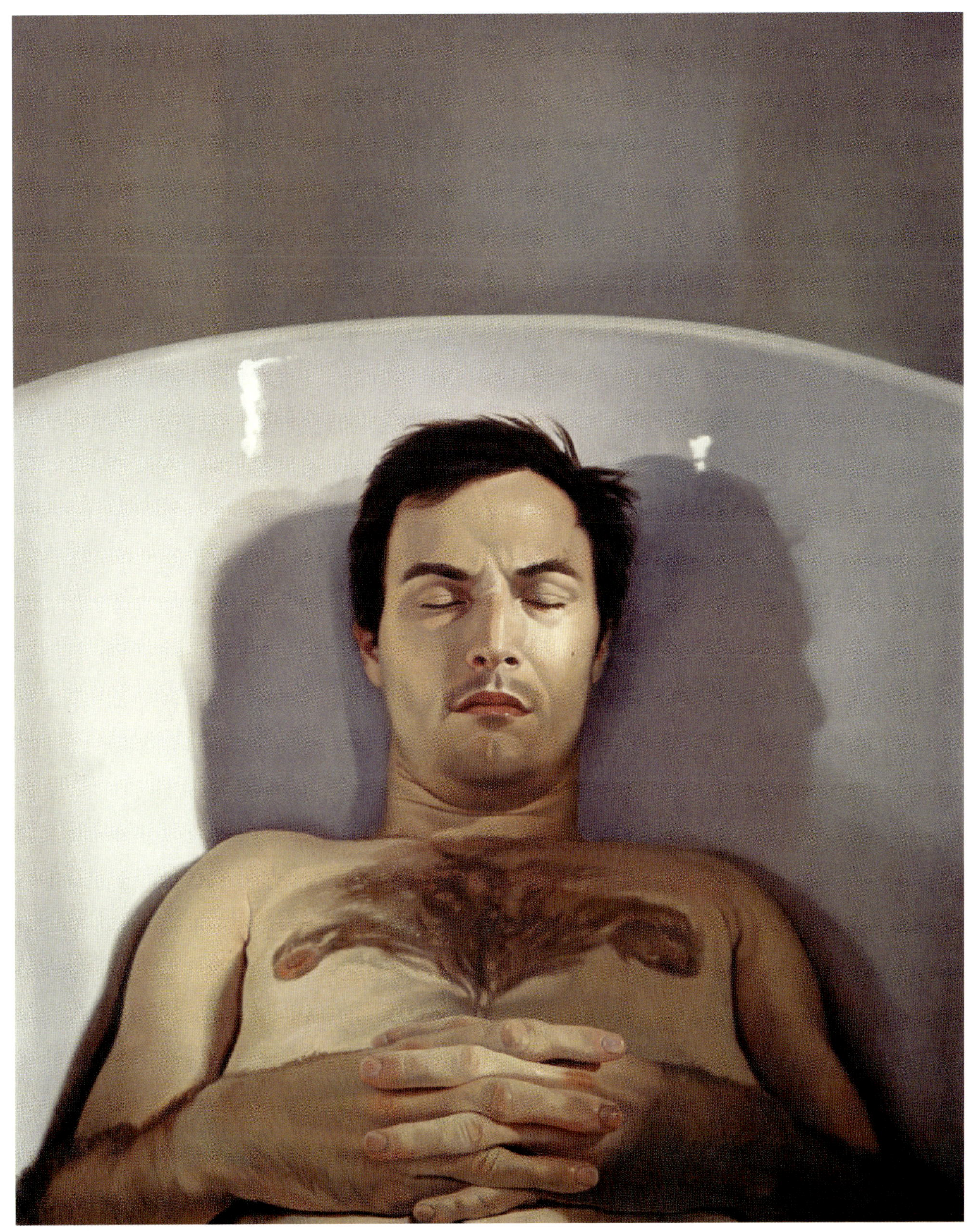

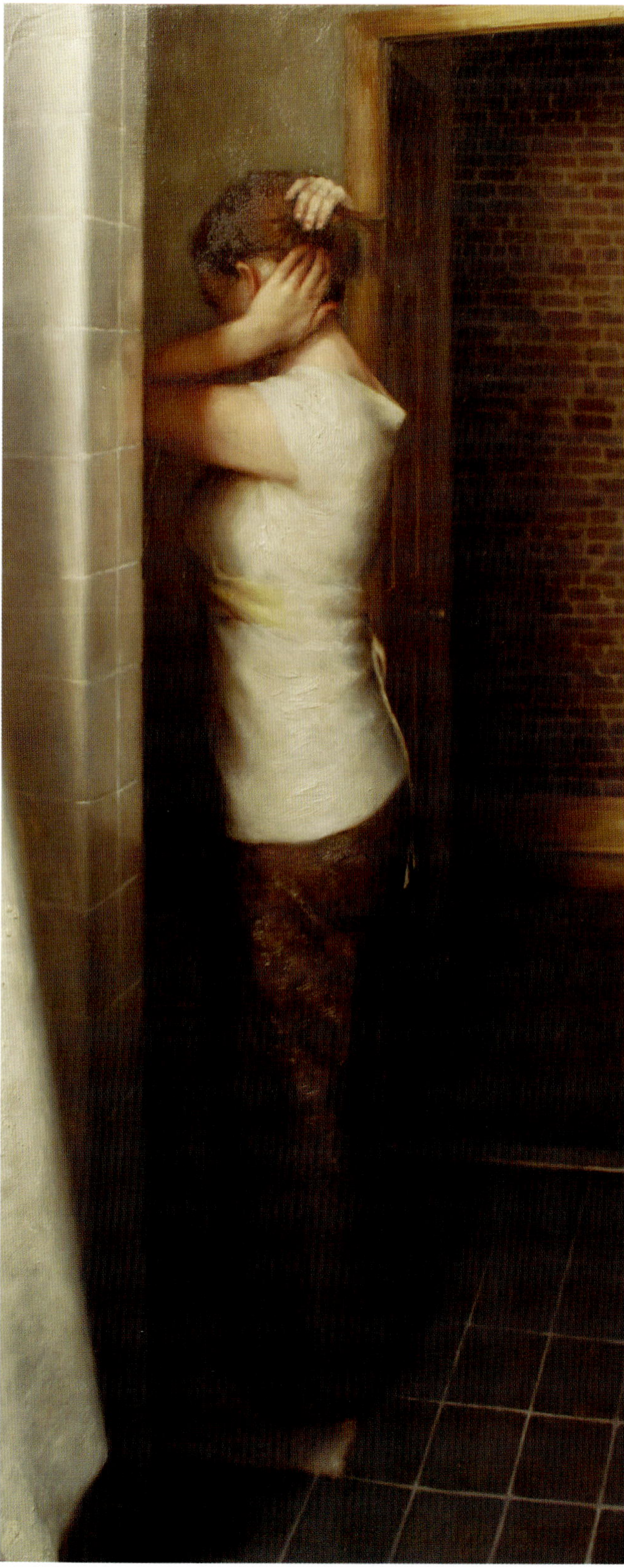

interlocking fashion. "Channel edges," slats placed on the top and bottom of thin panels, can be seen in Maarten van Heemskerck's *Saint Luke Painting the Virgin* (1553).

The indirect painting method of classical egg tempera used for smaller panels was as significant as fresco in the early Renaissance. Tempera refers to any water-based paint binder that creates an opalescent quality within a dried paint layer.[3] Like fresco, egg tempera painting did not lend itself to correction. The design, including any areas for gold leafing, and the anticipation of final color values, were carefully planned. (Gold leaf in religious works of art added precious value and reflective, mysterious effects.) Egg tempera pigments were ground into fine pastes, with water and wine or vinegar as wetting agents or preservatives. A natural emulsifier, the egg created a quick drying durable film on the absorbent gesso ground. Pigment pastes were premixed into a range of color values, tempered with a binder of egg yolk and water into a creamy consistency, and thinned with water for better handling. Small glass vessels, saucers, shells, or animal horns were used for storing mineral and organic pigments.[4] Egg tempera creates a semi-opaque film, even with opaque pigments. For a greater range of tone, color was placed over a fully rendered underdrawing in ink or metal point. Prior to adding full color, the underdrawing was reinforced with an underpainting in neutral gray hues, often a mixture of black, white, and yellow ochre called *verdaccio*. *Terre verte* ("green earth") was often used as underpainting for areas of flesh tone, evident in Sienese paintings like *The Maestà* (1308–11), Duccio di Buoninsegna's masterpiece. Artists worked separate areas, often back to front, overlapping forms for spatial effect.

Egg tempera dries quickly, so blending effects were achieved by multiple, successive brushstrokes in carefully premixed tonal ranges. Knowledge of the refractive index (the range of pigments' transparency to opacity) helped organize multiple layers as forms built up into beautiful clear hues. Glazes of transparent pigment washes intensified or toned down (using complements) body color. The egg binder in tempera doesn't yellow, so color harmony lasts, as in Sandro Botticelli's egg tempera masterpiece, *The Birth of Venus* (1486), a large canvas with gold accents. After the publication of a new twentieth-century Cennini translation, there was a resurgence of interest in egg tempera, evident in the work of George Tooker and Andrew Wyeth.

The transition from egg to oil paint progressed in an uneven manner during the Renaissance throughout Europe, following the development of egg-oil emulsion painting, *tempera grassa* or 'fat.' When egg was emulsified with a drying oil, sometimes with an added balsam or resin, the additional fat created a creamier consistency, facilitating blending. Incompatible pigments, like copper-resinate green, had previously been isolated in an oil-resin binder, applied as a separate glaze over an area of a dried tempera painting. Resins, natural extracts from various trees including the hard fossilized resins of copal and amber, oleo-resins or balsams, and the soft resins of sandarac, mastic, and damar, were also used as "final varnishes" to protect finished tempera and mixed technique paintings. Experimentations with treated oils and varnishes enhanced a tempera painting with a warm tint, but

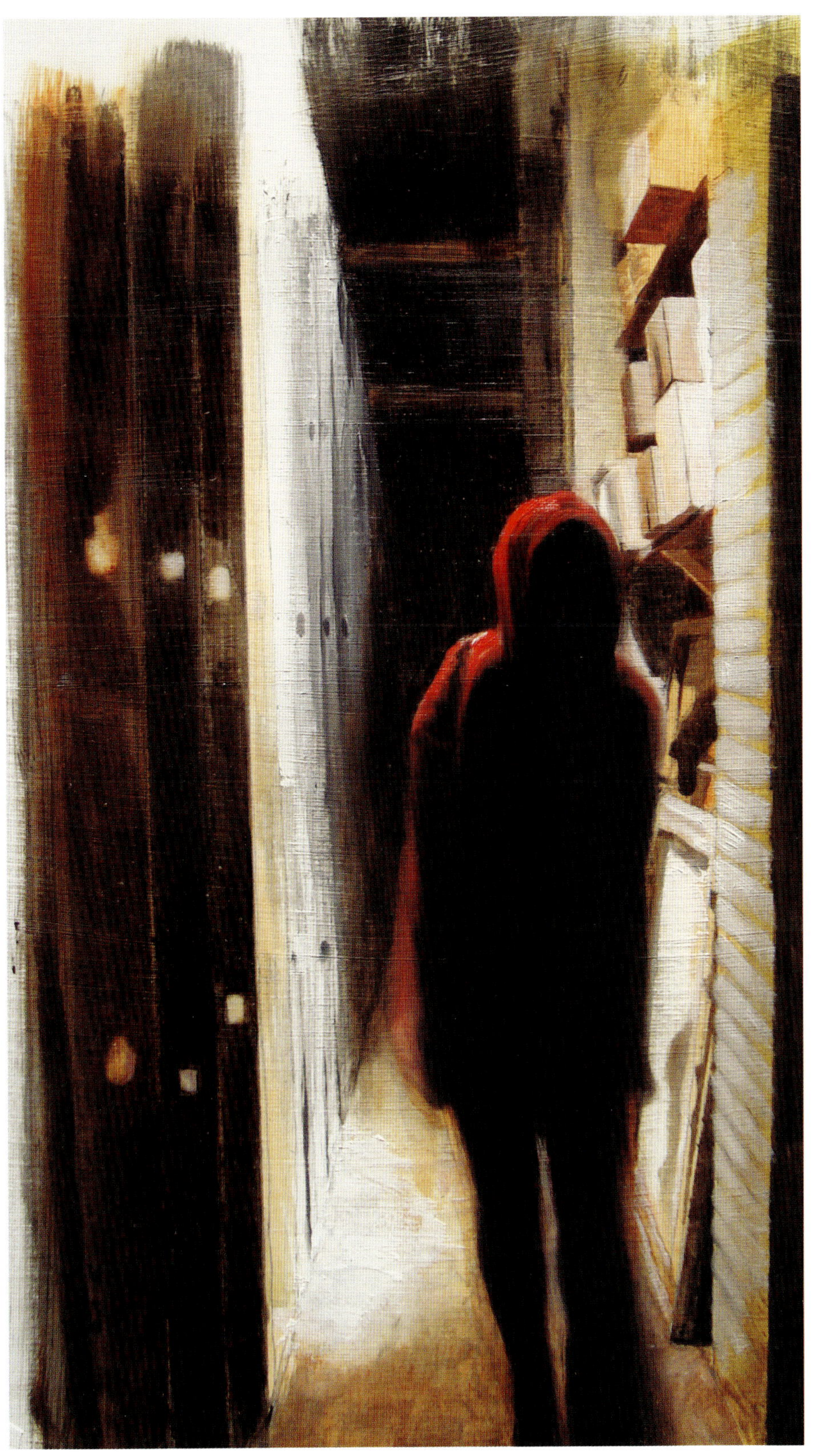

Tun Myaing
Hallway Study 1,
2010
Acrylic, oil on
paper
12 x 7 inches

(opposite)
Samuel Eversen
Morning, 2007
Oil on linen
30 x 12 inches

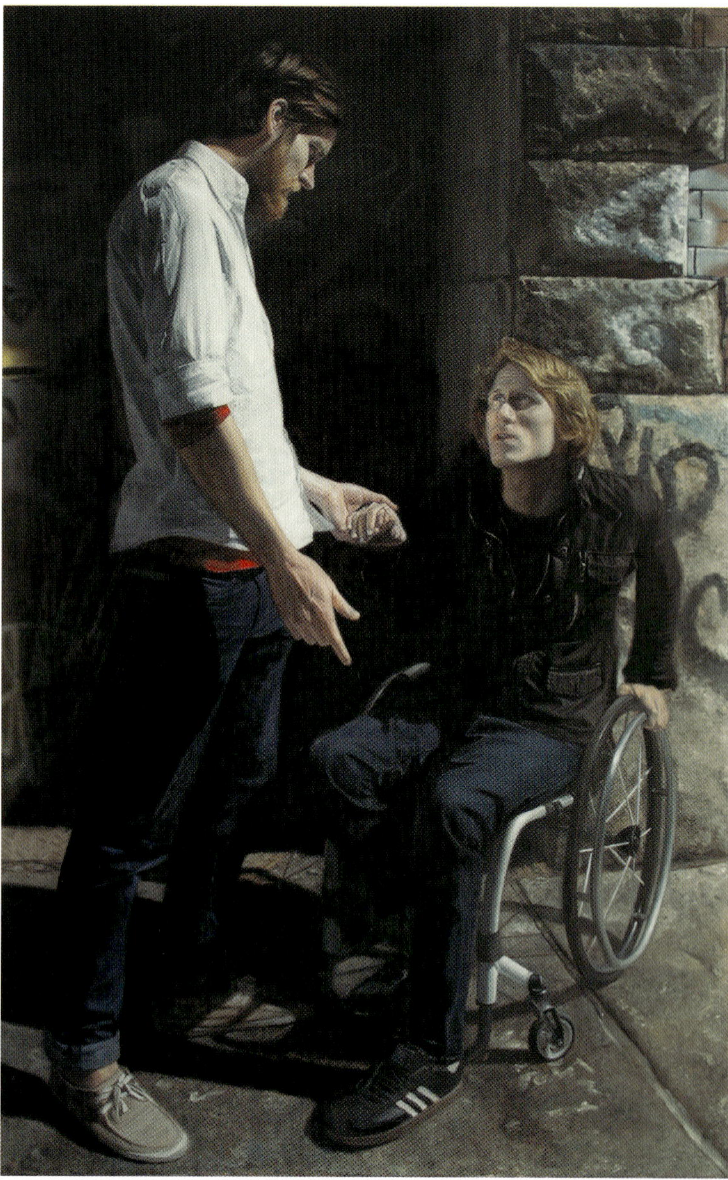

Adam Cross
Healing of a Paralytic, 2013
Oil on canvas
68 x 42 inches

(opposite)
Elisabeth Miller
Red Shoes, 2012
Oil on linen
84 x 40 inches

varnishing a finished egg tempera painting caused an uneven saturation of color if not properly tempered. Renaissance artists experimented with mixed techniques, working with layers of different mediums, or using indirect and direct methods within the same painting.[5] In *The Madonna of Mercy* (or *Misericordia*, c. 1460) Piero della Francesca used both egg tempera and oil paint on an absorbent gesso ground, whose high absorbency did not work well for oil areas, which have degraded.[6] Due to such structural problems, painters began to use an isolating layer, imprimatura, in between mediums to lessen the ground's absorbency, often a thin coating of a drying oil with or without resin.

In the High Renaissance the more versatile and flexible oil paint became popular. Jan van Eyck (1395–1441) of the earlier Northern Renaissance is credited with its first systematic use. Pigments, organic and mineral, have unique chemical and physical properties in oil binders: their absorption rate of oil, film quality, lightfastness, refractive index, covering ability, and drying rate. Layers of mixed pigment had to be logically structured, working the leanest and fastest-drying pigments below the layers of fatter and slower-drying pigments. This "lean-to-fat" principle kept the paint layers from cracking and peeling over time. Hand-grinding pigments with a drying oil created a malleable and slow-drying paint with varying effects, depending on the inherent properties of pigments, additives like resins and balsams, and the oil's treatment (processing). The drying oils of plant and nut extracts, such as linseed, walnut, and safflower, harden into solid films with diverse flexibility and strength. How they behaved when mixed with pigments depended on their processing from raw material: washed and filtered (cold pressed) or bleached and sun-thickened; heated in containers with oxygen (blown oil) or without it (stand oil, pale straw); or boiled with drying agents of lead (black oil) and mastic varnish (meglip). Each treatment affected the oil's properties—its drying rate, glossiness, viscosity, and whether it flattens in appearance. (All drying oils harden into films that eventually darken, becoming more yellow and brittle with age.) Ground paint was typically stored in small animal bladders, and for painting was placed on small wooden tablets (palettes) with handles or thumbholes.

During the period of transition from tempera to oil, as technical information spread, different regions and artists devised their own paint recipes and variations in process. The early work of Titian (Tiziano Vecelli, 1485–1576) show the mixed technique of an egg oil emulsion underpainting over an earth-tone ground on canvas. The growing use of a canvas support in oil painting added a textural element, allowing for the brushstroke and nibs of the textile to create visual interest and texture, such as "broken color" or "scumbles." As artists moved to oil from egg as a binder, the resulting paint needed a solvent such as turpentine as a vehicle. Hand-grinding made paint "longer" (more fluid and slower drying), which made new paint application techniques possible. Metal knives could mix paint on the palette, scrape away wet passages, or add and mix paint on the surface of a work. Thick impasto passages could catch the light and create well-placed accents for credible illusions of reality. "Feathering" with a brush (artist-made brushes from a variety of animal furs, hog, squirrel, and red sable), or reworking texture added to the sensual feeling of a painting. Painting "amendments," such as marble dust and ground glass, created special effects, seen in the richly bodied and glowing transparent oil colors and opaque impastos of Diego Velázquez's (1599–1660) or Rembrandt van Rijn's (1606–1669) paintings.

Different treatments for the traditionally white ground layer influenced the sequence of wet paint over dried layers in the indirect method. Grounds might be colored, toned, or glazed, with knife, brush, or rag. Van Eyck used brilliant white grounds, and linear metal point and/or ink underdrawings covered with a softly blended *grisaille* (gray tonal underpainting). This lay below rich, transparent glazes, light penetrating through them and reflected back to the eye. Gesso grounds with a lightly colored *imprimatura* in the Italian Renaissance began with careful *disegni* of earth-tone grisailles, while the later Venetian and Spanish schools used darker grounds. Light was established by adding semi-opaque *velaturas* ("soft veils") over the dark ground, and the buildup of dense layers of opaque, white underpainting. The ground's color established areas of shadow, influencing overall color harmony. Working through numerous glazes, Titian created complex, nuanced color, sometimes from a simple palette of black, white, red, and yellow ochre. As pigments in oil paint turn more transparent with age, evidence of a darker ground may diminish the overall color harmony, as can be seen in some works of Nicolas Poussin (1594–1665). In the eighteenth century, double grounds, separate layers of contrasting warm transparent colors and cool opaque grays, can be seen in backgrounds and incomplete areas of works by Jacques-Louis David (1748–1825).

Although their main purpose was to assist in planning the design and color scheme of an indirect painting, small directly painted oils by artists like Titian or Peter Paul Rubens (1577–1640) appear to the modern eye as complete works of art. Color tones were mixed directly on the palette and applied, often in a single layer and more gestural style in a *bozzetto*, a value composition painted with earth tones and white, or in a *modello, a* painting developed further in color and detail.[7] The direct method of *fa presto* ("make quickly") can be seen in Luca Giordano's (1634–1705) single-layer compositions of opaque and semi-opaque paint passages in varying thicknesses that interact with the middle-toned, warm ground.

Classic *au premier coup* ('at the first stroke') painting, as in the works of the seventeenth-century Rubens and Frans Hals (1580–1666) and the eighteenth-century Rococo Jean Honoré Fragonard (1732–1806), can combine direct and indirect methods.[8] Rubens's large, prolific workshop exemplifies an efficient process for complex, well-planned, commissioned works. Along with *bozzetti* and *modelli*, studies used by workshop assistants in the development of a final work, Rubens executed numerous studies from life. In these a swirling *imprimatura* of a light-toned ochre-to-gray glaze covered the white ground, the composition defined in linear marks and transparent layers of warm shadows. Wet-over-dry layers alternated between warm and cool palettes and transparent and opaque pigments, allowing for a purity of tones,

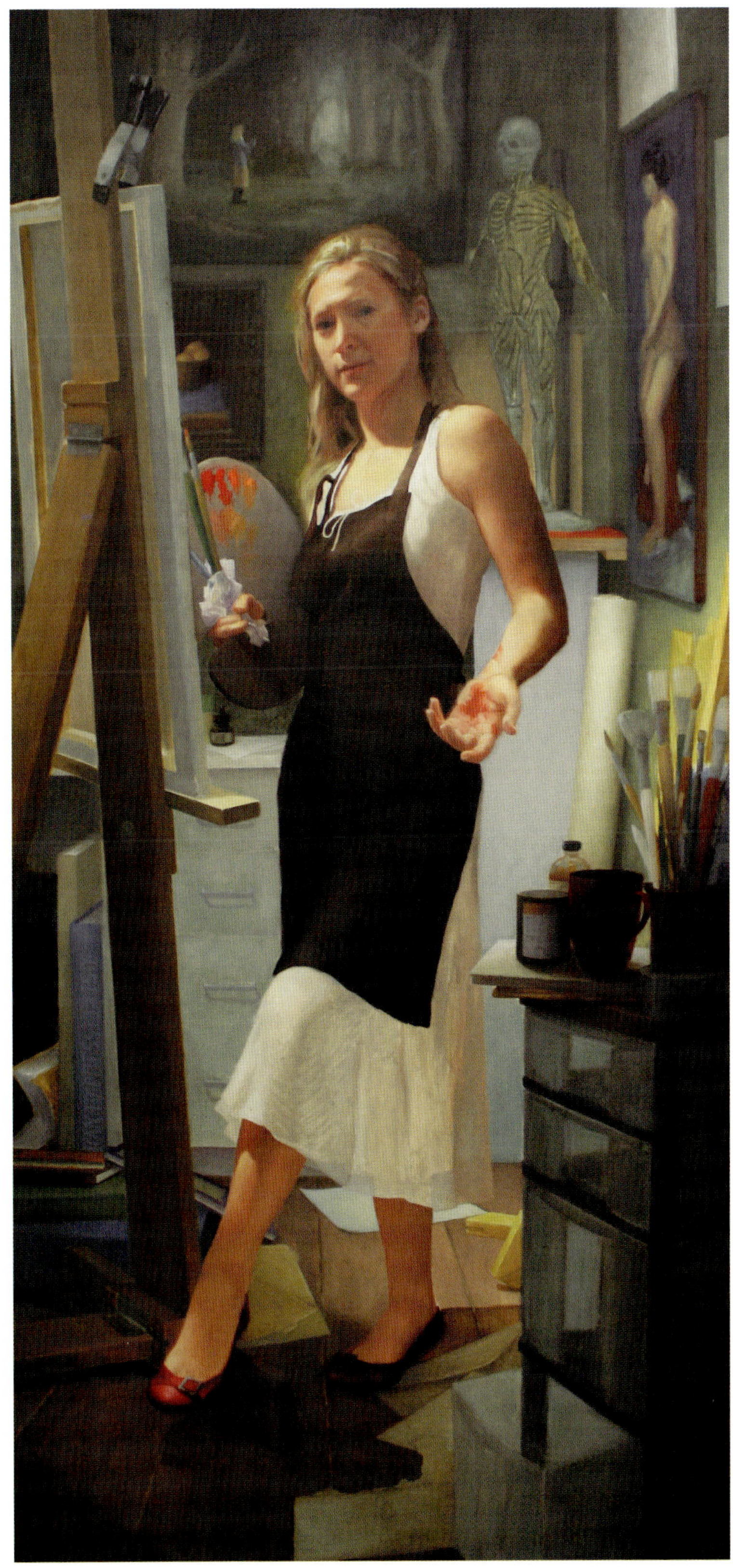

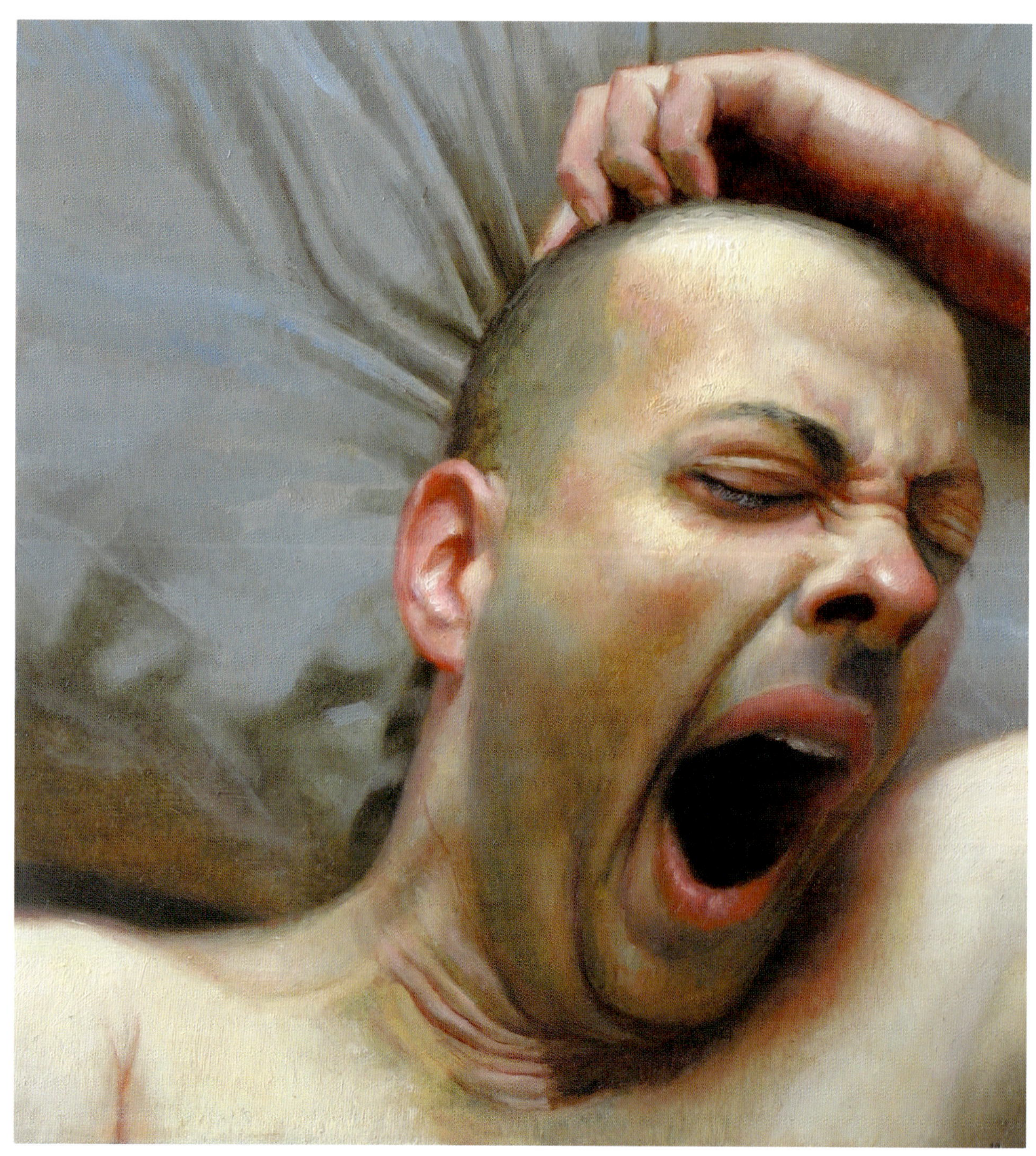

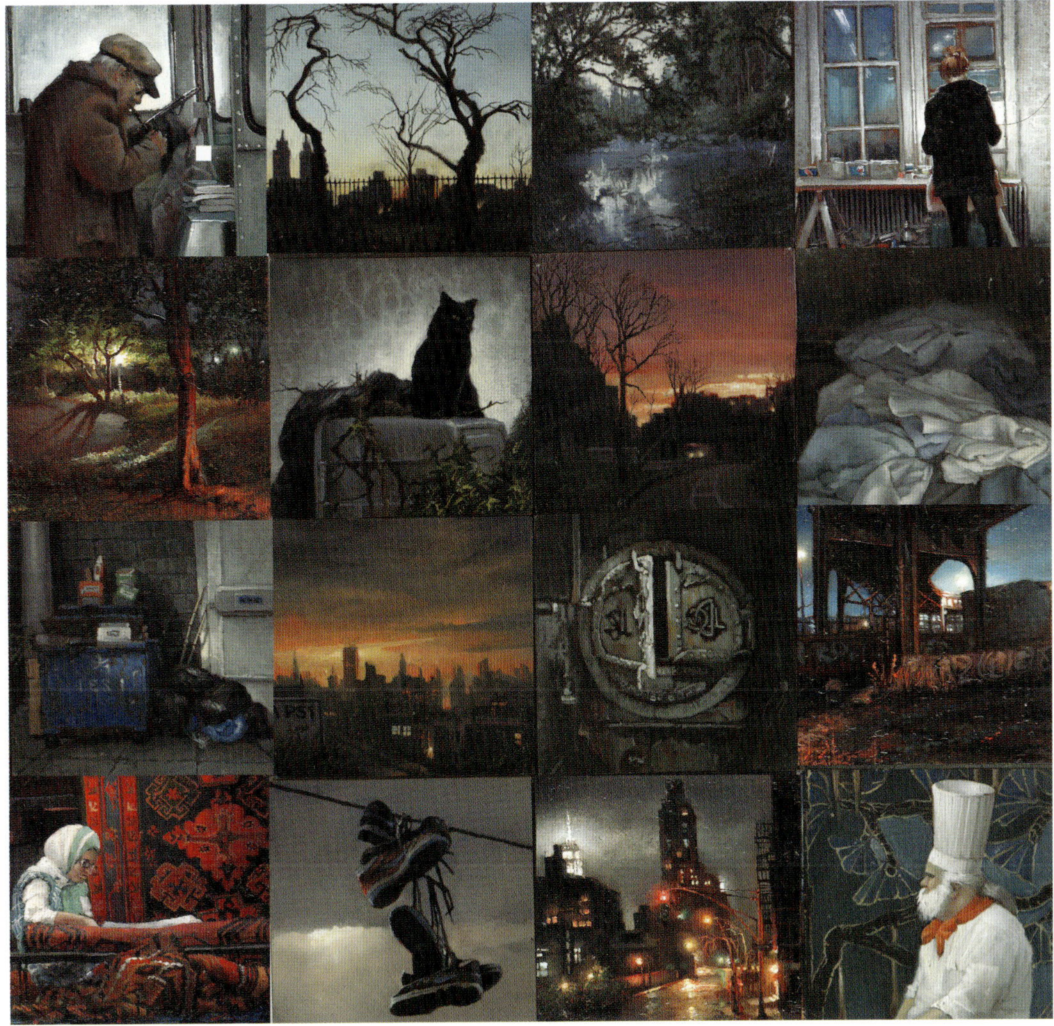

as paint passages did not directly mix together. Over this carefully prepared *doodvert* ("dead painting"), Rubens worked more directly, mixing tones for flesh areas, local colors, and reflected lights; final touch-ups were opaque, impasto accents and highlights, and fine veils of transparent hues.[9]

A more modern direct approach is evident in nineteenth-century Impressionist paintings. The Impressionist rejection of the multilayered, indirect painting processes of the French Academy resulted in wet-into-wet applications of paint on white grounds. The composition was developed in the act of capturing fleeting color and light with brushmarks that expressed the process.[10] The convenience of modern, commercially prepared oil paint stored in metal tubes would inspire experimental technique, as did new shapes of brushes. Traditionally brushes were "rounds" until shaped, manufactured metal ferrules became common for both soft hair and bristle.[11] Oil painting "mediums" were developed to change the standardized consistency of commercially prepared paint. Containing treated oils, resins, balsams, and driers, they modified the paint's handling, refractive index, texture, or drying time. The basic painting medium of turpentine (solvent) and a drying oil or "half-oil" made the paint longer, while cold wax pastes adding a dense opalescence "shortened" paint handling. Painting mediums from the past still hold great intrigue for artists hoping to find "secret formulas."

The studio practices and techniques, especially of the Renaissance and Baroque periods, continue to offer a rich variety of both reliable and experimental stylizations that contemporary artists combine with newer innovations in original ways. Mining the rich and fascinating world of historical materials and tools creates a shared sense of craftsmanship, connecting artists through time and uniting us in purpose.

Dina Brodsky
Jersey City, 2011
Oil on mylar on plexiglass
8 x 8 inches

(opposite)
Christian Fagerlund
Untitled, 2005
Oil on panel
5.5 x 5 inches

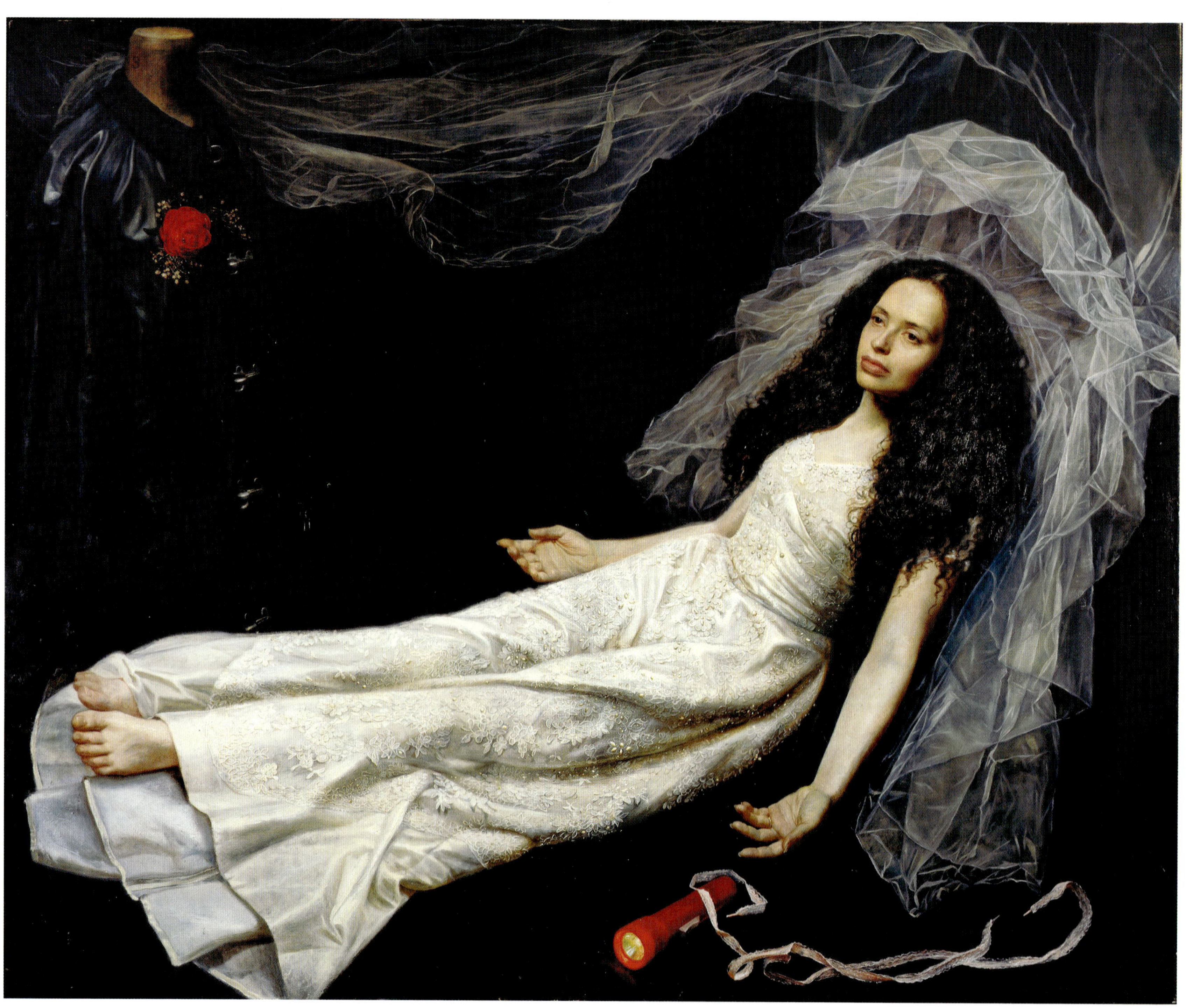

STEVEN ASSAEL

Painting the figure and narrative was not in high regard in college in the late 1970s, and anyone interested in the Old Masters and craftsmanship was considered conventional and retrograde. But what we rebel against we assimilate, and part of that methodology—an emphasis on the experience of process—influenced me. My habit of placing my palette onto the canvas comes from a teacher at Pratt, the Abstract Expressionist Joe Stapleton. He would make two paintings at once, one being his palette, the other his painting. Having colors right there in the image keeps me aware of flux and makes painting sensational—something to do with the play between conscious organization and subconscious response, which operates both conceptually and perceptually. I'm always aware of teetering equilibriums, symmetrical and asymmetrical relationships related to spatial parameters. Camus said, "Know your limits"; understanding the parameters of any medium lets one explore its possibilities, finding freedom within that framework. We can intimate universals within the confines and limitations of our perceptions, coupled with the finite rawness of materials and craft.

Every painting starts with an emotive urge or desire that may or may not be connected to a narrative idea. I'll have a sense of what I want, but am open to chance. I usually start with a visual, thematic idea—brides, for example—but once the narrative evolves, its subtleties are articulated as the painting develops. I allow the sitter's performance to interfere with my concept. I think of people posing as actors who reveal an outward formality and an inner history. Like a director, having a strong actor can steer the narrative in one direction over another. Moments embody the fullness of an experience; the advantage painting from life has is in the representation of what is expected or unexpected through the sequence of events. Chance cannot enter the process in this way using photographic reference. Photography can be helpful for general references, but for me it's all about how ideas are generated by memory, and the synthesis of experienced perceptions.

I've always kept a sketchbook, and because everything is in motion I tend to sketch quickly. Drawing trains memory and strengthens imagination by making experience tangible in the mind. My initial strategy is a kind of tempered planning, structured but still allowing for flexibility and change. I organize my composition from imagination, or based on ideas from my sketchbook and observations. Once I have a visual sense of placement, I grid the canvas, then draw in an underpainting with a color related to the overall color complexion. Without allowing for change, an overly prescriptive composition can deaden a painting's execution, like having too much bread before a main course.

I pay a lot of attention to texture, starting with how I prepare the canvas. I prime my canvas with rabbit-skin glue, then apply layers of lead white. It dries for several months, developing a lean surface that allows for a buildup of viscosity. I use various brands of paint, depending on what I need (viscosity, drying rate, etc.), such as Williamsburg, Old Holland, and Sennelier. My medium combines Venetian turpentine, stand oil, and a small amount of damar or mastic varnish. I think of all painting as direct painting, each act a prelude to the next, built on expectations and surprises of what's to come. I build thick and opaque layers in my lights and thin transparency in my shadows, sometimes allowing for ground to show through. Opacity projects toward the eye and transparency recedes away from the eye. When opacity builds up too much against a warm underpainting showing through transparent shadows, I might scrape it down using coarse sandpaper, a palette knife, or a razor blade. I want the painting surface to be seen as a remnant of process, and to evoke time—the feeling that what you see came from a previous experience. The excitement of the experience of painting is very important to me, and I want the viewer to feel it.

I paint on a colored ground because it enhances a feeling of dimension, and gives me something to react to. The dominant light will determine the imprimatura; if the light is cool I'll choose a warm ground and vice versa. Once I start with color, I clearly separate values as warm and cool. I start with shadow masses, considering value and temperature simultaneously. I don't think of color as identifiable as red or blue, but as light with temperature. Red can be cool depending on what's next to it; color is relative. I'll sometimes augment the drama of cool light and warm shadows with colored spotlights or gels. Light and color are powerful metaphors for illumination and revelation.

As a painting proceeds I refine the feeling of completeness, whole to parts, at every stage in proportion with color and value at once. I see everything together, but I would say a painting is never finished, only made sufficiently complete.

WADE SCHUMAN

My goal in painting is to put feeling into an object. I want to be able to leave a room, have someone else come into that room and look at the object and feel something. Hopefully that feeling has depth and resonance. That is the magic trick. Intellect and technique are part of it, but ultimately the goal is transference of feeling.

I have three basic systems for creating an image. They are not exclusive from each other but originate from different sources. One method is perceptual—observing objects or living things. To sit and look at length and then make a visual representation of that object can feel like an almost religious manifestation of conscious perception. The second approach consists of larger paintings or polyptychs that combine multiple systems of image making: perceptual, conceptual, and imagined. These images deal with issues of narrative or juxtaposition, somewhat like a novel to the short stories of the perceptually based work. They combine various sources, some photographic, some visualized, and some perceptual.

The third method of image making originates entirely from visualization—images created internally and then manifested as paintings. This work is different in origin than perceptually based work, but I want the veracity and depth of description perceptual sources offer. These internally created images are sometimes a cipher. I often need an investigative dialogue with the image to understand the root of why it is compelling me. I try to discover an underlying metaphoric language, and link that narrative to a larger artistic goal or concept.

I am working on a series of images on the concept of virtue. I am exploring the idea of virtue not from a traditional context, but thinking about what virtues we may hold in common—a meditation on what a virtue is. I have no set

(opposite)
Steven Assael
Bride I, 1993
Oil on canvas
60 x 72 inches

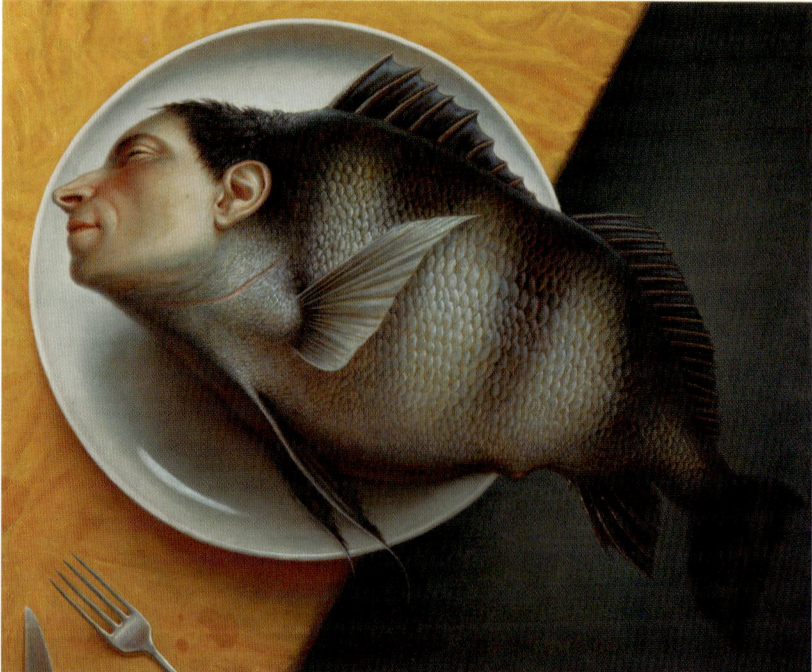

Wade Schuman
Virtue: Sacrifice,
2013
Oil on linen panel
25 x 30 inches

(opposite)
Angela Gram
Devolve, 2012
Oil on canvas
48 x 60 inches

preconceptions for these images. The first of the series is a fish with a man's head. The image came from a dream in which I saw a painting; I woke up and made a sketch of the image in a notebook. A year or so later I came upon the image and thought about it in regard to the series on virtue. Through sketches, I narrowed down the concept to a possible manifestation of the idea of self-sacrifice. The fish-man sits on a plate in a state of acceptance, willing to sacrifice himself literally. The plate rests precariously on the edge of a table and could fall at any moment. I wanted the image to be disquieting, and the creature to be supremely confident but also intensely vulnerable.

I wanted to construct the image in a palpable and concrete way. I brought in a friend and took photos, visited Chinatown and took photos of fish, and searched images of fish online. I did drawings using all these resources, trying to create a loose image that got to the essence of the feeling, gesture, and intention of the sketch from my head. I picked out a plate and a fish and found a taxidermist to mount the fish in position from my drawings. After he sent back the specimen, I made a prosthetic head out of Sculpey that slipped over the head of the fish. The final fish-man sculpture was a perceptual resource to re-create the image I'd visualized. This was important because tactile physicality is an essential part of expression in painting for me.

I used the sculpture to do a final finished drawing one-third the size of the painting, on toned paper in white and black ballpoint. Ballpoint allows a huge range of graphic expression, from loose to exact and refined. I love the intaglio-like oiliness of the ink and its common and humble aspect. It is the drawing tool of childhood, of doodling, and of the office. It's an implement emblematic of the twentieth century. I took a photo of the drawing and printed it on transparency paper, projecting it on a panel with an overhead projector. I then drew the image in ballpoint directly on the panel. The panel support is Dibond, composed of plastic sandwiched between two aluminum sheets. On top of this material I adhered medium-weave linen with acrylic matte medium. The priming is an initial coat of white acrylic over which are three layers of alkyd oil primer tinted a mid-value buff color, sanded between layers. This warm ground adds a sense of reflected light and a glow in the shadows.

A transparent red oxide imprimatura was laid thinly over the ballpoint underdrawing with linseed oil. The imprimatura is an important technical part of the painting; it establishes the essential composition, value structure, and most importantly the feeling. I worked it up in thin layers, building a glowing underlayer that can be seen in the finished painting's reflected lights in the shadows, and under the pectoral fins. The painting was finished with a full palette of many opaque, semi-opaque, and transparent layers, building impastos in the lights and preserving aspects of transparency in the shadows.

The image required changes as I went along: I had difficulty with the perspective of the floor, and trouble getting the tail to feel like it curved down in space. I worked from the drawings as well as the sculpted model. I wanted the detail of fantastically complex scales, but not have this overwhelm the form and solidity of the animal. I wanted a salient but gentle consciousness in the face. In the end I tried to create a painting that has presence and that compels one to decipher its intention and meaning. The idea is to create an image that can be looked at many times without exhausting subtle layers of expression.

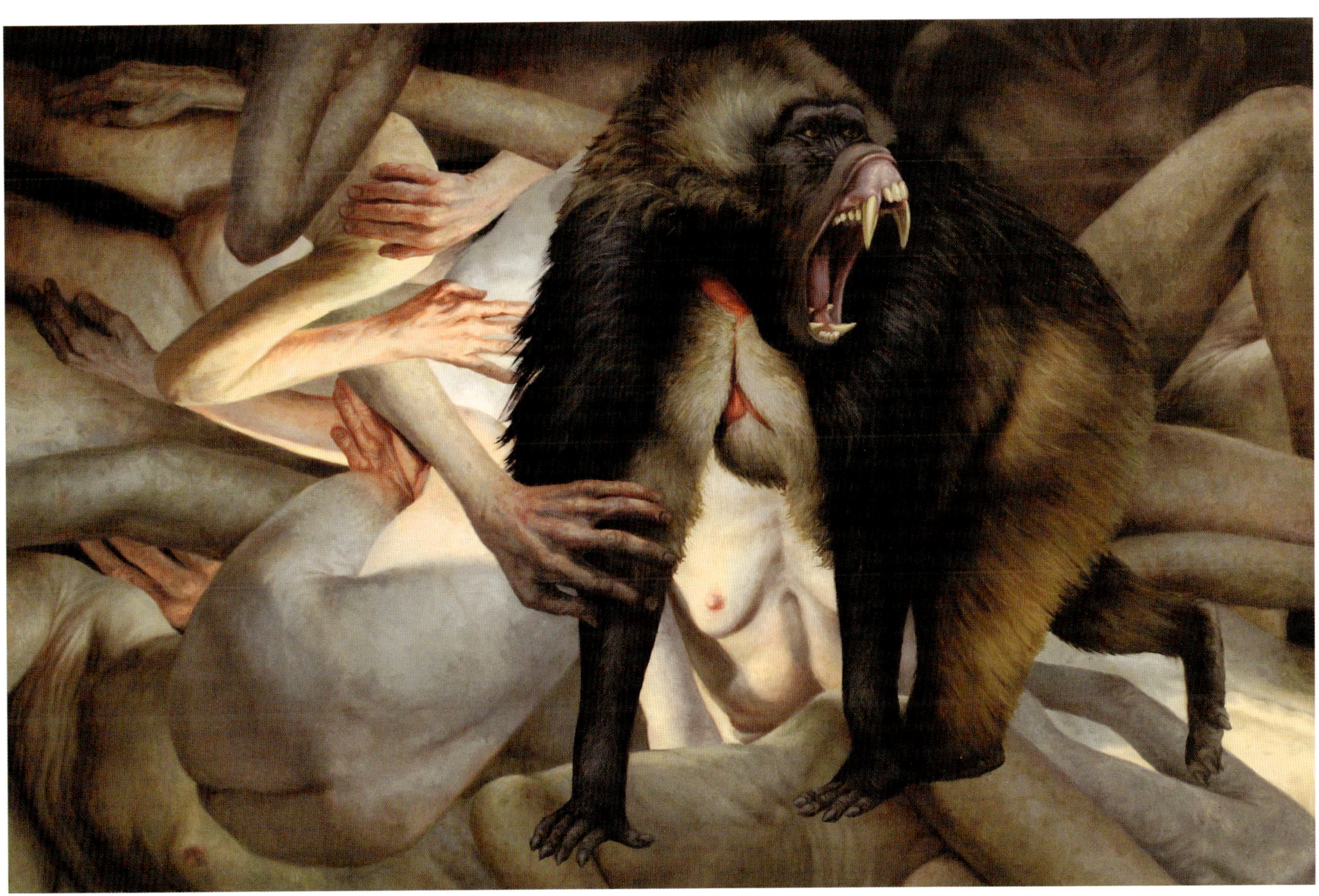

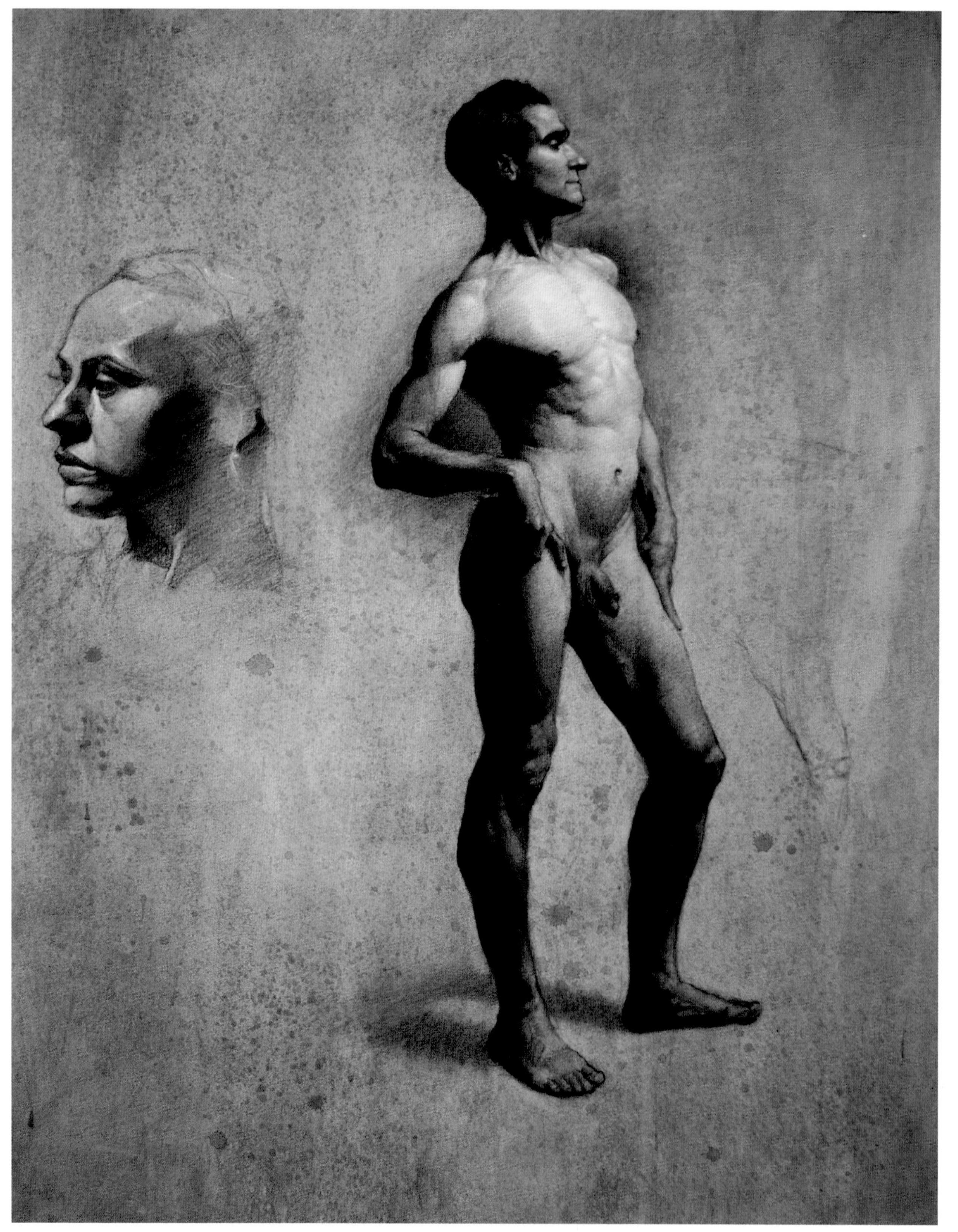

OUTSOURCING TECHNIQUE: MIMESIS, METHOD, AND METAPHOR IN FIGURE SCULPTURE

ROBERT SIMON

THE ADMISSION AREA OF THE DIA ART FOUNDATION in Beacon, New York, housed the work *Declaration of Intent* (1969), by Lawrence Weiner, a founder of Conceptual art. Consisting of a text in large typeface split among high walls under which the public circulates, like a fragmented portal inscription that sets the ground rules for all who enter, it read:

> *1. The artist may construct the work.*
> *2. The work may be fabricated.*
> *3. The work need not be built.*
> *Each being equal and consistent with the intent of the artist the decision as to condition rests with the receiver upon the occasion of the receivership.*

Declaration of Intent is at once an artist's manifesto and a work of art. It articulated a technical agenda that still influences art education and practice, including contemporary figure sculpture. For Weiner, the work is complete as an idea; thus it doesn't matter who produces its physical component, or whether that gets made at all. Around the same time, Donald Judd and other artists who *did* have need of the sculptural object began using fabricators to make their work. These developments constituted a departure from the formalist thread in Modernism that had led from Paul Cézanne to Abstract Expressionism. For a painter like Jackson Pollock, the direct encounter with the medium of paint was the defining characteristic of the work. Similarly, we think of his contemporary David Smith as a "welder," as surely as we think of Michelangelo as a "carver." By contrast, the work of Jeff Koons, which exemplifies the post-Conceptual current in contemporary art, is made entirely by assistants. However, it is not only in modern times that we find the sculptor removed from the production of the sculpture.

Sculpture is more laborious than the companion art of painting, and more dependent upon technical assistance. In sculpture, technique has two facets—one artistic and one mechanical. The mechanical portion of technique can be allotted to specialized artisans or tradesmen, generally without detriment to the result. Originally, their ranks included mold makers, foundry workers, stone carvers, the enlarger, the patinist, the kiln master, and so on. By the nineteenth century, sculptors were so dependent on them that Jules Dalou, a contemporary of Auguste Rodin, proposed that they be recognized with their own monument. With the evolution of sculpture in modern times, the field of support has expanded under the rubric of "fabrication" and now includes carpentry, model making, earth moving, metalworking—an entire steel factory in the case of Richard Serra—software operation and computerized prototyping. However, even when the skill level of such assistants exceeds that of the sculptor-in-chief, their role and status remain subsidiary.

The artistic portion of sculpture technique lies in the inception of the form and remains with the sculptor. It cannot be delegated, because it is embedded in the direct engagement with the medium and intrinsic to the work. Michelangelo's carving technique, for example, is inseparable from his ideas. The mechanical and the artistic iterations of technique may overlap in the singular effort of the sculptor, or separate through the introduction of fabricators. Conceptual work, on the other hand, doesn't recognize the distinction of artistic technique even for the artist; in the case of Koons, it dissolves in a factory of fabricators.

Given the present revival of the figure, Rudolf Wittkower's account of the technical evolution of Western sculpture is worth revisiting.[1] For Wittkower, carving and modeling dominated sculpture's technical narrative. He used the term "glyptic" to denote the irreversible process of subtraction

(opposite)
James Linkous
Standing Male Nude, 2012
Charcoal and white chalk on paper
28 x 21 inches

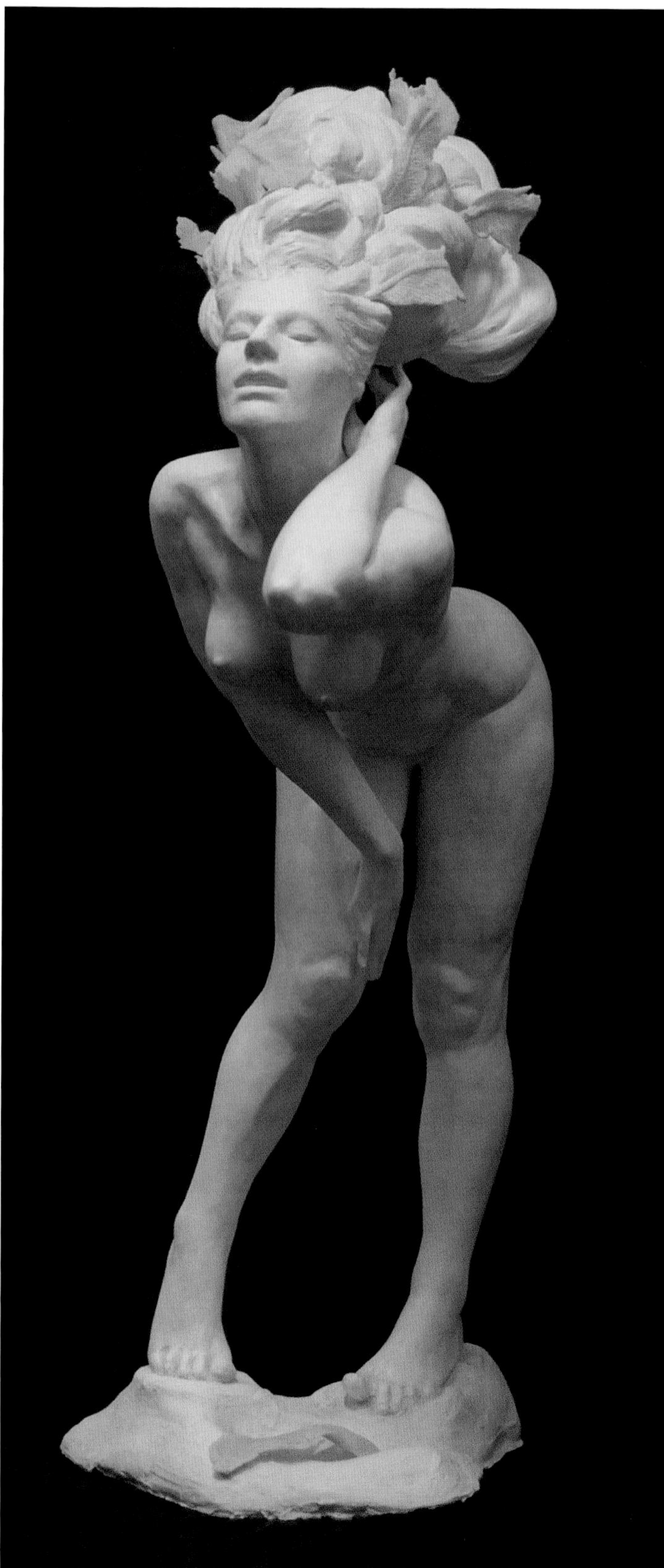

by which obdurate media like stone or wood are worked, and "plastic" for the additive procedure by which form is built up with a pliable but impermanent medium such as clay or wax. Carving may be direct or indirect. The direct carver works the stone from start to completion, drawing and redrawing the contours of the emerging figure as a guide for the chisel. In indirect carving, the figure is copied into stone from a preexisting model by a mechanical technique called "pointing." Pointing devices function as three-dimensional calipers to guide the carver to the surface of the new form within the block—as it were, blindly. Pointing was generally tasked to a laborer who remained anonymous despite being the maker of the final product. Today's computer-driven milling machines replace the original manual process.

Plastic technique is inherently indirect, because the inception of the work takes place in a different medium than that of the finished sculpture. A clay model must be molded and cast in a stable material such as bronze or plaster, or reproduced in stone via pointing. On the other hand, plastic media permit artistic experimentation throughout the creative phase of the work. Modeling clay on an armature affords the additional freedom to project forms into space. A cantilevered figure can be transposed into bronze because of the metal's tensile strength, whereas its replication in stone would require the addition of supports that are not original to the design. Clay sculpture can be made permanent by firing it in a kiln, but that was risky and rare for large work until recent times; and regardless, the heat shrinks and transforms the material so that the final product is not identical to the original.

The ghost of antiquity haunted later European sculpture, whereas painting of the same era had no extant precursors with which to suffer comparison. The statues that survived antiquity are predominantly marble copies of bronze originals. Bronze was the typical medium of non-architectural sculpture from the classical period onward, but very few bronzes remain, as in later times the valuable metal was melted down for other purposes. The statuary of archaic Greece exemplifies the rudiments of direct carving technique. To create a marble *kouros*, the sculptor first drew silhouettes of the front, back, and sides of a standing figure on the corresponding planes of a vertical stone block. He then removed the stone outside the lines, blending the silhouettes into a three-dimensional figure—albeit a somewhat blocky one to modern eyes. This shape may have honored the hero it depicted, as the philosopher Pythagoras, who had conceived of moral values in geometric terms, held that virtue was "four-square."[2] Later bronze statuary, which enjoys less formal constraint, was cast from models conceived in clay. Their subsequent copies in marble were not directly carved, but reproduced in stone by pointing.

During the medieval period and early Renaissance, the carver of figures was only a specialist within the lowly trade of stonemasonry. Stone carving and painting were then considered manual arts. Leon Battista Alberti, in his 1435 treatise *On Painting*, first proposed that the visual arts be reclassified with the liberal arts, in which case the social status of painters would rise.

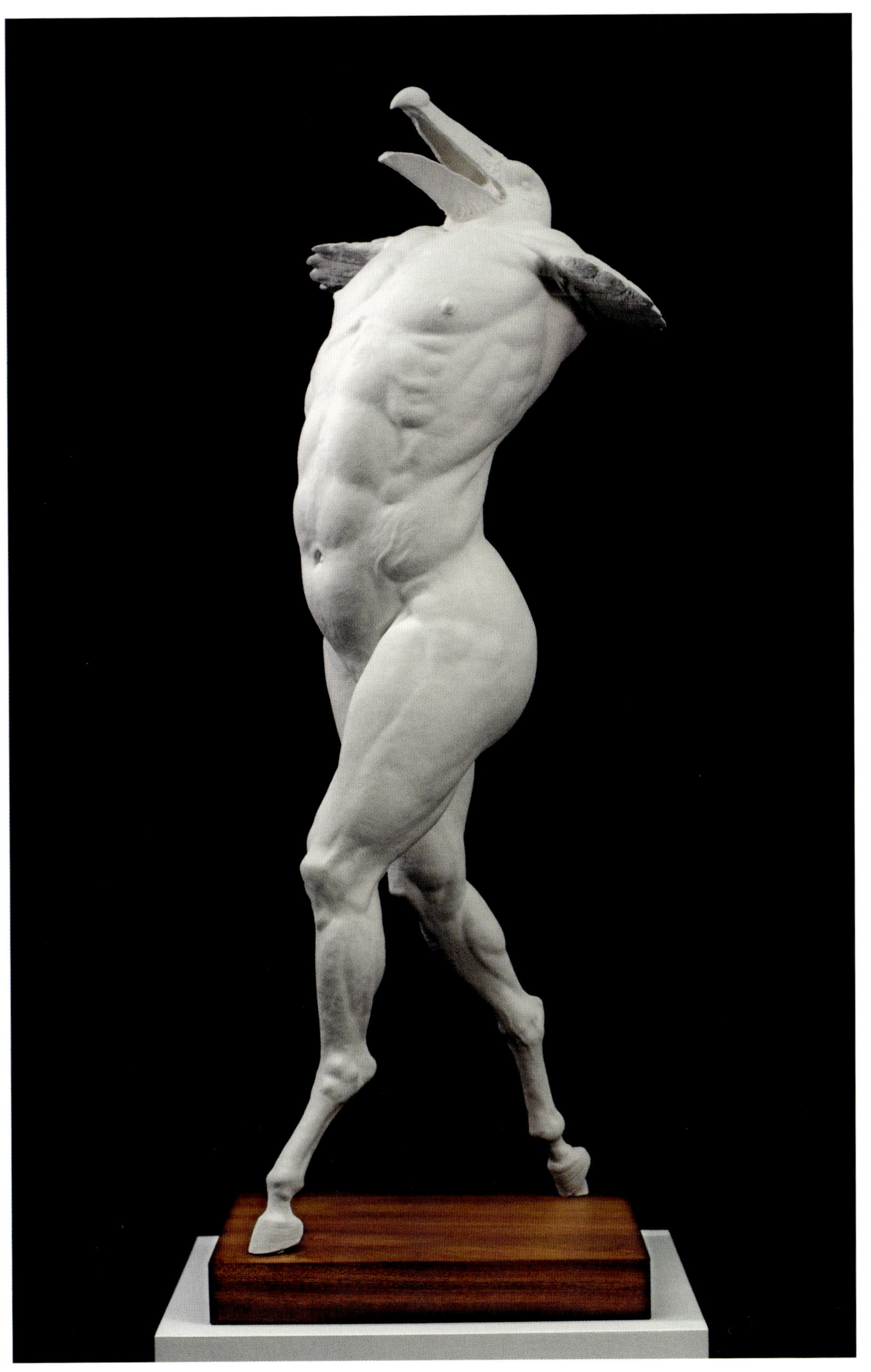

Jonathan Davies
Death Following a Young Woman Home One Night, 2005
Plaster
36 x 13 x 13 inches

(opposite)
Elyse Hradecky
Leda and the Swan, 2011
Plaster and mixed media
33 x 17 x 9 inches

However, the persistent stigma on manual labor held back the elevation of the sculptor and his métier. Sculpture lacked two of painting's additional calling cards: a patron saint, Luke, who had depicted the Virgin Mary, and the Latin poet Horace, whose dictum *ut pictura poesis* helped draw painting into the world of letters.

Alberti also wrote treatises on architecture and sculpture. The latter is brief by comparison with the others and exchanges their depth of concern with theory and aesthetics for a narrow description of pointing devices and their use. It infers that sculpture is measured into existence with engineering tools but does not specify whether the measurements are to be taken from a live model or another sculpture. This ambiguity within his *De statua* is a reminder that in sculpture, replication can be hard to distinguish from creation; the technologies of molding and casting are as old as sculpture itself. Reproduction is inherent to the medium, as surely as a painting is unique.

During the Renaissance, the comparison between carving and modeling was played out in the rivalry between Michelangelo and Leonardo. In Milan, Leonardo modeled a gigantic horse in clay, but he never cast it in bronze so within a few years it was destroyed. Michelangelo was dismissive of Leonardo's fruitless attempt to make sculpture by modeling and asserted that *true* sculpture is achieved only "by force of removal" in carving stone. Modeling, which proceeded "by means of putting," was akin to painting and hence inferior according to Michelangelo, who conceived his figures directly in stone. He rejected the common use of measuring tools—the demeaning implements of the stonemason—saying that he had "calipers in his eyes." Other carvers attacked the marble block simultaneously from all directions, but Michelangelo commenced from the front plane in bas-relief, and drew out a fully dimensional figure by depressing the background. He defined the emerging form with a chiseled version of *disegno*, its drawing in contours, the skill to which relief in any depth is bound. An ancillary meaning of *disegno* was "artistic concept." In essence, Michelangelo's carving technique refuted the inference of Alberti's treatise that sculpture is a mechanical process of copying and supplied instead a method by which a concept could be transferred directly from the mind into stone by way of drawing. Leonardo the modeler occupied himself instead with the engineering problem of pointing and designed a novel mechanism for that purpose. However, he also wrote that sculpture is only a manual art, in part because a copy shares all the same properties as its original.[3] Sculpture had become subject to a theoretic debate rooted in its technical aspect.

Despite Michelangelo's insistence that modeling is not sculpture, he invented a modeling technique that would become crucial to his successors. Michelangelo's few remaining clay models, or *bozzetti*, are three-dimensional sketches rather than finished pieces in miniature. Subsequently, the *bozzetti* of Giambologna (Jean Boulogne) attained an unprecedented level of importance; in fact, they were so admired that a new form of collecting arose around them. Wittkower observed that this new focus on modeling came at a price, because the sculptor's interest began and ended with the clay. To turn his *bozzetti* into monuments, Giambologna established a corps of artisans to enlarge the work and render it in marble by pointing, without his direct effort. The finished marbles do not exhibit quite the same twisting plasticity as the *bozzetti* of origin. Something was lost between the conception of the piece in one medium and its execution in another.

Gian Lorenzo Bernini's equal mastery of modeling and carving glued sculpture technique back together. Contemporaries marveled at his ability to "carve the stone as if modeling wax." The exhibition of Bernini's terra-cotta *bozzetti* at the Metropolitan Museum of Art in 2013 left no doubt that he was a prolific and unequaled modeler who made extensive use of preparatory studies to develop his ideas. But Bernini's working method was unlike that of his contemporaries in that he was able to move from the *bozzetto* to a full-size sculpture in stone without recourse to an intermediary full-size model as a pointing guide.[4] Sometimes assistants executed his marble enlargements, but this division of labor was necessitated only by the size and volume of his commissions. The bust of Scipione Borghese attests to Bernini's ability to work directly in stone without a preparatory model at all. After studying his subject in a series of quick sketches on paper, he moved on to carve the bust while the Cardinal posed for him.

After Bernini, plastic technique played an increasingly dominant role in the French Academy. For admission to the *Académie Royale de Peinture et de Sculpture* sculptors were required to produce a half-life-size marble figure. However, training and practice commenced with clay modeling. With the advent of Neoclassicism, sculpture achieved temporary ascendancy over painting through the artistic equivalent of an acquired pedigree. In H. W. Janson's account,[5] the sculptor's objective was to produce a "modern classic" in parity with certain statues from antiquity, such as the Apollo Belvedere, that were admired at the time. Though Antonio Canova superficially polished his marbles upon their completion, his work ceased in essence with the provision of the "original plaster," a cast from a full-size clay model that was not preserved. The finished sculpture was a marble copy of the original plaster, executed independently by craftsmen-carvers. As the exemplary statues from antiquity were also marble copies, and in modern times were reproduced again as plaster casts, sculptural form had taken on the aspect of a Platonic ideal that transcends its particular manifestations. Meanwhile, by the 1830s, advancements in metallurgy had rendered bronze cheaper than marble, and so accurate that there was no need for the sculptor to work on the final cast. Bronze reproduction became commonplace, and sculptors sold factories the rights to mass-produce their work.[6] Concurrently, society was in the grips of a "mania" to erect statues in every public place. Production techniques and prevailing taste coalesced to ensure that monumental sculpture could both thrive and be monotonous. Sculpture, while remaining figurative in character, had become industrialized in process.

Much later in the century, Rodin shook up the art establishment with a revolutionary approach to modeling both small and large work. His vast output of life studies absorbed and revamped the entrenched training exercise—the *académie*—of European art schools. Regardless, Rodin, like his contemporaries, employed others to execute his plasters in bronze or marble interchangeably. Though he was often dissatisfied with his marbles, he never sought to limit his production to bronze, perhaps to meet the demands of the art market. Hence throughout the nineteenth century, the sculptor's activity in the initial stage of design was thoroughly divorced from the technical disciplines of the final medium. The gulf between conception and execution first encountered in the output of Giambologna had become institutionalized.

A contemporary artist like Koons is even further removed from the finished product than the sculptors of the nineteenth century, but their early modern successors went the other way entirely. Constantin Brancusi, for instance, used traditional media (stone, wood, and bronze) but always worked them to completion. He turned bronze into a direct medium by abrading the cast metal, despite the technological advances that had rendered such effort non-requisite. On the other hand, the Constructivist sculpture of the modern period abandoned traditional technique entirely. From Pablo Picasso to David Smith and beyond, sculpture could be an assemblage of parts held together with welds, bolts, wire, screws, nails, and glue. Constructivist technique broke through the inherent limitations of carving and modeling, in part by allowing the sculptor to work directly in the final medium by addition and subtraction alike.

Figure sculptors of the early modern period, such as Antoine Bourdelle, Aristide Maillol, and Henri Matisse, stuck with traditional media and technique. In the mid-twentieth century, Alberto Giacometti was still modeling clay and casting bronze, even as he pushed the life study to its outer limits. However, the figure sculpture that gained notoriety in the 1960s was founded on completely different ideas and processes. George Segal and Duane Hanson made their work by casting from live models—a form of fabrication. Regardless of the subsequent artistic use to which the mold or cast was put, the work began with reproduction. The old hierarchy of artistic and mechanical technique inverted, easing the figure back into contemporary sculpture. One current in the present revival of the figure includes Hanson. It originates not in the formal academies of the nineteenth century but rather in the contemporaneous popular genre of the wax effigy and leads to hyperrealists such as Ron Mueck. Mueck's work combines traditional modeling technique with a modern casting material. He layers tinted resin into his molds—much as a canvas painter would superimpose translucent glazes—to create the illusion of human flesh. The technique originated in cinematic special effects to provide replacements for the bodies of live actors. Mueck changes the game by radically altering the scale of the figures while maintaining an uncanny optical illusion of their presence. It's an illusion that subsumes our awareness of the medium and the artist's manipulation of it.

The history of sculpture supplies a comparative study of formulas of mimesis that compensate for sculpture's innate propensity to imitate the real. A "speaking likeness" by Bernini, such as the portrait of Scipione Borghese, moves us in part by seeming to animate the marble. The medium and the artistic technique cohabitate with the referent, and the

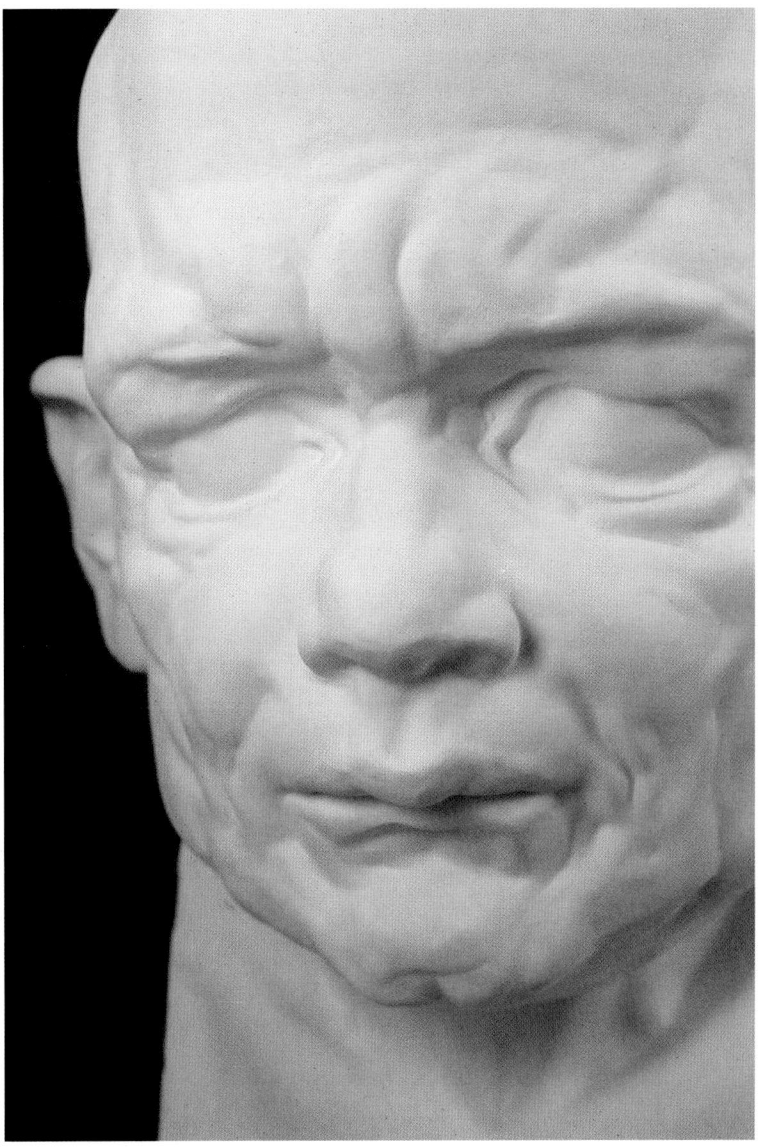

Jeff Hesser
Baby Head II, 2005
Hydrocal
43 x 25 x 16 inches

representation comes out ahead. Bernini's carving technique confers meaning through its plastic effect. The *Ecstasy of St. Teresa* unfolds on an anti-gravity stage in which Teresa's spiritualization in sainthood is allegorized by the apparent release of the marble from the burden of its own weight. The metamorphosis of the stone, evident as sculptural alchemy, helps to convey the viewer's imagination into the mystery drama enacted by the figures. The iconography is prompted by technical playacting in the medium of its incarnation.

With Michelangelo technique and intent are fused. Erwin Panofsky demonstrated that Michelangelo's *Captives* for the tomb of Julius II personify the struggle of the soul with the flesh that lies at the heart of Neoplatonism.[7] As they were left in various stages of incompletion, they document a carving process in which the sculptor appears to release the figures from their "prison" in the stone. The ideal form of the buried figure, which seems to exist in advance of its own creation, embodies the perfection of the eternal soul, while the stone matrix connotes its entrapment in base matter. Panofsky speculated that the emergence of the figures from the stone as tangible objects compromised the ideal of them in the mind of the sculptor, leading to their abandonment. Thus a conflict between Neoplatonism and mimesis itself was also played out in the arena of technique.

Rodin was a master of portraiture and life modeling, but his representations are grounded in invention. Rodin sometimes photographed his work in progress,[8] but his *St. John the Baptist Preaching* (1880), which appears to be walking, does not depict any instant in the course of locomotion that could be captured by Eadweard Muybridge's camera. Though he employed a posed model, he imbued the sculpture with an inexorable forward gait that is the opposite of stop action. Both feet fully touch the ground, which never occurs when walking; and the legs form a triangle that ought to confer stasis to the figure, were it not for the way the feet appear squeezed against the earth, as clay to clay. Thus the antithetical artistic objectives of movement and stability are reconciled through the handling of the medium. The roughness of the clay throughout the surface of the figure fuses with the character of the saint, an aspect of his modeling that Rodin preserved in plaster. He also turned that replicative medium into a direct one by cutting up casts to create new works. He combined fragments of bodies in different positions, then modeled transitions between the parts to create a single composite figure that, while anatomically impossible, nevertheless communicates a convincing sequence of motion. Such work in plaster does not translate well into the hidebound medium of marble; it took an industrial revolution in metallurgy to preserve it in bronze.

Giacometti challenged the premise of representation by driving the life study to its logical extreme. James Lord[9] reported that Giacometti claimed "the aims and frustrations of painting and sculpture are the same, or nearly so," and that "what I'm trying to do is just reproduce on canvas or clay what I see." But these assertions were accompanied by the counterclaim that "it's impossible to reproduce what one sees." Indeed, "to make a head really lifelike is impossible, and the more you struggle to make it lifelike, the less like life it becomes." Giacometti's immersion in this core dilemma within representation guaranteed that his work would remain unfinished. Lord's own portrait was an endless cycle of doing and redoing. At one point Giacometti told Lord his features were in a constant state of flux. Diego Giacometti, his brother's fabricator, terminated Alberto's sculptures by removing the clay models and casting them. Compared with the sculpture of Michelangelo, which is *non-finito* as a result of abandonment, Giacometti's is unfinished because of his inability to stop.

(opposite)
Robert Simon
Slump Head, 2009
Earthenware
12 x 12 x 11 inches

While Giacometti insisted that he only sought to show things as they appear to him, he also despaired "that he doesn't have the technique for doing so." However, his technique is perfectly suited to showing the predicament of his premise even if it does not supply a solution to it. Clay inherently resists completion. If kept wet, it can be added to and subtracted from indefinitely. Clay's infinite reversibility allows as many variants of form as there are sensations on the eye. The medium and the technique are intertwined with the artistic challenge posed by Giacometti's unique concept of sculptural representation disengaged from measurement. Giacometti's pursuit of appearances by means of the life study only underscores the instability of perception itself. There is no fixed reality to copy. A model constantly shifts position while holding a pose, and his or her appearance is further contingent upon changing light conditions and viewpoint, as well as the fluctuating receptivity of the perceiver. Prior to Giacometti, representation aimed to channel this chaos into a stable form, while endowing the form with the artistic power to "move" the imagination of the viewer. For Rodin, the life modeler, and Bernini, the spirit alchemist, the transaction between fixity and flux served as the entry point of the technical imagination within the requirements of mimesis. Giacometti threw out this balancing act for a direct encounter with the paradox that necessitates it.

In effect, Giacometti confronted the phenomenology of perception before Minimalism took up the matter on its own terms. Giacometti told Lord, "If only someone else could paint what I see . . . it would be marvelous, because then I could stop painting for good." It seems he yearned for a fabricator to take over his impossible task. But even a successful delegation of labor does not remove the story of technique. In Minimalism, the turn to fabrication was as inseparable from intent as carving was to Michelangelo. Despite Michael Fried's belief that Minimalism had revived a variant of sculptural anthropomorphism,[10] the work of Donald Judd and Robert Morris in fact relied on anonymous, machined surfaces to deflect the viewer's attention away from the construction of the object and the "relatedness" of its parts as a substitute body, toward the broader arena of viewing. Yet even as digital technology is added to the portfolio of sculpture technique, the artist and fabricator continue an ancient dance.

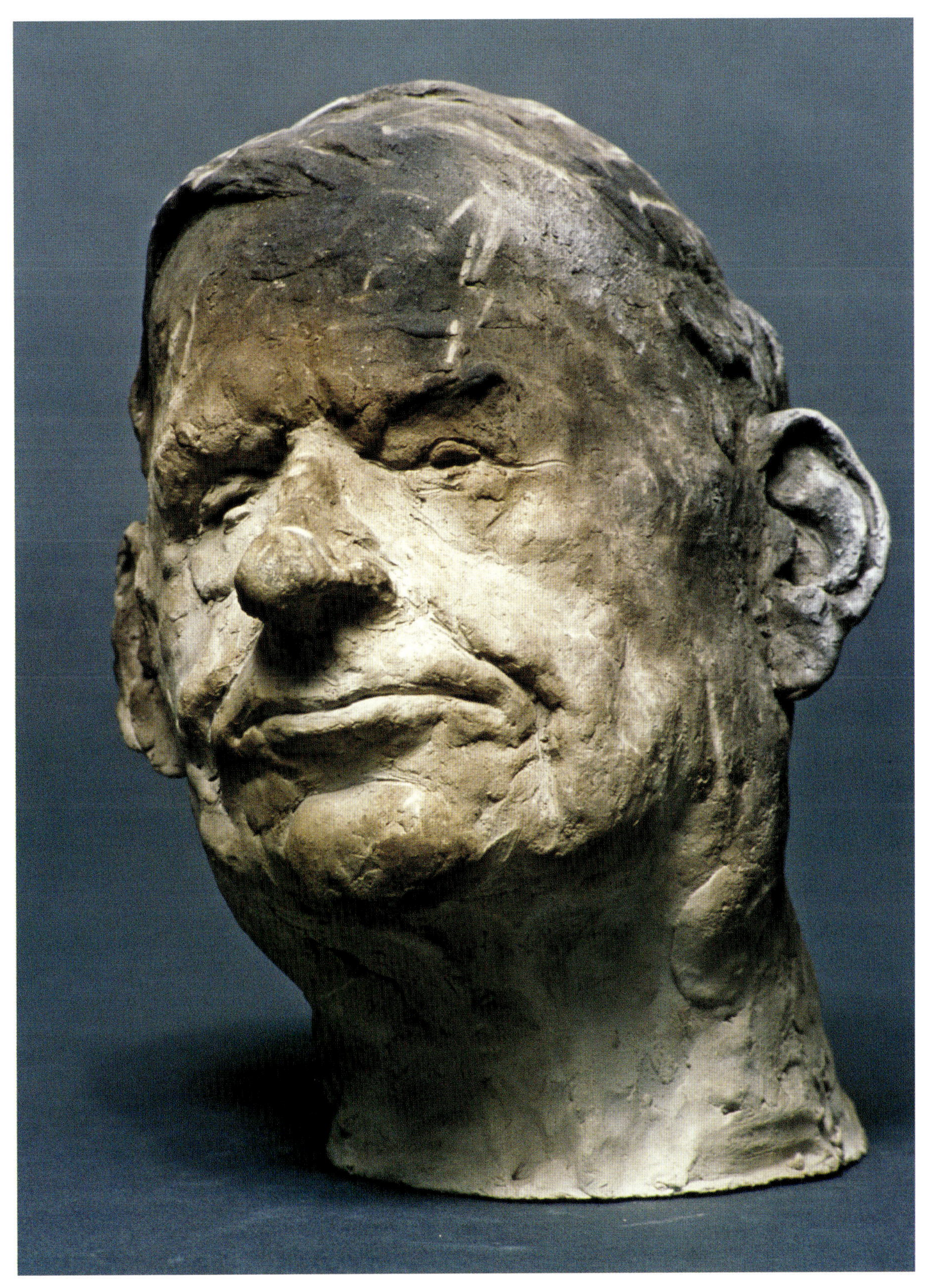

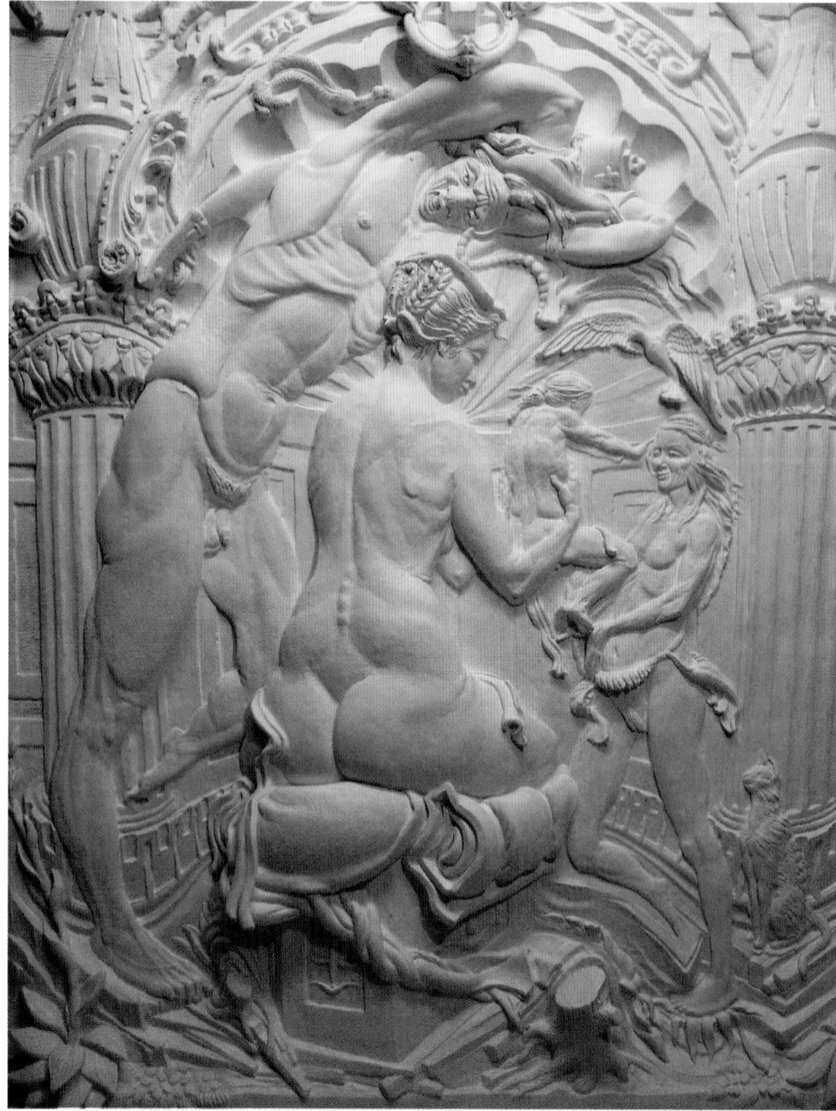

Randolphlee McIver
Slaughter of the Innocents (detail), 2013
Plaster
68 x 42 inches

(opposite)
James Raczkowski
Still Life, 2012
Oil on canvas
60 x 40 inches

RANDOLPHLEE McIVER

I formed my visual and analytical thinking in drawing and painting at Art Center College of Design in Los Angeles and later majored in sculpture at the New York Academy of Art. My work comes out of Greek and Renaissance classicism, which uses a similar abstract, visual language of basic geometric forms—the cube, circle, cone, and cylinder—to set forms in space. My method for relief sculpture was inspired by the late work of Lorenzo Ghiberti and Donatello's *rilievo schiacciato* (flattened or squashed relief), which I have combined with alto, or high, relief.

Slaughter of the Innocents has been in progress since 2005, inspired by news reports showing Iraqi civilians being bombed. It involves two standing figures with two relief panels. An "Image of Death" (male figure), represented on both sides of the two reliefs, lifts an axe to strike the unsuspecting family. In an arched alcove at one end, a life-size "Figure of Mourning" stands presenting her offering—a vase memorializing the loss of the innocents—to the dead.

The composition was established through drawing and in small maquettes; the piece is architectonic in structure. I start with an idea developed through many drawings of all four sides of the relief, and of various aspects of this sculpture. I use water-based clay with pliable wire armature for the sculptural model, a very fluid material that allows rapid compositional changes. When the clay model is completed, it is cast into a plaster positive. Its size and complexity prohibit it being cast in one piece, so I make a three-piece modular mold for a standing figure, a base for the entire structure, and two relief sculptures with alcove.

When the plaster-of-Paris model is complete, the process of enlargement into the finished sculpture begins. I make a plywood vertical structure to support the oil clay I will use for the relief. Oil clay allows better detail, which allows many changes over a long period of time. I use a string grid on the model and then make a grid with pencil on the enlarged panel, for placement of the appropriate masses of clay onto the panel. Soon the grid disappears, and I redraw the grid directly onto the clay while redrawing the images. This process can take up to a year.

The final synthetic marble stone sculpture will be subdivided and developed into six modules, each piece weighing over three hundred pounds. The modular molds are cast in silicone rubber, which gives me the option to finish the sculpture in various materials, such as wax for a bronze cast, or artificial stone cast in Hydrostone, Hydrocal, plaster, or synthetic marble. The final piece will be cast in synthetic marble stone, a liquid plastic made by Smooth-On. Various powders can be added to it to create the effects of metal, marble, porcelain, or granite. Synthetic stone is lighter in weight than solid stone, which makes it a lot easier to work with and transport. *Slaughter of the Innocents* is not a literal illustration of the actual event. My hope is that anyone from any nation viewing it will know its meaning through visual imagery alone—the massacre of innocents in homes, marketplaces, and workplaces—making words of explanation unnecessary.

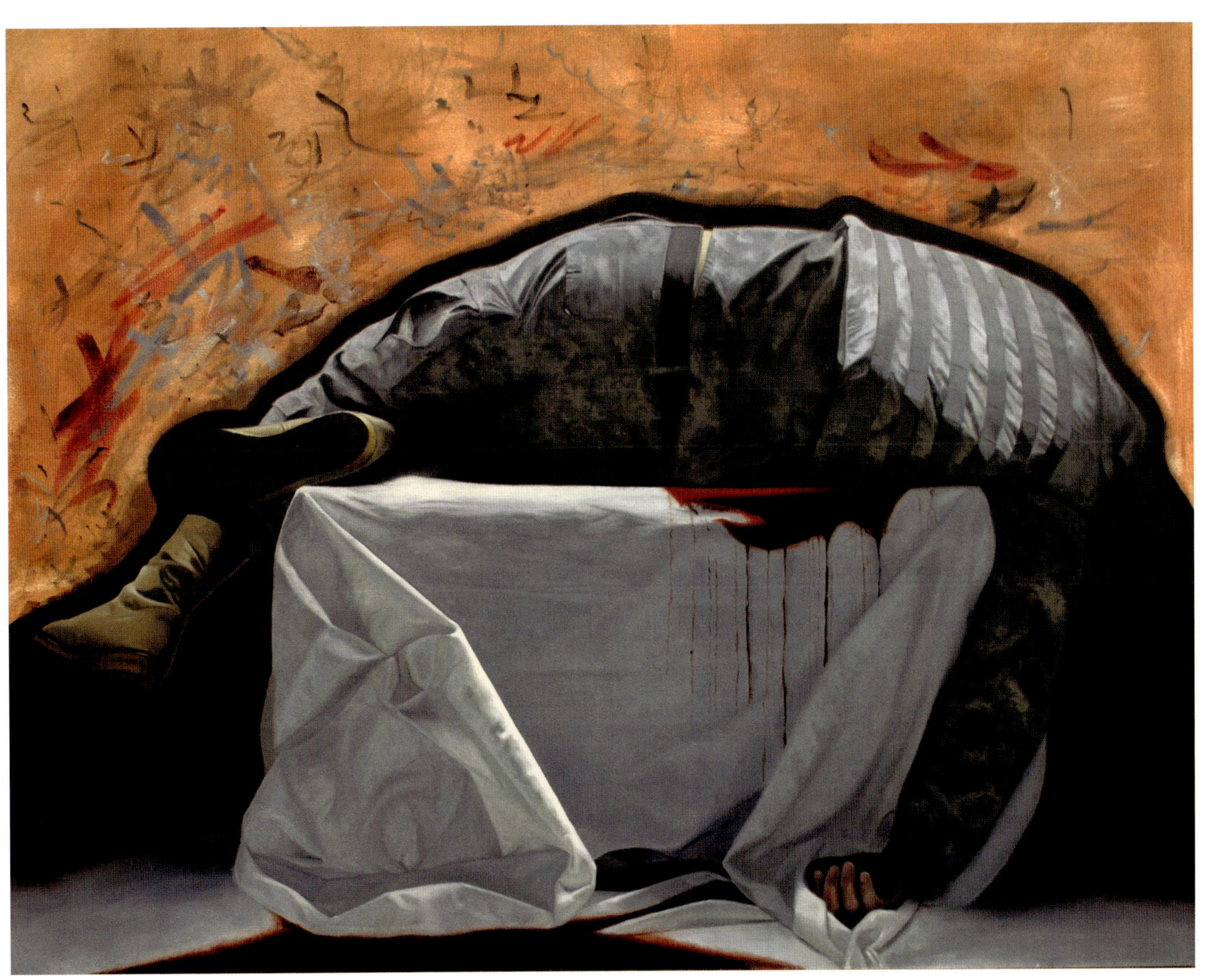

TOWARD AN ALLEGORIZATION OF METHOD

VINCENT DESIDERIO

EMBEDDED BENEATH THE MUTE SURFACES of paintings lie indications of theoretical matter intelligible to persons familiar with the technical practice of art. In some sense these constitute a body of discourse concerning technique as narrative, through which the ordering of effects reveals a story beyond (and sometimes at odds with) the staged drama. The manner by which these effects are organized and manipulated creates patterns of signification that run throughout the history of painting. Within the ongoing discourse of technical narrativity are arguments that conjoin painters of different times, of seemingly disparate natures. Identifying, decoding, and reconfiguring these patterns lies at the heart of the psychology of creation and the affliction described by Harold Bloom as "the anxiety of influence." Method becomes allegorized when painters revisit and explore the hermetic threads of an argument present but often barely discernible in the work of their predecessors. For artists, the allegorization of method is not mere quotation. It is an alignment of preexisting methodologies, reconfigured in the service of originality. It is an act of reification by which visual arguments are celebrated, even as they are reconfigured, deconstructed, and re-contextualized.

Perhaps the most significant of these allegories is perspective. Invented in the early Quattrocento, perspective has remained the central myth of visual arts for the last six hundred years. The arguments initiated by its early practitioners have given rise to the most original developments of Western art. Its program of spatial articulation, whether professed, subverted, or even elided from practice, remains the primary consideration of the artist. Discovering the history of how painters have allegorized perspective requires a certain degree of heuristic plasticity—the same creative interpretive methods used by artists for centuries.

With the invention of perspective we see the first demonstration of a kind of technical narrativity that we will call sequential. Sequential narrativity is a form of pictorial construction that privileges a continuity of effect linking the viewer, through the painting, to the artist and his intention. It creates a circuit of complicity experienced as a seamless fictive whole, characterized by a rapture or trance of viewing. The optical field opens before the spectator, inviting a kind of surrender to the picture's illusion (the illusion inclusive of all sensually transmitted visual ideas). As such he or she enters into a kind of optical complicity with the work and through this complicity participates in the picture' s narrativity. A visual experience of this nature suggests an orchestrated disclosure of intention (on the part of the painter) and an uncanny capacity to follow/participate in its unfolding (on the part of the viewer).

The optical field can also be made to shut down before the spectator, discouraging direct sensual participation. A visual event of this kind is marked with the sense of an object's removal from the sequence of its normal comprehension or cultural utility. This forces a detached reading, emphasizing a critical model of removal from any speculation in regard to intentionality. The activation of such an interplay between the picture and the viewer engages in a practice of erasure, whereby the expected meaning of an object and that meaning' s continuity with experience are rendered inscrutable in order to allow for re-representation or redefinition. This de-familiarization signals a rupture in the stream of sequential disclosure. Narratives of this type can be called emblematic in that they presume the isolated sign to be the locus of condensed cultural information.

As examples of technical narrativity, both sequentialization and emblemization are the fruits of perspective—of spectatorial privilege accorded or denied. A brief examination of how painters have allegorized perspective could serve as the basis for a general study of technical narrativity and the allegorization of method.

(opposite)
Vincent Desiderio
Redux, 2012
Oil on canvas
76 x 80 inches

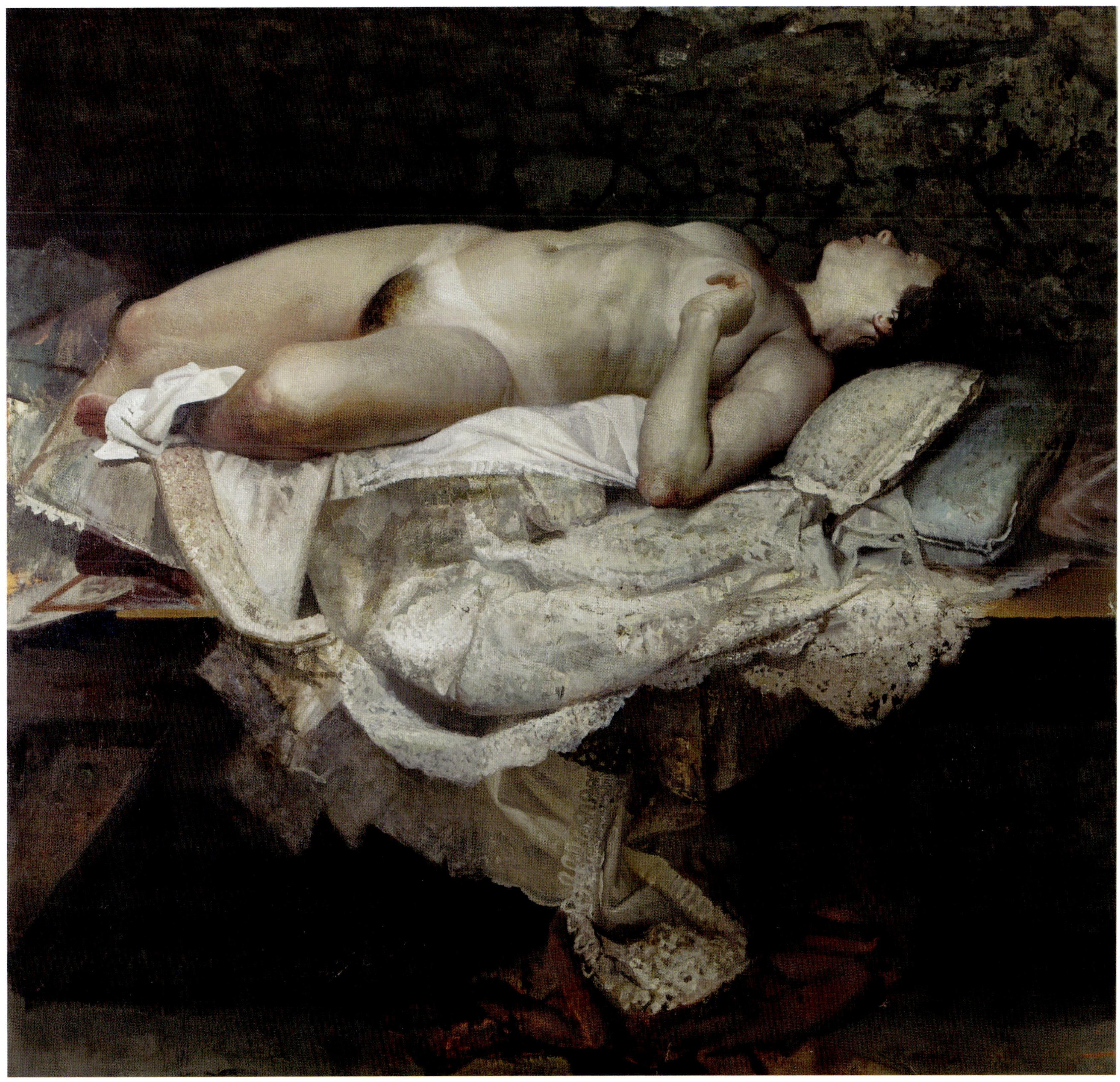

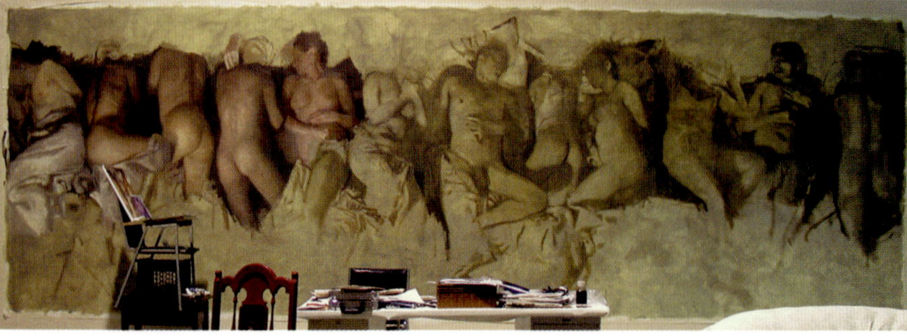

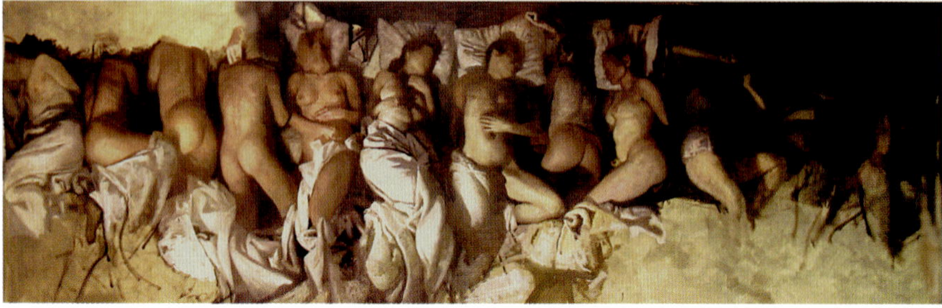

(top and bottom)
Vincent Desiderio
Sleep (early states),
2012

(opposite)
Vincent Desiderio
Sleep, 2012
Oil on canvas
52 x 252 inches

THE CIRCUITUS SPIRITUALIS AND THE SEQUENTIALIZATION OF SPACE

In about 1415, Filippo Brunelleschi created a foreshortened image of the Baptistery of San Giovanni on a small panel. Afterward, he drilled a hole through the panel at a point corresponding to the vanishing point of his perspectival construction. He invited individuals to view the surface of the panel from behind, through the peephole, while holding a mirror at arm's length so that the painted image was viewed as a reflection. The panel has long since disappeared, which makes it particularly mysterious and difficult to ascertain exactly how it was made. One thing, however, is clear: For his demonstration to work properly and prove the direct correspondence of the monocular view to the vanishing point, Brunelleschi drilled the peephole, necessary for viewers unaccustomed to viewing illusion as such in painting.

Most intriguing is that the viewer, along with partaking of the illusion, sees his own eye reflected back at him. He observes, in a single moment of viewing, the opening of a visual corridor connecting him with an infinite point deep within the virtual space of the picture. Because of their fixity within the logic of illusion, the viewing eye and the vanishing point share a place of privilege, for it is on their reciprocal gaze that the entire system depends. The reflective aspect of this moment indicates conditions of departure and return—in effect, a circuit is established. Most remarkable (and Neoplatonic) in this instant of alignment, the individual, by way of a rationalized optical field, participates in a kind of revelation. As such, perspective is a tool of contemplation or, as Leon Battista Alberti called it, "an aid to religion." It enabled the "flight of the soul" to traverse vast distance to a point where it can view itself in participation with divinity. The circuit links man with the ineffable, incomprehensible "other"—a mystery beyond all reason, yet a mystery into which reason is compelled to stare.

Alberti's celebrated treatise *On Painting* appeared in 1435, twenty years after the first documented demonstration of linear perspective by Filippo Brunelleschi. Neoplatonism and its relationship to notions of cosmic infinity were already part of the intellectual zeitgeist of Italy, so Gemistus Pletho's famous series of lectures on Platonism (1438) found a receptive audience among Florentine intellectuals. They inspired the creation of the Platonic Academy of Florence, whose leader, Marsilio Ficino, later codified the ideas into what is called Renaissance Neoplatonism. By the late fifteenth century, Cristoforo Landino was unequivocal about his illustrious relative Alberti's participation in Neoplatonic circles. Alberti's circle of like-minded friends included the mathematician and philosopher Nicholas of Cusa, also acquainted with Brunelleschi and Piero della Francesca through Paolo Toscanelli—who taught the young Piero mathematics and brought to Florence Biagio Pelicani's 1390 treatise, *Quaestiones perspectivae*. The importance of Neoplatonic thought is paramount to understanding the development of perspective in the early Quattrocento.

Understood in the Neoplatonic sense, perspective is an alignment with infinity that can never be reached, beyond the comprehension of man. Neoplatonic rational structure enforced the absolute importance of reason, argued Plotinus and Cusa, by understanding the limits of reason. A tool of contemplation, it focused the soul in its pursuit of the One, aiding its flight through contemplation of a geometric construction. In the traversal of vast distances to the point of participation with divinity, the circuit links the terrestrial realm to the threshold of infinity. There, the soul interfaces with the One and achieves the culmination of its quest—divine rapture—but remains free and mobile, its return possible through the corridor that connects the place of viewing with the vanishing point. Therefore perspective is a circuit akin to the *circuitus spiritualis*, described by Ficino later in the century. It "enlivened" in an all-persuasive web of illusion that, when experienced, locks the viewer into alignment with its systematic disclosure. Within the field of continuous space the painter places the *istoria*, narratives of momentous acts of virtue, nobility, devout patrons, and sacred mysteries. All are pilgrims on their way to rapture, exemplary models of devotion accompanying the soul on its flight to the Divine.

Perspective was the discovery of artists who immediately saw it as proof of their intellectual worthiness. By its use, Alberti claimed, the artist would be judged as "another god" by winning "perpetual fame." For painters, perspective was the essence of what would later be called the design and drawing, or *disegno* (still later, tonality or modeling), of a painting. It was the rational, quantifiable stability that formed the backbone of art. In fact,

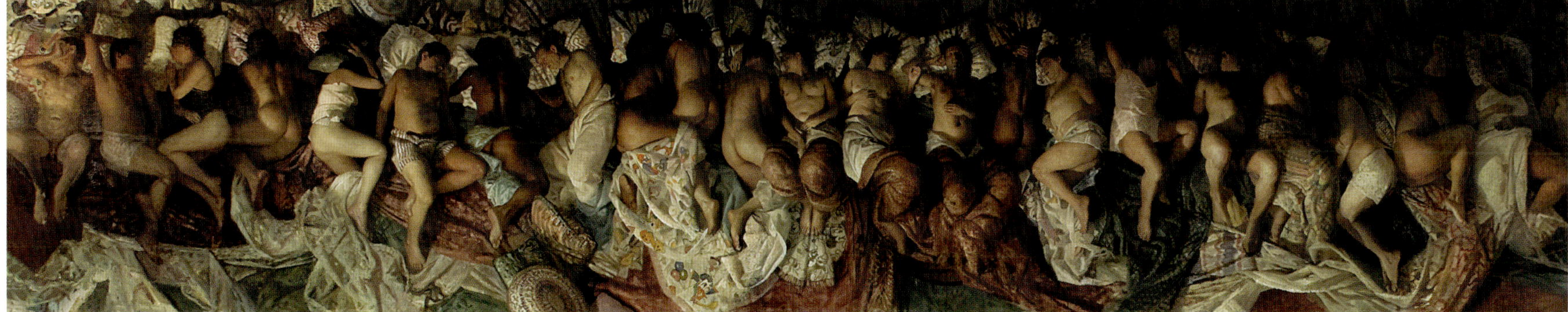

Alberti's *Della pittura* was a manifesto of sorts, announcing the emergence of the artist as steward of the *circuitus spiritualis*, its subtext replete with indications of the elevated importance of artists both intellectually and socially. Perspective would become the means through which painters sought entrance into the elite academic circle of the liberal arts. Yet a burgeoning animosity rose between artists and other intellectuals over the validity of the rational component of *disegno*'s "sensate wisdom," as Alberti called it. Deemed merely the product of sensation and not reason by many Neoplatonic theorists, painting was thought incapable of prompting the journey of the soul to the ineffable One, despite Leonardo's insistence that the "eye is the window of the soul."

In the sixteenth century, the clarity of perspectival corridors fell prey to irresolution. Mannerist inwardness—*disegno interno*—was a radical shift in codes of intelligibility, reflecting a privatizing of the artist's esoteric vision, one made available to a select audience of cognoscenti whose patronage inadvertently encouraged increasingly obscured theoretical manifestations. This was in part a self-protective measure, for under the scrutiny of intellectuals often unsympathetic to the artists' aspirations for a new kind of recognition, artists retreated inwardly. Inspiring a break in the symbolic continuity of pictorial space, Mannerism signaled a disturbance in the Neoplatonic *circuitus spiritualis*. It undermined perspective's monocular privilege, sublimating the rational foundation for the soul's flight to the ineffable One, and its analog in the vanishing point. Nonetheless, the Neoplatonic notion of perspective as Plotinus's "flight of the alone to the Alone," within which the soul contemplates itself, endured in the solitary, radical individualism of such artists as Jacopo da Pontormo, Tintoretto, and El Greco. And it is in El Greco's work that we see one of the most dramatic examples of the allegorization of perspective as a vertical flame.

THE OPTICS OF ILLUMINATION AS ANALOG

In the shadow of Mannerist doubt and paradox, Caravaggio found a synthesis in a world half seen, half obscured, through chiaroscuro. A momentary flash, an insight or epiphany, is perceived in what I term the incidence of reflection—the highest light of the light mass. In a space undefined by architectural orthogonals, this incidence of reflection is the prime indicator of the spectator's privilege, rendering illumination the equivalent of the vanishing point. Yet unlike the vanishing point, this highlight does not recede into infinite space but projects forward to the eye of the beholder. The velocity of light at that time was considered infinite—a claim on which, it is said, Descartes staked his entire philosophy. Thus the capture and focus of that light placed human presence within the mystery of the ineffable through a direct line of reflection, re-establishing the *circuitus spiritualis*.

Caravaggio's idea of illuminated mass constructed tonally, built upon Masaccio's and Leonardo's innovations in chiaroscuro, would serve as an important model for the description of form for centuries to come. This construction consisted of four key zones of illumination and shadow; in combination with chromatic shifts the desired effect of verisimilitude is achieved:

> *Light strikes the form at an angle that reveals approximately three quarters of its surface, creating an illuminated field—the light mass. As the form turns away from the light, but before it falls into shadow, an area of grayness appears to the eye, known as the turning- or half-light. Inside this light mass floats the incidence of reflection. Caravaggio's model manifests a progressive privileging of form—unadorned and isolated. In effect form became the embodiment of space.*

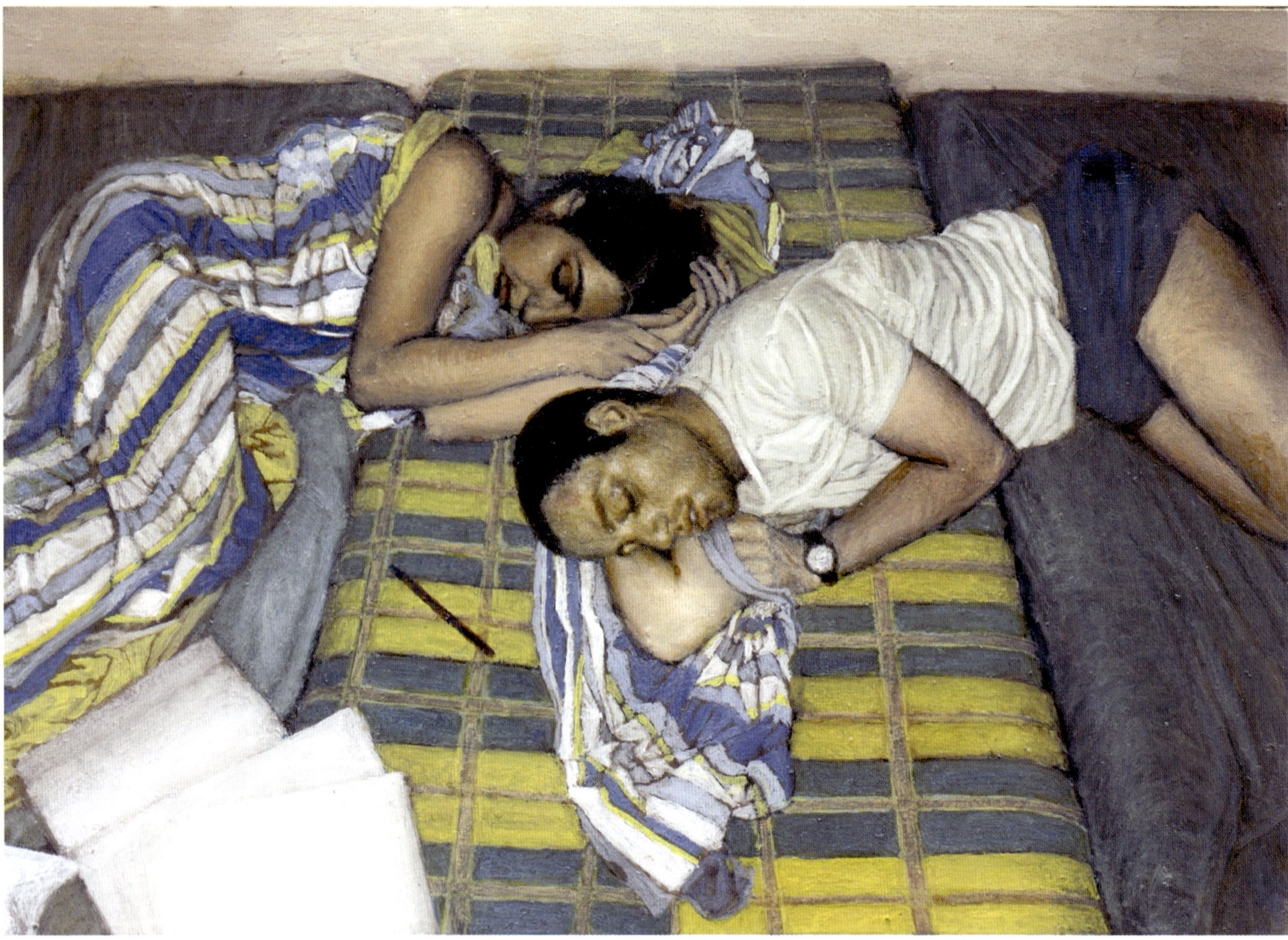

Maya Brodsky
Natasha and Yotam,
2011
Oil on panel
5 x 7 inches

(opposite)
Ian Healy
Pigs, 2011
Oil on canvas
80 x 96 inches

Unlike the hallucinatory ephemeral space shaped by *disegno interno*, this new method was grounded by the palpable structure of form. As defined by the optics of illumination, it became the culmination of the artist's intellect, embodying the "sensate wisdom" earlier described by Alberti. Through the visual discourse of the painting, form demonstrated the unity of reason and perception, and by the nineteenth century it occupied a central position in the curriculum of art students.

However, by the nineteenth century form had already enjoyed a variety of interpretations in the hands of artists. Chiaroscuro, transformed into a high graphic sense by Caravaggio and his followers, had given way to a livelier palette. Pictorial space in the work of Rubens and Velázquez was liquefied, sometime spilling into the linear confines of the form. In their work an ever-present quality of "passage" prevails, whereby the highly reflective propensity of shadows and halftones insinuates itself into less illuminated areas. Crucial to this manner of working is the locus of form's opening, always in the zones of shadow and half-light, described by Eugène Delacroix as "mirrors." Yet despite intrusions into its borders, form maintained stability, almost always privileging the light mass over the shadow—since form articulated by light became the reason of the painting, driving the focus of composition. Form exerted a kind of managerial control over how the image was understood—just as it was always already present in the conjuring mind of the artist—signifying "the discourse of the thing itself," in Plotinus's words.[1]

The opening up of linear confines within the elements of the picture, predicated on the intrusion of ground into figure, partly liberated the forms from their fixity within the pictorial field. This generated an effect of figures themselves spilling from imaginary space. The sheer fluidity of this pictorial field indicated a kind of surrender to the hypnotic suggestion of a vision continuous with the space of the viewer. In this way, Baroque artists dramatically expanded the inescapable web of illusion initiated by linear perspective. It was a position revisited later by Delacroix and the Romantics.

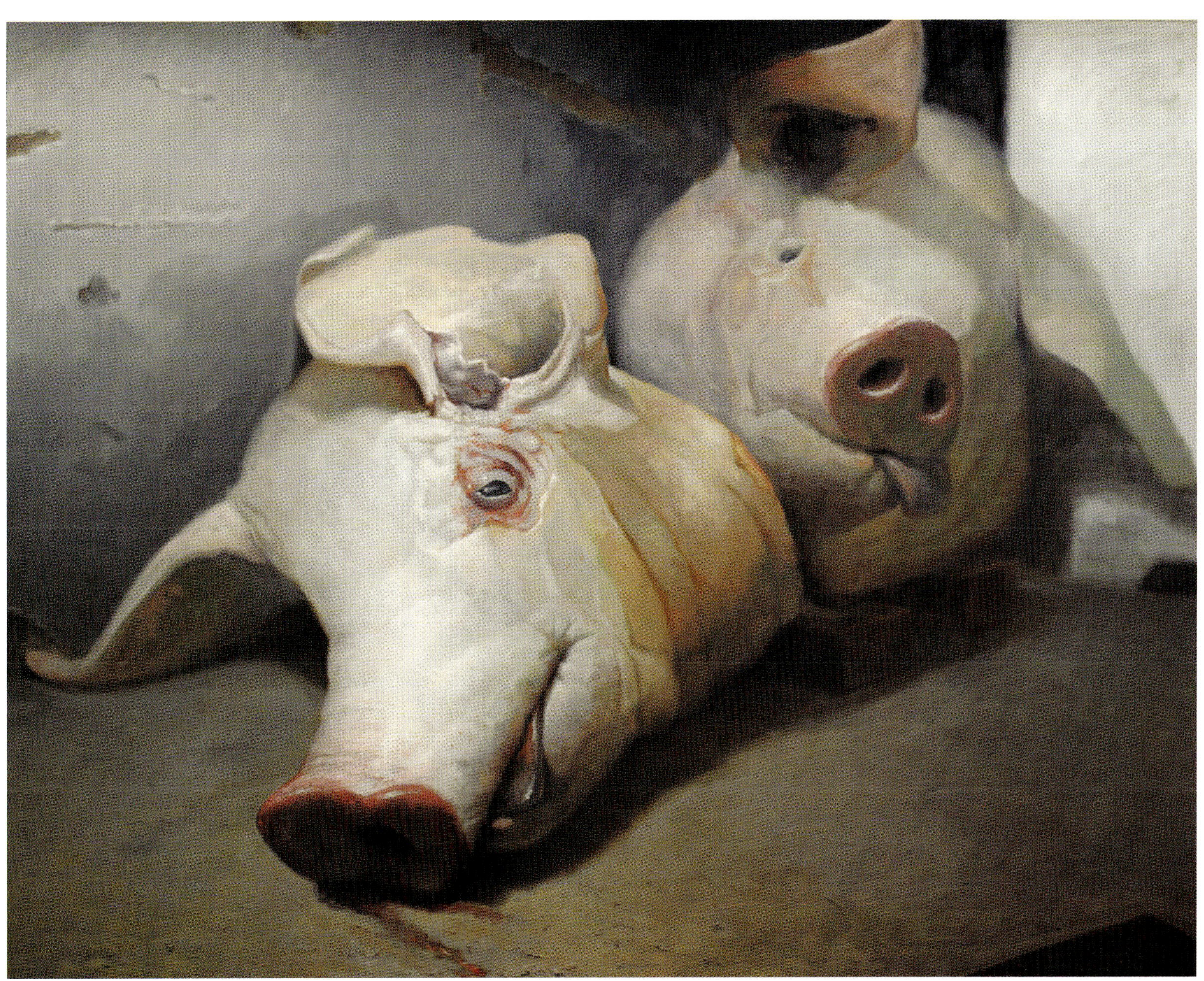

SPECTATORIAL DISTANCE AND NEOCLASSICISM

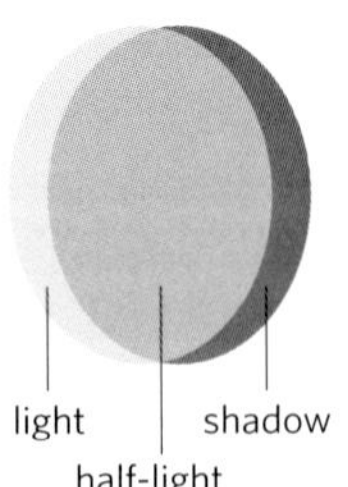

Yet by Delacroix's time in the early nineteenth century, another configuration of pictorial space favoring a more centripetal pictorial construction evolved. The precursor of this movement and its most influential model was Nicolas Poussin, an exact contemporary of Peter Paul Rubens. His long and active life was spent in Rome, where he absorbed, firsthand, the ancient forms around him. Eventually, painting of this sort found its greatest practitioners in the Neoclassical school of Jacques-Louis David. Neoclassical pictorial stability was evoked by a deep sense of order that was sequential and modular in the mathematical way that smaller relate to larger compositional parts. It indicated the projection and imbrication of form into a highly rationalized space. The object is contained within a field of regularity, predictability—a fathomable space illuminated to isolate the clear demonstration of masses and their interaction.

incidence of reflection

light mass

turning

shadow

We experience this visual field as if it were in a hermetically sealed box, distanced from our empathic involvement. We are thus held in a position of spectatorial distance—a place from which we can contemplate but not participate in the *istoria*. Consigned to a position outside of the frame, we behold the tableau, a "portable and self-sufficient picture that could be taken in at a glance."[2] The tableau is a painting wrested from site specificity, an embodiment of artistic accomplishment manifesting centuries of understanding, communicated through vectors of effect that recapitulate and celebrate the intellectual history of painters, whose empathic indifference establishes a purely spectatorial condition. It is a highly artificial construction predicated on form, its allegorization by the hierarchic events entombed, as it were, beneath the slick patination of a final varnish. Form, thus encapsulated within the newly fashioned citadel of the tableau, was publicly exposed in regular Salons, official exhibitions juried by the French Academy. Critical writing both in the press and in pamphlets accompanied these exhibitions, providing written appraisals and elucidations of exhibited works. Among the most notable were those of Denis Diderot.

Michael Fried draws an important connection between Diderot's advice to actors and the isolated narrative of a painting—a drama we are constrained to witness voyeuristically from the other side of the frame: ". . . think no more of the beholder than if he did not exist. Imagine, at the edge of the stage, a high wall that separates you from the orchestra. Act as if the curtain never rose."[3] The isolation of the viewer from the scene, or *istoria*, is critical to the function of such a construction. Compare it to Alberti's contrasting advice to painters of the perspectival field: "In an *istoria* I like to see someone who admonishes and points out to us what is happening there; or beckons with his hand to see; or menaces with an angry face and with flashing eyes, so that no one should come near; or shows some danger or marvelous thing there; or invites us to weep or to laugh together with them. Thus whatever the painted persons do among themselves or with the beholder, all is pointed towards ornamenting or teaching the *istoria*."[4] Here the beckoning of a viewer's participation in the optical and spiritual journey offered by Alberti's perspective aligns him or her with fellow pilgrims. Figures in the *istoria* anticipate the viewer's presence among them as they proceed to their destination—the (vanishing) point of infinite convergence. Conversely, the newer Neoclassical pictorial construction stresses his or her exclusion and participation only as a spectator.

(opposite)
Yunsung Jang
Portrait of Mother,
2013
Oil on canvas
96 x 84 inches

Form, as noted, had evolved as an allegorization of the Neoplatonic circuit of continuity to become the rational "marker" within painting. Its unity, constructed by the hierarchic portioning of light and shadow dispersed over an illuminated mass, culminated in the incidence of reflection's opening of the infinite corridor. French Neoclassical painting of the late eighteenth and early nineteenth centuries constructs moral lessons through hierarchically staged elements, from smallest detail to the highest emotion of the drama's climax.

Although the demand for pictorial unity preoccupied painters throughout the sixteenth and seventeenth centuries, eighteenth-century artistic interest turned to the action within the drama. Through dramatic narrativity, French Neoclassical painting illustrates form's symbolic manifestation. The visual moment of dramatic climax achieved—the *coup d'oeil* (glance, "stroke of the eye")—within a strict compositional unity is analogous to form's incidence of reflection within strictly organized zones of illumination. Perspective's epiphanic revelation, and its analog in Baroque light, are reified into "radical intelligibility"[5] in this new French painting. This reification occurs at the picture plane of the Neoclassical painting. Here a synaptic inhibition takes place, momentarily breaking the unified complicity of perception and reason. The sequence of fluid disclosure throughout the composition is stopped, as though interrupted by an authoritative, pedagogical voice, strongly suggesting how the picture should be viewed. It is tempting to see the tableau, a French creation, as a readymade, a box of pre-manufactured ideas corralled into a form institutionally recognized as art.

DELACROIX'S DECONSTRUCTION OF FORM

The structured authority of Neoclassicism and the institutional and critical prescriptions that enforced it were untenable to an artist of Delacroix's temperament. For him, the hermetic encapsulation of painting's technical narrative reified into formulas of disclosure, amounting to a co-opting of the painter's imagination. Painting's capacity to evoke an uninterrupted continuity of being, an alertness to the unfathomable sublime, stuttered in the moral strictures of Neoclassicism. The soul's "free flight" by way of painting's armature was impeded by the interruption of the plane of the picture. Neoclassicist closure stressed a past-tense viewing—a fait accompli—that objectified the experience. For the painting's organic function to be activated by present-tense visual complicity between painter and viewer, form had to be in a sense deconstructed. Among the Romantics, who frequently sought insight and inspiration in exotic places, terrifying emotional states, and the sublime exaltation of nature, Delacroix located this experiential narrative within the act of painting itself—specifically, within the optics of

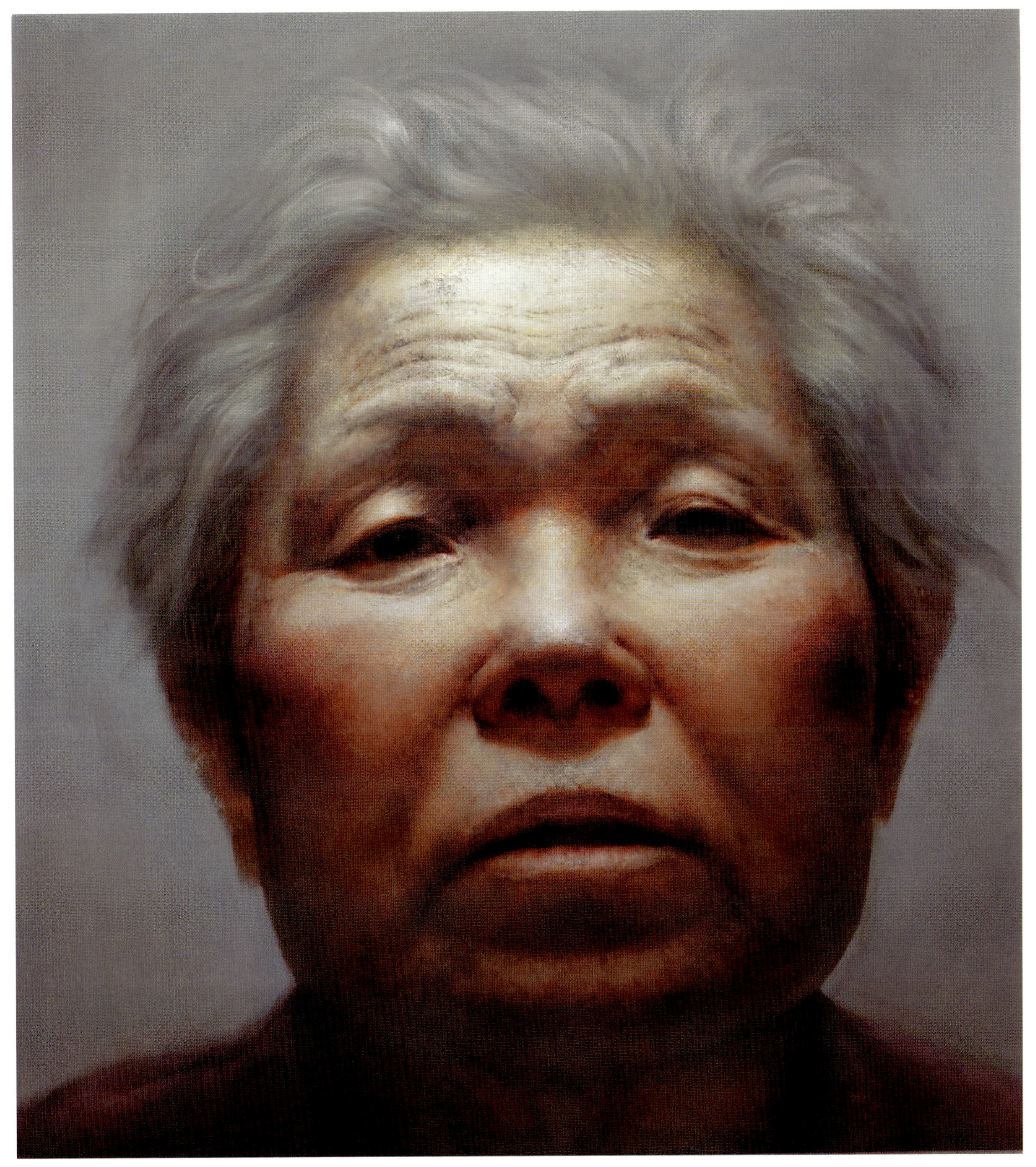

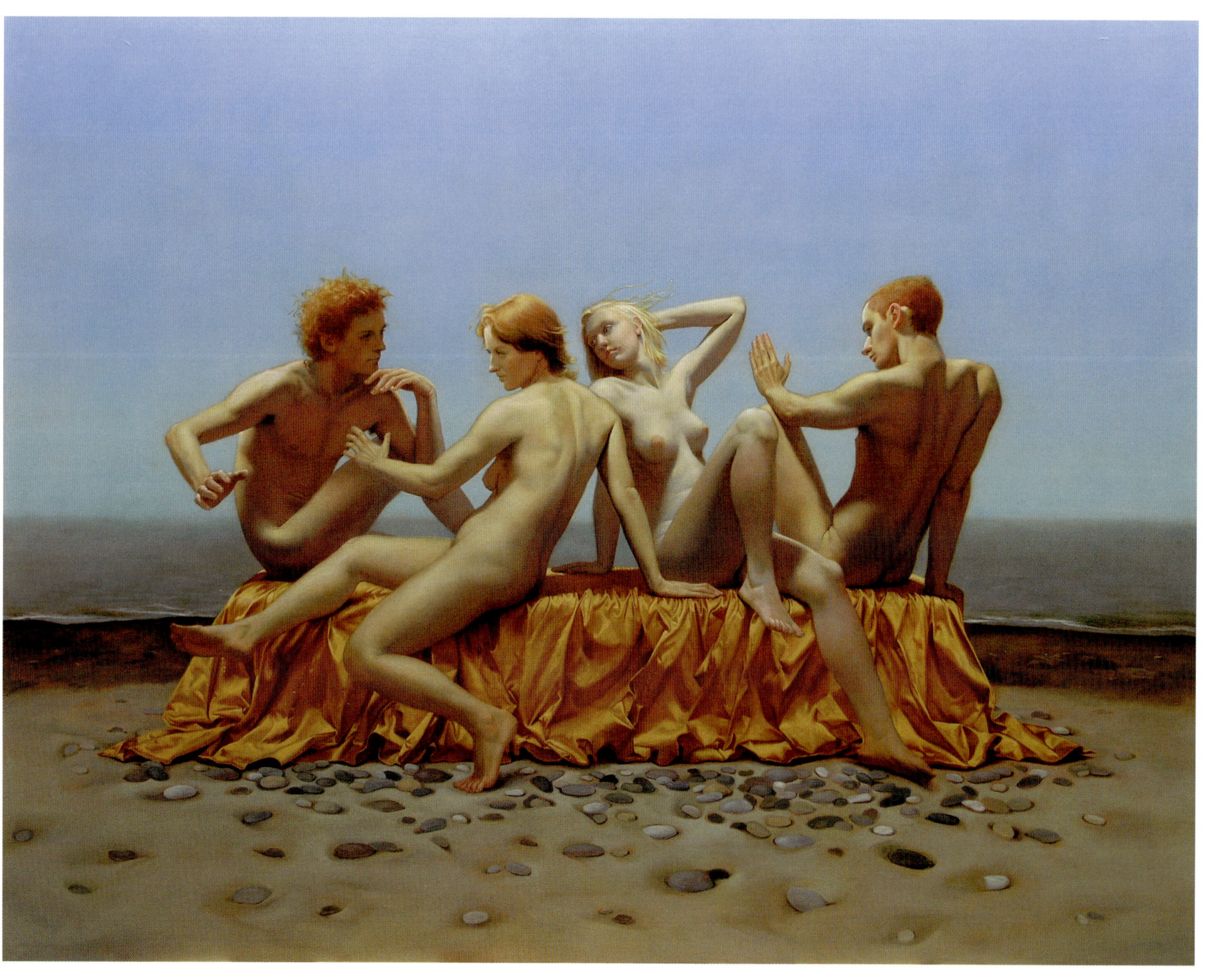

illumination's zone of greatest chromatic activity: half-light. Through its emphasis, Delacroix would enact one of the greatest disturbances in the continuity of form's privilege within the rational structure of painting.

In Delacroix's paintings, light filters onto scenes in a mottled fashion, punctuating a visual field already established in half-light. On May 5, 1852, he made a curious journal entry (see below) describing color relationships in terms of the optics of illumination, which anticipated the eventual subversion of form by color in avant-garde painting. Its substance is absolutely central to the artist's conception of color—both optically and as an allegorization of the exotic. For Delacroix, the half-light of a gray day represented an exotic realm where color was free to demonstrate its highly reflective propensity, undisturbed by incidents of direct light and shadow:

> *A picture should be laid-in as if one were looking at the subject on a grey day, with no sunlight or clear-cut shadows. Fundamentally, lights and shadows do not exist. Every object presents a color mass having different reflections on all sides. Suppose a ray of sunshine should suddenly light up the objects in this open-air scene under grey light, you will then have what are called lights and shadows, but they will be pure accidents. This, strange as it may appear, is a profound truth and contains the whole meaning of color in painting.*[6]

Delacroix's tempestuous *Death of Sardanapalus* (1828) is a manifesto of sorts, heralding the destruction of a system of pictorial stability. Taken from Lord Byron, the massive canvas depicts Sardanapalus casually reclining on his bed, watching dispassionately as the symbols of his wealth are destroyed. Rather than submit to surrender he orders his kingdom be decimated. The painting's even illumination allows full description of human forms being put to the blade; it is tempting to read into this Delacroix's dawning awareness of half-light's subversive, revealing nature, and the consequences his investigations into color would unleash.

The pure chromatic interface of light and shadow became the goal of the French Impressionists; the break into symbolic, expressionist color in Postimpressionism occurred on the heels of color's ascendancy. By the end of the nineteenth century, color had become completely dislodged from its moorings in tonality. In the paintings of Vincent Van Gogh, Edvard Munch, Odilon Redon, James Ensor, Pierre Bonnard, and Henri Matisse, a sense of Dionysian reverie prevails, and rationality is utterly destabilized by the suppression of tonal markers. Delacroix, concerned with the liberation of form in order to enable an unimpeded sequentialization of space, was not prepared to take such a move, but his rebellion against the shackles of tonal supremacy melted the icy box of spectatorial distance, allowing the viewer's sensation of immersion into pictorial space. Delacroix compressed the contemplative distance essential to the Neoclassical sensibility to a point of simultaneity of the subject with the object it presumed to observe. The inwardness of Delacroix's vision, allegorized by the infinity of chromatic variety within half-light, rendered him present with an exotic realm of the Self.

Romantic painting epitomized a perpetual state of becoming—an eternal present tense galvanized by the traces of the painter's brush. It represents the reclamation of the painter's authority over the continuity of visual thought, channeled through the autonomy of creative imagination. With the dismantling of form and its dissolution into the fluidity of creative imaginary space, an ultra subjectivity was born. Through heightened sensuality, activated by color's primacy, the painter forced an advance on the picture plane, projecting his viewer into the volatile convolutions of the artistic mind. The viewer becomes engulfed by the artist's imagination, in the genius of his hallucinatory vision. This would eventually lead to an absolute break with the sequential codes of disclosure in painting. For this to occur, painting had to elide the very medium through which this current flowed: space itself.

The sequentialization of space via perspective—the rational act of creating sensual perception of homogeneous space—formed the common ground of viewing for more than five centuries. It maintained the painter's distant memory of perspective's *circuitus spiritualis*, which unified reason and perception with the flight of the soul. It establishes continuity between painter and viewer and set the stage for, as Norman Bryson wrote, the "mutual work of signification"[7]: The painter organizes a sequence of visual events as vectors of intended viewing, coaxing them into alliance with an unfolding visual field. He manipulates these events to resist the eye's tendency to wander from the authoritative structure of the work, and their contingency within the visual field constitutes narrative formation. Whether that field empathically embraces the viewer by drawing him into the web of the painting's performance (in Romanticism) or delays his participation by hermetically closing itself off from fluid interaction (in Neoclassicism), the construction's intelligibility still requires that the viewer surrender to the artifice of its illusion, thereby establishing a circular practice of exchange. As such he enters into an optical complicity with the work, and through this complicity participates in the picture's sequential narrativity.

MANET AND EMBLEMATIC NARRATIVITY

The radical early work of Manet is the first example of the absolute break in the tradition of sequential disclosure. It signals the beginning of Modernism and the creation of the artist in full rebellion against society and its bourgeois codes of intelligibility. His work shows the nascent stages of a form of technical narrativity termed "emblematic." Emblemization requires a shutting down of the traditional channels of disclosure between painter and viewer. In this visual event, an object's removal from the sequence of its normal comprehension or cultural utility forces a detached reading. This establishes the need for formal critical analysis that omits any speculation regarding intentionality. The emblemized painting disemploys the viewer's expectation of homogeneous space, razing the enchantment of seamlessness. Intelligibility through mutual expectation on either side of the painting's membrane is re-circuited to mask the exact nature of the artist's meaning—privatizing it in a way that recalls Mannerist inwardness.

(opposite)
Martha Mayer Erlebacher
The Cycle of Life, Fire: Youth, 2006
Oil on canvas
64 x 80 inches

The development of emblematic narrativity in Manet's work is brilliantly demonstrated in his three versions of *The Execution of Maximilian*, all dated around 1867. In the first (at the Museum of Fine Arts, Boston) a full-blown Romanticism is evident in the dense, smoky haze and swift and brutal brushstrokes that speak directly to the violent death of the emperor and his aides. Borne on a whirlwind of empathic disclosure, its reality contrasts sharply with the second version (at the National Gallery, London), which is oddly dispassionate, suggestive of Neoclassicism. (We are reminded too of the coolly objective detachment that characterizes the optical stoicism of Diego Velázquez, a painter Manet greatly admired.) Our spectatorial view removes us from the brutality of their action. The technical narratives of both pictures offer no real surprises in terms of spatial expectation; both are firmly rooted in pictorial practices that would have been instantly recognizable to their viewing publics.

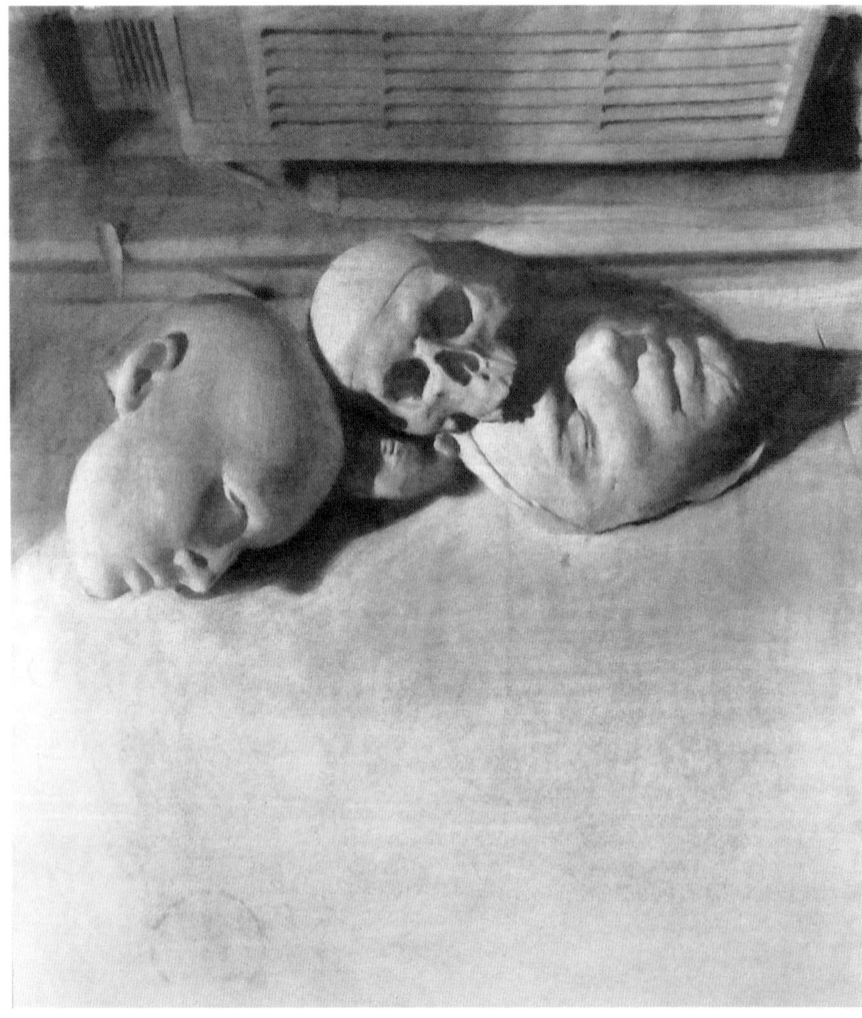

Michael Grimaldi
Windowsill Self-Portrait 2, 2010
Graphite on paper
18 x 14 inches

(opposite)
Will Cotton
Fairy Floss, 2009
Oil on linen
83.25 x 56.25 inches

The third version (at the Kunsthalle Mannheim) is a different story entirely and has inspired a good deal of commentary. The detachment already discernible in the London version attains a level verging on visual agnosia. The figures are pure synthetic creations, almost like decoupage, lifted from one context and reinserted into another. One might interpret the abbreviated brushwork as lively reductions of form in the service of optical illusion, the way a Velázquez or Frans Hals at close range dissolves into vigorous masses of color, while space is solidly established from a distance of a few feet. The forms in the Mannheim *Execution*, however, unresolvable at any distance, are marks isolated from their utility in the accomplishment of illusion (one is tempted to see them as signifiers detached from the onus of the signified—misquotations from the index of recognition). Aesthetically privatized and exclusionary, they suggest the artist's self-imposed exile—a tendency previously noted in the *disegno interno* of Mannerism and in Delacroix—within the work itself.

The Mannheim *Execution* is painting turned inward to itself. It strangely includes spectators absent from previous versions. The relative naturalism of these figures, amassed above a wall that separates them from the action they behold, contrasts sharply with the relentless flatness of the rest of the picture. Fried wrote that he regretted their superfluous presence in his reading of an allegorical drama,[8] and Juliet Wilson-Bareau called them the "only overtly emotional note in the picture."[9] I see their existence as historical markers, indications of the kinds of beings who once inhabited pictures—the figures in an *istoria*, depicted in a manner reminiscent of Francisco de Goya. They view the killing from the other side of the synthetic action we are privy to. Thus, for Manet, the execution can only be presented as an inscrutable phenomenon parenthetically mediated by the history of such depictions and our own incapacity to understand it.
In Manet's hands the defining operations of perspective—the illusion of spatial continuity and the capacity to visualize the flight of artistic soul to the ineffable realms of the sublime—are reified into an allegory of thwarted visibility. The terrifying indifference that characterizes the Mannheim *Execution* did not escape the notice of Georges Bataille, who stated that

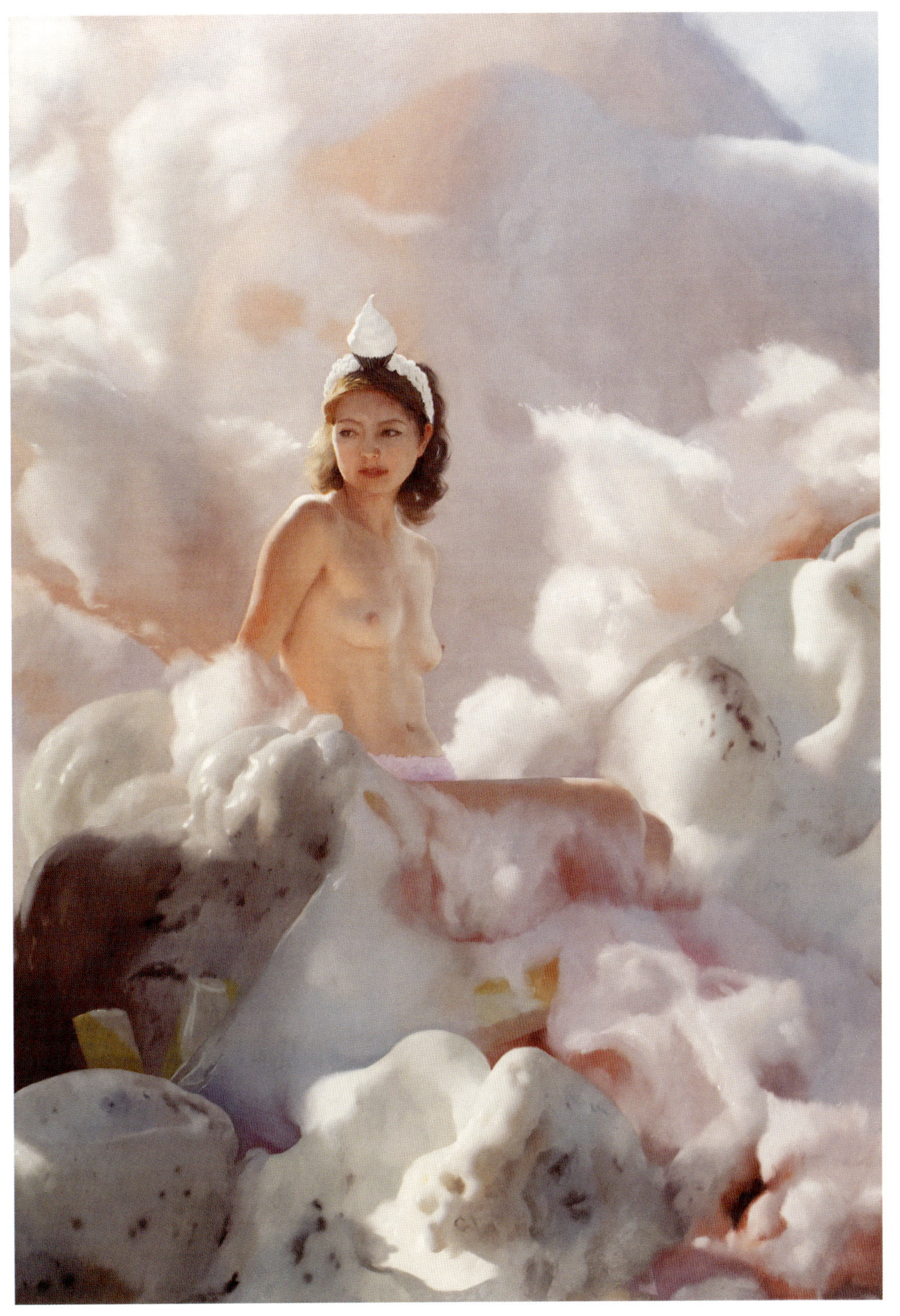

Manet depicted the murder of a man with the detachment of an artist painting a fish on a platter.[10]

The strangeness of this painting is to a large degree related to Manet's propensity for reshuffling preexisting shards from the history of painting and re-contextualizing them. Painterly effects and thematic materials are lifted from positions within an illusionistic paradigm, and reissued in ways that undermine illusion's seamlessness. The broken illusion draws attention to itself, calling into question the very necessity of its existence—and in the case of Maximilian's execution, the futility of human vision to identify truth. In this, the Mannheim *Execution* anticipates the creation of two entirely different works of art—both engaged with perspective and the futility of perception: Marcel Duchamp's *The Bride Stripped Bare by Her Bachelors, Even* and Gerhard Richter's *Baader-Meinhof* series.

No doubt Manet was perplexed at the public's reception of his work and sought, throughout his life, to gain the official recognition he believed was his due. The same was true of Delacroix in regard to the Academy. The ridicule to which his works were subjected caused his friend Zacharie Astruc to remark that his "paintings have a soul and that they experience in themselves the effects of that hostility."[11] The impact that this hostility had on painters of the next generation was profound. Recognizing the futility of public acceptance, painters once again retreated inwardly, as the Mannerists had. By radically changing the codes of intelligibility, Manet initiated the creation of the artist as fugitive—the Modernist in perpetual flight from the scrutiny of the critic—and set in motion a methodology for the avant-garde that continued for over one hundred years. The fugitivity of the artist has been indicated by the famous words of artists themselves: "Learn to paint from your imagination, then you will find your soul and avoid the scrutiny of the amateur" (Paul Gauguin); "The painting should be executed like the perfect crime" (Edgar Degas); and as Pablo Picasso remarked, "Art is a lie through which the truth is revealed."

No one alive today can recall what it must have felt like to act as an artist before the habitus of steady-state revolution, nor envision what the early years of Modernism meant for its participants. The exuberant and incendiary brilliance of early Modernist creations suggests that embarking on a refreshed program of visual thought must have been exhilarating. Still, one can see a tempered enthusiasm in avant-garde artists, for in all their revolutionary verve, they had not lost sight of the great land mass preceding them, which determined to a large degree the character of their revolution. They still remembered the hard-won struggle for artistic autonomy that had preoccupied artistic intention since the birth of perspective, understood as a circuit of revelation, an empowerment of artistic vision. Even as they dismantled and realigned its internal functions, changing, as it were, its code, they possessively guarded its ownership—for it was, after all, their invention. They did this even if it meant burying it under the ground of their subconscious, allowing it to effervesce from time to time in order to remind them of the rigor and profundity of visual thought.

(opposite)
Roxanne Ritacco
Child on Bed, 1998
Oil on canvas
60 x 79 inches

EDWARD SCHMIDT

In 1964 I began studying at Pratt Institute. Gabriel Laderman's class was transforming. His teaching was grounded in cubism and Modernism. He studied with Hans Hofmann and Willem de Kooning, and was among the New Realism painters in New York. My strongest influence then was Lennart Anderson. I was also influenced by Robert Beverly Hale, whose anatomy classes I attended at the League. I studied at Skowhegan with Philip Pearlstein and Walter Murch. I moved to Paris to attend the École des Beaux-Arts and studied with Roger Chapelain-Midy. I drew casts and made regular visits to the Louvre, looking at Poussin, Delacroix, Géricault, and Chassériau, and drew from the Puvis de Chavannes murals in the Panthéon. I painted figure compositions of contemporary street scenes and many small landscapes around Paris. In the MFA program at Brooklyn College, I studied with Alfred Russell, Joe Groell, and Jimmy Ernst. Russell and Groell were especially influential. In 1975, I was a founding member of a Pratt summer landscape painting program in the south of France. I painted scores of plein-air pictures, an experience very important for my later painting. I moved back to Paris to study engraving at Atelier 17, with the surrealist printmaker Stanley William Hayter, whose teaching of automatic drawing was an important influence on me. I won the Rome Prize from the American Academy in Rome and left in 1982 for two years in Rome, an amazing time.

I work in several modes when I paint and draw, and often have no plan to carry out a complete pictorial idea. I produce lots of possible images simply for the pleasure of doing it. Drawing is primary for me. I draw regularly and see, think, and imagine in terms of drawing. I practice drawing from memory and work in sketchbooks of all sizes and qualities. Working small, I like the clarity, sharpness, and strong graphic language of pen drawing. I do, at times, follow the tradition of pictorial development starting from small compositional sketches, working the most promising among them to a larger scale.

Exploring ideas and images, I prefer water-based media, often fabricating my own paints. I use brushes of all sizes and shapes. I also use sponges, pads, rollers, scrapers, etc., that I shape and cut to make various marks and patterns. I combine dry drawing materials with water-based paints. I work in washes of watercolor, or apply water to chalks, or use pigment washes (dissolved dry pigments in water) on heavy semi-absorbent paper. I also use thinned white paint (gouache, acrylic gesso, or a water-soluble oil paint) as a "body color" to establish a hierarchy of light. I may develop a small study in elaborate grisaille values to mimic the full tonal range of a finished painting.

On studies, I often work spontaneously to create compositions with brush and ink, tempera, or acrylic, and use a variety of brushes, some strange in character such as modified fan brushes or brushes with hairs cut away. At times, I am after the gestalt, a broad dark and light structure. Other times I work for complexity and richness of tone to stimulate visualization and the discovery of latent images, a tradition that extends from Leonardo to the English blot painters, to Victor Hugo and the Surrealists.

I also work directly on the full-size canvas or large-scale prepared paper. The direct "attack" on a large canvas is unfailingly exciting. This allows the discovery

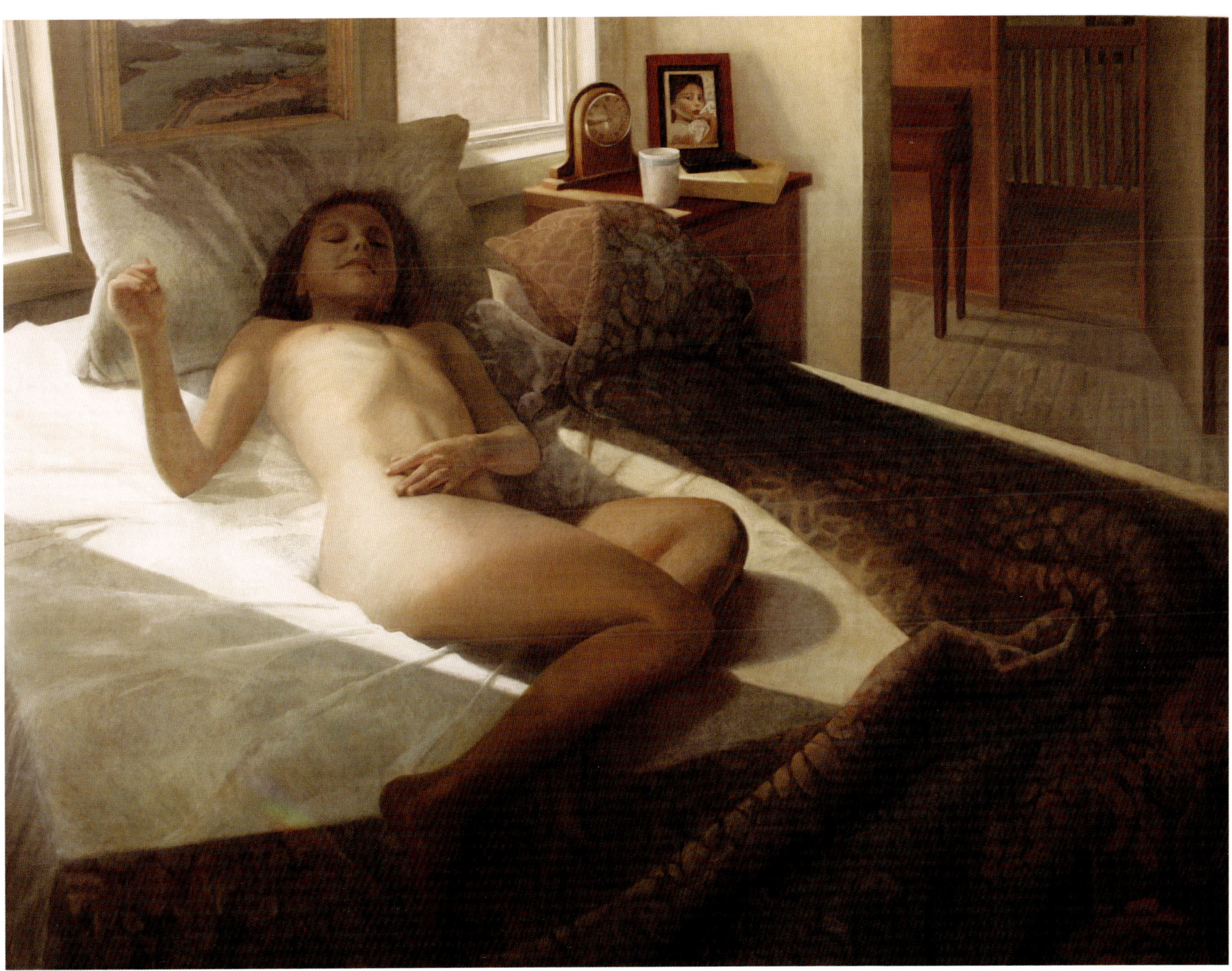

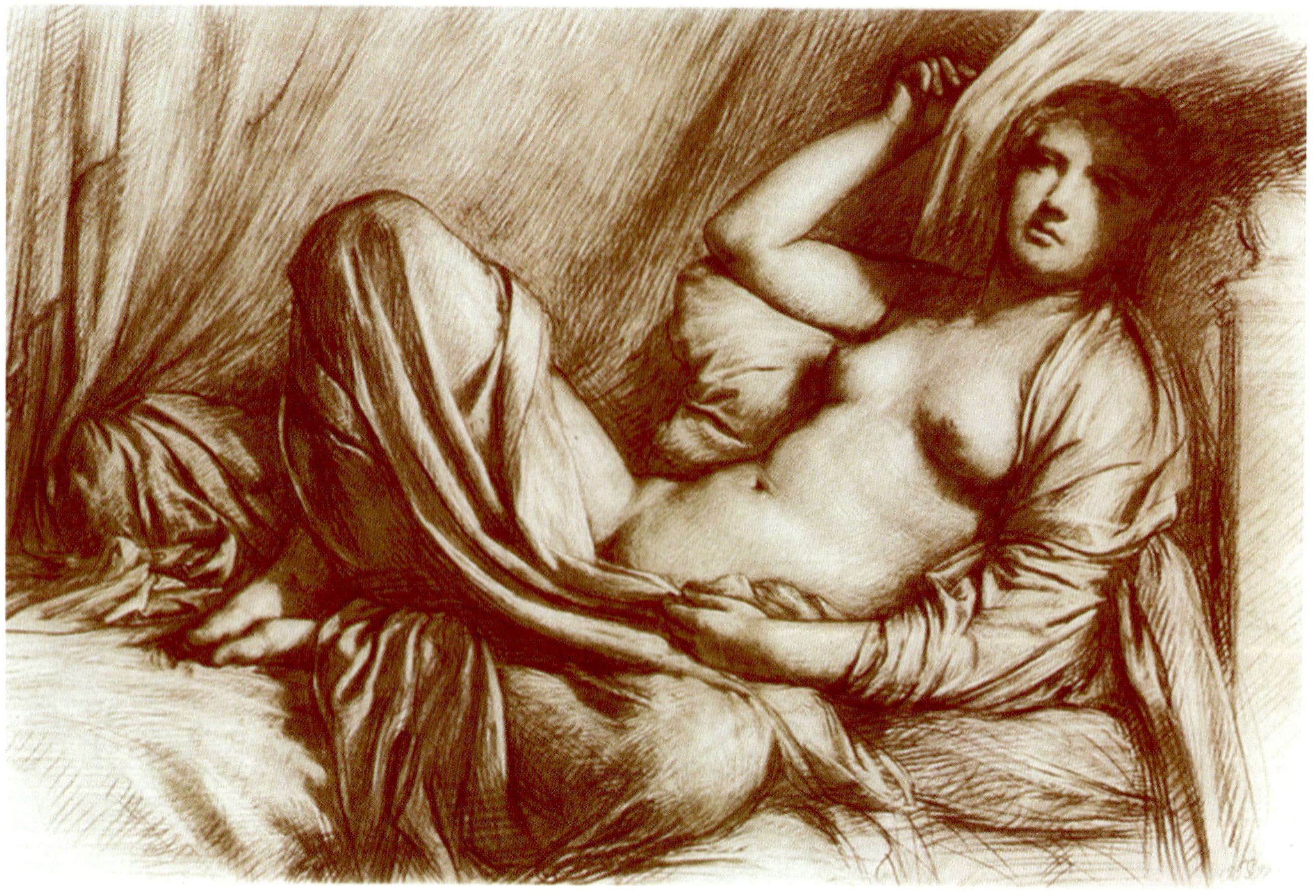

Edward Schmidt
Danae, 1997
Sanguine chalk on paper
32 x 45 inches

(opposite)
Edward Schmidt
Conversation (Diana and Callisto), 2003
Oil on linen
39 x 43 inches

of an image in the actual scale and support. I conceive of this initial stage as part of an underpainting, in which drawing, brushwork, colors, pigments, painting medium, values, shapes, edges, and details are all consistent with the technical requirements of the foundation layer of an oil painting. I especially like working when the distinctions between drawing and painting become blurred. Developing an underpainting is essentially a drawing activity for me. Transforming the picture into an oil painting is not the end of drawing. The brushwork, modeling, working of contours, surface description, and placement of details, all depend on drawing—the controlled movements of the hand and brush.

I do also work directly from models, painting and drawing on the canvas without a subject, freely changing the poses until a composition and narrative start to take form. A second pose may be added to find a formal and expressive counterpart to the first. My palette at this stage is restricted to a limited range of neutral warms and cools: venetian red, yellow ochre, ultramarine blue, lead or titanium white, umber, and black, with a medium of diluted Galkyd, working with large brushes. I am also drawing and correcting in charcoal or sanguine chalk. I use the contrasting temperatures of paint and drawing media to differentiate shapes of figures to ground, light to shadow, structural and spatial planes.

The next stages involve attention to the requirement of the composition as a whole. I will often return to making small drawings or oil studies to work out the picture's problems. I will again use models, refining poses and working the colors and light with more confidence and complexity. Each aspect of picture-making seems to become especially important at different times. Presently, spatial construction and pictorial structure are occupying my thoughts and research.

Photoshop and the scanner are marvelous tools I often take advantage of. I collect images and references from everywhere, transform them through Photoshop and file them. I use Photoshop playfully and find it useful in exploring possible compositions. I don't have much interest in projection. Deciding when a painting is finished has never been an easy question. I like the Arshile Gorky quote: "When something is finished, that means it's dead, doesn't it? I believe in everlastingness. I never finish a painting—I just stop working on it for a while."

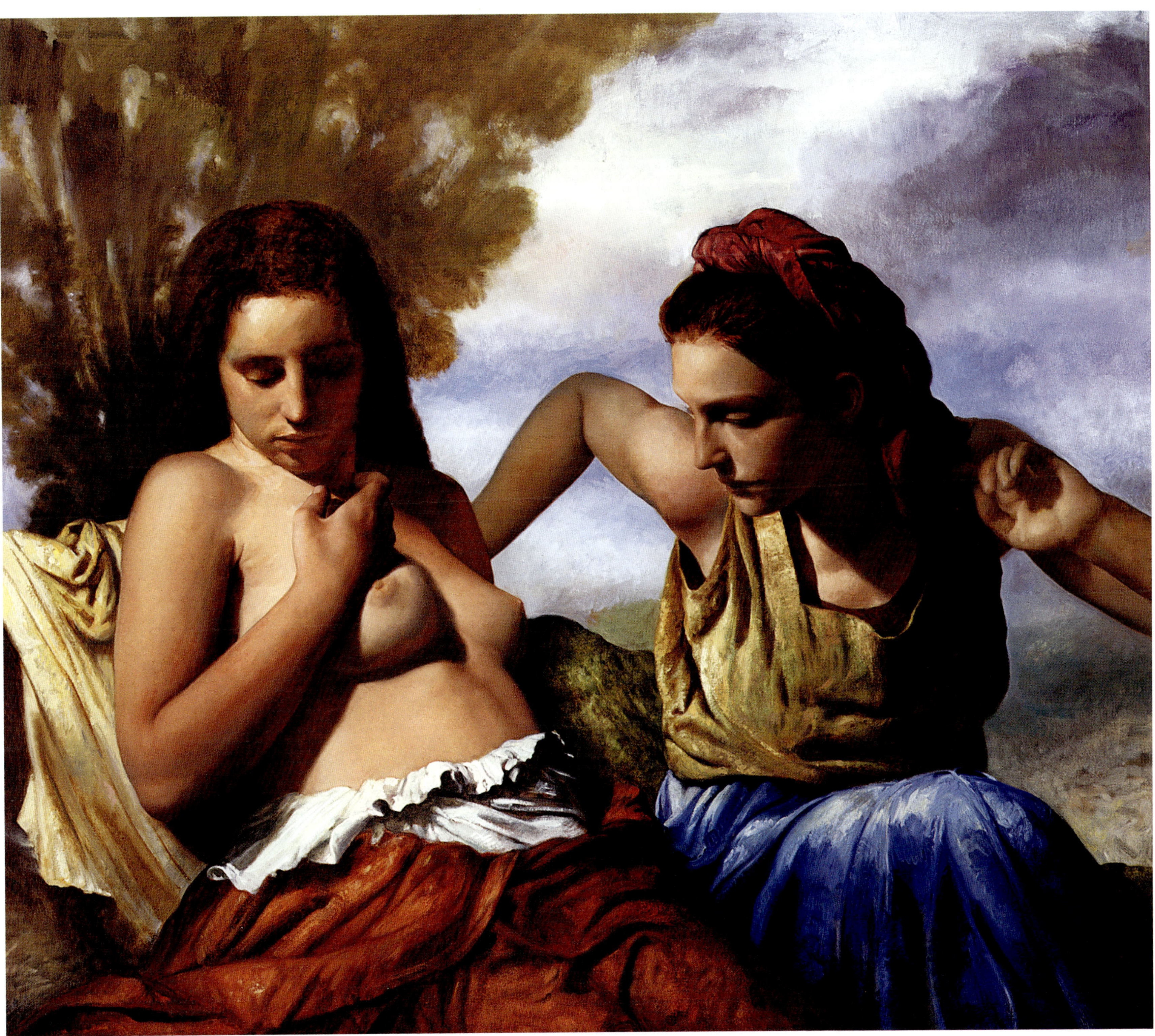

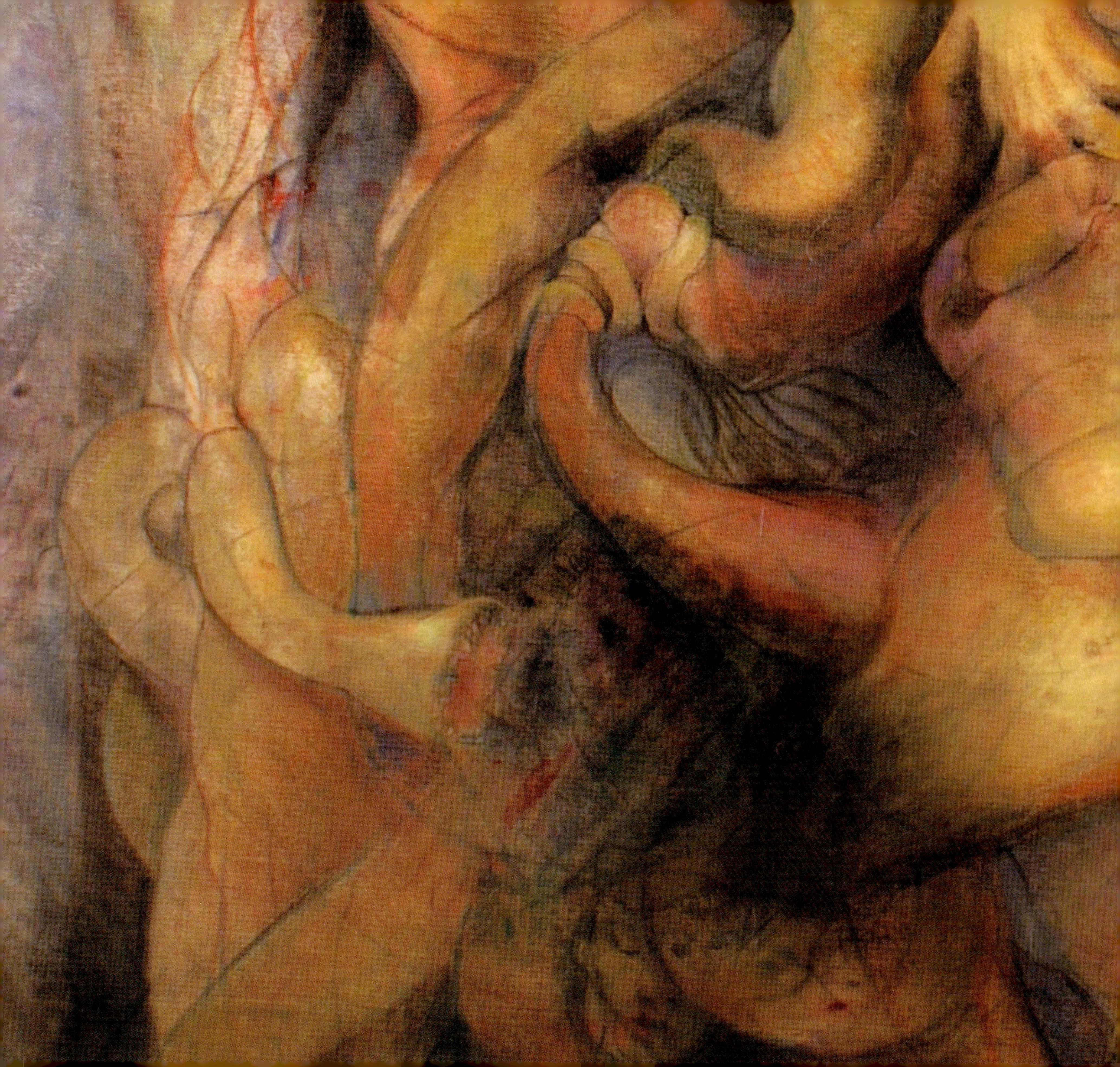

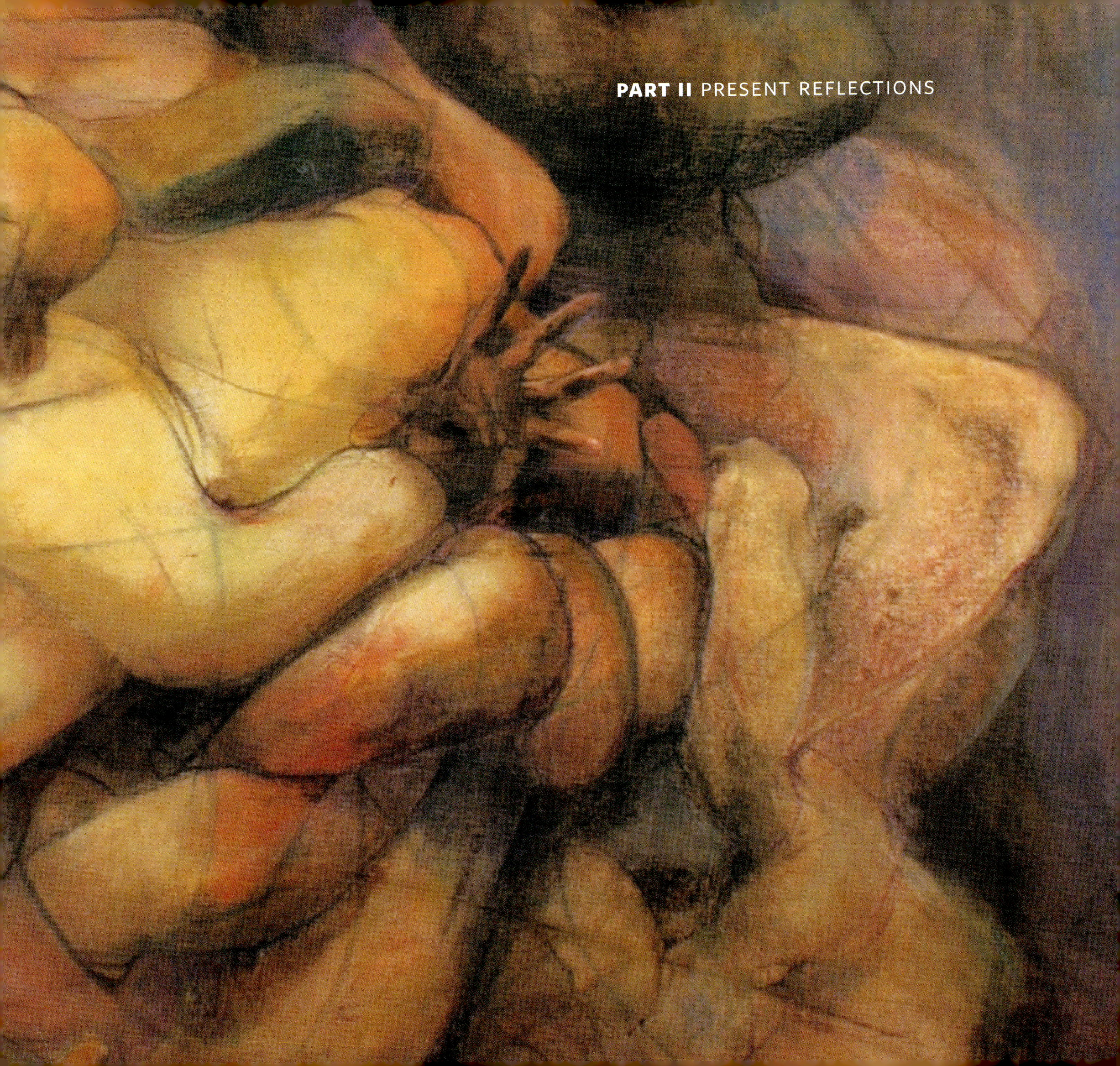

PART II PRESENT REFLECTIONS

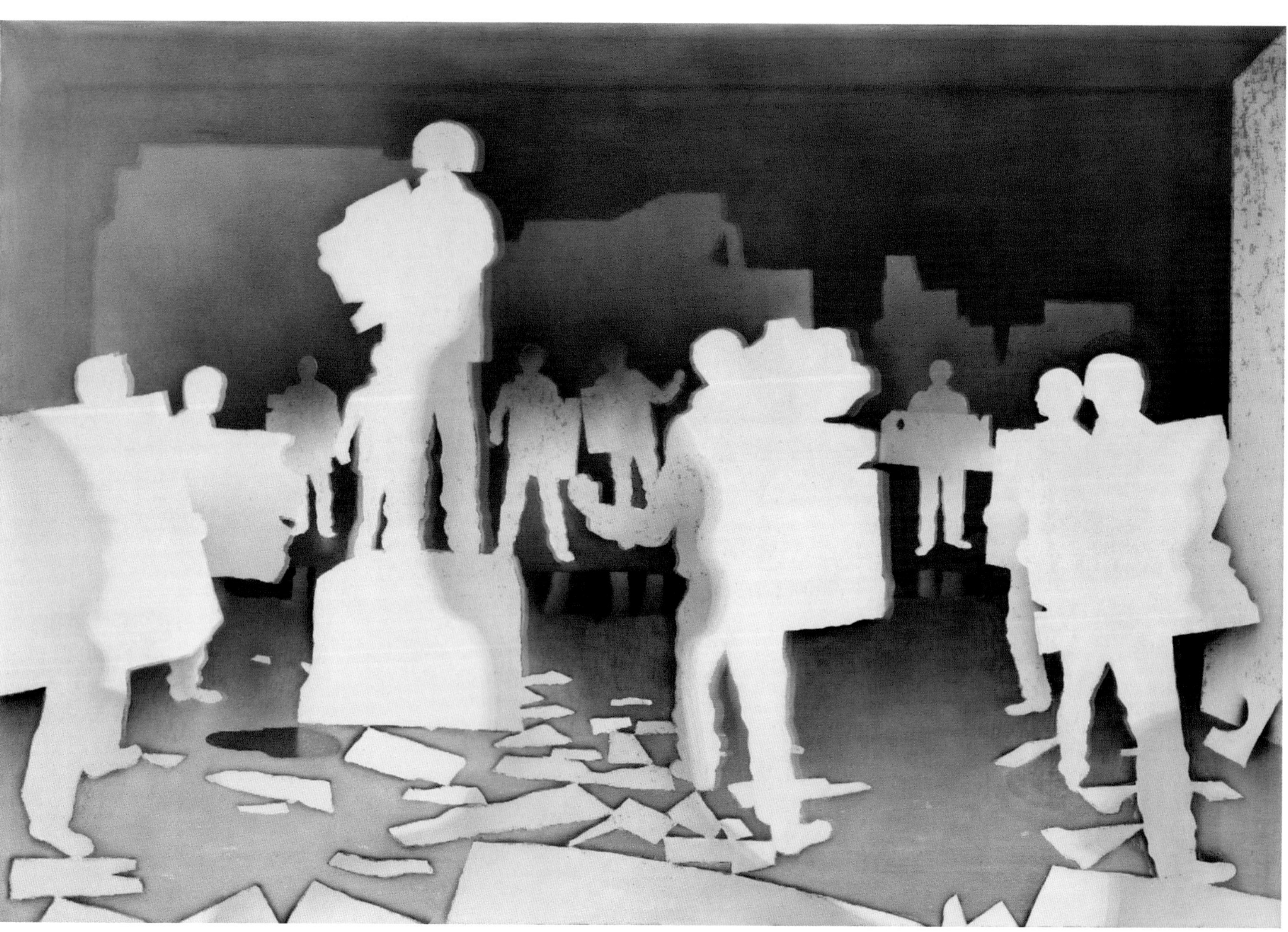

THE INVENTION OF CLUMSINESS: PHOTOGRAPHY AND MODERNISM

ALEXI WORTH

ONE EVENING IN MAY OF 1853, after a walk in the forest with two old friends, Eugène Delacroix asked them to participate in a little experiment. First he passed around a set of unusual pictures, daguerreotypes he had just taken with his friend Jean Durieu. In these small silvery images, a naked man and a woman appeared in conventional art-school postures, staring warily back at the lens. Among the first human beings to be photographed nude, the couple didn't exactly impress the great painter and his companions. "Poorly built, and oddly shaped in places," as Delacroix put it, the two models were "not very attractive generally." After his guests had spent some time examining the daguerreotypes, Delacroix asked them to examine a second set of pictures, ones that should have been much more appealing. These were engravings by the celebrated Renaissance draftsman Marcantonio Raimondi—including perhaps his *Adam and Eve* (circa 1520), or the famous *Judgment of Paris* (c. 1515), both figure compositions based on designs by Raphael. Like Paris himself, who contemplates three nude goddesses in Raimondi's print, Delacroix's guests were asked to make a fraught comparison. When it came to a key subject of Western painting, the unclothed human body, how would the new "machine art" fare against human skill? How would Daguerre's unflattering nakedness compare to the Renaissance's idealized nudity? The result was decisive. Looking at the older nudes, Delacroix's group saw them with new eyes: the Raimondis were no longer admirable. They were clumsy, even grotesque.

> *We experienced a feeling of revulsion, almost disgust* [Delacroix wrote in his diary] *for the incorrectness, the mannerism, the lack of naturalness, despite the quality of style—the only thing one could admire. Yet at that moment we could no longer admire it.*[1]

Those few words record both a private social occasion and a historical watershed—the moment when photographs defamiliarized the art of the past. Delacroix and his peers had grown up in an era when human nakedness was memorialized by prints, drawings, and paintings. To their eyes, the look of photographed bodies seemed abnormal and unattractive. As of that evening though, *so did Renaissance draftsmanship*. Western visual culture was beginning its shift to new, less artisanal foundations, and for an awkward transitional moment, both new and old norms were insecure. Photography, as Delacroix put it, had begun by rendering a "detestable" service: "without completely satisfying us, it spoils the masterpieces."[2]

Almost two centuries later, we're apt to think of the birth of photography as initiating a long history of anxiety about painting's future. For Delacroix, the opposite was true. The past was shadowed, while the future looked brighter than ever. In the following months, he would arrange more modeling sessions with Durieu, and eagerly make drawings from the results. Over time, he felt that photographs would contribute to a new and improved kind of painting. In his journal, he ended his account of the evening's experiment with a confident glimpse into the future: "Truly, if a [painter] of genius should use the daguerreotype as it ought to be used," Delacroix prophesized, "he will raise himself to heights unknown to."[3]

What kind of "heights" did Delacroix imagine? If future viewers shared the new, almost painful sensitivity to incorrectness, perhaps photography would become a sort of proofreading tool. The painters of the future would use it to eliminate the old faults and mannerisms, assimilating photography's impressive objectivity—while (of course) steering clear of its potential unattractiveness. This kind of prudent assimilation was in fact the hallmark of the next generation's leading painters, people like Jean-Léon Gérôme, Alexandre Cabanel, and Jean Meissonier in France, John Everett Millais in England,

(opposite)
Alexi Worth
Square II, 2013
Acrylic on nylon mesh
48 x 68 inches

and Frederic Edwin Church in the United States. A bland accuracy, akin to photography in its finish and meticulous detail (but not in its frankness), paralleled the growing availability of photographs themselves. Some critics claimed that by 1859, "the majority of artists" were already working directly from daguerreotypes, "their most precious aid."[4] We'll never know if that's entirely true, but it doesn't matter: whether or not they were drawing from them, virtually all mid-century painters were looking over their shoulders at photographic effects. And we know that even a brief exposure could induce the sensitivity that Delacroix had first described, the disgust and revulsion at a pre-photographic "errorfulness." What we now think of loosely as "academic painting" was in effect the first broad response to this sensitivity.

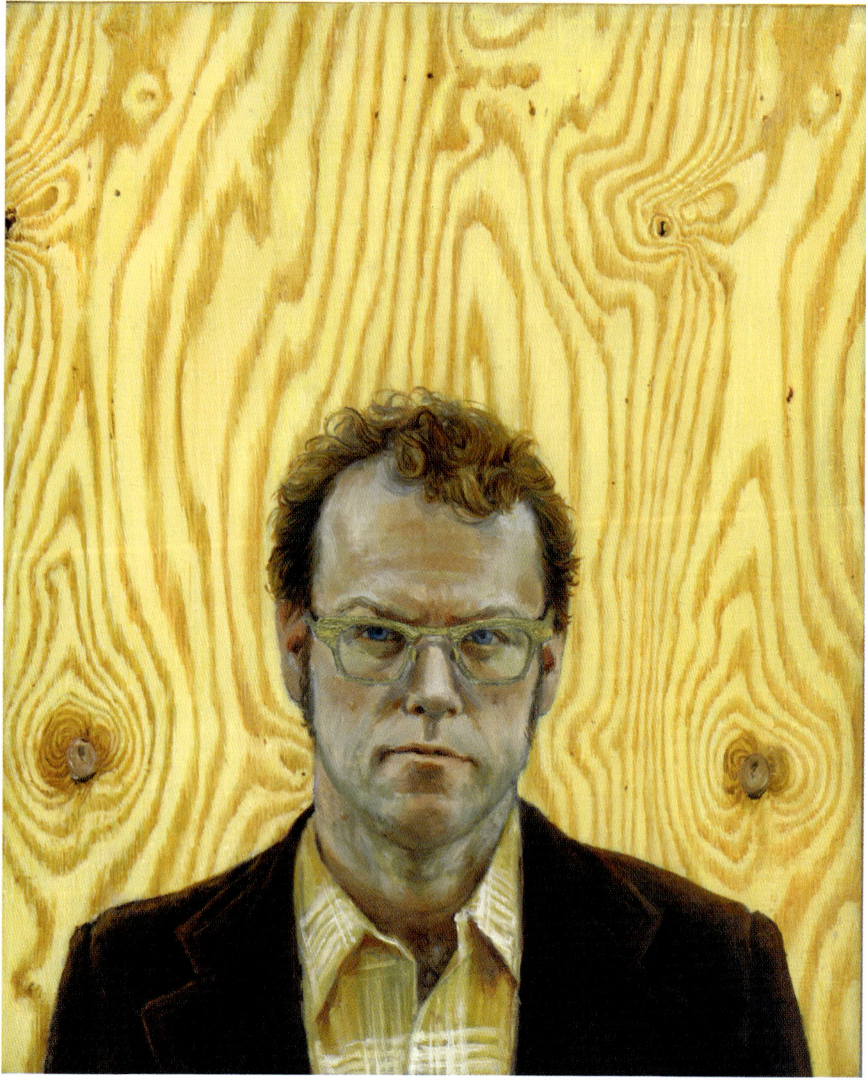

Alexandra Evans
John Jacobsmeyer as Master of His Piney New World, 2011
Oil on panel
10 x 8 inches

(opposite)
Amy Bennett
Exposure, 2006
Oil on panel
8 x 10 inches

Delacroix may have felt that sensitivity keenly in May of 1853, but he was no prophet of academic painting. On the contrary, he was its most outspoken opponent, with a lifelong distaste for technical qualities he associated with an imagination-stifling literalism. Chief among these was overabundant *detail*—the meticulous, minute, seemingly infinite detail that was also seen as the most dazzling and characteristic feature of photography. In an essay written a few years after the Durieu experiment, Delacroix defined photographic vision in terms of detail. As he saw it, photography was quintessentially "a medium for giving a completely exact rendering," for showing us "all the leaves on a tree, all the tiles of a roof." Its unrelieved exactness struck him as unnatural and unselective: "When a photographer takes a scene," he complained, "the edge of the picture is as interesting as the center . . . the subordinate parts as dominant as the main subject."[5] Even correctness, which seemed to captivate Delacroix the evening of the Durieu experiment, was a conditional virtue. In the first instant of recognizing Raimondi's inferiority, he was careful to say that the engravings' "quality of style" was still visible, although not "at that moment." Implicitly Delacroix anticipated a time when correctness would matter less. "The grandeur of the masters," he later declared, perhaps thinking more forgivingly of Raimondi, "does not consist in the absence of faults." He was close to taking the next logical step, that is, historicizing errorfulness as part of older art's quality of style.

In short, Delacroix's aesthetic made him a very peculiar enthusiast of photography. While academic ideals dovetailed (all too readily) with clear, successful photographic prints, Delacroix's ideals were much trickier to reconcile. If you were a young ambitious Delacroissian in the later 1850s, deciding *how* to use photography "to raise painting to new heights" would have been a formidable challenge. Still, it's clear that your paintings would need to depart from Salon photo-naturalism in both subtle and obvious ways. They would be less detailed, more simplifying. Their execution would be uneven, differentiating central from subordinate subjects. And they would likely have a new relationship to traditional painting—a relationship based on a more sympathetic, possibly even affirming, view of its faults.

Ten years after Delacroix's experiment, such a painter did appear. His work was singled out for precisely these qualities: for its brusque simplifying manner; for its strange unevenness of execution; for its marked echoes of Old Master painting; and for its sometimes glaring, unapologetic

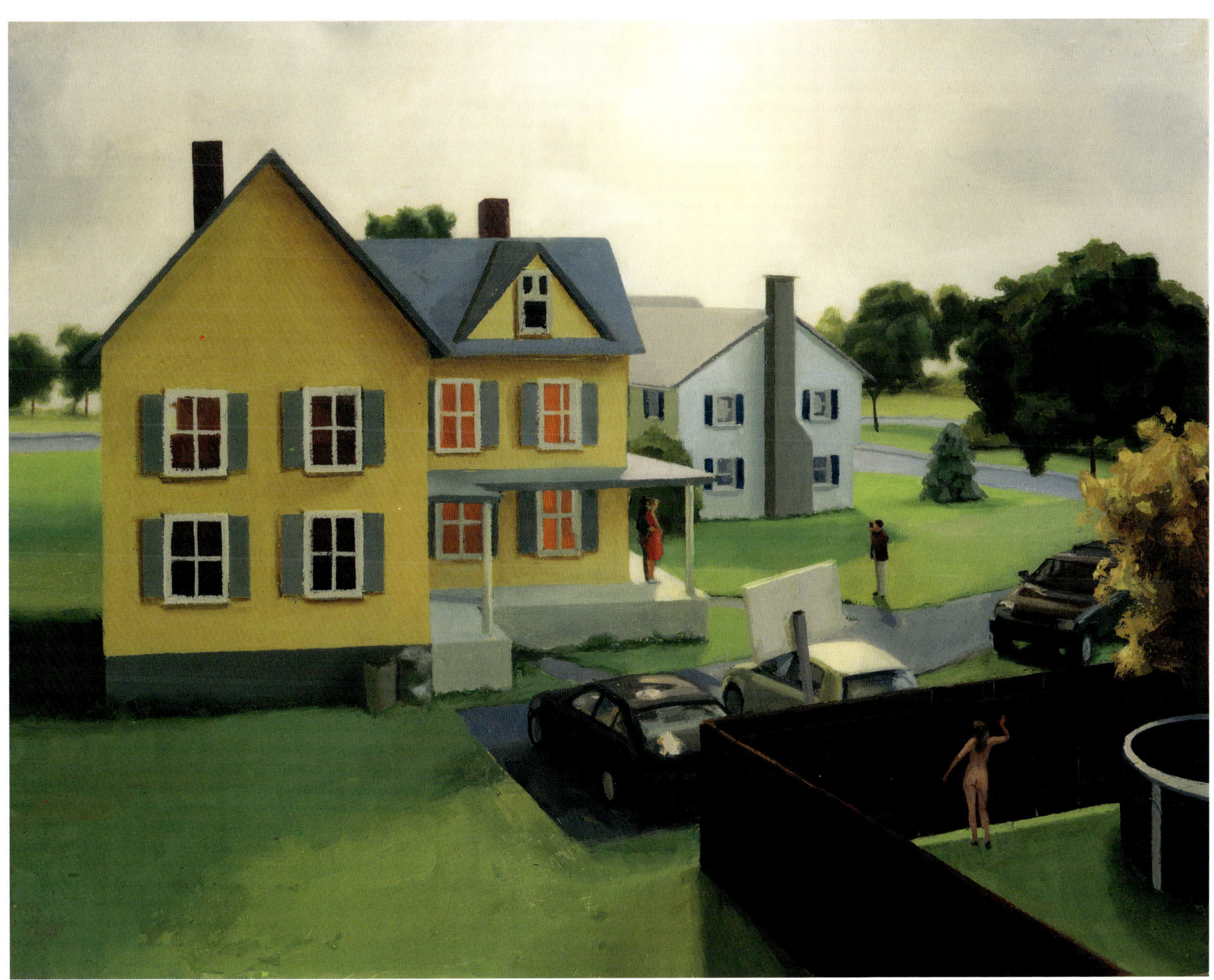

incorrectness.[6] But the connection does not end there. One of his paintings recalls, in very specific and suggestive ways, the story of Delacroix's experiment. That painting, Édouard Manet's *Le déjeuner sur l'herbe (Luncheon on the Grass*, 1863), combines a forest setting, nakedness, a visual quotation from Raimondi, and a pair of male friends, one whom seems to be pointing toward the disrobed woman across from him, as if the subject of their discussion was precisely the quality of her nakedness. And the quality of that nakedness is unusual: Though her pose echoes Raimondi, her chunky short-limbed proportions are akin to those of the figures in the Durieu/Delacroix daguerreotypes—as is her viewer-accosting stare. There are (as I have argued elsewhere)[7] reasons to believe that this figure was painted with the aid of photographs staged by Manet himself. Her nakedness may have been conceived as a specifically contemporary, *photographic* nakedness. It's possible, in other words, that the *Déjeuner* is an allusion to, or even a quasi-reenactment of, Delacroix's experiment. Having heard the story (perhaps from Delacroix himself), Manet may have set out to fulfill Delacroix's prophecy in his own idiosyncratic ways.

One confirming circumstance is the famous reaction of Manet's audience, which responded to the *Déjeuner* with emotions not unlike those felt by Delacroix and his dinner guests. To their eyes, Manet's figures seemed oddly shaped and unattractive ("The nude hasn't a good figure, unfortunately"), but also mannered, and incorrect ("Is this drawing? Is this painting?" asked one reviewer) despite their grudgingly conceded "quality of style." In other words, the *Déjeuner* functioned as a conflation of Durieu and Raimondi, eliciting the negative reactions associated with both sides of the photographic/pre-photographic divide. To his own short-term detriment, Manet chose a kind of "imprudent assimilation," affirming not only the awkward truths of photographic nakedness, but also the fictional freedom of pre-photographic nudity. To early audiences, still suffering from the first wave of post-photographic sensitivity, that combination amounted to little more than ugliness and clumsiness. But to later eyes, it offered an escape from the narrow impersonality of photo-naturalism, and access to the surprisingly wide-open realms of counter-normative figuration, soon to be inhabited by Paul Cézanne's bathers, Henri Matisse's dancers, and Pablo Picasso's *demoiselles*. For audiences who could appreciate their coarse, clumsy bodies as avatars of will and freedom, Manet had in effect reversed the results of Delacroix's experiment, turning revulsion into appetite.

All this, however, depends upon an unpopular and widely discredited idea. In standard histories of nineteenth-century painting, photography is at best a ghostly presence, understood as playing a minor, simple, and mostly unconscious role. Kirk Varnedoe wrote a celebrated essay that outlined this view, arguing that the few documented occasions when Manet, Edgar Degas, Édouard Vuillard, and others made use of photographs were insignificant. Any source photographs, Varnedoe insisted, were "terminally utilitarian," and "totally dissolved in the creative process." He called on his peers to categorically "set aside the idea of the influence of photographs."[8] Art historians have largely heeded his call.

(opposite)
Bryan Drury
Jann, 2011
Oil on wood
24 x 18 inches

What if Varnedoe was wrong? What if photography's role was formative, complicated, and conscious—despite being largely unacknowledged? It's at least possible that many early modern painters, uneasy about the aesthetic and ethical issues raised by photographic use, kept silent about it—and that art historians have been collectively misled by that silence. Manet is among the most thoroughly studied artists in all of Western art history. Sensible minds will resist the idea that our understanding of his development could really be subject to what is, in effect, a giant blind spot. And yet all accounts of Manet's career glide past what should be unignorable facts: that he came of age just at the moment when photography first became widely available; that he made his first submission to the Salon in 1859, the year of the enormously controversial first photographic Salon; that he was on close terms with the three most important figures in that controversy—Nadar (né Gaspard-Félix Tournachon), Charles Baudelaire, and Delacroix; and that his early breakthrough paintings make use of lighting effects that appear almost simultaneously in the work of photographers like Nadar. Manet lived at the center of a fierce, unprecedented debate—not about Spanish painting or Japanese prints but about the meaning and consequences of photography.[9]

Overturning Varnedoe's dismissal has interesting and welcome implications. It would link Manet to new research on artists like Picasso and Vuillard, who kept archives of thousands of postcards and photographs they took themselves, and whose production in both media is increasingly visibly intertwined.[10] It would require, above all, a fresh infusion of historical modesty—a new sense of how little we understand about the art of the last 150 years, despite so much concentrated scholarly attention. Modernist painting is an argument with photography. This phrase sounds too simple, but it sounds simple only because so much of the breadth and intricacy of the argument have only begun to be mapped.

This essay is indebted to the work of Aaron Scharf, Beatrice Farwell, and Anne McCauley, and to conversations with Svetlana Alpers, Alexander Nagel, Carol Armstrong, and Blake Gopnik.

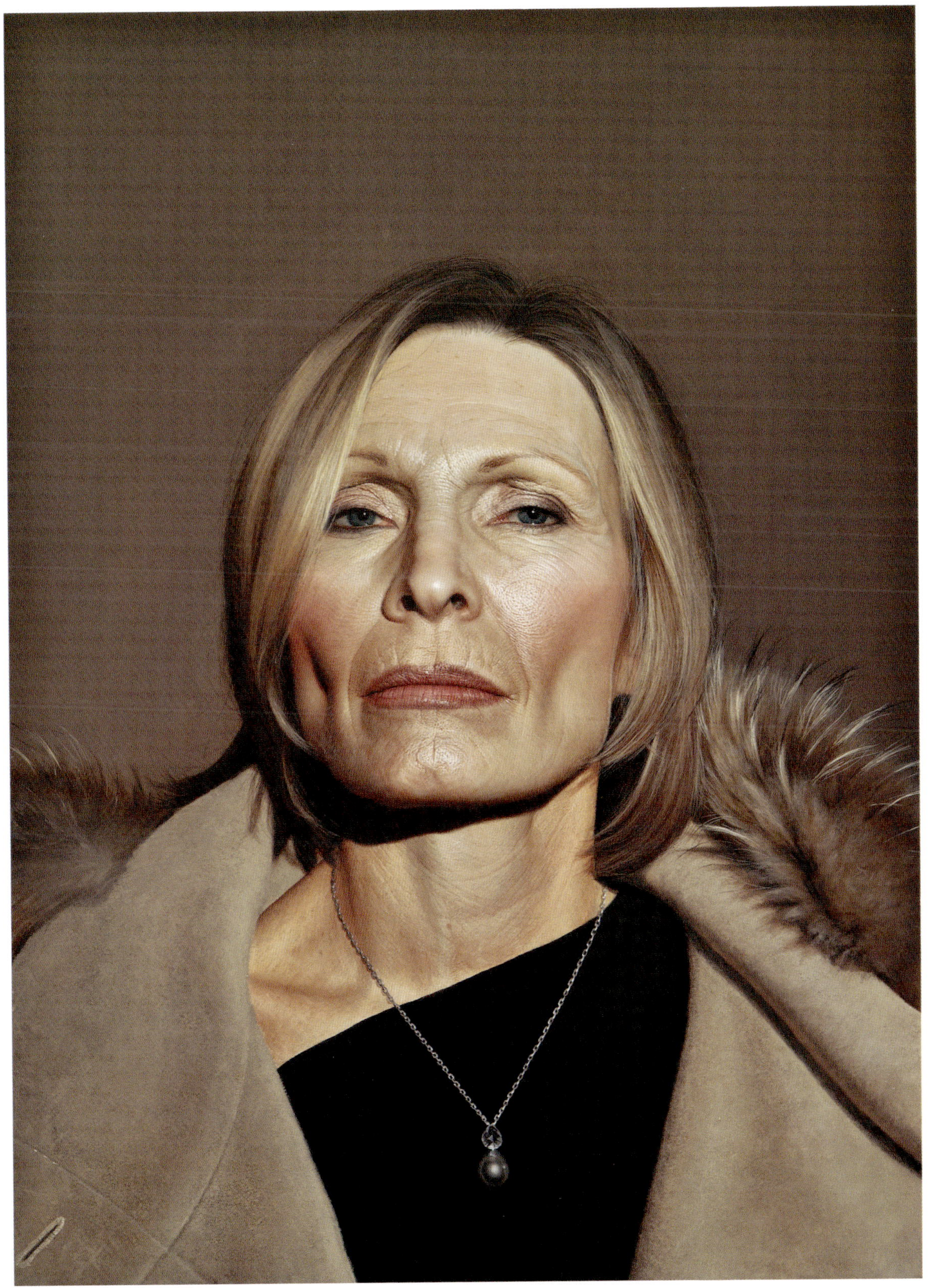

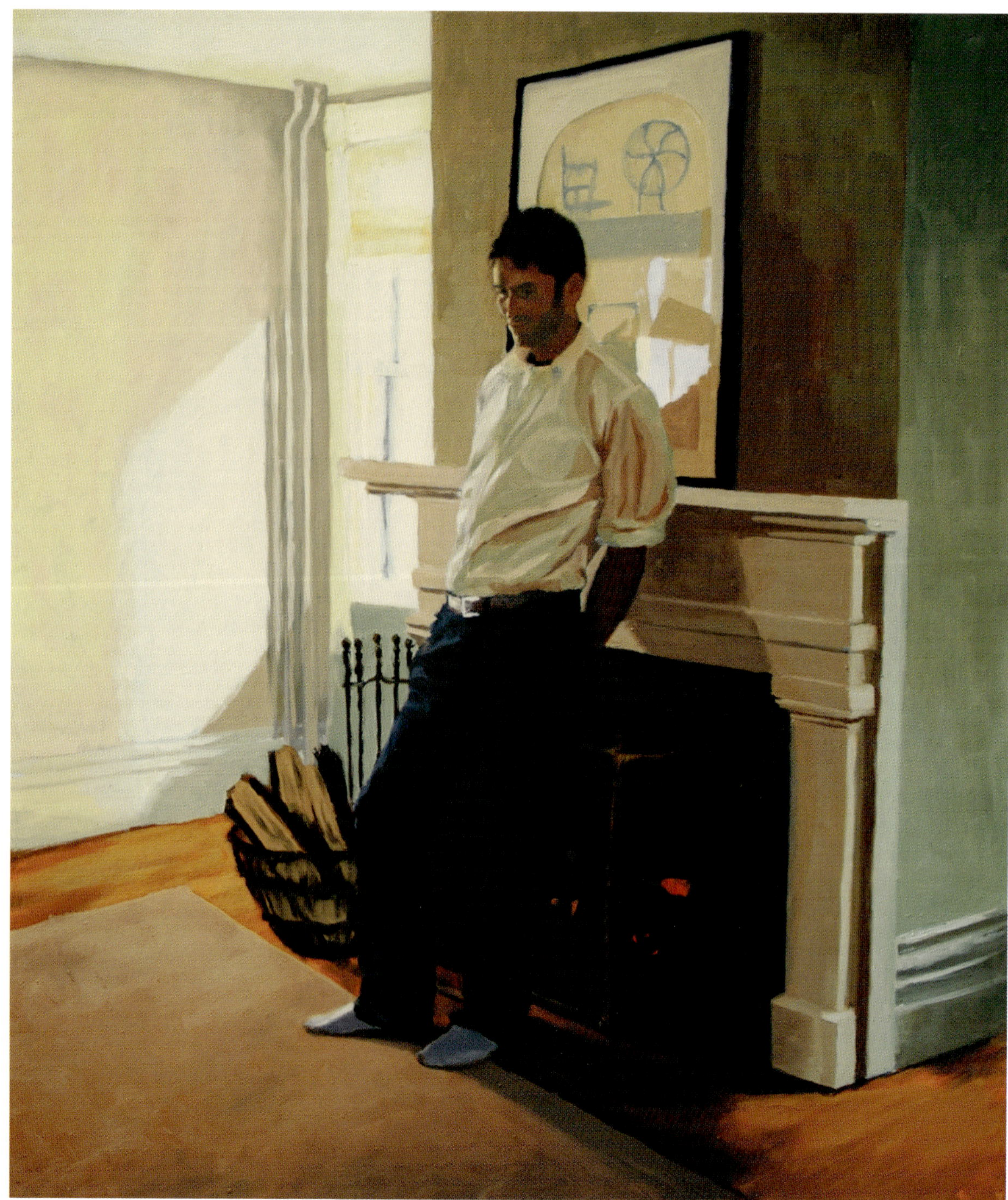

David Kratz
Evening, 2008
Oil on canvas
36 x 30 inches

(opposite)
Bryan LeBoeuf
Age of Man, 2003
Oil on linen
50 x 48 inches

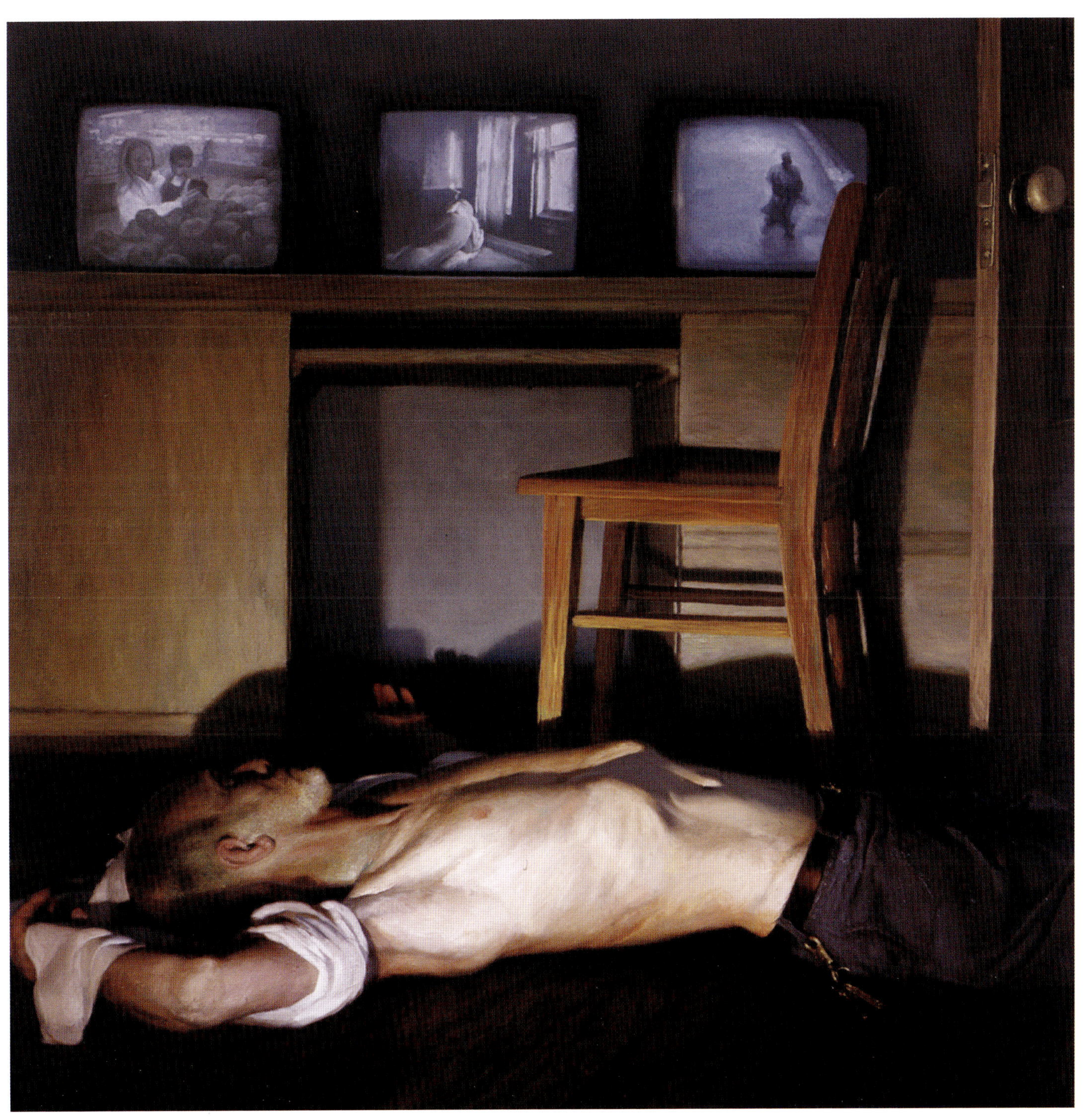

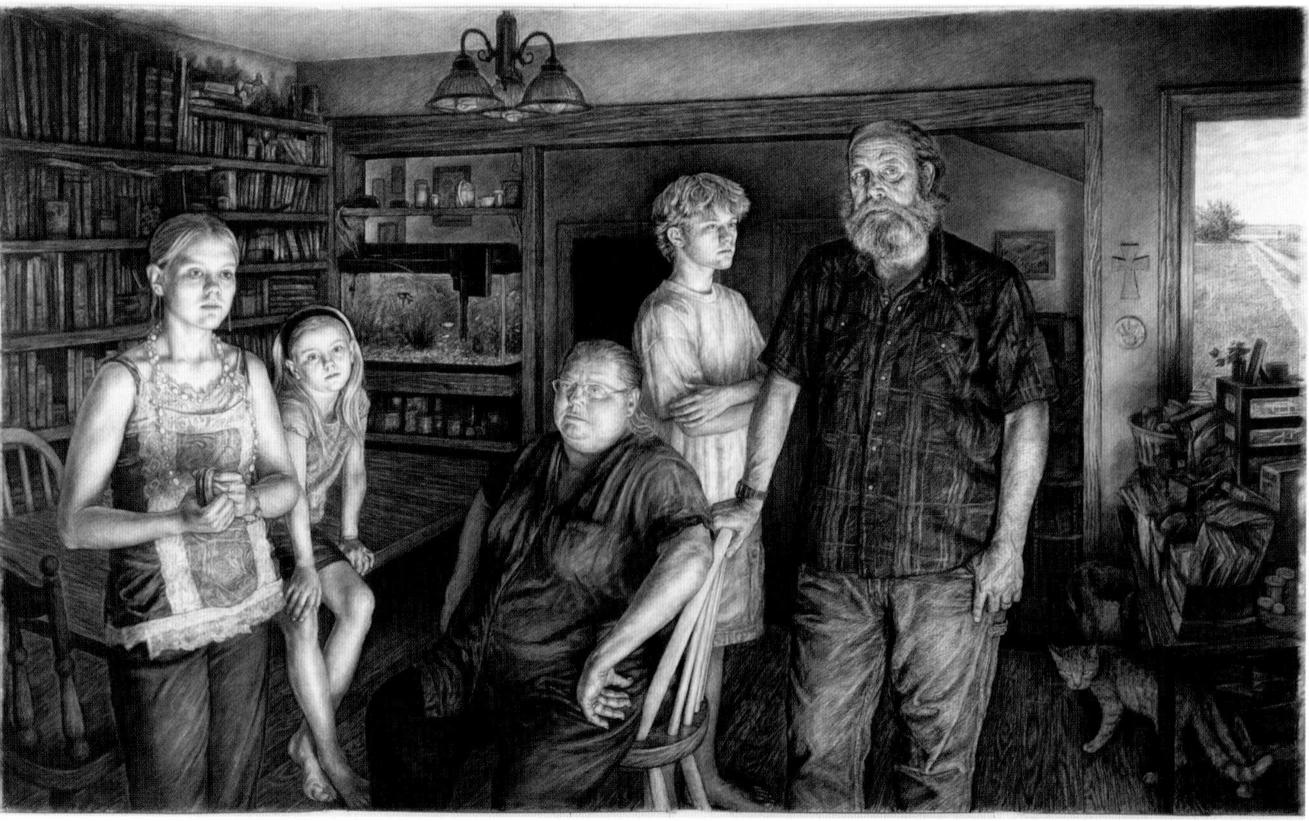

Edgar Jerins
Daina & Doyle at Home with Anita's Children, 2007
Charcoal on paper
60 x 96 inches

(opposite)
Jeanne Kenney
Bryant Park, 2005
Oil on canvas
36 x 40 inches

EDGAR JERINS

Life was very practical in Nebraska where I grew up, focused around farming. I spent a lot of time in nature; the Great Plains has lots of sky, and the Nebraskan Sandhills are strange and beautiful. I liked pioneer stories, and was also influenced by World War II stories I heard growing up in a Latvian community—the Russian invasion, stories of flight, the fire bombing of refugees in Dresden, the day the Iron Curtain came down, etc. People talked about this magical place that had been devastated, probably a mythology common to diasporas. Although art was not a big deal in general, my grandfather had been a scenic painter in Latvia, and my mother painted, so they encouraged us. I learned traditional oil painting methods from my older brother, a great talent; his high school art teacher brought us to Dimitar Krustev for classical training. From the moment I drew my first nude, I knew I wanted to make art about people.

Early on I'd responded to the sensuality of Goya's portraits, and also to his darkness. The *Third of May 1808* (1814) is composed in such a way that the firing squad becomes a faceless machine, and you become that man about to be shot, thinking about what it might be like to know you're going to die. I was also influenced by New Objectivity's honesty—Beckmann, Schad, Dix, Nussbaum, Grosz—and how these artists portrayed the nightmare of war. Through my studies at the Pennsylvania Academy of the Fine Arts, my work continued to be influenced by the Old Masters until a discussion with my first New York dealer, Peter Tatistcheff, who encouraged me to create work that delved into my past. So I spent a few months clearing my head, avoiding museums and galleries, not looking at art, and decided to do a drawing of my surviving brother, Tom, in the house we grew up in. That led to my first drawing series, *Men in Their 40s*, narratives of men facing adversity. I want the viewer to feel that they have entered these people's lives, so the drawings are large and horizontal, for a cinematic, temporal effect. Sticking to black and white heightens the drama.

I start a drawing with a feel for the narrative. I stay with my subjects—they are all people I know—and take hundreds of photos. They wear whatever they want; some get dressed up, some don't. Multiple reshoots help capture them relaxed and candid, unaware of the camera. I control the lighting carefully and may alter elements in the environment for definition and dramatic effect. Often I light people from below to create strong shadows, increasing the sense of isolation.

Back in the studio with the photographs and the visit fresh in my memory, I lay in the composition's major elements in vine charcoal on heavy paper, drawing freehand in one- or two-point perspective. Once the composition is set up, I tape

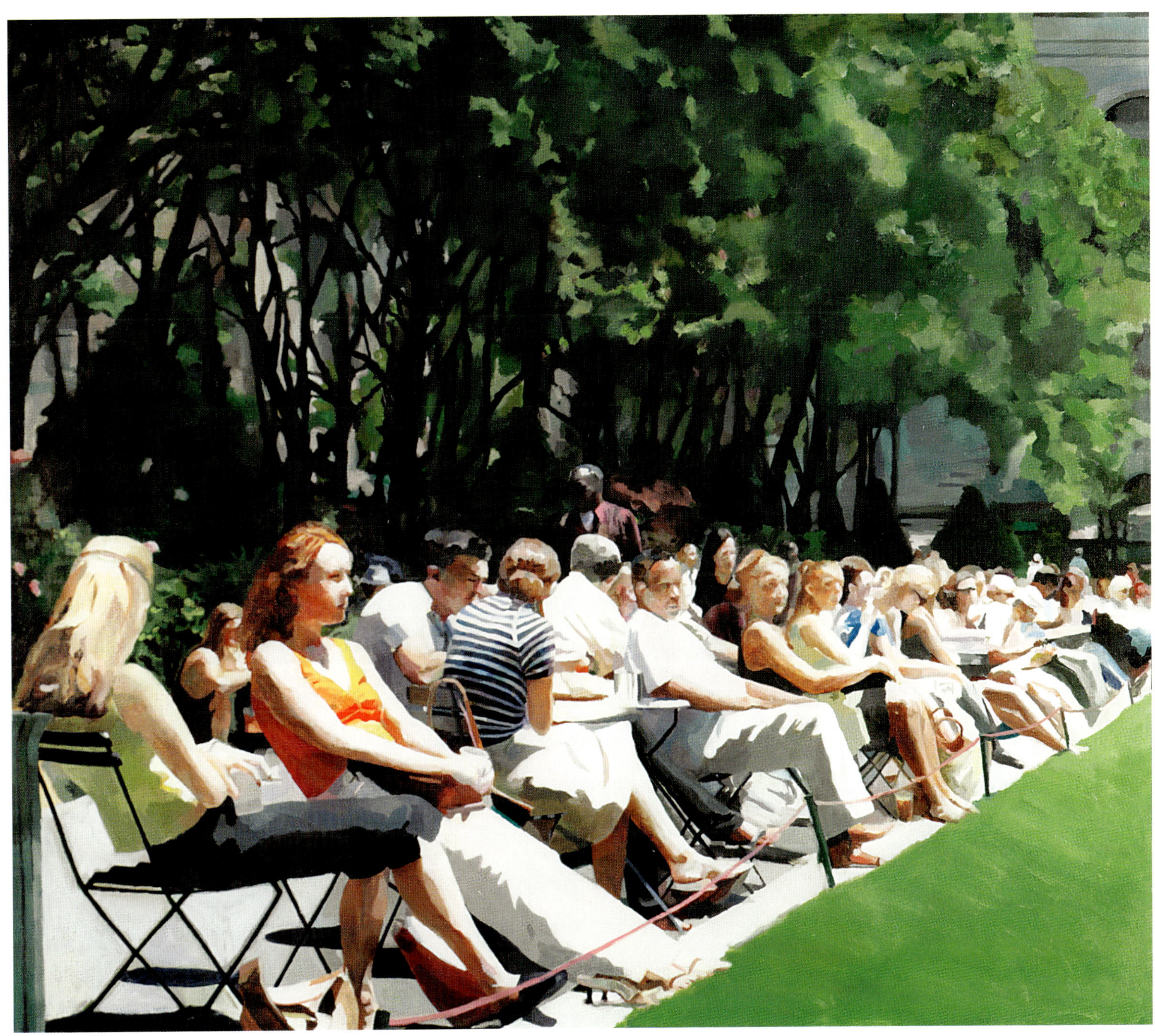

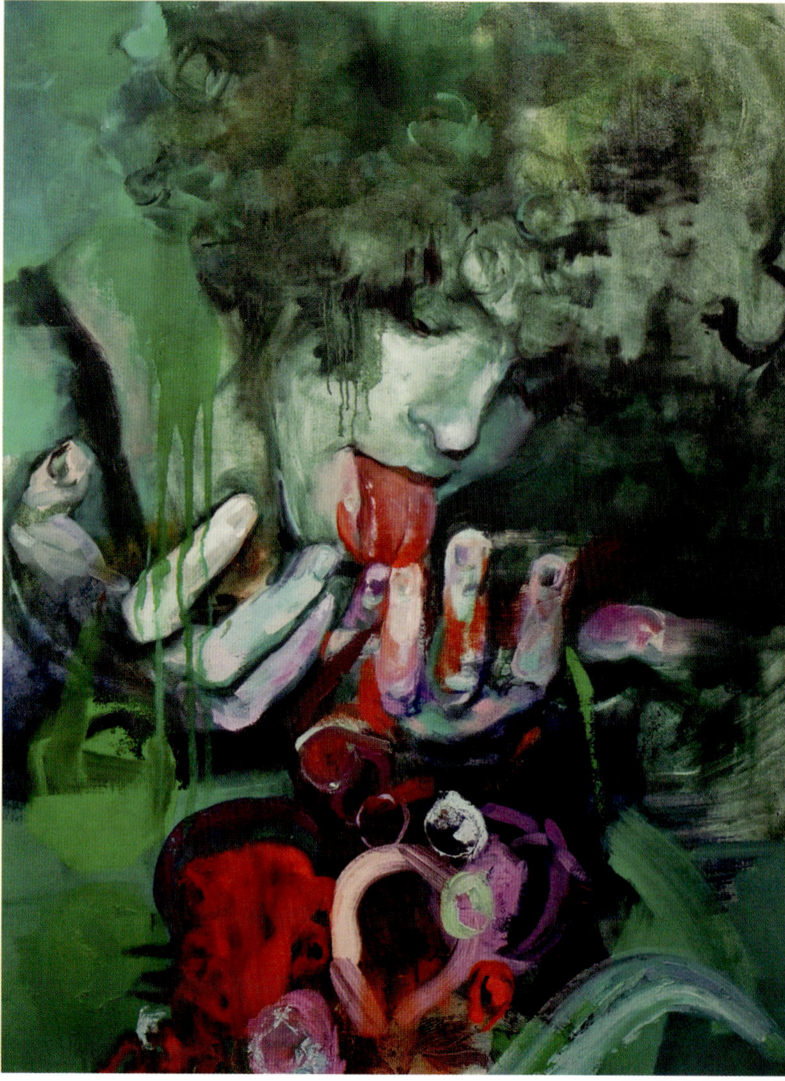

Megan Ewert
Sweet/Tart, 2012
Oil on canvas
48 x 36 inches

(opposite)
Alyssa Monks
Purple, 2011
Oil on linen
8 x 12 inches

a string to the vanishing points to check all my angles. If perspective is off, people may not notice, but they'll feel it. I don't project photos but utilize their information individually, in a composite fashion. When I was doing more academic work I wouldn't have included a Coke can or a lawn mower in a picture, because doing so would have dated it. But every object evokes personal history, so I include references natural to the subjects' lives; I want the portraits and environments to possess equal expressive power. Figures are positioned with attention to the psychology of viewpoint. For example, I asked one model to hold his gun where he could quickly shoot me, so even though in the drawing he is holding the gun down, the pose is subtly uncomfortable.

As the vine builds up, I remove it with compressed air, and refine imagery with charcoal pencil, paper stomps, and an electric eraser, which I also draw with. Everything is focused, but darks and value contrasts dominate the foreground. Controlling light is hugely important to creating a seamless flow among artificial sources, so the scene looks natural. As the drawing nears completion, I use white gouache for the liquid highlights of eyes. I always try to leave some pure paper for a luminous quality. The drawing stays very fluid and I change things around until the very end—which occurs when there are no more problems.

I'm interested in a general public audience, like the Regionalists were. I tell stories of people who would never expect to be in a narrative picture, but whose stories should be told. My aim is to be sensitive to human frailty, to express hardship in a way that isn't hopeless or sentimental. Evoking a particular place and time pulls people into art—and if you create a compelling narrative, people will respond.

ALYSSA MONKS

For the last twenty-six years, the unpredictable nature of oil paint has both fascinated and frustrated me. I was introduced to a studio full of grown-ups when I was nine in an old barn in New Jersey, and to the intoxicating smell of linseed and oils. My curiosity was piqued when I was told this stuff was very serious, expensive, and like nothing else I've ever tried. It was messy. It was hard to control. It was beautiful, poisonous, and permanent. It was limitless. I was determined to tame it, although all too often I would indulge in its spontaneity and rawness. At the New York Academy of Art, I learned the skill of creating a two-dimensional reality made of this slippery, sensual dirt and oil. My instructors also taught me something else: the value of a beginner's mind, remaining always a student, always curious, always fascinated. In other words, learning the skill to control the medium could potentially kill my fascination and curiosity. The closer I got to accuracy, the more I learned that imagination must guide skill.

I use various techniques, which will surely evolve in the coming years as I search for new tools. My goal is to keep myself curious, creative and not reliant upon technique, always experimenting mindfully and openly. The one constant is that the destination must remain unknown. The photograph, with sufficient lighting, accurate white balance, and high resolution, is a starting reference. I take thousands of photographs to get a full range of ideas and possibilities, using different filters—water, steam, glass, petroleum jelly, makeup, vinyl—to create enough illusion for the viewer to grasp, while on the verge of slipping away into abstraction

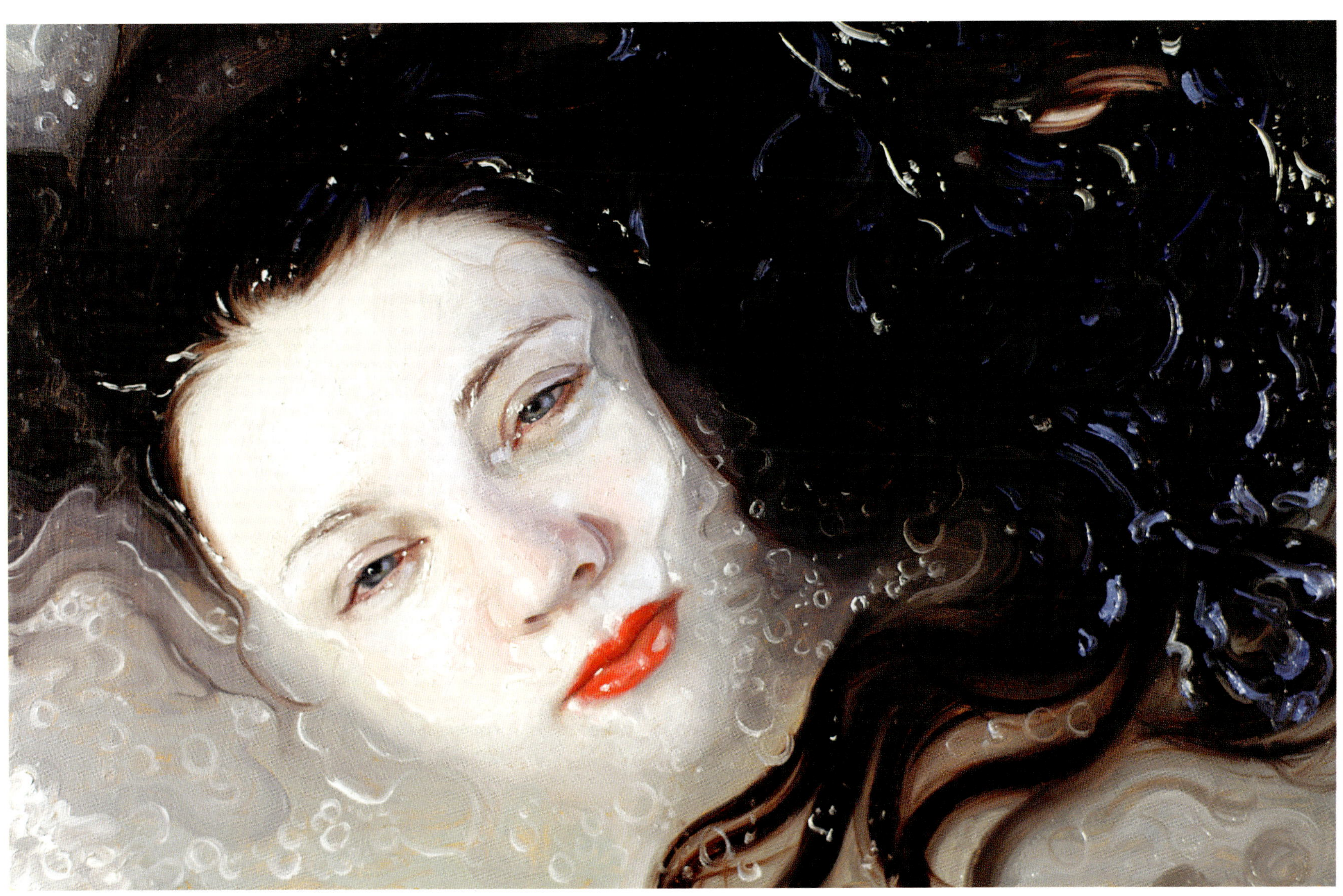

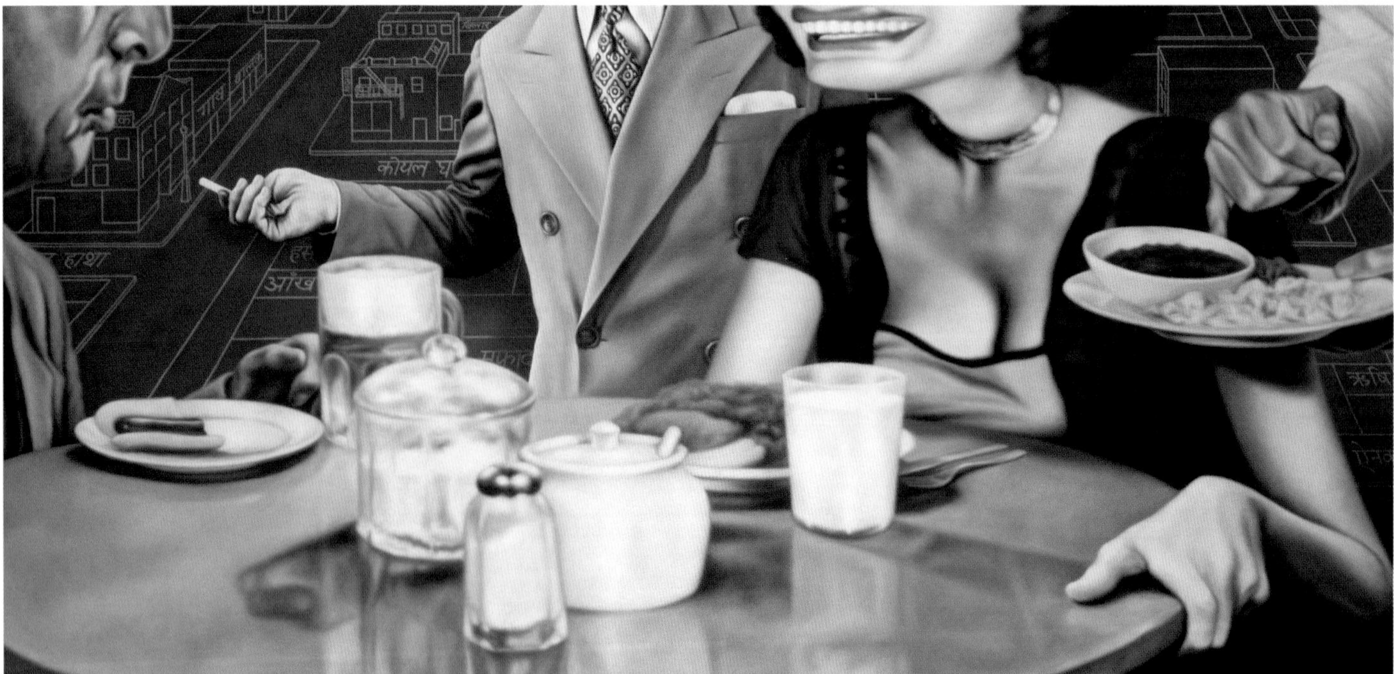

or revealing artifice. Drawing from photographs, imagination, and life helps me investigate under the skin, beneath the visible surface. I use oil-primed panel or linen surfaces, and draw the composition in with a transparent wash in raw sienna or yellow ochre, so that a golden glow vibrates through subsequent paint layers. Mixing a large amount of colors before I begin frees me up to paint thickly without stopping to mix again. I prefer large flat and round brushes and use a damar medium mixed with linseed. After I create accurate proportions, measuring and refining, I distill the composition down to its most intriguing moment: an illusive expression or sensual shape, a lip curl or some strange ambiguity. Most exciting is discovering the texture that would best describe the subject and how it resonates with me. I push that further by exaggerating, enhancing, or obliterating forms, and inventing new ones. When it's all working well, I create a painted world of an abstracted reality, with some controlled technique juxtaposed against delicious moments of invention.

In the early stages of a painting, I work with what initially attracted me—a composition or expression I feel connected to, or a shape or color I want to expand upon. Then it becomes about my experience and my world. About halfway through, it takes on its own momentum and compels me in different directions, beyond what my original intrigue was and into unfamiliar territory. It is at this point I stay present, even if the unpredictability makes me nervous or frustrated. This is the crucial moment to sustain; embracing this discomfort will reap great moments of surprise and mystery. A new color relationship or texture can reveal itself, a new technique or accidental effect can change the whole direction of the work for the better. Possibilities I could not plan or predict are revealed just because paint misbehaves so easily and often. Maintaining a mindful presence in this stage is important, or such possibilities could easily be painted out and lost. To create these moments, I have to risk as much as possible. The technical system and control I've learned to get me from the blank canvas to a finished painting have to be challenged and deconstructed repeatedly. Falling into a painting trance only suffocates the potential of anything significant or engaging happening in the studio, and makes me a disconnected machine manufacturing a product. I want to be seduced by the paint, and ultimately surrender to it.

Obfuscating the subject in places makes the moments where the body is clearly visible more satisfying, and the moments it is not more engaging and titillating. My work has evolved toward creating a symbiotic relationship between abstraction and realism. The point in time where one becomes the other fascinates me, where raw paint strokes and dabs become something else. My goal is to suspend that moment where, as in life, one gives up control and surrenders to the present. In that vulnerable stillness it is possible to create empathy. To create this in paint I utilize an "open circle." If all the forms and details are seamlessly resolved, there is no room for the viewer to interact with and "finish" the painting in their mind, with their own solution or experience. But if a bit of the circle is left unfinished for the viewer to complete, it creates a space for empathic connection to occur. Finding that sweet spot of "just enough" resolution is my challenge. When it succeeds, the viewers find themselves, their story, their mortality.

Eric White
Intermezzo, 1999
Oil on canvas
36 x 72 inches

(opposite)
Chris LaPorte
Funeral, 2011
Graphite on paper
48 x 72 inches

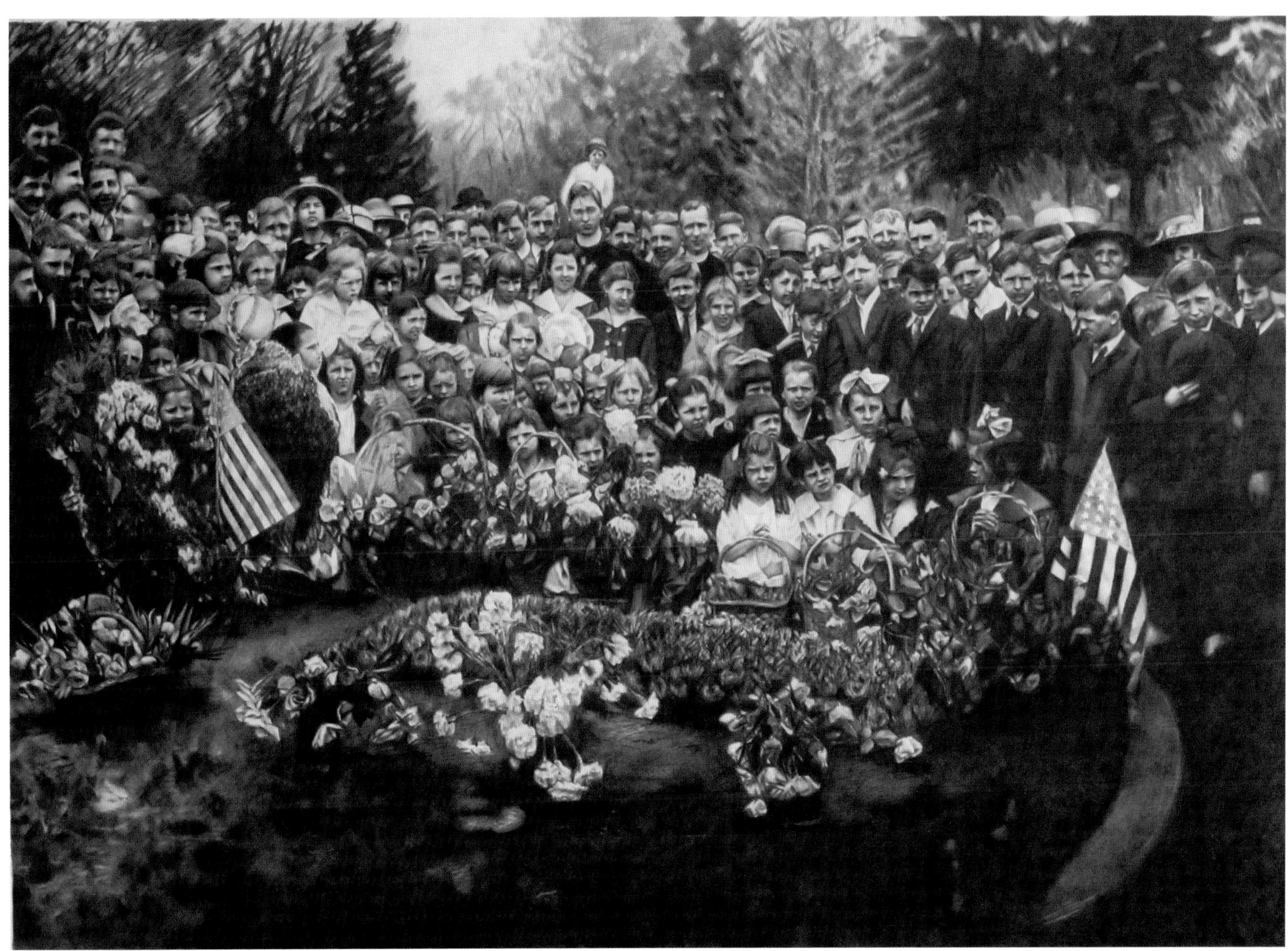

REFIGURING HISTORY PAINTING: REPRESENTATION MEETS MODERN TECHNIQUES

MARGARET McCANN

HISTORY PAINTING ENGAGES PEOPLE WHO MATTER via the power structures that make that determination. Memorialized ambitiously in paint, significant secular or religious events become cultural symbols. For centuries Michelangelo's Sistine Chapel (1512) was one of few thrilling man-made sights, and aspiring painters, along with aristocrats on the Grand Tour in Rome to catch the ruins, made pilgrimages to study it. Michelangelo quickly mastered fresco, while Leonardo's difficulty in finishing his *Last Supper* (1498) involved a dislike of the technique's quick drying (thought Sigmund Freud), so he "chose oil colors, the drying of which permitted him to complete the picture according to his mood and leisure."[1] Oils' flexibility would increasingly enhance such personal inclinations as painting contended with Modernist experience and techniques. History painting permutated into twentieth-century eclecticism, and in conjunction with photography can be seen to calcify into Socialist Realism, and transmogrify into post- and meta-modern ambiguity.

Rightly prized for its high degree of difficulty, history painting (hailed by Leon Battista Alberti in the Quattrocento as the most difficult form of painting), topped portraiture, genre, landscape, animal, and still life painting in the academic hierarchy that fell apart in revolutionary France. Depicting numerous proportional forms in believable space and light artfully, as in the quiet manner of Piero dell Francesca or the anti-gravitational one of Paolo Veronese, still expresses visionary athleticism. History painting's prime mover, the human form, a vehicle for divine action in humanistic/hubristic times and places, generally follows the Western example of the Greek nude. Based on mathematical canons influenced by the unchanging ratios of Egyptian stone forms, and perhaps by Zeuxis's composite method of combining perfect human parts into an ideal whole, "The Nude" has been periodically revived, moving Leonardo's *Vitruvian Man* (1490) to manifest the Roman architect's ideal proportions. Unlike the figure's more organic role in traditional Eastern art, the classical Western figure embodies architectonic persuasion over, rather than harmony with, nature.

(opposite)
Jerome Witkin
Taken (panel 3), 2002–03
Oil on canvas
108 x 94.5 inches

History painting's form was largely shaped by erudite content in the French Academy, which codified the genre's particularly Italian achievements. Students learned subject matter, ancient history and literature, and the technique of compositely engineering the successive steps of indirect oil painting: the *croquis* (preparatory compositional sketch), *étude* (study), and *equisse* (painted sketch). The *ébauche* (earth-colored, thin underpainting) on the final canvas mapped the major light and tone masses of the composition, colored glazes were then mindfully applied.[2] (The European term for an art opening, *vernissage,* hails from the vivid reveal of the image's tones, colors, and detail after a final varnishing.) Although the blueprint of the underpainting allowed only reasonably extemporaneous execution, the beauty of studies/sketches—Leonardo's notebooks, the proto-expressionistic drawings of Anthony Van Dyck, John Constable's meteorologically attuned landscapes, Jean-Baptiste-Camille Corot's Rome—had been valued. Yet their function was basically private, preparatory research for a larger, more permanent purpose. History painting's backdrops made nature a stage set, the way a Claude glass superimposed theatrical grandeur on an ordinary vista.

REALISM AND MODERNIZATION

The populist sentiments of Romantic history paintings like Francisco de Goya's *Third of May 1808* (1814), Théodore Géricault's *Raft of the Medusa* (1819), and Eugène Delacroix's *Liberty Leading the People* (1830) rendered not past but contemporary events heroic. Venturing further, the grand scale and inclusion of a nude in Gustave Courbet's 1855 self-portrait, *The Painter's Studio: A Real*

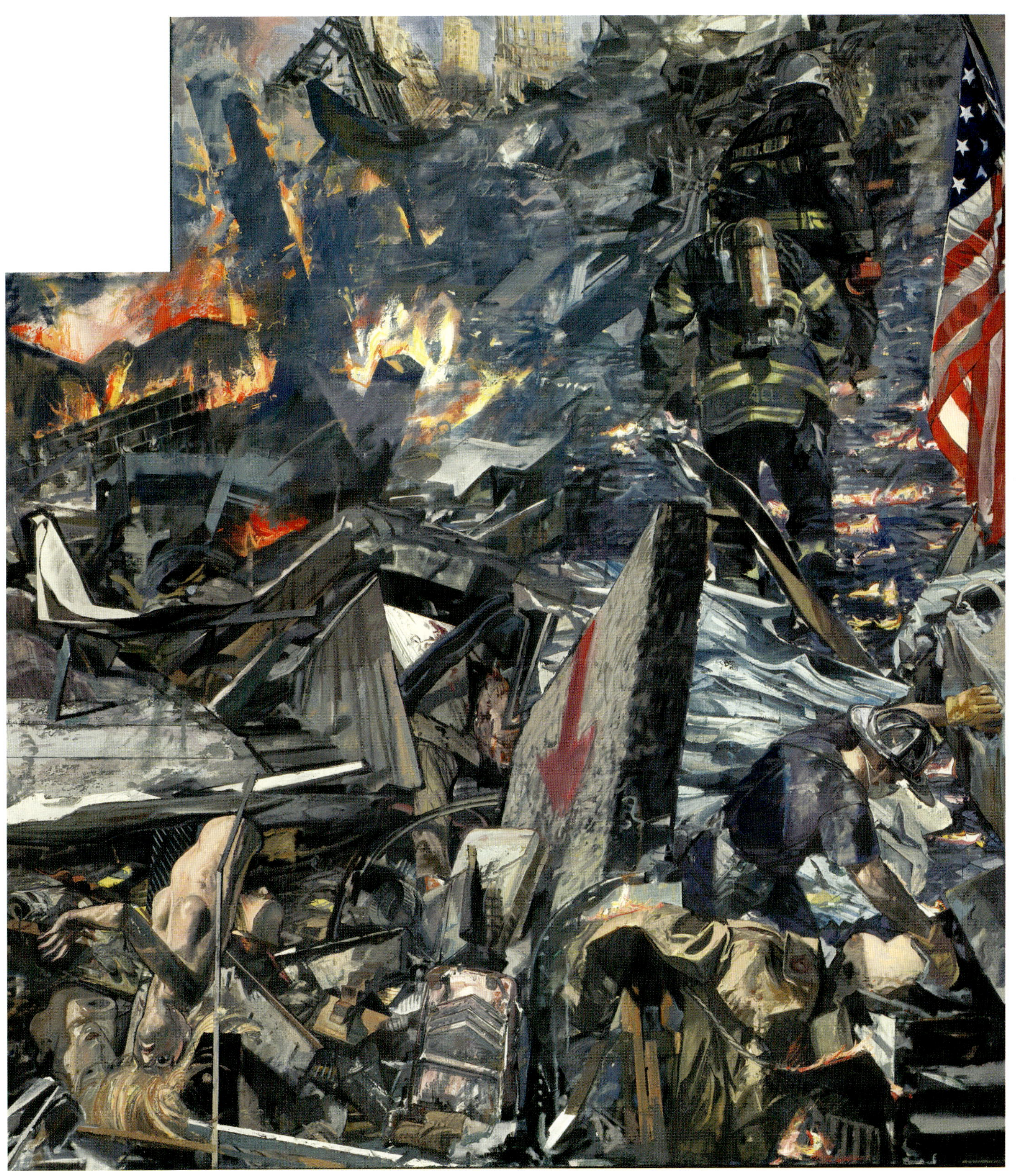

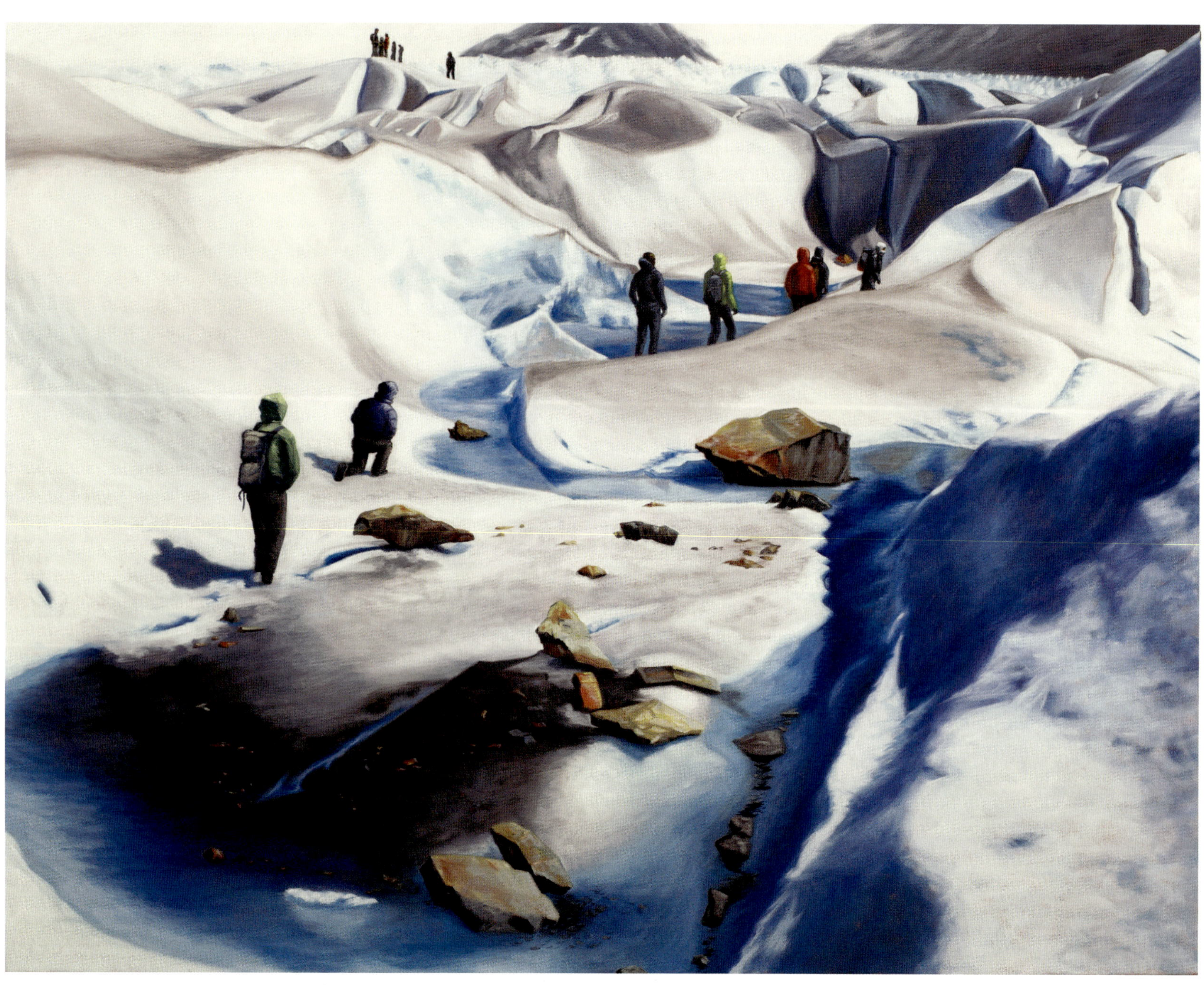

Allegory of a Seven-Year Phase in My Artistic and Moral Life not only invoked history painting but dramatically privatized it. The Pre-Raphaelites' whimsical clouding of genre boundaries conveyed artistic independence, but Courbet engaged the hierarchy's implicit class divisions; Realism brashly appealed to common rather than learned knowledge in a time when scientific facts were multiplying. His gigantic but local *Burial at Ornans* (1850) abandoned past significance for mundane reality; as religion's steady demise discharged death as the commencement of afterlife, hardship became primarily tragedy without reward, a problem to be solved.[3] His oversized *Stonebreakers* and *After Dinner at Ornans* of 1850 lack the vast space of history painting that rendered working class toil timelessly picturesque, or the diminutive scale of genre painting that rendered it quaint. Subversively composed, Courbet's large foregrounded peasants irreverently turn their backs on the viewer.

Charles Baudelaire advocated the painting of "modern life" in 1863, as mass media—journalism, art criticism, photography, kitsch—was consumed by an escalating middle class empowered by Enlightenment ideals, open to invented stories like those the novel proffered. The hold patrons of history painting had on facts, opinion, and possibility was slackened by the proliferation of printed matter in a volume and velocity unmanageable to non-draconian oversight. Realism's compositional innovations, like cropping, synecdoche, and inclusion of the random, reflected the influence of Japanese prints, photography's indiscriminate gaze, and the naturalism of novels, in which "like life itself . . . protagonists were often left in midstream . . . to continue their struggles outside the work of art."[4]

Historical values lost further traction against the intense modernization of Paris by the Industrial Revolution in general, Baron Haussmann in particular, between 1853 and 1870. "Paris impressed the idea of modernity on all who lived in it by the spectacle of the symbols of the physical past being swept away and replaced."[5] The new sewage system cleared sidewalks, empowering the *flaneur*'s peripatetic observations. A revolutionary electric grid catalyzed nightlife; people started bicycling around. Casual venture in new public spaces—parks, gardens, and art museums (the Louvre opened in 1798, the Jeu de Paume in 1851)—increased interaction among strangers. Europe's new train system rapidly moved large populations, as well as the middle class (and landscape painters) on day trips to the country or seaside. An influx of immigrants to the rising city included recently freed gypsy slaves from eastern Europe who, along with flaneurs, rag-pickers, and other Baudelairian "modern heroes" appeared in popular illustrations, and in paintings like those of Courbet, Henri Rousseau, and Édouard Manet.

DIRECT PAINTING AND EXPERIENCE

Courbet was motivated by leftist politics, unlike Baudelaire's friend Manet, who wished to change the Academy, not overthrow it as the Impressionists did. Manet's technically progressive teacher, the *juste-milieu* painter Thomas Couture, had his students sketch in the Louvre and on the street, focusing on the spontaneity of the *croquis*. Manet extended Couture's emphasis on the *ébauche* (underpainting) in a painting's final stages by substituting local color, like green for grass, for earth tones:

> *Manet's paintings . . . were regarded as unfinished because they were seen as elevating the* ébauche *to the status of the finished surface . . . one* ébauche *superimposed over another . . . [T]his innovative technique was construed by the public and critics as signaling a more general attack on established notions of competence with the values they evoked. As [with] Courbet, this kind of affront to decorum was taken as a typically "modern" departure . . .*[6]

To regular Salon-goers, Manet's unmodulated forms, heralding the start of painting's flat fate—according to Clement Greenberg, whose descriptions in essays like "Modernist Painting" became prescriptions—probably looked less like the start of something new than like absurdly giant sketches. Such effrontery echoed the derision of popular illustrators like Honoré Daumier; Linda Nochlin suggests reading puzzling paintings like *Luncheon in the Grass* (*Le déjeuner sur l'herbe*; 1863) as "monumental and ironic put-ons, *blagues*, a favorite form of destructive wit of the period . . . pictorial versions of those endemic pranks which threatened to . . . profane and vulgarize the most sacred verities of the time".[7]

Following Manet's iconoclastic merge of history and genre painting with sketchy irony, Impressionism pushed Realism's elevation of non-epic human action (genre painting), still life, and landscape, and granted the study/sketch permanent status. Through varied influences—of Dutch *alla prima* landscape painting and Johan Jongkind's on Eugène Boudin, who painted with Claude Monet; of J.M.W. Turner's on Monet and Constable's on the Barbizon School; of Corot's on Camille Pissarro, who taught Monet and Paul Cézanne—Impressionist *plein air* painting became an end in itself. The exploratory character and formerly pointless transience of perception took on modern meaning. Shifting light in a painting indicated passing time as time's temperament was changing, sped up by mechanical efficiency, slowed and expanded by leisure; Impressionist paintings with trains traversing a landscape express cultural transformation. The prediction of Karl Marx and Friedrich Engels, that capitalism's changes would make "all that is solid melt into air,"[8] resonates with Baudelaire's aesthetic description of *modernité* as "the ephemeral, the fugitive, the contingent, the half of art whose other half is the eternal and the immutable."[9] As imitation in painting was interrogated by direct experience, painting became

> *. . . a continual search and learning to paint the often-agonizing process of a lifetime, not a set of rules to be mastered in a series of graduated stages within an academy. The rejection of "values" as the basis of painting in the progressive art after Corot can thus be interpreted both in the pictorial sense of an abandonment of under-painting, a fixed, hierarchical scheme of abstract light-and-shade predetermining the final meaning of the work—and at the same time, as the rejection of the social, moral, and epistemological structures which such a pictorial scheme presupposes . . .*[10]

(opposite)
Carrie-Ann Bracco
Following Robyn, Perito Moreno Glacier, 2012
Oil on canvas
32 x 40 inches

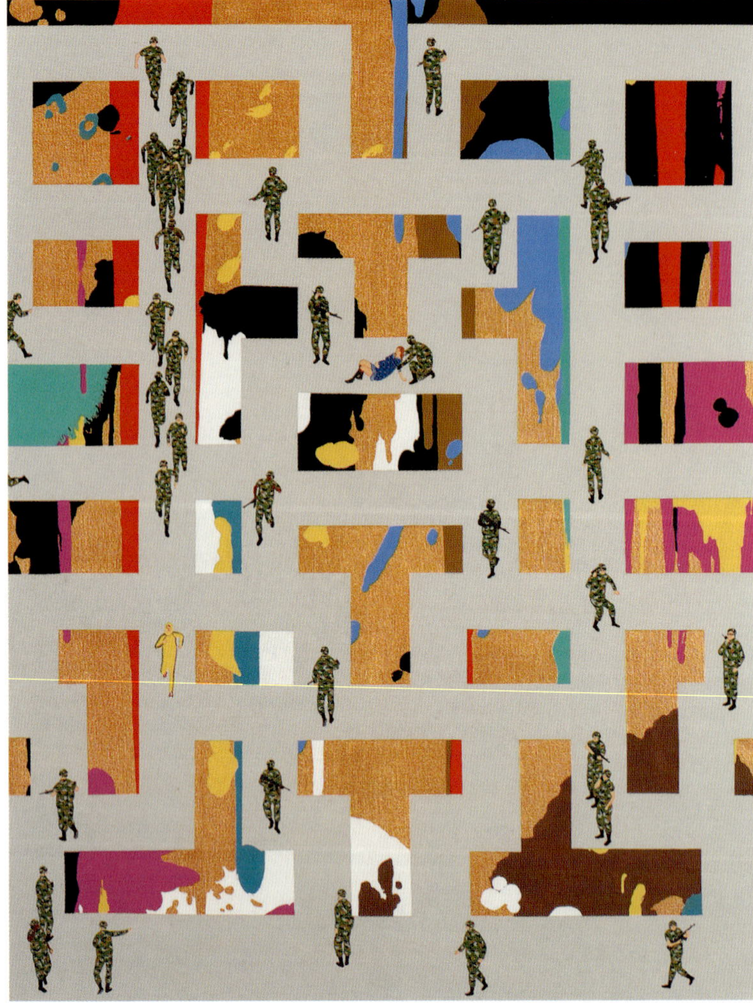

Tat Ito
Toyotamahime,
2009
Acrylic on canvas
24 x 18 inches

(opposite)
Megan Marlatt
LeRoi's Toys, 2009
Acrylic, oil on linen
52 x 62 inches

This fundamental transition in technique from indirect to direct painting was facilitated by one of the multifarious effects of mass production and better chemistry: ready-made artist materials. A greater variety of premixed, re-sealable metal-tubed oil colors allowed portability and spontaneity. Renoir said, "Without colors in tubes, there would be no Cézanne, no Monet, no Pissarro, and no Impressionism."[11] Tone ceased predetermining composition, the blank slate of a white canvas replaced the brown ground; colors were not placed over but contained tones. "Don't paint bit by bit, but paint everything at once by placing tones everywhere," advised Pissarro.[12] The color theories of Goethe, Michel Chevreul, and others played out by Impressionists, Neo-Impressionists, Paul Gauguin, the Nabis, the Fauves, and Wassily Kandinsky's abstractions, for example, would eventually entirely emancipate color from description. Impressionism's transfer of Realist objectivity onto optics also encouraged haptic responses to the swift capture of changing color-light. Texture and touch, suppressed in the smooth "high finish" of timeless history painting, could enjoy itself. The mark's personality, paramount in the paintings of Vincent van Gogh, James Ensor, the Nabis and Fauves, also inspired by primitive art, fully flowered in Expressionism. Ultimately, the viewer's re-experience of the Abstract Expressionist's eye, mind, and hand would turn form into content, a "Greenbergian" progression toward self-determination.

PHOTOGRAPHY AND PERCEPTION

The elephant in the room of Modernist painting, the mass-produced camera's mimetic power encroached on painting's historical pride, cultural identity, and market. Making a likeness everyone could agree on, photography insinuated that the painter's visualizing talent and training in perspective, proportion, planar structure, anatomy, light, and shadow were unnecessary. Seeing a daguerreotype in 1839, the Neoclassical painter Paul Delaroche exclaimed, "From today, painting is dead!"[13] Twenty years later, Baudelaire cautioned:

> *Let photography . . . enrich the traveller's album, and restore to his eyes the precision his memory may lack . . . save crumbling ruins from oblivion, books, engravings, and manuscripts . . . all those precious things, vowed to dissolution, which crave a place in the archives of our memories; in all these things, photography will deserve our thanks and applause. But if once it be allowed to impinge on the sphere of the intangible and the imaginary, on anything that has value solely because man adds something to it from his soul, then woe betide us!* [14]

To its discredit, photography fostered unstudied, un-experienced representation, encouraging insensitivity and superficiality, as in exploitative Orientalism. But it also offered painters something new: In first enchantingly blurring, then freezing, time, photography afforded a new scrutiny of light, movement, shape, expression, and gravity-defying, haphazard gestures—availed by Delacroix, Edgar Degas, Thomas Eakins, and countless artists since. Access was granted to unknown moments, people, and places,

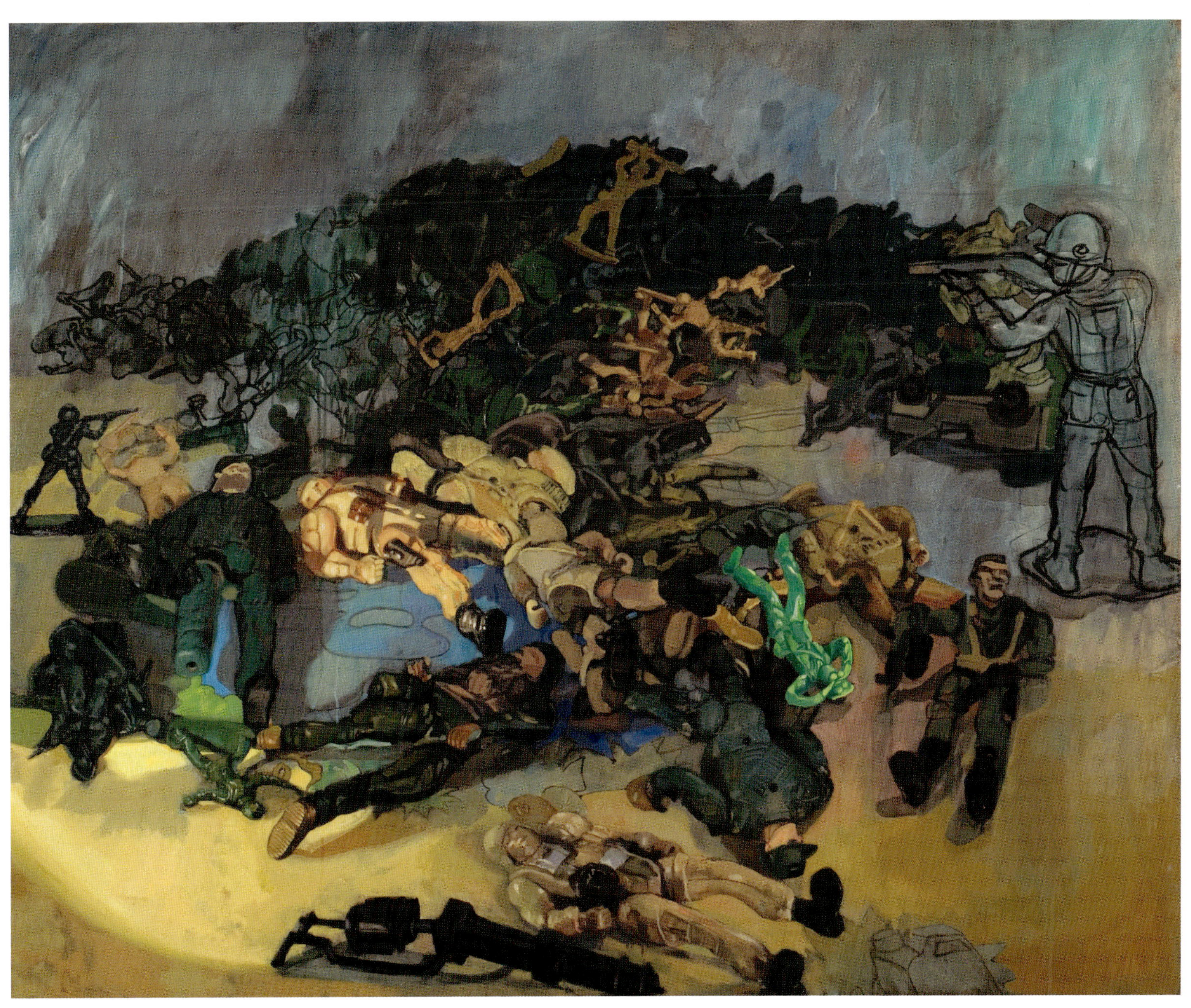

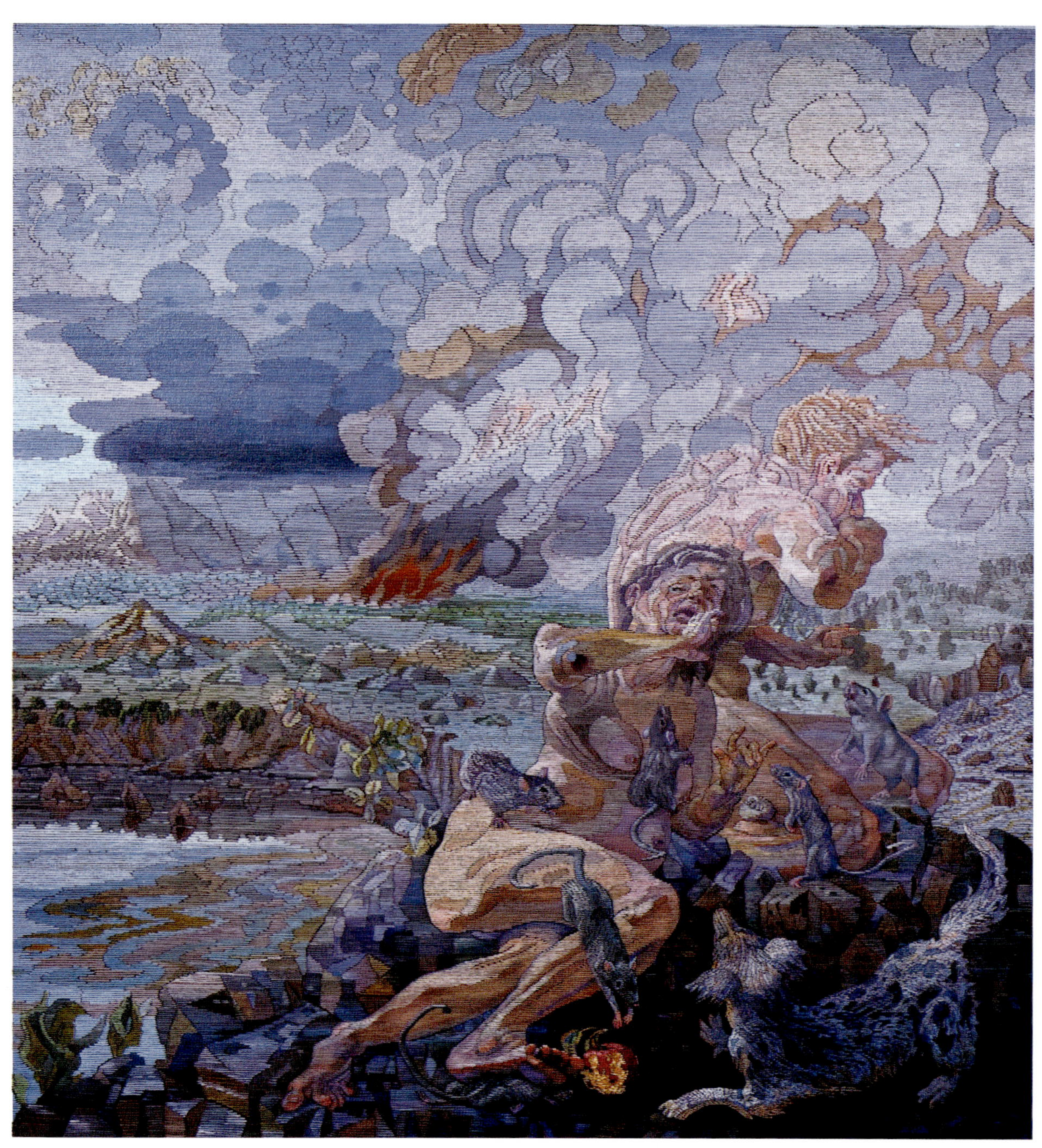

resulting in voyeuristic close-ups, heightening the dark views of Walter Sickert and the "intimacy once removed" of Pierre Bonnard. Photography made the strange available and familiar.

Decreasing mimetic expectations also let earlier stages in a painting be ends in themselves. Distancing itself from photographic illusionism, progressive painting stressed originality. Aaron Scharf argues:

> *Common to all Post-Impressionist styles was the concerted and active rejection of the material world as seen by the camera. . . . The human touch, the intuition and a more abstract conception of reality were now considered fundamental to art. To exceed the limits of the lens became imperative . . . . [When the artist] declared the subservience of the visible to the invisible world, he entered into a realm of consciousness . . . no photographer could discover and no camera could record.*[15]

Yet the formation of the fragmented nineteenth-century "period eye" and "cognitive style," to use Michael Baxandall's terms, as manifest in Impressionist broken color, and Neo-Impressionist divisionist technique, and personified in the flaneur's fleeting and peripheral vision, was far more than a reaction to photography. Realism was not the common mode of seeing until a small group of avant-garde artists disrupted it, argues Jonathan Crary. The replacement of a geometrical visual model with an optical one, inspired by the empirical investigations of Goethe, John Ruskin, Turner and others, preceded photography's impact:

> *The collapse of the camera obscura . . . was part of a process of modernization, even as [it] had been an element of an earlier modernity, helping define a "free," private, and individualized subject. . . . By the early 1800s, however, the rigidity of the camera obscura, its linear optical system, its fixed position, its identification of perception and object, were all too inflexible and immobile for a rapidly changing set of cultural and political requirements.*[16]

Baudelaire's famous 1859 metaphor characterizing the flaneur as "a kaleidoscope gifted with consciousness" was timely, for optical illusions (the magic lantern, phenakistoscope, etc.) were popular entertainment. Most were developed for scientific experiments, but David Brewster intended his stereoscope to democratize the "secret knowledge" of optics. Widely consumed (one London company sold over five hundred thousand between 1854 and 1856), it is not hard to imagine the influence the composite, artificial stereoscopic image, with its emphasis on binocular disparity, had on Cubism. Stronger microscopes and telescopes also deepened the transparency of appearances for observational painters. Gustav Fechner's research, defining perception as temporal and sequential resounds with Cézanne's search, "not a logic of contemplative distance, of perceptual autonomy, but rather an account of a nervous system interfacing with a continually transforming external environment."[17] Articulating new physiological responses to new realities, painting could be a kind of visual thinking.

Beyond perception, the study of visual afterimages (several scientists damaged their eyes staring at the sun) led to concepts of an abstract optical vision, as the machine aestheticized physical forces. The Eiffel Tower's machined structure (built as a temporary entrance arch to the 1889 World's Fair), and the novel visions of the landscape's geometric patterns it offered from above (as described in Robert Hughes's *The Shock of the New*) were radical sights. Pure invention in painting perhaps compensated for the diminished human role (of both represented figure and artist) following the rise of machines—as would be personified by Alberto Giacometti's twentieth-century "disappearing man," and overcompensated for in Socialist Realism's industrial-strength figuration.

HISTORY PAINTING, EAST AND WEST

Despite its diminished status after Modernism, history painting continued through post–World War One Mexican and WPA murals. An elliptical, Courbet-like sociopolitical content persists in Ashcan School works like George Bellows' *Cliff Dwellers* (1913), in Social Realism, and in the "magic realism" (an evasive moniker) of Peter Blume's *The Eternal City* (1937) or George Tooker's *Government Bureau* (1956). In Otto Dix's *Flanders* (1936) and Picasso's *Guernica* (1937) war's tragedy rather than triumph is conveyed; the postwar Expressionist figuration of Renato Guttuso and Philip Guston's sad, satirical Klan paintings from the Civil Rights Era take on social struggles. Like Guston, Georges Seurat's paintings are usually interpreted formally, yet *A Sunday on La Grande Jatte* (1886) could be a subtle expression of modern dystopia, a "sardonic view of the New Leisure."[18] Such "abstracted" figuration is often seen as primarily heralding a formalist endgame of recusal from representation. Yet the figure's emancipation from the academic canon and its engagement with both perception and abstraction, as in the work of Max Beckmann, Francis Picabia, Edwin Dickinson, Fairfield Porter, Alice Neel, David Park, and countless others, has sustained a vigorous run since its inception. The overblown opposition of figuration and abstraction is further belied by the many strictly perceptual painters (Stanley Lewis, Lennart Anderson, and George Nick, for example) who started abstractly.

Nonetheless, as historical narrative largely relocated to the silver screen in the twentieth century, and the figure to television's sitcoms, talk shows (and eventually reality television and YouTube), Western figurative painting did make some bad choices, getting mixed up with low taste, reactionary agitation, and Aryan delusions. As history painting reacclimated eastward, it served Socialist Realism's visionary more than commemorative purpose, "The Nude" updated, as it were, to an "ideal common type." Employing anecdotal (genre painting with historical pretense) and inspirational storytelling in the Soviet Union and Eastern bloc, it was exported to China and elsewhere to contradict indigenous painting, serving Cultural Revolution iconoclasm—and propaganda, as history painting often has. Understandably, savvy Western painters "avoid[ed] subject matter like a plague."[19]

(opposite)
Alexandra Finkelchtein
Expulsion from Paradise (right panel), 2012
Oil on canvas
58 x 53.5 inches

Greenberg had presumed, as did Joseph Stalin, that it was too difficult to inject propaganda into avant-garde art. Yet even when avant-garde artists did detach from society, "repudiate[ing] revolutionary as well as bourgeois politics . . ."[20] their art had an unintended aftermath. Nelson Rockefeller, who commissioned Diego Rivera's huge mural in New York City—tragically destroyed in 1932 after the artist refused to paint out his provocative portrait of Vladimir Lenin—called Abstract Expressionism "free enterprise painting."[21] The CIA collected and planned exhibitions of Western modern art throughout Europe, Cuba, China, and other countries during the Cold War[22] over hearts and minds; Abstract Expressionism "was the kind of art that made Socialist Realism look even more . . . rigid and confined than it was."[23] As the struggle against Euro-Communism through CIA post-World War II "stay behind" entanglements[24] comes to light (one retired general described the Marshall Plan as "counterinsurgency"[25]), uncertainty is underscored. Thus to ideologically reject, for partial GDR Communist function, amazing works like Werner Tübke's *Early Bourgeois Revolution in Germany* panorama (1976–87), in which history painting engages non-classical figuration (more naked than nude, in line with Grünewald or Dix) would paint with too broad a brush.

The Western vanguard's self-purge of the figure and narrative also distanced itself from photography, playing out its Parisian inheritance—Baudelaire lamented that photography undermined genius—that exalted first perception, then imagination and emotion over imitation. But while photography had abruptly trespassed Western history painting's mimetic legacy, both were fairly new forms in the east. In Russia, Western-style painting collided with traditional icon painting; the 1757 founding of Russia's first Academy preceded early photography by less than fifty years. Photography was established in China by 1838: Only later did Chinese artists studying in Paris incorporate Western perspective into traditional painting. Indeed, Socialist Realism made ready use of photography's convincing verisimilitude, exemplified by the giant billboard portrait-icons of Communist heroes in Tiananmen Square; Mao's is based on a 1964 black-and-white photograph, *No. 4 Standard Picture*.[26] Andy Warhol's Mao paintings, also based on this photograph, likely read more politically where Postmodern nihilism is less pervasive.

Conversely, the use of photography in American figurative art, aside from conceptual idioms like Pop art and Photorealism that were disconnected from the Impressionist instigation of "pure painting," has been seen until recently as a travesty. Exceeding the usual mystique surrounding method, painters from Neo-Expressionism to appropriation who used technical devices—photography, projection, Photoshop, etc.—have hidden or denied it, although David Hockney's "Secret Knowledge" implicitly connects the contemporary use of such modern conveniences to a longer history of artists using technology.

(opposite)
Jennifer Presant
Blue Room, 2007
Oil on linen
48 x 72 inches

MECHANICAL REPRODUCTION AND CYBERSPACE

Nowadays, however, many figurative painters working in Western idioms do so from trajectories that did not pass through figurative painting's nineteenth-century revolutionary quandaries or its identity crisis regarding verisimilitude, and thus don't fret over the photo. Contemporary Chinese painters such as Liu Xiaodong make photo-based and painterly images with little deference to perceptual "truth." Moreover, for younger painters anywhere television, cameras, computers, and smartphones are prevalent, daily living seems inherently second-hand. Kitsch may be "vicarious experience and faked sensations,"[27] but vicarious experience doesn't necessarily beget kitsch; mirror neurons show remote learning may develop empathy. Manet's flippancy may have forecast alienation and a Greenbergian rarity, but it perhaps prefigured our trans- or meta-modern, cybernetic experience of the artificial as "natural" as well, in which the divide between direct and indirect experience shifts like a lava lamp, and people travel primarily through cyberspace.

Despite Susan Sontag's fair description of its neutralizing effects, photographic images of huge historical events like September 11 (explored by Jerome Witkin in his polyptych *Taken*, 2003), even viewed ad nauseam, still haunt. The credible strangeness and porous boundaries of oblique experience come through Luc Tuymans's eerie *The Secretary of State* and Michaël Borremans's blatant use of photography; Marlene Dumas's expressionist use of the photo is praised for "capturing her human subjects in their own moment in history."[28] Photographic mimicry creatively interpreted by painters such as Colin Chillag, Jonas Wood, Matthias Weischer, and Mamma Andersson, sometimes including the displacement of montage, may express a recollection of, or longing for, authenticity and immediacy—Jorge Luis Borges's "nostalgia for the present"—via the armchair wanderlust gazing at photographs inspires. The photograph in painting can metaphorically convey the limits and distortions of memory and knowledge ironically or transcendentally. Like any other painting skill, tool, or technique—perspective, the camera obscura, optical mixtures, projection, Photoshop, etc.—photography may be used artfully or not.

Painting will never have the power it had before the last two centuries' explosion of mass media and technology, but the culture wars of Cold War–era painting that plagued American figure painters (at least) seem over, and Postmodern cynicism perhaps waning. Via the twenty-first-century global value of "quality in variety," figurative painting may persist in the orbit Courbet and Manet launched (given the influence American and thus French art has had), qualified by Symbolism's personal mysticism, interfacing public and private, naked and nude, past and present. The diverted or suppressed historical urges of Gauguin's *Where Do We Come From? What Are We? Where Are We Going?* (1897) indirectly persist (through Mark Tansey's ironic shadowings), sometimes by way of self-portraiture's point of view—like variations on an "allegory of the studio" theme. Perhaps the vaguely hopeful Sims-like characters poetically suspended in many contemporary meta-narratives are in search of a bigger picture. Plenty of untold "people's histories" such as women's, Native Americans', and African Americans' await depiction—and dispersion over the democratic field of the internet. Cyberspace's atemporality and ghostly denial of our physicality may embolden the memorializing power of figurative art.

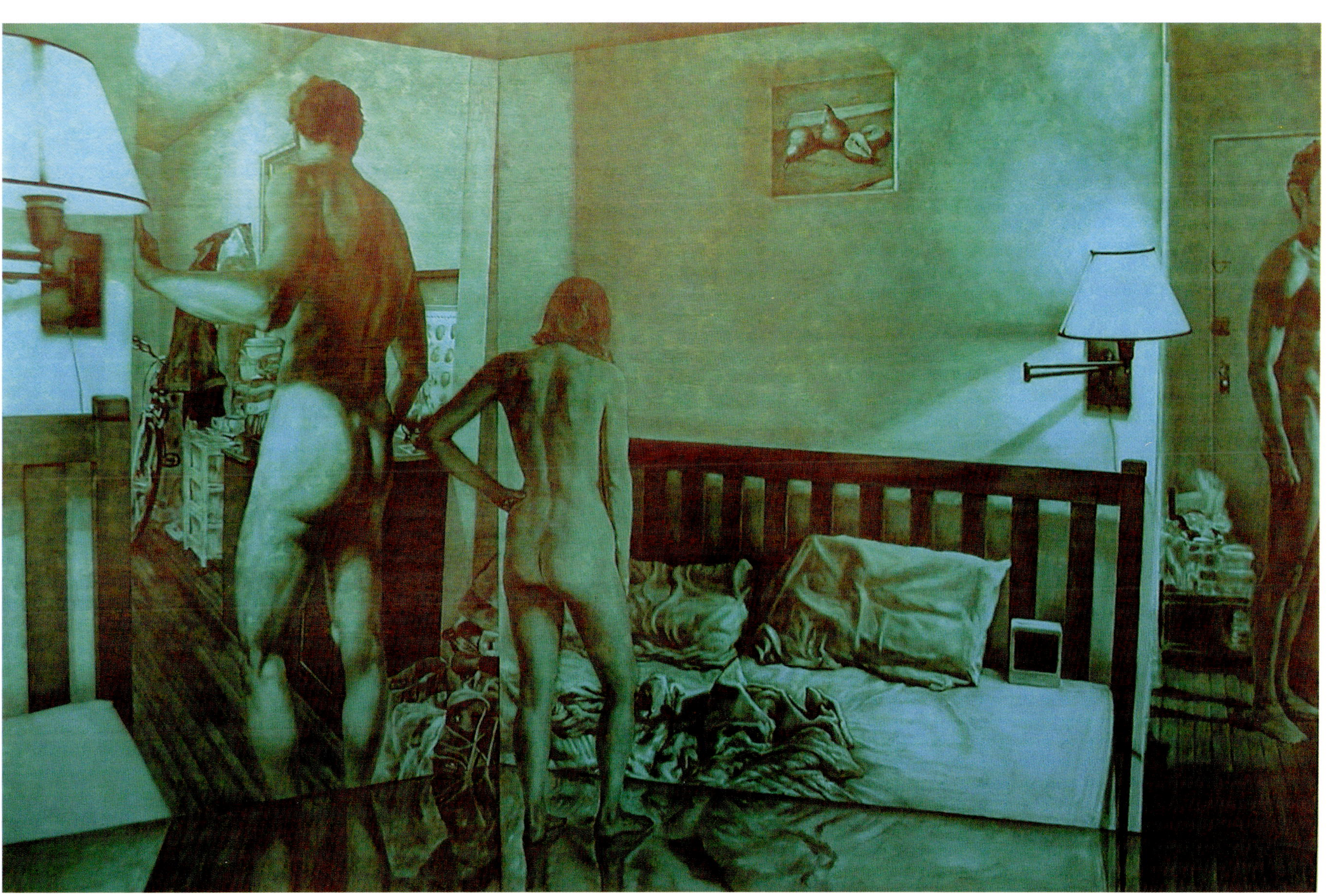

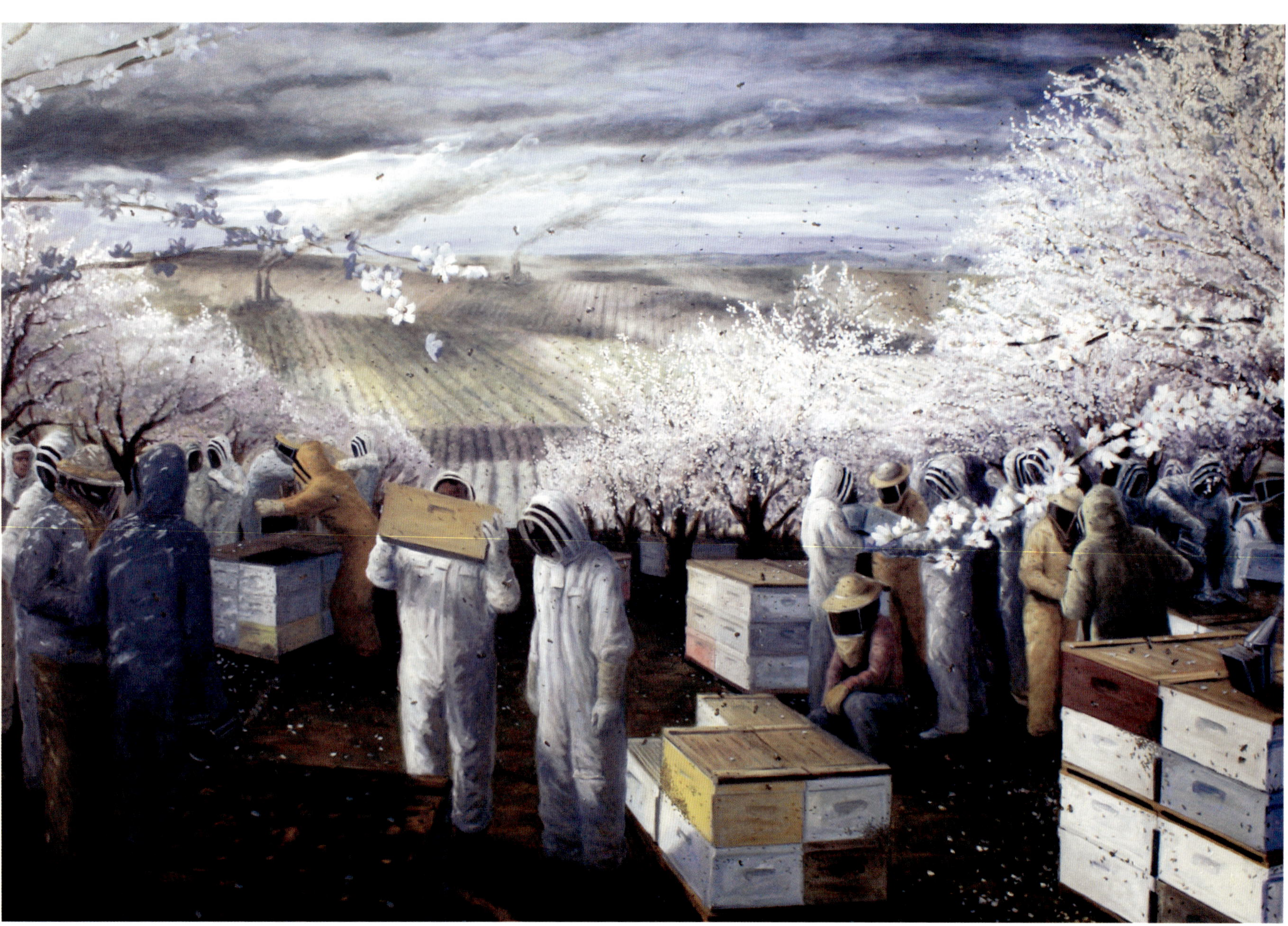

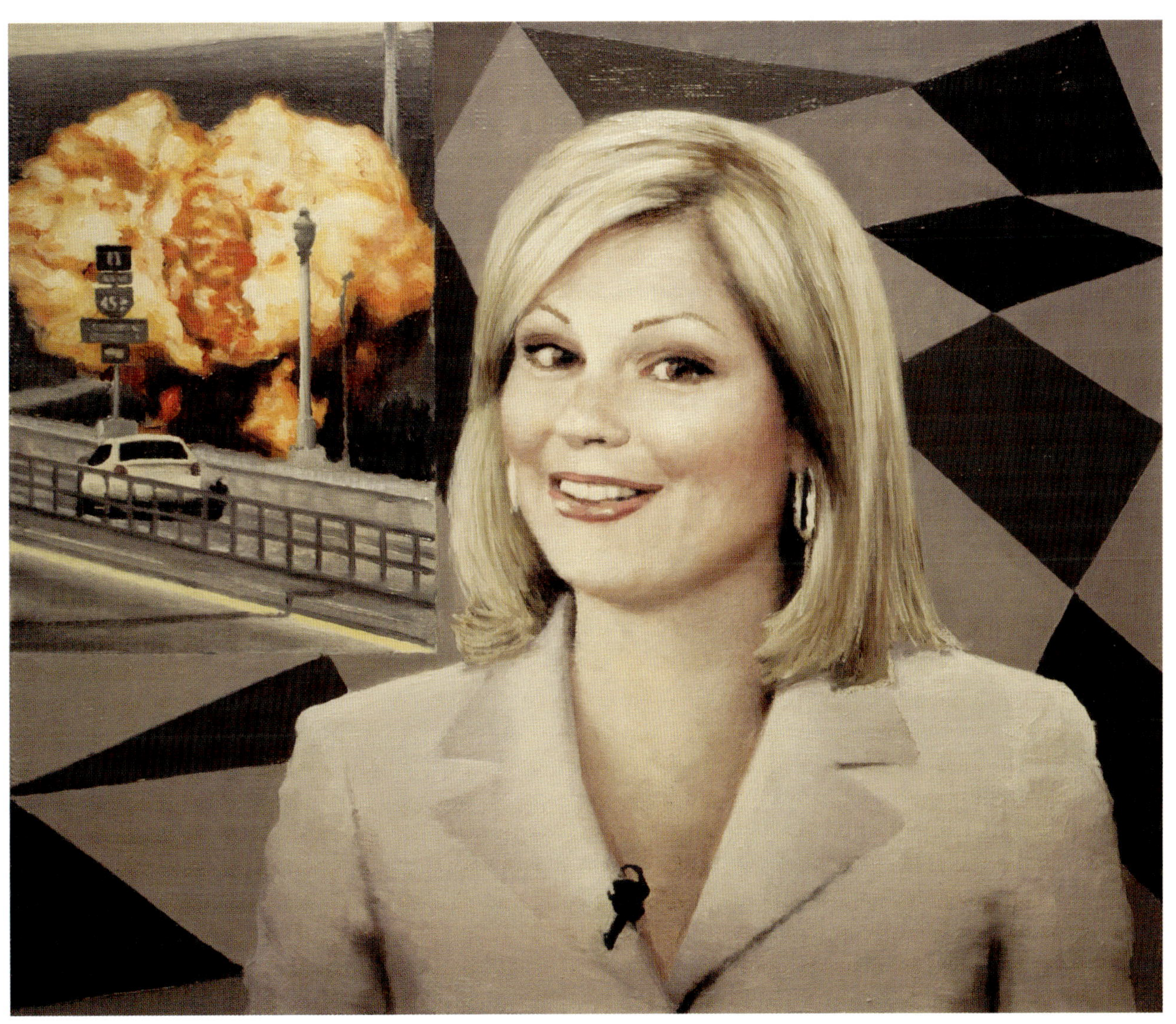

Robert Selwyn
News, 2009
Oil on linen
20 x 23 inches

(opposite)
David Pettibone
Monoculture Pollination, 2012
Oil on canvas
60 x 84 inches

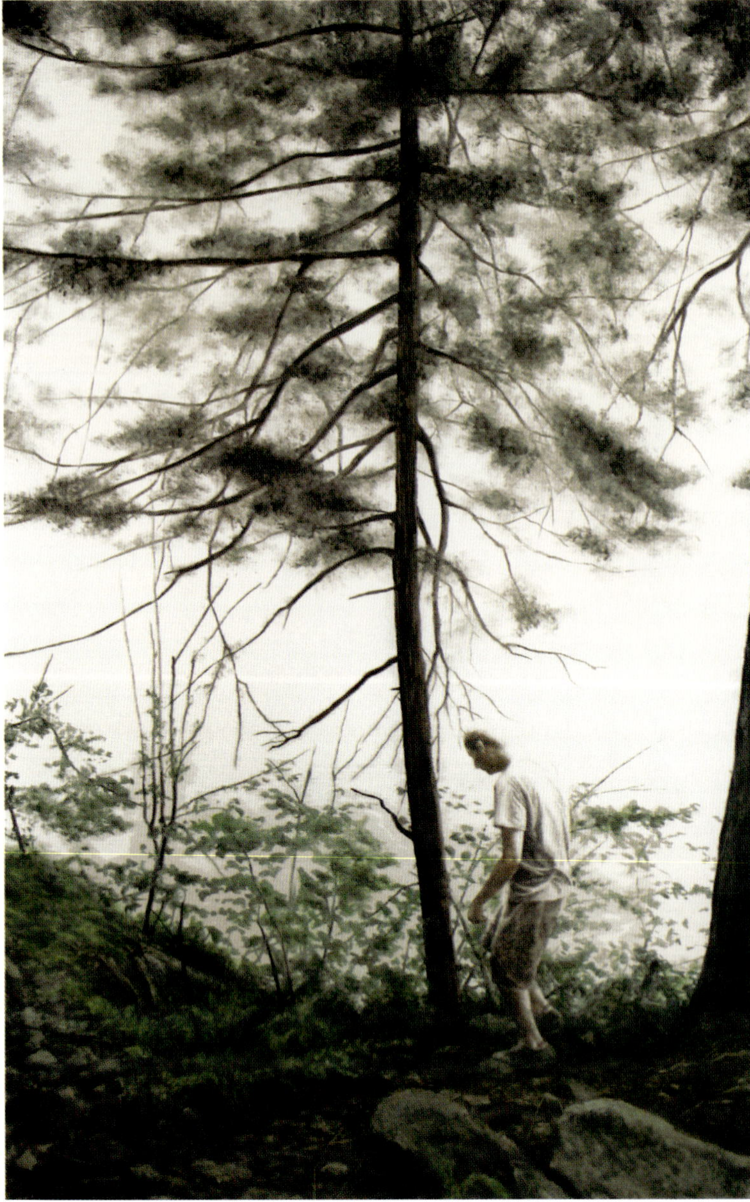

Lisa Lebofsky
Threshold, 2008
Oil on aluminum panel
16 x 10 inches

(opposite)
Steve Mumford
Empire, 2010
Oil on linen
96 x 122 inches

STEVE MUMFORD

I think of myself as a modern-day history painter of American wars. Since 2003 I've made many drawing trips to the combat zones of Iraq and Afghanistan, drawing from life for various publications and also looking for subjects for larger studio paintings. I felt that it was crucial to witness and draw my subject matter directly rather than rely on received wisdom from the media or other sources, to avoid predictable and clichéd ideas. In 2008 I was embedded with an infantry unit from the Fourth Division in Mosul, Iraq. The city was relatively calm and on the patrols I joined I saw no shots fired; however, one evening on the route back to the combat outpost in their armored Humvees, the platoon was diverted to provide extra security for a prisoner movement at Diamondback, the military airfield. The sun had set and we encountered an extraordinary scene: hundreds of bearded, blindfolded, and shackled prisoners being unloaded from buses, arranged in long lines, squatting on the tarmac, then led up a huge ramp into the brightly lit belly of an enormous C-17 for transport to some secret destination. I was told by guards there that the Geneva Convention prevented me from taking photographs, but that I could draw, which I proceeded to do as fast as I could, spilling no small amount of ink on the tarmac.

Two years later I organized a photo shoot on the roof of my studio in New York City to get the details I needed for a convincing painting of the scene I'd witnessed in Mosul. I have never been able to make up or remember much in the way of realist details: I always need source material to work from, whether from life or photographs. I hired half a dozen Arab models through Craigslist and recruited as many of my friends as were available. I ordered orange prisoners' jumpsuits and leg shackles for the shoot, and already had an extensive inventory of military uniforms and Airsoft rifles from previous paintings; I built a plywood ramp and had strong construction lights to mimic the look of the bright raking lights of the C-17's interior.

I had my models run through the action: as prisoners waiting in lines, then with the guards guiding them carefully up the ramp. These kinds of photo shoots invariably turn into a kind of art performance in themselves, the models often experiencing the intensity of the roles they're in, especially when there's some duress—in this case, negotiating the ramp in the darkness, blindfolded, and legs shackled to each other, as well as the nagging feeling of guilt experienced by the "guards" from the power imbalance inherent in the scene. We went through many repetitions of the events, while I took high-resolution photographs with a 50mm lens and a tripod. I only loosely choreographed the positions of the models, instead instructing them to move as naturally as possible while I shot photographs.

With Photoshop I created multiple crowds and lines of figures, liberally repeating my small cast until it swelled to dozens. This becomes an exercise in careful selection and combination of hundreds of different photographs to achieve the right balance of realism and a poetic rhythm of figures. I also needed clear pictures of the interior of a C-17, at approximately the right angle, or close enough to extrapolate from. These were found online, in news photographs or amateur photos of air shows on military bases.

I spent a month creating the composition, loosely based on one of the drawings I'd done on the landing strip. I tried many different combinations of figures, until I eventually worked out the final composition. I then decided what

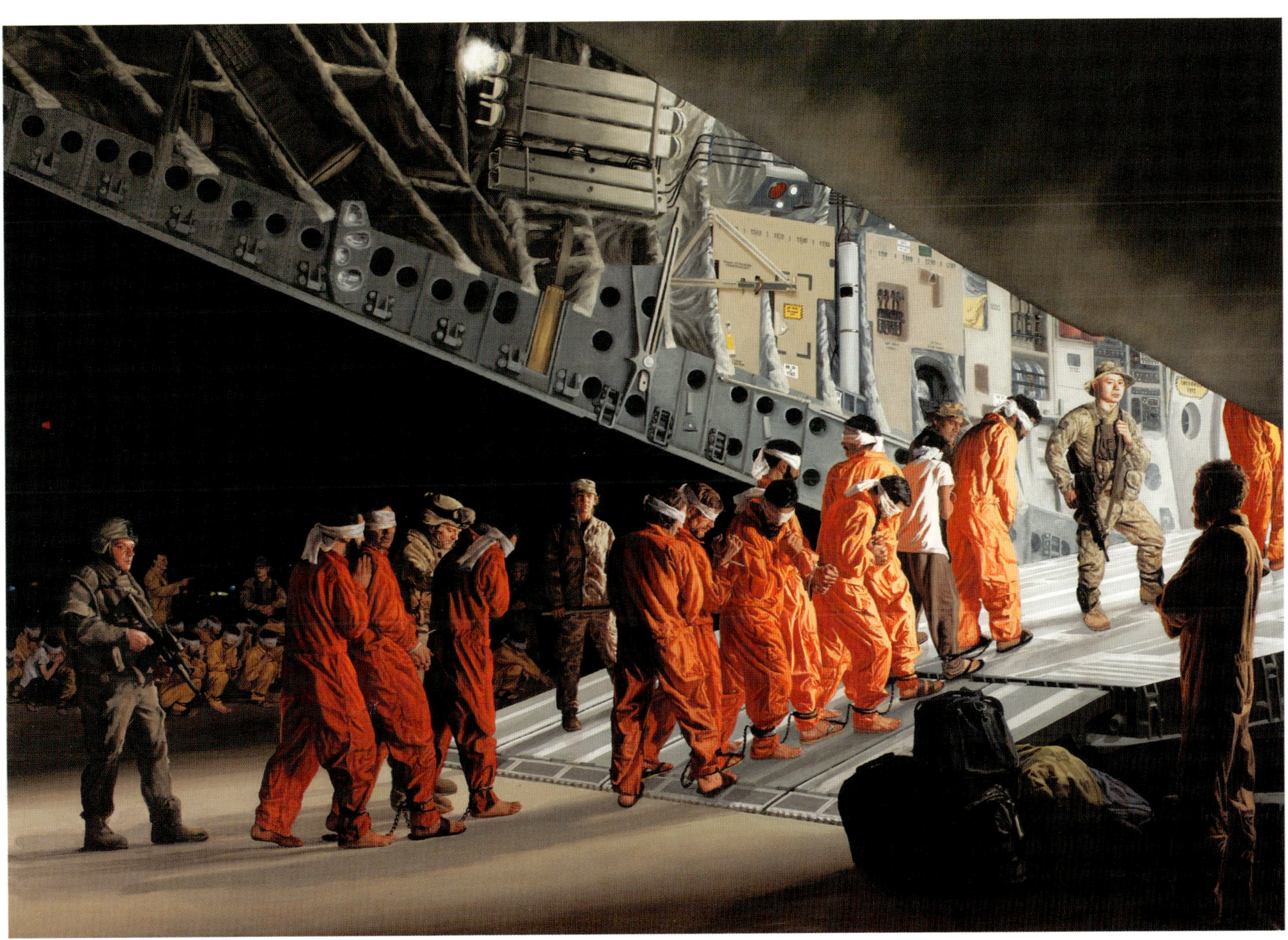

size canvas the image should be. I settled on 8 x 11 feet; in keeping with the public spectacle inherent in traditional history painting, I tend toward larger canvas options. For this size I needed to build a simple scaffolding, which consisted of three sawhorses with several ten-inch planks spanning the width of the painting. I work with a smallish palette table on wheels, which I placed on the scaffold planks when working on the upper sections.

One of the salient points about history painting is that the specific subject depicted can act as a metaphor for a larger theme. The scene I'd witnessed in Mosul was moving both for its scale and human drama, but also because of the unease I felt in seeing so many prisoners of war who might well be incarcerated indefinitely in places like Guantanamo, or subjected to torture in Iraq or one of the "black sites" maintained by the CIA in other countries. This struck me as a price that each U.S. citizen pays in moral capital, to guarantee our country's commitment to power and thus safeguard the political status quo: the price, in other words, of empire. In this way I arrived at the painting's title, *Empire*.

To transfer the basic composition to the canvas I printed out the final composition on a small size that fits over the plate of an opaque projector and premixed about a dozen oil colors for a quick, painterly approximation of the image. These represent a spectrum of values so that I can easily establish the darks and lights of the image, as well as clearly mark the placement of broad details, such as the general features of a figure. Then, working at night for best resolution with the projector, I rough out the whole image, covering the entire canvas with paint. This takes one or two nights depending on the size of the canvas. At the end of each session I lightly scrape down the canvas with a large palette knife to get rid of any paint buildup, allowing for revisions down the line. When I'm ready to paint the image after the compositional preparation is complete, I utilize many printouts of digital images for details necessary to capture the believability of the scene. I first paint the deep space, and work my way forward to the nearest objects. As surfaces dry, I may add glazes to heighten color or value. As the whole surface gets considered and painted, changes are often required: I sometimes scrape out and repaint substantial parts. Sometimes the painting merely requires a series of adjustments.

I prefer to live with a painting for several months before deciding that it's finished. I want my paintings to be more than simply depictions of occurrences within the historical context of the war, but to convey deeper themes about our shared humanity. When one seems ready to enter the world on its own, I give it a final retouch varnish and, if I'm lucky, send it on its way.

MICHAEL ANANIAN

My paintings' surfaces are scarred, rubbed, scratched, built, destroyed, and rebuilt. I'm as interested in bold, vigorous paint handling and execution as I am in particularity of description and nuance of form. I want the rough, raw treatment of paint and form in my work to echo the visceral reactions and mental states of the people depicted, with the end result a fusion of visual and psychological elements. My subject matter has been influenced by literature and film dealing with duality, opposites, shadows, and the uncanny. Novels such as *Peter Schlemiel, The Secret Sharer, The Double,* and *The Shadow*, and silent movies such as *Warning Shadows, The Cabinet of Dr. Caligari, Nosferatu,* and Antonioni's 1975 film about the doppelganger, *The Passenger*, have been important references.

(opposite)
Michael Ananian
Presto!, 2010
Casein on paper
22 x 26 inches

Counterpart is a seventeen-painting story in casein about the doppelganger, which took me four years to complete. It expands upon leitmotifs about duality, multi-personality, multi-identity, and doubling that are more submerged in earlier work. My sustained focus on sequential narrative is unusual in the world of contemporary painting. My enthusiasm for visual storytelling I attribute to the few illustration courses I took as an undergraduate at the Rhode Island School of Design—courses that concentrated on the communication of an idea, something taboo to my Modernist education in graduate school at Yale. I have probably learned the most about constructing sequential narratives from graphic novelists, principally in how they use exaggerated perspective, drastic scale shifts, dynamic points of view, and differences in frame size to control the frame-to-frame movement and pacing of the plot. My biggest traditional influences have been late medieval predella paintings and early sixteenth-century German limewood sculptures. Hogarth, Masereel, and Ward have helped me with character development and psychological content. Paula Rego's pastiches of fairy tales and Gabriel Laderman's short but fantastic sequential narratives in oil have been important contemporary influences.

Counterpart was specifically influenced by *A Short History of the Shadow* by Victor Stoichita. After reading it, I drew charcoal portraits of the two main characters, trying to make their outlines as distinctive as possible so that their silhouettes alone could identify them. Next I drew studies of shadows, then sketched thumbnails on 5 x 7-inch note cards. I created a storyboard on a wall so that I could edit—arrange, rearrange, add—scenes. On the wall I noticed something else, a meta-composition that corresponded to the meta-structure of the narrative: The last four paintings were loose reflections of the first four paintings—like shadows, reflections are a significant element in double stories; the first and last four paintings framed the out-of-time, dreamlike subsequence of the middle eight paintings.

After this preparatory research I was ready to paint, from both invention and observation. I used myself in a mirror for my main characters, and a foot-tall artist's mannequin for one of the characters, making it as large as the human characters. I started using casein in my work twenty years ago because I wanted a medium that dried quicker than oils so that I could speed up my revision process and make a lot of changes in a short amount of time. Casein handles much like oils and dries faster than acrylics, but has its own technical challenges. When registering values in casein, I have to guess what they will be when dry because lighter values dry darker, and darker ones dry lighter. Casein's lighter-than-normal, restricted value range and dusty, matte glow played a vital conceptual role in *Counterpart* by emphasizing the dreamlike, surreal aspects of the narrative. Hot-press watercolor paper, 140 pounds, is the best support for casein because it warps less than board or canvas. To keep the piles of paint from drying out on the palette, I mix the casein with a little bit of water in jars, using a tear-away wax paper palette to mix specific colors. Because casein is predisposed to subtle drawing techniques and fine detail—and not to pushing paint—I use only round, synthetic sable brushes. I scrape paint off the painting's surface with razor blades to get unusual textures and painterly effects.

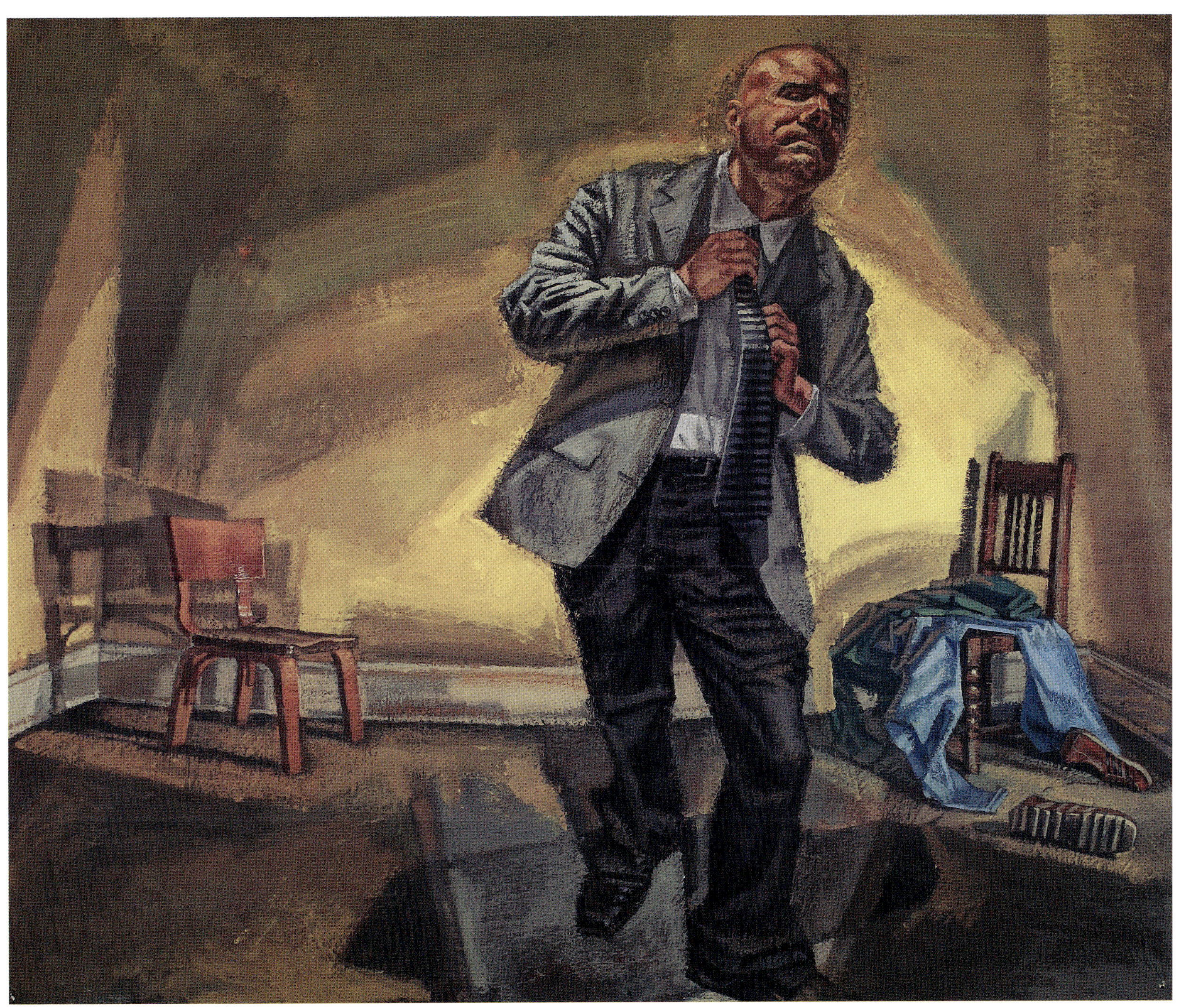

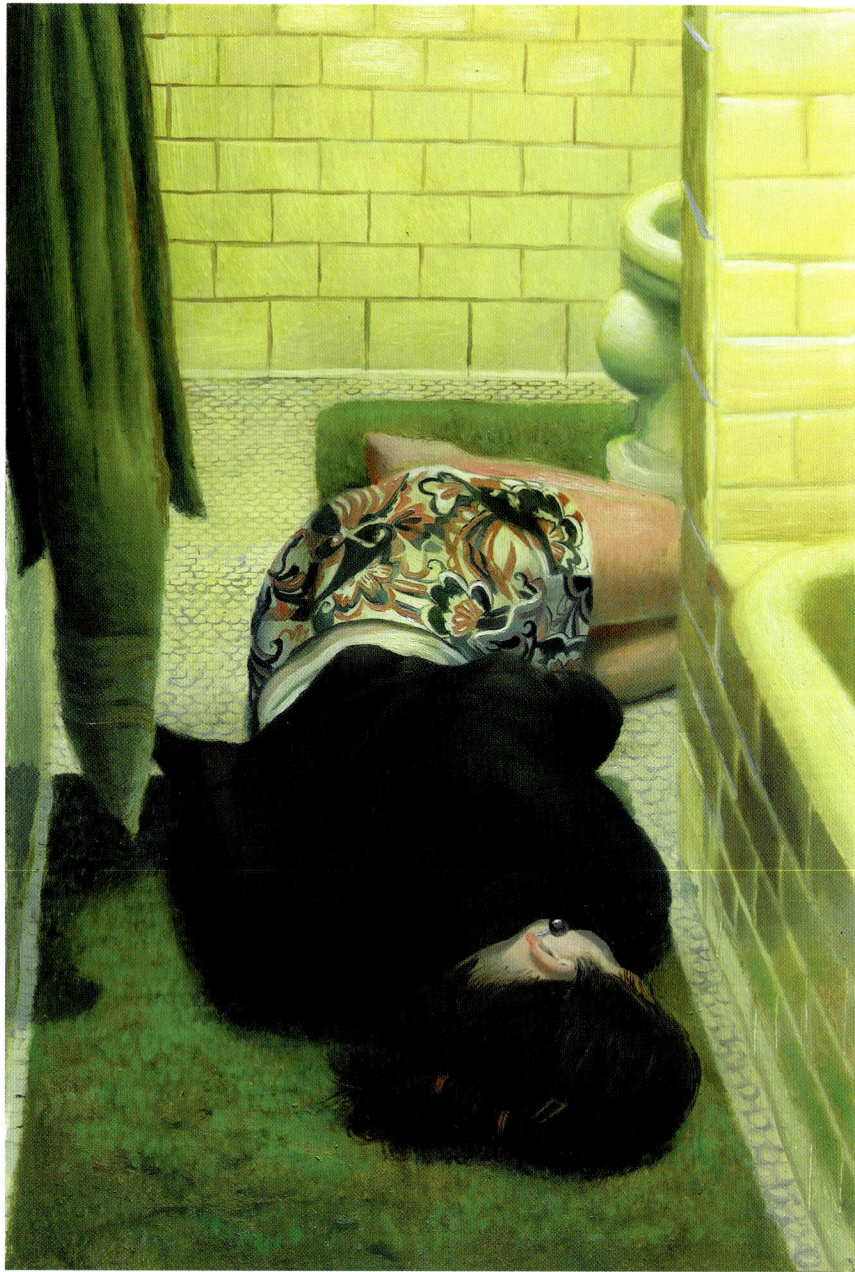

Thomas John Carlson
Passed Out, 2007
Oil on wood
15 x 10 inches

(opposite)
Margaret McCann
Believe It or Not!, 2012
Oil on linen
50 x 50 inches

Each painting in *Counterpart* took about three months to finish. I knew a painting was done when my editorial process no longer produced improvements. This was the painting's way of telling me that it would be better to address any remaining questions by beginning a new painting.

MARGARET McCANN

I started painting giant figures in the late 1980s, inspired by the monuments of Rome. I landed there on a Fulbright grant to study depictions of saints, fascinated by their equally neurotic and sublime qualities. I spent a lot of time staring at Roman ruins and experiencing the city's cornucopian and sculptural qualities while teaching on-site drawing. Rome's heavy sense of history made daily life feel like a de Chirico painting. I began to understand how American I was when I took my students to draw Constantine's giant foot on the Campidoglio and the first thing it reminded me of was not that emperor but Claes Oldenburg. For my classes I assigned projects like "draw an object as a monument" and "self-portrait as a monument," and then started doing them myself. I set up still lifes, placed objects, then sculptures, and then figures in them.

My understanding of color grew from studying Sienese, Venetian, and other artists like Piero, Filippo Lippi, Signorelli, and Morandi, from noticing subtle temperature shifts of the warm cityscapes against the sky, and from having to figure out how to teach, specifically how to apply Albers's minimal schemes to the complexities of perception. A Lucian Freud show at Palazzo Ruspoli in the early 1990s was a revelation in terms of his color and handling of edges. I often took my students to see Caravaggio's many masterpieces in Rome, and have been greatly influenced by his sense of form and handling of cloth. (I've begun painting cloth as water in many boardwalk paintings straddling still life and landscape.) I greatly admire Brueghel's skills, complexity, and humor.

Growing up in the middle of ten children in the tumultuous 1960s, my brain probably developed habituated to a visual field with a lot of moving parts; the multiple viewpoints of Cubism feel familiar. My sense of space tends toward horror vacui and I resolve compositional variables into an order just this side of chaos. Trying to harmonize diverse, even contradictory elements (in both form and content) reflects my eclecticism; I made many collages as an undergrad at Washington University in St. Louis, where I also studied with a terrific figure drawing teacher, Barry Schactmann. At the New York Studio School I learned about space and light from Gretna Campbell, and developed an intense engagement with the vicissitudes of process. At Yale I learned to love abstract painting, but in the 1980s discussion regarding figuration barely ventured beyond whether it was valid. Analytical discourse was captivating but could revolve around things like whether a drip could be non-expressionistic. So living in Europe was a welcome profundity.

My paintings change a lot but start from a conceit, a visual idea or a title. Still lifes are based on perception and on themes. I like being close to what I'm painting so my eyes "feel around" the form. I'm a direct painter and spend a lot of time mixing and adjusting color with a palette knife, and focus a lot on edges, form, and color harmony. I often scrape out what I've painted, responding to new descriptive and textural conditions. I may use photos for specific information in places but I

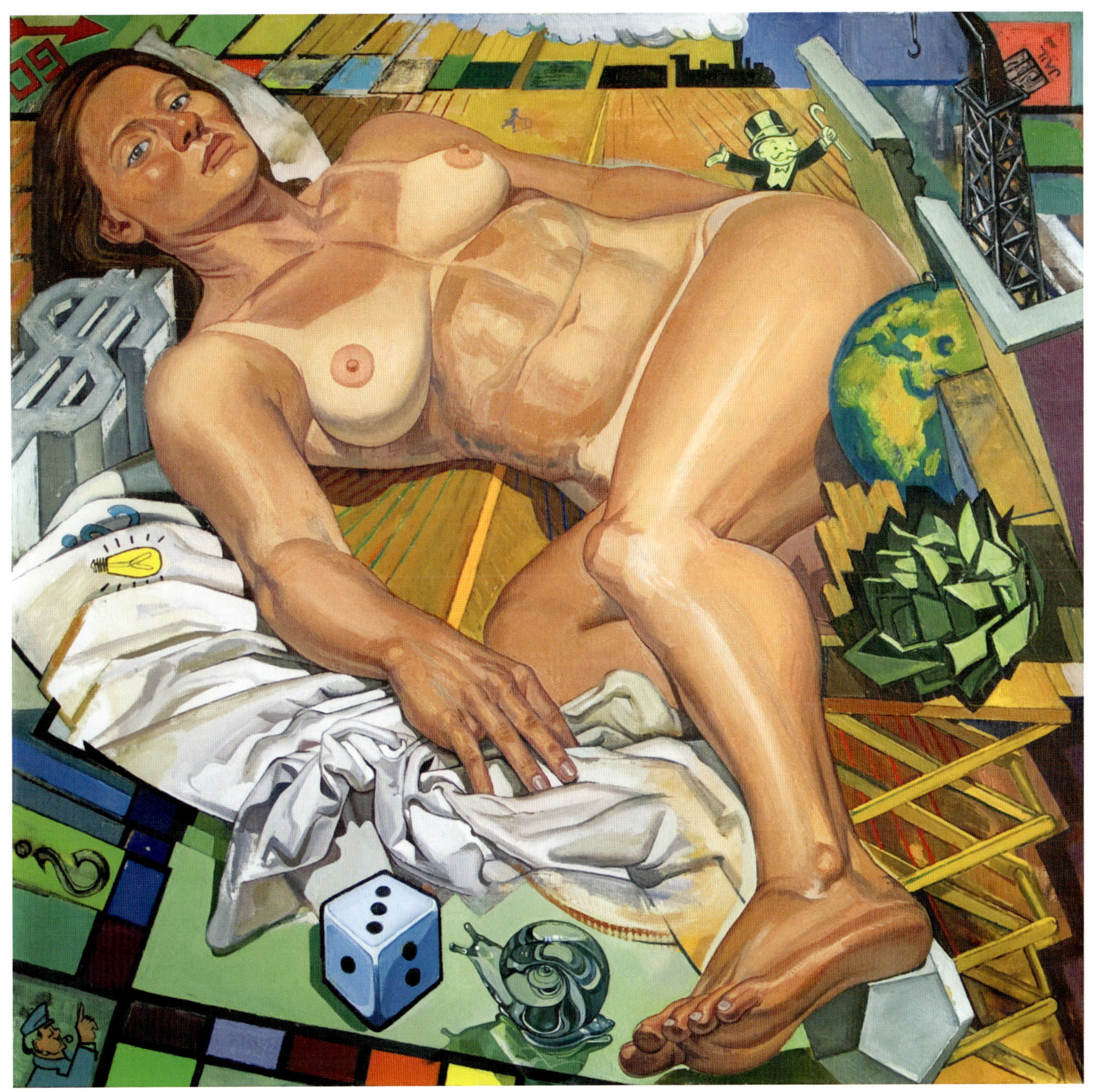
GO

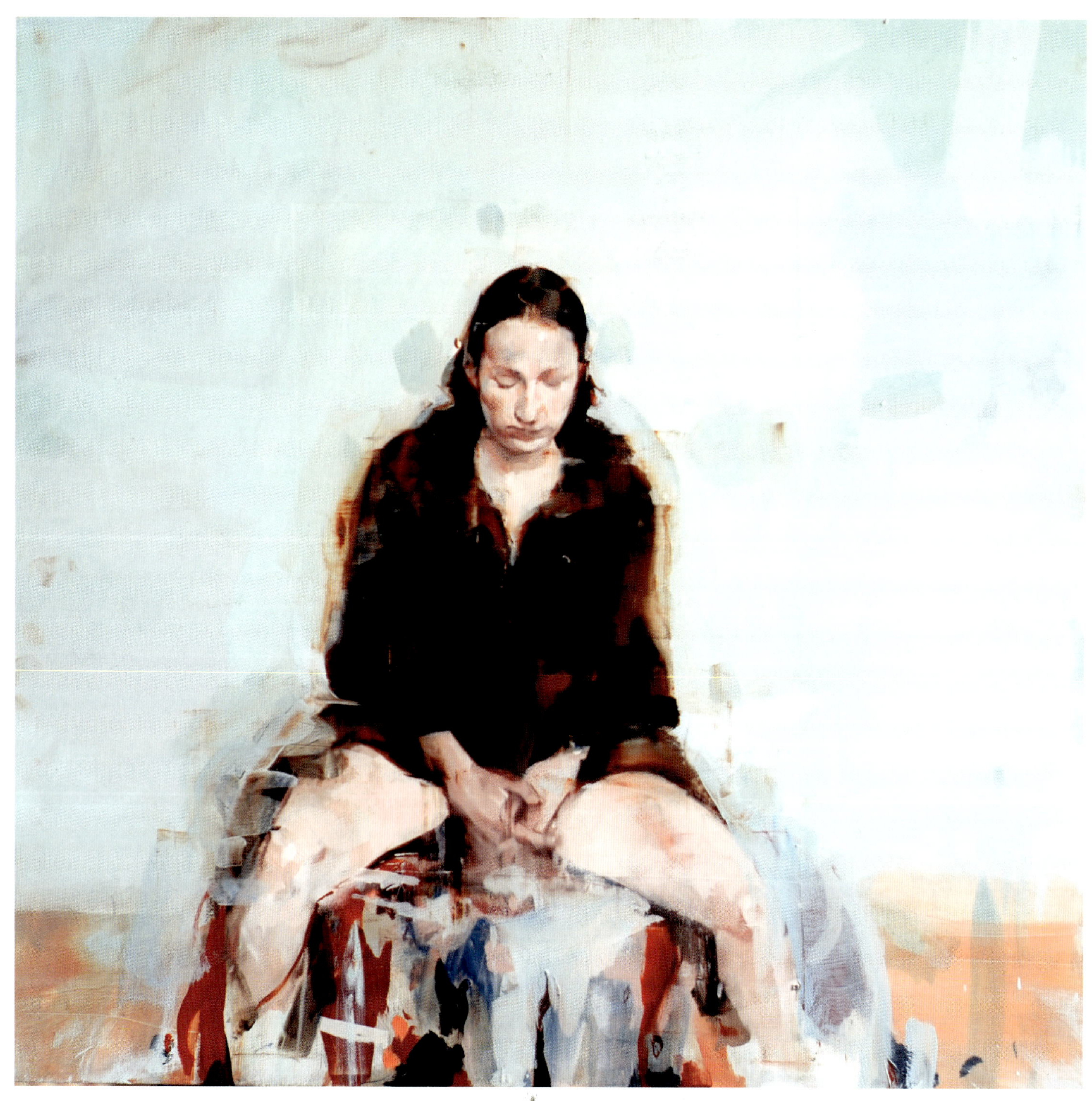

can't make convincing light and volume without observing. A series I've worked on since grad school, self-portraits with stuff piled up on top of my head, like Marge Simpson's beehive or the Guggenheim, are more psychological, like surreal saints. The head is painted from observation but the rest flows from seeing where playing with the paint and imagery leads.

Giant paintings start with the figure, then I see what kind of environment it suggests. I prefer foreshortened poses because the forms create deep space while simultaneously stacking up on the picture plane, so flat shapes also contain volume. For *Believe It or Not!* I wanted to include the Ripley's Museum on the boardwalk of Atlantic City, where I lived for four years, a surprisingly beautiful place; compared to Rome it's an ephemeral mirage. I started the painting in the late spring, so over the summer as the model's tan got progressively darker there was a lot of repainting and the figure became disjointed. So I emphasized spatial dislocation as I went along and added almost untenable contrasts in saturation, codes of description, and texture. This painting took about six months to complete, but I often work on a painting for years—as Andrew Forge said, "A painting is finished when the reservoir of energy attached to it is drained"—but it's done when all compositional variables achieve a homeostasis that reads like a satisfying "eye-pinball" game.

ALEX KANEVSKY

I was born in Rostov-na-Donu in Russia. Nobody in my family was an artist, as far as I know, but my parents had a nice big collection of art books. That was a major influence. By the time I was ten years old, I could tell Cézanne from Manet and had many paintings permanently imprinted in my mind. My own first painting was an effort to copy a van Gogh landscape with farmhouses. I thought at the time that it came out pretty well, almost as good as the original in the book. I gave it to my mother who promptly hung it over the kitchen stove, where it luckily didn't survive very long. I didn't really see any actual paintings beyond the usual official drivel about workers and peasants engaged in heroic toil, done up in the style of the time, both bombastic and sentimental, heavy on dappled sunlight and Popeye-esque forearms. My father described this Socialist Realism style as "well-fed horses striking the pavement with their hooves."

Only when I was fifteen years old and my family moved to Vilnius in Lithuania did I see the kind of paintings that had the capacity to both trouble and impress. There was a fairly dark and expressionistic school of painting in Lithuania that didn't seem to have any interest in realism or the social issues. That was an eye-opener. I realized that paintings could find the reason for their existence within themselves rather than being merely a decoration or a propaganda tool. From that point on I was hooked. After I came to the United States in 1983 I studied at the Pennsylvania Academy of the Fine Arts, which didn't give out degrees at the time, so I don't have one.

My influences after that have been wide-ranging and not limited to painting. Certain major principles in art easily cross over between literature, music, and visual art. All these are often influenced by the vernacular culture. The following are in no particular order and come from many fields: Giacometti, Auerbach, López-Garcia,

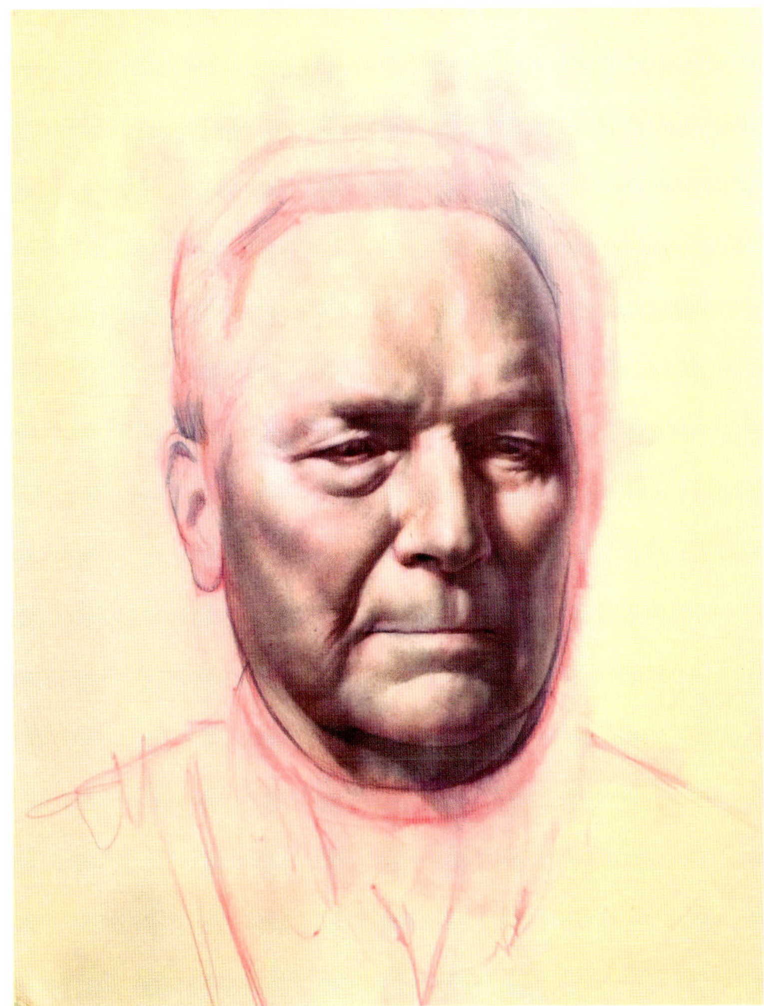

Raphael Sassi
Old Man Looking at Kate Middleton's Portrait, 2012
Ballpoint pen on paper
17 x 11 inches

(opposite)
Alex Kanevsky
J.F.H., 2010
Oil on wood
24 x 24 inches

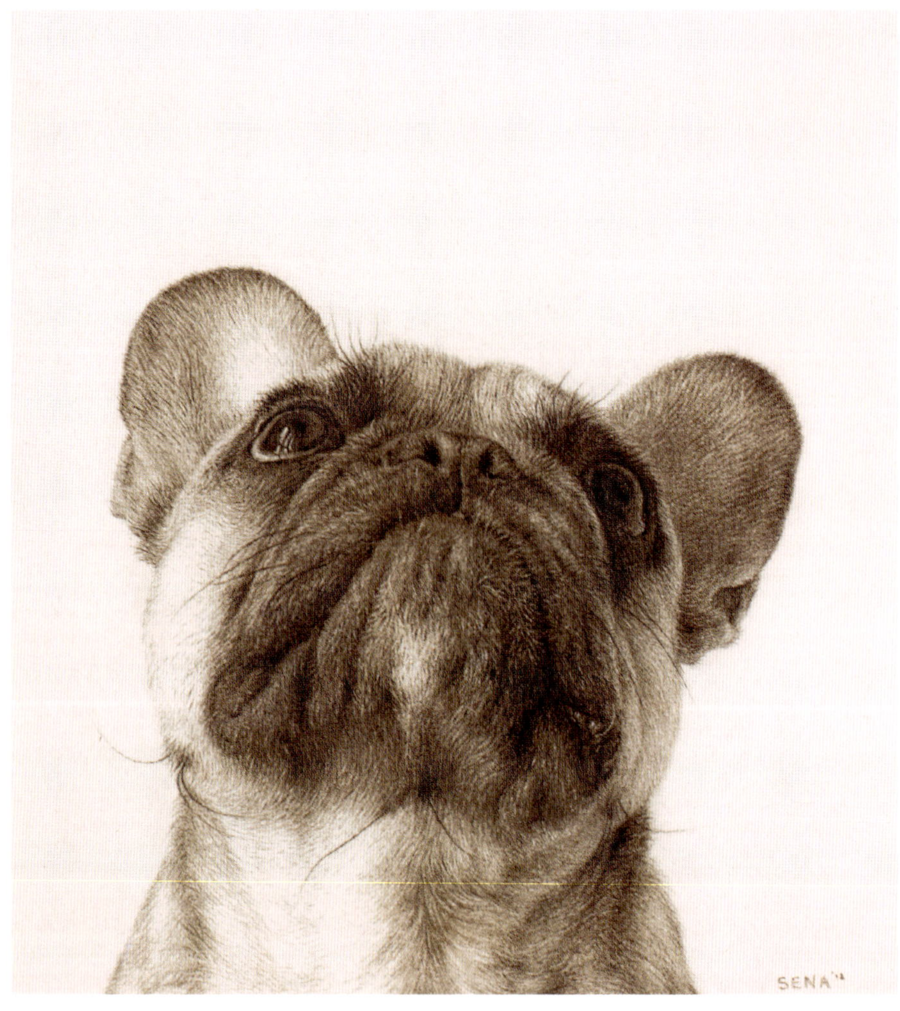

Amber Sena
Chosen, 2012
Pastel, charcoal on paper on wood
8 x 8 inches

(opposite)
Shangkai Kevin Yu
Portrait Sketches, London, 2010
Oil on canvas
24 x 35.5 inches

Seurat, Beuys, Twombly, Uglow, Rembrandt, Velázquez, Ingres, Diebenkorn, van Gogh, Soutine, Lucian Freud, Francis Bacon, Cecily Brown, Jenny Saville, Tolstoy, Joyce Cary, James Joyce, Wallace Stevens, Ezra Pound, Joseph Brodsky, Cormac McCarthy, Shostakovich, Alfred Schnittke, William Eggleston, Nan Goldin, Aki Kaurismäki, Andrei Tarkovsky, Korean and Japanese potters, D. T. Suzuki.

I don't have a set procedure. I begin with a visual idea that corresponds to a situation or an event that I find compelling. Like everyone else, I have my own unique view of the world. As an artist I try to arrive at the extreme clarity of that view and then try to find visual means, capable of expressing this clarity. I begin working directly on a board or canvas. I paint mostly on birch plywood unless the size is too big for that. Then it is stretched linen. I use all kinds of oil paint—Guerra, Mussini, Holbein, Rembrandt, Classic (Triangle Coatings)—and I use Liquin as a medium.

Sketches and preparatory drawings are not very useful to me since most of my paintings undergo numerous compositional changes as I go. I do draw from models once or twice a week simply because I enjoy it, as a stand-alone activity unconnected to painting. I find the extreme level of abstraction that drawing is to be fascinating. I also enjoy their one-time-deal aspect; you either have it at the end of the day or you don't. For the fairly slow painter that I am, this is very fresh and liberating. Some of my drawing discoveries have recently begun filtering into my painting. I didn't intend for this to happen, but it is very interesting to watch and participate as a medium begins asserting itself outside of its usual parameters.

When I paint directly from life, the composition results from what I see in front of me. It changes, as what or who is in front of me changes, and also as my vision of the painting becomes clearer to me. I consider all formal aspects as I paint: light, form, space, color, texture, scale, etc. The painting progresses in a series of layers, each one almost a complete painting until I manage to create a layer that satisfies me, which becomes the top or final layer. Toward the end, the

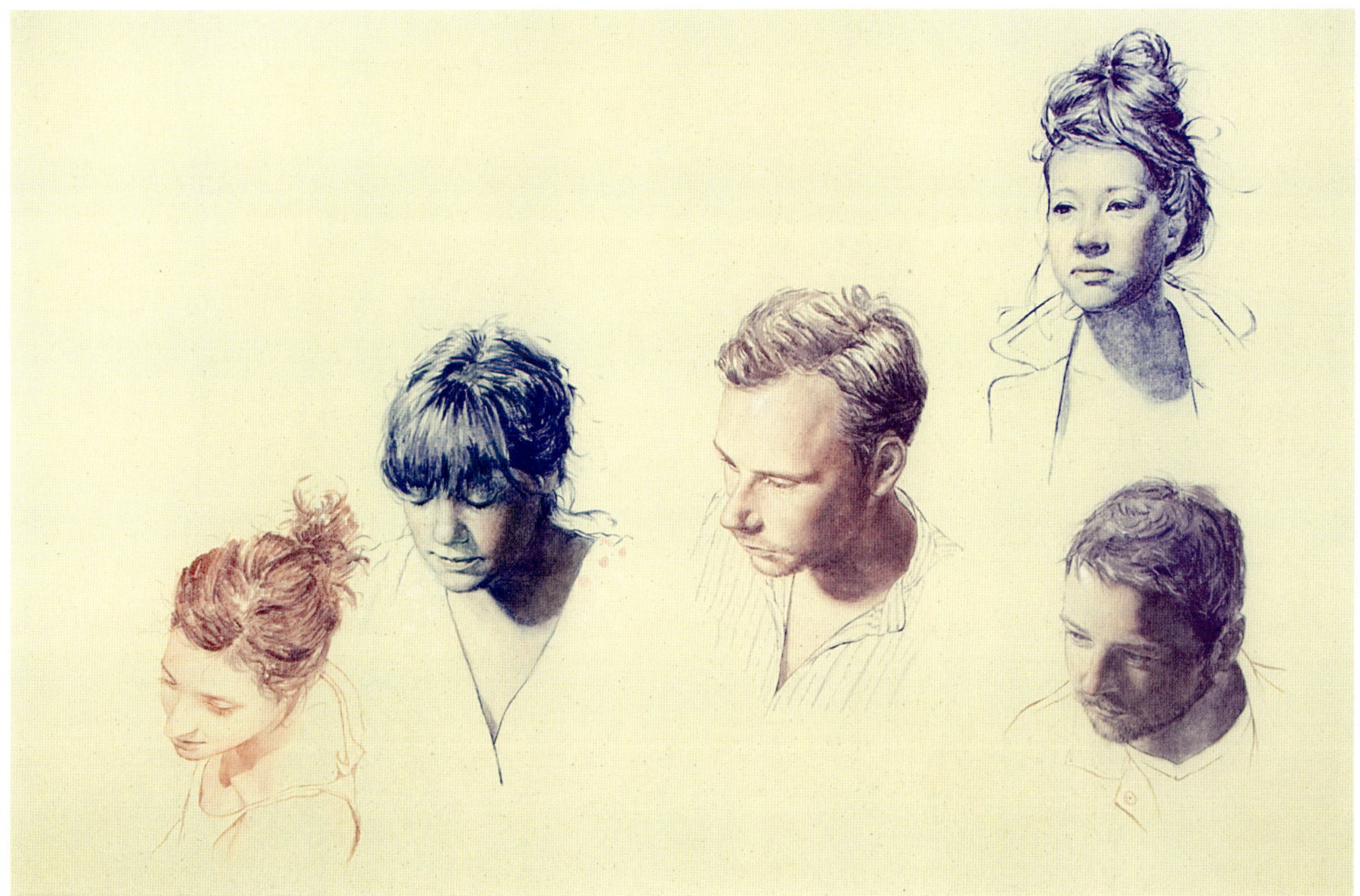

layers begin to resemble Swiss cheese; they have large holes through which the successful passages of the previous layers are visible.

Sometimes I use photos, usually my own, in addition to or instead of direct observation. Beyond having a good-quality digital camera there is not much craft involved; they are essentially unadulterated, minimally composed snapshots. I take them all the time with no particular painting in mind. Photos are inferior to direct observation, but they also have some desirable qualities: they show fleeting situations, momentary events, and produce unintended artifacts; they also remove me as an observer a step or two away from reality, sometimes necessary for personal reasons. I use Photoshop sometimes to mix a few photos together, again in a very low-tech fashion. I don't use projection to transfer images to a painting surface because I feel the need to have a loosely linked chain of image permutations. Photography is dangerous that way—it is easy to lose the "room for failure" that makes painting so interesting.

A painting is finished when I am happy with a painting, when all the potential improvements will only do harm. When any roughness and awkwardness left in it ceases to be a shortcoming and becomes a vital part of composition. Or when a painting is irretrievably lost (finished in a different way). Paintings do let us know when to leave them alone. Artists often overlook these signals, being so focused on imposing their will. I don't think of painting as something I do to a canvas. To me it is a complicated relationship of equals. A form of conflict. When we reach some sort of agreement that makes everyone satisfied it is a good time to leave it alone.

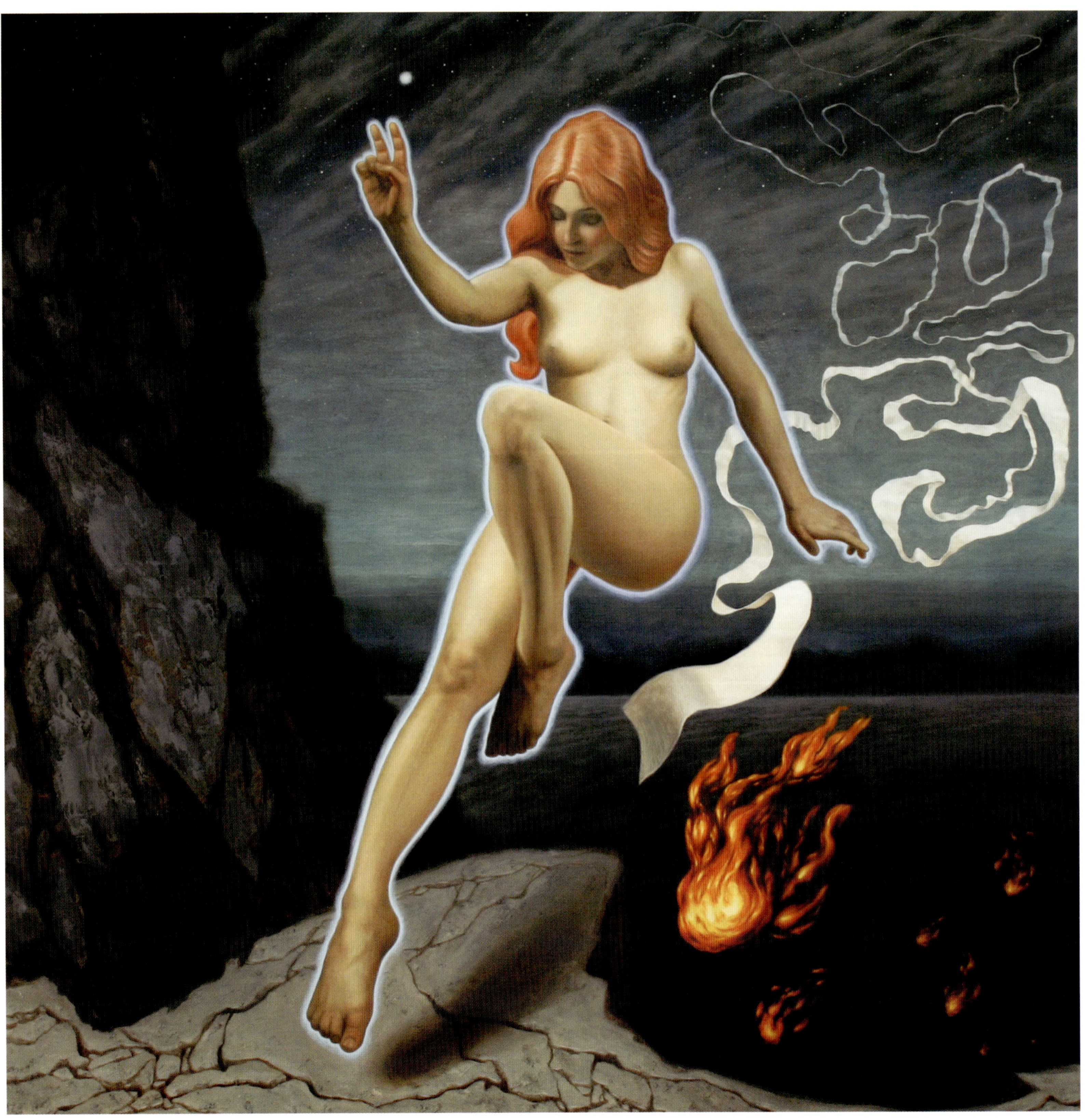

FREUD AND THE ETERNAL FEMININE IN MODERNIST PAINTING

DONALD KUSPIT

Faust is the model for Freud's patients, for Faust, reaching the limits of his culture, and seeking to escape those limits, first had to escape that culture, including—as in the classical Walpurgisnacht—the past of that culture. He had to resist the temptation of the hypostatized moment, the temptation to be a monadic personality. He had to reach the point of accepting the eternal feminine, the eternal not-I, the eternal otherness which draws us forever onward.
—Morse Peckham, "Reflections on Historical Modes in the Nineteenth Century"[1]

The irresistible pressure of Freud's ideas has led to an increasing measure of agreement that sexuality is the world's motivating force. . . . Freud had no hesitation in considering all the manufactured objects which surround us to be sexual symbols and in separating them, as such, into masculine and feminine categories.
—André Breton, *Surrealism and Painting*[2]

At least since Odilon Redon's *In the Dream* (1879), the notion that a work of visual art could be a dream image, representing figures seen as though in a dream—and thus peculiarly fantastic, distorted, and strange—became acceptable if not widespread. Without it Gauguin's remark in 1888, that "art is an abstraction . . . from nature while dreaming before it,"[3] seems inconceivable. But it was not until André Breton, in *The First Surrealist Manifesto* (1924), acknowledged Sigmund Freud's theory of the "omnipotence of the dream,"[4] that the idea that figures and objects in visual art had to be "dreamlike," as Dalí said,[5] and thus "enigmatic," as de Chirico argued,[6] became de rigueur. It was what differentiated modern from traditional art, where, however dreamlike, the figures were "real."

More particularly, the figure had to convey the enigma of sex, for, following the early Freud of the *Three Essays on the Theory of Sexuality* (1905), and Freud's even earlier *Studies on Hysteria*, written with Joseph Breuer in 1895, Breton was convinced that "sexuality is the world's motivating force." The enigma of sex was embodied in woman, more particularly in female hysteria, for all the hysterics in Breuer and Freud's book are young women who had sexual problems. They acted out their frustrated sexual feelings in their bodies, gratifying them by theatrically somatizing them in a dreamlike state. Quoting Rimbaud, a proto-Surrealist poet, Max Ernst described a dream as a "simple hallucination."[7] He often dreamed—with compulsive repetitiveness in *La femme 100 têtes* (1930), in effect his orgiastic Walpurgisnacht—of hysterical young women. He hallucinated them into visceral immediacy with his technique of frottage, ironically reminding us that frottage is a "sexual perversion in which orgasm is induced by rubbing against the clothing of the sexual object."[8] The material—smooth paper on grainy floorboards or grainy paint on smooth canvas—that he used to make his touchy-feely rubbings symbolized woman's clothing and even the skin underneath it. A *frotteur* is "one who gains sexual excitement through the sense of touch,"[9] suggesting that for Ernst the aim of art was to generate sexual excitement, and that it was animated by sexual feelings.

As Ernst suggested, the rubbings were essentially masturbatory. The "hallucinatory succession of contradictory images" they generated derived from his "childhood memory" of the "hypnagogical visions" that magically appeared on the "false mahogany panel facing my bed" as he masturbated. He regarded the panel as a version of what Breton called the "paranoid wall" in whose "spots" and "smudges" Leonardo da Vinci "saw" many "fantastic" and "bizarre" things.[10] What Ernst "saw" was "amorous," as he said, indicating that he knew Freud's theory of infantile sexuality and that

(opposite)
Dave Wagner
Noli Me Tangere,
2013
Oil on canvas
72 x 72 inches

he was hallucinating—dreaming, as it were—while masturbating. Like Breton, he had studied Freud, and like Freud he regarded the dream as a wish fulfillment, particularly of infantile sexual wishes, polymorphously perverse—like frottage—from an adult point of view. Following Freud, he regarded art as a wish-fulfilling dream, but one made in a hypnagogic state of mind rather than during sleep. Hypnagogic imagery occurs "during the stage between wakefulness and sleep, that is, just before sleep has set in,"[11] suggesting that art spontaneously occurs—we automatically hallucinate—in the mental space between consciousness and unconsciousness. For Freud, and the Surrealists who were his followers, what Freud called the "dream imagination" and the artistic imagination are essentially the same. "Dream work" is "artistic work," Freud said,[12] and the artist is a person who gives his or her private dreams publicly acceptable form, ironically reminding us that the content of all dreams, especially "amorous" dreams, is universal, and all dreams are peculiarly "surreal."

For Ernst the images produced by the masturbatory process of making art were so many orgasms. Ernst became the standard bearer for Modernist frottage painting in all its variations—for richly textured, ultra-personal process painting, so-called "signature painting," often expressionistic, with hallucinatory figures embedded or implicit in the "bold" painterliness. It involves an intense rush and hallucinatory discharge of sexual energy, a sort of narcissistic response to imagined figures; or, more precisely, to what psychoanalysts call internal objects to which one is emotionally attached and devoted, seemingly inescapably, and thus, as Freud said, seem to "possess" one, take over one's life (and art). Thus Expressionism—Figurative Expressionism, from Kirchner onward through Francis Bacon, and Abstract Expressionism, from Kandinsky onward to Pollock—as well as Surrealism, is heavily indebted to Freud's theory of sexuality.

Ernst Gombrich makes the point when he uses Freud's distinction between the ego and the id— the former the site of "the forces of control," the latter "the most primitive layer of our mental life, identical with the instinctive drives"[13]—to understand the influence of primitive art on modern art, more or less beginning with Picasso's treatment of the female figure in the canonical, trendsetting *Les Demoiselles d'Avignon* (1907). For Gombrich, primitivism involves submission to "the anarchic tendencies of the unconscious"[14]—what Gauguin, in 1903, called the "savagery" and "barbarism" of "instinct."[15] But letting the genii of instinct loose resulted in works that were a "sum of destructions," as Picasso said.[16] As Gombrich noted, when uncontrolled—unsublimated, unsocialized, uncivilized, as Freud said—the instinctive drives "manifest themselves in insanity."[17] There is something insane about *Les Demoiselles d'Avignon*; they are among the first of what might be called the "insane figures" typical of modern hallucinatory representation. What Gombrich called "the lure of regression" to the primitive instincts—primitive art was thought to symbolically represent them—cannot help but lead to symbolic insanity, that is, the symbolization of insanity by way of bizarre hallucinatory figures. Woman became the symbol of insanity by reason of her supposedly inherent hysteria—sexual hysteria, suggesting that there was something insane about sex for the modern male artist. And about his dependence on woman for sexual satisfaction, and the sexual satisfaction she got from hysteria, which made her independent of him. For the misogynist male artists, woman both represented insanity and drove them insane, that is, made them aware of their inner insanity.

(opposite)
João Henrique Brandão
Occupy, 2012
Mixed media on canvas
97 x 65 inches

What the regression destroyed—dehumanized and denaturalized—was the figure; it was reduced to abstract rubble, more particularly, to what psychoanalysts call part (body) objects, supposedly given "artistic form," and then randomly reassembled into a freakish semblance of a figure. *Les Demoiselles d'Avignon* was supposedly sexual in import, but what Freud called the sadistic component of sexuality was let loose and emphasized, suggesting that Picasso's painting had more to do with what Freud called the disintegrative death instinct than the integrative life instinct. It set the model and tone for future sadistic destructions of the figure—especially the female figure, as became transparently clear in Picasso's abstractly surreal female figures of the 1920s. A sum of parts that do not add up to a human whole—however artistically novel they may be—their vicious absurdity appears again and again in Modernist fantasies of the female figure, from Hans Bellmer to Willem de Kooning.

The sadistically destructive attitude to woman typical of many modern male artists reaches a kind of nihilistic climax in Alberto Giacometti's sculpture *Woman with Her Throat Cut* (1932). It is a radically negative vision of woman—in contrast, say, to the positive vision of her, as a symbol of happiness and joie de vivre, in Renoir, and earlier, in antiquity, in the idealized female body of Venus. She is clearly a source of pain rather than pleasure in many Modernist images. She is ugly rather than beautiful; she is not exactly a sex object—Picasso desexualizes her by turning her body into a geometrical contraption—suggesting that what is unconsciously at stake in modern male representations of woman is castration anxiety. What the psychoanalyst Wolfgang Lederer's called man's "fear of woman"[18] is transformed into hatred of her, acted out through art. The modern male artist defends himself against woman, who unconsciously symbolizes castration, by mutilating, murdering, and dismembering her—artistically raping her, as it were, and disposing of her body after he has cut it up into parts. It was as though he had no need of her after he had used and abused her, which was his perverse way of showing his need for her—and his power over her. In *Celebes* (1921), Ernst turns her into a headless hollow shell, a lifeless empty vessel whose pale, skeletally thin arms, with sexually suggestive red wrist bandages, beckon us to follow her to our deaths. Freud thought hatred was more primitive than love, suggesting that modern male artists were indeed emotionally primitive.

The seductive "dream woman" the male artist may have seen in his sleep is not the same as the nightmarish "dream woman" he tended to construct when he was awake. The artistically "simulated dream," as Dalí called it, is not the same as the spontaneously occurring dream, however much that may be its model. Both involved seemingly free association, what Breton, following Freud, called "the disinterested play of thought . . . in the absence of any control exercised by reason, exempt from any aesthetic

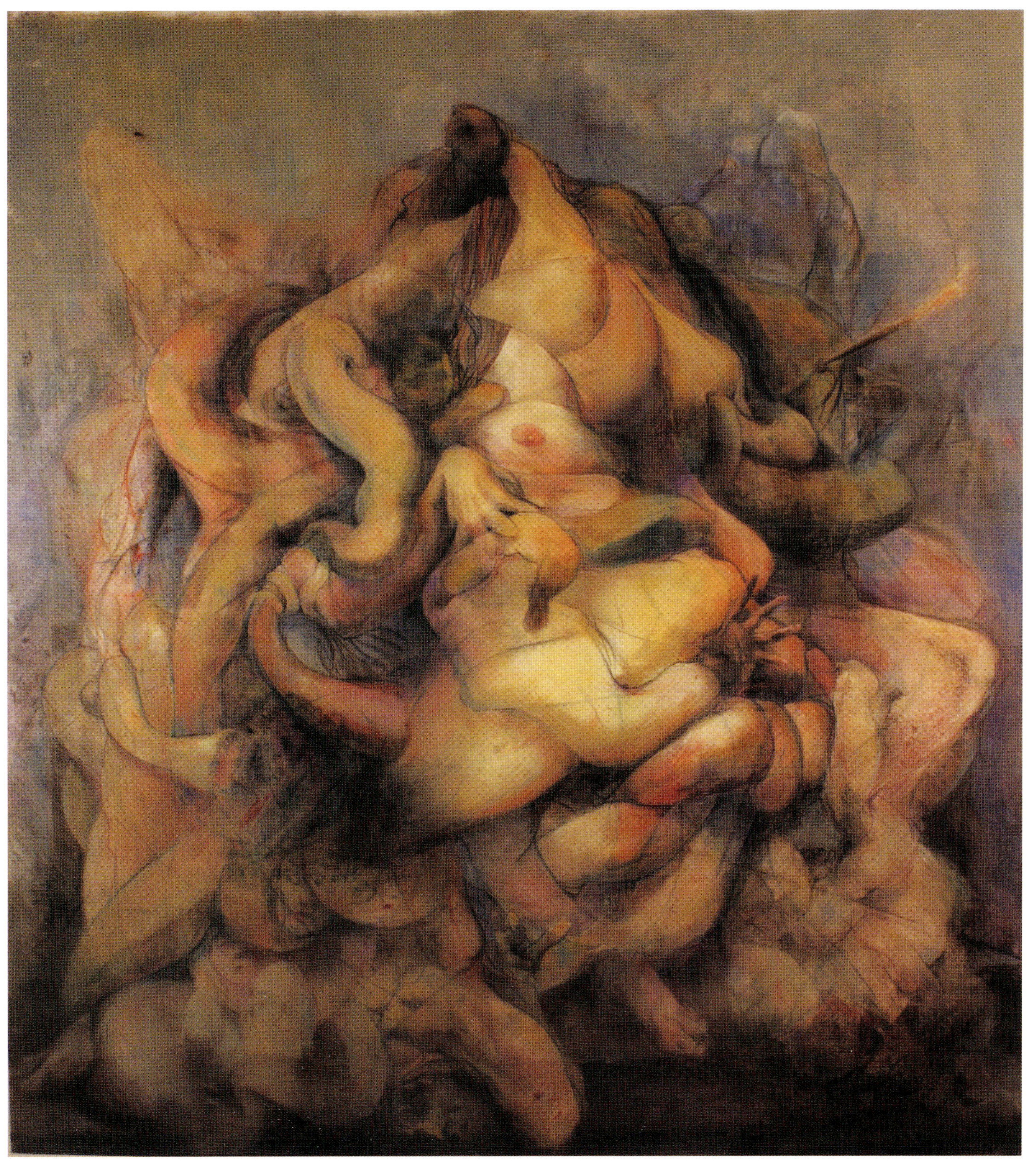

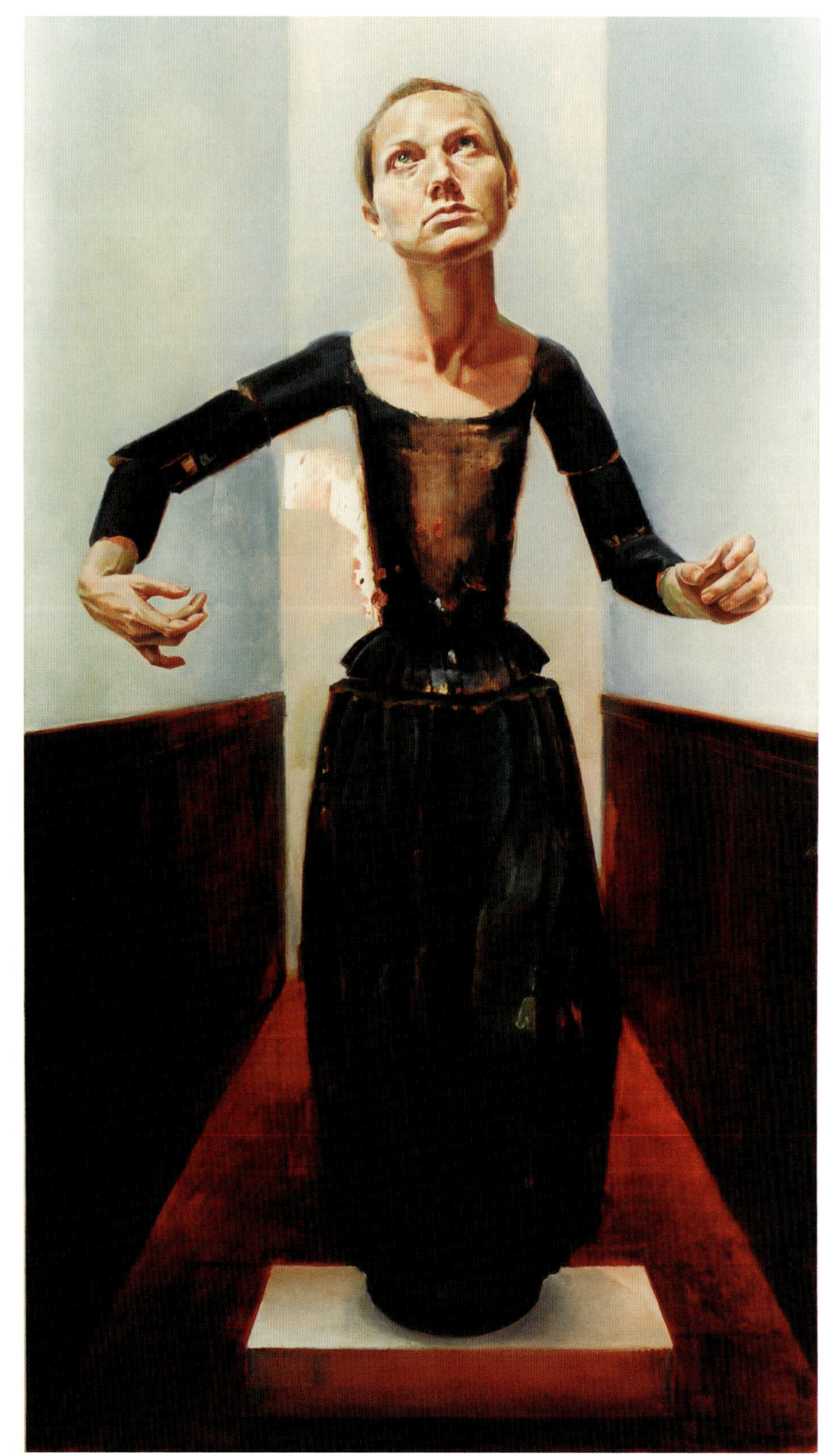

or moral concern."[19] Thus what Ernst called "the magistral eruption of the irrational" in art by way of what Breton called "psychic automatism in a pure state."[20] (He plagiarized the term from Pierre Janet's *L'Automatisme psychologique* [1888].) The modern task of art was to make the irrationality latent in life manifest—to make the insidious, pervasive, insistent influence of the irrational in "the private life of individuals, the public life of nations" self-evident.[21] Ernst's irrational figures seem to be automatist hallucinations, like the irrational figures of the German Neo-Expressionists that follow them, perhaps most noteworthily those of Georg Baselitz, Rainer Fetting, and Markus Lüpertz.

The method of the construction of dream figures was supposedly by free or "chance" associations, as Ernst called them. Collage was his preferred method of free associating, but, as he well knew, following Freud, as Breton did, that seemingly free or chance associations were unconsciously determined, and as such were hardly free, that is, did not occur by chance. They made unconscious sense, however nonsensical they seemed to consciousness. The Surrealists were following the topographic model of the psyche Freud elaborated in the last chapter of *The Interpretation of Dreams* (1900). He distinguished between the unconscious, preconscious, and conscious. The preconscious mediated between the unconscious and the conscious. Unconscious wishes—instinctive wishes defensively repressed into the unconscious, where they remain active, potent, and profoundly influential on conscious behavior (such as making art)—appeared, in disguised form, in dreams, often by way of some seemingly insignificant, trivial, but emotionally telling day residue that lingers in the preconscious. However changed in appearance by the artistic dream work so that they lose their conventional meaning, they become charged with instinctive meaning: Thus the "forbidden" wishes emerge into consciousness, in whatever compromised form, through the unconventional appearance of the dream. It has to be interpreted, and so do Surrealist dream works—more broadly, the many modern dream works, whether abstract or representational in style, or some combination of the seeming opposites.

Freud thought of the dream as a wish fulfillment, as noted. The repressed wishes are its latent content; the experienced dream, with its air of what Breton called "immediate absurdity" and de Chirico called "sudden revelation,"[21] is its manifest content. The psychoanalytic task—and the task of psychoanalytic interpretation of art, particularly modern art, which presents itself more or less explicitly as a dream work motivated and informed by the dynamic unconscious—is to make us conscious of the latent content of the dream by interpreting it, in conjunction with the dreamer's associations to it and life experiences. Both involve figures, usually what psychoanalysts call primary objects, however much they may be disguised as secondary objects. As the psychoanalyst Michael Balint argues, even abstract artists relate to their forms as though they were figures, in whatever complicated relationships.[22] Many, even most, theories of art put forth by modern artists are apologetic rationalizations of their dream works. They are civilized excuses for their uncivilized dreams about other human beings, and sometimes themselves.

Through the ages male artists have represented the female figure—it has been said that the archaic sculptures of fertility goddesses, including the *Venus of Willendorf*, are among the first works of figurative art—but perhaps not with such frustrated vengeance as during the Modern period. I suggest Freud's idea of castration anxiety, and with it the infantile view of the female as a castrated male, a male who has lost his penis and become a woman, and thus "powerless," underlies much of the modern fear and hatred, not to say mistreatment and misrepresentation, of woman evident in modern art, from Cubism and Surrealism onward. I suggest that so-called pure abstraction, with its rejection of the figure—however implicitly figurative—is informed by unconscious terror and rejection of woman and her body. Nonetheless, the obsession with the female figure implies that the modern male artist is in pursuit of the eternal feminine, to use Goethe's term. It was the saving grace that drew Faust onward at the end of Goethe's drama. But the fact that she is distorted into hallucinatory grotesqueness when the modern male artist holds her in his grasp implies that she has become devilish and deceptive, as though announcing that she will castrate him, damning him to creative failure and sterility. The modern artist's brutalized female figure is a sort of morbid memento mori of the classically beautiful female figure.

And yet, despite his negative attitude to the eternal feminine, she continues to draw the modern male artist onward, fascinating him because she remains fixed in collective memory. She is the archetype of eternal otherness in the male, preventing him from hypostatizing his maleness as the be-all and end-all of human existence. To use Jung's distinction, she is the *anima* within him, trying to unite with his *animus*, if never quite let alone easily doing so. For the Surrealists, she was symbolized by *Gradiva*, the title of a 1902 novel by Wilhelm Jensen that Freud famously analyzed in a 1907 essay entitled "Delusion and Dream in W. Jensen's 'Gradiva.'" Freud's word *Wahn* has been translated as "delusion"; it is the German word for "madness" or "insanity." In German, *Wahnsinn* means "nonsense," that is, having no sense, and as such insane. Jensen's hero Harold was fascinated—virtually hypnotized—by the figure of a young woman pictured on a Roman bas-relief, serving as a tombstone, he had seen in Pompeii. The young woman is Gradiva, which in Latin means "the woman who walks." The bas-relief depicts a young woman who lifts the hem of her robe as she strides forward. There is such a bas-relief in the Vatican Museum; Freud saw it in 1907, and kept a copy of it in his study. Harold came to realize that the Gradiva of the bas-relief was Zoe Bertgang, his childhood playmate, for whom he had sexual feelings. *Gang* means "walk" in German; Harold unconsciously associated the fictional Gradiva with the real Bertgang by way of their names, youth, and femaleness. The story is about a repressed memory, a "mad dream" of a real woman, and Harold's conflicted sexual feelings about her. It is, to recall Ernst's words, an "amorous childhood memory."

The bas-relief is an artistic dream work. Bertgang haunts and informs Gradiva for Harold, giving the fictional woman hallucinatory presence, all the more so because he unconsciously feels that she is walking toward him, that she was "made for him," or rather that he made her, if only in a dream.

(opposite)
Daniela Kovacic
Black Virgin, 2013
Oil on canvas
88 x 48 inches

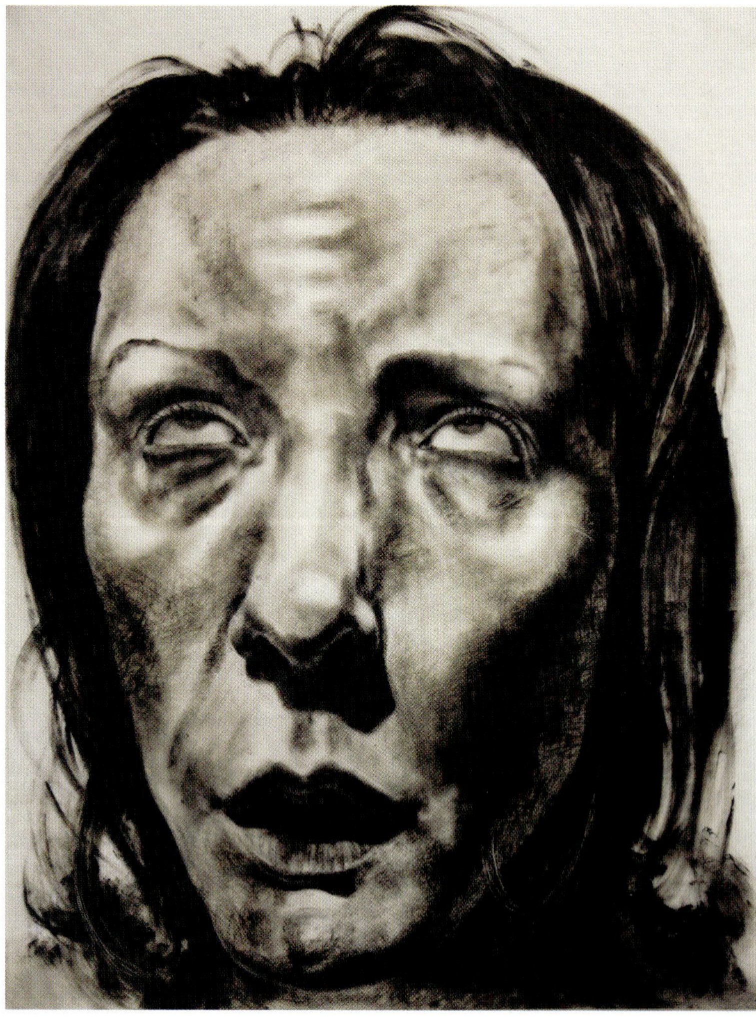

Clara Lieu
Self-Portrait No. 5, 2011
Mixed media on plastic
48 x 36 inches

(opposite)
Amanda Scuglia
Idle Hands, 2011
Oil on canvas
60 x 36 inches

Bertgang endures in his unconscious—she's as permanent and as eternally youthful as the dream girl Gradiva, the eternal work of art that is the bas-relief, an ageless work of art that retains its youthful freshness. Bertgang is the latent content of the manifest content that is the bas-relief of the lively, graceful Gradiva, reminding him of his lost youth. The bas-relief is a day residue, and Zoe represents Harold's repressed sexuality. It is worth noting that he was an archaeologist, and Freud initially thought of psychoanalysis as a kind of archaeological excavation of the forgotten past, remembered only in the unconscious, in whatever dream form. Hysterics, as he famously said, suffered from "memory traces"; Harold seems to be a male hysteric, like many modern male artists—certainly the Surrealists, who argued that hysteria was a state of being not a mental illness.

Dalí called his wife and muse Gala "Gradiva," and used the figure of Gradiva, in whatever distorted—unclassical—form, in many works, for example, *Gradiva Finds the Ruins of Antropomorphos* (1929). She is the subject of many Surrealist paintings. Masson's *Metamorphosis of Gradiva* (1939) influenced many male American Abstract Expressionist painters, among them Gorky, Pollock, and de Kooning. Their paintings seem to be in perpetual metamorphic process, suggesting the mercurial character of paint, and with that of their dream work. In 1937 Breton opened an art gallery in Paris, naming it Gradiva. It was designed by Duchamp, with a door in the form of a doubled shadow of a female figure. Clearly the eternal feminine, in the fictional form of Gradiva, casts its shadow on modern art, even if it doesn't always do her justice; that is, even if male artists remain conflicted about her effect on them. The female body may epitomize irrationality to the modern male artist's eye, but its irrationality is what draws them to it, putting them under its spell, for the artistic better or worse.

Freud had a direct and indirect influence on the representation of the female figure—and the figure in general, as Victor Brauner's array of sexually indeterminate figures makes clear—in modern art, and continues to have an influence. This is by way of the notion of the "male gaze," as though envious epistemophilia, not to say perverse scopophilia, was unique to male artists, which is not the case, as Sylvia Sleigh's "female gaze" at the youthful nude male body makes clear. Woman's self-conscious unconscious is clearly at narcissistic work in the expressionistic surreal vaginas, each the symbol of a famous woman—her name and significance are part of the work—in Judy Chicago's *The Dinner Party* (1979). The vagina, in its eternal otherness to the penis, is the entrance to the eternal feminine. For some male artists, to enter it is to leave all hope behind, a message that Dante said was inscribed above the entrance to hell; for other male artists it is the pearly gates of heaven—a promise of salvation. It is often ambivalently both for modern male artists, especially those unable to make peace with the woman inside them, that is, to confess and own their eternal femininity.

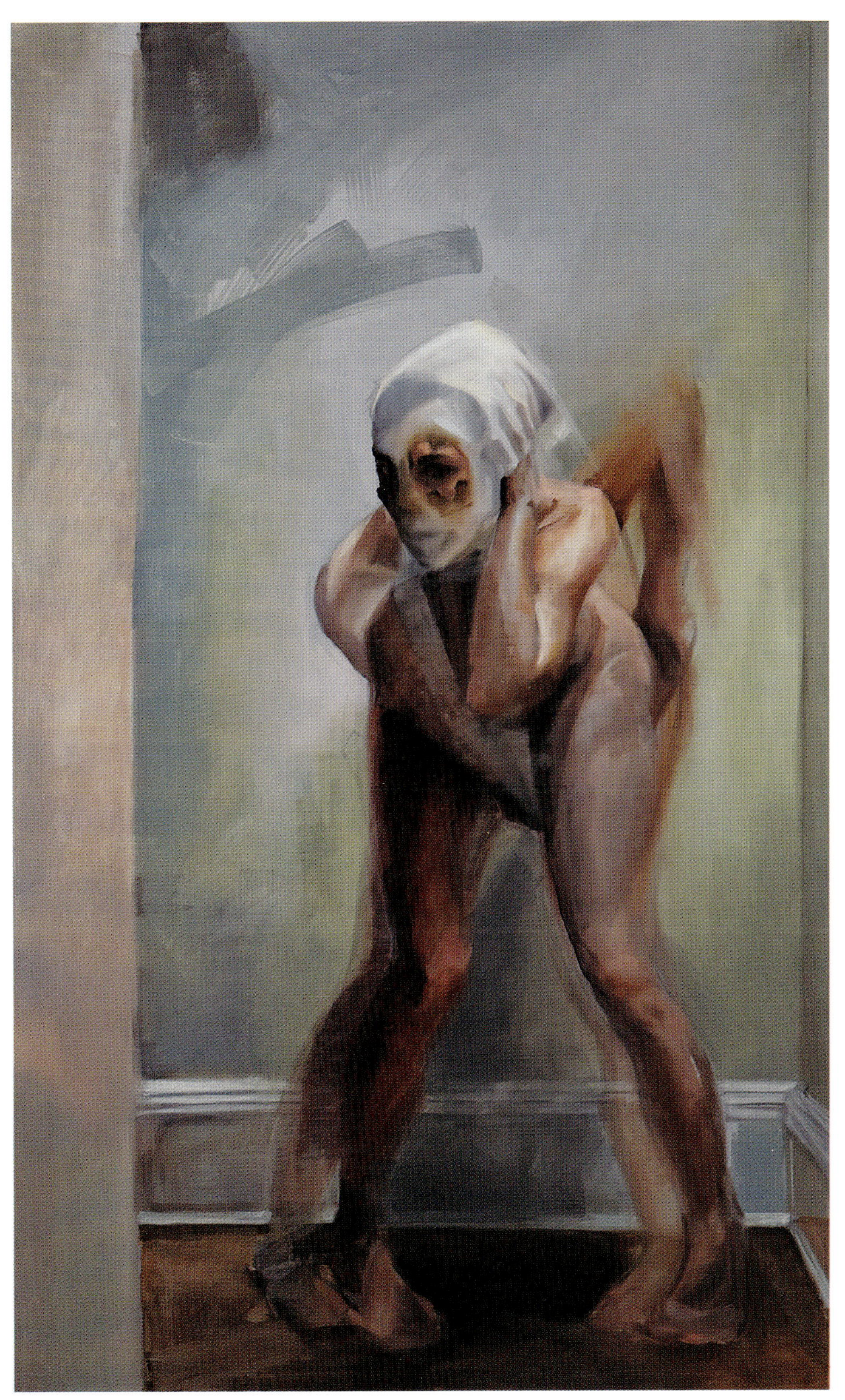

F. SCOTT HESS

I am by no means in love with the act of painting. After a ten-hour workday in the studio I can be a very grumpy man. For this reason the content of a work is critical to me. Making the resonant vision in my head "real" in the world is the point. I feel the purpose of art is, and always has been, to create meaning in a meaningless universe. The job of an artist, therefore, is a very important one.

I started drawing at age seven to magically control my world through images. Concurrently, my parents' divorce had me living with my mother. By the time I entered college, I'd drawn thousands of naked women, bound up or in jail. After studying Freud and psychology, I realized the intent behind these bondage drawings was to prevent my mother from leaving, too. As my artistic style evolved, it was driven by a subconscious impetus to control: The more realistic the rendering, the more powerfully the image bent reality to my will. Though my need to create overtly erotic subject matter lessened by my mid-twenties, the desire to explore my own psychological makeup, and that of my fellow humans, remains the main thrust of my artistic content to this day.

I serendipitously enrolled in the Academy of Fine Arts Vienna and studied there from 1979 to 1984, drawing figure studies for hundreds of hours and learning about our insides at the Anatomy Institute. The former involved live bodies in the auditorium where Egon Schiele had drawn, the latter, corpses and body parts, which seared anatomical knowledge into my brain. Though trained at the Academy to paint in alternating layers of egg tempera and oil glazes, I taught myself to paint alla prima in a quasi-Impressionist manner; my colors on the canvas were vibrant, laid down in patterns of small strokes that caused a sensation of movement across the surface. That changed in 1998, when I was hired to teach the actor Jason Patric how to paint and draw like Rembrandt . . . in one month! So I researched how seventeenth-century Dutch paintings were constructed. Using their minimal palette of about sixteen extant colors led to a profound change in my painting technique, especially regarding the importance of tonal relationships and how effectively limited color can deliver meaning.

Today I utilize a combination of all these methods. I might sit at the easel with one technique in mind, but the painting decides on something else. I am more aware of what I shouldn't do (layers that will crack, wasting bright or expensive colors in underlayers, faulty drawing, etc.), than bound to what I should do. Learning to draw and paint from life is critical to the process of seeing in paint, but working from life can trap artists who become dogmatic about it. There are mountains of dull life paintings and pits full of badly copied photos. The juice of figure painting lies in the artist's ability to translate and invent, whether the source is life or another image. I still do life-painting demos in class, but in studio works I generally employ photography for the figures. I paint the still life elements from life and invent the environments. Though I can invent a reasonable human figure, it never provides the specific surprises that reality, observed or captured in a photo, can.

My ideas generally spring into my head automatically, and I rarely remember how or when they arrived. When I'm suddenly aware of the image, I don't write it down; I try to forget it. If the idea keeps coming back then I know it is psychologically important and I'll follow through. When ideas are absent (as in Yeats's poem, "The Circus Animals' Desertion"), I have a couple of methods to force the issue. One is to appropriate and transform an art historical reference. I've absorbed so many images from my European travels that they often resurface subconsciously as part of an automatic vision formation. Or I'll take a painting I'm obsessed with and work it up in my own way, learning a lot about the original piece in the process. Another method involves sorting through my thirty-year-old "morgue" of ten thousand photographs, which functions as an external subconscious. I pull out anything of interest and place the chosen ones into thematic groupings—like people climbing ladders or men fighting—which shape ideas.

I draw out my ideas on paper, and transfer them via grid indices or projection. Once painting, I'm very conscious of turning forms with color, to avoid photographic flattening. Nowadays my laptop is always next to my canvas, to study a photo source or reference desired objects and details. I can Google a running horse, for example, and find a shot from the angle I want, perfectly lit. (Years ago I'd have searched an encyclopedia for images, and invented the angle and lighting.) I'm inspired by the panorama mode of my iPhone camera, which is actually closer to the way we see than traditional perspective is; our eyes and head move across a vista when we look, and with each shift, perspective changes. This helps to create dynamic movement across the canvas.

I arrange colors on the palette in a wheel, with the umbers and ivory black plopped down between the reds and blues, but as I paint, they have no names; they are cooler, warmer, richer, paler, etc. The visual surprise of color carries tremendous emotional charge, so I'm thrilled when I can use a bright color right out of the tube without destroying the fabric of the composition. A pure vermilion sets sexual fires, just as emerald green in leaves wafts oxygen from the canvas. A painting is finished when the entire surface reaches a consistent level of the reality I am inventing. The presentation must be seamless, no distractions from the content of the piece. If disturbances in the fabric of this reality create little holes through which the meaningless universe slips through your eyes into your head, then I've failed to do my job as an artist.

(opposite)
F. Scott Hess
Self-Portrait with Upturned Collar,
2011
Oil on aluminum panel
24 x 18 inches

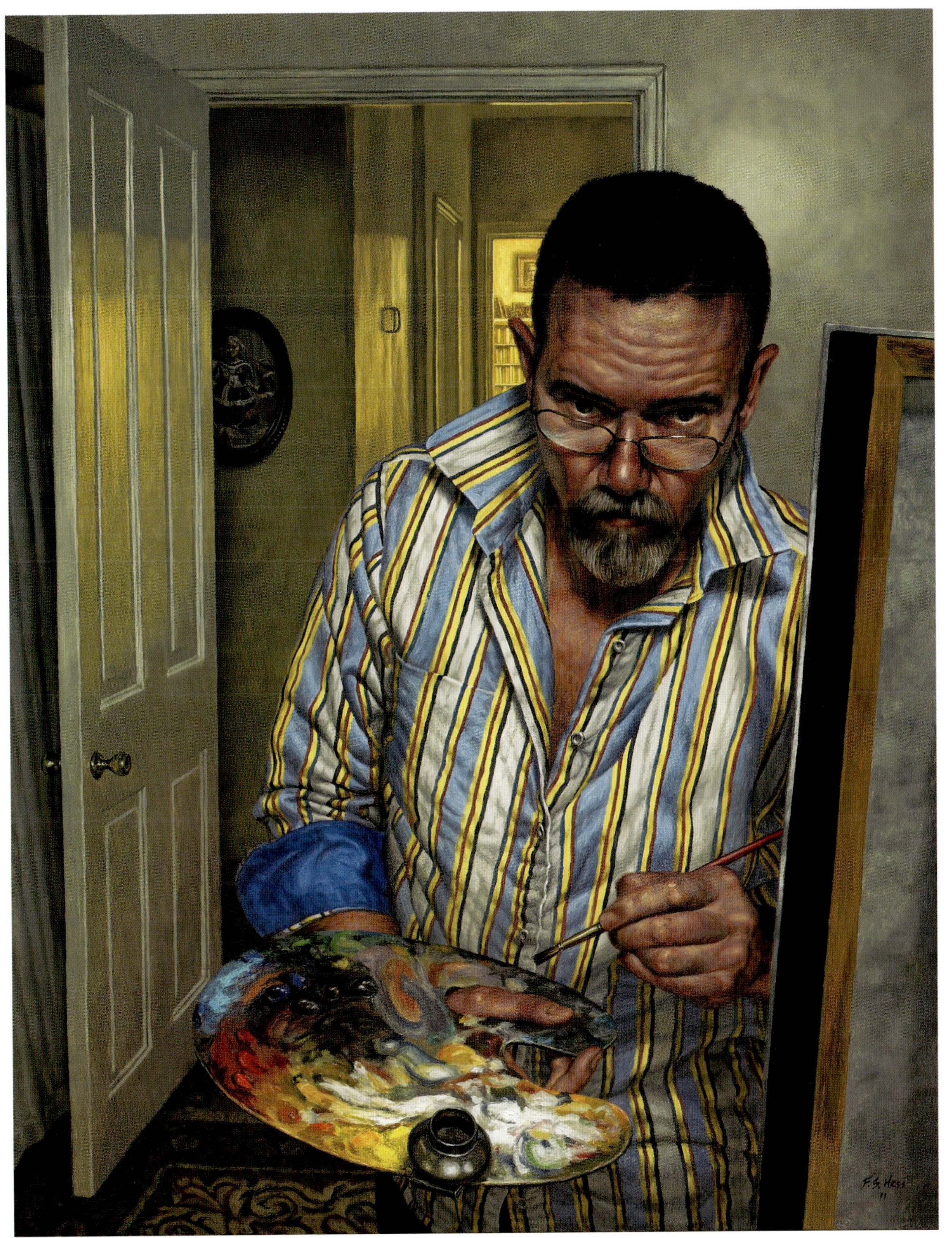
F.G. Hess
'11

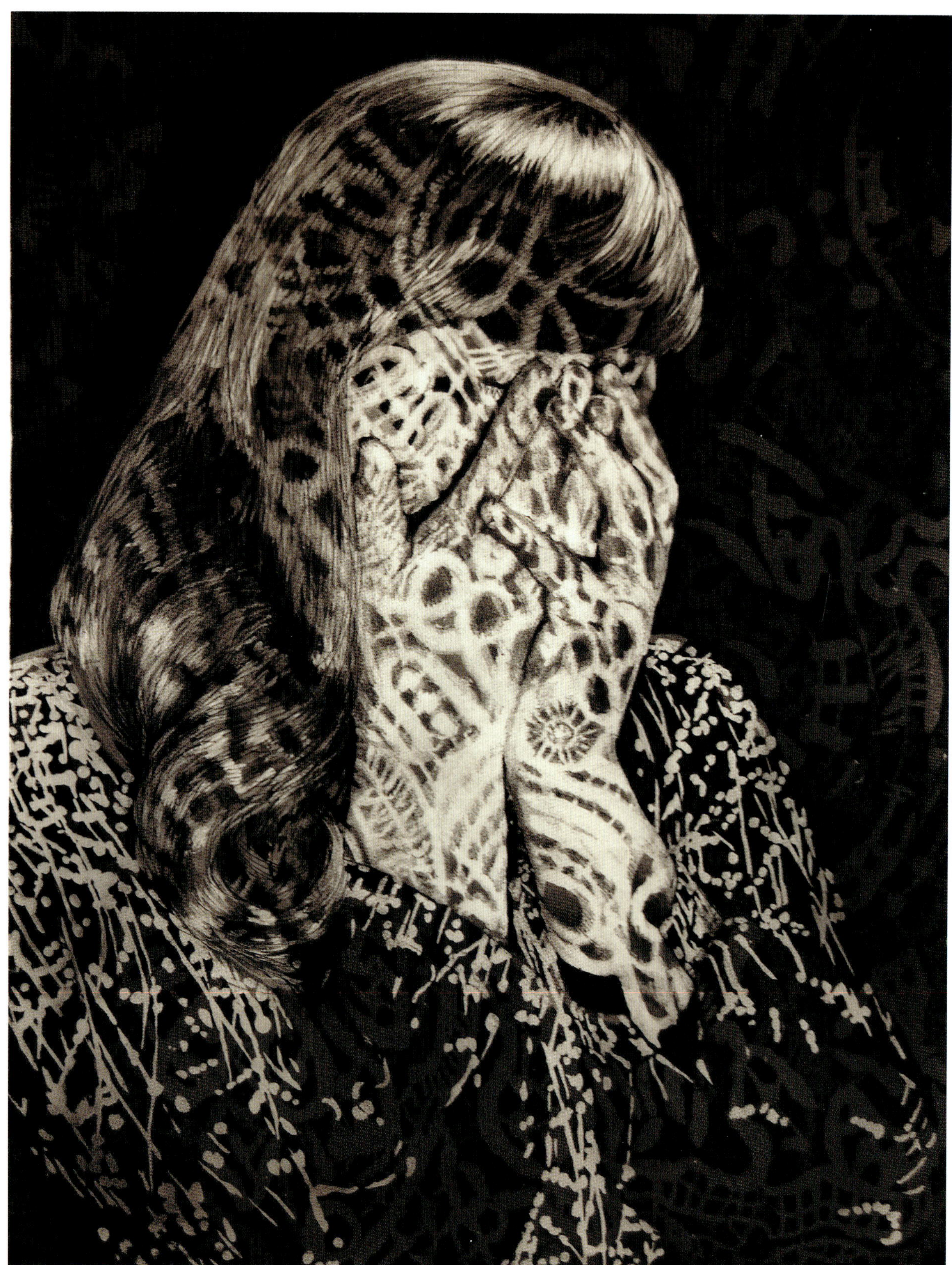

Holly Ann Sailors
We Found Her Hidden, 2012
Intaglio
12 x 9 inches

(opposite)
Daniel Bilodeau
Pile 1, 2013
Oil on linen panel
56 x 40 inches

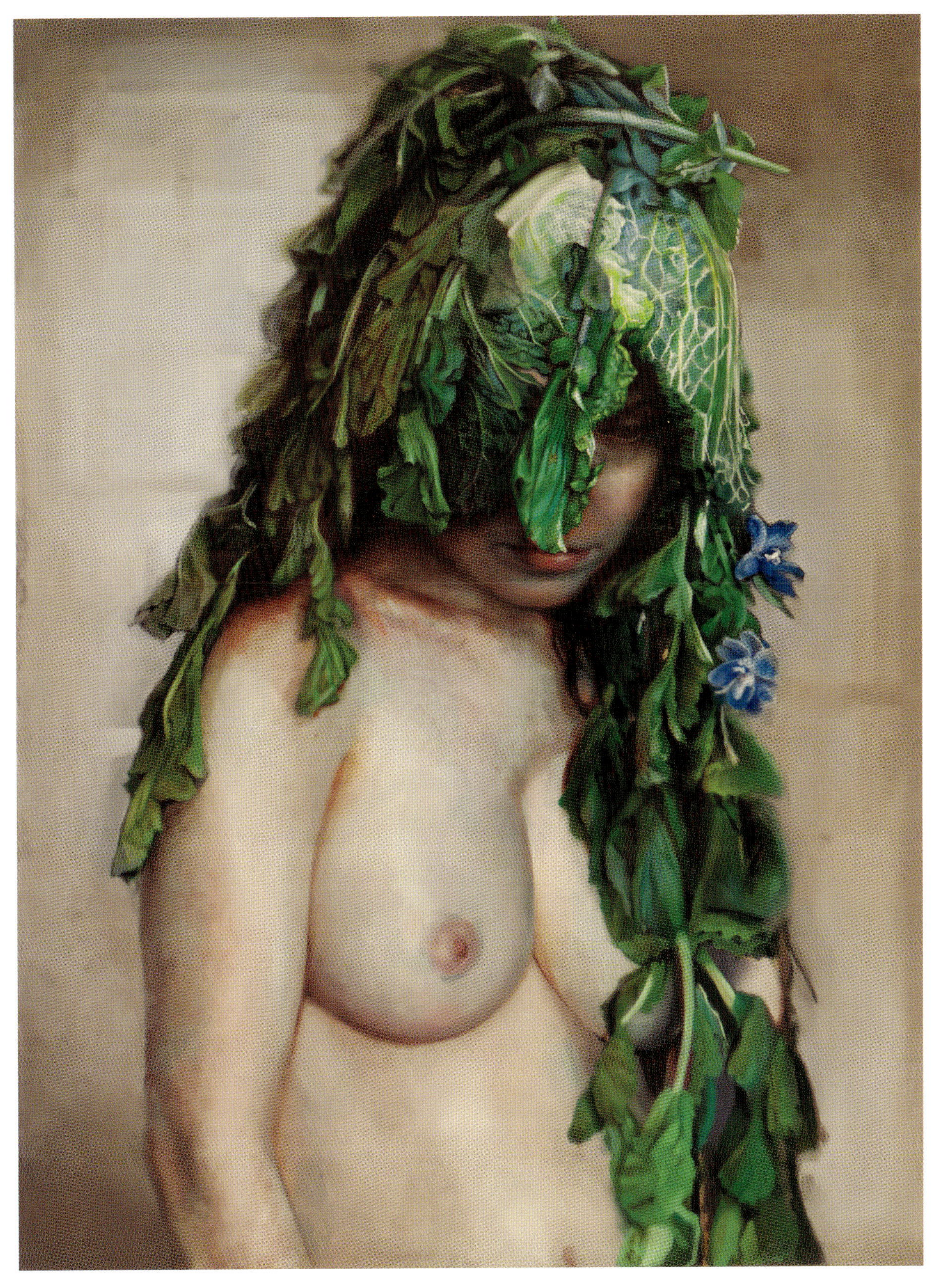

REPRESENTATIONAL ART AND KITSCH

KURT KAUPER

SINCE IT FIRST CAME INTO USE IN THE 1860S, the word "kitsch" has been associated with representational art.[1] Ferdinand Avenarius, for example, traced its etymology back to a German mispronunciation of the English word "sketch."[2] Matei Călinescu claims that it originated with artists and art dealers in Munich, and was used to describe landscapes that were cheaply and quickly produced in order to satisfy the demand of a new type of upper-middle-class tourist usually from England or America—who wanted to return home with the cultural validation that only fine art could provide.[3] While the concept has expanded to include a range of other cultural forms, it remains associated with representational art up to the present day. In a recent review of Pre-Raphaelite painting published in the *New York Times*, Roberta Smith condemned artists in the movement for contributing to "the onset of kitsch," and listed Maxfield Parrish, Norman Rockwell, and Thomas Kinkade as descendants of the kitsch lineage.[4] Her correlation between representational art and kitsch wasn't unusual: If one searches for her uses of the word "kitsch" or "kitschy" in *New York Times* reviews dating back to 2007, she is without exception referring to representational artists. Odd Nerdrum, a traditional painter based in Norway, has attempted to rehabilitate the word by embracing it as a positive description of art that privileges aspects of classical representation that he claims—with little justification—have been abandoned by the modern "artist" and "intellectual," both being terms he uses with some contempt.[5]

In this essay, I'd like to look at the history of kitsch, and propose that its relationship to representational art is tenuous, and always dependent on shifting historical circumstances. In spite of Roberta Smith's and Odd Nerdrum's assertions—echoed by countless others—kitsch cannot be understood as necessarily aligned with representational art, nor as a stable category. Representational art may qualify as kitsch depending on a specific set of circumstances, but so could any other approach to making art. The persistence of reflexively equating kitsch with representation renders the term dead, and prevents it from being used as a tool for critical analysis today.

Before considering the history of kitsch and its relationship to representation, I'd like to revisit two foundational aspects of its original meaning that in recent decades have been ignored, thus reducing the word to simplistic notions of good and bad taste. In the 1930s, three major essays were written on the subject: Theodor Adorno's "On Kitsch," in 1932; Hermann Broch's "Evil in the Value System of Art," in 1933; and Clement Greenberg's "Avant-Garde and Kitsch," in 1939. While there are differences between the essays, all three agree on the defining characteristics of kitsch: its dependence on various modes of mass production, its imitative, derivative nature, and its attempt to conjure an illusion of culture from the remnants of outdated and abandoned creative forms. For each writer, kitsch was a subject deeply embedded in the desperate political and cultural situation of the period. Near the beginning of his essay, Broch wonders if "intellectual and aesthetic problems" can be taken on in the midst of the "most pressing current question: 'do we have enough to eat?'"[6] And when he says "it becomes the mission of kitsch as an aesthetic phenomenon to be the representative of the ethically evil";[7] or when Adorno declares that the job of kitsch is to "deceive people about their true situation," and notes that "all kitsch is essentially ideology,"[8] both are referring obliquely to that which Greenberg devotes the last four paragraphs of his essay: Hitler, Stalin, and Mussolini's use of kitsch as a delivery system for totalitarian propaganda.[9]

Adorno's essay differs in an important respect from those of Broch and Greenberg. He makes a claim that isn't addressed explicitly in the other texts, and has received almost no attention at all in the subsequent literature:

(opposite)
Jamie Adams
Niagaradown, 2013
Oil on linen
78 x 83 inches

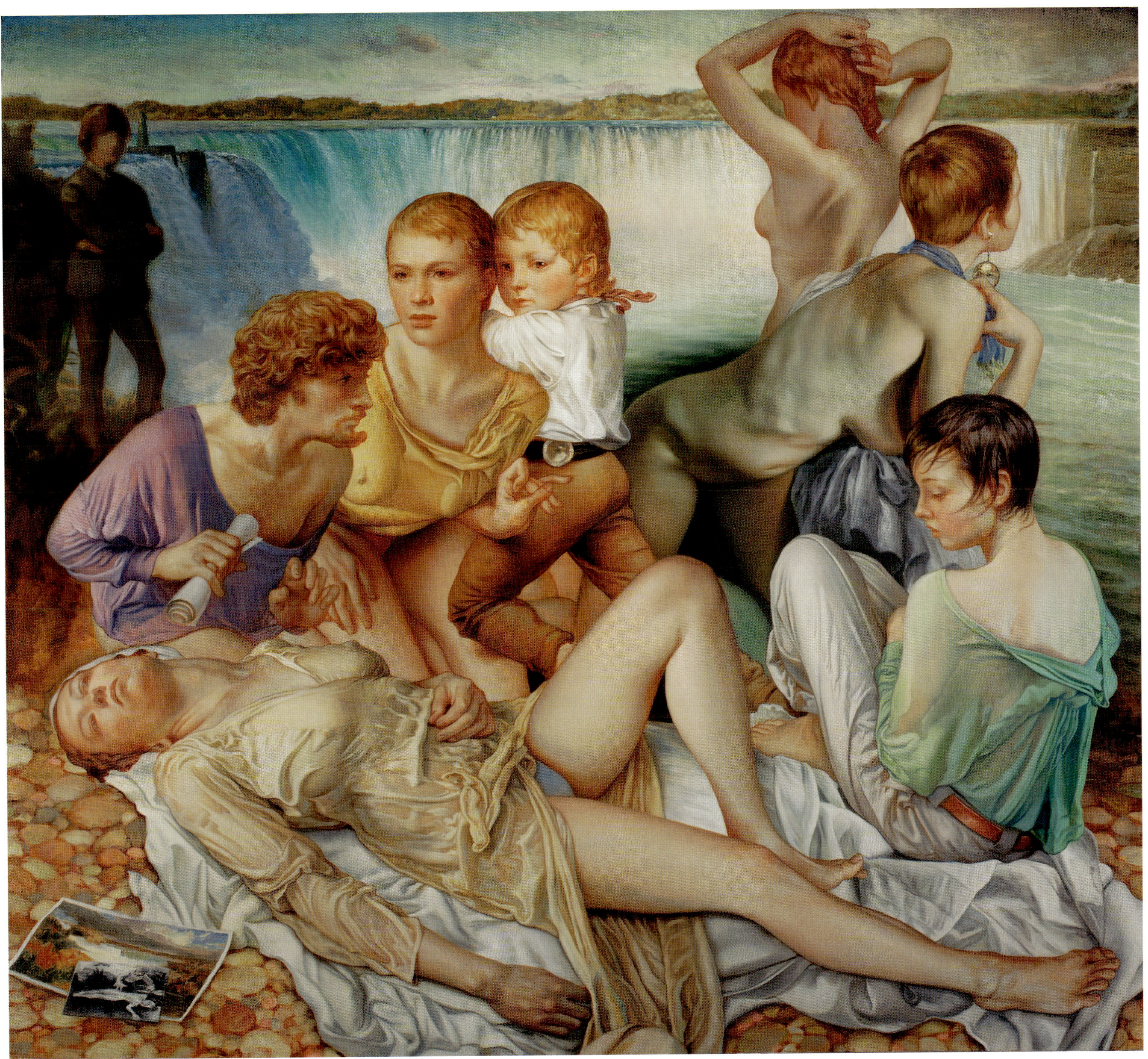

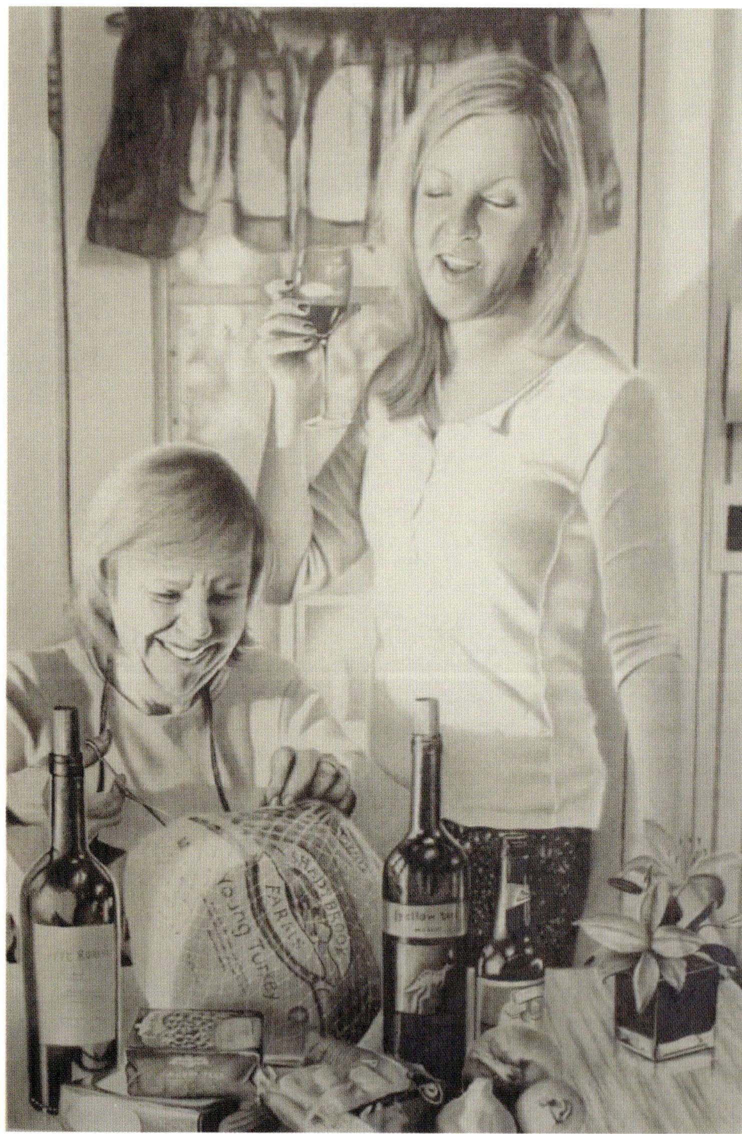

Mark Paczkowski
Pardon, 2013
Graphite on paper
30 x 20 inches

(opposite)
Kurt Kauper
Derek, 2005
Oil on wood
93 x 58.5 inches

> *There is no general criterion for kitsch, for the concept is itself a frame that is always only filled historically and has its actual justification only in polemics. Today, the term has long since been adopted by the juste milieu and has, itself, become an ideological means of defending a moderate "culture" of the musical that no longer possesses any power. Thus the talk about kitsch itself begins to be kitschy, as it succumbs to the very historical dialectic from which its object emerged.*[10]

Kitsch, for Adorno, wasn't a stable category, but was entirely dependent on the specific "polemics" of a historical period. He says earlier in the essay: "[It] is impossible to grasp 'kitsch' in a free-floating aesthetic way. The social moment is essentially constitutive of it."[11] And while Greenberg and Broch don't say so explicitly, the historical contextualization of the "problem" of kitsch in their essays implies that they, too, saw kitsch as historically determined.

These two aspects of kitsch as defined by Adorno, Broch, and Greenberg—its use as a delivery system that masks corrosive ideological content, and its unstable, shifting nature—became lost as the subject continued to be a topic of aesthetic and cultural consideration throughout the twentieth and into the twenty-first century. Midcentury artists and critics such as Ad Reinhardt and Dwight Macdonald addressed the topic in terms of the polemics of high versus low culture, but even for them the pathos and political urgency evident in Adorno, Greenberg, and Broch's essays are absent, and discussions of kitsch had calcified into clearly defined, stable categories of, as Milan Kundera would phrase it, "the sublime and the paltry."[12] By the time the Italian art historian Gillo Dorfles published *Kitsch: The World of Bad Taste*, in 1969, kitsch, in both popular and critical consciousness, had become exactly that which Adorno said it couldn't be: a free-floating, hierarchical designation of so-called bad taste, removed from a specific cultural situation.[13] Dorfles's book is a catchall, indiscriminately labeling a wide range of advertisements, films, romantic art, architectural proposals, tourist objects, eccentric home décor, various cultural activities, spiritual yearnings, and countless other items as kitsch, without offering a set of cultural circumstances that would justify such a broadly ranging category. And if the cultural implications of kitsch for Adorno, Broch, and Greenberg were totalitarian politics and the destruction of civilization, for Dorfles it's little more than a "lack of elegance . . . cultural retrogression . . . industrial and artistic non-up-to-datedness which is often equivalent to out-and-out bad taste."[14] With Dorfles's book, kitsch had become a meaningless term, devoid of the cultural and political urgency it had in the 1930s.

While flaws in scholarship are easy to identify in Dorfles, more serious treatments of the subject also fail to take into account the political and cultural urgency at the core of the original definitions, and Adorno's insistence on the historically determined nature of kitsch. Barbara Kirshenblatt-Gimblett, for example, dedicates a chapter in her book *Destination Culture: Tourism, Museums, and Heritage* to an analysis of the Modernist critique of kitsch, which, like Dorfles, she conflates with the more general term "bad taste." She critiques discussions of kitsch—primarily those of Clement Greenberg and Milan Kundera—for what she sees as their insistence on stable categories of high and low that do little more than confer status on those making the distinctions, and deny the value of any cultural production except in the realm of what she ironically labels "the legitimate arts."[15] She doesn't mention the urgent politics in the background of either writer's analysis of the subject. And while she goes to great lengths and makes a convincing case that distinctions between good and bad taste are unstable and historically determined, she fails to take note of the fact that Adorno himself insisted on the very same thing in reference to kitsch. And finally, the use of kitsch as subject matter in contemporary art—Jeff Koons's career would be a good example—makes the very same mistake: assuming that kitsch can be understood as a stable category of bad taste.

In spite of the innumerable pages devoted to critiquing historical treatments of kitsch as being based on unjustifiable hierarchies of high and low taste, a cursory analysis of the original definitions of the term reveal that it is a much more complex phenomenon. Kitsch is a term attached to an object or a set of objects that can be identified as contributing to mass delusion: images, films, news stories, advertisements, and art that propose one reality—both palatable and easily understood—but in fact deliberately conceals a pernicious and socially corrosive core. From the 1960s on, when critiques of the Modernist analysis of kitsch first appeared, it would have been more illuminating to consider kitsch in the form of the pseudo-events described by Daniel Boorstin,[16] or the society of the spectacle articulated by Guy Debord,[17] instead of its caricature as a simplistic and snobbish hierarchy of taste.

But if kitsch can't be understood as a stable category, and if therefore representation can't reliably be equated with kitsch, there is nevertheless a history that gave rise to the common, if misleading, association between the two. Late nineteenth-century academic art was flourishing when the word "kitsch" first came into use. By the early years of the twentieth century, it was generally equated with kitsch. In recent years, it's enjoyed something of a resurgence in popularity and scholarly interest. But it's easy to see how, at the end of the nineteenth and into the early decades of the twentieth century, the most celebrated art of the European Academies—by William Bouguereau, Alexandre Cabanel, and Jean-Léon Gérôme in France; Lawrence Alma-Tadema and Frederic Leighton in Great Britain; and Anselm Feuerbach and Ferdinand Keller in Germany, for example—could be condemned for a number of failings. While ostensibly producing work that was intended to ennoble the viewer, artists associated with the official academies were producing paintings and sculptures that pointedly ignored the complex realities of an increasingly industrial and consumer culture, plagued by enormous social inequities and political stasis. Their highly polished, absurdly imagined historical, religious, and mythological scenes, romanticized depictions of contemporary life, bucolic tableaux populated by peasants with impossibly rosy cheeks and soft hands, and outright state propaganda, contributed little to the development of the art of the time. Ideas outside of

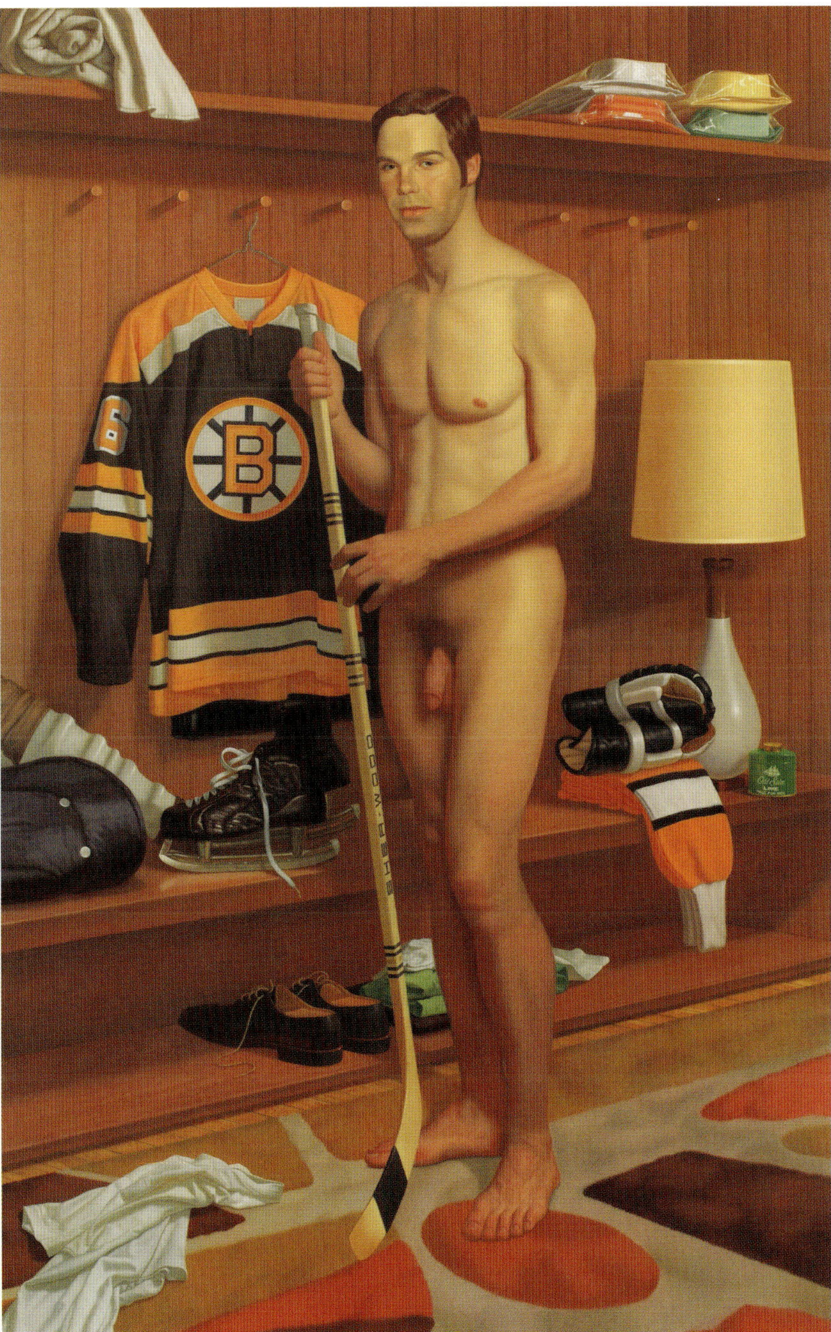

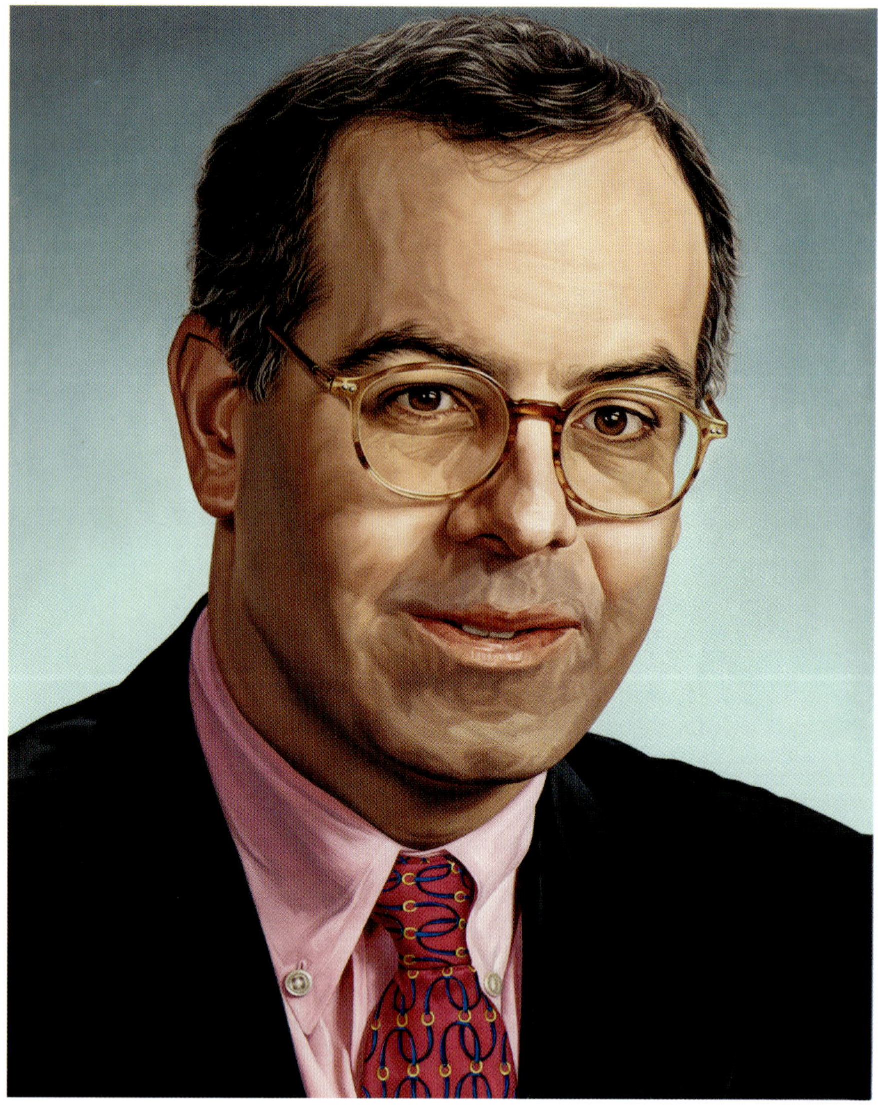

Mathew Cerletty
David Brooks, 2009
Oil on linen
19.25 x 15.25
inches

(opposite)
Gary Murphy
Rêveur, 2010
Oil on linen
16 x 12 inches

the finer and finer development of craft were entirely neglected. Formal and narrative developments of past masters were refined and gentrified to be as commercially palatable as possible to the new millionaires, particularly from the United States. Add to that the industrial-like efficiency with which the academies were, by the mid-nineteenth century, producing highly trained but creatively interchangeable artists, and the correlation between late nineteenth-century academic art and kitsch is clear.

Concurrent with the flourishing of the academies, another and more insidious source of kitsch in the form of representational art was rapidly expanding: advertising imagery. By the mid-1880s, the advertising industry in Europe and the United States was well on its way to being a major influence on mass culture. The "popular, commercial art . . . chromeotypes, magazine covers, illustrations, [and] ads"[18] that so horrified Clement Greenberg were proliferating across Europe and the United States. Advertising artists such as Jules Chéret, a gifted draftsman and designer who had assiduously studied major figures of Western art and incorporated into his work the same principles of classical representation taught at the academies (in an admittedly economical way), was producing drawings for posters that were widely disseminated throughout Europe. The techniques and pictorial strategies of classical Western art could now be seen every day on the streets of Paris, London, and other urban centers, in advertisements for plays, burlesques, light operas, and consumer products of all kinds.

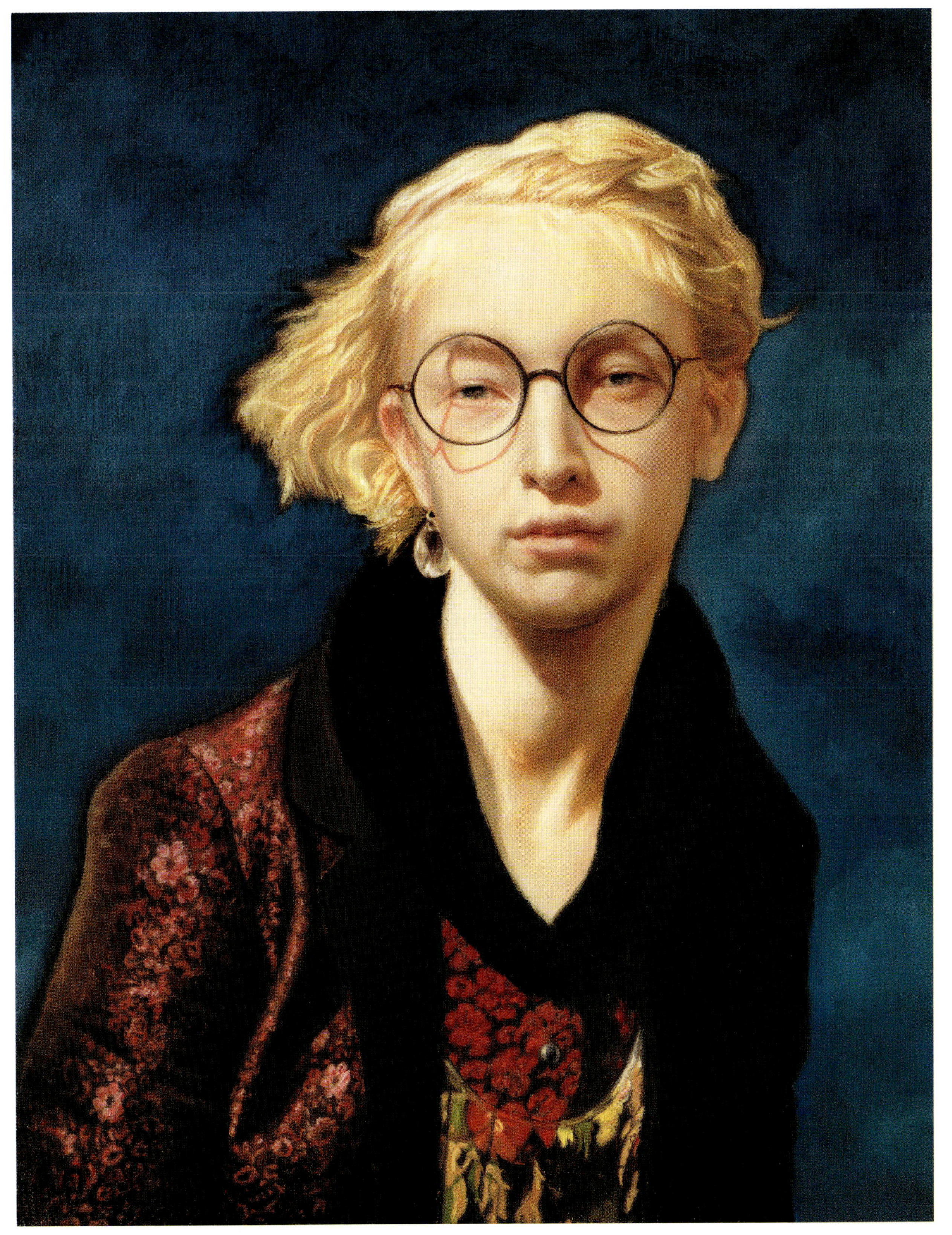

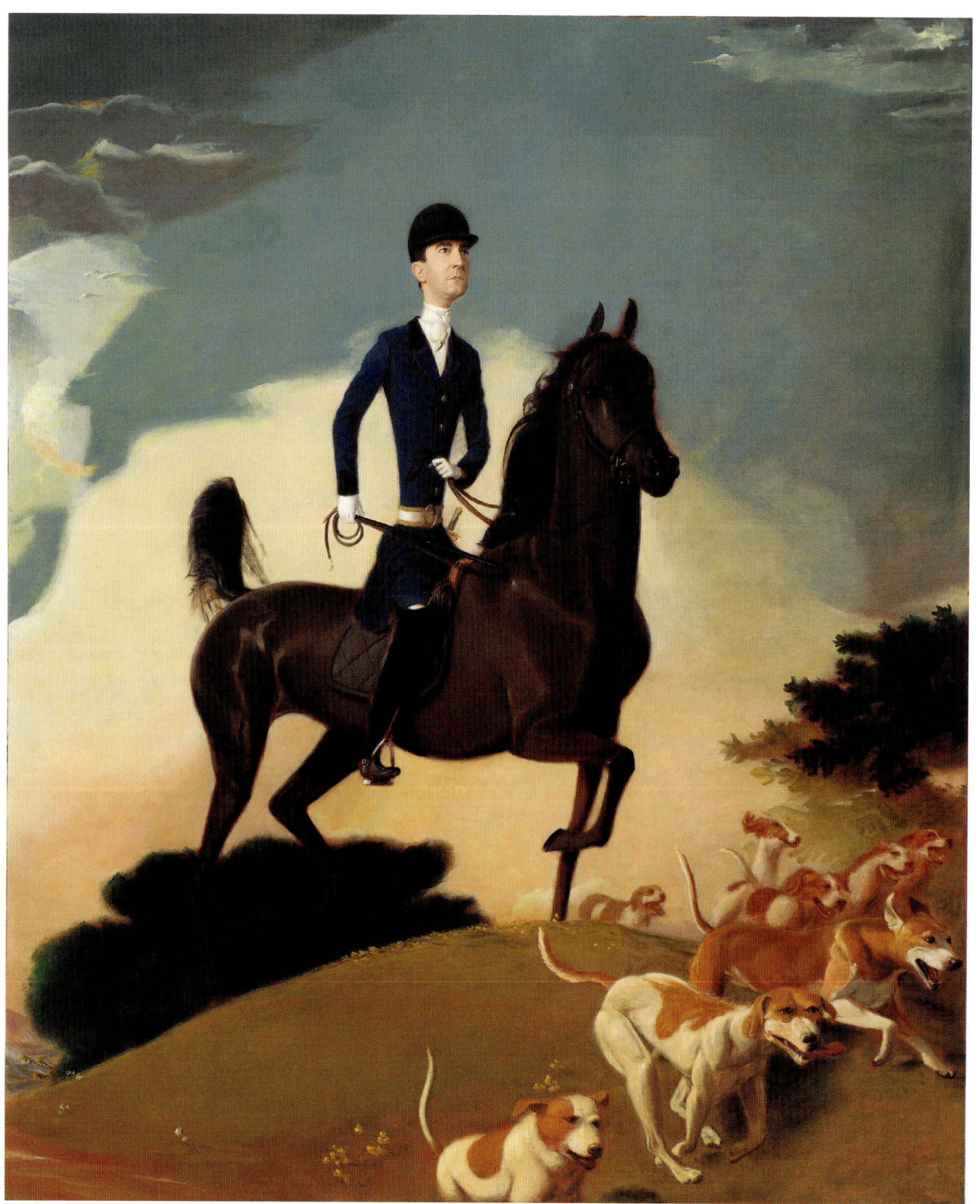

Confusing the boundaries between traditional painting and advertising images was the marketing masterstroke that earned Thomas J. Barratt the nickname "Father of Advertising."[19] In 1886, his company, the A&F Pears Soap corporation, purchased the Royal Academician John Everett Millais's 1885 painting *A Child's World*, which shows a young boy intently watching a soap bubble float through the air. They also purchased the copyright. Barratt put his acquisition to very profitable use: The image was engraved for reproduction—with the addition of a bar of Pears soap in the foreground—and widely reproduced as an advertisement for the company's product. It was the first appropriation of a painter's work for use in advertising. Millais was widely criticized for allowing his painting to be used in such a way. His friend, the novelist Marie Corelli, attacked what she saw as his acquiescence in the corruption of his work, complaining that the painting—which now had a second life as an advertising image—could no longer be viewed with "the veneration that befits all great art."[20] The advertising industry had erased the distinction between classically derived representational art and kitsch.[21]

As early Modernists such as Édouard Manet, Edgar Degas, Paul Cézanne, Auguste Rodin, and Medardo Rosso began to redefine representation in painting and sculpture—which would lead to the radical inventions of early twentieth-century masters—advertising artists picked up and continued with the techniques and strategies left behind. By the early decades of the twentieth century, traditional representation was primarily the domain of discredited academicians, advertising artists, and illustrators. Furthermore, the narrative and compositional strategies, elaborate costume design, and use of pantomime that had been the domain of traditional history painting was absorbed by silent Hollywood film. Traditional representation shared more with standardized forms of culture than it did with what was being widely accepted as the most advanced painting and sculpture being produced at the time. In the decades that followed, periodic returns to traditional modes of representation, such as the Neue Sachlichkeit (New Objectivity) movement in Germany or American Regionalism, for example—no matter their genesis or intent—could too easily be aligned with popular culture or the official art of the Nazi, Soviet, and Italian Fascist regimes to entirely escape the accusation of being kitsch. Even artists with impeccable Modernist credentials such as Max Beckmann, Pablo Picasso, and Francis Picabia—when their work too closely approached traditional representation—were, according to some critics, tainted by association.[22]

The Picabia paintings that have been the object of such criticism are, of course, the nudes of the 1940s. Portraying fit and happy young women basking in comfortable interiors or natural settings, they are disturbingly similar to official Nazi compositions. Seen after the war as ghastly forays into the most discredited kind of traditional painting, they were roundly dismissed as kitsch embarrassments and omitted from all but three of the numerous exhibitions of his work held between 1947 and 1976.[23] It took decades, and the interest of painters such as Sigmar Polke, to reframe the paintings so that they could be seen as continuations of Picabia's ongoing

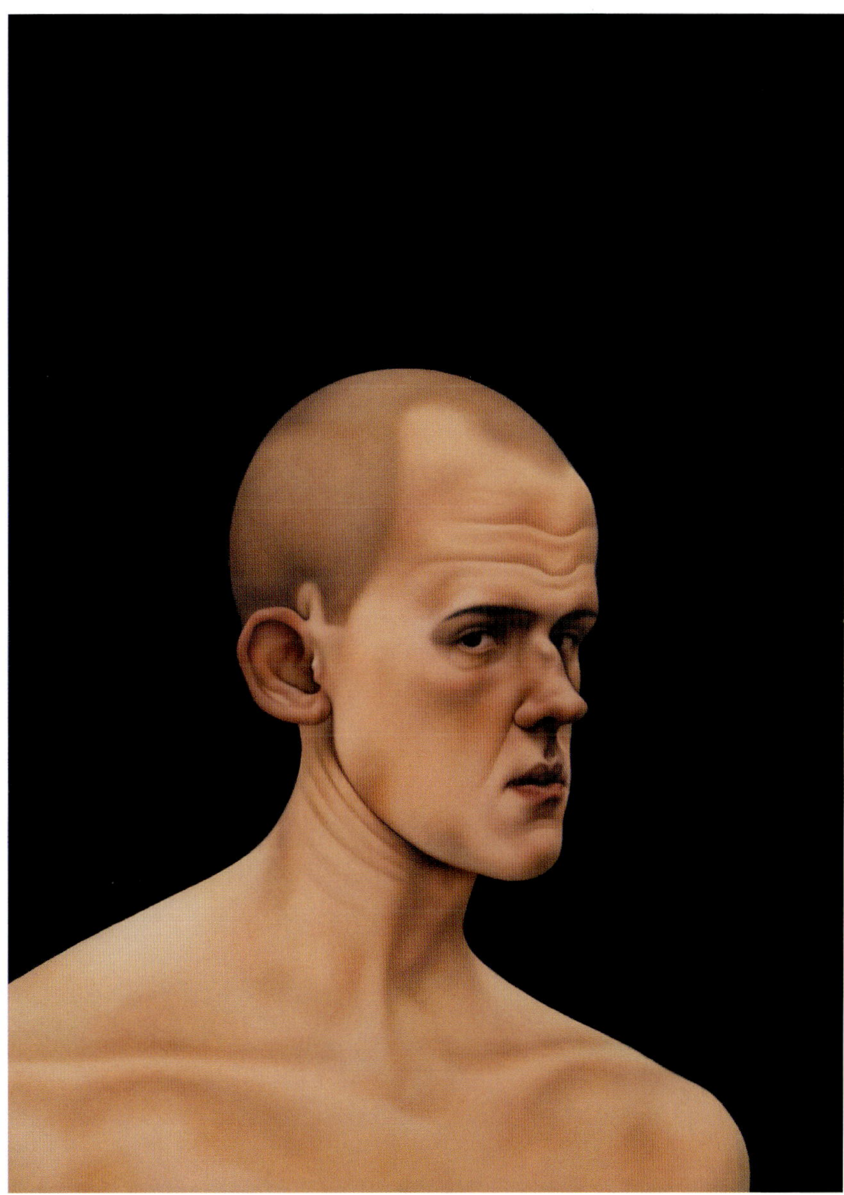

Matthew Miller
Untitled, 2013
Oil on panel
36 x 24 inches

(opposite)
Jansson Stegner
The Foxhunter, 2013
Oil on linen
84 x 66 inches

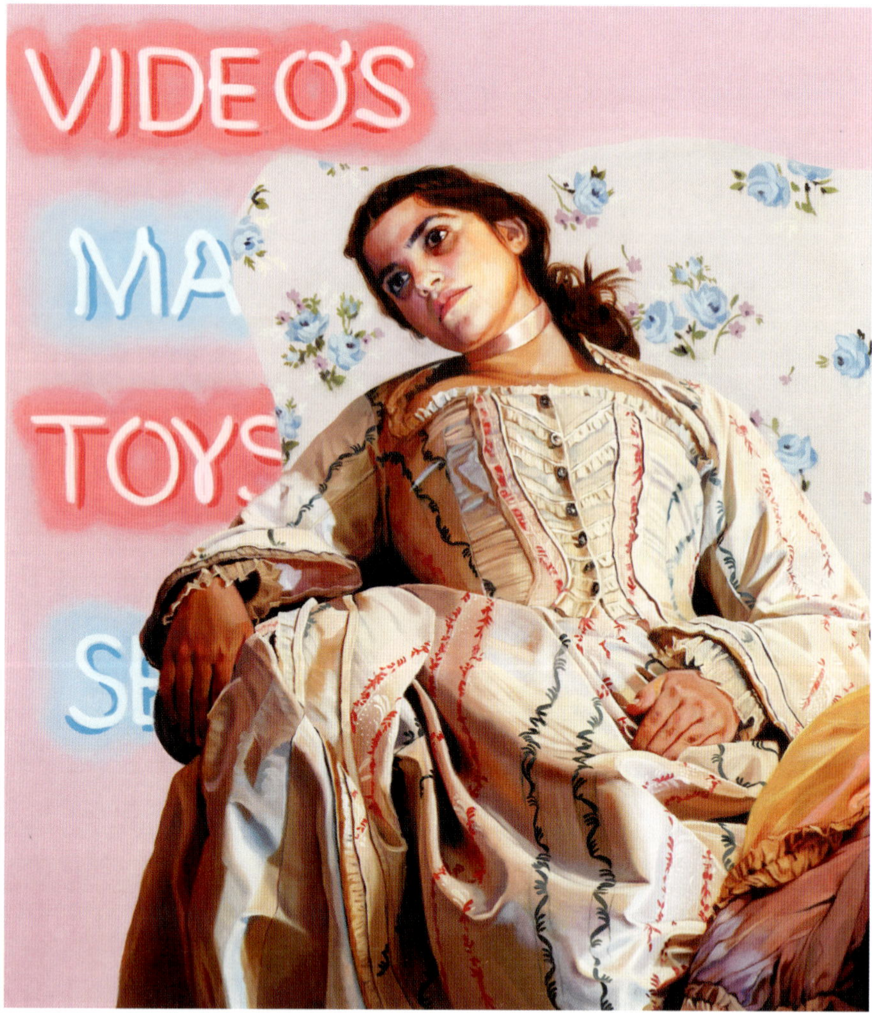

Panni Malekzadeh
Tara Playing, 2010
Oil on linen
34 x 32 inches

(opposite)
Heather Morgan
Sourpuss, 2011
Oil on canvas
56 x 42 inches

search for subversive, Dada gestures. Not only did Picabia choose to paint traditionally rendered nudes, but he delved deeper into the taboo world of kitsch by basing the figures on soft-core photographs of naked women found in mainstream magazines such as *Mon Paris* and *Paris Match*. Far from regressing into a traditional sensibility, Picabia used kitsch imagery layered upon kitsch imagery as a way of performing a double critique: First, as Alison Gingeras has noted in her essay "Subversion of Kitsch," he re-presented mass market images as unique, auratic paintings, symbolically undoing the standardized identity formation enacted by the magazines;[24] second, through his use of degraded forms of imagery to achieve radical ends, he mocked the strict hierarchies of Modernist art and showed that if formerly kitsch images could be used subversively, then formerly subversive images (Modernist abstraction) could become kitsch.

Picabia's paintings were quickly forgotten, and by the 1950s there was no longer an urgent conflict between representation and more experimental forms of image making. If for no other reason, representational art had faded into critical oblivion. That's not to say that representational art wasn't being made. Obviously, it was. And examples of representational artists working during the height of midcentury Modernism are too numerous to list. But with the ascendency of Abstract Expressionism by the middle of the 1950s, a younger generation of more experimental artists—from those associated with the Situationist International to Jasper Johns and Robert Rauschenberg—were reacting, at least in part, to its firmly established position as the apogee of Modernist achievement. They paid no attention to representation—particularly traditional representation—which was at best an eccentric, antiquarian practice hovering around the periphery. It was essentially irrelevant.

It wasn't until the 1960s that a new generation of artists would use the marginalized status of representational art to destabilize mainstream paradigms of avant-garde achievement. Andy Warhol is the most well-known example of such an artist, although the radical nature of his methods and source materials often leaves him outside of discussions of representational art. But there were many others whose profiles were much lower than Warhol's, and whose work wasn't fully appreciated until much later. In 1992, Mike Kelley wrote an essay titled "Death and Transfiguration," in which he questioned why Paul Thek labored in relative critical obscurity from the 1960s until his death in 1988. He focuses on Thek's 1967 installation *Death of a Hippie*, with its pink sculpture of a rotting, dead hippie as its narrative center. Kelley describes it vividly as "a pink raspberry shitsicle in answer to [Walt Disney's] porcelain-white vanilla bar."[25] He describes Thek's work in general as "truly embarrassing, calling to mind crafts more than art. Bunnies, Bambi, Bojangles, stomach-churning, sweet hippie, and middle-American kitsch are combined in sometimes horribly melodramatic situations."[26] Kelley is of course contraposing Thek's aesthetic of decay to Walt Disney's falsely purified vision of American culture. But more relevant to this discussion are the mainstream histories of 1960s American art that, according to Kelley, collude with the likes of Walt Disney in propagating that vision. He claims that

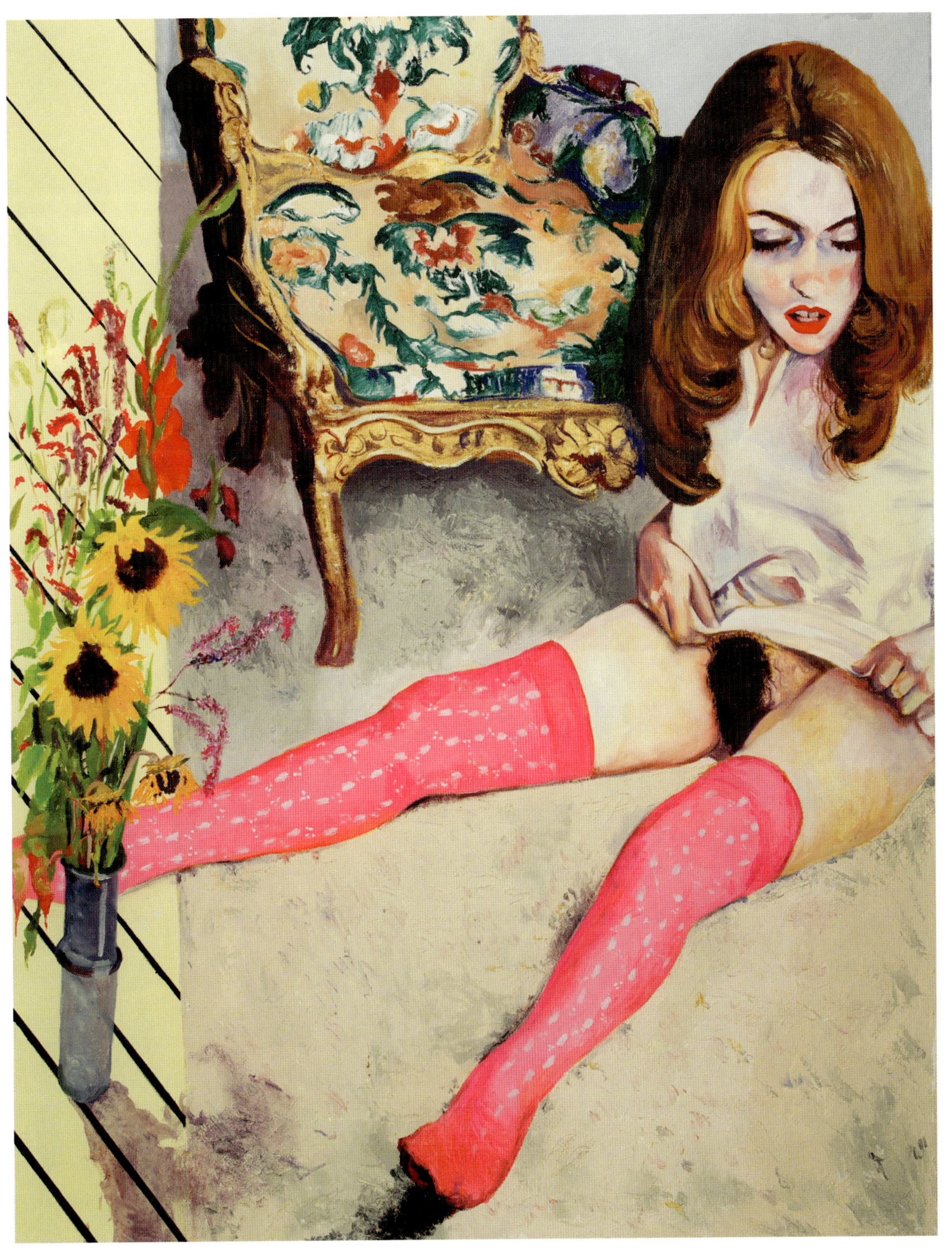

conventional art histories represent the 1960s as "a glorious, almost classical epoch. Art was cool, reasonable, and in touch with the national identity. The '60s was the last golden age of Modernism, before the fall orchestrated by Postmodernism."[27] He goes as far as to claim that such histories are "spookily aligned with Reagan/Bush ideology."[28] Mainstream Pop art with its slick, polished surfaces; Minimalism and its pure forms; and Conceptual art's desiccated privileging of the linguistic, represent, for Kelley, a purified vision as false as Walt Disney's: a vision of American society that intentionally omits the baser elements in the culture. The "decadent aestheticism"[29] and unforgiving narrative content of Thek's hippie statue act as reminders of the ugly truths that lie behind the cultural façade. Like Picabia thirty years earlier, Thek is embracing figurative forms and narrative devices—adding his own excesses such as the installation's pink color—that are linked with conventional definitions of kitsch. But also, like Picabia, Thek saw through the conventional understandings, and realized that his forms and narrative devices were no more intrinsically kitsch than the increasingly academicized emphasis on visual and conceptual purity that was the legacy of Modernism; which isn't to say that Pop, Minimalism, or Conceptual art were kitsch, just that they could be.

The 1960s were a period in which a wide range of other representational artists working in noncanonical ways provided alternatives to what were becoming overly familiar and therefore potentially kitsch approaches to making advanced art: R. Crumb, Öyvind Fahlström, Peter Saul, and Tom of Finland all come to mind. While these artists are "representational," their representation derives in part or entirely from nontraditional sources: camp, comic books, pornography, beefcake, psychedelia, hippie, and other countercultures. By drawing on forms that were conventionally dismissed as kitsch and thereby mucking up its relationship to persistent notions of the avant-garde, their work provided a vividly decadent alternative to the formal and narrative purity of the 1960s canon. Their example opened up a potential approach for artists working in more classically derived modes of representation. Kelley's essay on Thek might lead to a reconsideration of those artists from the same period associated with a more classical turn in representational art: Could they be seen in a similar light? Some traditional artists did, after all, incorporate base subject matter or counterculture narratives into their work. For example, in 1972, Harvey Dinnerstein painted a large-scale narrative painting entitled *Parade*, in which a procession of nude figures representing members of various counterculture groups move in ecstatic revelry across the canvas; and in 1977, Odd Nerdrum painted *The Murder of Andreas Baader*, a Caravaggesque scene showing the tragic leader of the Baader-Meinhof Gang being shot through the head by a member of the German Secret Police. But despite similarities to their less traditional peers—in terms of cultural influence, themes, and subject matter—both artists' work is neutered by its reverence for classical pictorial structure and modes of expression: It overwhelms all else. Reverence for tradition becomes the content, never allowing the potentially subversive subject matter to be a meaningful part of the viewing experience. Almost without exception, the same can be said of the innumerable traditional representational artists who emerged in the 1960s and '70s.

(opposite)
Phillip Thomas
Portrait #3, 2013
Oil on panel
29 x 29 inches

Not until the early 1990s did artists again pick up on the subversive use of representational art as kitsch, elaborating on the examples set by Picabia and Thek: Monica Majoli's polished, intimate sex paintings; Lisa Yuskavage's expert combinations of low-decoration, soft-core pornography and the light, form, and space of classical masters; the technical, formal, semiological, and narrative heterogeneity of Kerry James Marshall's work; and John Currin's gleefully grotesque re-imaginings of traditional painting are probably the best examples. All four artists embraced traditional representation and mastered its pictorial language; they didn't simply deploy signs for traditional representation, as artists from the Pictures Generation did. And they counterposed their carefully crafted traditional language with entrenched cultural paradigms—artistic and otherwise—in order to undermine them. It was, perhaps, the last time that the correlation between representation and kitsch could be utilized as a subversive gesture: Since then, "low" and "subculture" sources that lent representation its subversive edge from Picabia until fairly recently, and that constituted a previous definition of kitsch, have been completely assimilated into mainstream art practice and critical discourse—an assimilation that was years in the making and is now complete.

Kitsch still exists, to be sure: Wade Guyton's retrospective at the Whitney, with the artist's use of exhausted Warholian and Conceptual gestures masquerading as progressive, nicely fulfills Adorno's description of kitsch as "serving up past formal entities as contemporary . . . to allow intentions that suit some powers or other to appear to them in a fairy-tale glow."[30] And Alix Rule and David Levine's essay "International Art English," from a recent issue of the online journal *Triple Canopy*, reveals the curious language of art world press releases to be a textbook example of kitsch, both in form and function.[31] But today representational art rarely, if ever, appears as kitsch. It has become too common a pictorial and sculptural mode, yet not dominant enough in recent critical discourse and visual consciousness to have the importance—for good or bad—that kitsch has always had.

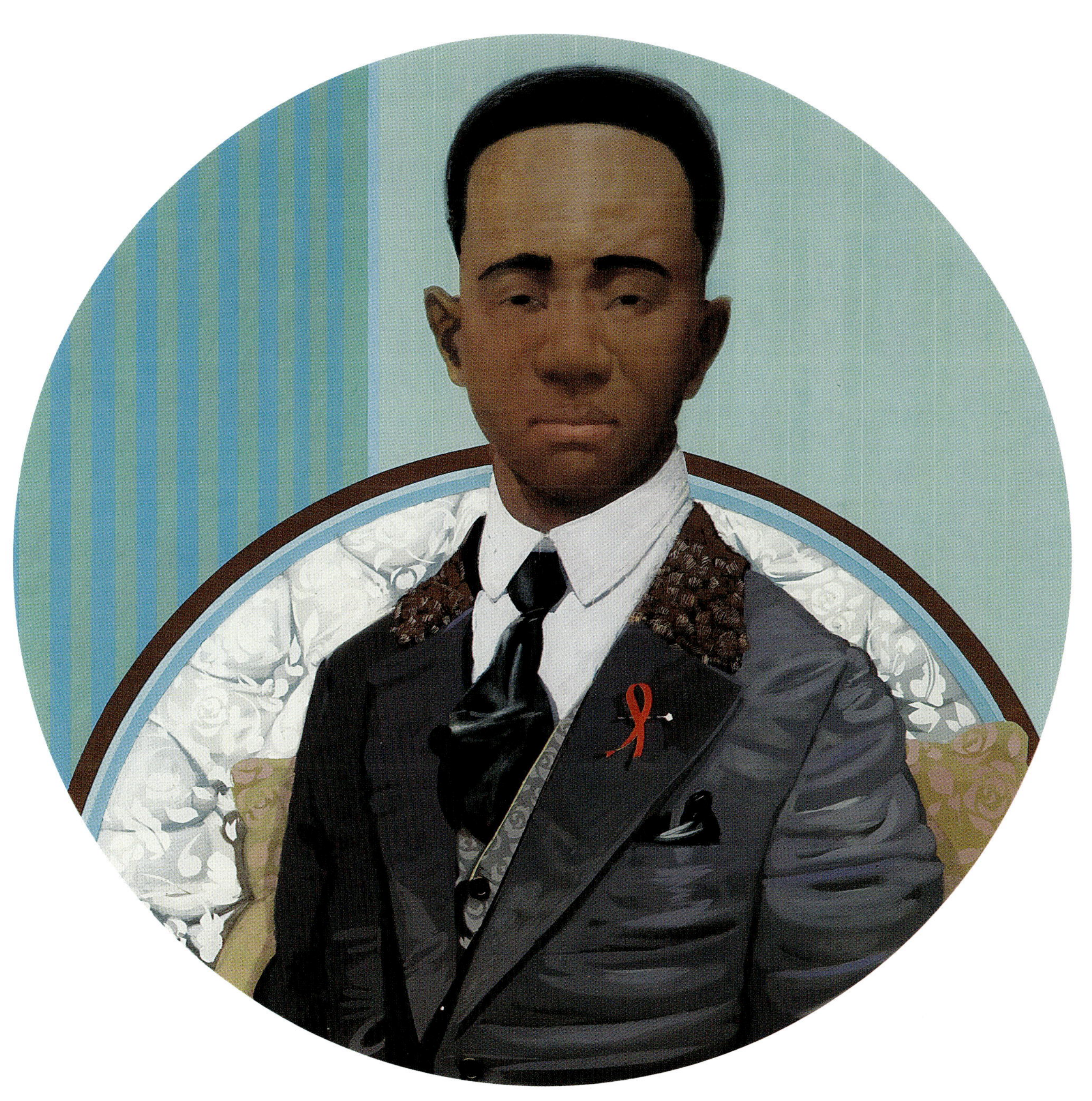

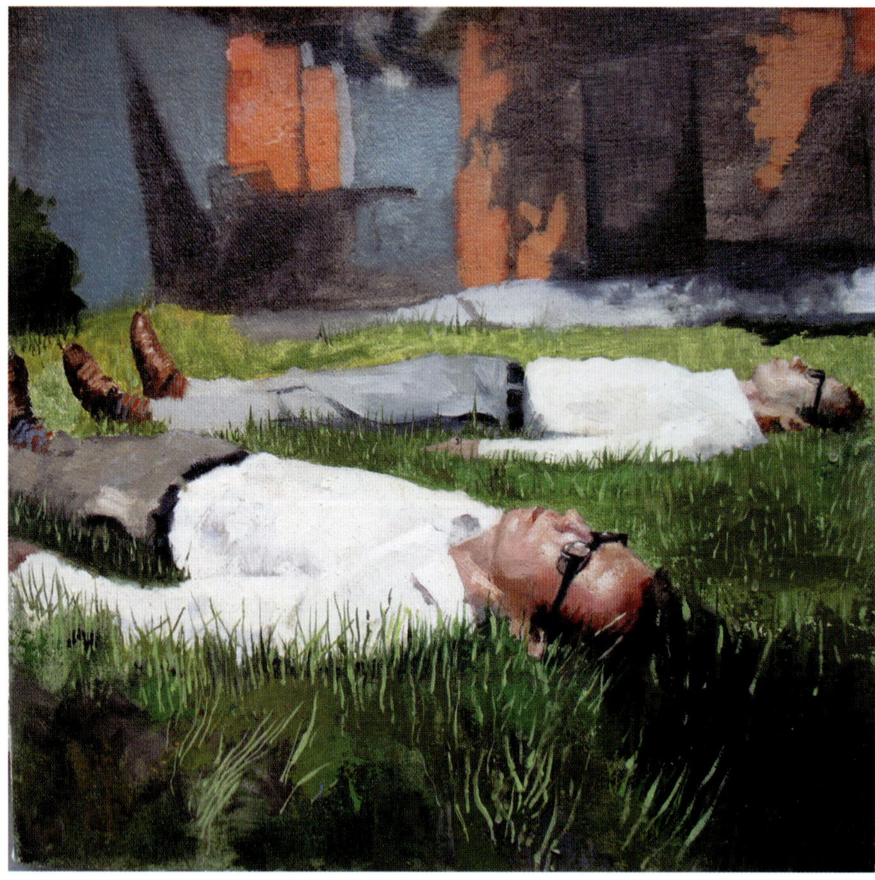

Caitlin Hurd
Somewhere Else,
2013
Oil on canvas
12 x 12 inches

(opposite)
Peter Drake
Parade, 2008
Acrylic on canvas
58 x 77 inches

PETER DRAKE

As a child I was walleyed. After corrective surgery at the age of seven, I began drawing and painting almost constantly. My older sister taught me painting, and we would copy anything from Hallmark Christmas cards to Picasso's *Three Musicians.* I remember faithfully copying one of Picasso's still lifes and only realizing after I was finished that it represented something more than hypnotic lines and shapes. Being able to draw and paint as a child had its advantages: In fourth grade a fellow student named Kathy approached me and gave me the option of making her a drawing of a horse for a quarter, or getting punched in the face. Kathy was bigger than I was. I took the twenty-five cents.

In my teens I was fortunate enough to travel in Italy and France with my family. On the night of our arrival in Florence my father took my brother and me for a walk to prepare us for seeing the sculpture of David the next day. He wanted us to know that what we were about to see was something beyond sculpture, something that had moved men and women for generations. When I saw it I felt Michelangelo could hear my thoughts. I made drawings of his sculptures for the rest of the year. Later at Pratt I tried to expose myself to as much as I possibly could. This was during the 1970s and much of the academic norm at the time was focused on Reductive Abstraction. I was always interested in narrative and metaphor and so was drawn to artists like Joe Smith and Rudolf Baranik, who were teaching at Pratt at the time. I also made a point of taking one illustration class every semester to stay in touch with popular culture and artists who were interested in storytelling.

My life as an artist started on the Lower East Side in the early 1980s. I was living in an apartment that was the size of a pizza oven. I slept on the floor and had to roll up my bedding to make room to draw. One night while making some pen-and-ink drawings I ran out of white ink. In order to alter the drawings I started to sand into the paper. This was a sort of eureka moment; instead of painting shadows I was painting light. Eventually I started to work subtractively on everything. It just made more sense to me. I would lay out a roll of paper, sometimes twelve feet long, cover it with black sumi ink and start sanding into it, usually starting with the source of light and then just moving across the surface. I used everything from rasps to very fine sandpaper, sometimes tearing through the paper entirely. This method had the added advantage of creating an unfamiliar and weirdly abused surface. I had been looking at a lot of Giotto and Masaccio and felt a connection between the ragged surface of my drawings and the sense of passing time in decaying frescoes.

Most of what I am interested in pictorially is somewhere between the real and the unreal. I spent most of my early career trying to find some way to describe the surreal aspects of growing up in the suburbs. I was raised in a beautiful town an hour outside of New York City. There were many stately nineteenth-century homes that looked like they were right out of a Hopper painting. The reality of the town, however, differed dramatically from its appearance. One of my neighbors lit her hair on fire as she was trying to kill herself in her oven. Another neighbor had her head blown off by her estranged husband. My Sunday school teacher—the priest who confirmed me—hung himself in the Sunday School playground as a Long Island Railroad train was pulling out of the station. At that time I worked entirely

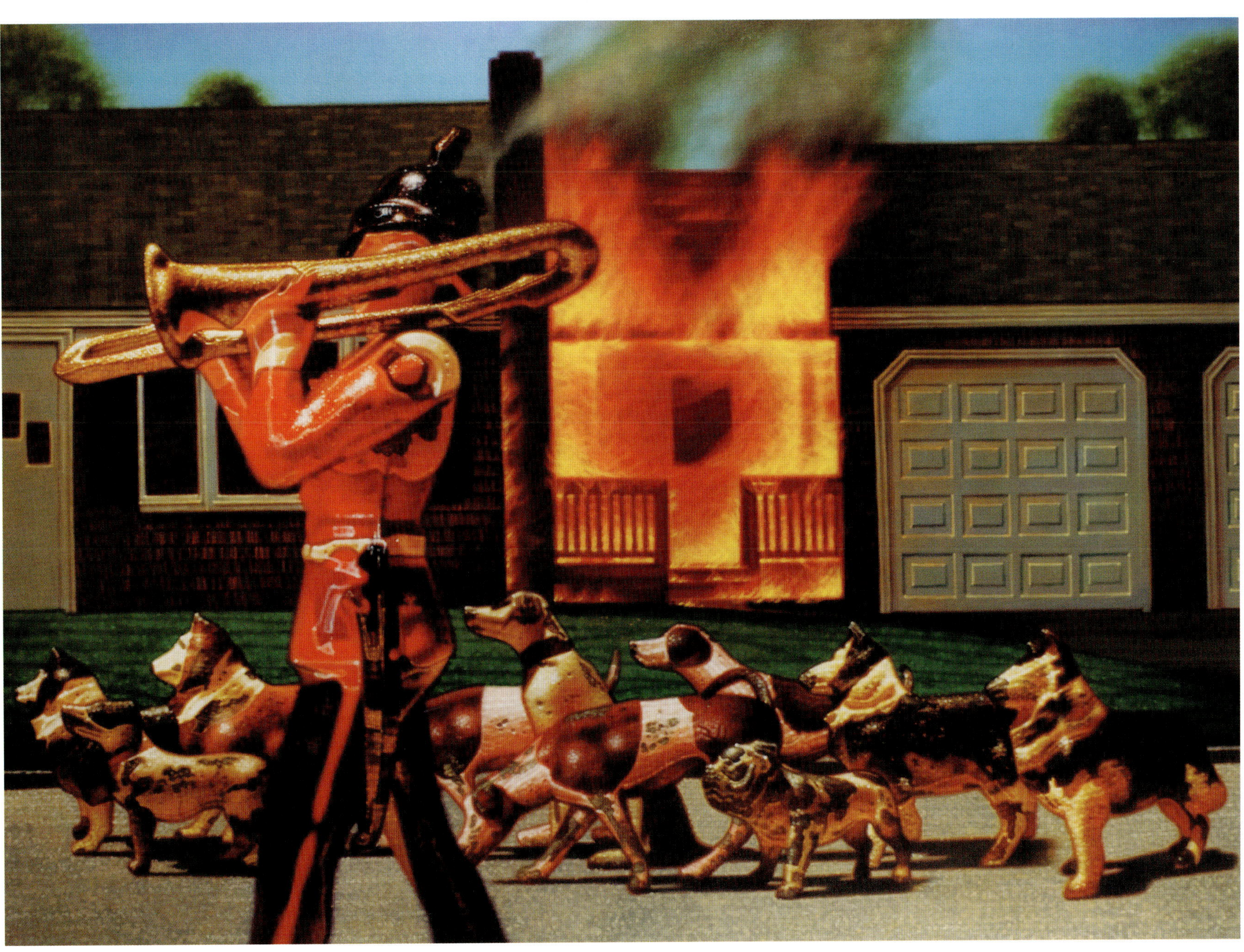

from my imagination, and would try to find visual equivalents to the sense of unease that marked my childhood. I tried to strip the paintings down to their barest essentials. I think that this is why I was so drawn to Giotto; there is a very shallow stage space that is populated with only the things that are absolutely necessary for the story.

As my imagery progressed, so did the technical language I used to realize it. I started to work on layers of modeling paste that were built up and sanded down to create a surface that felt like a decaying wall. I would cover the surface with layers and layers of various colors, so that as I sanded through them unexpected chromatic events would occur. By this time the images that I was drawn to came directly from my subconscious. I became incredibly adept at remembering and recording my dreams every morning, sometimes ten or fifteen dreams per night. I have always struggled with insomnia so waking up frequently and fusing the dream in my memory became the norm. Dream imagery has the added advantage of being utterly unselfconscious and surprisingly revealing.

My studio life is fluid; every seven years or so I need something completely different from my painting. Currently I've been looking outside myself for what I see as the unreal in the real world, which has taken many forms. I have collaged images from magazines that were popular during my childhood and made images that I think of as just "off." I have worked with images of lead toy soldiers set down in real environments that seem at odds with the toys' origins. I have used animation to generate paintings, and made paintings that have resulted in animations. I believe artists should follow their instincts when it comes to change and personal growth in the studio. This can be disturbing for professional relationships and disorienting for yourself, but in the end it creates a more dynamic studio life.

DIK LIU

I think of myself as an observational painter. My work is obviously realistic, but that is the outcome of figuring out what I am seeing in the world, rather than of a procedure of rendering realistic images. I don't paint for the viewer and I'm not really interested in making a picture. My work concerns itself with problems intrinsic to painting, such as the conflict between being loyal to perception, and developing a painting's own "argument." I need painting to not just give pleasure but also be intellectually engaging and visually challenging. I like art with a bit of discomfort that offers new ways of looking.

My undergraduate teacher, George Nick, helped me develop facility at Massachusetts College of Art and Design, but at Yale grad school I discovered how mesmerizing it is to question skills, and for many years afterward I painted abstractly. Over time, I realized I am most engaged working from direct observation. My primary concern is the light/dark arrangement of the color. The high chroma and shallow subject matter camouflage any antiquated painting concerns I have, and poke fun at tastefulness. I've been influenced by Velázquez, Rembrandt, Vermeer, Cézanne, and also by more obscure painters like Edwin Dickinson, Martin Johnson Heade, Joseph Decker, and Priscilla Roberts. I dislike the elegant predictable formalism of Chardin, and the easily accessible beauty of Matisse.

(opposite)
Dik Liu
Woman Eating a Steak, 2004
Oil on panel
28 x 28 inches

When I paint still lifes, I spend a lot of time setting up the motif because while painting I don't edit what I see. I begin with an imprimatura, usually ultramarine blue, and block in shapes and tones to locate the composition. Once I have something on the canvas to react to, painting becomes a thinking process involving many discoveries in my responses to light, space, and color relations. Observational painting is more complex than mere copying, because the visual world presents a spatial envelope too deep for the canvas, and a multitude of color relations too vast for the pigments on the palette. As I paint I compress the visual world into the canvas, negotiate color possibilities, accepting some and rejecting others.

Mark making expresses moments of confidence, and also doubt. I'm always conscious of the picture plane, and make brushstrokes that may be spatially incoherent, even mechanical looking, but that hold a pure response to light. The contrast between artifice and authenticity interests me. Some marks become reference points, springboards and signposts that move me in one direction instead of another, articulating questions the painting will try to resolve. Blending for me would be intellectually unchallenging, so I additively follow the tones as I engage them. Each stage relates to the inherent visual magic and integrity of pictorial construction à la Hans Hofmann, that push-pull thing. Perhaps I'm a covert romantic. But I'm not into French existential fixations; Giacometti-inspired methodology can be a shtick, a fake romance that uses "The Struggle" as premise, process, and style. I prefer the way López-García toiled to find a solution. His paintings look like he had all the time in the world to resolve them.

When I work from the figure, I use oil sketches and photos as references. The sketches determine the sense of light and tonal range I am after. Working from photos poses its own challenges, because photos lack three-dimensional information—the form, the air, the palpable sense of space between the artist and the motif. The light has already been interpreted by the camera; the original light is gone. So I need far more imagination to fill the gap between what I know of the visual world and what the photos before me can show—a process more like working from imagination than from direct observation.

When Henry Ford had his employees look for broken Model Ts, and assessed the broken versus working parts, he concluded that the parts still working were unnecessarily well made, so he tried to design all parts to fail simultaneously. Most things in life are pass/fail in this way, but painting can focus on lasting quality—even if realistically we have no idea what will endure, because we don't know what the future will need. That painting can be so terribly inefficient is amusing, and part of the content of my work. Maybe I want people to say, "He sure spent a lot of time painting something goofy really well." I may want the viewers to see my paintings as ridiculously well painted, or too well painted, like the still-working parts of a broken Model T, and to wonder why—but I'm not concerned with why I might want them to wonder. My paintings pose questions, and I'm very comfortable with not getting any clear answers.

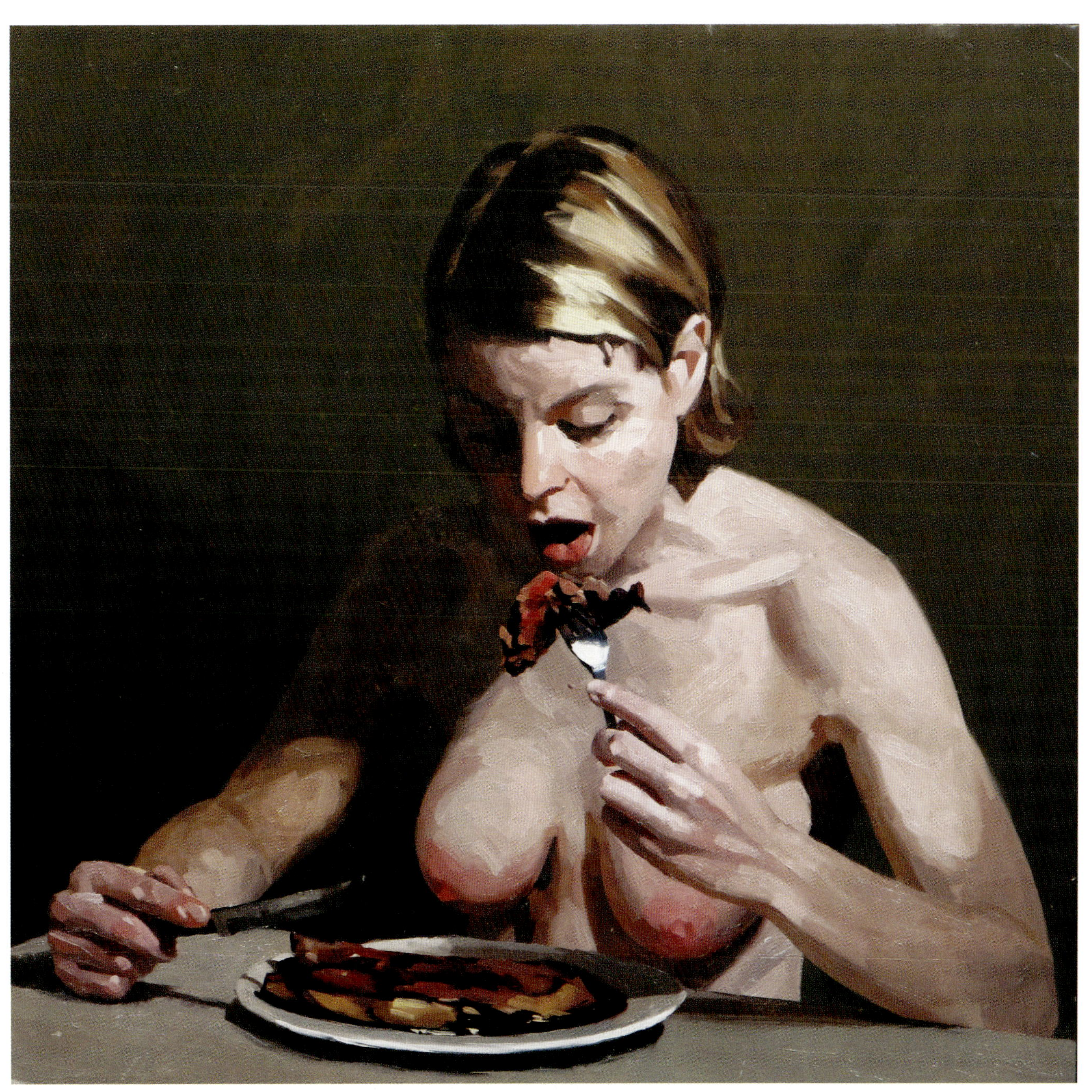

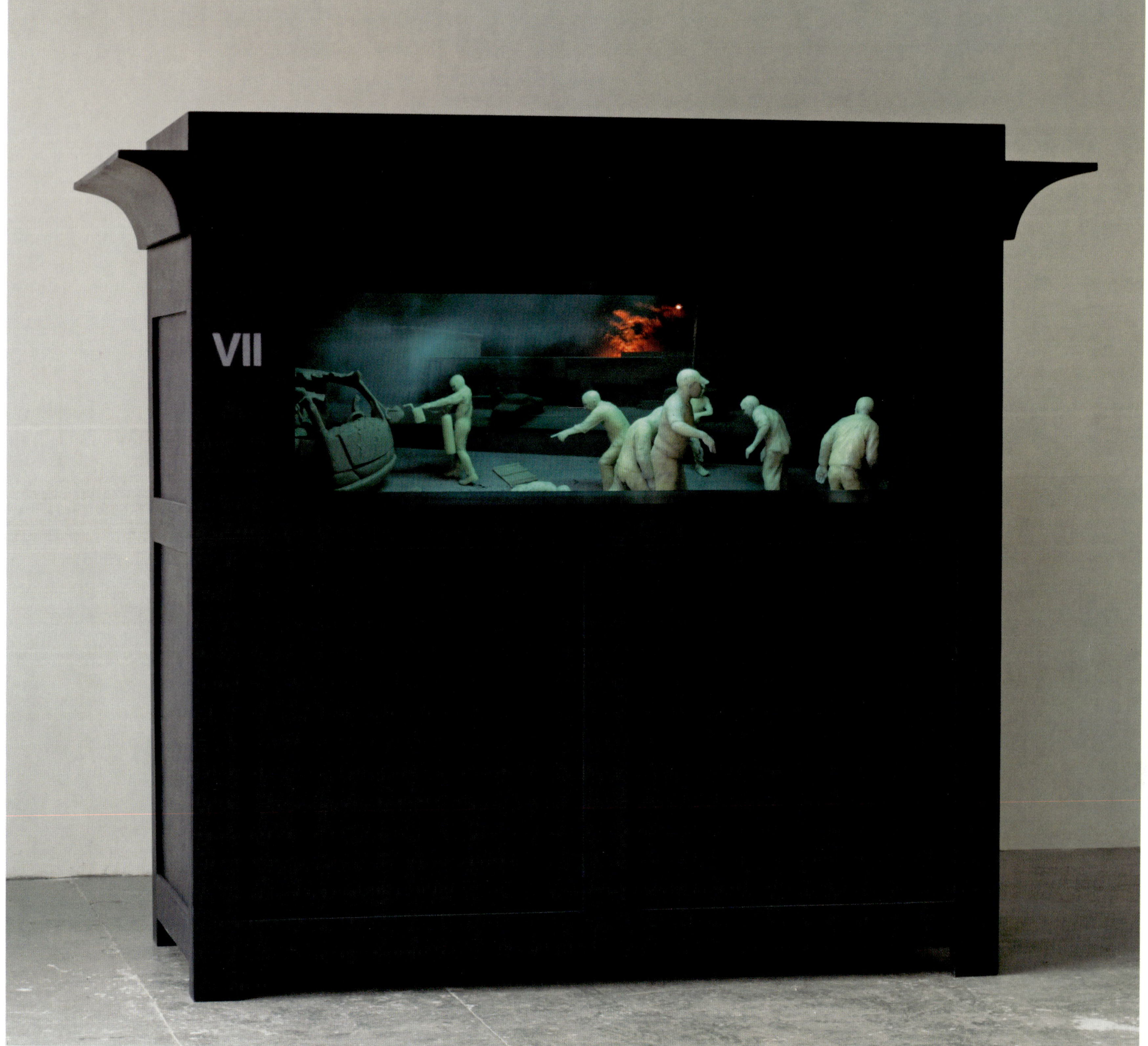
VII

TWENTIETH-CENTURY FIGURATIVE SCULPTURE

ROBERT TAPLIN

IN 1988 JEFF WALL PUBLISHED A BRILLIANT ESSAY in which he discussed the sculpture of Stephan Balkenhol, one of a number of sculptors who were at that moment gingerly testing the possibilities of a return to figuration in contemporary sculpture. Wall described Balkenhol's roughly carved wooden sculptures as "pale monadic figures, isolated from both universality and concrete social individuation, [who] usually appear before us simply attired, in a dress or trousers and a shirt. They are like people who have recently come out of a hospital after a serious illness, who cannot yet really return to active life but who can get dressed normally and face things again."[1] Wall labeled these "monads" a "counterexperimental form obliged to interrogate the language of experimental sculpture . . . from the viewpoint of the familiar human body."[2] Thus, figurative sculpture stepped back into the light of day after the extended near-death experience of Modernism. Subsequent years have seen a halting acceptance of the notion that representational sculpture could regain enough health to do more than address the weaknesses of the experimental forms which, over twenty-five years later, still dominate the discourse about contemporary sculpture.

The Constructivist movement in the early years of the twentieth century was the blow that shattered the dominance of the figure in sculpture. Picasso's experiments with Cubist construction opened the way for the radically open, abstract sculpture of Vladimir Tatlin and his Russian contemporaries as well as the Futurists in Italy, which in turn unleashed a torrent of activity that carried right through the twentieth century with Julio González, David Smith, and Anthony Caro as leading lights. The midcentury embrace of a cloying racist idealism by the Nazis further tarnished the position of figuration in the eyes of most observers. And yet, even in the face of the overwhelming Modernist drive toward the geometric, the mechanical, and the industrial, there were important ways in which the figurative tradition survived, particularly in the interwar period.

In the 1930s, the heyday of Dada and Surrealism, wildly hypersexualized work such as that of Hans Bellmer, done in defiance of the Nazi war against "degenerate" art, provided a keystone for the investigations of Kiki Smith, Jake and Dinos Chapman, and innumerable others who became associated with the new representational sculpture of the "abject body" in the 1980s. Marcel Duchamp's *Large Glass* (1915–23) and the later *Given: 1) The Waterfall, 2) The Illuminating Gas* . . . (1946–66) also form parts of this thread of Dada figuration. In contrast, the "Return to Classicism"[3] that drew many artists after the devastation of the First World War provided a basis for some of the most horrendous Fascist art, but also motivated Picasso and Matisse, as well as Marino Marini, Arturo Martini, and others. They rejected the vapid idealizing classicism of their Fascist contemporaries for a deeper, archaic one that seemed to offer a point of stability and humanity in a world that was spinning out of control. Some of their efforts have a surprising affinity with recent sculptors such as Judith Shea or Diana Moore, who took up the problem of classicism in the 1980s in a new context of feminism and post-colonialism. Another thread of figuration that survived the Modernist onslaught was a decorative, linear, folk art–influenced sensibility found in Nadelman, Manship, and to a lesser degree Lachaise and even Brancusi. In the 1980s this line of attack found a vigorous proponent in James Surls, and more recently in artists such as Claudette Schreuders and Folkert de Jong. And then there was Giacometti, whose ephemeralized, extenuated figures seemed to be more about the instabilities and anxieties of perception than about depiction as such. He exerted enormous influence throughout the mid-twentieth century. Two relatively unheralded British sculptors, Raymond Mason and Reg Butler, did fascinating work in the 1950s and '60s

(opposite)
Robert Taplin
VII: One Nation Rules (Fortune), 2008
Wood, resin, plaster, lights
84 x 94 x 52 inches

as they looked for ways to escape the shadow of Giacometti's achievement. Particularly, Butler's passingly strange cast-resin figures of the 1960s prefigure many of the preoccupations of the figurative revival of the 1980s.

Giacometti's example notwithstanding, it is striking that nearly all of the significant representational sculpture of the twentieth century, including most of that of the figurative revivalists of the 1980s, was anti-naturalistic in form and non-observational in method. There were a few exceptions including the great Spanish realist Antonio López-García, Robert Graham, and later Judy Fox. It is also often forgotten that a great abstractionist like David Smith held on to the practice of drawing from the nude and exhibited large figure drawings with his abstract sculpture in the 1960s, and that Anthony Caro and Mark di Suvero exhibited figurative works early in their careers. In contrast, many of the first wave of representational sculptors of the 1980s and '90s seem to have been working as lapsed post-Minimalists. Balkenhol, Magdalena Abakanowicz, Antony Gormley, Katharina Fritsch, and even Juan Muñoz all used the figure as a unit or cipher that was placed either singly or in repetitive groupings to build a place or location, functioning in a similar way to the units of a Judd or Andre. Narrative action, individual presence, or any sense of the figure as an individual protagonist in a psychological or physical drama was suppressed in favor of an abstract occupation of the sculptural field, and a focus on material and process. The hidden anthropomorphic presence of the statue that Michael Fried had detected in Minimalism came forward, but stopped short of taking on illusionary human characteristics.

Much of the activity of the 1980s was seen in the context of Neo-Expressionism, and Expressionism is another vital thread in the web of twentieth-century figuration. Gauguin, Kirchner, and Baselitz were each representatives of a particular generation of Expressionists all making figures, usually carved in wood, done in direct emulation of tribal or ethnic prototypes. (The current Expressionism of Huma Bhabha and Thomas Houseago is done more in emulation of Picasso and Giacometti than of the original tribal artifacts.) Rejection of the sullied Western canon and the embracing of a primitivizing style in the hopes that it can capture the true angst and isolation of the modern psyche seems to founder repeatedly on doubts about the validity of a willful or faux naïveté and questions about an essentialist reading of tribal art. The recent turn of a committed formalist like William Tucker to a species of expressionist abstraction clearly based on the fragmented figure is a more interesting development.

The Postmodernists posed an ostensible challenge to the principles of Modernism, but despite their decades-long dalliance with illusion and narrative there remains a deep-seated distrust of the fundamental illusion of presence, perhaps even of representation itself. The basic thrust of Modernism, embodied in a pioneer like Cézanne, was an attempt to find an unadorned reality, a direct access to the world. Cézanne's inquiry into the somewhat disembodied, flickering instabilities of his "sensations" and the fractured, papery (Hopper's term) quality of his representations seemed to insist on their status as records of perception, not illusions of reality, and became a touchstone for most Modernists. A representation that did not seem to question its own validity became associated with the hegemonic regimes of the past, particularly the history of European and American colonialism and imperialism. Much of the imagistic work of the Postmodernists took this a step further and dedicated itself to exposing the principle that representations were not to be trusted, that the task of the artist was to expose the lie. Jeff Wall, in a discussion of the problem of fragmentation and the unified subject, labeled this work "iconophobic representation,"[4] and claimed that all representations now had to "rebuild themselves with a different legitimacy."[5]

In this context, the figurative revival of the 1980s has run up against a strange kind of glass ceiling where figuration that takes a ribald or satiric approach (Ed Kienholz, Paul McCarthy, Maurizio Cattelan), claims a conceptual pedigree (Charles Ray, Jeff Koons), or stays firmly in the realm of fairy tale or fantasy (Kiki Smith) finds some qualified acceptance because all these approaches decline to commit fully to an illusionary human presence. They also studiously avoid anything that could be characterized as virtuosity in rendering, another Modernist taboo. Even that perennial also-ran, hyperrealism, such as practiced currently by Ron Mueck and Evan Penny, pushes its photographic illusionism to the point where the whole "effect" collapses in a sudden return to the materiality of silicone rubber and fake hair.

At the end of the day, there have been few attempts to fully activate the naturalistic presence of the figurative statue, to hazard what Jeff Wall seemed to propose in 1988, "a thoroughgoing restoration of the idea of the socially emblematic human figure as it must really live, work and suffer"[6] in a contemporary world. This amounts to a call to abandon both a tainted idealism and the focus on surface verisimilitude, and take up the deeper historical task of realism—a call that remains at this moment largely unanswered.

(opposite)
Nicolas Holiber
Trophy, 2013
Wood, mixed media
65 x 15 x 9 inches

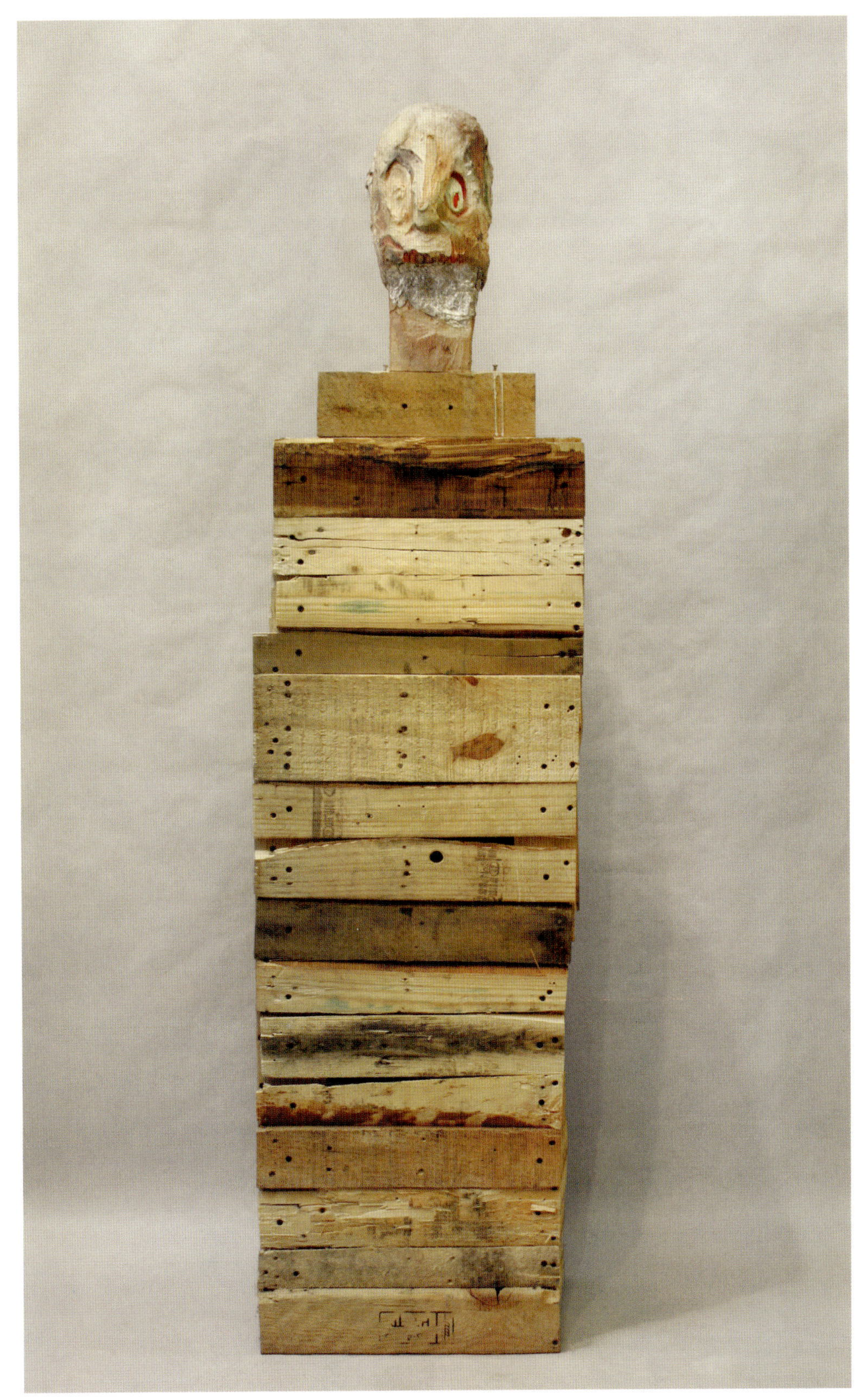

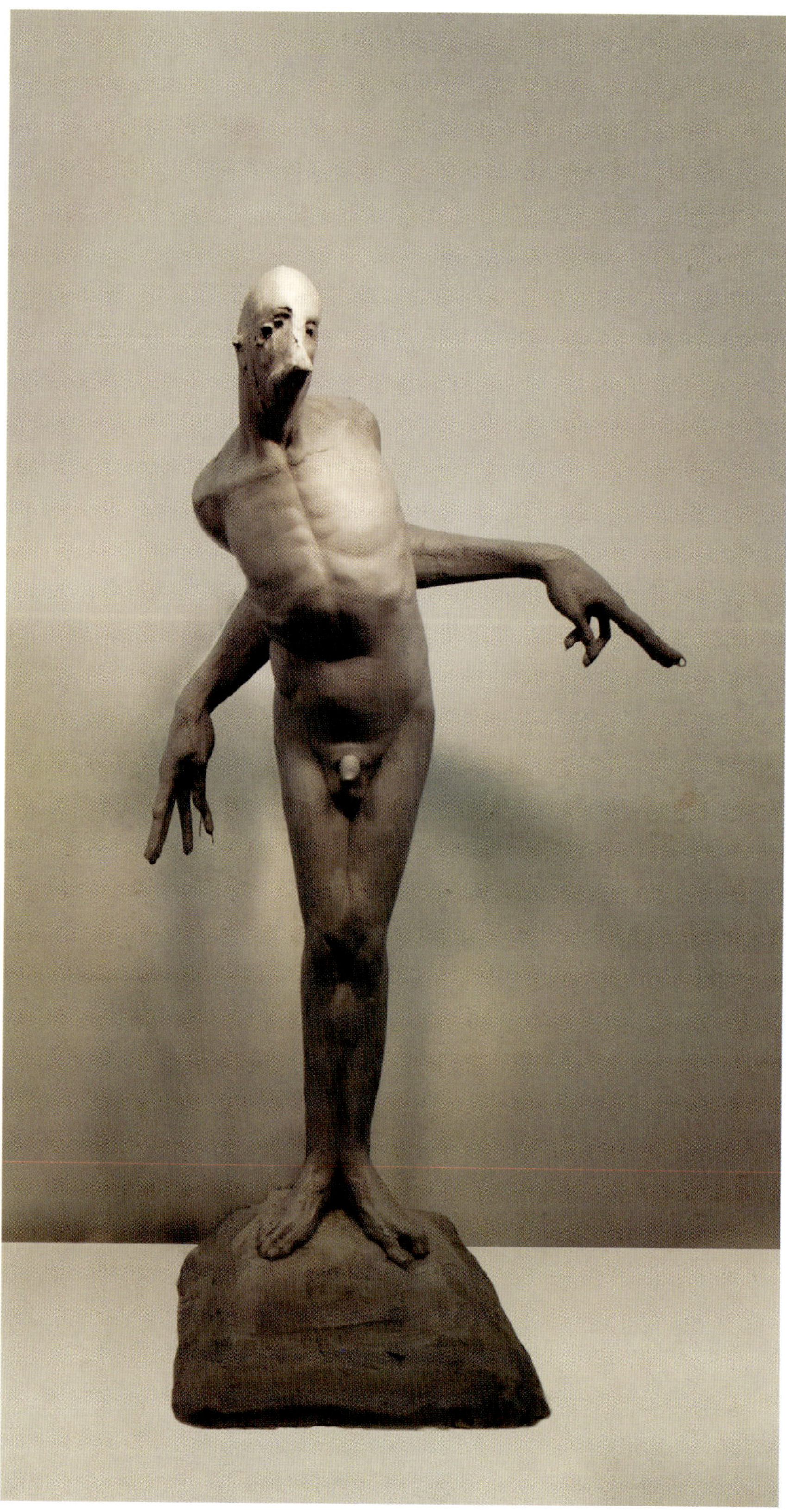

BRUCE GAGNIER

If I make a good figure, then perhaps I will have made a sculpture. Sculpture as content is of no interest to me—the figure is. Its ability to move creates metaphorical movement in and out of meanings. My work is Modernist, but any particular separation of art into categories is absent in me, and not criteria for evaluation. My statues comprise fragments of figures, pieces that may not belong together, recovered through memory, but without awareness of specific instances or place. All are welcomed into the work without historical re-qualification.

I draw constantly from the model and memory, combining two methods learned from teachers loyal to their own histories but dedicated to the fundamentals of plasticity. One described the abstractions behind illusion with deference to Cubism, and pushed us to create autonomous forms. The other analyzed appearance using a perceptual method based on measuring bilateral parts from point to point to discover relative depths. My sculptural practice is largely self-taught. In my first clay sketches from the model I closely observed the outline, like a carver would. Eventually I learned how to move the clay in a painterly tactile way, "off the edge," from Rodin. Study in museums, committing to memory how figures were formed, is central to my continuing education. The disinterred quality of the National Gallery's basement's collection of unfinished sketches by Rodin and Degas especially interested me.

I start a sculpture usually with a study as a guide until unconscious, unpremeditated actions take over. When I'm sculpting, I'm drawing the clay rhythmically in a manner that recalls Celtic ornament, Byzantine arabesque, and Renaissance figure drawing. I insert details early on, before the whole is in place, and move parts around like a collage. Anatomy, often flawed, is pieced together, remembered as encountered in each area of the figure. Tools intervene, a rake made from a kitchen knife, a wire, a butcher knife, a chisel-like tool of my own making, something to smooth with—and as soon as possible the clay's identity and beauty are killed for its rebirth as flesh. These persons of clay do not build up in regular stages from start to finish. Instead each seems to advance and compress itself around its persona—but perhaps it has simply passed through all of mine.

During what is an empirical and approximate technique, body parts are repositioned in response to character suggesting itself. If the image begins to approximate any given, it is altered toward the experiential. These liberties are not all arbitrary, but express legitimate modes of experience in relation to the artistic task—will, faith, desire. Content is written into these bodies via the physical work of making them, which can feel oppressive from a lack of skill and the elusive path ahead. The turmoil of modeling in clay leaves a record specific to each experience behind, which greatly determines their final look and feel. Also built into the process are guesses and welcome mistakes. I would like to think that as these figures merge with the terms of the space they create around them, they express their own inner life on their surfaces, and in what becomes partly a psychic space.

As I model I also envision the clay in bronze, paying close attention to "hills and valleys"—how I describe Donatello's bronze David's painterly effects. Created in a tactile way, using pressure to work inside the form, light appears in valley surfaces. Seen through solids, the play of light is illusionist, almost watery, dissolving

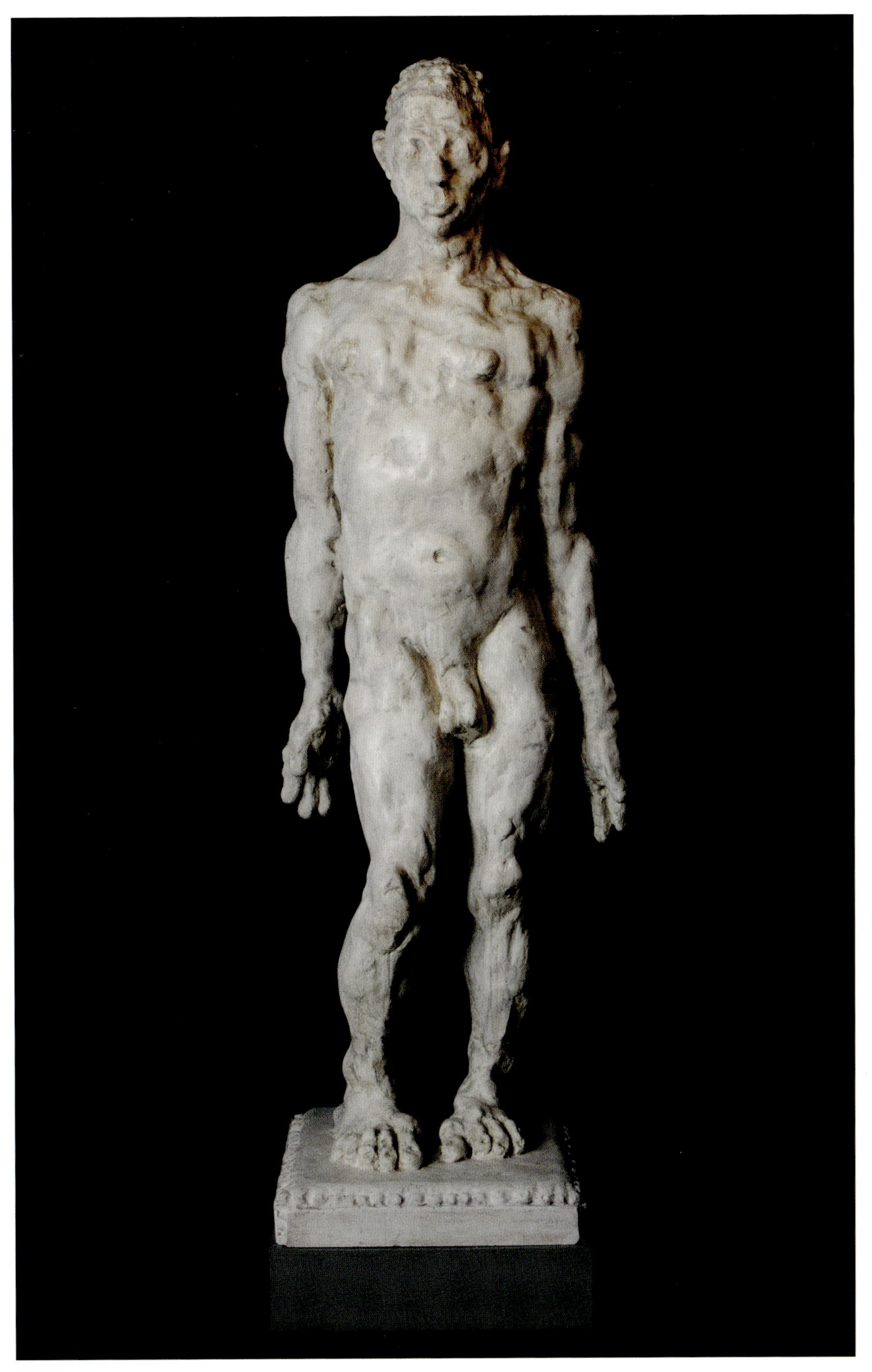

Bruce Gagnier
Les, 2013
Hydrocal
74 x 23 x 20 inches

(opposite)
Alfred Rosenbluth
Mocking Bird, 2013
Clay
75 x 36 x 24 inches

tactile substance and replacing it with space—this part of my process takes most of the effort in the evolution of the final image.

My sculptures might appear to the normative vision as mere distortion, or an exaggeration of patterns. They require viewers to bring to their appraisal an understanding of culture, a knowledge of clay modeling, an openness to seeing something they assume to know so well afresh—and thus not resort to things like illness and other physiological reasons to explain variations in relation to the desirability of perfect smoothness. Perhaps my figures would prefer to immerse themselves normally and easily into the outer world, but they know themselves through me as I get to know them, and our situation together can't allow this as a legitimate solution. In truth all their positions and anatomical combinations adjust in avoidance of this, due to the ever-present suspicion that falling into line with any replica of meaning might promise success, but only guarantees defeat. The edge I am trying to describe is from inside reality as it defines itself to the outside.

The political aspect of the content of my figures could be my approaching them without presupposition, so they can define themselves beyond expectation. More important to me is the role of a plastic consciousness, which on some days regrettably feels partial or absent altogether—and beyond that, a plastic conscience, always nagging, without which there could be no final assault on a compelling projection of the image. When the various parts harmonize in a whole that equates with the personality of the being, a kind of existential moment, I withdraw from the work and they are on their own. But these are provisional people, each one trying to arrest the process at a moment that will help the next figure better engage my notion of content. They might be best judged not through an understanding of values outlined by Modernist concepts of sculpture, but by whether or not one has a feeling of affection for them as people who have survived an onslaught of pressures with some measure of internal identity.

MICHAEL FERRIS JR.

My most recent sculptures are freestanding pieces, often over six feet in height. Making one is a complicated process that involves many stages. The most compelling aspect of making my artwork revolves around the question of how to charge inert material with life and emotional power that transcends the inanimate. Over the years, I've developed a set of personal techniques that have helped my work evolve toward those ends.

I constantly collect various discarded wood, from raw lumber to used furniture. The majority is pine, which usually gets cut into basic blocks for use in a sculpture's structure or undersurface. When I find wood with a particular color like oak (light brown), poplar (light to dark green), or walnut (dark brown), I put it aside to be cut for later use in the overlaid surface. I cut much of this wood into basic geometric shapes on a band saw. For the more complicated and unusual shapes, I first run wood though a router. I then sort the pieces into Ziploc bags, which are pinned to my studio wall for systematic use according to shape, size, and color.

I create many pencil or ink drawings that run the spectrum from accurate carefully rendered portraits to more analytical form-based studies. These serve the overall purpose of informing my sculpting process intellectually, but more importantly, they connect me emotionally to the sculpture I am constructing. They help me get into a more meditative, focused state of mind. The analytical drawings are measurement drawings. Their sole purpose is to provide very accurate proportional information, much like blueprints for architecture. Initially they served as the only conduit between the accurate planning stage and the actual sculpture, but over time I realized that while measurement drawings provided a huge amount of useful information to the sculptural process, they weren't quite enough. While the drawings were to scale between 1-to-1 and 1-to-4 ratios, shifting back and forth between the smaller 2-D plane to the much larger 3-D form felt awkward.

I needed another stage to bridge the gap, so started making what could be considered a drawing-maquette, a very accurately rendered 3-D model of the sculpture being planned—simply put, a 3-D version of the measurement drawing. Eventually I arrived at designing the maquette half the size of the sculpture, a 1-to-2 scale relationship, thus making size transitions between the maquette and the sculpture direct and simple. The incorporation of a maquette into the process compartmentalizes specific metrics, so I no longer concern myself with how to transform 2-D into 3-D while sculpting, which makes it more reactive and less cerebral. As I work, I continuously add and subtract wood to hone in on an accurate sense of human likeness, and of form.

Once I complete the structure, I overlay the surface with complex patterns of wood pieces, adhered with color-tinted glue. The color decisions I make are fully integrated with my choices regarding pattern, value, shape, rhythm, etc. I know I am going in the right direction with a sculpture when I see all of these elements come together and start to visually vibrate. The last stage of my process involves synthesizing the nuances of the underlying form with the complexity of the patterned surface. Before I know a sculpture is complete, I have it in my space for a long time, sometimes sitting and looking at it for hours. Other times I don't look at it directly at all and just pay attention to it peripherally. The whole process is very intuitive and unstructured so it's hard to explain, other than to simply say that I know a sculpture is completed when it feels good to me.

At the core of my methodology is a simple and personal interest. I want every sculpture to have a more realized emotional humanistic quality than the one I made previously. This sometimes feels very daunting and mysterious. After all, it reflects a drive to capture an ever-deeper psychological and emotional state in a static three-dimensional form. The only way I can begin to comprehend my goal is to engage in a basic learning process of recognizing any skill-based shortcomings. When I embrace this attitude, something important and emotional always sparks within me, and as I work to improve a sculpture, this feeling is naturally expressed in the artwork. In other words, a sculpture's presence is built one "brick" at a time.

(opposite)
Michael Ferris Jr.
Toufic, 2010
Wood, pigment
76 x 37 x 23 inches

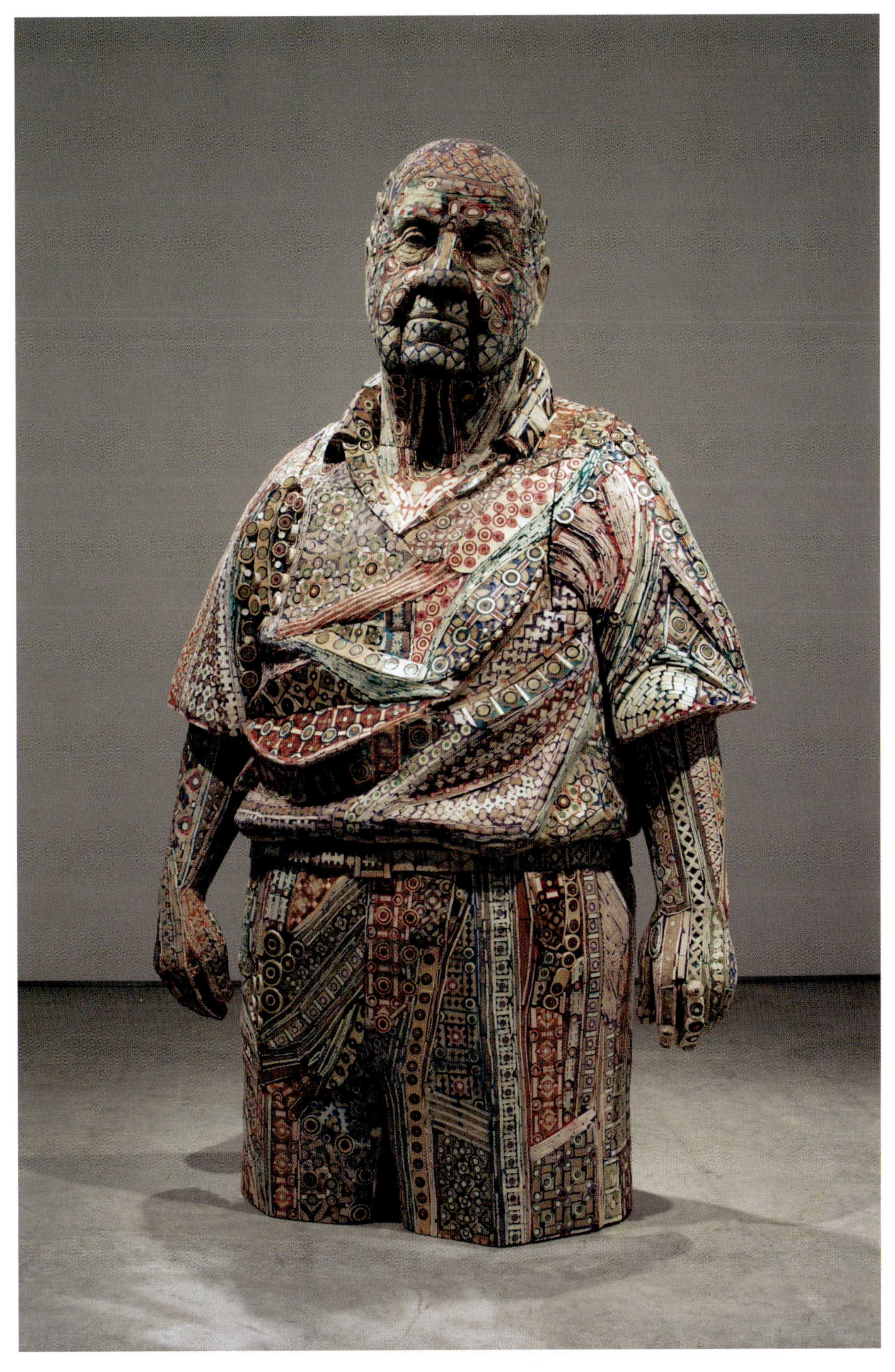

REPRESENTING AVANT-GARDE REPRESENTATION: FROM PAINTERLY FIGURATION TO MATTER-OF-FACT REALISM 1950–70

IRVING SANDLER

(opposite)
Tun Ping Wang
Vague, 2010
Pastel on paper
60 x 40 inches

IN THE 1950S, COMPARED TO ABSTRACTION, figurative painting was often denigrated as backward looking and academic. Clement Greenberg, for example, wrote in 1954 that today, the object and the image can be put back into art only by "*pastiche* or parody" and can only be secondhand. But a growing number of avant-garde painters, the most influential of whom was Willem de Kooning, paid Greenberg little heed.[1]

Artists who employed figuration in the 1950s were divided into two groups. On the one hand, there were gesture, action, or painterly painters, who relied on the improvisational *process* of painting and revealed it in the finished canvases. On the other hand, there were realists who were intent on depicting the actual appearance of their subjects. In emphasizing the *image*, they curbed the evidence of facture.[2] The gesture painters, both abstract and figurative, stressed, as Meyer Schapiro remarked, "the importance of the mark, the stroke, the brush, the drip, the quality of the substance of the paint itself, and the surface of the canvas as a texture and field of operation," all of which were signs of the artist's active presence.[3]

De Kooning's *Women* (1950–52) showed the way. Intent on revealing his subjective feelings about his subjects, he depicted them with balloon busts, staring eyes, and bared teeth, at once voluptuous, imperious, fierce, and humorous. As Thomas B. Hess commented, they are "queens . . . rulers of a country that names its hurricanes 'Hattie' or 'Connie.'"[4] Among younger figurative gesture painters Grace Hartigan stood out. In 1954, she found new subjects in New York City, such as the mannequins of brides in downtown store windows. They attracted her because they expressed what was "vulgar and vital in American modern life."[5] In contrast to Hartigan, contemporaries of hers such as Alex Katz, Fairfield Porter, and Larry Rivers were verging toward a factual realism, even while they included subtle painterly details in their canvases. Of the three, at the time, Rivers was the most specific, notably in his *Double Portrait of Berdie* (1955), his aged mother-in-law. His scrutiny of the "obnoxious detail" of her naked body, as Leo Steinberg described it, was widely considered outrageous and perverse.[6] But Lawrence Campbell hailed Rivers's notorious double image "unabashed, unidealized nakedness [as] an entirely fresh note."[7]

Jasper Johns developed another novel variant of painterly realism in the 1950s. He represented everyday objects and images—targets, numbers, letters, maps—the most memorable of which was the American flag. His image was an original development of Marcel Duchamp's readymades except that in contrast to Duchamp's rejection of retinal art, his pictures were beautifully painted. The most persuasive rationale for Johns's painting was provided by John Cage. Cage said that Johns's kind of artist had dissolved the distinction between art and life. Moreover, instead of focusing on the artist's inner life and emotions as the figurative gesture painters had, Johns looked out at the world and aspired "to open up one's eyes to just seeing what there was to see."[8] His purpose was to make people alive to their surroundings. Johns's painting would lead to Pop art in the early 1960s.

In the late 1950s, Alex Katz took a critical look at figurative gesture painting and asked: What were the figures doing there? Were they anything other than tokens in paintings that were essentially abstract? What was the responsibility of the artist to the human subject? What would make figurative painting contemporary? How could ideas culled from abstract art be used in figurative painting? And wasn't there just too much smudged and scumbled, slapdash painting around? It all seemed both commonplace and formulaic ("dead on arrival," Katz quipped, in conversation), concluding that if figurative art was to be renewed, it would have to become more literal. By 1960, Katz had deflected the course of figurative art toward a New Perceptual Realism, suppressing loose brushwork because it obscured the details of

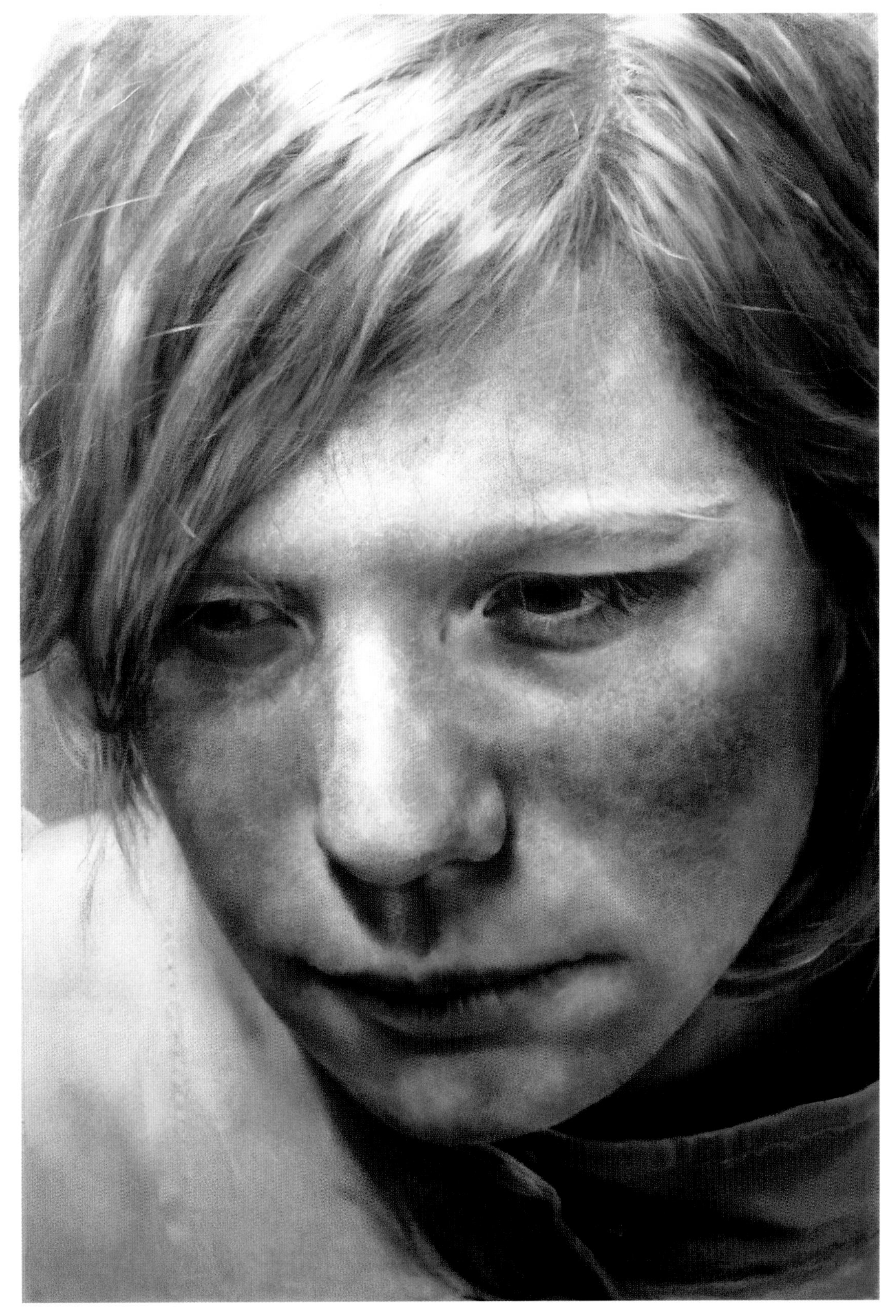

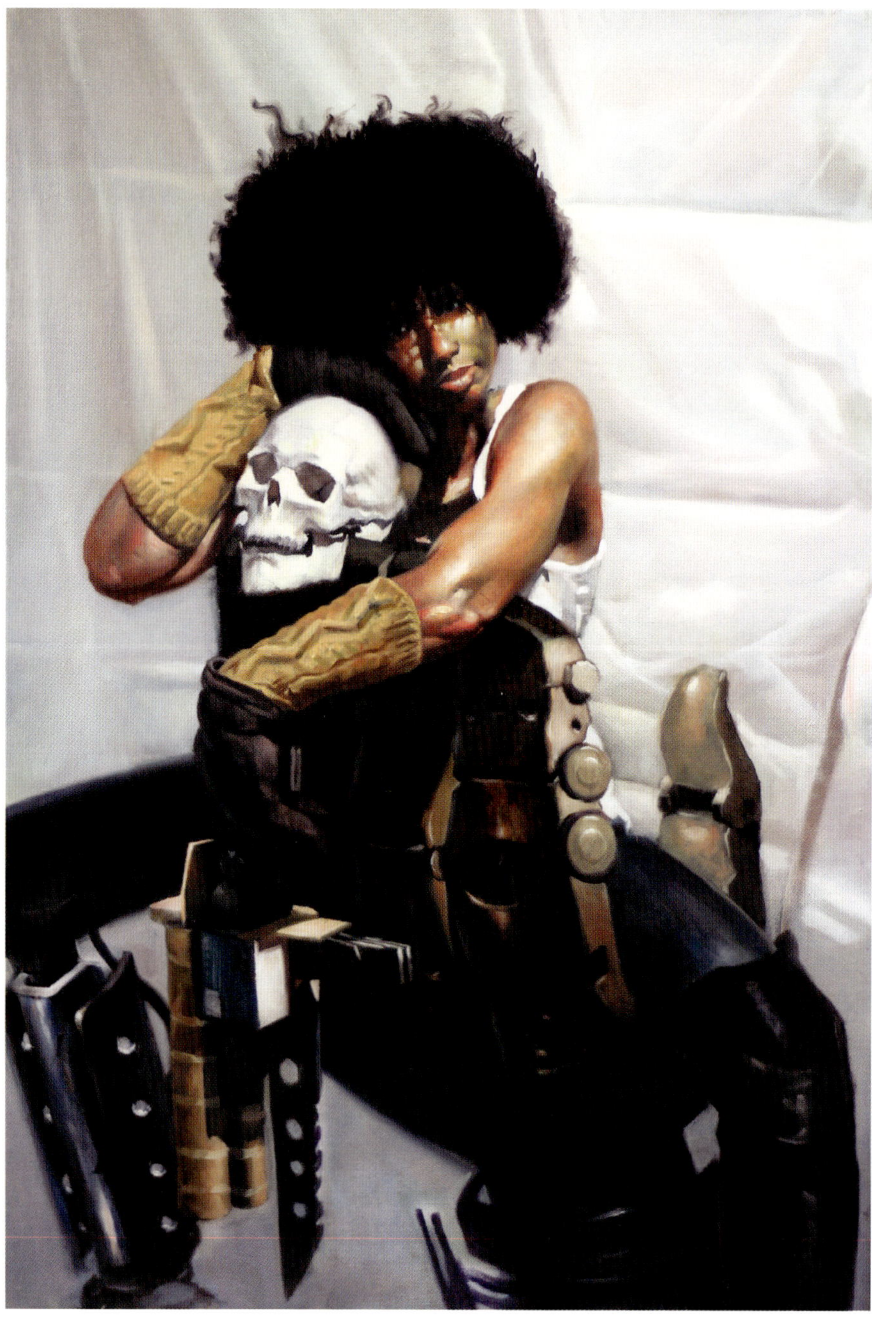

Eric Telfort
Maya, 2010
Oil on linen
24 x 18 inches

(opposite)
Stephen Vollo
Vanitas, 2013
Oil on canvas
48 x 36 inches

observed subjects. Instead of using traditional modeling to create the bulk of his figures, he adopted Matisse's Modernist method of using flat planes of color in conjunction with contour drawing to achieve a convincing illusion of volume and depth.

Developing a New Perceptual Realism was only one of Katz's contributions to figurative painting. Another was the innovation of the "Big Realist Picture." His ambition was to have his paintings compete in visual impact, muscle, and grandeur with the new Color Field, Hard Edge, and Minimal abstraction. But, anticipating Pop art, he also had an eye to contemporary mass media, large-scale billboards, and wide-screen movies. From the 1950s on, Katz's primary subject matter has been portraiture. He has depicted his family and artist, poet and dancer friends, and above all Ada, his wife and favorite model. Katz has sought to make his painting of them *contemporary*, and as their appearances kept changing, so did the pictures. This is clear in the transformation of his impecunious sitters from the Eisenhower 1950s to the affluent Kennedy years, when they become stylish, looking at ease and assured.

Philip Pearlstein soon joined Katz in the development of a matter-of-fact New Perceptual Realism. He too suppressed ambiguous painting that blurred the figures. Pearlstein's primary subject is the naked female model—naked, not nude. He paints her, as he said, "conceived as a self-contained entity possessed of its own dignity, existing in an inhabitable space, viewed from a single vantage point."[9] Pearlstein is not interested in his models' psychological and social attributes, nor indeed, in any kind of interpretation. His subjects have no distinctive personality traits, no narrative, and no name except *Naked Female*. To make his figures new and not merely a rehash of used-up figurative styles, Pearlstein reviewed the history of Western art, in which, as Kenneth Clark commented, the female nude is the central subject. As Pearlstein saw it, none of the earlier realist styles were truly factual. Even the naturalism of Courbet was tinged with Romanticism. His kind of realism had been relegated to the dustbin of history by Modernists. Pearlstein proposed to rehabilitate true-to-life figuration, but he would go beyond Courbet and try to be unequivocally objective. Although Pearlstein's model is unlike any of her predecessors in Western painting, she insists on being included in their company, if only to highlight the differences between them and her.

Younger New Perceptual Realists influenced by Katz and Pearlstein are Rackstraw Downes, Janet Fish, and Robert Berlind. However, unlike the older painters, Downes has portrayed urban garbage dumps, sewer mains, and rural landfalls. His best-known subjects are panoramic views of the Texas plains. Downes's on-site sweeping vistas of the prairie are closely observed but nonetheless the heirs of Jackson Pollock's and Clyfford Still's abstractions evoking the American Great Plains. Berlind's canvases reveal the visual poetry of natural forms that won't stop moving, such as tree branches swaying in the wind or fugitive reflections and refractions of puddles, ponds, and streams, often at night. Fish's "portraits" of shrink-wrapped fruits and glass jars and bottles containing pickles and the like are distinguished by

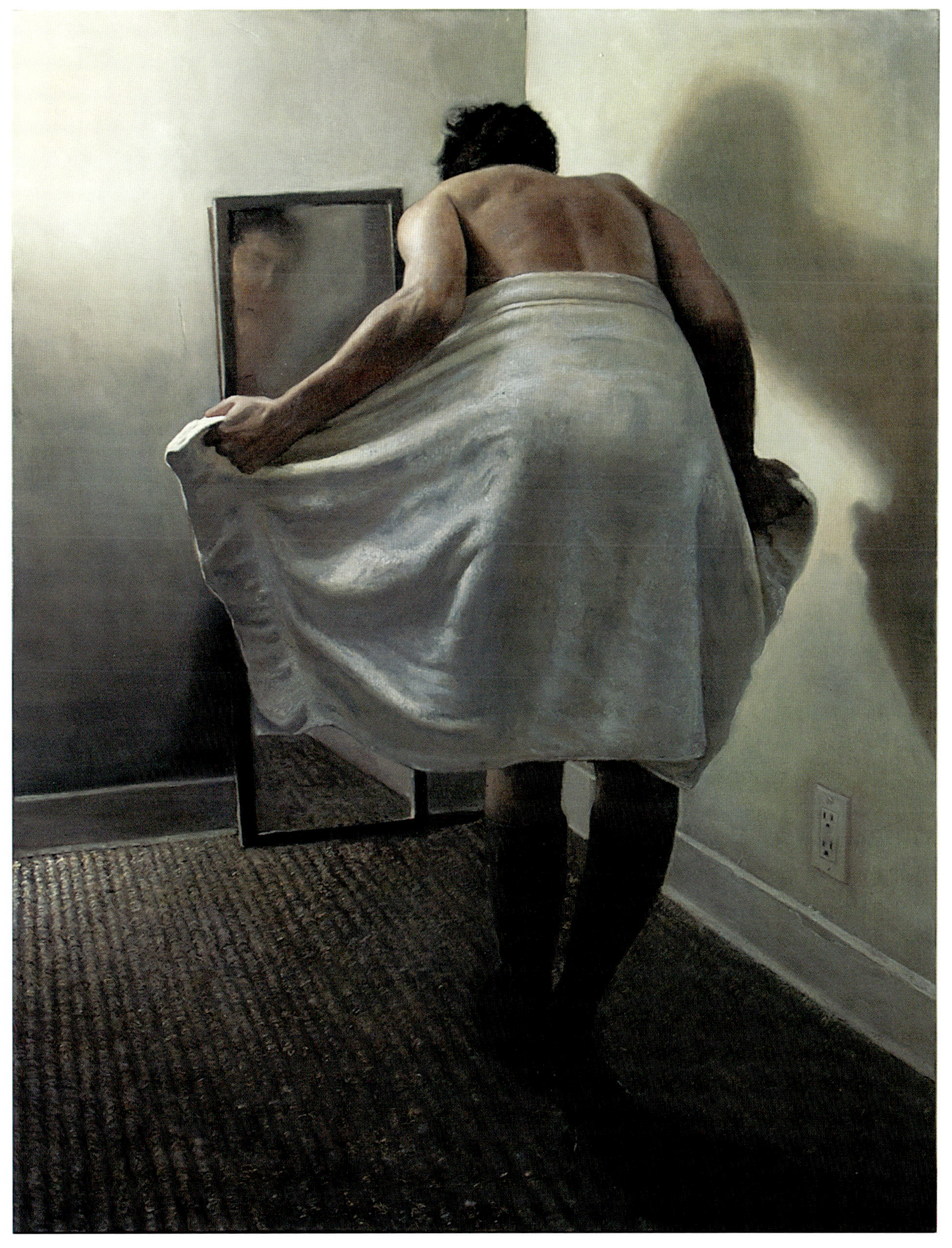

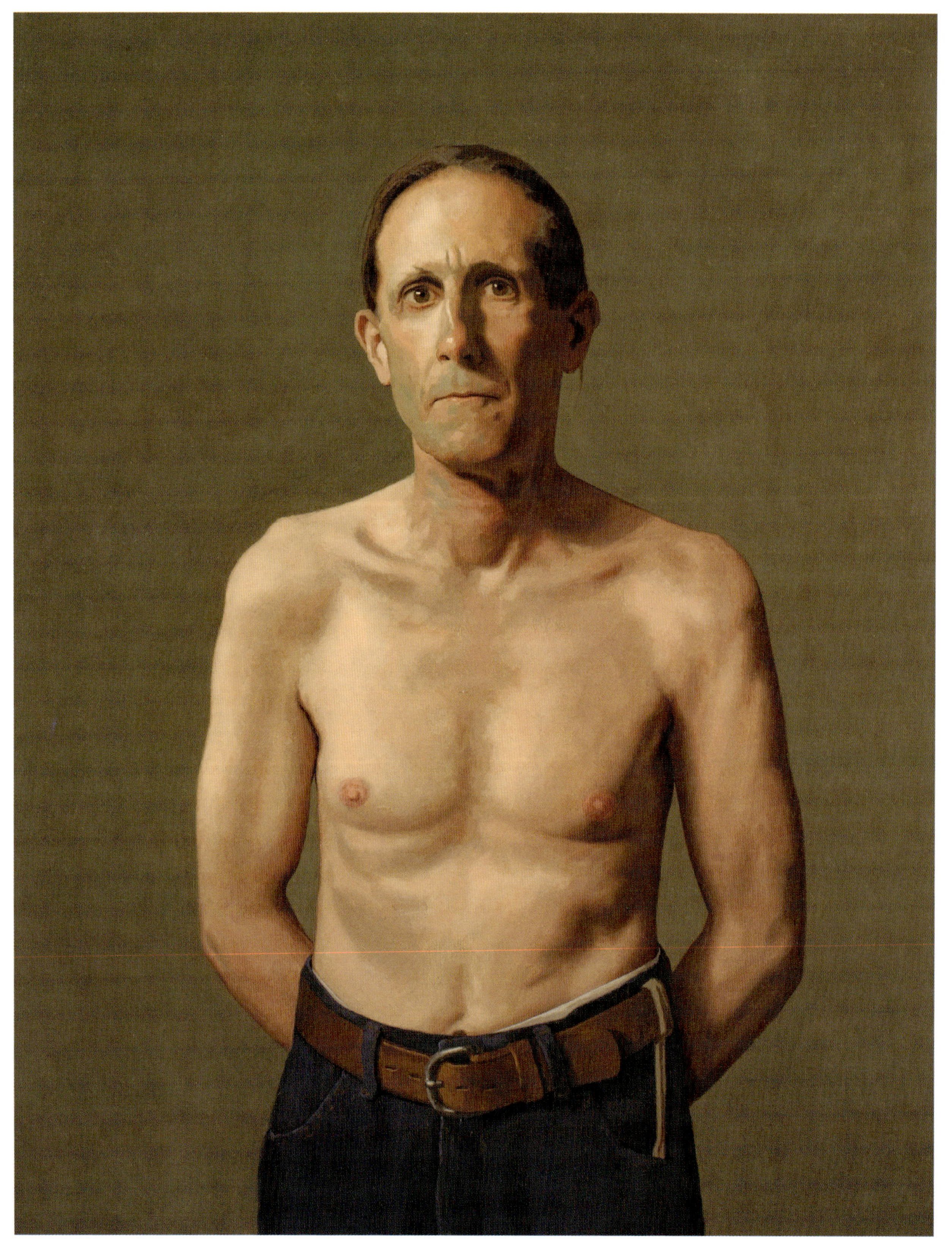

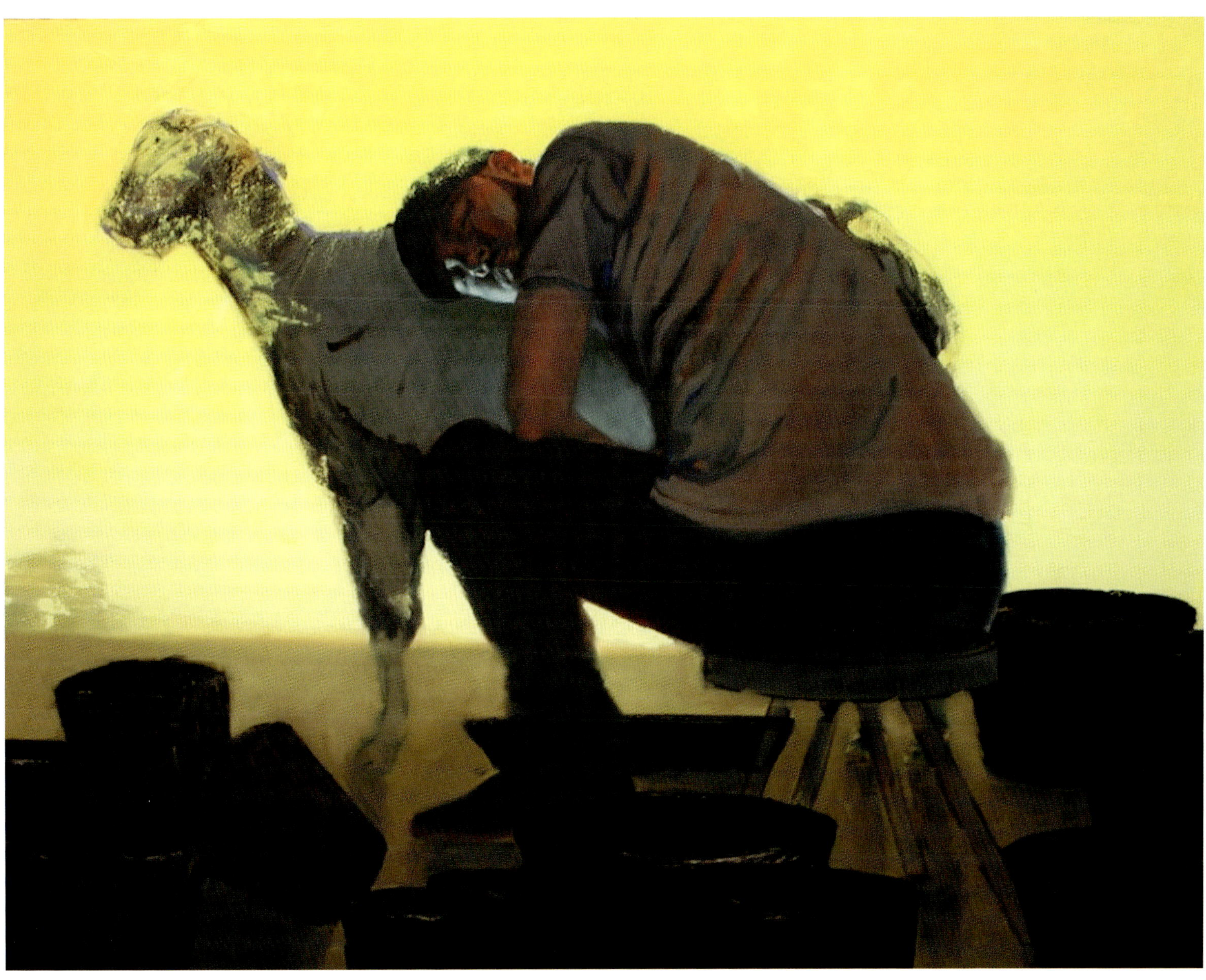

Nicolas V. Sanchez
Search: Top Ten Ways to Milk a Goat, 2012
Oil on canvas
60 x 84 inches

(opposite)
Robert Armetta
Ted, 2006
Oil on linen
36 x 27.5 inches

their virtuoso play of light as it passes through glass and liquid, and the way in which the flow of light is translated into the flow of pigment.

The New Perceptual Realism was part of a pervasive style change that began to develop in avant-garde painting at the end of the 1950s, a change that also included Stain Color Field and Hard Edge abstraction, Minimal painting, Pop art, and Photorealism. Like the New Perceptual Realists, the most interesting and gifted artists of the 1960s, both figurative and abstract, reacted against what they considered a glut of gesture painting, declaring it sloppy and self-indulgent—enervated, outworn, and academic. Artists of the 1960s purged signs of the touch or the hand as signifiers of their subjective, personal experience and creative process. Improvisation, exemplified in visible brushwork, became taboo. In fact, the very appearance of avant-garde art changed. Instead of the dirty, ambiguous, and subjective direct-from-the-self look of 1950s art, 1960s art had a clean, clear, and objective distanced-from-the-self look. The "hot" expressionist look of gesture painting gave way to finished surfacing that was in a word, "cool."

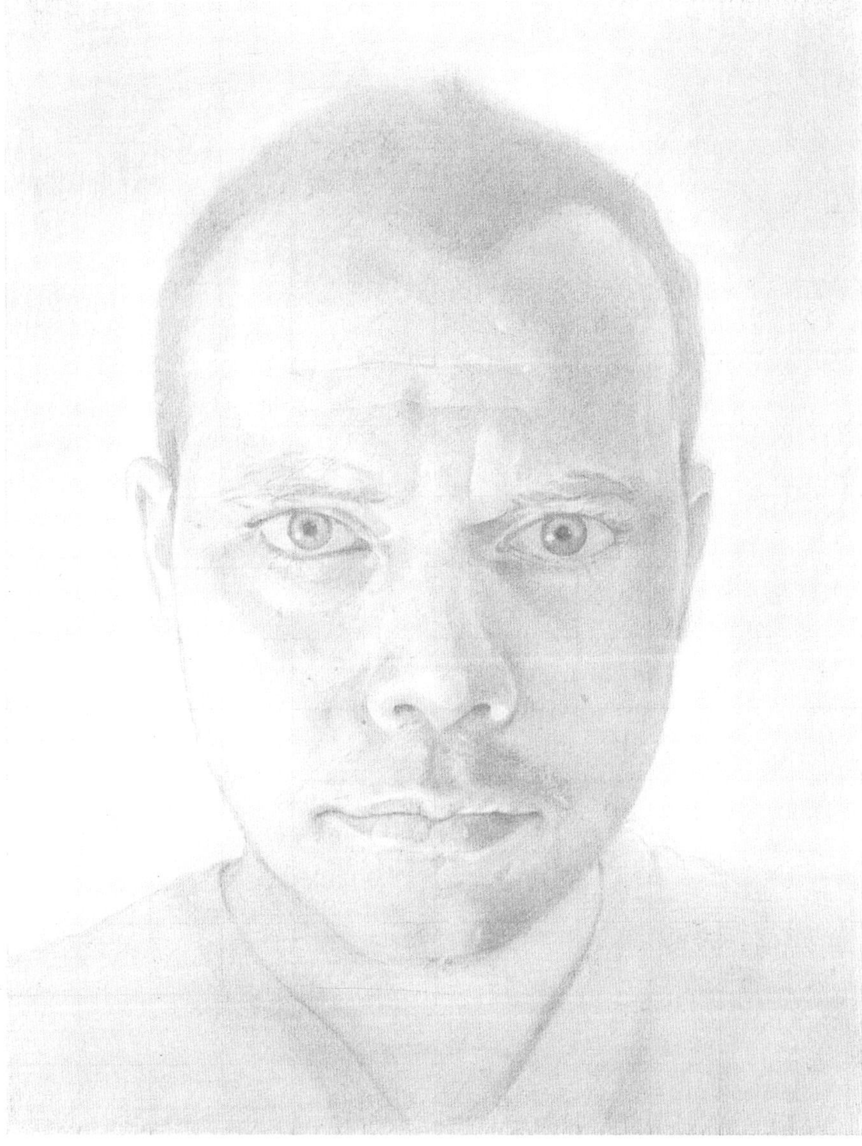

Grayson Ronk
Self, 2012
Graphite on paper
8 x 6 inches

(opposite)
Jesse Stern
Self-Portrait, 2012
Oil on panel
20 x 16 inches

Pop art exploded with a WHAM on the New York art scene in 1962. Its leading artists, in particular Andy Warhol, Roy Lichtenstein, and James Rosenquist copied advertisements, comic strips, billboards, and the like. As Warhol said, they "did images that anybody walking down Broadway could recognize in a split second—comics . . . celebrities . . . refrigerators, Coke bottles—all the great modern things that the Abstract Expressionists tried so hard not to notice at all."[10] It is significant that all the original Pop artists developed their styles independently—each responding to something in the air, as it were. Indeed, only in the 1960s was it possible for artists to even imagine borrowing subjects from popular culture with the intention of creating high art. This would have been inconceivable during the Depression 1930s or wartime '40s, when consumer goods were not affordable by, or available to, the great mass of Americans.

However, the United States had changed radically during the dozen years after World War II. Two revolutions had occurred: one in newly automated production, the second in mass communications, notably the growth of television. The upshot was an affluent post-industrial or consumer society, defined by an abundance of commodities and fueled by the ever-expanding mass media. This led artists to believe that media imagery had so drastically and irrevocably changed ways of seeing the world that it had to be dealt with seriously in art.

Pop art was a novel development not only because its subjects were culled from popular culture, but because it borrowed its techniques from commercial art, namely Lichtenstein's Benday-dotted stenciling, Rosenquist's billboard-like rendering, and Warhol's photomechanical silk screening. As for their subjects, Warhol depicted what he called "products"; Roy Lichtenstein tackled big themes, such as love and war, but for fear of sentimentality, counteracted their human drama ironically by pirating his images from comic strips; and Rosenquist depicted fragments of billboard images, which because they were often unrelated, evoked a mood of strangeness reminiscent of Surrealism. Pop art may be viewed as a critique of consumerism, as exemplified by Rosenquist's famous mural-size *F111* (1965). Named after the warplane, it exposes the interrelationship between the military-industrial complex and consumer society. Lichtenstein referred directly to popular culture in his appropriation of comic-book images. Warhol was a consumerist addict, so enamored of his appropriated commodities that he presented them without modification. This was a radical move aesthetically, since artists, except for Duchamp in his readymades, traditionally had transformed or interpreted their subjects.

Pop art looked new at a time when novelty was prized: It seemed avant-garde in that it muscled into "high" art the subject matter and techniques associated with "low" commercial art; it seemed socially relevant; it seemed aesthetically pertinent in its moment since its clearly defined, unmodulated forms resembled those of Minimal and Hard Edge abstraction. Moreover, Pop art was scandalous, and it riveted art-world attention, engaging both those who reviled it for celebrating vulgar kitsch as well as those who praised it for its insights into contemporary America. Lichtenstein, Rosenquist,

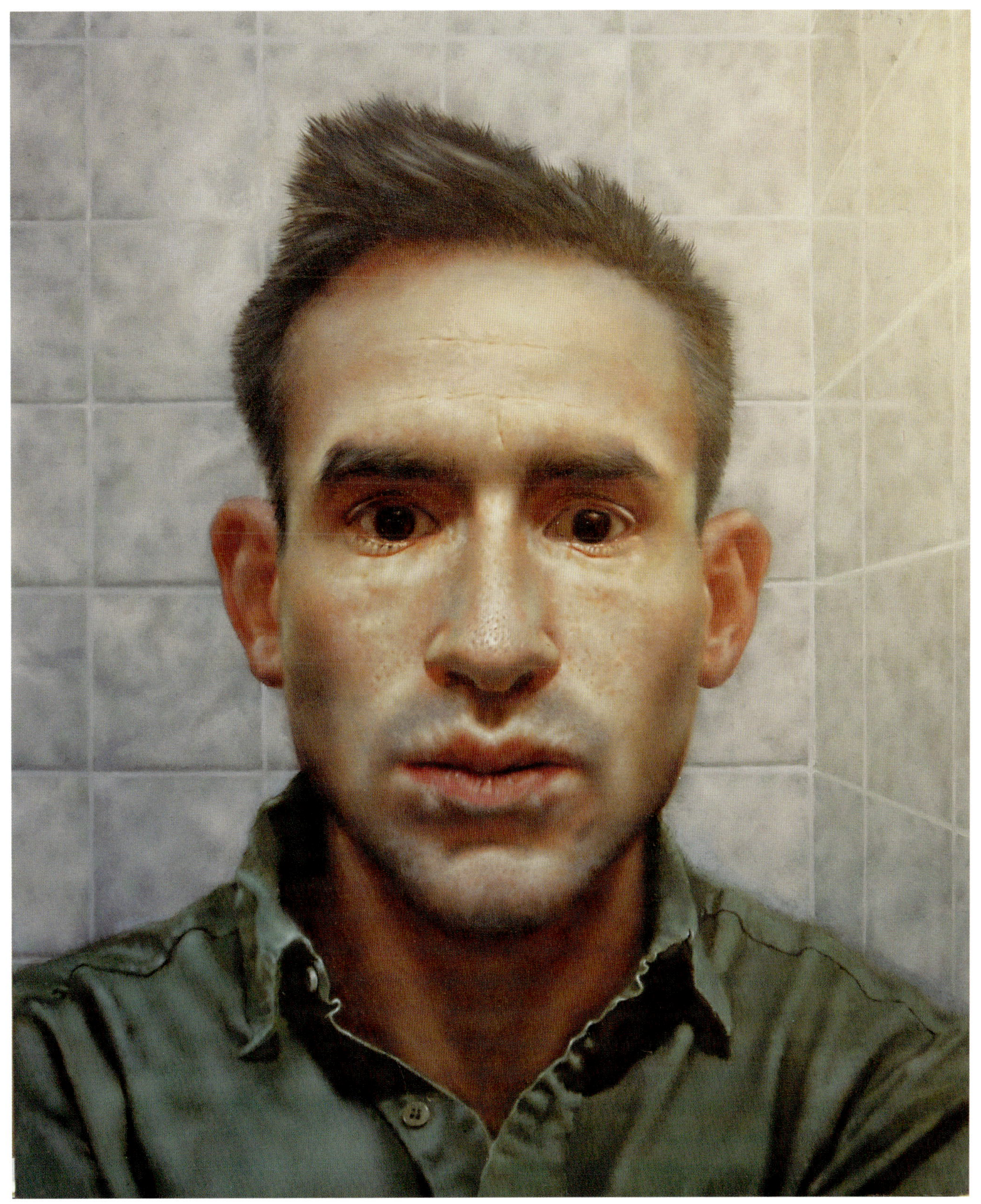

and Warhol have been called "hard-core" Pop artists, because they rendered their images in the depersonalized techniques of commercial art. Not so the Pop art of Claes Oldenburg, which stands apart. Instead of representing his ordinary objects in a deadpan manner, he transformed them imaginatively. In this sense, Oldenburg is a Pop Expressionist, extravagant and fantastic.

Photorealism, notably that of Chuck Close and Malcolm Morley, emerged in the late 1960s, somewhat later than the New Perceptual Realism and Pop art. These artists used painting to replicate photographs, a new approach in realist painting. This practice was especially relevant because photographs had become ubiquitous in modern life. A primary component of our visual reality, they ranged from candid snapshots and home movies to Hollywood films, TV programs and commercials, illustrations, and images and advertisements in magazines and newspapers. It may be that photographs have impacted contemporary perception so pervasively that the very way we see the actual world is mediated thereby. It is no surprise then that artists would use camera images as the subjects of their paintings.

Richard Estes remarked that the Photorealists had "a cold, abstract way of looking at things, without any comment or commitment."[11] In their literalism, they were related to the Pop artists and New Perceptual Realists, if more to the former, since they made images from media images and often used the airbrush, a tool identified with commercial art. As contemporary artists, the Photorealists on the whole preferred to paint subjects associated with our time: urban scenes, brand-new automobiles and motorcycles, diners, drive-ins, and, in the case of Morley, ocean liners. In contrast, Chuck Close painted traditional portrait heads, but nine feet high, a most unconventional size. Indeed, he was the innovator of the "Big Photorealist Painting." Close and Morley stand out among Photorealists in that they have dealt intensively with the relationship between photography and painting. They have emphasized the painted surfaces of the canvas as well as the represented photographic image. Morley cut up color postcards into little squares and then painted each "abstract" square independently. In his huge paintings, Close was able to render photographic images accurately while calling attention to subtle variations of the facture.

To sum up: What was exceptional about avant-garde realist art in the 1960s was not only that it was new but that it encompassed so many engrossing and productive variants—and outstanding artists.

(opposite)
Andrew Lenaghan
Self-Portrait in the Garret, II, 2009
Oil on linen
82 x 60 inches

ANDREW LENAGHAN

My life paintings are homages to actual light; I try to be specific and attentive. My plein air paintings are also meditations on a place. I thrive on the interaction with the actual subject; it focuses my attention and is all around me as I work. I watch the sun pass through a location, see who peoples it, hear the noises, smell the smells. Weather, the light and color of atmospheric conditions, time of day, and how the moving sun dramatically changes what it falls upon are key. I work primarily in midday when the summer sun is more or less from above, or do a morning painting and an afternoon painting, or different versions of the same place in different light. If it rains I'll paint from an underpass, and have even conducted painting campaigns from an automobile to beat the weather. I sometimes photograph locations to remember them as potential painting sites, and cannot help being influenced by how the lens composes them. But I complete paintings on location, from start to finish. I never revise or touch up in the studio.

My paintings generally have three stages. First, I draw the composition in line with paint. I paint on white MDF board, which has a flat and smooth surface; I love the way brush marks show up right away on it. When paintings are more than four feet long, I'll use canvas. My paintings almost always involve perspective, and in larger paintings I use a carpenter's snap line to establish it. I've gradually moved from strict one-point and two-point perspective with perfectly vertical and horizontal levels to a looser, more idiosyncratic approach. Second, I block in colors in thin paint. My palette consists of nine high-intensity oil pigments and white. The paint remains relatively thin, with white elements the most thickly painted. My brushes are nylon—flats for big shapes and blending, liner brushes for finishing passages. I frequently employ a flat nylon brush dragged alongside edges to achieve straight lines. To keep my hand off wet portions I use a maulstick—it's in my left hand most of the time. I use no medium other than an odorless thinner. Third, I move through the painting slowly, observing and rendering detail. The first two stages are fast and the third stage takes longer. The paintings are inevitably a collage of different moments in time wedded together, but I remain true to the motif; in my quest to tell its story faithfully, I don't change what is there. My paintings are in part documentations of my process.

My studio is where I analyze my paintings' progress, and when it's too cold to paint outside I paint interiors. Window light, and the exterior-versus-interior contrast, is a lighting challenge I find intriguing. Interiors have more consistent light than exteriors so require less strategizing. *Self-Portrait in the Garret* was painted in winter, in the small studio at the top of my house. The light is diffused daylight coming through the window I was facing as I looked in a mirror. The canvas depicted in the painting was originally the painting itself, as it appeared in the mirror. But this image proved difficult and this painting within the painting kept looking like a mirror, so I painted it out. But it looked empty. Then I had the inspiration to paint one of my daughter's paintings, which was on the wall in the rear of the room, on the canvas instead. When I put the orange jug of paint in, and the orange dab of paint on the brush, suddenly it all came together. Even my startled expression, painted long before, sort of went along with the emerging narrative—a realist painter painting a self-portrait while painting a child's drawing. It was a

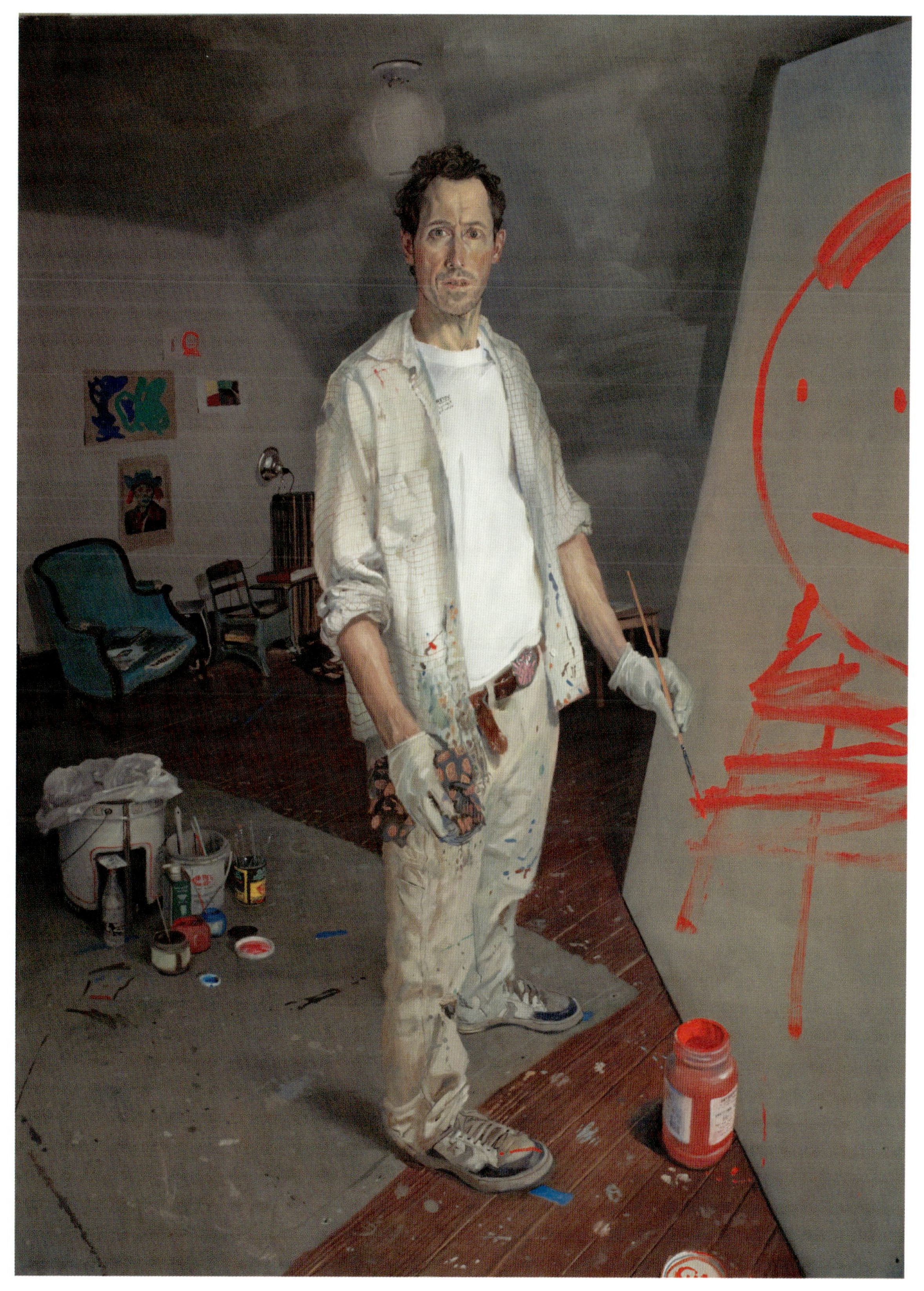

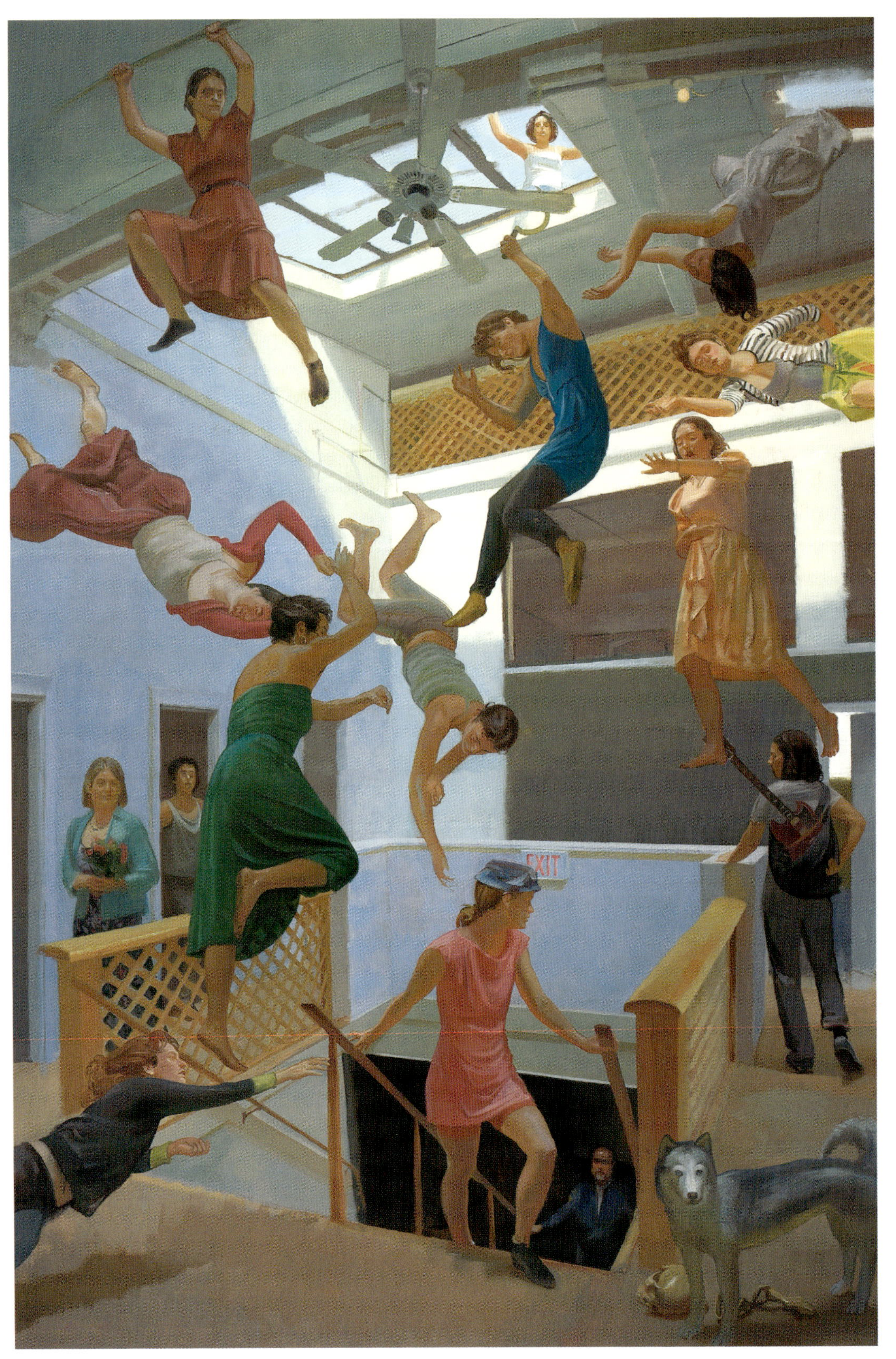
EXIT

great example of a painting teetering on the edge of failure and then suddenly and quickly resolving itself. Very satisfying indeed.

SCOTT NOEL

Drawing and painting as a child involved fitful efforts to invent figures, and much time selecting and transcribing the appearances encoded in photographs of athletes and musicians. Studio classes at Washington University in St. Louis introduced me to the excitement of figure drawing, awakening an obsessional love for working from life that has shaped my painting practice to this day.

My earliest critical categories separated drawing and painting the figure into two inquiries. Drawing the figure was concerned with finding equivalents for the felt experience of mass, movement, volume, and space, all very well described by Kimon Nicolaides in *The Natural Way to Draw* and in the books of Robert Beverly Hale. Painting located the stimulus of the figure in questions of context emphasizing light and atmosphere, which translated into problems of color and tonality. Over time, the tension that seemed to exist between the act of inventive construction in a figure drawing and the problem of responding to an envelope of color light began to resolve itself around the theme of shape organization. I admired the draftsmanship of Degas inordinately. His example of massive, gestural figures distilled to silhouettes in contre-jour dance class compositions persuaded me that shape and volume belonged together in pictorial thought.

My youthful practice of drawing from photographs cultivated a sensitivity to the way shapes map an appearance. But the immersion in gesture, mass, cross contour, plane conception, perspective, and anatomical structure developed in the life class made me critical of photography as a source for figure painting. Degas's blend of observation and invention had the power to illuminate the great figuration of the past, and the evidence was that observational realism only went so far. A painter had to look, remember, invent, and poetically construct to get anywhere near Titian, Velázquez, Ingres, and Delacroix. Charles Hawthorne's teaching narrative of direct painting, using the "spot of color" approach for finding color value relationships in a visual field, has been equally important to the development of my thinking. I like to look, to address appearance empirically, and improvise through the pressure of direct observation toward the pictorial qualities I find meaningful. For me, meaning unfolds in shape-gesture, color ensemble, and scale, whether I am painting the figure or a cityscape.

Blending observation and improvisation tends to simplify a painter's technique, and my painting mechanics are pretty spare. Working from life, I try to come to definitive phrasings in each sitting. When the paintings are large, an alla prima attack is physically challenging. My biggest investment is preparation for addressing the painting. This involves working mostly on lead-primed linen supports that I prepare myself, and the use of large quantities of very good oil paint. I favor what might be called a low-intensity palette: Italian earth, yellow ochre half-burnt, yellow ochre pale, jaune brilliant, flesh ochre, caput mortuum, purple brown, transparent gold ochre, golden green, greenish umber, manganese blue, Payne's gray, blue gray, and lots of flake white. Flake or Cremnitz white is critical for its incomparable mixing qualities and its versatility in achieving opacity and transparency interchangeably in a single passage of painting. Flake white dries fast, can be overpainted almost infinitely, and gets more beautiful over time in any paint film. Flake is also weak in tinting strength, thus a wonderfully delicate instrument in finessing small shifts in tone when painting wet into wet.

Direct improvisational painting for me involves finding a realization of forms wet into wet like Hals or de Kooning. In attacking a painting, a large amount of accurately mixed color has to be put down, and to do this a good trowel-type palette knife is indispensable. The color is carefully mixed in quantity to discover what Edwin Dickinson called the "large spots" that key the tonality of a composition. As my paintings have grown in scale, often over eight or nine feet and up to twenty-two feet, I've taken to using house painter's brushes and brayers to move the paint into place. Once the color notes are truly struck, smaller brushes are deployed to pull out the features of a face, or the windows on a sunlit building from the color mass.

Although I use observation as a stimulus and test for my pictorial judgments, I'm a little uneasy calling myself a realist. I paint appearances to discover something I want to see. I want painting to transform the fabulously contingent occasions of the visible into a durable pictorial rhetoric. My continuously renewed engagement with figure drawing, mostly in pastel, and my passions for contemporary painting keep me marinated in ambition and desire. My pictures seem right to me when the world has become something beautiful and abiding, having passed through the arbitrary and distorting lens of my longing.

RICHARD PHILLIPS

The image that inspired *Large Nude* (1997) was found in a basement store formerly in the East Village, owned by the former child actor and model Michael Gallagher. It specialized in vintage fashion magazines that attracted the elite of fashion world photographers and designers, and provided an invaluable resource of historical imagery and information. I spent hours looking at fashion imagery of the late 1960s and early '70s, and came across an overlooked, small collection of vintage soft-core gentlemen's magazines. Within the pages of an early 1970s magazine I found the images that would inspire *Large Nude* and later *Tongue*. Both had dynamic perspective that placed the viewer in a subordinate position. The pose for *Large Nude* was aggressive, self-possessed, suggesting both taunting display and an outright challenge. The decision to add this image to an upcoming exhibition was immediate, and the process began as soon as I got home.

Home was a studio apartment on East 7th Street between Avenues A and B, and my studio was a twelve-by-twelve-and-a-half-foot front room with a nine-foot ceiling, facing Tompkins Square Park. In order for the perspective to work the painting had to be the maximum possible size. The exact dimensions were deduced by first cropping the magazine page to amplify the dramatic impact of the pose, anticipating my height in relation to it. Clear acetate was placed over the image, gridded into sixteen sections. I made a small charcoal drawing on gray-tone paper corresponding to the correct ratio of the 103 x 78-inch painting. Then I stretched a 16 x 20-inch canvas to focus on the portrait alone, to understand how to approach it while working up on a ladder, with my palette clamped to it. The drawing

(opposite)
Scott Noel
Eurydice, 2012
Oil on canvas
148 x 96 inches

established a tonal scale for reference during the painting of the grisaille. I worked from the darkest darks up to the midtone of the paper, then created a further scale of highlights with white chalk.

While the drawing was in motion the preparations for the canvas began. Choice of linen was important because the coarseness of the weave needed to be enough so that dragged soft edges could be made without too much trouble, yet not so rough that edges and surfaces would have obvious texture. This subtlety was achieved by selecting T-linen from New York Central Art Supply. The sizing, two coats of animal glue sanded in between each coat, made for a taut and compliant surface for the primer, which needed to be of the correct density to fill the weave, as well as the right absorbency to accept the imprimatur and the grisaille. I achieved the right consistency by thinning Fredrick's lead paste with turpentine and adding calcium carbonate. Applying the primer with a large palette knife was easy, but living with the fumes in the middle of winter with the windows open and a fan blowing was not. My bed was a futon in the kitchenette area, next to stacks of drying canvases. Once the primer was dry I took a large house-painting brush and applied the imprimatur. It was tricky to mix the right amount of raw umber oil paint into turpentine with enough medium for it to flow easily on the surface, and also be easily rubbed in without big streaks or blotches.

Once the work was dry, a pencil line grid was drawn corresponding to the divisions on the charcoal drawing and the photograph, and the same steps were followed as in the small study. The small painting allowed me to adjust the mixture of oil, damar varnish, and turpentine to the surface, and to create the palette for the flesh tones, floppy hat, and background. When the surface was ready, the grisaille began. Starting with a small mongoose-hair brush, I used a half-cut version of my stand-oil medium to draw a detailed linear drawing of the whole image, using the grid for references, also painting freely across it. This method differs from standard photorealistic dissociative "filling in of squares," as it allows for a more responsive visual result. Once that dried I began laying in tones of the raw umber grisaille. The process of working from the background to the model's hat, face, and breasts allowed for a fair amount of detail to be articulated from the outset. The painting of her hands, stomach, and thigh required solid drawing and management of close value tonal relationships. The charcoal drawing provided reference points for each section. As with all my grisailles, the painting had to look finished in monochrome.

At the time, my palette was a narrow kitchen table I put on wheels, with a glass surface and four plastic paint buckets across the far edge. My choice of brushes was important to create the uncanny presence of flesh well beyond human scale. I used filbert-shaped natural bristle brushes from the largest to nearly the smallest sizes, to have the greatest versatility of drawing edge to spreadability. For soft details I used a range of mongoose-hair brushes, and for blending, badger-hair brushes. A friend recommended I use the largest brushes for as long as possible until it became necessary to add detail. This economy of brush usage remains an invaluable piece of advice.

Each painting session was planned according to what could be accomplished in a specific time frame, much in the way a fresco painter must plan. So finding edges to "blend out" was quite important. At the time my standard medium was meant to become mostly dry overnight. Quick drying medium allowed for opaque alla prima painting that could be resumed by scumbling over a brushed-out edge. The translucent raw umber grisaille allowed for a thinner and less opaque application of paint when painting the flesh tones out from the shadows. Warmth in the shadows was therefore accomplished easily, and with the drawing as a tonal guide, I focused on subtle color and temperature changes across the form. This raw umber base tone was also important for the background. Warm green was mixed in two versions that were distinctive in their temperature and hue. The darker warm tones were painted first, then the cooler, more opaque tones were laid in wet into wet, blended with a stiffer bristle and then the softer badger brush.

(opposite)
Richard Phillips
Large Nude, 1997
Oil on canvas
103 x 78 inches

In each section of the painting this method of working from dark to light and transparent to opaque gave a visual and textural sensation of form that heightened the colossal presence of the model. Focusing on changes within shapes and across form, the experience of looking is activated as one adjusts the eye from one range of values to another, coupled with the dynamics of the physical density of the paint. The major shapes of the model's form now established in both chromatic and physical terms, control of edges then introduced the quality of local atmospheric perspective. In the background a slight halation of light was pre-painted, anticipating the need to differentiate tonal boundaries. The overall restriction of the palette led up to a culminating moment on the beads using Prussian blue for shadows and manganese blue for the light. This slight addition of color within the context of the warm green background and the siennas and yellows of the flesh completed the painting.

When *Large Nude* finally arrived at the Turner & Runyon Gallery in Dallas, Texas, it was clear the painting would take the central wall, which faced the street. It was viewable through the glass doors day and night. Later I heard that Billy Gibbons, lead guitarist for ZZ Top, had been in to see the show and had responded strongly to the work, saying "I don't know a lot about art but I sure do like this painting. I'm going to go play the Super Bowl this Sunday, but when I get back I want to talk more about *Large Nude.*"

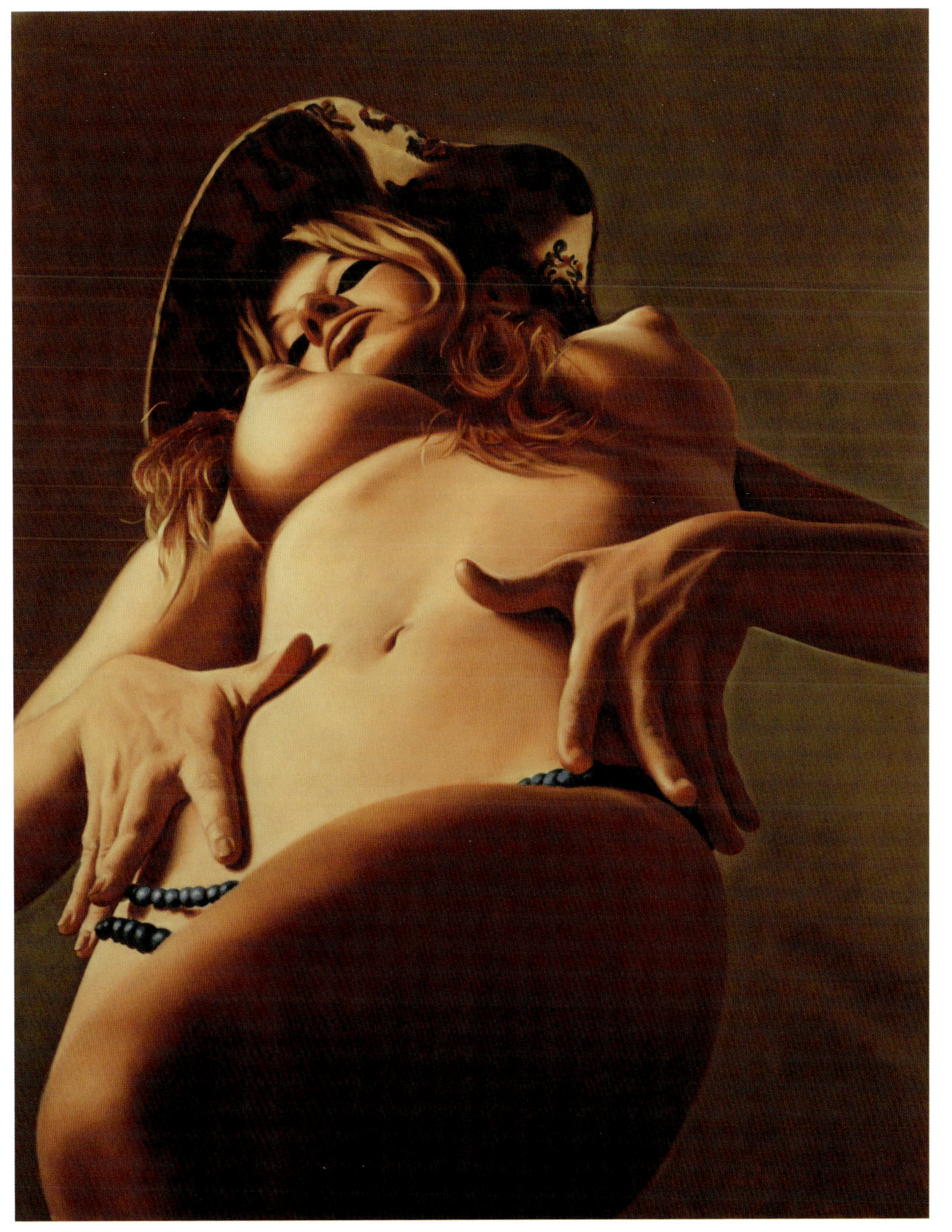

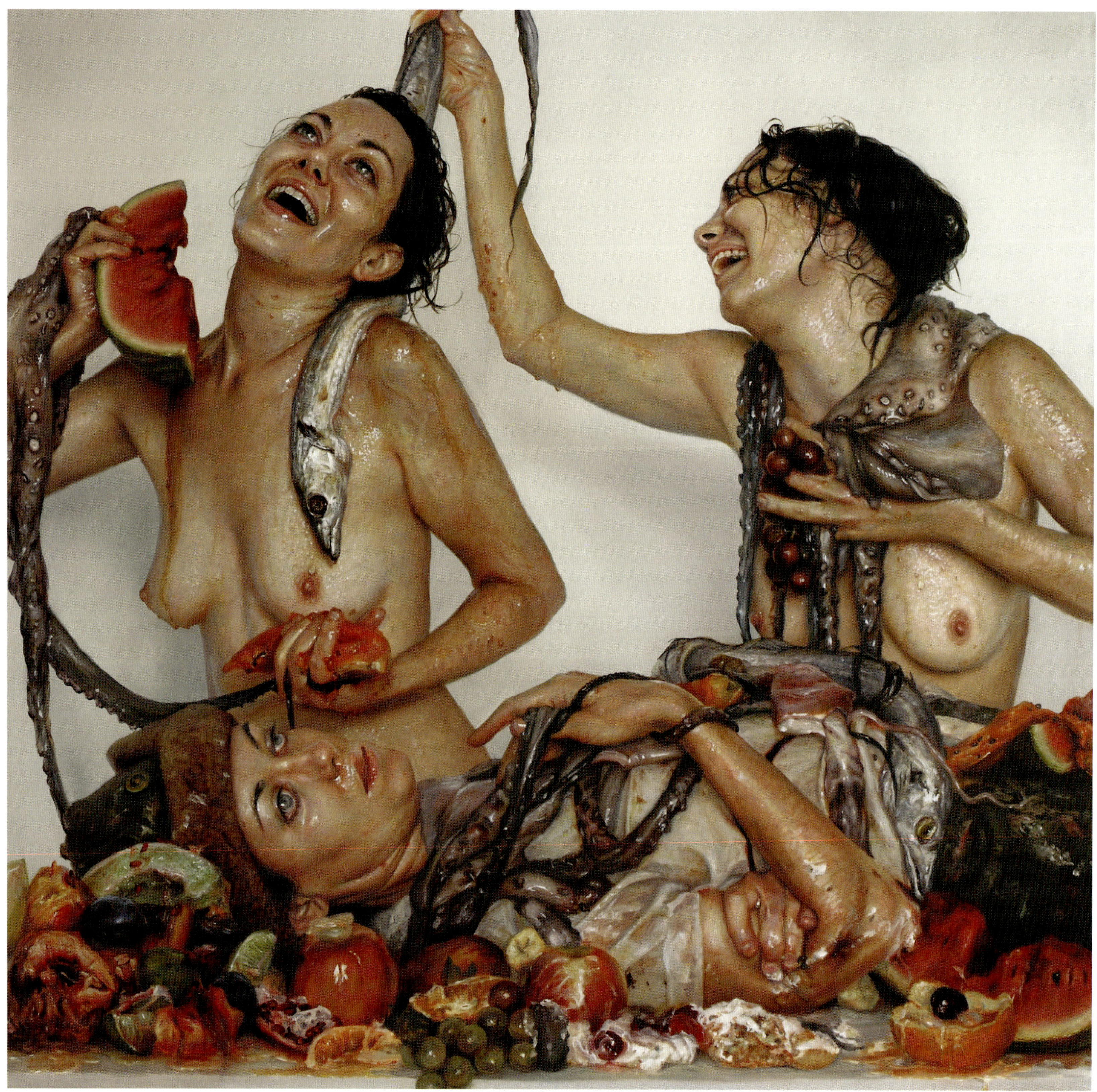

MONSTERS RULE:
THE GROTESQUE IN CONTEMPORARY PAINTING AND SCULPTURE

DAVID EBONY

IMAGES OF DISFIGURATION, ENTROPY, AND THE ABJECT, plus a wide variety of displacement, distortion, and abhorrence, pervade recent art. The anti-form attributes of the Ugly, it would seem, have supplanted the long-revered formal characteristics of Beauty. Indeed, the grotesque has become increasingly prominent in art over the course of the past century. This peculiar manifestation of cultural expression is more admired than ever and often celebrated in the contemporary art world. Practitioners of such works are frequently well regarded critically, handsomely rewarded financially, and periodically dominate the scene. Why is this so? What are the roots and aims of the grotesque? This vast and complex subject presents a formidable challenge to critics and observers in search of a credible analysis and clarification of the phenomenon.

In choosing the grotesque as his theme for SITE Santa Fe 2004, curator Robert Storr explains in the exhibition's catalogue that

> *One might reasonably conclude that the present era is inherently grotesque. I will not dispute that except to note that in Dickensian logic the best of times is always accompanied by the worst, so that there is nothing special in saying that this is a grotesque time, since all periods are lived as a series of contradictions, which, by their nature, foster their own characteristic grotesques.*[1]

For the sake of elucidation and simplicity, the present study below is subjective, as it focuses on only a few select examples of the grotesque in recent Western art, mostly American and British painting and sculpture, and all centered on the figure. I am not attempting here a comprehensive examination of the grotesque in all fields of artistic endeavor. In deference to limitations of space and time, it is necessary to sidestep examples of the grotesque in video, installation, performance, photography, and photo-based works, including those by prominent artists in these areas today, such as Paul McCarthy, Matthew Barney, Nathalie Djurberg, Ashley Bickerton, Kara Walker, Andres Serrano, Joel-Peter Witkin, Wangechi Mutu, and numerous others, whose efforts have generated a great deal of interest—and controversy—over the past decade or more.

BIRTH OF THE GROTESQUE

The grotesque as a genre of contemporary Western art can be traced to the Renaissance. Roman artists of the sixteenth century were fascinated by the monstrous figures decorating the ancient walls of Nero's golden palace, Domus Aurea, the long-buried ruins of which had been recently discovered at the end of the fifteenth century. Leonardo, Raphael, Michelangelo, and others referenced these figures in some of their works. According to art historian Alessandra Zamperini, "The grotesques were called grotesques from their having been discovered in underground grottoes. . . . In a sense, the grotesque was liberating, seemingly eliminating the constraints imposed by the more traditionalist current of Classical theory. The grotesque could be understood though only partially and conditionally as an expression of a liberating anti-classical spirit."[2] In a brilliant amalgam that well illustrates the dichotomy, Italian painter Carlo Maria Mariani, known for his reimagining of Neoclassical art, appropriated Leonardo's drawings of the grotesque. In Mariani's compositions, such as *Monsters of Grace* and *The Source of Anxiety* (both 2008), he superimposes several of Leonardo's deformed faces on androgynous nude figures representing classical ideals of beauty.

The grotesque in recent art is part of the legacy of the angst-ridden postwar period. In the last years of World War II, as Nazi atrocities came to light and atomic bombs exploded over Hiroshima and Nagasaki, human

(opposite)
Monica Cook
Sprouting Potatoes,
2009
Oil on canvas
36 x 36 inches

self-regard was radically altered. Extensively documented in film and photography, humankind's capacity for inhumanity and its unbridled capability for self-annihilation became integral components of everyday reality. Eventually, the era evolved—or devolved—to an age of nihilistic self-immolation as well as, contradictorily, one of great prosperity. The grotesque may be viewed as the work of a cynical generation that sees no future and seeks to sublimate any impulse toward idealistic self-reflection. Or it could be simply a necessary symptom of cultural advancement. Social and cultural development has always depended on those who could thwart convention and challenge the prevailing notions of good taste, beauty, and truth. On one fundamental level, the grotesque aims to provoke, to cause outrage intended to upset the status quo; and its manifestation typically coincides with social upheaval, political strife, and war.

SENSATION

Almost precisely one hundred years ago, on the eve of World War I, the notorious Armory Show in New York instigated a seismic cultural shift. American art audiences encountering for the first time works by European Modernists like Pablo Picasso, Henri Matisse, and Marcel Duchamp were shocked by these artists' apparent disregard for conventions of form, space, and most of the laws of logic that hitherto governed the understanding and depiction of the empirical world. Later, in 1938, as Europe was about to implode once again, Duchamp curated a key Surrealist exhibition at the Galérie Beaux-Arts in Paris, in which his novel installation of works by Salvador Dalí, Max Ernst, and Man Ray was decried by some observers as a hideous grotesquerie. In hindsight, of course, this perceived cultural aberration was nothing compared to the heinous grotesqueries of Nazi atrocities that were then about to unfold.

More recently, an outcry comparable to that accorded the Armory Show was ignited by *Sensation*, an exhibition of contemporary British art that appeared at the Brooklyn Museum in 1997. A number of museum goers were offended by the freakish distortions of the human figure presented by artists such as Jake and Dinos Chapman, Marc Quinn, and Marcus Harvey. Above all, they were incensed over Chris Ofili's reputedly blasphemous work, *The Holy Virgin Mary* (1996), which many deemed grotesque merely from written descriptions of it in the press. City officials briefly shut the exhibition down in response to the protests. A large canvas with a glittery, golden hue, *The Holy Virgin Mary* is actually a rather sweet, Africanized image of the mother of Christ, albeit made of hundreds of fragments of photos taken from pornographic magazines. The canvas frame rests on glitter-covered balls of elephant dung, a number of which are also attached to the surface of the canvas. Some members of the public heard about the use of pornography and shit in a religious image and condemned the work as indecent and an affront to Christian doctrine. Today it seems quite tame, but at its debut it was by far the most incendiary artwork of the day. In its historical context, the work coincides with the rising influence of Christian fundamentalism on secular politics, and anticipates by only a few years the West's ongoing battle with radical Islam.

Sensation also introduced to U.S. art audiences the work of British painter Glenn Brown. Mimicking classical painting techniques, Brown produces startlingly iconoclastic reinterpretations of Rembrandt, Gainsborough, and Fragonard, among other Old Masters. Using slick, nuanced surfaces of serpentine lines in garish colors, Brown demonstrates, in works such as *Death Disco* (2004)—inspired by Rembrandt's 1634 portrait of Saskia as *Flora*—impressive technical dexterity as well as a rather deviant sensibility. His subjects appear to be melting or decomposing. As critic Michael Bracewell has observed: "Just as Basil Hallward's portrait of Dorian Gray, through some perverted act of transubstantiation, reveals the decay and corrupting soul of the sitter while Dorian himself remains eternally ageless and handsome, so in Brown's art we see a fateful contract between painting itself, the history of art and the processes of aesthetic putrefaction."[3] While Brown may be engaged with deconstructing his original models, he manages to maintain a sense of lyrical beauty, almost, but not quite, in traditional terms.

The grotesque as it appears in postwar British figurative art has a long and unique legacy. Graham Sutherland's 1946 *Crucifixion*, a commission for St. Matthew's Church in Northampton, is a seminal work. Here, the elongated, twisted figure of Christ set against a garish field of acid orange and purple references the victims of Nazi concentration camps as well as Matthias Grünewald's Isenheim Altarpiece. Sutherland's work in turn inspired *Painting* (1946), an even more horrific treatment of the figure by his close friend at the time, Francis Bacon. This famous painting, now in the Museum of Modern Art's collection, shows a decapitated man in a business suit under a black umbrella, flanked by carcasses of beef, complete with a teeth-grinding magenta background. At once compelling and repelling, it remains one of the most unnerving images in all of art history.

Lucian Freud, one of Bacon's cohorts in the so-called School of London of the 1950s, produced some of the most audacious portraits and figure studies of recent decades. While keenly observed and painstakingly wrought, Freud's paintings, such as *Leigh Bowery Seated* (1990) and *Benefits Supervisor Resting* (1996), highlight the billowing flesh of the hefty models in an intentionally unseemly manner. Freud's idiosyncratic approach to the human figure has had a broad influence on younger generations of British painters, including Jenny Saville. Born in Cambridge in 1970, Saville often uses herself as a model in large-scale photo-based paintings focused on tight, unflattering close-ups of her face and nude body. Visceral brushwork and exaggerated foreshortening bring her wildly distorted features to life.

Corresponding to Saville's two-dimensional sleight-of-hand, Australian-born, London-based sculptor Ron Mueck employs myriad illusionistic devices in his hyperrealist painted resin sculptures. Like many of the artists under discussion here, Mueck produces works of considerable beauty. Yet his works often cross the line from the alluring to the repugnant primarily by means of a perversely twisted sense of scale. Despite the ostensible realism, works such as the monstrously outsized, seven-foot-tall seated *Big*

(opposite)
Tim Buckley
Vacation, 2013
Oil on canvas
64 x 54 inches

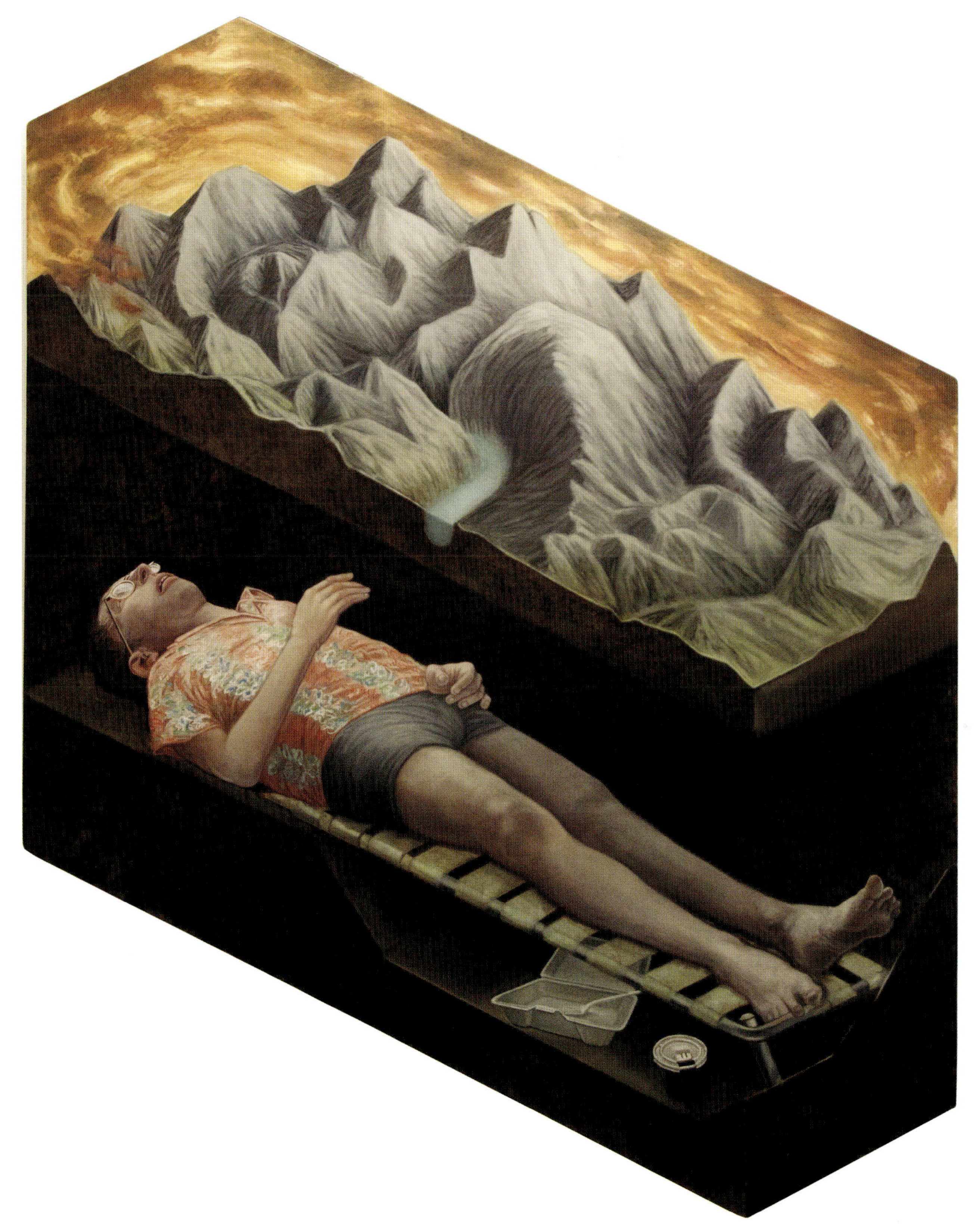

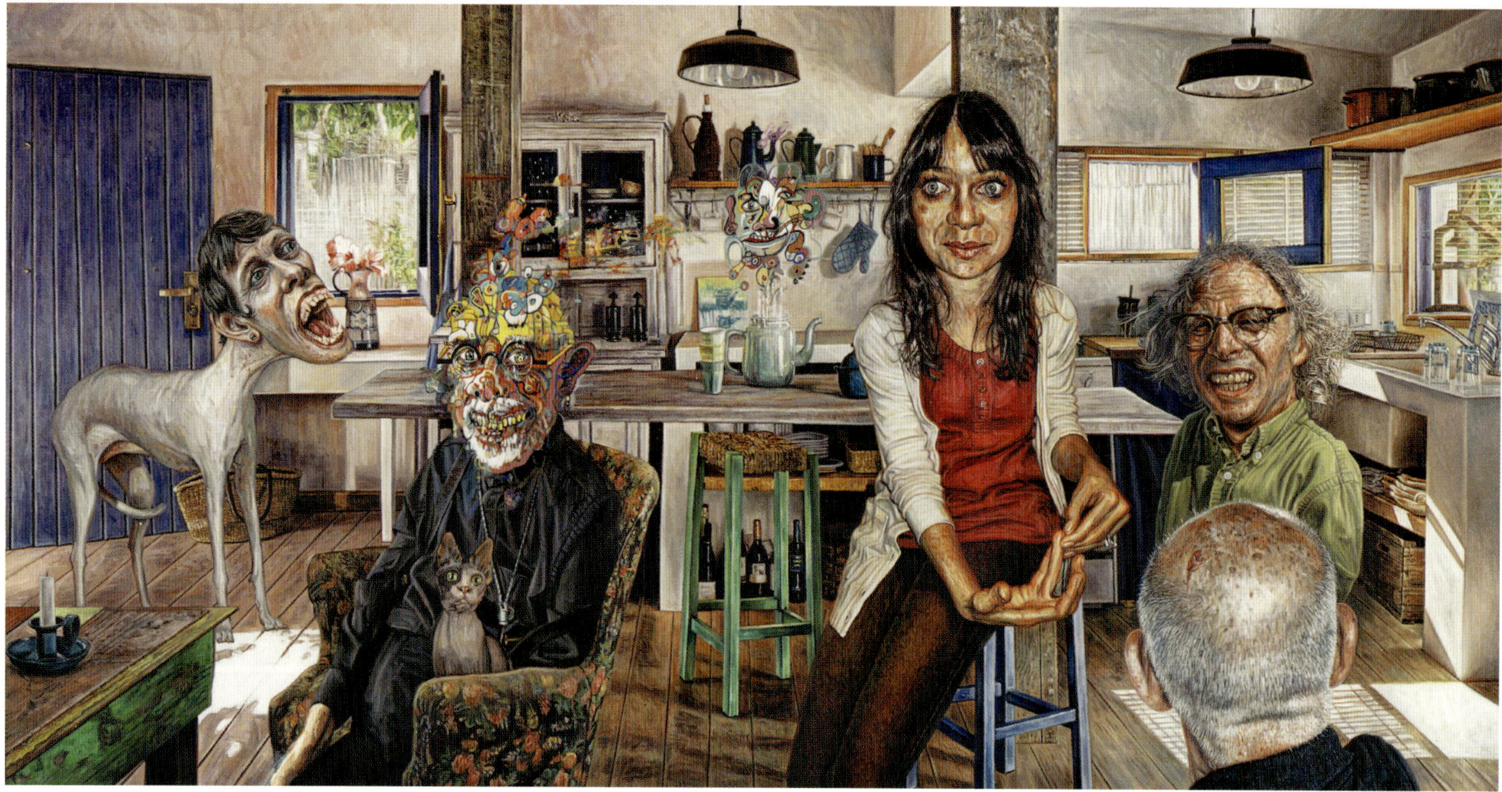

Mark Greenwold
The Banker's Daughter, 2010
Oil on linen
20 x 38 inches

Man (2000), in the collection of the Hirshhorn Museum, and the creepily diminutive *Two Women* (2005), at barely three feet tall, unnerve viewers like the stuff of nightmares.

GROTESQUE AMÉRICAIN

Best known for his bitingly satirical depiction of American society in the 1930s and '40s, painter Paul Cadmus (1904–1999) often advised artists to "exaggerate or no one will notice." Exaggeration is certainly an understatement with regard to key Cadmus works such as *The Fleet's In!* (1934), in the Navy Art Collection, and *The Seven Deadly Sins* (1945–49), in the Metropolitan Museum of Art's collection. In these paintings, he uses classical techniques to describe the figure in repulsive physical terms in order to condemn America's hypocritical social constructs and the misguided moral codes of the period.

Even more excessive in his exploration of the grotesque, Ivan Albright (1897–1983) painted the figure in minute detail, exaggerating to an extreme degree every flaw and wrinkle. He chose to highlight any abnormality his subjects might possess. Correlating with earlier works by German Expressionists like Otto Dix and George Grosz, Albright uses lurid colors and harsh lighting to create horrific images of decay and dissolution, such as *The Farmer's Kitchen* (1933–34), in the Smithsonian American Art Museum, and *Picture of Dorian Gray* (1943–44), in the Art Institute of Chicago. The latter shows a tall, standing figure, whose decrepitude has apparently evolved into a putrefied state of being. The frightening image drew significant public attention to Albright's work after it appeared in the 1945 MGM movie of the Oscar Wilde story directed by Albert Lewin, who had commissioned the painting.

TODAY'S GROTESQUE

One could make a case that the grotesque in contemporary American art begins with Willem de Kooning (1904–97). Specifically, his notorious Woman series of 1952–53 paintings scandalized the public and press due not only to the fact that these figurative works signaled a stunning departure from Abstract Expressionist doctrine, but also because of the savagery of the images as well as their execution. Misogynist accusations aside, in each of these paintings, the violence of the brushwork intensifies the overall ferocity of the picture. The advent of Pop art in the early 1950s ushered in a new wave of the grotesque. Andy Warhol led the way with his Death and Disaster series of the early 1960s. Silkscreen paintings of car-crash victims in *Saturday Disaster* (1964), in the Rose Art Museum, and *Suicide* (1963), from the Dia Art Foundation collection, were intended to shock, and they did.

Cartoon imagery proved to be fruitful source material for a number of artists in the 1960s, who gleefully introduced a new and appalling nadir of taste to art audiences. The sinuous drawing style and attendant humor-driven script characteristic of popular cartoons has had a lasting impact on fine art, and continues to gain currency today. Some artists, such as R. Crumb and Robert Williams, directly appropriate cartoon-style figuration as well as the format of captions as commentary on the images. Others have taken great liberties with the genre. Peter Saul, for instance, has developed since the early 1960s a uniquely acerbic brand of cartoon imagery. The San Francisco–born artist parodied Abstract Expressionism in his early paintings, and later confronted de Kooning directly in his work. Saul's *Woman with Bicycle* (1976) reimagines and redefines de Kooning's "Woman," transforming the figure into a super-slick, glossy version of herself by means of a refined painting technique that eschews all traces of Ab Ex gesturalism and texture. In an interview with Robert Storr, Saul illuminates his tongue-in-cheek attitude toward Abstract Expressionism:

> *Lately, I have become more broad-minded and more interested in abstract painting. And particularly found out that, much to my absolute amazement, I like de Kooning's later painting when he's losing his brain much better than the earlier famous paintings. I have a feeling that Abstract Expressionism was caused by a certain nervousness that came about because of World War II. I think everybody was drinking coffee and smoking, and it made everyone so jittery they couldn't paint buttons and noses and things, you know; they just couldn't do it. Their patience was shot by the war.*[4]

Cartoon imagery has inspired a younger generation of American artists, including George Condo, Elliott Green, Thomas Woodruff, and Jon Pylypchuk, whose works are often at home in the realm of the grotesque. Condo obsessively deconstructs and reconstitutes the late works of Picasso in a jarring process of transmogrification, while Green and Woodruff, with a greater emphasis on drawing, create mythic scenes. Frequently these settings are populated by freakish beings, part-human, part-animal, arrested in a state of metamorphosis. Using collage techniques, hand-scrawled texts in balloon-like cartoon captions, and a painterly approach to the canvas, Pylypchuk anthropomorphizes small furry creatures who spout out droll witticisms and, more often, banal absurdities. In the more traditional visual idiom of realism, painter Mark Greenwold populates his canvases with family and friends. But these would-be homey presences morph into macabre characters; they appear to play out nightmarish dramas in familiar, carefully defined domestic interiors. In one recent work, *The Banker's Daughter* (2010), a group of figures gathers in an ordinary suburban kitchen. A ferocious dog on the left bears a growling human head. To the right, Greenwold's friend, the artist Chuck Close, sits for a portrait. His barely discernable features, however, disintegrate into minute abstract shapes in garish colors and seem to dissolve into thin air.

Corresponding to the discordant imagery in works by provocateurs such as John Currin and Lisa Yuskavage, Dana Schutz produces outlandish figure studies that often appear as portraits, except that the features seem to implode or explode before one's eyes. *Face Eater* (2004), for instance, is a horrific image showing a head with a huge mouth apparently in the act of devouring its own eyes, ears, and tongue. Schutz also alludes to art-historical precedents in works such as *Presentation* (2005), in the Museum of Modern Art's collection, ostensibly depicting an autopsy session with medical students crowded around a corpse. The imposing canvas recalls Rembrandt's *The Anatomy Lesson of Dr. Nicolaes Tulp* (1632) but is executed in a style reminiscent of James Ensor.

The grotesque also thrives in avant-garde sculpture. In his use of unorthodox materials as well as novel formal strategies, the Canadian-born David Altmejd pushes the boundaries of what defines the figure and its meaning in relationship to the environment. His work often evokes a natural-history museum diorama gone awry. Altmejd's outlandish, large-scale humanoids made of wood, epoxy, clay, and horsehair merge with sprawling installations that suggest haunted landscapes and urban environments. *The Index*, for example, a site-specific work that filled the Canadian Pavilion at the 2007 Venice Biennale, contained mirrored walls and sculptures of disconcerting figures and animals that immersed viewers in an infinite, otherworldly space. Sculptors Huma Bhabha, Thomas Houseago, and Matthew Monahan gravitate toward slightly more conventional mediums of bronze and plaster, and approach their works in terms of discrete objects. But the results of their individualistic experiments with the figure are equally disquieting. Houseago aims for a heroic scale and feeling in large-scale pieces like *Baby* (2010). Poised like a football player ready to spring into action, this nearly nine-foot-tall phantom in white resin has a stylized skull for a face and one arm clad in what looks like protective armor. This "baby" is far more threatening than cuddly. All three of these artists share a strategy perhaps best described by Monahan in a recent lecture:

> *To make the body exist at all in art, it has to be subjected to a series of shocks and fits, failures, exaggerations, and bodily mortifications. And its only sign of life is sad and broken—unable to fire its arrow—it does not matter: at least we have tried. It is about the discovery of our hands—the simple contact of skin and paper that emerges from a subterranean, muddled story of catastrophes and fusions.*[5]

Monahan's statement implies a kind of resolution, or at least a temporary truce with the abject that lies in the creative act itself. Dispelling the notion that the grotesque stems from a pessimistic view of humanity or a nihilistic take on the world and its prospects, these comments proffer the realization that in the process of reconceiving the figure one might discover the promise of humanity's revitalization. This way of thinking would make the grotesqueries of everyday life seem far less offensive.

TRENTON DOYLE HANCOCK

"The Mound" is not your average avatar. He is black. He is white. He is happy. He is not happy. He is beaten down. He is mythology and methodology.

I've used the Mound as the central figure in my work for years. His character developed as a result of my introspective search for something essential in figurative representation. This generated a personal analysis on race and religion and an awareness of universal connections. I have always sought solutions to visual problems using my innate understanding of my own body, its limitations, and its proportions. By examining these, I was able to internalize and then broadcast my findings visually through painting. To have a body is an irreducible fact of existence, and our inhabitance of this body is the factor that allows us to empathize with others. It is a call to service to deal with the figure and the issues that sculpt our perception of the self, most notably the invisible gazes that construct identity. The Mound acts as a test subject in examining these gazes.

Before I had a deep understanding of the histories of art, I knew I wanted my artistic legacy to somehow be defined through the characters that I created. Early on I thought this would be done solely by means of the comic book or the graphic novel, but these modes of making proved incapable of encompassing my varied influences and concerns. Tales of heroes from comics, biblical parables, Greek mythology, and film fueled my desire to contribute to the landscape of figuration. The common thread throughout all these modes of expression was a need to propel a figure (a mobile surrogate of the self) through a narrative or psychological space. The ordering of figure and ground, action and consequence, was appealing to me, and the prospect of creating a character that was relevant to it exciting. I sought the power, flexibility, and agency that the human form had through pictures.

Eventually I created many new humanoid creatures all bound by a narrative, and at the center of my super-narrative was the Mound. This creature is pathetic yet proud, one forged out of the materials of existing myths. His species is generally described as plump, jovial, and ignorant, with a body covered in oscillating black-and-white fur bands, interrupted by pink fleshy sores. The Mound didn't start out looking this way, but evolved from a general humanoid template into his current mound shape. I created him in the year 1996, the result of a year's worth of intense introspection and formal investigations. While I was an undergraduate at East Texas State University, my aspirations to create an essential form guided my brush to paint figuratively. I thought a lot about da Vinci's Vitruvian Man and its depiction of a perfect human geometry. This classic representation of the body was entirely unrepresentative of any real state of being, so I decided to pluck the arms and legs from my figures, leaving them as "bowling pin" forms. These vulnerable wobbly figures felt relatable but still were merely skeletons upon which to drape skins. Projecting human qualities onto objects and ideas gave me a new understanding of the possibilities of figuration.

While searching for appropriate cosmetic traits for the Mound, I learned of the teachings of W. E. B. Dubois and his theory of double consciousness. Dubois argues that Blackness in America is characterized by a schism in vision. One strain of consciousness understands the world through an African eye, another through a Eurocentric eye, creating two overlapping and competing viewpoints within the same head. At the time it was comforting to hear this theory, because it was a confirmation of how I felt as a black man who both celebrated and was critical of Western, particularly American, culture. When I merged this idea with my existing designs, the Mound appropriately developed the black-and-white furry bands that cover its body.

Over time, I have come to very specific breakdowns of what the Mound's stripes might stand for. It's difficult to speak about his coloration without mentioning my inheritance of a Christian spirituality, a colonial Western model I remain hyper-critical of, yet am indebted to, having been raised on Southern Baptist ritual. The white stripes can suggest the Western order imposed through Christianity. The black stripes are like black skin and all it entails. My grandmother's favorite Bible verse, Isaiah 53: 5, indicates another reading: "But He was wounded for our transgressions, He was bruised for our iniquities: the chastisement of our peace was upon Him; and with His stripes we are healed." Of course, the biblical stripes refer to the evidence of Christ's flagellation and His commitment to absorbing the physical and emotional pain of humanity. For the Black American community, Christ was an untouchable, incorruptible symbol of hope in an otherwise hopeless condition. An ideology centered around a man who was persecuted, whipped, and tortured to the death was very appealing and relatable to a group of people who endured similar degradations on a daily basis. Not only that, but there was the promise of retribution and eternal rewards for a life of suffering. Ultimately the Christian church became a meeting place for black people to codify and exchange ideas among themselves. A new hybrid language was invented, and at its heart were community, symbolic refuge—and sometimes actual refuge.

My Mound character could be a kind of tortured Christ figure, but it's of no interest to me to adapt Christian tales for the purposes of moral propaganda. However, I am interested in continuing the legacy of the Christ form, or hero, as depicted in Western art. Perhaps this lends another reading of the black-and-white bands of the Mound. The Mound has helped me to connect my history as a junior deacon in the Baptist and Pentecostal faith with my study of countless images of Christ (Grünewald's being my favorite) peppering every other page of my art history books. The Mound has helped me to examine other aspects of culture and the self from a stable, safe vantage point.

The term "mound" describes not only the genesis of the characters of my painting mythology but also how the paintings are conceived and ultimately constructed—their methodology.

> MOUND definition
> *noun; a rounded mass projecting above a surface*
> *verb; heap up into a rounded pile; to pile (up)*

My paintings usually take form following an accumulation or a buildup of textual and physical material. These source materials range from researched themes, scenes from films and my dreams, passages from writings and poetry, scavenged bits from artworks (past and present, mine and others'), and drawn/painted notations. Other materials are of a physical nature such as paint, scraps of paper

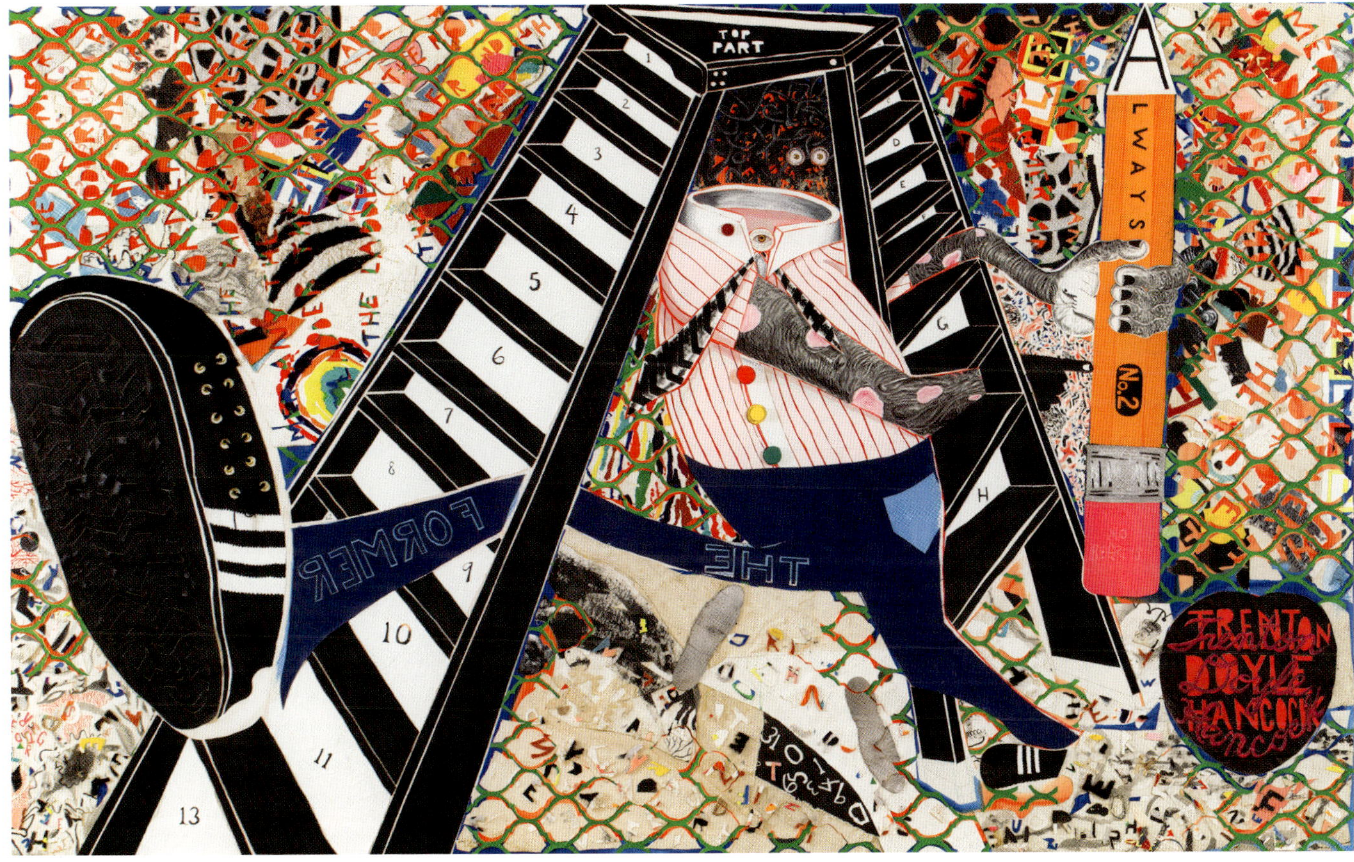

Trenton Doyle Hancock
The Former and the Ladder or Ascension and a Cinchin', 2012
Acrylic, mixed media on canvas
84 x 132 x 3 inches

and canvas, Odor Eaters, napkins, hair, fortune cookies, dirt, etc. The accumulation, piling, and shelving of all of these reference materials falls under the heading of "mounding," my way of organizing and keeping track of materials. The units within any given mound are grouped according to some defining characteristic. As similar materials are lumped together, a kind of living organism starts to form. After the mound absorbs a certain number of units it begins to feel alive. It starts to undulate with potential. I don't always immediately know how the materials in the mound will be used in a painting, and let the mound mature for weeks and sometimes years. My understanding of a material's transformative function isn't always readily apparent, and there is usually a considerable wait time before I can use them with any amount of efficiency. My studio is like a computer database, but instead of compressing information into micro-folders, the information remains visible and exposed, spilling out into the working space. Sometimes the boundaries of these mounds are compromised by the contents of another mound. In these instances I sometimes make visual connections between disparate materials, and transfer that relationship directly to the painting process. In other cases, the mound itself becomes the art and there is no need to transform it.

I paint mounds even when I'm not trying to. It's simply how I organize. Looking back over my oeuvre, I notice many of my paintings involve heaps of information, oftentimes forming in the middle of the canvas, another application of "mounding." I'm drawn to conical forms apexing with a rounded arch, and exhibiting a certain stubborn gravity. This is habitual and intuitive. My 2012 painting *The Former and the Ladder or Ascension and a Cinchin'* is a slight variation, culminating at the center top of the work with the last rung of a ladder. The ladder form assumes the place of the mound, functioning as the painting's central architecture. I'm not sure why centrality and an almost bilateral symmetry fascinates me so much. Perhaps I internalized this compositional strategy after seeing Richard Dreyfuss playing with his potatoes in *Close Encounters of the Third Kind*. Or maybe I'm trying to build my own version of Brueghel's *Tower of Babel*. Maybe, just maybe, I wasn't breast fed long enough. I'm not sure.

It's a curious thing to repeatedly answer the call to produce form. It's even more curious when that seemingly stable form shifts its permutations right before my eyes from painting to painting. Figuration in painting is a result of a need to locate ourselves in a continuum and pinpoint existential coordinates. For me, the Mound fulfills this need in a very basic way, providing a platform for future cultural and personal analysis and discovery.

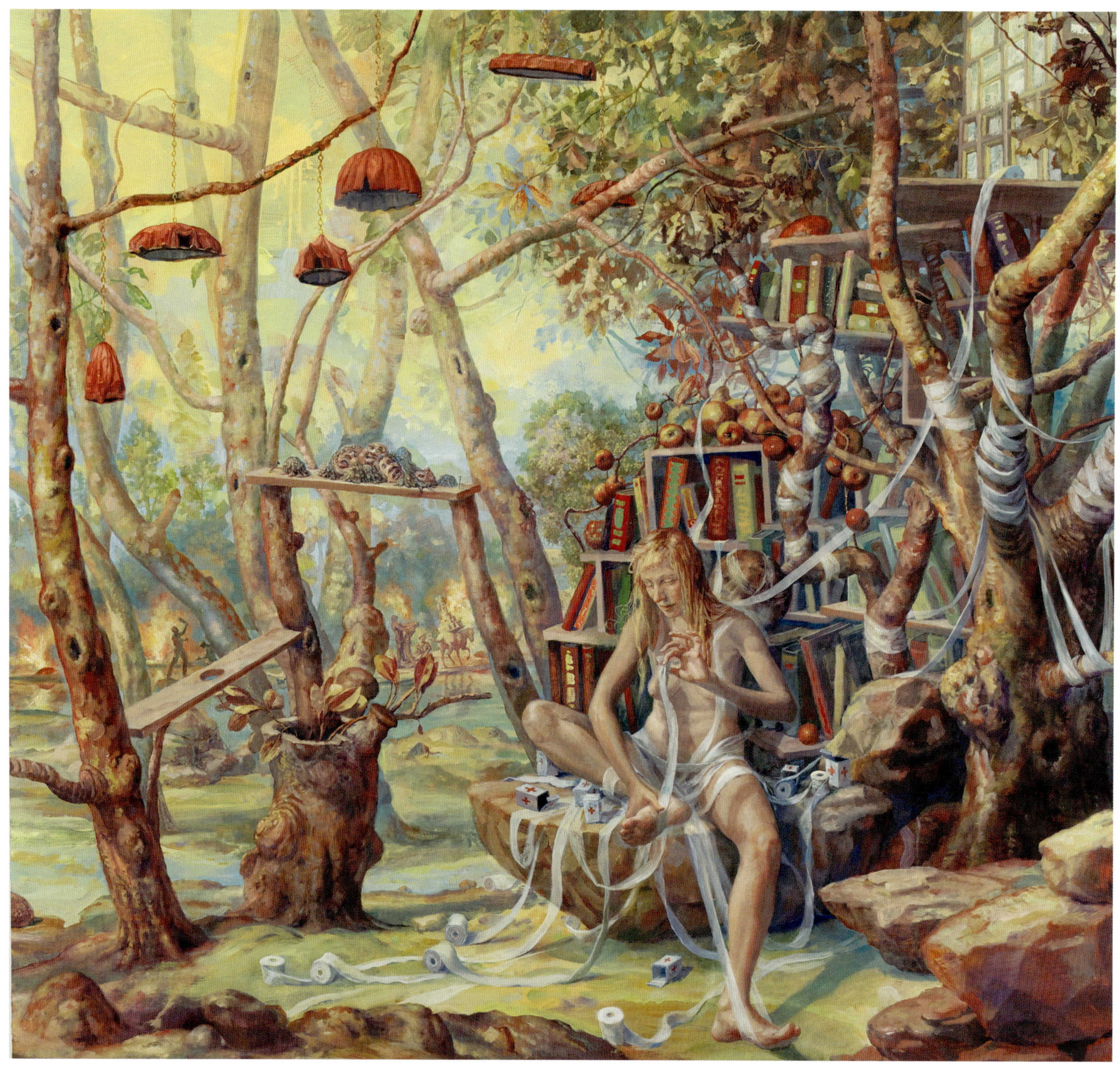

LOOKING BACK AT THE MALE GAZE

JULIE HEFFERNAN

WHY THERE ARE NO NUDES IN THE LASCAUX CAVES we can never know, but surely, given the evidence of hundreds of rooms in museums all over the world, there are few subjects in art more enduring or compelling than the female nude. Be it narcissism, horniness, mother desire—we just can't stop looking at her. As a Catholic girl on the hetero end of the spectrum, I never saw one until I found a *Playboy* magazine under my brother's bed, but I still remember those large, enthralling breasts of Tiffany. I don't recall feeling ashamed (this was before "gaylord" became a taunt in the schoolyard): I just loved those breasts.

The 1980s came along and I became a serious painter, but by that point, it wasn't okay to paint breasts anymore. Women were beginning to actively protest their minority status in the art world, notably in the actions of feminist groups like the Guerrilla Girls and through Linda Nochlin's inquiring essay, "Why Have There Been No Great Women Artists?," which questioned the historical strictures on art education for women. And Laura Mulvey's 1975 groundbreaking essay about the male gaze in film, "Visual Pleasure and Narrative Cinema," questioned the very act of looking at the nude, such that few artists took figure painting seriously anymore. Mulvey's essay elucidated how point of view, privileged screen space, and eroticized organization of film elements presented women for voyeuristic pleasure. And I, watching Marilyn Monroe's photophilic ability to portray a dumb blonde (and a witty satirist) in *Gentlemen Prefer Blondes*, discovered via Mulvey's essay my own complicity in a voyeurism Freud had gendered as intrinsically masculine because it involves active viewing. "The masculinization of the look responded to the feminization of spectacle,"[1] as Mulvey later put it. After reading her essay I recall feeling guilty for my unwitting implication in a process damaging to women—as well as for the keen visual pleasure I had taken in paintings like Titian's *Europa* (1562) or Rubens's *Abduction of the Daughters of Leucippus* (1618). Like Tiffany, those images were offering me something quite different, which Mulvey wasn't addressing.

Titian, Rubens, and Bonnard certainly didn't lay claim to female experience, but they did provide a partial view of what being female might be about. Their female figures did not primarily exist, to my mind, for anyone's voyeuristic pleasure, but rather for the access they allowed to greater depth of experience, as in paintings like Titian's *Mary Magdalene* paintings (1533, 1565). This painting tells a story about suffering and how it dis-integrates us, captured in the way Magdalene's hair transforms into consuming fire. We experience the pain of her suffering as we locate ourselves in the realm of the imagination and take on her identity. This fundamental empathic phenomenon is central to a good narrative—the assumption of the body of another. Empathy is, at its core, imagination. In painting this occurs through the tactile imagination, the ability to feel through our eyeballs.

Until the end of the nineteenth century, societal strictures forbade women to paint the nude. In rare instances Renaissance women artists like Artemisia Gentileschi developed important artistic reputations, although often through the aid of a male relative. Artemisia's *Judith Beheading Holofernes* (1599) is one of the most tragic of Judiths: an activated, emotionally wrought character, unlike Cranach's cooler, more distant version. And no wonder, since Artemisia was herself publicly objectified as a curiosity because she dared to participate in the prosecution of her rapist.

My very first drawings were of Breck girls, and I loved painting the nude in school. But I later found my way around the impasse elucidated by Mulvey in paintings I made of fruits with interior images, which I called "self-portraits" since they were reflections of my interior self. I returned to the nude after my own body malfunctioned. An ectopic pregnancy had left a bandage on my groin and suddenly I was catapulted into the very center of

(opposite)
Julie Heffernan
Self-Portrait Dressing Wounds, 2012
Oil on canvas
67 x 70 inches

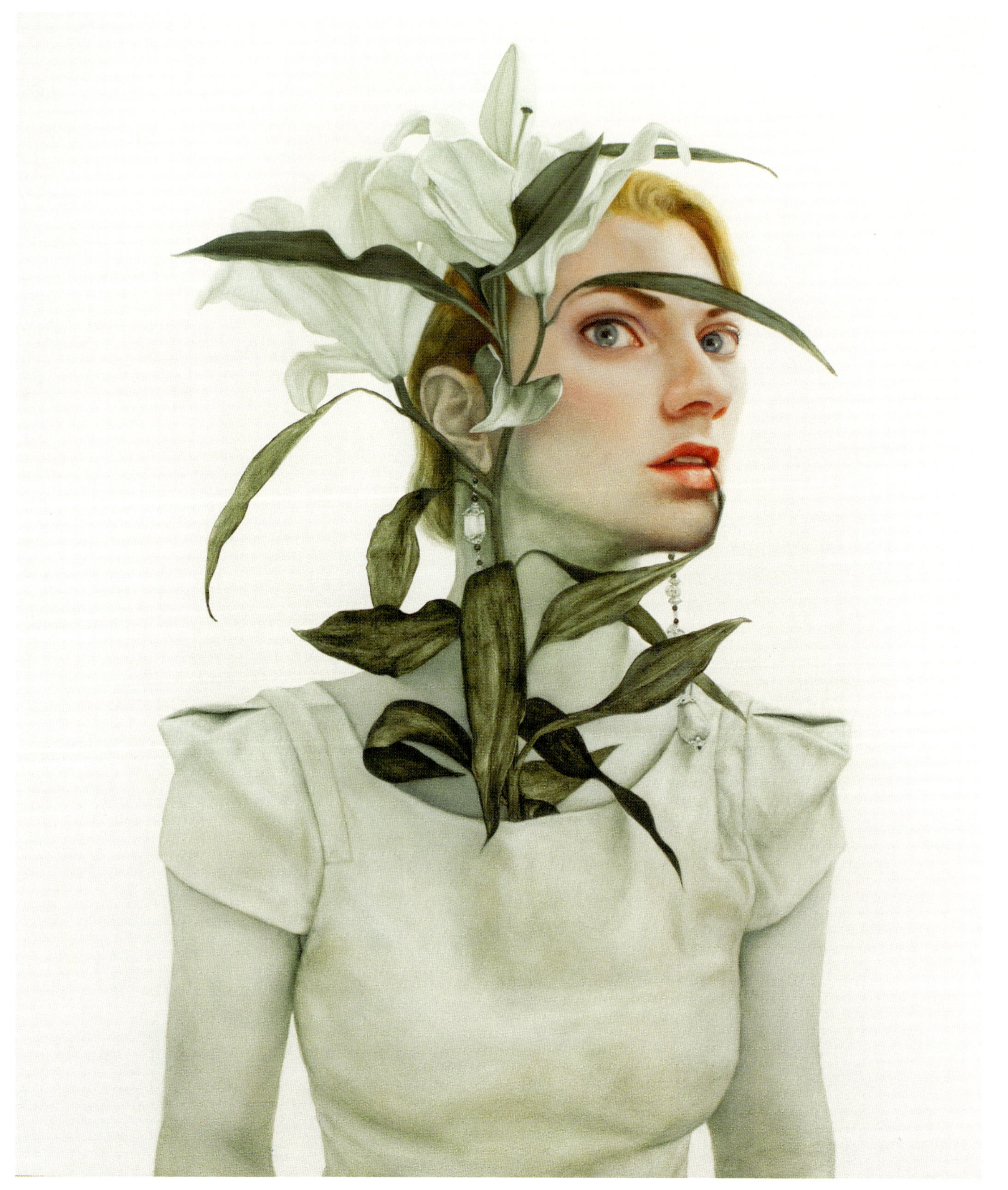

women's history, since before modern medicine ectopic pregnancies could be fatal. Though I had had real concerns about conspiring with the Gaze, after this experience the female body for me was no longer an object of it but the site of a physical communion with women of yore, dead from similar reproductive mishaps. In the wake of this emergency, I was able to use what could have been a traumatic experience and re-experience the female nude from my own and my sisters' perspectives, as a body—just a body—with the scars of life written on it. If feminism has done anything for women, it has allowed them to question the maxim that mere biology is destiny.

What I realized was that Mulvey's thesis was a call to arms: not to stop painting the nude but to imagine a different kind into existence. As a female painter, I have a different orientation not only to the nude, but also to the ranginess of sensual experience and how we imagine it into art. A lot of women painters today tell their stories of incandescent interiority from this entirely different, non-masculinist perspective, as did certain male artists before us. Regardless of any strict art historical accuracy, certain paintings by men seem to me to evince a distinctly proto-feminist understanding of women as actors, embodying will and complexity, or to contain narratives investigating taboo aspects of femaleness. Fragonard's *The Swing* (1767), with all its rococo ooze, depicts the main female character within a quintessentially feminine space, described by Dave Hickey as a space that invites entry, like Tiepolo's vast empyreans. (Caravaggio's *Conversion of St. Paul* of 1601 typifies masculine space, protruding into the viewer's realm.)[2] *The Swing*'s space is deep and moist—a rebuke to Baroque swagger; its central female figure presides magisterially but humorously over the man below her (most likely looking up her dress). She is within the deep space of the trees and humid air, a ruckus of swirling pink folds, throwing off constraints of sexuality symbolized by her cast-off shoe. She reminds me of Jane Campion's depiction of the inner character of Isabel Archer in her film *Portrait of a Lady* (1996), where Isabel's complex interior life is metonymically captured in the sensually swishing folds of her long, elaborate skirt. Snaking over the ground like some exquisite swamp thing, her skirts hold qualities of complexity, fluidity, and multivalency.

From a different perspective, many of Bonnard's paintings show a partly hidden female figure subsumed by her environment, as though he understood intrinsically the repressed state of women then. Bonnard often painted his emotionally remote wife in the womblike, female space of a bathtub, where she spent a lot of time due to illness. *Nude in Yellow* (1931) makes a radical departure from the familiar theme of "woman at her toilette." An initially indecipherable foreground shape becomes knuckled fingers holding something scribbled red, with clots, which might in fact be, as Robert Berlind hypothesized (in a conversation with me), a menstrual rag that Bonnard was investigating via paint in order to know his wife more intimately. In my view Bonnard, and by implication the viewer, is not looking at his naked wife in an objectifying way but seeking to engage with her deeper mysteries via an object closely identified with her Otherness, and with the mess and mortar of female experience.

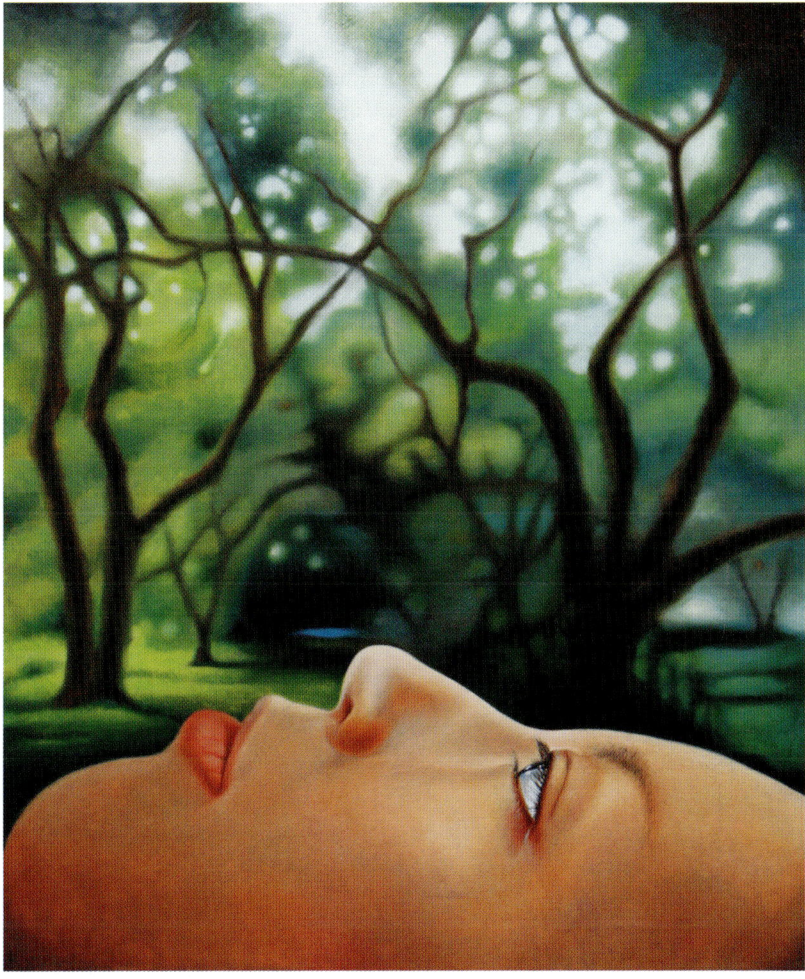

Kim Zack
Dream, 2011
Oil on canvas
24 x 20 inches

(opposite)
Julie Elizabeth Brady
Lily, 2013
Oil on wood
24 x 20 inches

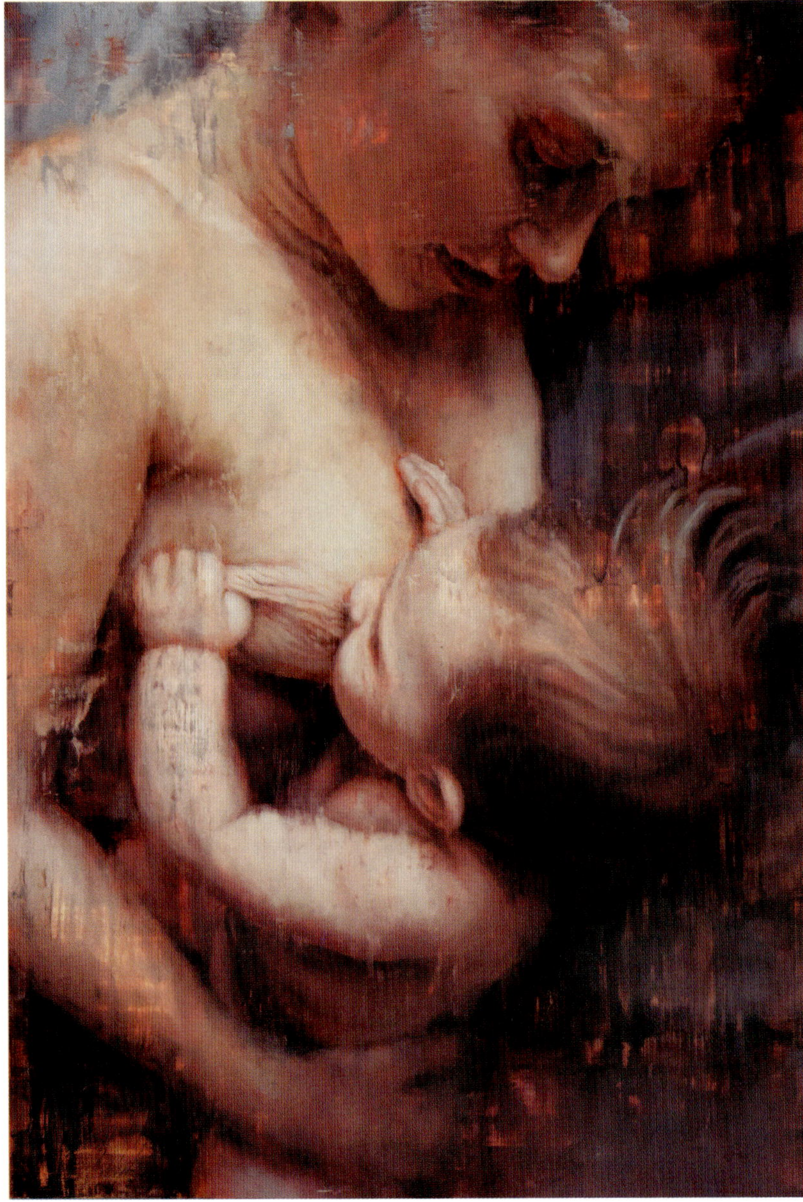

Modernism didn't engender nearly the number of female painters as one might have hoped. Women's engagement in the workplace and acquisition of greater financial security did not necessarily gain them entry to the wild frontiers of Modernist innovation. Female Surrealists were generally sidelined by their more prominent husbands, though I would claim Surrealism's psychoanalytic penetration of surfaces inspired a new generation of women painters. The marked subjectivity in the work of some younger contemporary female painters like Cecily Brown, Inka Essenhigh, and Hilary Harkness could be traced back to Surrealism's inward look. Any so-called feminine perspective has now been redefined through Postmodernism to encompass many new fields of inquiry (e.g., narrative art, outsider and feminist art)—all repudiations of Modernism's utopian impulses—and resists the tyranny of the mirror, as it frames and objectifies.

There are of course many painters who objectify women, John Currin being the most obvious example. His earlier work, however, provocative as it may be, isn't exploitative; it illustrates how fetishized portrayals can aspire to more. The bulge of a hip or elongation of a neckline set off by a cantankerous slash of negative space shifts the emphasis from body parts to the boisterous language of shape. Conversely, in his porn series he provides too much specifically genital information and loses sight of the polymorphously perverse, multifaceted nature of sensual experience. Kama Sutra paintings are not pornographic because they create metaphors for sensuality in their rich environments of ornamental arabesques and pattern, echoed in the intertwining of lovers' limbs. Unlike, say, Courbet's simplistically frank *Origin of the World* (1866).

Today one legacy of Mulvey's article is a new generation of people privy to the oppressiveness of the male gaze, but also with access to the liberating nature of their own sensorial peculiarities. Armed with a multitude of tools and freedoms wrested from the tumult of the feminist movement we (in the Western world) are freer than we've ever been to define how we see ourselves and escape the confines of our anatomies. The self-determined nude in all her fabulous nakedness has come back with more power than ever to move us, to arouse us to an ecstatic appreciation of her subversive beauty, and to help us imagine fresh pathways toward a transcendent, liberating physicality.

Michelle Doll
Mother Child, EE1, 2013
Oil on board
30 x 20 inches

(opposite)
Buket Savci Atature
Untitled, 2011
Oil on canvas
24 x 28 inches

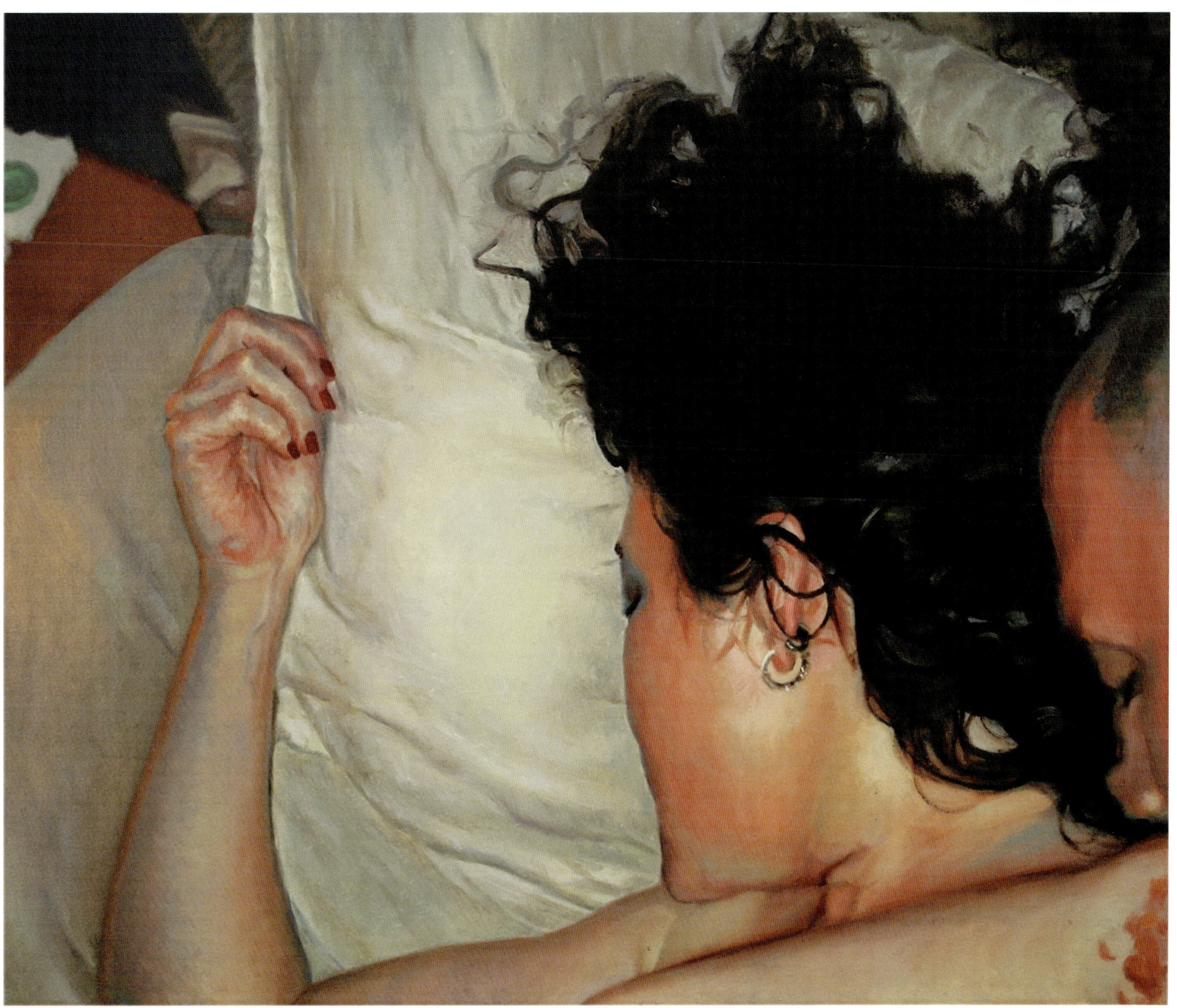

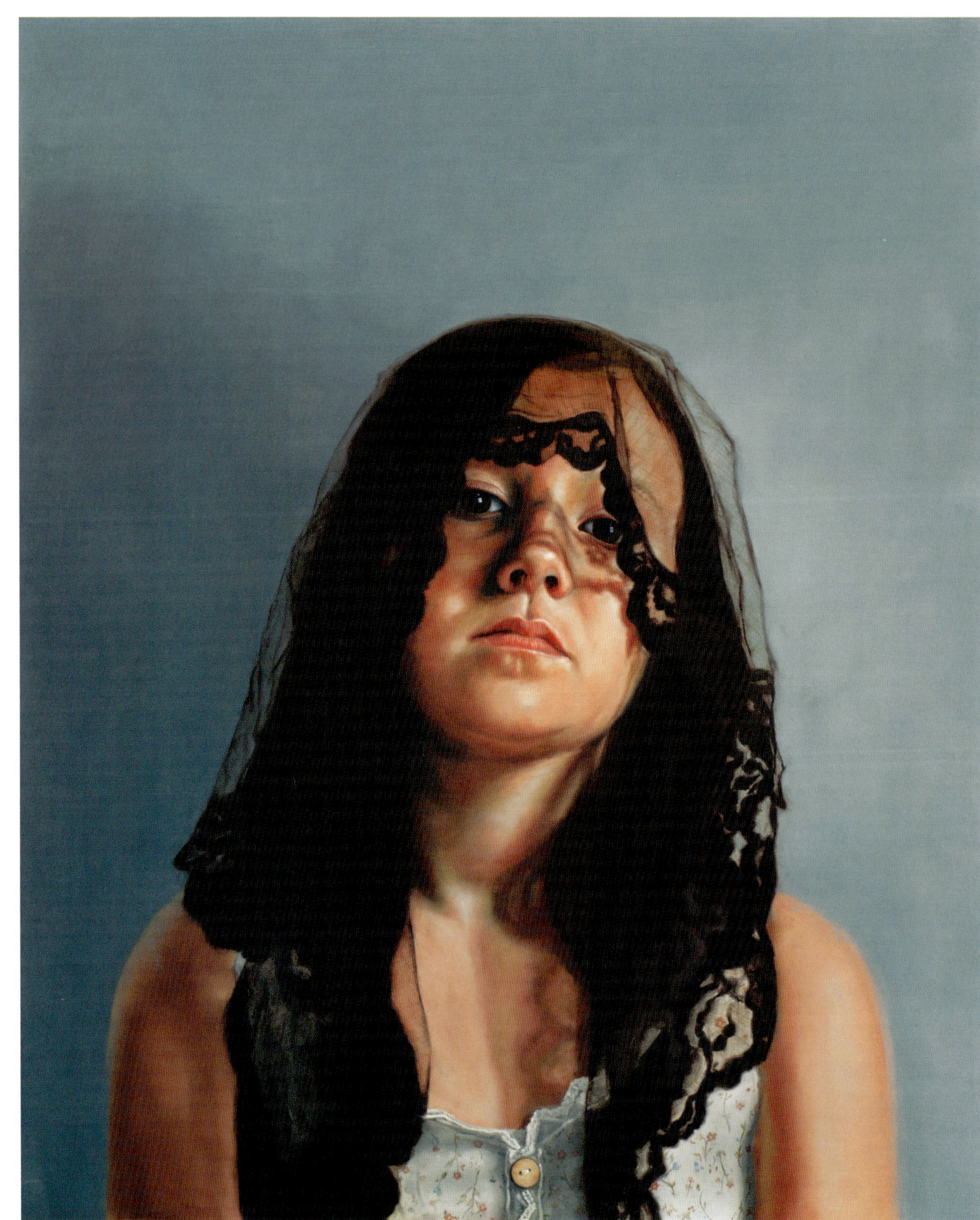

Maria Teicher
Alexis and the Veil,
2013
Oil on canvas
30 x 24 inches

(opposite)
Margaret Bowland
White Fives, 2012
Oil on linen
84 x 70 inches

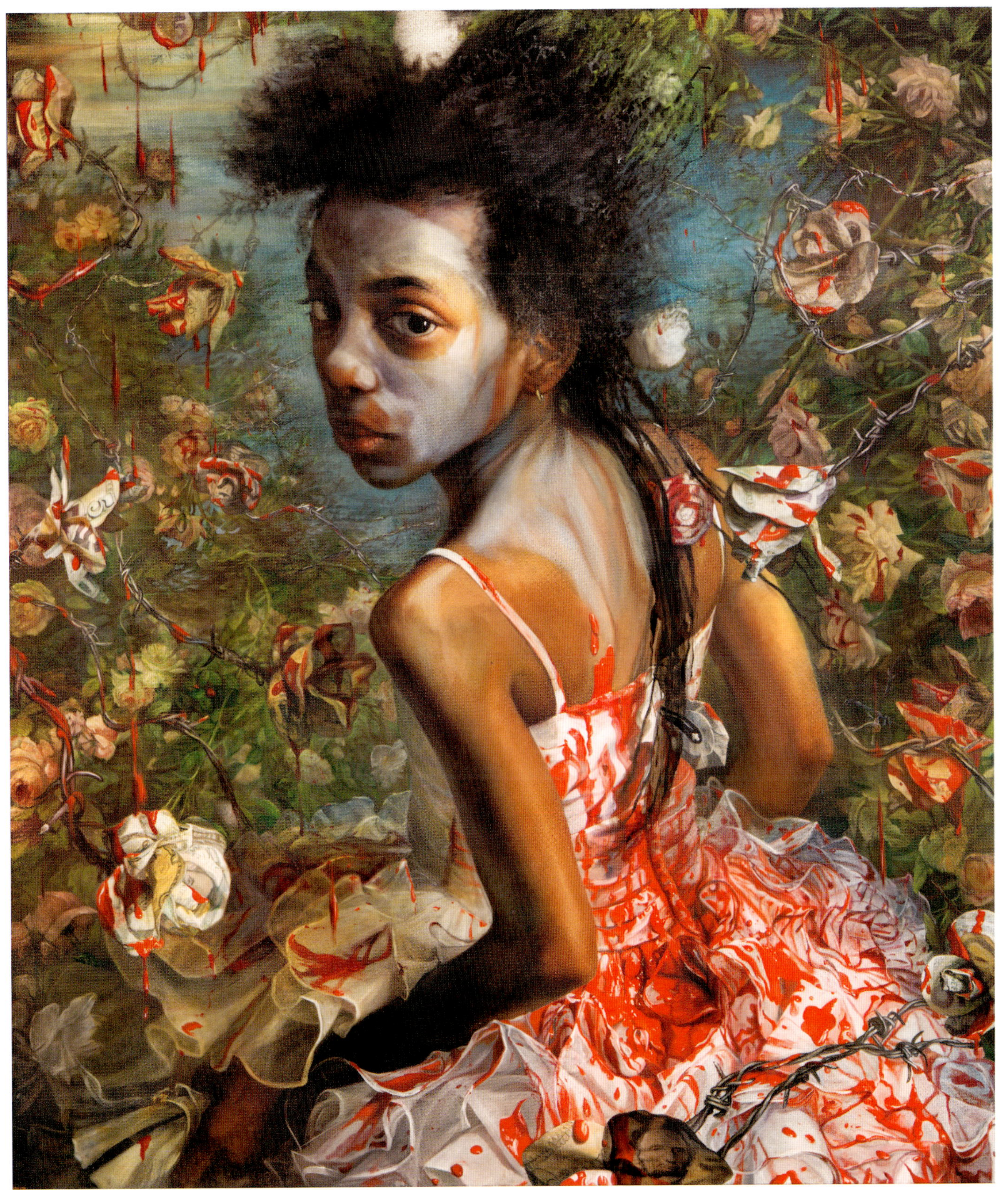

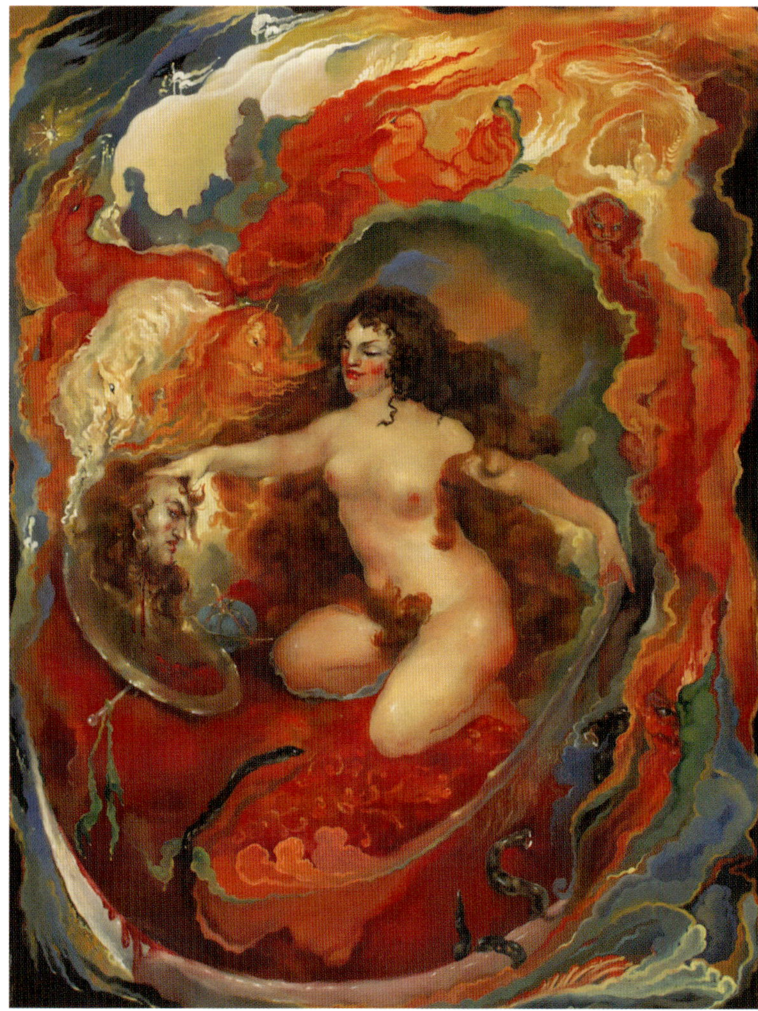

Olesya Udovidchik-Sentypal
Lust, 2010
Oil on canvas
48 x 36 inches

(opposite)
Anne Harris
Portrait (Pearls), 2001
Oil on canvas
36 x 30 inches

ANNE HARRIS

When I'm asked, usually by polite non-artists, "What kind of paintings do you do?", I respond (awkwardly), "Sort of like portraits, only the people don't exist; self-portraits only they don't look like me; freaky self-portraits . . ." Actually, I like to make very specific paintings that can't be nailed down. I want them to have what great portraits have—a mesmerizing tractor-beam hold, emotional complexity and intensity, plus highlights in the eyes—but not be about what's conventionally expected—rendered likeness, telltale signs of the soul of the sitter, my own angst, or the attributes of biography. I've come to realize the key to the shifting experience I want lies in the way the paintings are painted. My hope is that contradictions built into them between paint and illusion, form and material, subject matter and idea, figure and ground, will allow them to function broadly and deeply, that the meaning of the work will unfold gradually, in layers, in a way that parallels the process I use.

I begin by looking at myself or at a model, but soon the painting goes its own way. I don't have a final image in my head, but rather a broad idea, a feeling I'm after, a kind of intensity. I usually work on paintings in groups, over a long period of time, sometimes years, not because they technically require it, but because I keep going over a cliff—too contrived, too mundane, too much meaningless facility, or some nuts-and-bolts painting issue is giving me grief. I often spend more time on the space around the figure than the figure itself; my "backgrounds" physically sit in front of my foregrounds. The air the figure is embedded in is so fundamental—the difference between an academic exercise and a meaningful painting. When that painting begins to breathe, when it looks back at me, when the wall around it and the air in front of it are charged, I know I'm on to something. I'm done when anything I do to it makes it worse, when it lives on its own. When I don't know how I did it.

The paintings are built in layers starting with the ground—gesso scraped thinly across linen, then sanded to feel like skin. Working translucently, I'll begin with neutral warms, usually raw umber, and pull lights in with white. Then temperature shifts occur: relative cools, warms, optical grays. I use a very limited palette, mainly warm earth colors, often no blues or greens. Raw umber functions as blue or violet (it's amazing what context and layering can do). I also use multiple whites; small differences in temperature, tinting strength, viscosity, and opacity become huge when the range is narrow. A sample base palette: Old Holland Cremnitz White and Zinc White, Williamsburg Zinc Buff, Old Holland Raw Sienna, Burnt Sienna and Mars Orange Red, Winsor & Newton Raw Umber. Depending on the painting, I'll have occasional hits of something more intense, like zinc yellow, which are usually buried under future layers of paint. In the end, I'm aiming for something I can't name, something I don't look at, but look through.

This process is akin to my pale skin: layers of translucent non-color through which light passes and bounces around, concealing and revealing structure, creating luminosity and shimmering gray-blue veins—both the glow and the blue are illusions produced by light passing through veils of barely pigmented skin. I'd like my painting to function as my skin does, a translucent, semipermeable membrane, shrink-wrapped around its contents, displaying and hiding what's physically and emotionally inside.

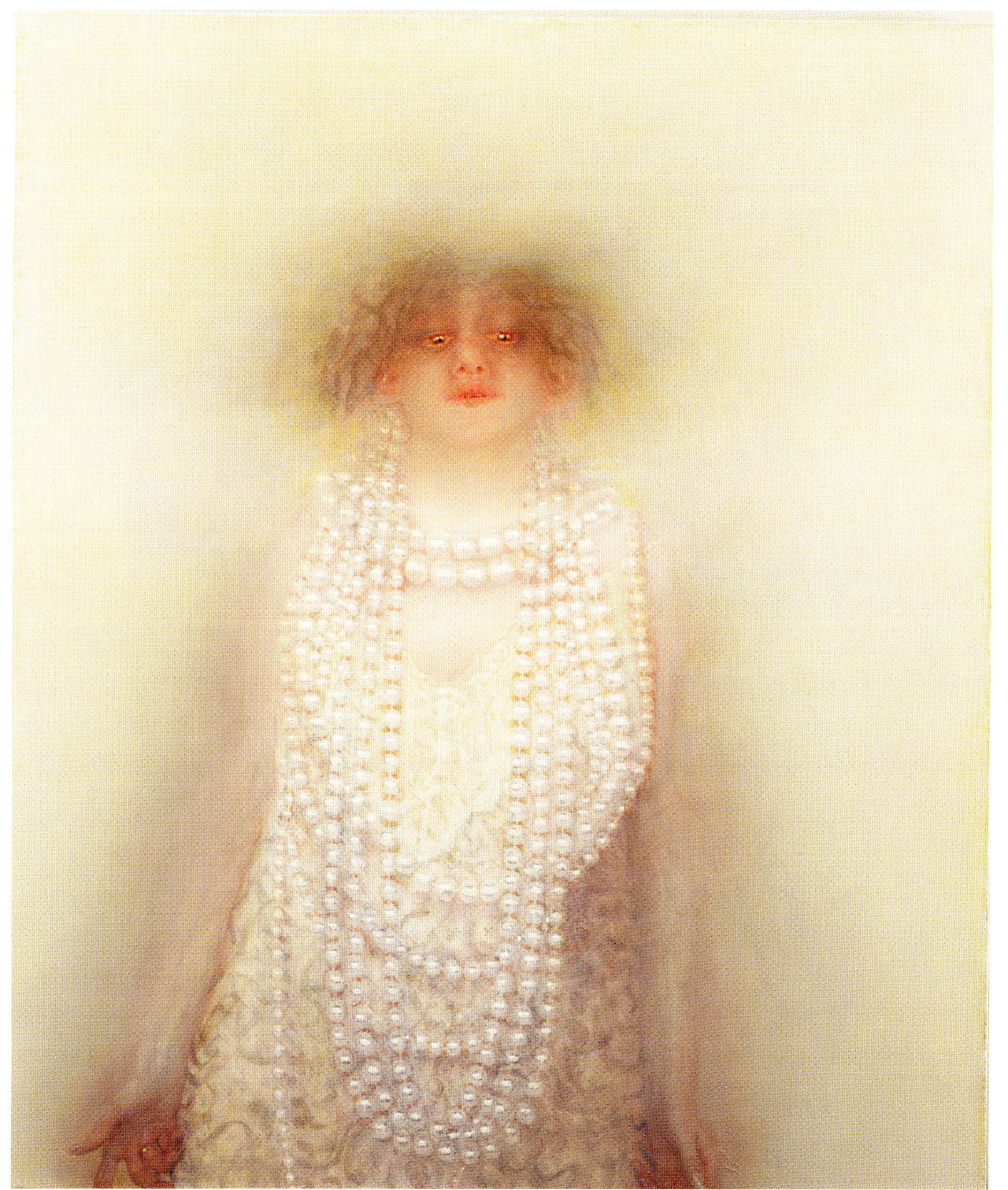

Always, while painting, drawing is in play. In fact, I've been trying for a long time to learn to paint the way I draw. Basically, drawing is almost everything. The distinctions that belong to painting—the skin of paint, luminosity generated by color, the physical weight of a painting—are stretched around drawing. By this, I mean drawing not just as linear design or formal structure, but something more fundamental—an organization of marks that transform a ground. That transformation is the key. It's everything. How does mark shape surface? How does figure shape ground? How do we shape our world? How does our world shape us?

That fundamental paradox—that figure and ground exist only in concert with each other—pulls us back to the substance of paint. Pigment. Essentially, historically it's dirt. It's earth. We make marks on a ground with the ground; and in that process we turn that ground into a world. So dirt smeared on a cave wall twenty thousand years ago still, today, transforms into antelope racing across a plain. This amazes me. And in the end it's all I want—to take this ancient stuff and make the same magic.

HILARY HARKNESS

For me, the foundation of painting is story. When I was a child, drawing and painting felt like subsets of lucid dreaming. My father worked in a paper mill and kept my playroom closet brimming with paper samples and art supplies to accommodate my habit of spending entire days at a time painting and drawing. The images that I drew were coming straight from my dream world, courtesy of a visual culture that included *World Book Encyclopedia* photographs and illustrated books by Richard Scarry that I assimilated while sprawled on a sofa. But, in my playroom there were no piles of photographic references through which to sort. Not like there are today.

Today, I'm still after story but with a greater sense of responsibility as a storyteller than I had in those early days. I still rely upon my imagination to determine the types of compositions I want to create, but I want images that ring true for my viewers. I want images that have a strong relation to reality. The realities from which I draw inspiration aren't typically found in my family's photo album, but they are very much inspired by my family. A number of my paintings explore events leading up to and surrounding World War II because of the rippling effects my grandfather's service had on my family. Yet, instead of relying on photographs of my grandfather, I often find myself rifling through mechanical specs of battleships. And for at least one of my pieces I was influenced by the musical *South Pacific*, which centered on that war. The first moments of creating a composition are about things larger than specific images.

For example, in *Flipwreck* (2004), I took notions about race and commerce expressed in *South Pacific* and turned them, at least sideways. Like many of the worlds in my works, the world of *Flipwreck* is a world without men, but it is not a world without war, because conflict is inescapable when the stakes are high and people go morally adrift. In my story, the Polynesians have turned the tables on both the American and Japanese warring parties. The sinking American ship has sunk the Japanese aircraft carrier, and sailors of both nationalities are washing ashore. The Polynesians need money, so they imprison the Japanese sailors and prostitute them to the Americans, who think they are buying the services of the Polynesians.

(opposite)
Hilary Harkness
Flipwreck, 2004
Oil on panel
13 x 22 inches

Still, even once I had this story in mind, I didn't go straight to film stills of the cinematic production of *South Pacific*, which would have undoubtedly had some photographic references that I could have considered. I wanted more information to play with, so I consulted maps and then the Internet, systematically looking through pictures of every beach that could possibly fit the specs to match the story in my head, from Bermuda and the Caribbean islands to Tahiti and Hawaii. Perhaps not surprisingly, the best beach for my purposes ended up being the north shore of Kauai, just a few miles from the location where *South Pacific* was filmed.

While playing around with the composition to make the beach even more like a cove (the setting I had culled from my imagination), I referred to photos pulled from multiple sources on the web, including random images of what looked like vacation photos of people I will never meet. Eventually, I transferred my drawing to a lead-primed linen-wrapped panel and began painting in earnest, but within weeks became restless because my reference photos didn't contain enough information to allow me to bring my invented landscape to life. I reluctantly canceled an upcoming trip to Paris—I needed to go to Kauai to paint studies on location.

During my trip, I found that direct observation gave me infinitely more of the critical information needed than photographs do. I saw the opacity of the surface of the ocean change relative to the angle of the sun. Waves broke far from shore on invisible reefs and wrapped themselves around large jutting lava rocks close to shore, the water gradually resealing as they passed. I snorkeled at dawn and discovered the depth of the ocean as its waters transitioned from turquoise to cobalt blue. I painted on beaches and discovered that yellow ochre and not iron oxide yellow is the best pigment to create tropical sand at dusk.

After returning to Manhattan with several beach paintings packed carefully in an old-fashioned hard-case valise, worthy of the *Mad Men* props department, photos I took during the trip served as reminders as I reconstructed the imaginary scene on the original panel. This time, the combination of painting from life in addition to using photographic reminders enabled me to make my imagery simultaneously more specific and more abstract. I remained true to my desire not to end up with a painting that feels photographic and therefore readable as an "objective" document, but rather something that might pull the viewer into the trancelike state of my childhood studio.

The experience of using Kauai for *Flipwreck* as a site where I painted from life has served to add the island to my internal landscape not as an actual place, but rather as a site with endless possibilities. Earlier this year, I returned to the island with my suitcase and easel, and a new story in mind that needs to be told. It's about a beach, a wooden ship, and a woman. A voyager. It's a version of a story that you might remember from the history books, particularly if you like biology. There are plenty of photos of the actual beaches, ship, and voyager. But the painting's reality will not come from setting up my easel on top of a giant tortoise or resting my tripod on its shell. At least not for now.

For now, the story will remain the foundation for me. Along the way, I may need to rely upon another trip somewhere else and some additional photographic references to be the type of storyteller that I want to be. And for me, this is okay. My easel is larger now; my hope is that my imagination will continue to keep pace.

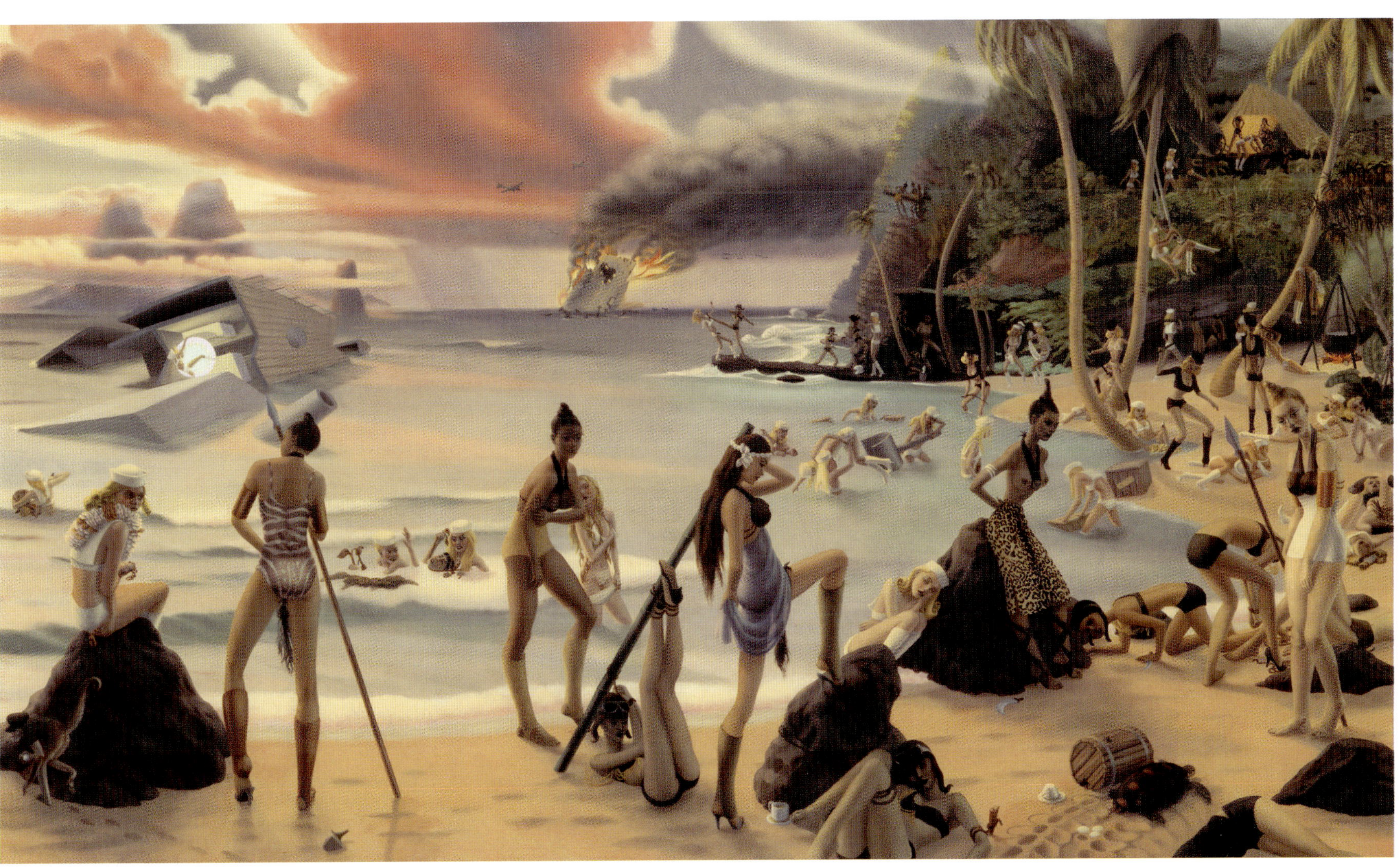

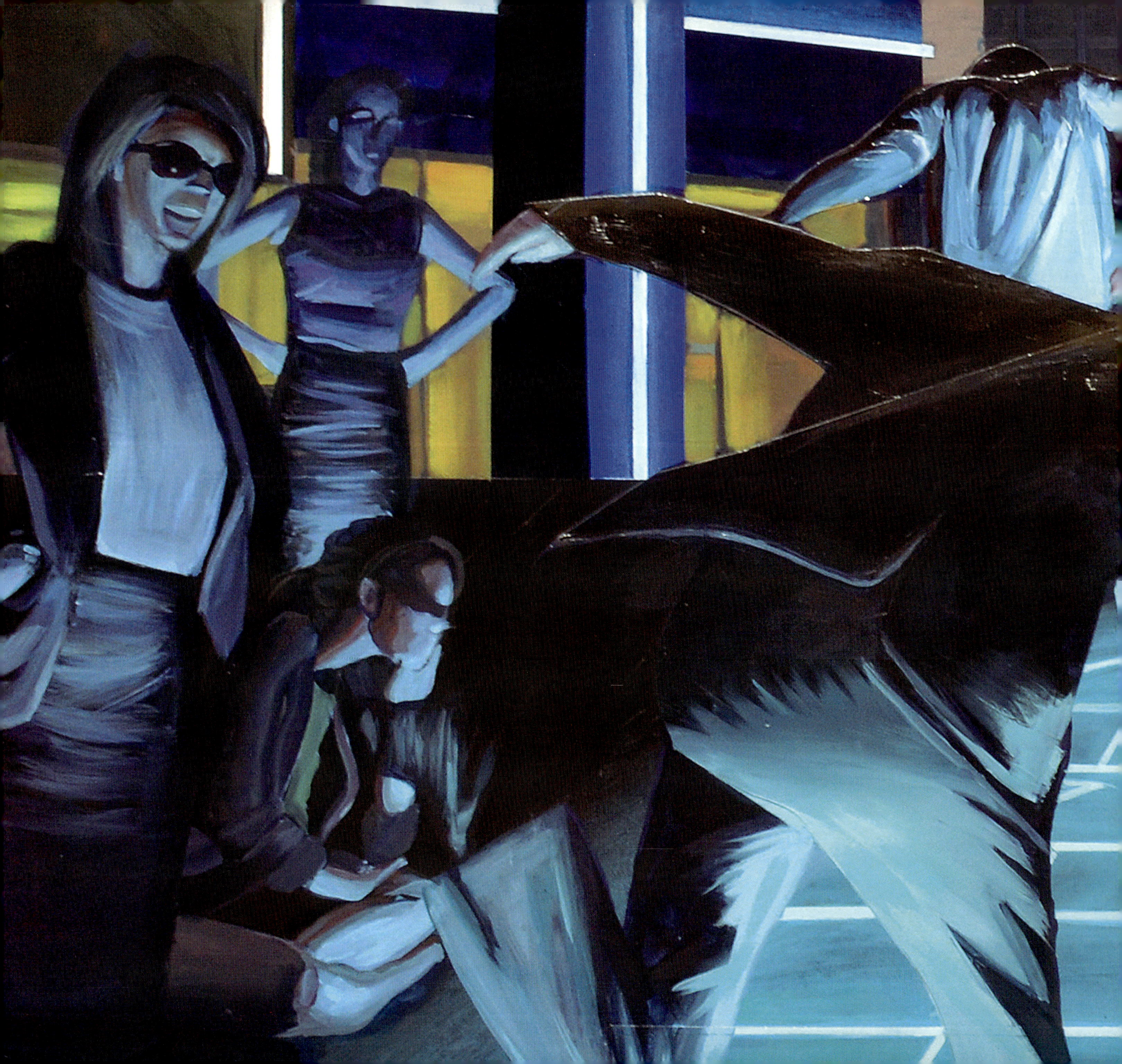

PART III FUTURE CONTINUUM

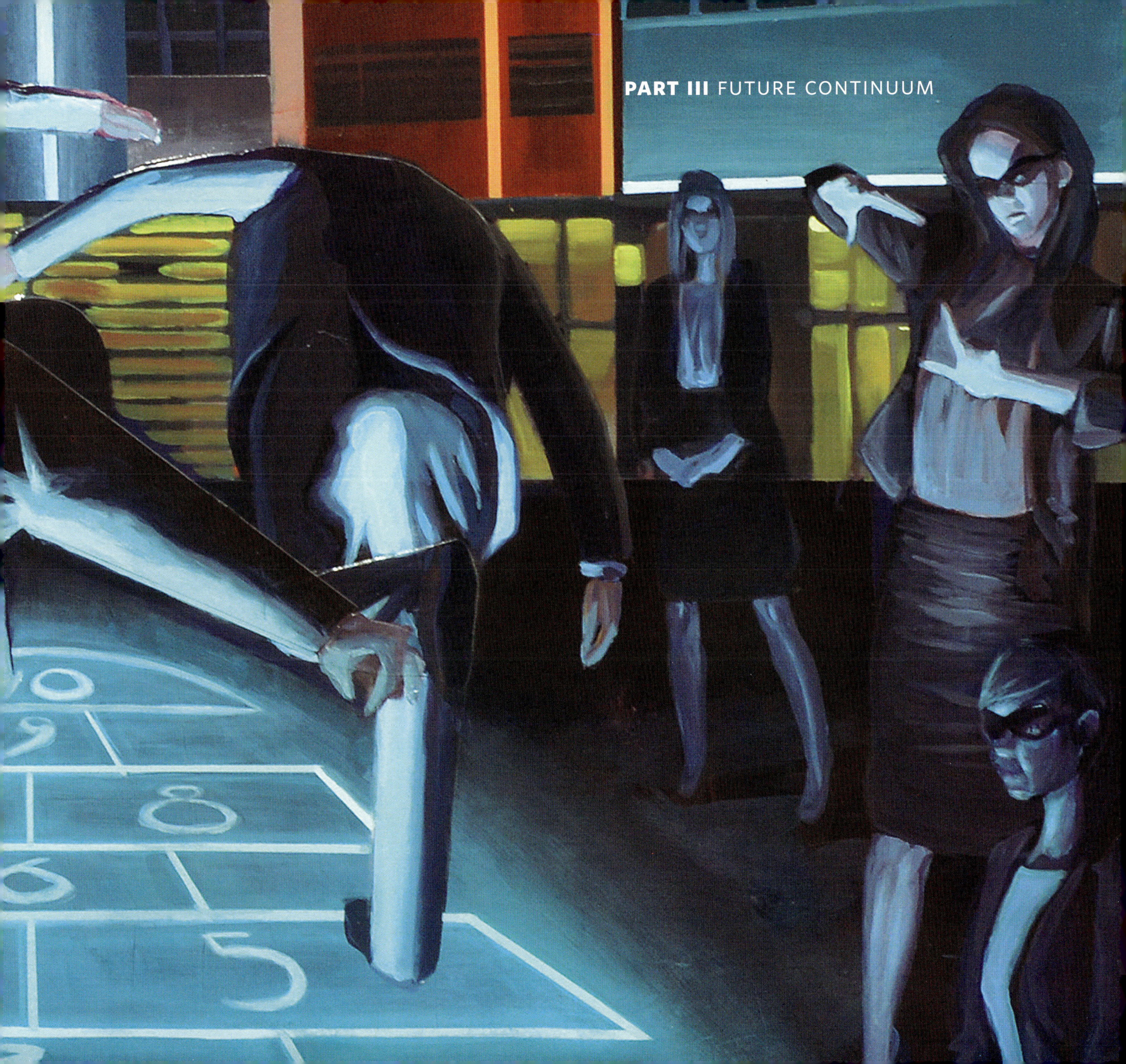

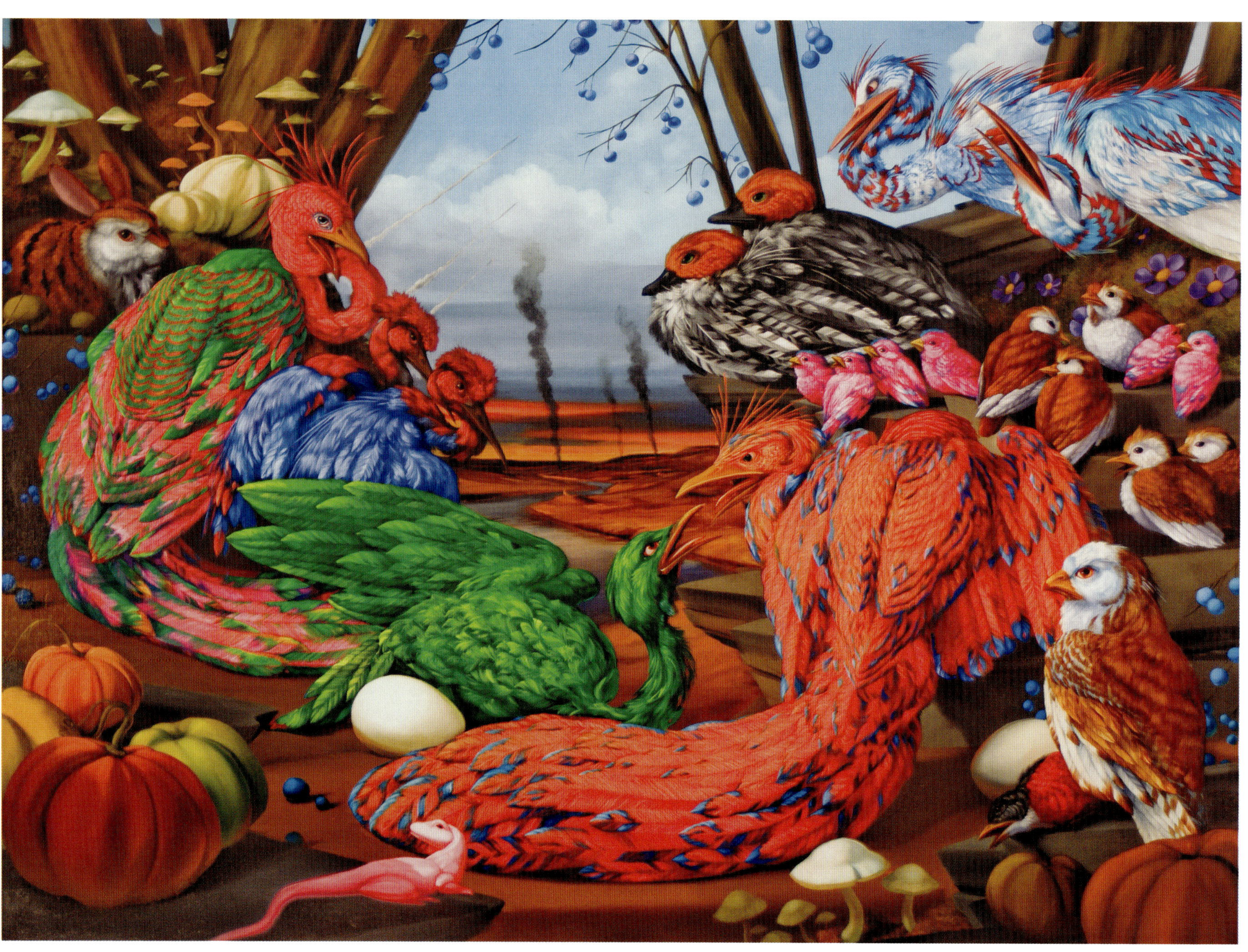

THE ECHO IN THE PICTURE:
THE SOCIAL POTENTIAL OF REPRESENTATIONAL PAINTING

LAURIE HOGIN

LIKE A TREE STRIVING IN A HARSH ENVIRONMENT, painting as a set of historically informed activities has spread across the broad, rocky slope of markets, institutions, audiences, and systems of delivery present in this stage of global capitalism. It has sent up far-flung shoots, some of which have grown into hothouse flowers or stunted suckers—thin, rangy, and striving until strung out, aspiring to make meaning according only to their own internal, terminal logic. The branch of representational painting is reestablishing relevance. The rise of Neo-Realism, the critical acknowledgment of contemporary figurative painters like Lisa Yuskavage, Walton Ford, Bo Bartlett, Julie Heffernan, and Vincent Desiderio, and the crossover of artists from the Lowbrow movement, or Pop Surrealism, like Barry McGee and Mark Ryden, into various realms of sustainable art economies, signal a new understanding of representational artistic strategies in rapidly evolving global culture. Popular magazines like *Juxtapoz* and *Hi-Fructose* and the proliferation of paintings in digital reproduction on the Internet suggest culturally resonant alternatives to institutionalized twentieth-century ideas. These developments contradict the long-reigning stances of "dead" (figurative) versus "avant-garde" (modern) painting, as well as the oft-repeated death of painting.

Painting persists today in academia, museums, commercial galleries, artist-run exhibition spaces, and the hobbyist's atelier, its only immutable fact the use of pigment in a fluid medium. Any painting's meaning is hypothesized through aesthetics (Greek for "feelings"), which describe an artwork's inherent qualities to locate its content, social use, audience, and therefore its ideology as a communicative object; and in the study of culture and cognition—phenomenology, psychoanalysis, and other Modernist discourses regarding meaning and metaphor. Prestige, and its origins in the psychological imperative for social status seemingly present in social animals, manifests, in questions of human aesthetics and the market, as philosophies of "taste" and judgment, which not only justify but require the valorization of certain social groups (and their stuff) and the marginalization of others (and theirs). The prestige accorded elite art discourses accounts for some marginalization of figurative painting in the history of institutionalized art.

Partly because of its legibility to the uninitiated, its democratic accessibility, and its affiliation with premodern aesthetics and problematic social structures, representational painting has been accused of vulgarity, corruption, low-mindedness, decadence, and right-wing sentiments, enduring periods of relative marginalization and outright banishment. But representational painting can only be so avant-garde. It harkens back to communicative strategies championed in the institutional structures of the bourgeois, pre-Modernist individual, and reclaims skills and techniques judged in accordance with the embrace of patriarchal authority and tradition. The avant-garde of the early twentieth century, embracing innovation and the anti-aesthetic, was necessarily political because it sought to destroy the oppressive social and cultural structures reflected in celebrated art of the preceding era. The notion of progress in formal and conceptual iterations of the painted object meant logically that if painting is subject to the same forces propelling other technology toward the unspoken techno-utopias of Modernist teleology, then as a field of expertise, painting aspires primarily to express new material strategies.

Past innovative art practices invented new forms of representation, added to the vocabulary of visual languages, dismantled authoritative representational conventions, revealed latent political or psychological content, and undermined the messages of dominant cultural structures in their times. But the ontology of paint has led to further painting investigations that, however critical of painterly works canonized in immediate precedent, are

(opposite)
Laurie Hogin
Darwin's Dream (Habitat Diorama with Critical Threshold Survivor Species), 2012
Oil on canvas
36 x 48 inches

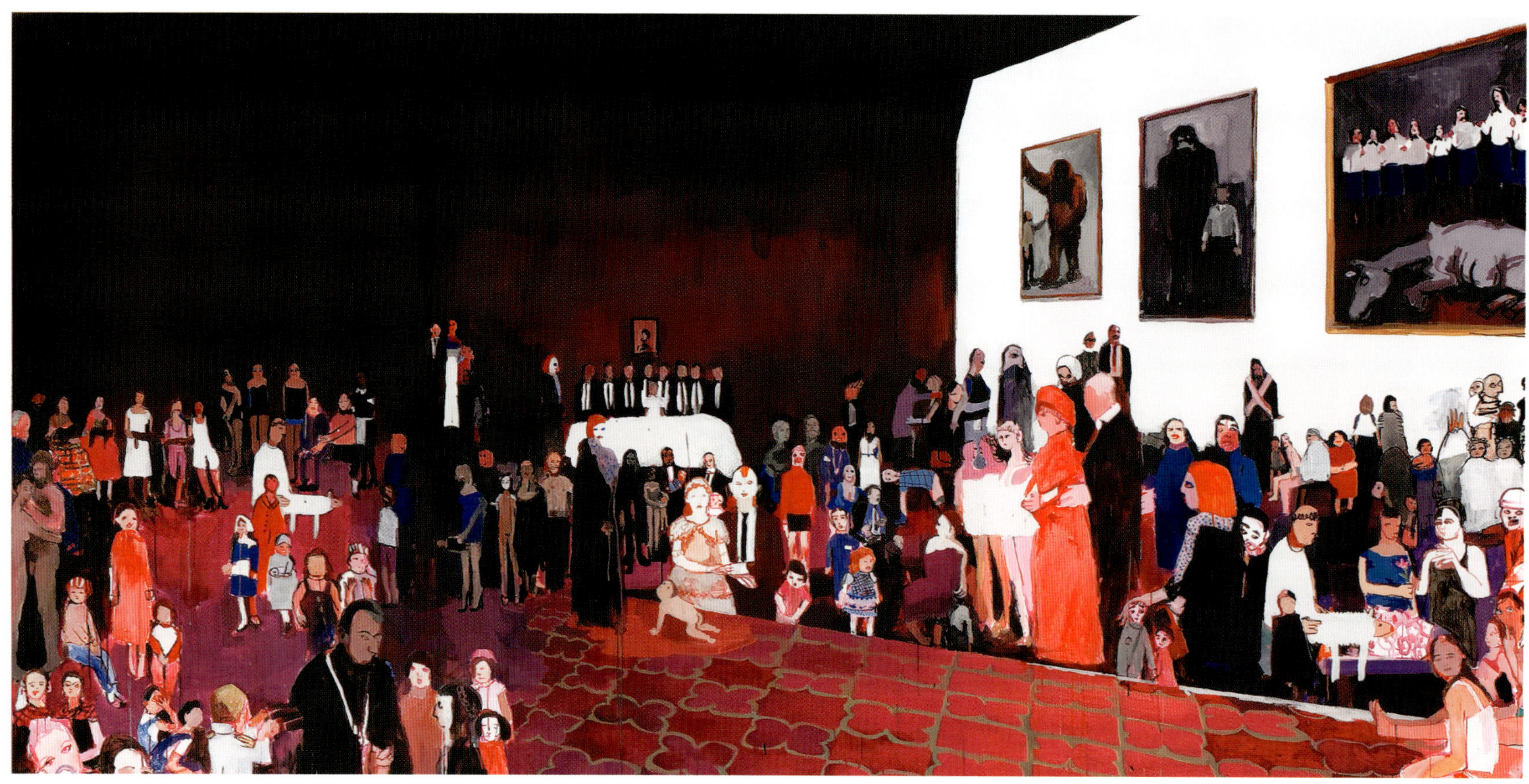

Helen Verhoeven
Event Two, 2008
Acrylic on canvas
82 x 164.5 inches

(opposite)
Alexander Barton
Trilateral, 2012
Oil, shellac, tar on linen
70 x 54 inches

not enough to encourage changes in consciousness, no matter how insightful and smart. The resulting self-referential ideas and values determining much contemporary theoretical and critical discourses in painting represent no political, social, or aesthetic rupture. In *The Return of the Real*, Hal Foster argues that "creative critique is *interminable*"[1] and utterly necessary, and that the "ambitious art of its time" feels historical pressure. He importantly asks: If avant-garde practices are aesthetically progressive, and transgression of earlier forms is status quo within institutions and academies, how do artists reinvest their practices with political meaning, relevance, and revolutionary potential? In the Postmodern era, the avant-garde model of cultural rupture, invented to serve the cause of democracy and the destruction of authoritarian forms, seems largely obsolete; even institutional critique has itself become institutional. The Modernist aesthetic and the avant-garde process are no longer change agents. Abstraction, Conceptualism, and Minimalism, iconically modern art strategies, are now genres or styles, self-referential visual puzzles and games, or official, corporate and governmental public art.

Establishing the historical significance of artworks through the mechanisms of curatorial and collector practice and describing the socio-intellectual movements and networks they represent are important to understanding broader history. A Marxist analysis of the art object and critique of decadence and pleasure in the commodity, once necessary to a radicalization of culture, has become a form of Puritanism demanding the art object be a cryptic, historically self-referential thing, decoded via extensive museum didactics in safe, regulated spaces, to predictably serve and reproduce existing power structures. The very notion of *the innovative*, now an institutional requirement, is the ultimate value in late capitalism: Institutions, academies, governments, and especially corporations have accommodated the process of rupture in visual invention. Their authority domesticates those objects

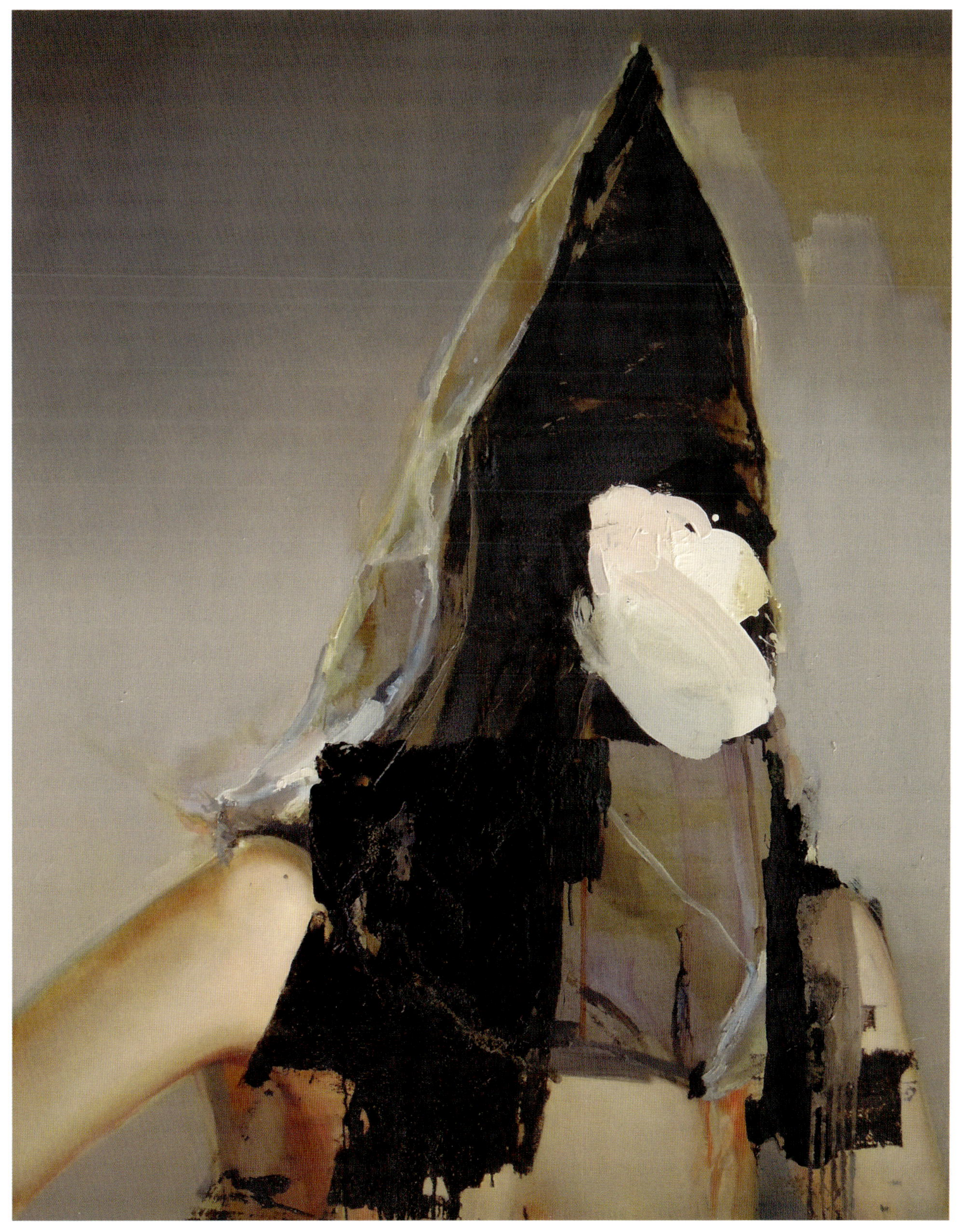

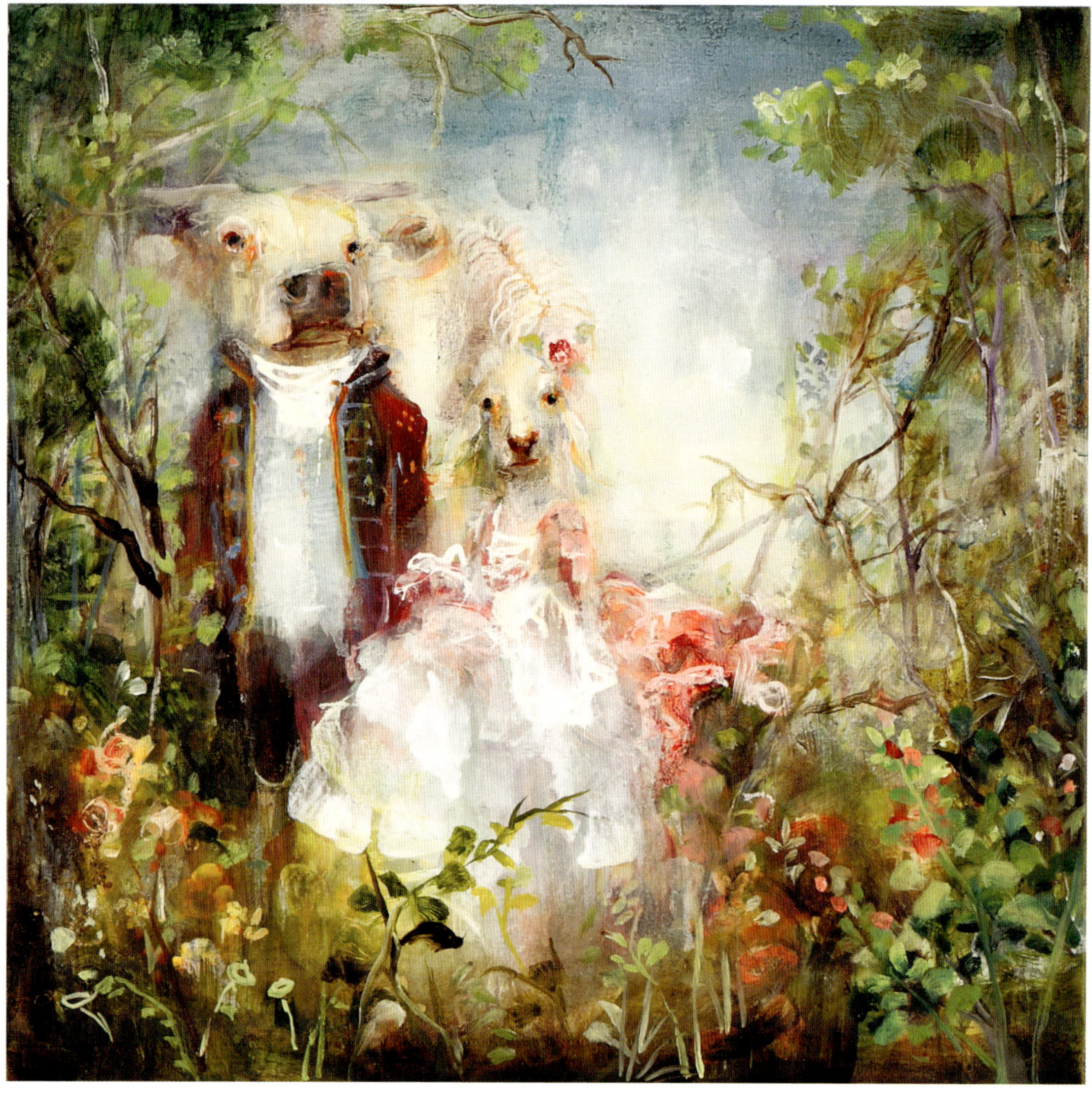

Susan Siegel
In Pink, 2012
Oil on canvas
8 x 8 inches

(opposite)
Catherine Howe
Proserpina (Winter), 2010
Oil on canvas
66 x 60 inches

and makes them didactic in hermetic, mandarin discourses, limiting them as boutique objects for the initiated, according to vested interests. ("Survival of the fittest" means "survival of the best adapted"; what a Petri dish best accommodates is not necessarily a potent agent in other ecosystems.) What exists now in the habit of aesthetic innovation is not *anti-aesthetic* in the sense of cultural rupture, but *anesthetic* to the body politic.

Having now determined contemporary discourses, Modernist explanations assume an undeserved political efficacy. One theory assumes that formal and material innovation is inherently radical or disruptive to existing social structures. Another argues that abstract formal qualities represent a universal aesthetic related to primitivism, the art of children, as well as a simplistic, binary interperetation of "instinct" and individual drives and "society" and civilization. Semir Zeki's 1999 book, *Inner Vision: An Exploration of Art and the Brain*, utilizes abstract paintings to explain the function of neuroanatomical structures in the visual cortex's responses to color, motion, line, and form. While new observational technologies in neuroscience and cognitive psychology allow scientists to observe, record, and measure the brain's responses, the ways in which the human subject *interprets* visual sensation remains hypothetical. Current study of how storytelling relates to the neurobiology of memory suggests that aesthetic responses are very complex, based in both evolutionary biology and in the human brain's plasticity through language and environment; even

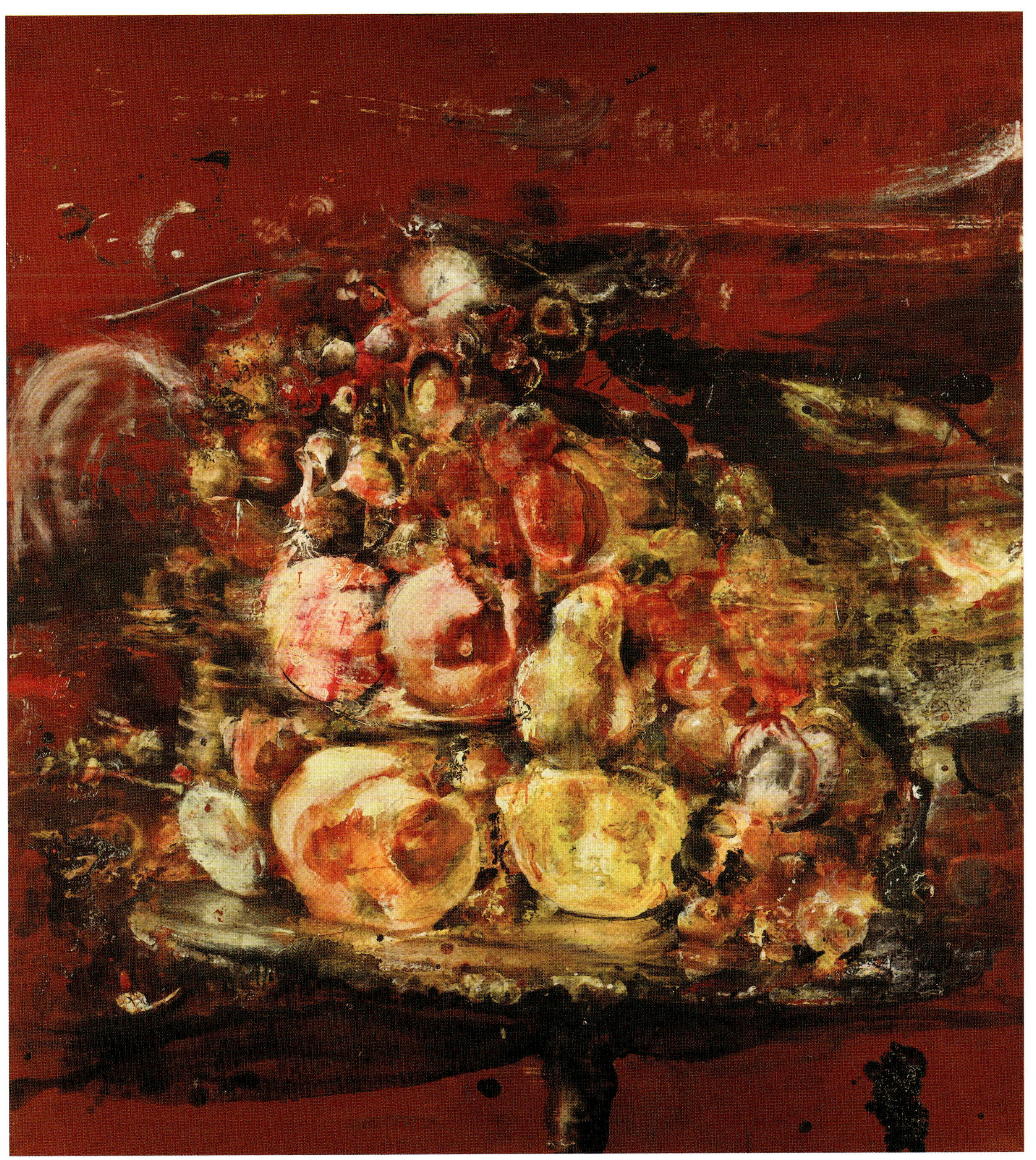

abstract painting has referents in narrative and sensory memory. Still, crude descriptions of the relationships among sense, memory, and language posit sensory experience as involving the response of the body and brain to stimuli in the moment: light, space, air, touch, movement, scent, taste, and the pain or pleasure derived from the situation, often preceding the verbal and naming. Narrative memory arranges such experiences in history and culture through language, contextualizing sensory experience, emphasizing some aspects and eliminating others, creating meaning. A story makes meaning out of nonsense. We are a storytelling species, and in the telling of stories we transmit social subject matter.

The rough points of this essay were written as an e-mail to myself from my phone, as I walked through Lake of the Woods, a nine-hundred-acre preserve of prairie and woodland situated among industrial corn and soy fields, tracts of suburban sprawl, and patches of rural poverty in central Illinois. The Sangamon River, which runs through it, was at record flood stage, and the woods full of growth—tiny violet bundles on redbud trees, wild phlox, acid-green shoots, and arabesque tendrils—and the usual sprinkling of public park pastoral: beer cans, plastic bags, cigarette butts. Shreds of holographic silver Mylar fluttered in a tangle of twigs; its refractions made the responsive cells of my visual cortex fire, initiating electrical and chemical processes along dedicated pathways of memory and association. Other experiences sprang from memory to mind: sun on soap bubbles; a rainbow oil slick on blacktop and petroleum scent in the summer heat; a spectrum of color in the spray of a hose; a child's silver pinwheel spinning in the breeze on a silent beach. Certainly, this garish little flutter of garbage had its own narrative history—evidence of entire worlds of production, movement, commerce, pleasure. As with aesthetic experiences in the presence of art, the sensory phenomenon invokes other subjects, other places, other stories—including ideas for this essay—that echo with social, cultural, and personal experience.

Framing this experience literally—a story on the quadrangular screen of a smart phone—reinforces how pictures invoke narratives, which frame experience. Culture is full of quadrangles into which are projected the imaginary spaces of memory, arranged by narrative. The frame itself is an act of language: Like the edges of a picture, it delimits the chaos of the world, whose pieces are internalized and made part of the worldview and being of the embodied subject. Everything framed by the edges of the picture becomes meaningful; everything present in the picture adds to the story. In her book *Chaos, Territory, Art: Deleuze and the Framing of the Earth*, cultural theorist Elizabeth Grosz addresses the impulse toward art: "Framing is how chaos becomes territory. Framing is the means by which objects are delimited, qualities unleashed and art made possible."[2] The painting's picturing of an imaginary space thus represents simultaneously the interiority of sensory memory and the exteriority of narrative language and naming, functioning as a social statement: I am here; this is what I see.

The architectural impulse to posit a difference between "out there" and "in here" frames experience in narrative memory, defines that apparatus as a conscious, cultural, social subject, and makes *subjecthood*—the sense

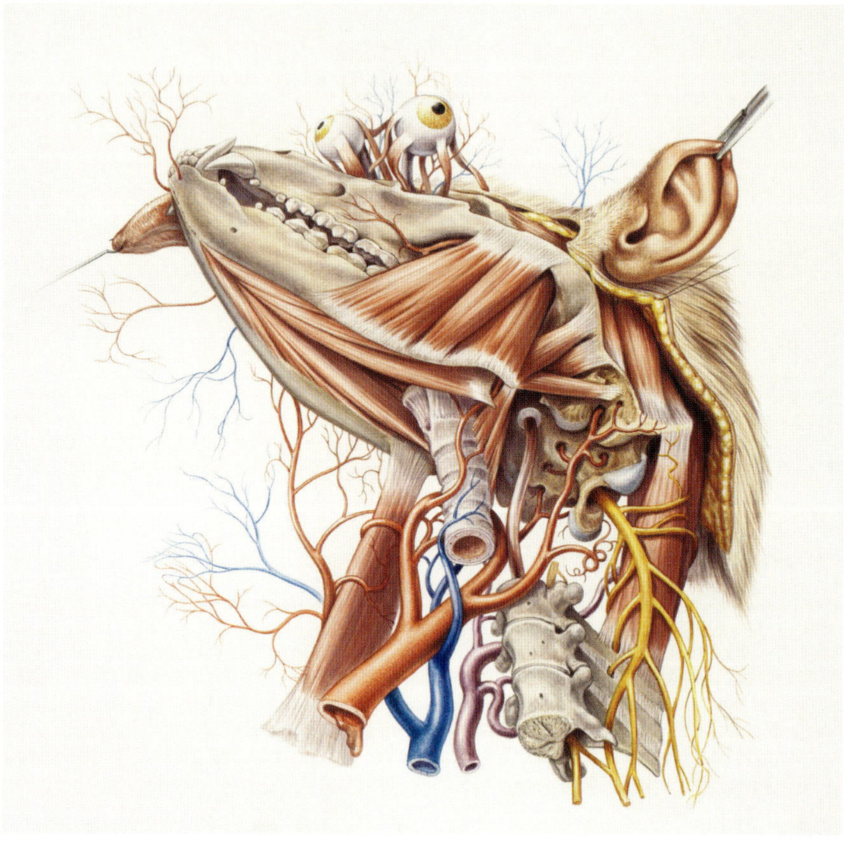

Roberto Osti
Deconstruction of a Werewolf, 2007
Watercolor on paper
16 x 18 inches

(opposite)
Ali Banisadr
The Devil, 2012
Oil on linen
16 x 16 inches

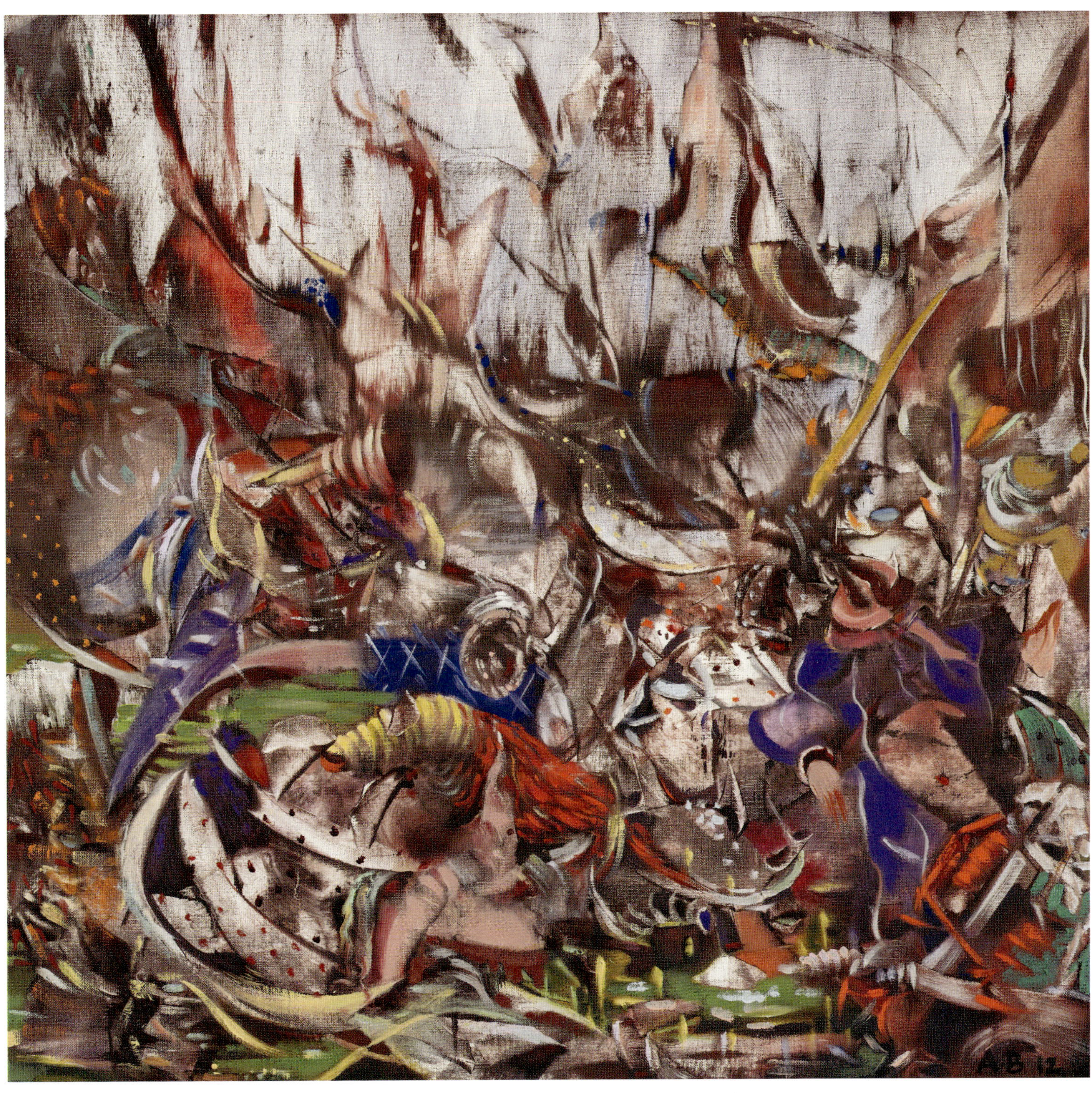

of being a consciousness located in, or inherent to, a body—possible. The subject, whose mind and body make memories in space and time, then reproduces memory as narrative—feelings and senses are recalled, named, and described. This descriptive language of narrative representation profoundly informs the Western pictorial tradition. The naming of things in imaginary space conspires with re-presentation of sensory experience through various formal means, including color, line, gesture, spatial illusion, and the rendering of objects in value. The result amounts to a request, on the part of the viewer, to identify with the subjecthood of the object's maker—a pictorial politics of identification. Unlike mechanical means of producing imagery, the surface qualities of or mere implication of the hand in a handmade art object reiterates the bodily presence and gestures of the maker in the moment of making. This evokes *kinesthetic empathy*—the excitation inherent in watching other human beings in time and space—no doubt related to the neurobiological phenomenon "mirror neuron" activation, in which regions of the brain are activated in concert with the actions of an observed body (perhaps explaining the efficacy of spectator sports, images of violence, and pornography). This begins to describe how the pictorial and *narrative* together make meaning—telling stories with content both manifest and latent, suggested by visual phenomena as much as by language. These meanings define and orient the subjective consciousness in social life, which describes and determines identity, sense of self, and relationships to other human beings.

Art is material evidence of the human cognitive apparatus. Representational painting entails the illusion of nameable objects on any flat, painted, discrete surface, reproducing visual (and thus sensory and linguistic) neurological phenomena in an imaginary space, as might be experienced by a single, embodied consciousness. Avant-garde discourses have erroneously conflated representational painting skills, strategies, and styles with conservative ideologies and politics. From memoir to narrative documentary to personal accounts in the description of social trauma, injustice, and war to accounts of psychological trauma and assaults on the dignity, identity, and freedom of the modern individual to speak without ostracization, the notion of embodied subjecthood coupled with narrative has always been a viable location for political awakening. This does not refer to the primacy of a constructed or ideological "individual" in culture, nor to patriarchal cults of heroic individualism—cowboy, athlete, soldier, inventor, entrepreneur—that permeate Western mythologies and attendant disparities of wealth and power. Nor does the notion of embodied subjecthood describe ideological "humanism" (as a belief in an ahistorical and metaphysical human essence) or what Derrida called "logocentrism" ("a tendency to refer all questions of meaning . . . to some singular presence assumed to be behind them—'author,' 'reality,' 'history,' 'zeitgeist,' 'stucture,' 'nature'"[3]). Rather, embodied subjecthood, acknowledging our material and social being, asserts the necessity of empathy, an awareness of the consciousness of the Other, and is necessary to the origin of fairness and the valuation of political equality. The retold story of embodied subjecthood present in any narrative (which presumes a speaker; a story must have a storyteller) has vital political uses including myth, history, propaganda, and the social message of the individual. This last is inherent to democratic philosophies, and valuable for its acknowledgment of the speaking subject, the individual, the author, as the subject's *uniqueness*. This basic tenet of rights accorded in the politics of modernity is an essential component of human rights movements.

(opposite)
Patrick Romine
Willie Gets a Beatin', 1995
Oil on linen
38 x 40 inches

Only recently has critical writing since the nineteenth century begun to value mastery of craft in painting, which is oddly marginal in the visual arts. Most other fields of creative or technical endeavor—musical performance, sport, science and technology, literature—have standards regarding achievement, and systems of prestige and profit; the prizing of skill inspires aspiration to imitate and identify. The Marxist critique of the object has often confused pleasure in mastery with the brutal systems of production and unequal power and wealth that produced nice commodities—and no wonder, as the media has revealed the horrors of the globalized labor market and reigning consumer aesthetic as clearly one of excess. A critical analysis of beauty and craft as an obfuscating sign was politically necessary—as is a new understanding of its relevance to the politics of empathy and inclusion today. Our current cultural context is one in which free markets promise stories, experiences, images, and commodities to fill every conceivable human need and desire. Objects, commodities, images, and works of art that provide pleasure, invent or reify social identity, and evoke or express desire are therefore both problematic and of great political and social potential. They participate in the organization of our psyches, the cognition behind our actions; they attract attention by providing pleasure or other kinds of cognitive or emotional satisfaction; and they communicate ideas.

Thus representational painting as an image-making practice has unique political and social potential. Even in reproduction—conversion into digital technology and distributed online or in print, published and dispersed—the painted image maintains its reference to embodied subjecthood, merely in the knowledge that it is a painting. It speaks an experience, communicating with all the various means inherent to its material strategy; these are the origins and essence of all social life. Certainly, the subject positions most commonly embraced and valorized through history have mostly reproduced power structures, such as the well-trodden theoretical territory in the feminist critique of scopophilia. But new social conditions and the manifestation of subject positions beyond patriarchy and heteronormativity, coupled with new means of mass distribution of these positions in electronic text and images, now require a theoretical reassessment of pleasure and the gaze, pioneered by neuroscience as well as recent feminist and queer theory. The political potential of first-person experience—and works of art full of the senses of material, time, space, nature, and the real—still speak powerfully for alternative perspectives of the cultural Other. Inclusion of the formerly excluded is the true current location of politics in art. This is a subjecthood that agitates for social and cultural change, and the representational is the best current option for a politicized aesthetic.

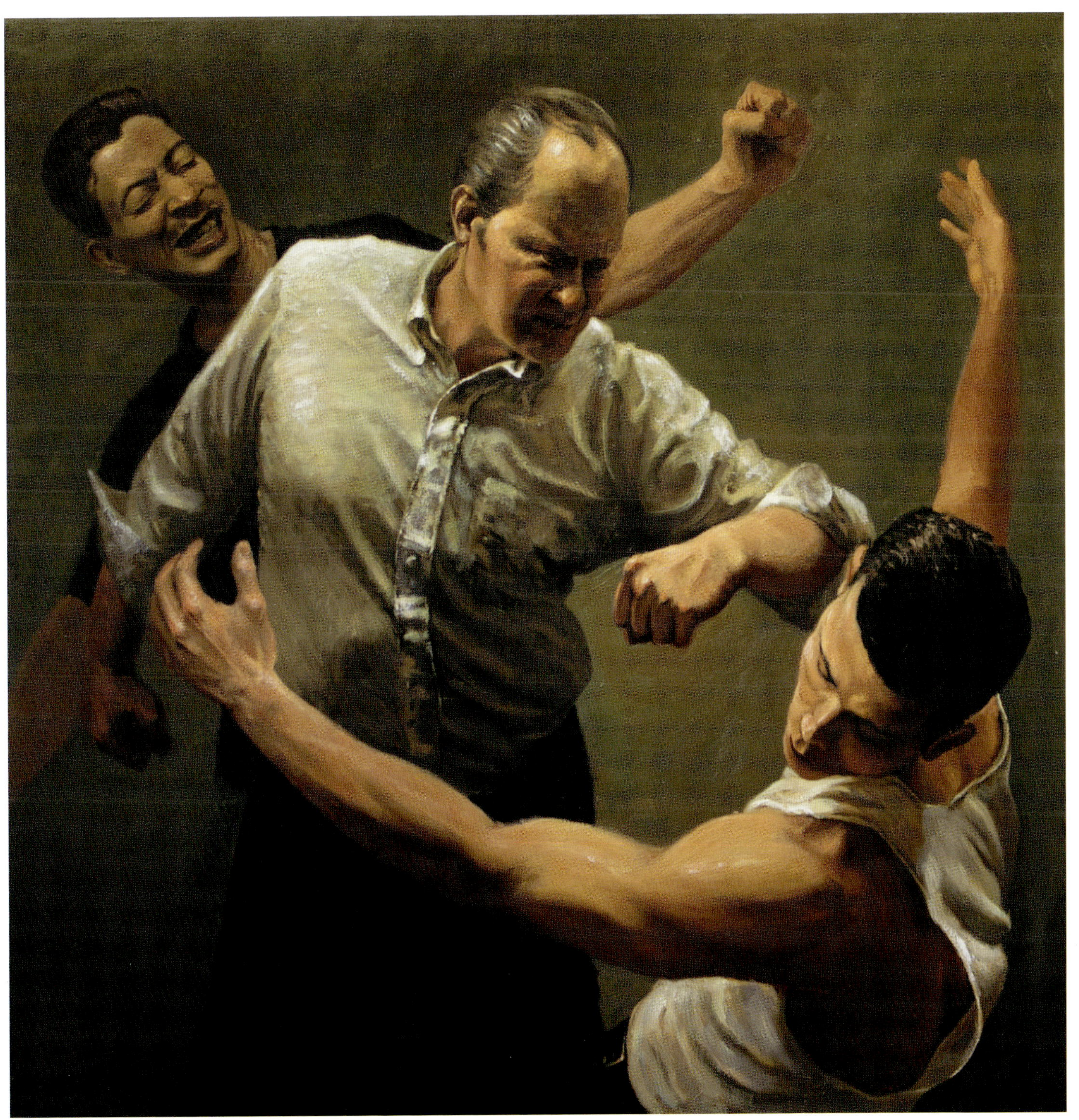

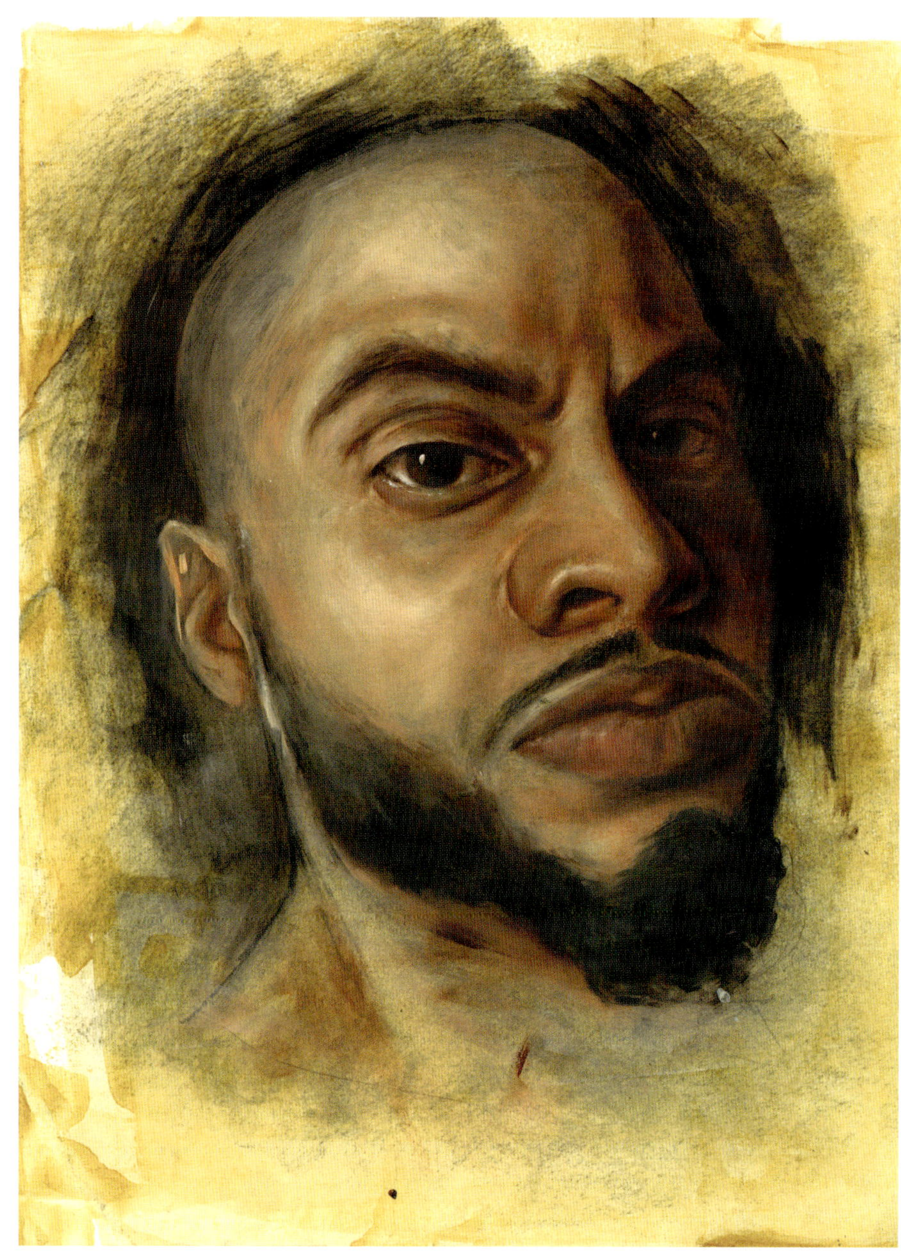

Robert Plater
Portrait of an Artist,
2012
Mixed media on
paper
14 x 11 inches

(opposite)
Sean Hyland
Chris Laughing, 2011
Oil on panel
6 x 6 inches

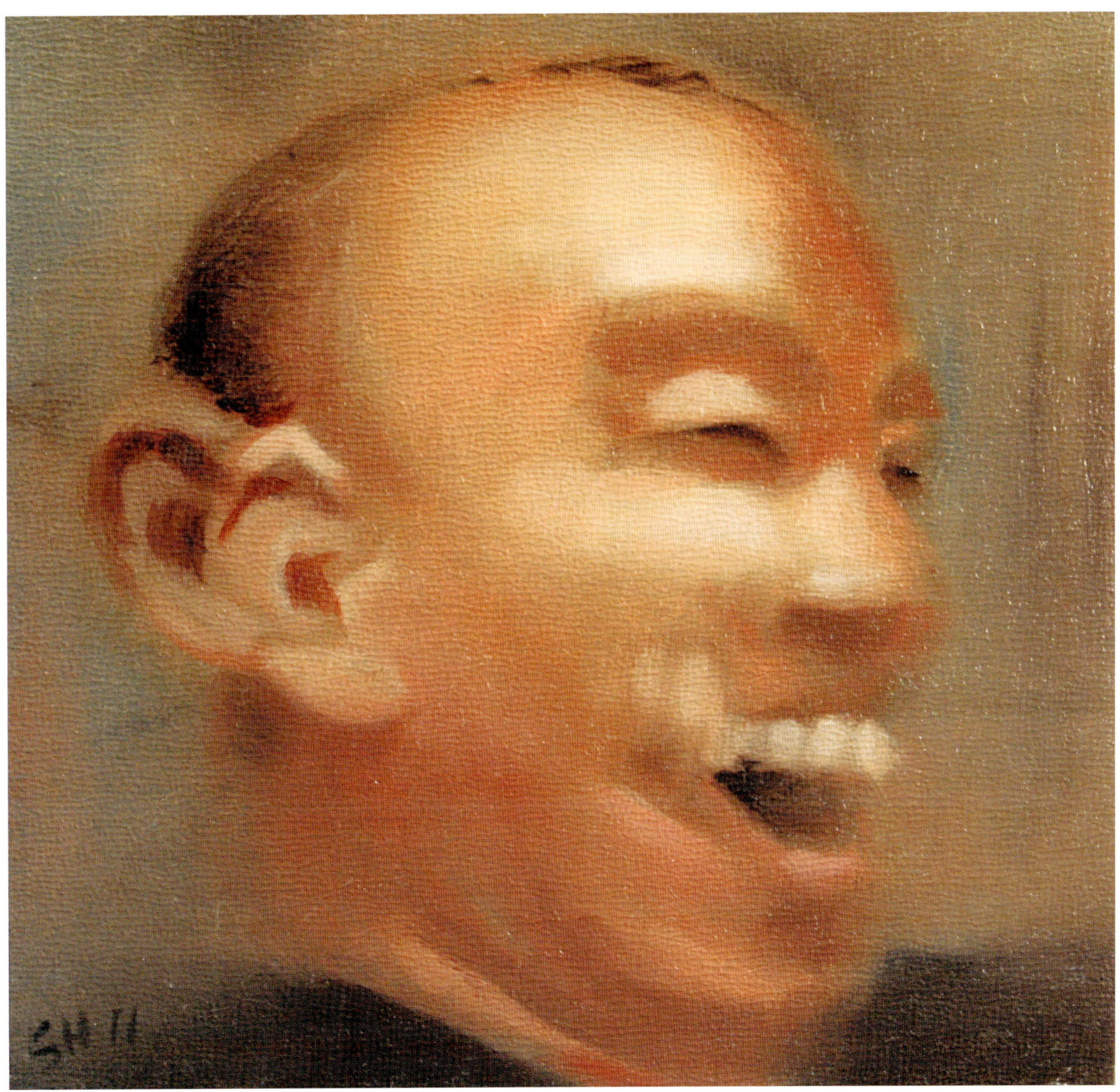

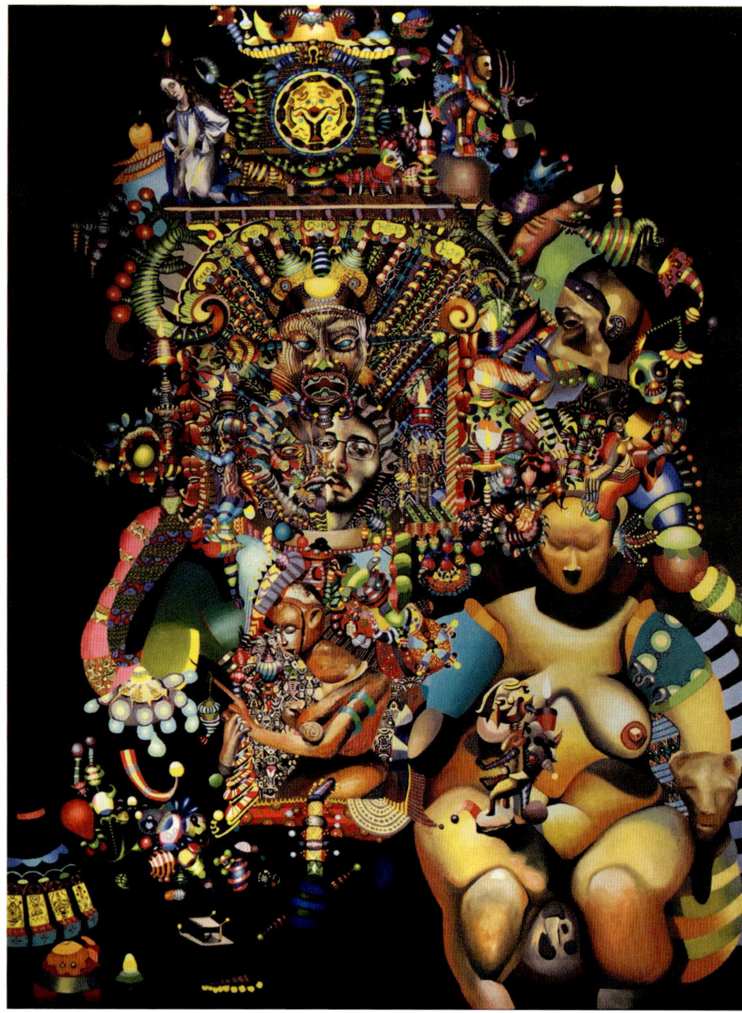

Jacob Hicks
Venus and Time,
2012
Oil on canvas
60 x 48 inches

(opposite)
Natalie Frank
Woman, 2013
Oil, enamel, collage
on board
76 x 54 inches

NATALIE FRANK

The figures that populate my paintings are in between worlds, genders, and sexualities. They exist between animal and human form, painted illusion and abstraction. I begin with stories, whether they involve multiple figures engaged in invented narratives, or a single portrait that reveals a story through its face and body, or the architectural space surrounding it. I look at a combination of sources to create these figures and scenarios—including books on the Ballets Russes and World War II, medical encyclopedias, and imagery of carnivals and mythology—to yield bodies and scenarios that span genres and histories. I look for environments, too: interiors from home décor magazines, period homes, empty institutional spaces. I also light, dress, and photograph models and people I know. I take hundreds of photographs of hands, feet, and eyes. I combine all these sources, and through imagination these pictures form.

I used to work in oil on stretched canvas and make sketches that I scaled to a finished drawing or painting, but my painting process is changing. I still use the figure within the mode of traditional painting as one tool to express narrative, but the medium itself has become a strong voice in the storytelling. Now figuration disintegrates into abstraction, passages of flatness and decoration; bodies hold together the reality of the painting, with just enough weight to insist on their own reality. The rooms people inhabit also have become a part of their bodies, as their forms flicker in and out of illusion and presence. The surfaces are important to me: often, I collage old canvases on top of an underpainting to bring texture and disruption to the top layer of paint. Sometimes, this collage comes off the edges of the board, asserting the autonomy and abstraction of the forms. I am combining enamel, oil, collage, and the bare surface of the board.

There's greater improvisation in the smaller paintings; these change rapidly. I plan the larger paintings with an umber sketch, laying in the figure and space. Still, the final painting is based on a loose idea and becomes the final image through a continual process of application and reaction. I prefer to work on oil-primed boards, made of composite wood, that I first prime with multiple coats of gesso, without sanding. I apply Williamsburg Titanium Oil Ground with a cake knife; I enjoy a marred surface and nonabsorbent ground. After two weeks of drying time, I put down an abstract painting in oil-based enamel. This gives me a surface to react to, and a purity of color that I can excavate toward and always return to. Sometimes, I will use Jade glue to affix layers of canvas of my old paintings. At times this imagery will not be covered with further coats of oil, becoming a part of the finished image. I also often remove the collage to reveal the underlayers of paint. More and more, I create three-dimensional structural components. I build screen-door attachments that open to reveal figures, frames that follow the irregular shapes of the painting.

I am always thinking of art historical precedents: Ensor and Goya's grotesquerie; Kitaj's flattened and drawn spaces; Tiepolo's and Degas's materiality; Kienholz's and the COBRA's integration of painting with sculptural materials; Picasso's definition of the figure and its relationship to personal and meta-narrative. The finished scenes themselves are iterations, characters reenacting age-old narratives of power: relationships that pivot around sexuality, mortality, and identity.

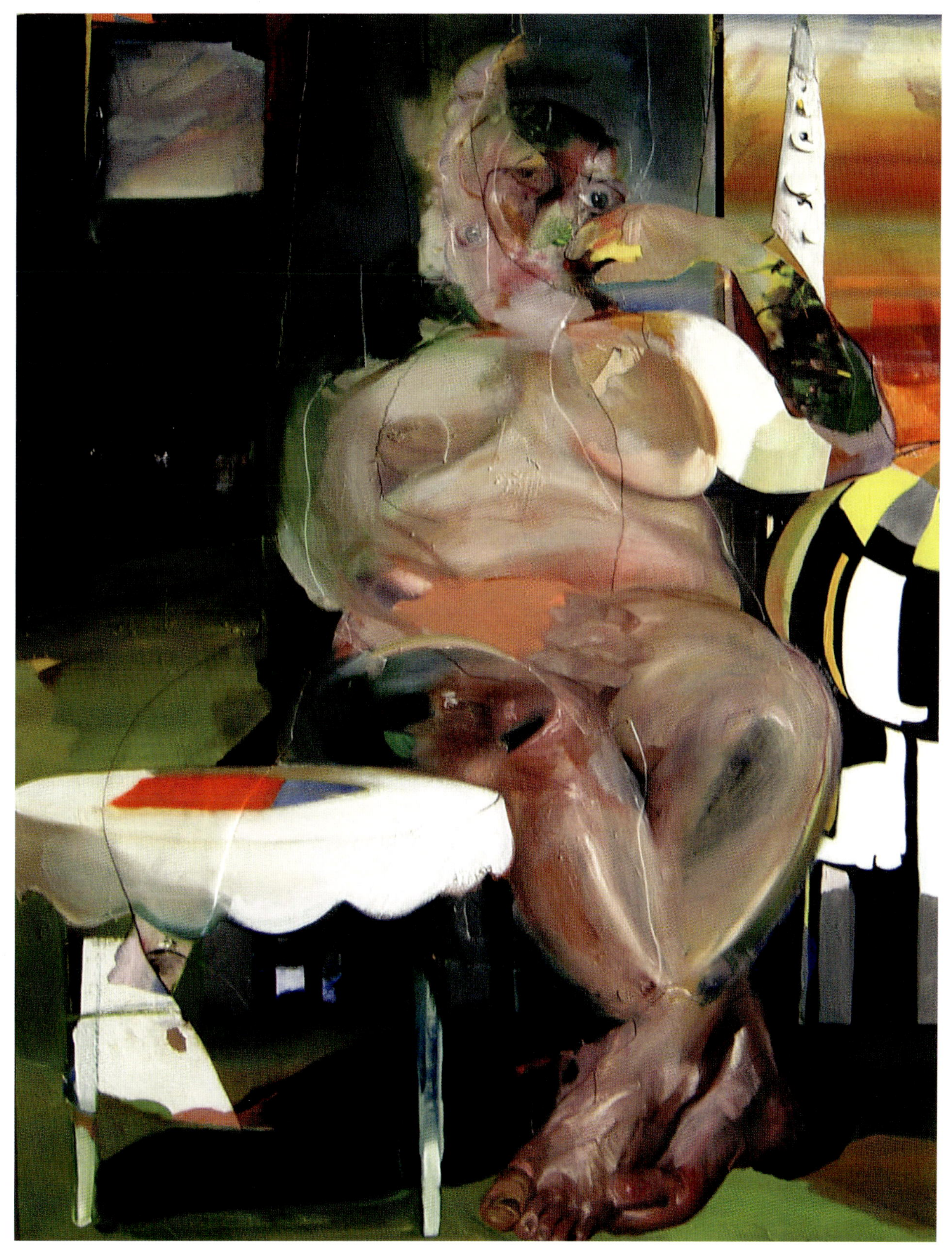

SCALE, MATERIALS, AND SELF-PERCEPTION IN CONTEMPORARY FIGURATIVE SCULPTURE

MARK MENNIN

LANDMARK CHANGES CAME EVERY FEW HUNDRED YEARS in the cycles of Greek statuary—archaic, classical, Hellenistic, late Hellenistic—and premodern European statuary—medieval, Renaissance, Mannerist, Baroque, etc. But major twentieth-century postwar movements have lasted twenty years, then fifteen, then ten, five, now maybe three. The upside is not too much remains irrelevant for very long, as nothing remains relevant. Only historical constants have repeated significance in cycles, and the beginning of the twenty-first century has re-established the figure as one. This re-morphing of human self-perception has not been bound to a scale, but has occurred in all sizes, from the figurine to monumental public works.

Two sculptors bear the major responsibility for keeping figurative sculpture relevant from early Modernism into recent history. Process and material as well as sculptural narrative played a role in the work of both Rodin, the obvious protagonist, and Medardo Rosso. Rodin had the hubris required to bring the traditional into the modern age on his own terms; he redefined figure modeling with his models in motion, rendering the kinetics of the body like no other. But if Rodin was the revolutionary warrior, Medardo Rosso was the spy, his impact subtle but enduring. Rosso's approach degraded the rules and formats of traditional figurative statuary. His frontal characters and narratives are not dramatic but antiheroic, pathetic, and mostly static, pensive, and quiet.

A master of the casting process, Rosso gave performances in his studio for small audiences (and in gesture, not unlike Richard Serra's early fecal, lead-flinging fiestas.) Lacking Rodin's patronage, Rosso cast less often in expensive metal, so his pieces remain in their primary wax and plaster. At first a limitation, it eventually became a choice. Translucent yellow foundry wax, which provided a warmer skin and captured and contained light in ways that challenged cold, impenetrable bronze, defines his work materially.

(opposite)
Ann Hirsch
Watchers, 2003
Polychrome plaster, hydrocal
24 x 18 x 18 inches

Rosso's influence has also been about making sculpture about the image of it, as much as about the actual object. His pioneering studio process showed the earliest glimpses of material experimentation, performance, and photography as sculptural assessment. Capturing transience of movement and light, often requiring a specific point of view (rather than seen in the round), he brought two-dimensional values to three-dimensional practice. His naturalism undermined the heroic and monumental. These subtle values led to the limitlessness of modern sculpture, figurative or otherwise. Rodin pushed a practice to its limits; Rosso quietly took limits away.

Public figurative sculpture was also a beneficiary of critical mood swings that followed many of Rosso's empathic cues. Before the late nineteenth century, the figurative monument was no study in humility. Heroic statuary dominated three-dimensional presentations—war memorial, mythological/biblical storytelling, and portraiture. Mussolini's Foro Italico (designed by Enrico Del Debbio) exemplifies empty Neoclassical hubris. A reduced caricature of the classical amphitheater is littered with thoughtlessly formed athletic statuary. Neoclassical romance with revolution, and the simple elimination of the decorative fungi of the Rococo, was sullied in such work. But after two world wars and various genocides, man's self-perception had changed drastically from that of the High Renaissance (not that he wouldn't miss those celebrated days of his own magnificence and perfection, but the self-aggrandizement probably felt a little less appropriate following some horrible truths). In more recent years, figurative sculpture has not only demonstrated this self-doubt but endured critical insignificance, indignant re-morphing, and for some periods of time, almost a total absence, which effected self-perception, studio practices, and material choices.

By the 1950s, New York had replaced Paris as the cultural capital of the world while the latter licked its physical and psychological war wounds. With

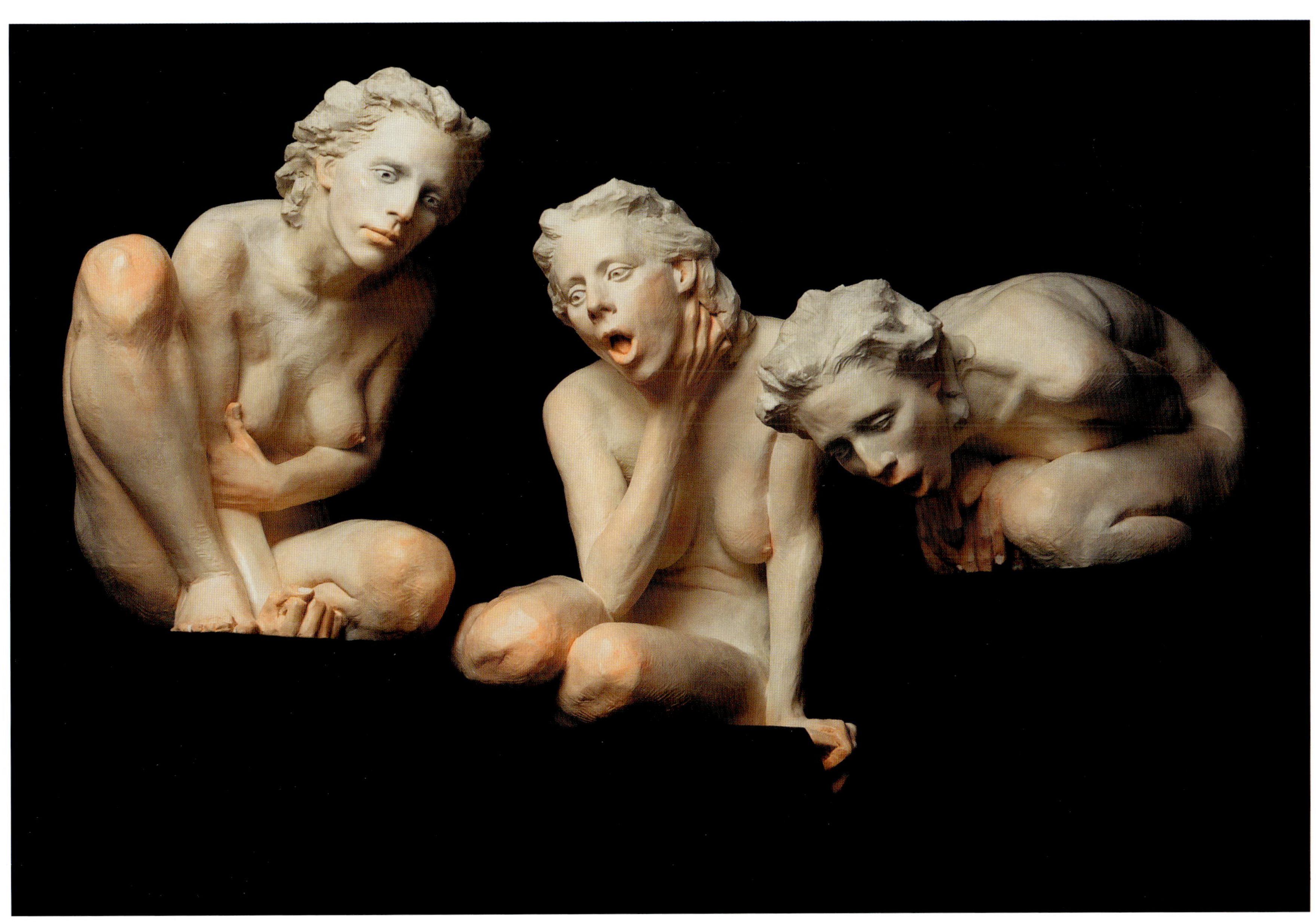

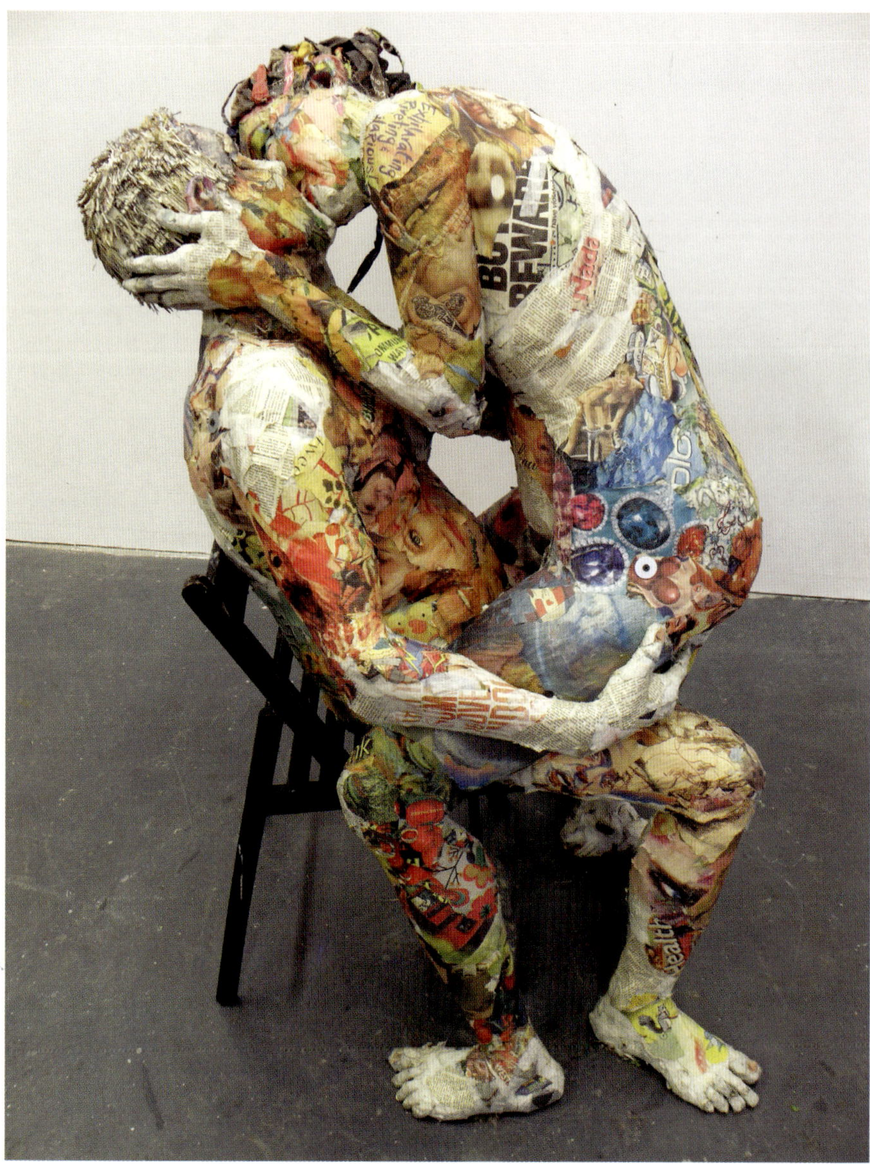

Will Kurtz
Coming Together, 2013
Wood, wire, newspaper, mixed media, wood chair
51 x 33 x 32 inches

(opposite)
Nina Levy
Couple, 1999
Plaster, steel, oil paint, resin
84 x 76 x 178 inches

a fresh slate, America backed its own brand of nonobjective art. It was a critical monopoly. In sculpture, direct metal welding eclipsed figure modeling—the sculptor traded in beret and smock for goggles, leathers, and cigars, used as much to ignite a torch as to inhale. David Smith, seeing the work of Julio González in Spain, became the icon of this practice in America. European welders like Theodore Roszak anthropomorphized stainless steel and nickel structures; César Baldaccini stayed within even more literal figuration before being swept up by Nouveau Realisme and its post-Duchampian trappings. In the larger arena the figure wouldn't reemerge until it was noisy and facile enough, in its unfortunate representation in early 1980s Neoexpressionism, but the rendered figure may have survived nonobjectivism best during the West Coast Funk movement. Whether because of an innate lowbrow approach or through some blue-chip rebellion, permanence in material was not at a sculptural premium. Though Manuel Neri carved marble and casted bronze, his direct plasters, ceramic figures, and odd resins and plastics show how materials brought his early figures to life. In their relative seclusion from New York, Bay Area artists were able to avoid international categorization, and maintained a particular autonomy, perhaps through irreverence and fierce provinciality.

A postwar figural version of mold making, the body cast, was not new. It was a medical and sculptural device long before Rodin was accused of using the process in his *Age of Bronze*, when presented at the 1877 Paris Salon. But body casting, standing on its own in Pop art and Photorealism, brought an unmodeled manifestation of the figure back. George Segal, Duane Hanson, and John De Andrea cast and patinated to a scary degree of reality, and yet breath seems to have left the body. Others employing some of this process were able to reel in the mimesis of the mold, giving figures back some life, with vital surfaces and the given virtues of their chosen materials. Magdalena Abakanowicz's multiple-figure narratives with burlap body casts provide a pathos missing in the bronzes. Likewise Kiki Smith seems to have used body casting more loosely, relying more on the buildup of modeled materials like wax to maintain the sculptural vitality of her narratives.

The 1980s frenetic dance between progressive and retro-classical cultures saw many new materials beyond the primary clay, plaster, wood or secondary materials of cast metal and stone. Perhaps owing to Italy's Arte Povera, lead, wax, latex and, yes, Styrofoam were all well investigated as alternatives to traditional materials. It is no coincidence that these materials were always used in part of a larger sculptural process like casting, mold making, or even art moving and storage, in the case of some plastics. Michelangelo Pistoletto's giant stacked Styrofoam figures were originally carved directly as models to be cast in bronze or carved in marble. Eventually, like Rosso, the figures were just kept in the primary material. Giuseppe Penone experimented in similar ways by cutting the foundry or firing process short and resolving pieces while in process.

With Marc Quinn and Jeff Koons we leave the arena of the hands-on figure modeler altogether. (The honesty of the complete disclosure, however,

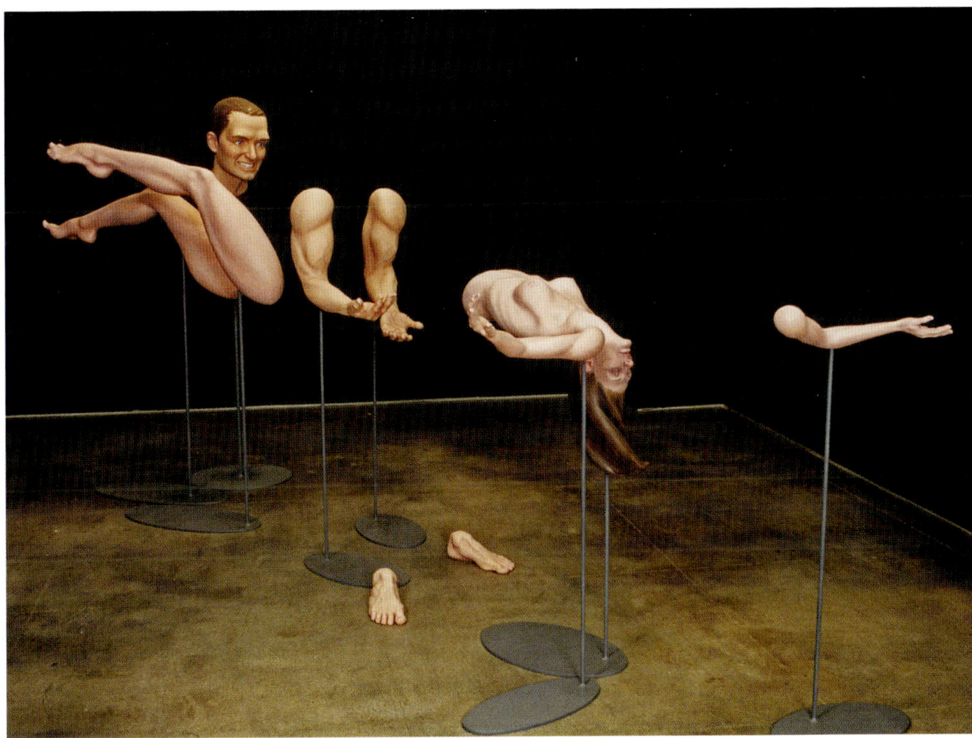

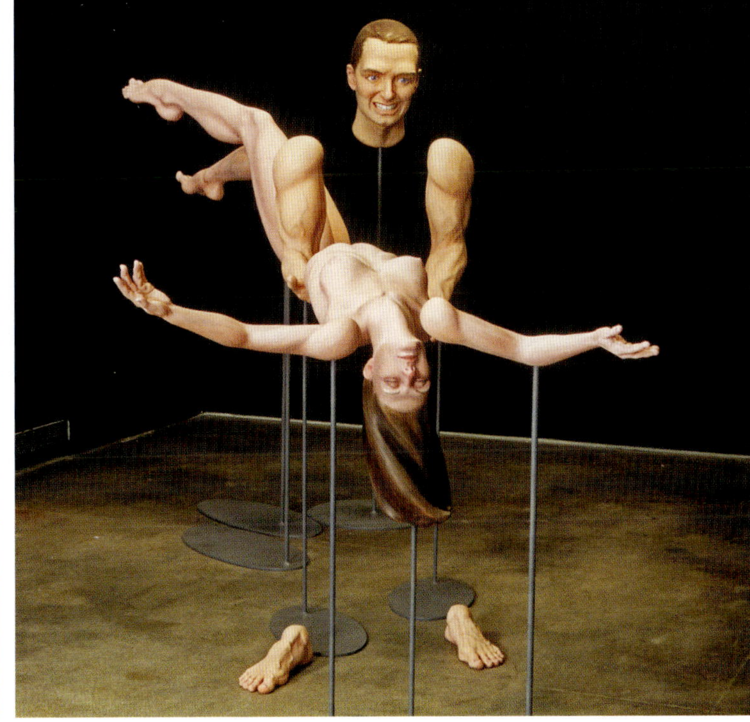

draws appropriate applause.) With fabricated stone and cast stainless steel, taxidermy now moves on to the cryogenic preservation of popular images. This sterilized quality is intended, but it's also the product of a factory process and many hands. Likewise the marble figures of Marc Quinn don't strive for the warmth of an earth material. With his use of stone, there are suggested affinities with heroic statuary, as with his models who suffer the effects of thalidomide. Their abbreviated bodies relate to antiquity's truncated heroes. Though the hands-off process may trivialize the physical plight of the models, the priority of pathos over idealization recalls the Rosso spirit.

A recent further step away from the verb "to sculpt" comes in the form of digital rendering. Here the tools are 3-D scanners and CNC (computer numerical control) machines. In most cases where there is integrity to the original model, the process differs little from any other farmed-out one. When a rendered figure is routed out in a synthetic material or compound, it is ethically the same as sending a model to a foundry. But material has meaning, and its relationship with the artist is meaningful. The more an artist manually divorces him- or herself from the process, the less significant he or she must become. There are always layers of decision making that need nuanced attention throughout the execution of a sculpture, especially with a figure. For example, as has happened in the digital world, an artist can choose a random found image and scan it three dimensionally, then have it executed in a material on a CNC machine—said artist successfully rendering

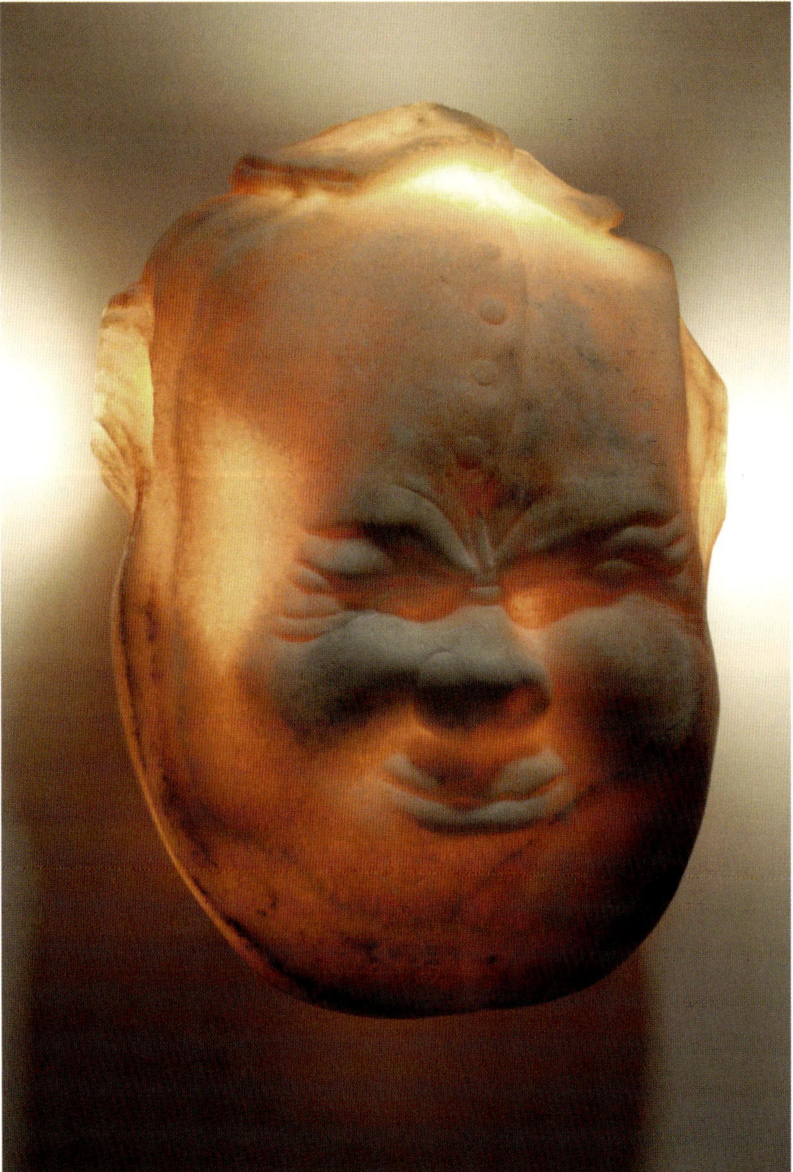

him- or herself completely insignificant within the context of his or her own work. This reinforces man's self-criticism that he works so hard to make himself extinct. Other than this existential danger, new technology can serve figure rendering well, in roughing out or routing out during layers of the process where extra labor serves no particular goal.

At its own scale, the figure has maintained sober self-investigation, the narrative and process working as partners in the hands of a thoughtful artist and craftsman, we presume. Yet we can imagine a giant factory-scaled process in the fabrication of monumental work such as Vera Mukhina's eighty-foot figure group, or an army of carvers and drillers rendering presidents on Mount Rushmore. The technical goals of public art have always been about permanence, grandeur, and the enduring vanities and legacy of patronage. The twentieth-century collapses of pretending dynasties brought a new humility to public memorial, however, and changes to patronage in post-industrial times. The memorial could project a newfound humanity, as though finding its more sensitive, feminine side. The speed of new information, which does not allow much time to digest current events or recent histories in the arts and gives only a shallow overview, lets the contemporary public artist evade an over-celebrated self.

Recent successes like Maya Lin's Vietnam Memorial or the 9/11 Memorial at the World Trade Center do not include rendered figures. However, the figural procession through these architectural projects, as well as the figural reflection and even absence, become as relevant to memorial as the inclusion of statuary. An earlier prototype might be Jules Dalou's tomb of Victor Noir in Père Lachaise Cemetery in Paris. A fallen martyr journalist lays slain by entitled Bonaparte spawn, as occurred during the peak of the Second Empire, when inbred royalty would be served no justice. What is significant is that the hero is no glorious conqueror but a man of letters without vindication, save his tomb. Such change toward the approach to memory can be seen in its best museums—monument cemeteries of Paris, Milan, and Genoa. Executed mostly by anonymous, highly skilled artisans, there is also unsigned statuary by modern masters, which makes for a great tourist game.

After the idea, material has always defined sculpture. The imagined process is what embellishes the experience of confronting a rendered figure. Dialogue between the object and viewer has most vitality when the dialogue between the object and its creator has imaginable vitality as well. All the mood swings of sculptural protagonists, materials, and processes have prevented figurative sculpture from remaining monolithic throughout the ages. After having achieved a degree of exterior perfection in permanent materials, looking inward at our own fragility can re-humanize this practice. Finding suitable materials and processes that convey such fragility can perhaps continue to keep the sculpted figure human.

MARK MENNIN

My decision to become a stone carver came long before my decision to be an artist, though without the latter goal, I never would have been compelled to actually pick up a hammer. The exposure to the magic of Renaissance and Baroque carvers is not a unique story. Mine was when I was nine years old in 1969 on a family trip to Italy. However, the energy in my father was indelible as he described each stone narrative in all the usual locations. He was a composer who knew about as much art history as anyone I've known since.

I never went to art school but studied art history at Princeton. I never really got my hands dirty until taking ceramics there from a fabulous Asian-Hawaiian sculptor, Toshiko Takaezu. I fell in love with the process and started lifelong dialogues about the figure and function and contact with an earth material. After graduation I started carving stone at the Art Students League and talked some Texans into commissioning me to copy Greek statuary. No, I didn't know how to yet, but it proved to be a good baptism by fire, and I was able to send myself to Italy and learn everything I could consume while honing the finer skills. This gave me ease with stone, even in the largest-scaled pieces.

Few contemporary carvers have had a significant influence on my work, but there are many giants in history both anonymous and known whom I admire. I also fear and admire cataclysmic geological events, as well as building endeavors that dwarf sculptural ones. The sculptors who have been most interesting to me straddle categorizations, or have redefined or undermined previous sets of rules. Isamu Noguchi and one of his mentors, Brancusi, probably nurtured along much of the multi-practice and multi-cultured values I admire. The work that fascinates me most is where nationality, religion, material, and gender remain only background components to a more universal statement. Though neither James Turrell nor Richard Serra is a carver, their statements are about some sublime achievement that defies language, and that's the only reason I can think of to become a visual artist.

I was able to make a living in Europe and spend many cycles of time in Italy and France, executing large projects and exhibiting. The travel was healthy though New York never failed to recharge me. When I got more involved in larger scales and construction, the tools not only got bigger and the process more physical, but mental preparation became more intense. It can be much like the prep for a daily athletic event, where eight to ten hours of hard labor await you, and if you squander the day, you lose . . . time.

In pursuing works of increased scale, I continue to consider historical examples, and this includes a larger geological history. Considerations of the site, sculptural punctuation of the landscape, and architectural circumstances have become very involved. Preparation drawings have become more about schematics than rendering. When Photoshop came along, it greatly helped with "siting" pieces, placing them in hypothetical, specific places.

So the beginning and the end of a larger carved form has become like a travel experience. I have relationships with some quarries that let me root around in places and choose specific blocks of stone. The block usually corresponds to an idea formed from a drawing. When the flatbed shows up at the studio, now a barn and some land, I offload the blocks with a forklift and arrange them to work on. Then the real labor begins. The use of pneumatic drills, jackhammers, and a wonderful water-fed diamond blade, which runs off a tow-behind diesel compressor, makes the initial stages of carving go quickly enough. This affords me some of the spontaneity of a modeler, and is most gratifying, if exhausting. It's a wrestling match with the machine as much as the material.

The complete physical involvement of direct carving is necessary to me, though models and prep drawings help practical execution. It's hard to be efficient in delegation when you really love a material; for me that would feel like hiring a surrogate lover. Thus I don't farm out the process except for polishing, which though satisfying, no longer changes the form and thus brings no great surprises.

In Italy there were always amusing bits of braggadocio at the bar, about the hardness or value of the stone a sculptor was carving, or about having found the "perfect block" . . . that would eventually get butchered or over-polished anyway. Now I only use the plentiful local granites that we see in curbs or building foundations, or I reuse stones that have had former functional lives. This affords me the hubris not to feel any of the preciousness or the delicate surgical process that many carvers suffer through. Carving has simply become the courage to remove, and the wisdom not to change that which I can't improve.

RONA PONDICK

I am very physical and touch everything. I can't walk past anything without touching it. I am a lover of objects and I am a maker who thinks with my hands.

When I graduated from the Yale School of Art in 1977 and returned to New York, I drew from Egyptian and Greek art at the Metropolitan Museum of Art as a way to understand my likes and dislikes. I discovered my artistic roots in Egyptian, Etruscan, and African art as well as in works by Brancusi and Giacometti. Over time, I discovered other artists who are important to me, like Riemenschneider and Bernini.

In 1995 I was approached to do a large outdoor sculpture for a private collection. I didn't think my materials, imagery, or the scale I had been working on would make sense outdoors. Since the late 1980s I had been working with ephemeral materials: wax, paper, heat-sensitive plastic, and found objects like shoes, baby bottles, and teeth that I chose because they felt metaphorically suggestive. I eventually decided to take the commission on and made big image, material, and scale changes. This is when nature entered my work and I made my first tree/teeth sculpture cast in aluminum.

This commission inspired me to further change my imagery and materials while my interest in symbolism and metaphor remained. I began making animal/human and tree/human hybrid sculptures. It all started with a life-cast from my head. I was looking for good detail with accurate skin texture and decided to use medical silicone to produce it. I didn't want to distort the form of my nose so I chose not to use straws that would help me breathe easily while my head was encased in rubber and plaster—which meant I could have possibly suffocated in the process. While my head was coated in silicone and plaster for several hours I felt the effects of sensory deprivation and freaked out. It was a horrible feeling to be encased like that, but I got what I wanted.

(opposite)
Mark Mennin
Sleepy Hollow 2,
2011
Onyx
16 x 13 x 10 inches

To date, every head in my sculptures derives from this same head. I change the scale of it with the use of computer technology while altering parts of it by hand. Eventually, I made life-casts of my hands, arms, and legs and altered them in similar ways.

Dog was my first animal/human hybrid sculpture and I had to remake it five times until it felt right. I was dissatisfied with modeling the dog's body in wax, which felt too soft and didn't hold the form crisply enough. So I started working with a claylike material that I could model, and once it dried it had the consistency of stone, which meant I could also carve and grind it. It was a little like combining Giacometti's process with Brancusi's.

When I first combined my head with the animal body, my thoughts were about mythology and the use of the hybrid image in art. Animal/human hybrids and monsters have a long history, beginning in neolithic times and continuing through the Egyptian, Greek, and Roman periods. It doesn't end there. Monstrous hybrids appear in the work of Bosch, Goya, and Redon, and into the present day. I wondered if I could make hybrids that were tied to history but remained relevant in my own time.

As I worked on *Dog*, I was also making *Monkeys*, a baroque tangle of monkeys climbing over each other. I hand modeled the animal bodies and their heads but I wanted the cast human arms, hands, and heads to feel like they had been directly removed from my body. I wanted to change the scale of the life-cast of my head so it was the same size as the monkey head. A physicist suggested I use reverse prototyping to scan and output a smaller version of the life-cast head. This is easy now, but was difficult in 1998 because the technology was new and I wanted such high resolution. The files were so big the computers kept crashing and it took a year to build. Once I succeeded at reducing the size of my head I started incorporating this technology into my sculpture making, but only when I wanted to change scale.

In my hybrid sculptures I may combine hand modeling, carving, chasing, mold making, and metal casting with cutting-edge 3-D scanning and building. In my life-casts I maintain a high level of detail in the skin-textured areas, rendering large parts by hand. I model the animal bodies by hand so they are highly refined and polished. I want the human, highly detailed skin texture to merge naturally into the refined and polished surfaces of the animal bodies. The physical posture of each animal and the human gesture help merge these two foreign bodies. I go to great lengths to make my hybrid sculptures feel effortless. I am very comfortable using old and new technologies to accomplish this.

In my tree/human hybrid sculptures I replace buds or ends of branches with miniature versions of my own head or hands. More recently I am merging life-size body parts with trees. I construct my own trees, which I love doing. I spend endless hours trying to seamlessly weave together hundreds of parts I have hand modeled with actual tree parts so that it looks like nature made it. But the trees are complete fictions. I always compose in the round and with the trees it's like drawing in space.

I am happiest when I am in my studio lost in my work. For me, it is a little like magic—a sculpture appears. Half of the time I have no idea why I have made a sculpture, and I have become totally comfortable with that. Sometimes it takes me many years after making a piece to understand why I made it. Sometimes I never know.

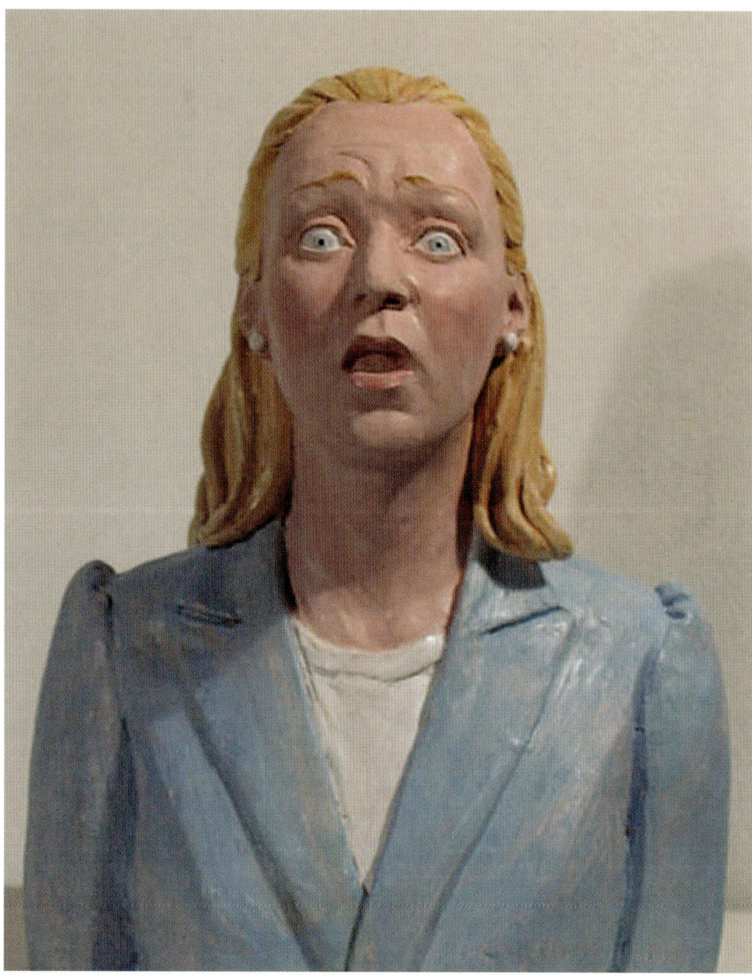

Cynthia Eardley
Witness (1), 2002
Hydrocal, casein
8 x 6 x 4.5 inches

(opposite)
Rona Pondick
Dog, 1998–2001
Yellow stainless steel
28 x 16.5 x 32 inches

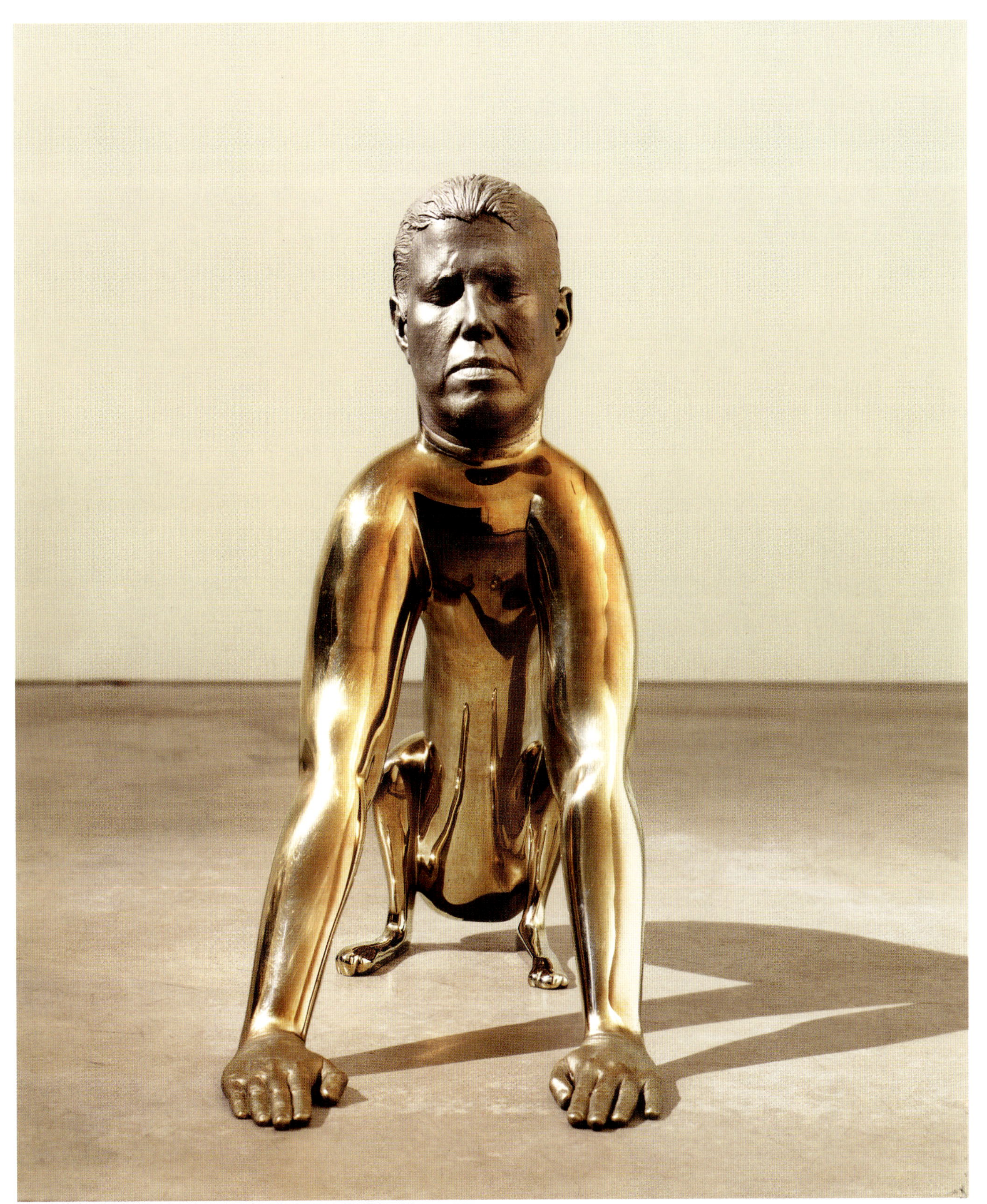

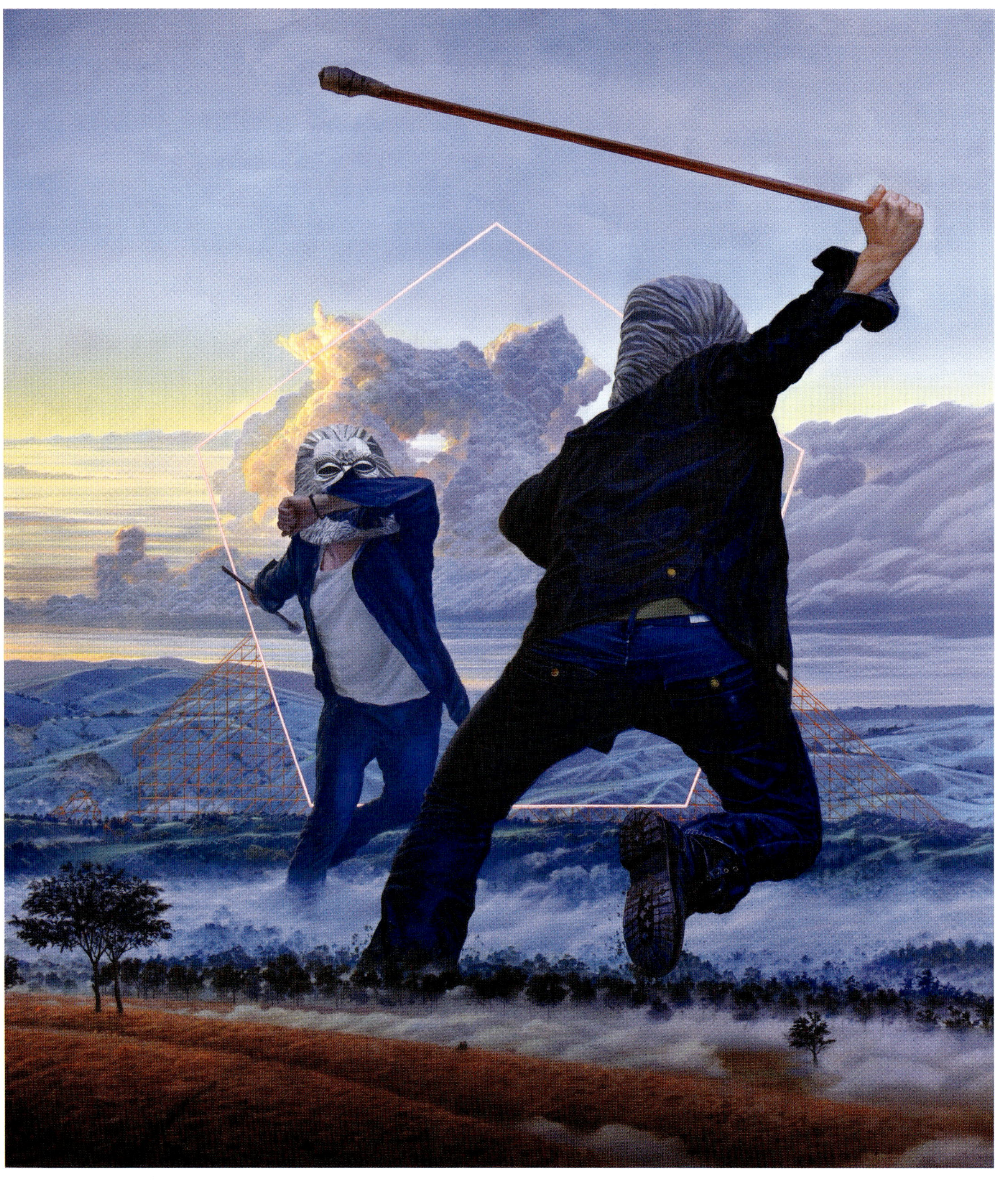

PAINTING AND DIGITAL TECHNOLOGY: FROM FILM TO PHOTOSHOP

JEAN-PIERRE ROY

AS A PAINTER I RARELY USE DIGITAL pre-visualizing precisely because of how much I have had to use it commercially, in the film/TV/advertising industry as a matte painter, concept artist, and production designer. Historically, the concept phases of most forms of design and media, from film to car production, have begun with pencil and paper, clay and paint and migrate slowly up the material chain to finished product. But there is today an almost ubiquitous need for visual products to end up digitally. The Internet has decentralized the production chain, and artists and designers find themselves working across time zones, languages, and national boundaries. To allow for this fast pace of visual informational exchange, sketching, color studies, and 3-D maquettes are almost all done in the virtual realm from the get-go.

I have developed a fluency with Photoshop and digital methods of production, which in painting has created a feedback loop that allows for commonality of thinking between 2-D "digital" and "analog"—digital as in generated and/or displayed on computer or monitor, and analog as in generated and displayed in a nonelectronic medium. Developed mostly for the fields of industrial and entertainment design, a new generation of software and hardware over the last thirty years has created a near-seamless integration between traditional picture-making concepts and practices and the digital realm. This generation of digital tool sets mean that if I can do it in Photoshop, I can do it in paint, and vice versa.

Photoshop, the industry-standard graphics editor, is used in film, graphic design, photo studios, corporate offices, and scientific and medical labs. It is pretty much required for preparing artistic images for the modern electronic workplace. But it can also be a powerful tool for the studio artist. Photoshop allows artists, designers, and creative professionals and amateurs alike to manipulate digital photographs and create raster and vector images. Raster, or bit-mapped, images are visual files with a finite level of pixel density, or resolution. Vector-based images are mathematically derived and can be blown up to any size without loss of resolution. Photoshop allows the combination of any sort of digital image to be layered into complex, authored composition; all files are made up of a mix of these raster and vector graphic elements. While Photoshop is the most commonly used, some artists use Painter, a program that more specifically mimics the grammar of traditional media, like virtual paint wetness and digital canvas texture.

The true power of Photoshop and Painter comes from their being the first image-making tools capable of making marks using light itself as the medium. Artists have always been obsessed with analyzing and expressing light in personal ways. Much of Western painting technique has focused not only on the analytical codification of the illumination of form, but also on the radiant properties of illumination. But painting light is a translation, a simplification and distortion of actual light, because physical pigments are a subtractive color-mixing system; each color added to the mix subtracts possible colors that can reach the eye. Light itself is an additive mixing system; each added color adds possible colors that can reach the eye. Before *Opticks*, Isaac Newton's groundbreaking treatise on light, artists, philosophers, and scientists thought that white light was colorless, a supposition that kept them at an unseeable distance from their subject. Through experimentation with prisms, Newton revealed that white light is made up of all of the colors of the spectrum, each of which can be split through refraction into individual chroma, or colors. This revelation has granted artists an unprecedented viewpoint from which to further their studies of nature, and inspired an entirely new set of media for artists to express their visions in.

The pinhole camera's projection capabilities have been around since the early Greeks (albeit without a recording plate), but its effects were ephemeral. The invention of the digital projector in the late twentieth century

(opposite)
Jean-Pierre Roy
To Break You Must Be Broken, 2013
Oil on canvas
72 x 62 inches

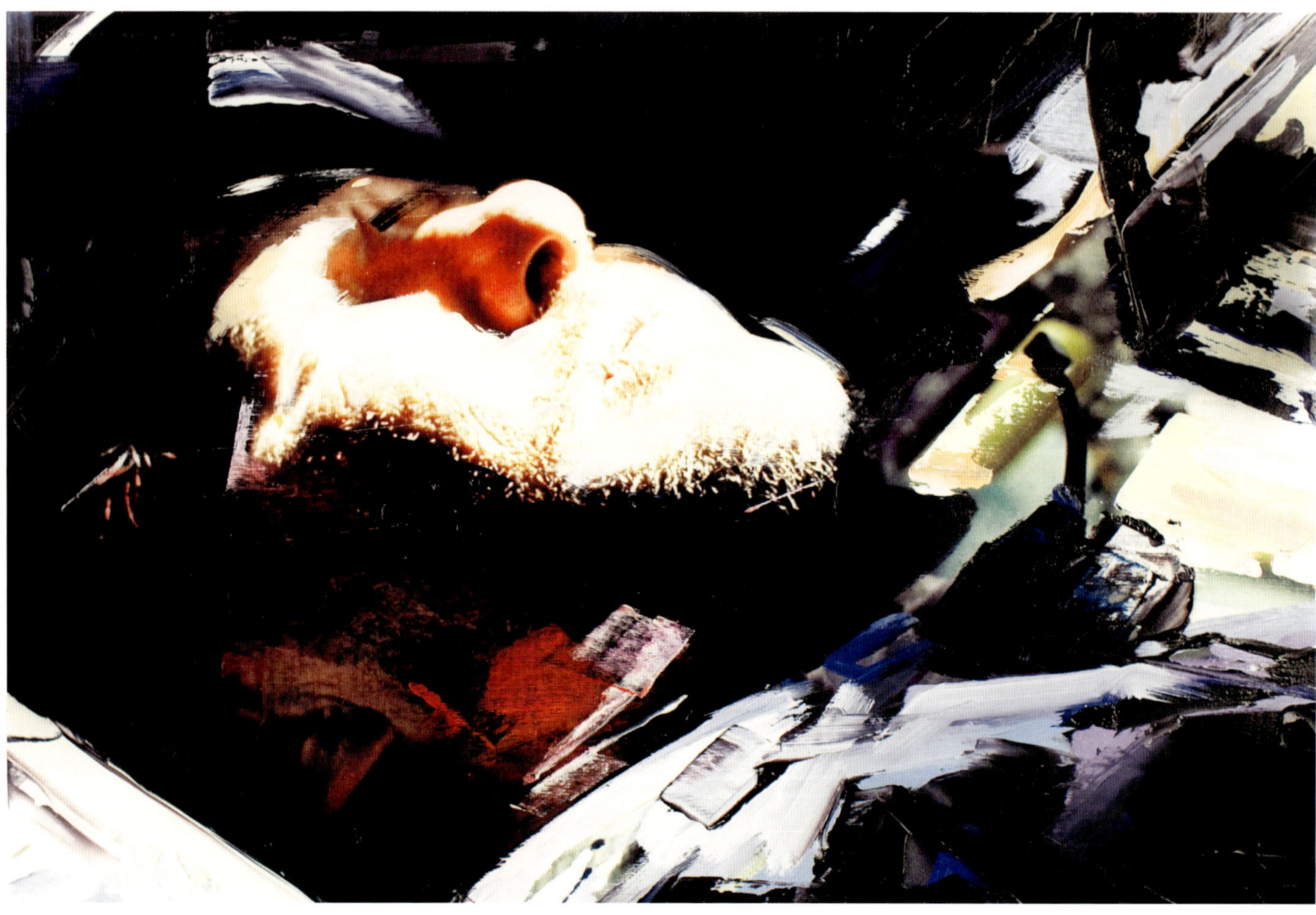

Michael Kagan
The Hold, 2009
Mixed media on canvas
13 x 19 inches

(opposite)
Debra Goertz
Downdraft #2, 2009
Oil on canvas
36 x 58 inches

let artists project and transfer transparencies, drawings, photographs, or collages to canvas, often manipulating images in Photoshop first. While Andy Warhol and other Pop artists used mechanical means of image production as both the process and content of their paintings, today many contemporary artists, from traditional painters to multimedia artists, use projection. Some artists make light itself the medium, as in James Turrell's optical compositions, which use projected light shapes for stunning illusionistic effect.

Since its birth, traditional photography has never been a thoroughly mechanical process. Early photographers, often master draftsmen, created images in which the line between the handmade and mechanically lensed was seamless. The idea of photo-manipulation wasn't even a postproduction studio fix; still photographers set up pieces of glass in front of the camera on which to paint out offending telephone poles or street car lines, to embellish everything from real estate photos to governmental propaganda—as when, after Trotsky became an enemy of the state, Stalinist censors manually painted him out of a famous photo of Lenin's May 5 speech.

In 1907 Norman Dawn put this same technique to use in a motion picture in the film *California Missions*, which depicts the Spanish missions of Southern California. Dawn used this glass-painting or "matte" technique to restore decayed buildings to their former beauty, and a new type of cinematic illusion was born. With the onset of Modernism, many artists were drawn to the possibilities of illusionism in the new film industry, which welcomed

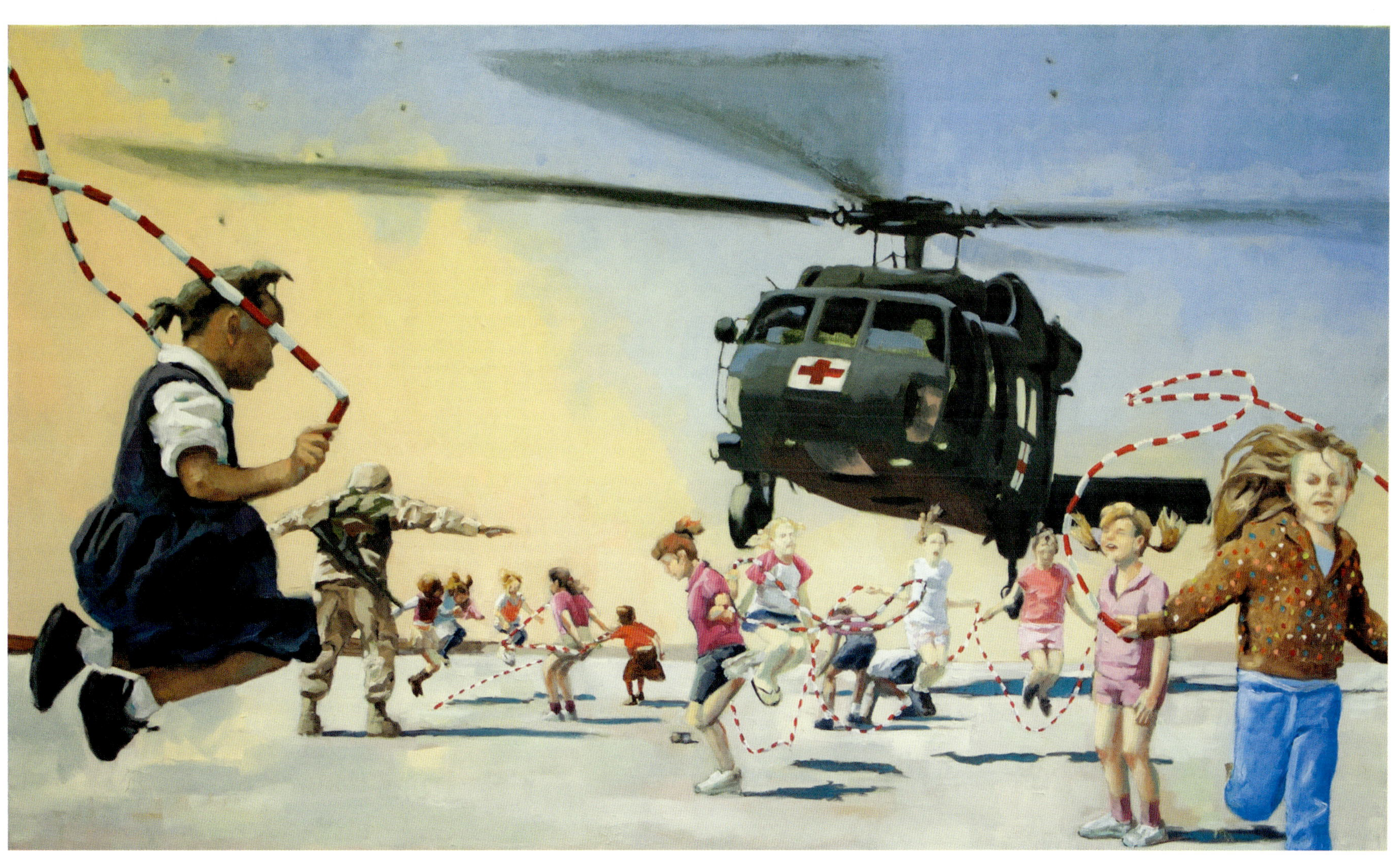

the representational skills of artists like Ferdinand Earle, who had studied with Whistler, and Walter Percy Day, an Orientalist painter. By midcentury, artists like Albert Whitlock, a trained sign painter (as was Pop artist James Rosenquist), Peter Ellenshaw, and Ralph McQuarrie combined the hand-painted with more advanced mechanical trickery. The results became a cinematic high point of illusionistic revelation, culminating in 1974's *Earthquake* (Whitlock), 1964's *Mary Poppins* (Ellenshaw), and 1980's *The Empire Strikes Back*, each of which included a revolutionary interaction of static and animated effects composited into a single shot.

But, as in the past, with advancing technology such tools didn't seem to see deep enough into the ether, and a new generation of optical manipulation appeared. In 1987, the Knoll brothers (Thomas and John) began the development of a program that became Adobe Photoshop. This robust 2-D digital imaging tool gave artists the optical clarity of the analog photo, allowing a dynamic authorship of the image, merging the languages of the photographic and handmade. The pixel (from "picture element") was the smallest piece of visual differentiation in an image, and could represent color, line, and value. When the stylus and tablet came along, allowing for a manual, brush/pen-based input into the computer, handmade decisions took center stage in the 2-D digital image pipeline. In a world where most images, both analog and digital, were being viewed on flat screens, texture was now a part of digital visual grammar and exploration.

Digital matte artists Michael Pangrazio and Yannick Dusseault used these tools to evoke the pre-cinematic, grand imagery of Hudson River School landscape painters Friedrich, Bierstadt, and Church in films like *Raiders of the Lost Ark* (1981), *The Dark Crystal* (1982), and *The Lord of the Rings* (2001–03). Craig Mullins showed that a digital tool set could compete with the impact and life of traditional 2-D materials, or at least begin turning heads toward new possibilities, by challenging the "closed form" language of digital imagery with his phenomenal virtual brushwork's push into the realm of "open form," long exclusive to the real world. Using stylus on tablet, mimicking the soft-touch of brush and pencil, artists could now use advanced processing power and software to move beyond the hard-edged, binary, graphic imagery that had given computer graphics its signature look in the 1980s. Digital tablets and pens, like the Wacom tablet, used pressure-sensitive surfaces to allow for tiny degrees of articulation, overriding the on/off mouse-click approach.

Color, long a shifting island of perceptual instability, now had an entirely new way of being explored. Photoshop allowed artists to isolate individual colors and selectively adjust their value, saturation, and hue, opening a whole new set of chromatic relationships without the need to repaint the image. Artists could explore color theory with the multitude of colors available on computer screens, and 2-D imaging software could deal with color and form on a rarefied, purely conceptual level. With the power of both subtractive and now additive color, light, as classically depicted, was not just symbolic, but material. Artist Daniel Rozin's projections use digital imaging and software manipulation to great effect in his interactive installation *Snow Mirror* (2006). The piece allows for a portrait of the sitter to slowly develop over time, digitally "painted" from the accumulation of virtual snowflakes. Beau Lotto's optical illusions use digital color in novel ways to reveal fascinating truths about our perception of color and how we make and view art. Alongside these virtual practices, more traditional artists are using these tools as a starting point to further push the boundaries of painting through a new understanding of color, detail, and light. Painters can paint observationally with Photoshop, a medium that speaks the same language as the photons beamed from the object to the eye—every color pure, every time. Painted Photoshop images can remain just that, projected and communicated via the Internet, or they can be downloaded and printed, or projected and copied with paint on canvas.

The perceptual world seems on another precipice of revelation. Alongside the 2-D, the engineering and architectural needs of the modern world have given rise to AutoCAD, which allows industrial designers and architects to model 3-D mechanically accurate prototypes. Advanced 3-D rendering and animation systems in the film and interactive worlds more fully meld the imagined with the real. "Gollum," filmmaker Peter Jackson's realization of J. R. R. Tolkien's tragic character, was a groundbreaking demonstration of these technologies in the service of emotionally charged storytelling. Ultra-high-frame-rate cameras, with an HD frame rate of 2,000 frames per second, allow the detailed examination of movements and events, permitting artists to visually explore a world previously unseen to the human eye. These technologies seem set to reveal a whole new layer of the natural world, straightening out even more of the subjective kinks in our perception of it, much like Eadweard Muybridge and his photograph plates did a hundred years ago. With Photoshop, a medium for imagery and—more importantly for painters—a medium for understanding, artists can now re-author this knowledge back into traditional mediums, literally shining a new light on the making of imagery.

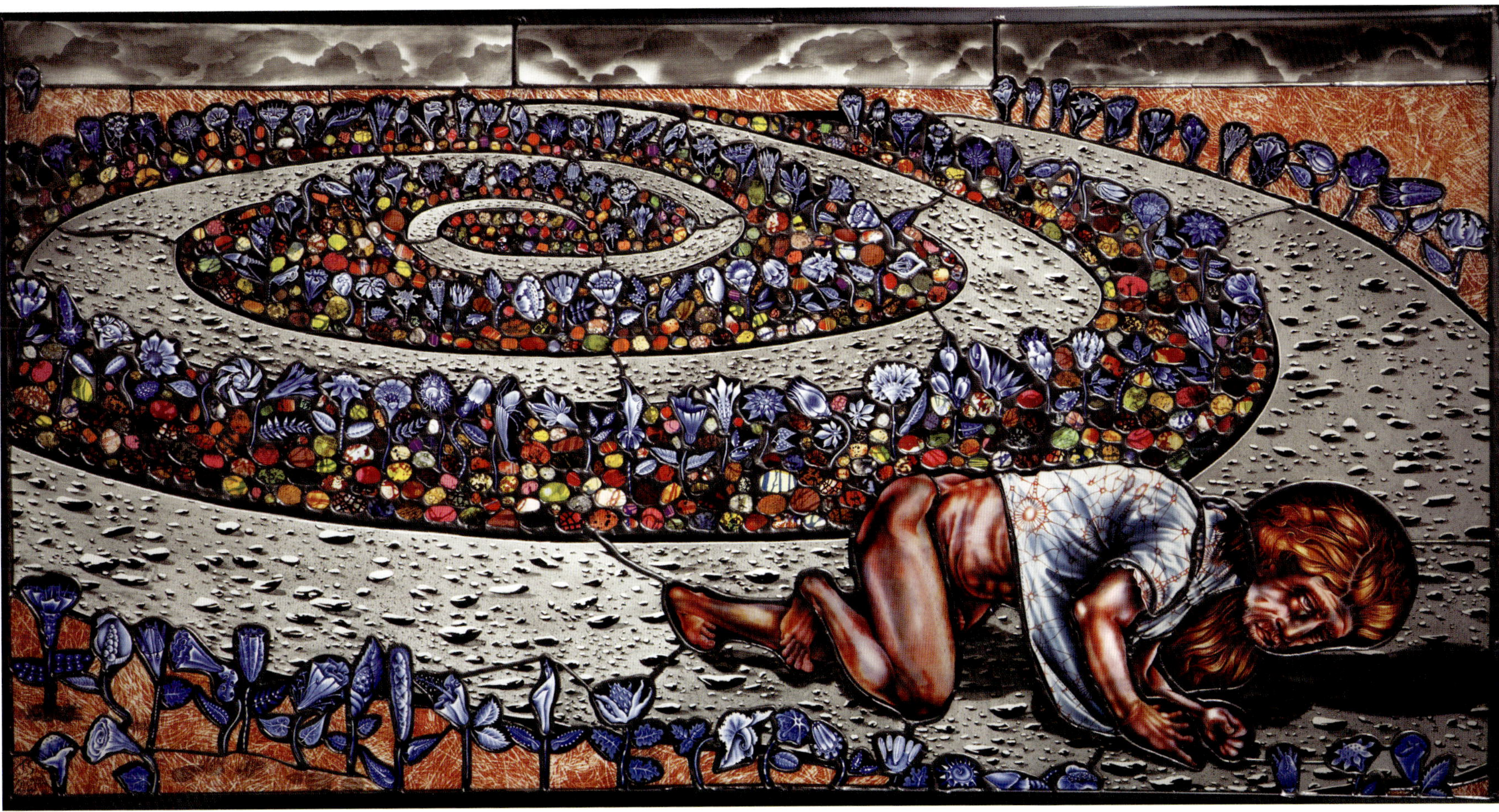

JUDITH SCHAECHTER

I've always been a big doodler. Growing up I went to Boston's Museum of Fine Arts regularly; my parents were very encouraging and open-minded. I liked Picasso and was a big fan of Gothic art, ancient Egyptian and Byzantine art, and the colorfully patterned textiles and tapestries. *MAD Magazine*, *Archie* comics, and popular TV also shaped my aesthetic. I went to the Rhode Island School of Design intending to be a painter, but took an elective in stained glass and knew immediately I wanted to devote my life to the medium. I felt "in sync" with glass—I like to keep my nervous hands busy, busy, busy, and the tedium factor and the variety of processes allowed me to focus my mind and concentrate for a change! The time it took to make a piece fit better with how often I had ideas worth making. Stained glass seems like a medium requiring great preplanning, but that isn't true—my working method is pretty spontaneous and experimental. A stained glass window is entirely dependent on transmitted light, and must be sensitive to that as a design and conceptual element; light and color are literally part of the content whether or not one chooses to work with them.

I am most inspired by the process of drawing. The more distracted I am the better, as all my best drawings are accidents and mistakes. Television, lectures, talk radio, music, and telephone conversations all help me work. I draw mostly heads and sometimes figures, paying careful attention to facial expressions. For a finished piece I'll pick only the most interesting faces, those that are "all wrong in all the right ways"; distorted to the verge of ugly yet beautiful; expressive of a range of emotional possibilities yet ambiguous; universal enough for a lot of people to relate to and not just specific to me. I like them exaggerated, original yet familiar, extraordinary yet recognizable, and down to earth. Sometimes I want them to have humor.

Judith Schaechter
The Sin Eater, 2009
Engraved stained glass
25 x 46 inches

I use Photoshop as a compositional tool to scan my doodles, clean them up, manipulate them—then arrange them to try out different compositional ideas. I transition to glass once I've generated enough creative material. Usually that's just a rough sketch of the figure, which I print out full size in order to make a cartoon (a cutting pattern). All other variables—background, patterns, details—are figured out in glass, each step predicated on the one that preceded it. I constantly change and revise the image. The look of the piece arises through the making and my responses to that process, so I rarely use assistants.

The stained glass I use most is flash glass, a handmade glass with a paper-thin veneer of intense color. I cut it with a steel wheel cutter and also use pliers to help shape it. Then I do any sandblasting if needed, a process that removes the colored (flash) layer by applying a stencil made of a material resistant to the sandblasting process. I usually hand cut this stencil, but occasionally use stencils made photographically from my drawings, using Photoshop to generate a black-and-white negative, which is then used to develop a film, which can then be applied to the glass (not unlike the photo silk-screen process). I only use this technique when I absolutely must, because it is cost prohibitive, and the glass has to be manipulated afterward to remove any clumsy, machined look. After sandblasting, I engrave smaller details with a flex shaft. I also file into the flash with diamond files, which make very beautiful tonal variations in the color.

The next step involves painting using vitreous paint. The only colors I use are black and silver stain (silver stain actually "stains" the glass yellow hence the term "stained glass"). I paint it on and fire it similar to a ceramic glaze. All other color is layered, up to five layers of flash glass. Once all the parts are done for a window, the last step is assembling the piece using copper foil, then soldering it together. I like to not know what the piece will look like until the very end! I know it's finished when I'm no longer fighting it.

JERRY KEARNS

Braque and Picasso brought collage to art around 1906. Paralleling Einstein's thinking in physics, time and space relationships were mutable in these artists' works. Collage's disparate elements, juxtaposed in multiple layers and viewed from multiple perspectives, still offer a shifting, overlapping vocabulary for contemporary painting and sculpture, an alphabet for articulating the slip-sliding-time-space-realities I experience. Like Dr. Frankenstein, I stitch together body fragments, only mine are taken from magazines, not criminals' graves. Actually, my process is more reminiscent of playing paper dolls with my sisters when we were kids.

I was born a Southern working-class baby boomer. During the 1950s, my family lived beside the tobacco factories in Winston-Salem, North Carolina. Life was extreme—poverty and alcohol violence shaped the days and nights. In the middle of the chaos, the Baptist church offered another possibility, another storyline, and another set of images. Predictably, from my childhood experience, I have a hyper-vigilant personality: *Y'all need to come look outside! There's a monster hiding in the tree line! It sure is a beautiful bastard! Wolf! Wolf! Wolf!* Gothic midcentury Southern storytelling is in my DNA, like country music.

(opposite)
Jerry Kearns
One Trick Pony, 2013
Acrylic on canvas
72 x 92 inches

My generation was the first to be raised by television. Nature and culture morphed together in our minds. We were zygotes, carrying the web in our bodies. Early on, I began merging television, movie, and comic book images with Christian Bible iconography to draw and collage simple comic strips. Today, I live with multiple millions of Americans who are rather equally occupying media fantasy and direct experience. Our history has left the subsoil for generations of cyber babies. Most of them will be proto-bio-bots, carrying the culture's dirty laundry.

Some years ago, I replaced photocopies and glue with Adobe Photoshop, a fantastic tool for shaping and storing images. All of my recent images are computer manipulations of newspaper photos, cartoons, television, film, fine art, and upscale fashion ads. There is always a wide spectrum under production in the studio. I select what interests me from media sources, and give them to my studio assistant, Amanda Tiller. She scans my plunder into Photoshop. Then she cuts the images apart and archives the results: Feet, Hands, Heads, Female Bodies, Male Bodies, and so forth. We talk about ways to reassemble the clothing and body parts into hybrid characters. I think of these as actors whom I cast in paintings. Amanda also archives a wide variety of interior and exterior photographs, which we cut apart and reassemble into environments. The work process is collaborative. An active back and forth, that leads to the creation of multiple models. Some of these eventually lead to my making a painting.

My painting images generally start with one or two actors. I select four or five possible environments, and add actors to the compositions. Thus begins a lengthy process, involving multiple models, that leads to a final image I like enough to paint. The transition from computer model to painting often takes one or two years. To begin, I project a slide of the selected image onto the canvas, and make outline drawings of the composition. I turn the projector off and apply the principal paint areas. Currently I use seven to fifteen colors to define the major shapes, and apply two or three coats of each color in mid-values. Drawing remains important throughout, and is instrumental to the look of the finished work.

The composition continues to change during the painting process, which plays out over a number of months, sometimes years. I generally work on several canvases simultaneously, developing each one in states or steps, working one area after another, constantly changing colors and evolving forms. Making a work over a lengthy period permits revisiting the image—which is what I do, always looking for the next layer to reveal itself. Over time, the painting slowly gains the solidity and density of form and image that I feel comfortable calling finished.

Day into night, birth to death, we are flooded with images. Cartoon or photo, print or telecast, each type and form carries a great deal of information about the culture that created it. Standing in the flow, I work as an editor. I take images apart and recombine them into amalgams of age, race, and gender. The buried nature of my characters' psyches has been shaped under years spent in the deep ravines of my troubled mind.

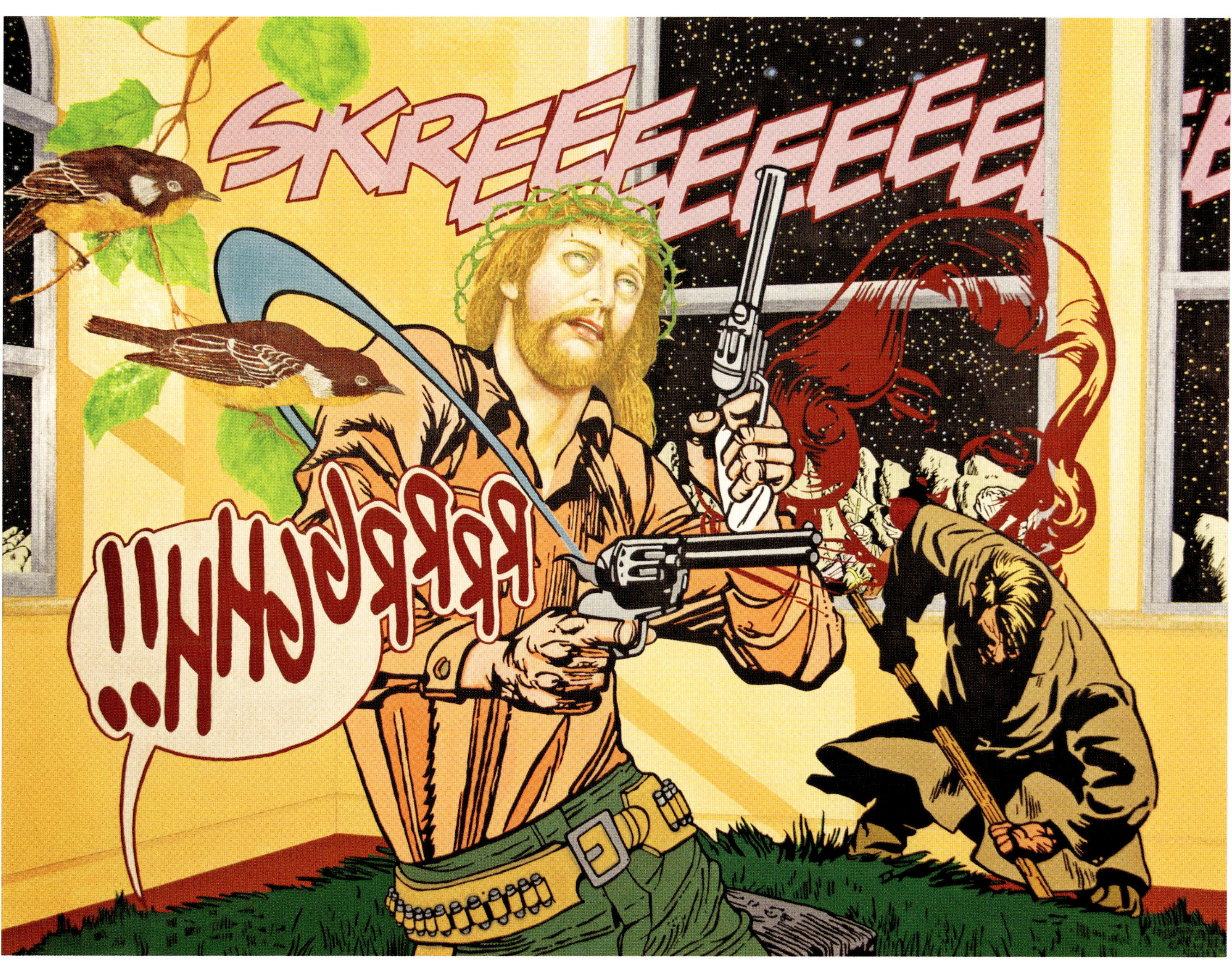
SKREEEEEEEEEEE

PICTORIAL SPACE ENTERS VIRTUAL REALITY: FROM PERSPECTIVE TO 3-D MODELING

JOHN JACOBSMEYER

CHARTING THE DEVELOPMENT OF SPATIAL THINKING in the Western pictorial tradition, from the origins of linear perspective to digital 3-D modeling, reveals a host of poetic and syntactical variations. The height of spatial artistry arguably occurred in the mid-seventeenth century with *Las Meninas* (1656) by Diego Velázquez, a narrative composition that achieves a dazzling level of complexity. A seemingly innocuous tableau of princess and artist discloses, through perspective and scale change, the revelation that you the viewer are royal, spectral presences in a distant mirror. While the brightly illuminated *infanta* stands as the central axis of her retinue, further examination reveals, from the shadows to the architecture, that the entire pictorial space pivots on the artist himself, who has usurped the traditional role of the sovereign in this state portrait. The exchange of pictorial dominion from sovereign to infanta to artist takes place in the sequence of shifting "blocks of air" that surge and collapse throughout the space, a choreography owing much to Venetian masters.

Since Velázquez, many styles and trends have cycled through the art world, with few focusing so rigorously on the poetic use of narrative space. Yet recently we've seen a reemergence in the use of spatial cues in painting and drawing, chief among them linear perspective. Twenty-first-century artists are creating elaborate spaces that rival in aspiration and execution the achievements of pre-Modernist history painting. This development runs concurrent with the growing role of 3-D modeling technologies in mass culture. Since the 1970s, video games and other computer-generated imagery (CGI) have notably reintroduced perspectival systems as a matrix for pictorial construction. By way of the first-person shooter (FPS), gaming has made the anxiety-producing "subjective view" (as in the viewer being the sovereign in *Las Meninas*) an ubiquitous aspect of our visual culture. Navigating *Las Meninas* requires an active eye responsive to spatial cues, a process similar to game play. Post-baby-boom artists have grown up participating in the expansion of this cultural phenomenon, from its early incarnations in arcades to the sophisticated virtual reality effects of *Call of Duty*. Contemporary artists have internalized many of gaming's qualities including its graphical perspective systems. The specific technologies best suited for the creation of complex compositions are the same ones used for video game design, and they are growing in use among studio artists.

The Autodesk program, Maya, and Cinema 4D are uniquely beneficial for figurative artists. They can construct 3-D environments based on a polygonal spatial language originating in the Italian Renaissance. Maya can eliminate the tedium of performing the complicated math of linear perspective and can create a model of the Velázquez studio in the Alcázar palace and determine the exact viewing point from which *Las Meninas* was painted. Other 3-D programs proven extremely useful include Smith Micro's Poser, which enables a vast array of figure manipulations from posing to texturing. These tools are fueling a shift from a largely Photoshop-dependent studio practice to a space-building methodology, one encompassing a broad range of spatial cues linked to each other through cause and effect. (For example, an object casting, or causing, a shadow is also an effect of a larger system of light zones, specular reflections, and shadow zones.) Virtual reality (VR) tools are specifically designed to simulate the systemic relationships in nature that artists have endeavored to represent since the beginning of the Western tradition. The VR environment seems to be replacing the Modernist notion of the picture plane as the foundation of pictorial space in an increasingly cybernetic culture.

Critical among these 3-D tools, chiaroscuro (the light-to-dark shading that gave volume to early Italian Renaissance forms) and linear perspective enabled Renaissance artists to organize disparate, volumetric elements and

(opposite)
John Jacobsmeyer
John Jacob-Jingle-Heimer-Schmidt,
2010
Oil on linen
26 x 22 inches

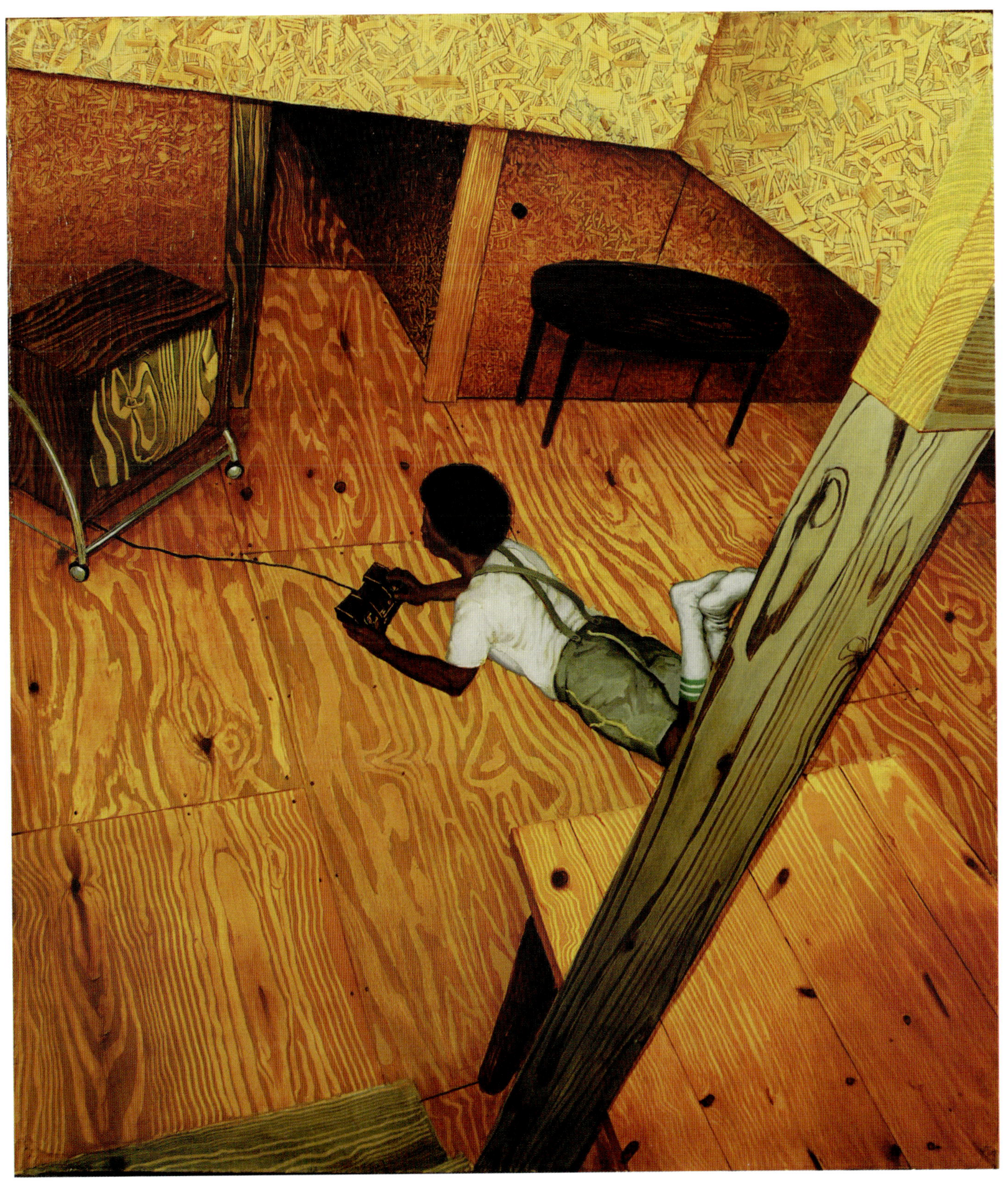

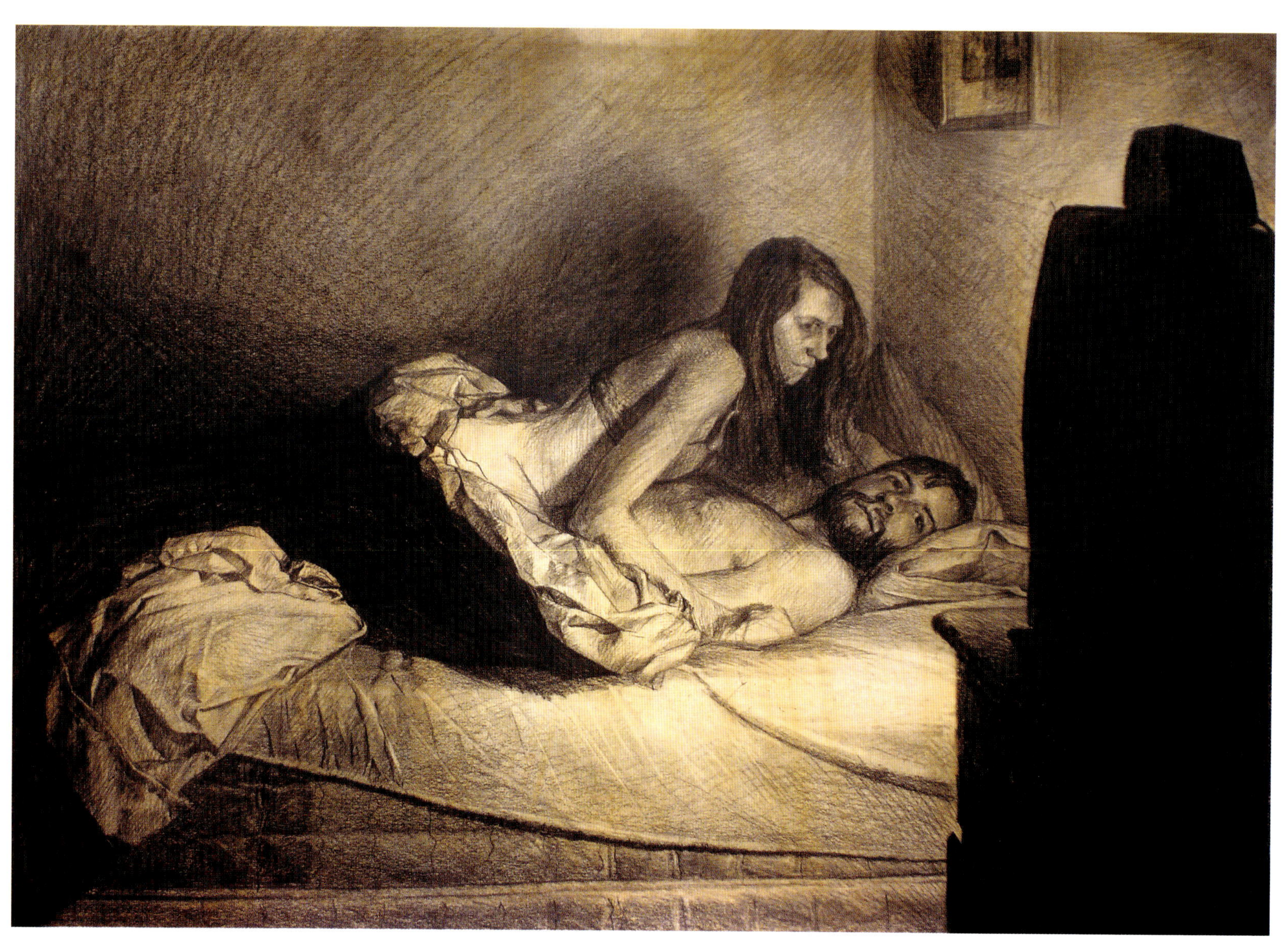

set a stage for these objects to be eventually causally linked. Giotto, the first great master of chiaroscuro, carved out credible volumes for the human figure with the most nuanced gradations. His chiaroscuro without true perspective gave volume to figures without fully addressing background space. A century later Masaccio surpassed him, subtly combining chiaroscuro in the human figure, and using cast shadows, with a new spatial system based on geometry, Brunelleschi's linear perspective. Codified by Leon Battista Alberti in *On Painting*, it proved a very useful system for rendering architecture, placing figures rationally within space, and for the figure itself, as in the foreshortened figures of Uccello and Mantegna. In fact Uccello's drawings resemble the polygonal web of most digital 3-D models today. The precision of Andrea Mantegna's foreshortening in the *Dead Christ* (1480) is as convincing a perspective view as one created with Poser.

The Florentine embrace of a pictorial hierarchy favored the human figure above all else. This prevented a major advancement toward fully integrated compositions, as did occur in Venetian painting, which seems to visualize the dialectic forces inherent in nature. With the exception of Leonardo's sfumato, complex pictorial principles were not exploited by the Florentines. Giorgio Vasari, in *Le vite* (*Lives of the Artists*), began the longstanding debate between drawing and color, Florentine *disegno* and Venetian *colore*. He highlighted the poetic and naturalistic features of Venetian "open form" and abundant color, but failed to fully recognize the sophisticated mechanics of the Venetian pictorial engine.[1] Newton's third law of motion, "for every force there is an equal and opposing force," seems prescient in the Venetian sensibility. In movement a body displaces air, pushing other air into the space left vacant. Giovanni Bellini, Giorgione, and Titian understood these dialectic principles as they applied them to space and light within their paintings.

In the Venetian system blocks of air and mass perform a contrapuntal dance, a holistic version of the classical model of dynamic balance, contrapposto. Like the norm in filmic sequences and FPS gaming today, Venetian artists placed the figure off to the side, leaving the center of the painting (not vacant but occupied by air) an invitation to diagonally enter the space. A characteristically Venetian figure, the nymph pouring water at the left of Titian's *Fête champêtre* (1510) functions as both a framing device and a major axis around which the central block of air rotates. This block opens the scene, steered by the sloping plane of the hillside, continuing up and back. There the viewer encounters the concert group, whose planar structure redirects the viewer back to the shepherd and adjoining trees. Not unlike the navigation tools in VR, in which one moves from one channel of air to another, traversing every zone of the pictorial fiction, the viewer eventually returns to the foreground. This circuitous journey through space, a distinctly Venetian invention, served as a general compositional scheme for most narrative painters thereafter and up to Edgar Degas, eventually entering cinema and gaming. Tintoretto's cycle of twenty-seven paintings, *Scuola Grande di San Rocco* (completed 1588) demonstrates nearly every spatial cue developed before photography, functioning simultaneously in fully integrated systems: overlapping, scale change, linear perspective, open and closed form, contrast, chiaroscuro, and zones of light. With these tools at their disposal, Baroque masters like Velázquez and Peter Paul Rubens were able to make the most believable pictorial fictions in increasingly individual styles.

A comprehensive pattern of cause-and-effect relationships in painting did not truly manifest until the late sixteenth century, when Caravaggio revolutionized the representation of action in painting. His tenebrism (extreme light and shadow) finally broke open the hermetically sealed and normatively lit figure of the Florentine mode. Caravaggio's great invention was laying out the action of light in a sequence of logical, specular reflections that merge initially incongruous elements into a thoroughly coherent tableaux. More truly causal sequencing is evident in his *Judith Beheading Holofernes* (1599), when the idea of naturalism for the purpose of identifying with the picture's subject was given a higher priority than symbolism during the the Counter-Reformation. It boldly captures the act's gruesome reality, every ounce of Judith's strength dedicated to the effort.

This heightened standard of verisimilitude was embraced by the Dutch Realists. Pieter de Hooch, Pieter Saenredam, and Johannes Vermeer used a linear perspective method similar to that developed by Gian Battista Alberti with, however, a significant difference. The perspectival pyramid (from the viewer's eye to the picture plane) became shallower, so the viewing point (station point) encroaches on the scene. What was once a very distant view, as though looking at the scene from several yards away (a narrow cone of vision much like a telephoto lens) moved closer to the scene, as if in the same room. This widening cone of vision resulted in obvious distortions that did not bother the artists or their audience; at the time painting was very much involved in a discourse on perception, and myriad optical distortions were being examined by Carel Fabritius and Samuel van Hoogstraten, among others. Saenredam's distortions are not optical but perspectival, and largely the result of an overtaxed perspective model in that his cone of vision was very wide while the centric ray (from the vanishing point) is obliquely positioned.[2]

Vermeer and Fabritius incorporated phenomena offered by the camera obscura into their painting language. The camera obscura, in existence since the time of Aristotle, and its more recent cousin the camera lucida, have been the subject of much debate recently for their potential use by artists for tracing. Pop artist David Hockney initiated a controversy by suggesting artists like Bellini and Jean-Auguste-Dominique Ingres needed such optical devices to achieve an accurate likeness. But what truly distinguishes Hockney's age of Pop and Imagism (which often used traced projections) from premodern pictorial language goes beyond devices. The spatial qualities in Vermeer and Fabritius attributed to the camera obscura did not come from tracing or from using it as a rendering device, but from observing the "live image" on the frosted glass of the device,[3] as can be seen in the coordination of Vermeer's soft or blurry edges with sharp-edged impasto applications of paint, separate from the surrounding color gradation. These idiosyncratic qualities in Vermeer correspond to the soft focus in the camera obscura's

(opposite)
Michael Meadors
Connected, 2010
Graphite, shellac on paper
15 x 22 inches

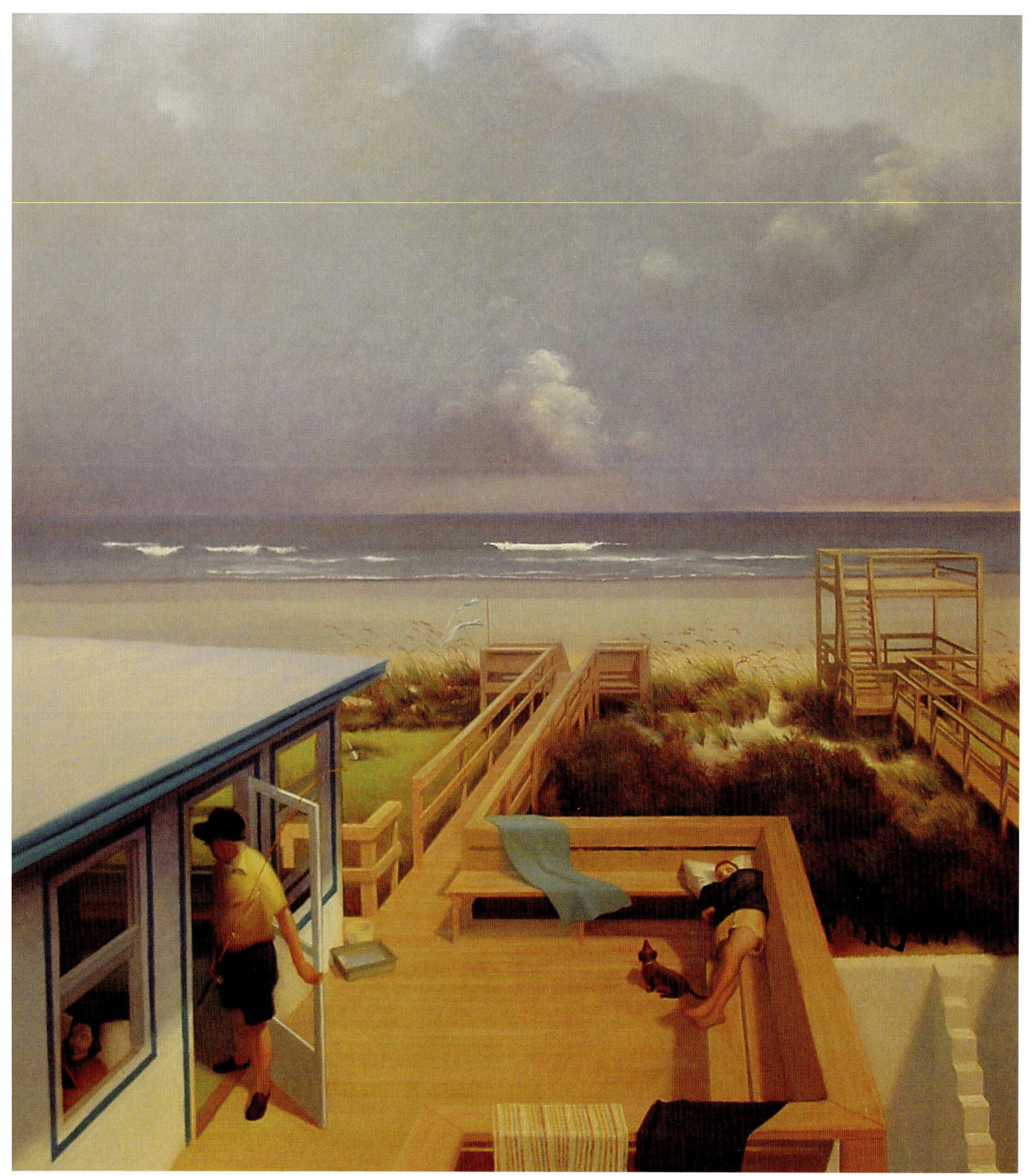

narrow depth of field, a spatial effect not unlike Leonardo's sfumato, which caused softly focused forms to recede. The impasto highlights, on the other hand, jump forward, not to a foreground space but to the very surface of the painting itself, as though the picture plane was the frosted glass through which we observe the scene.

The eighteenth and early nineteenth centuries saw fewer technical developments in the vocabulary of space, but a heady discourse on its application. The theory and model for pictorial space were the subject of much debate. Nicholas Poussin's work inspired French Academicians as early as 1700 to consider painting's ideal form to be a tableau, an overall sense of the image as an integrated centralized grouping. His use of clay models and linear perspective as tools for painting demonstrated a robust spatial thinking that helped sustain the academic idiom for generations. Roger de Piles, the seventeenth-century French author of *Dialogue sur le coloris* ("Dialogue on Colors"), called for a greater attention to realism, with its requisite array of spatial cues, exemplified in Rubens, thus extending Alberti's *disegno*-versus-*colore* debate to the Academy, which continued up to the mid-nineteenth century.[4]

In the late nineteenth century, the perspectival pyramid nearly collapsed with Édouard Manet, Degas, and Paul Cézanne, bringing an end to Western painting's spectatorial edifice, a system based on the subject/object dialectic. Manet exposed "assemblage" practice in narrative painting by not synthesizing his compositions. In *Le déjeuner sur l'herbe* (1863) the figures appear cut and pasted together with diminishing concern for logical spatial relationships. The woman bathing is too large; the sitting woman appears to be pasted in; the landscape is likely an allusion to Antoine Watteau.[5] Recent studies of Manet's methodology reveal a more radical heterogeneity in his form sense that suggests his process incorporated photography, art historical quotations, and perceptual painting. By making narratives so disjunctive, Manet attacked the unifying principle of the tableau. The result is montage, which positions him almost as a proto-Dadaist, Dadaism being characterized by diverse cultural references without logical organization.

Degas radicalized what had already emerged from the Dutch Realists, the shrinking of the perspectival pyramid. His use of perspective pushed the viewing point intimately closer to the subject. Reflecting the growth of photography in the 1870s, he widened his cone of vision to 90 degrees or more, as in many of the bather images, based on photographs. (Photography's impact on two-dimensional art since Degas has been to flatten pictorial space; although such an accurate record of empirical information might also be a tool for more spatial acuity.) Finally, Cézanne took a contrary position, and developed an original, alternative painting language very different from photography and most Impressionism. His *optique* (personal system for analyzing light and space) was the first major development since Caravaggio's tenebrism to break with notions of an object's integrity. Cézanne's spatial language was built on local edge relationships; his chiaroscuro inferred volumes emanating from edges, not enveloping the entire form, which resulted in a sequence of constantly shifting tonal and color relationships.

Georges Braque and Pablo Picasso saw in Cézanne a new spatial language that had escaped notice during the Symbolist years. Through Cubism they expanded on Cézanne's breakup of the symbolic figure. Cubist space is a fugitive and relentless phenomenon, but in essence a variation on the same dialectical construct that defined classicism. While Greek classical form utilized a system of contrapuntal movements within the figure, as in Polykleitos's *Doryphoros*, Cubist form was de-centered. There is no whole figure or ground, only relative shifts in space. Further developments in Synthetic Cubism move away from edge shifts, toward a system of overlays with far fewer spatial cues. After Cubism the avant-garde moved in the direction of poetic economy, the reified picture plane, and semiotics, retreating from the spatial rigors of pictorial composition. At midcentury Hans Hofmann voiced an attitude against illusionistic painting that was very influential: "[If] two-dimensionality is lost, the picture reveals holes and the result is not pictorial, but a naturalistic imitation of nature."[6] Pictorial space was tied up with plastic form in ways that precluded illusionism. Many early American realists resisted Modernism's push toward abstraction, but its impact can be seen in the Impressionist tendencies of Thomas Eakins, or later with the Cubist influence in Thomas Hart Benton.

Over time, robust varieties of pictorial space would become marginalized in the domain of "low-art" forms of comics and book illustration (as in N. C. Wyeth), while the high-art forms of Neoclassicism and Social Realism persisted as somewhat discredited. Yet Giorgio de Chirico experimented with non-normative perspective, followed by Surrealists Max Ernst and Remedios Varo, who experimented with frottage and decalcomania, new techniques exploiting random accidents and forms in nature, thus creating an almost limitless pictorial space for the new terrain of the subconscious. Many modern figurative artists continued combining elements of Cubist spatial construction, like Max Beckmann and Diego Rivera. Giacometti, however, applied the unfashionable polygonal language of perspective to his deeply subjective analysis of the figure in space. Edward Hopper and Balthus also found currency in a perspectival space for more theatrical aims.

A new approach to representation in the late 1960s and '70s by American Realists such as Jack Beal, Sidney Goodman, and Janet Fish embraced a fuller vocabulary of space, showing a preponderance of frontal planes that owed much to Cézanne and Hofmann. In Europe a number of artists were applying premodern modes of description in selective ways. In the 1980s, artists who re-engaged narrative space include Odd Nerdrum's masterfully painted tableaux, with backdrops of Nordic myth and desire; Anselm Kiefer's grand stage of history painting, scaffolded with linear perspective; Neo-Expressionists like Jörg Immendorff and Eric Fischl, in pursuit of a full spectrum of composition and content. Yet few painters were creating unmitigated spatial illusion. Dynamic narrative constructions could still be found, however, in the illustrations of Stan Lee and Jack Kirby for Marvel Comics, and in the *Lord of the Rings* calendars of the Brothers Hildebrandt.

(opposite)
Luke Allsbrook
Edge of the Ocean, 1999
Oil on canvas
48 x 42 inches

During the 1990s, the new figuration from post-reunification Germany of Neo Rauch, David Schnell, and others offered myriad spatial and narrative elements. These works are fractured, figural and non-figural impulses competing for dominance within the picture. In America a different mode of fracturing occurred; the work of Kerry James Marshall and Mike Cockrill presented the semblance of narrative space, but like Dadaist collages, the space is fugitive. While organizing disparate sources in a montagist way, the practice of many Postmodern figurative painters is shaped more by Manet and Duchamp. Cutting, pasting, assembling, and juxtaposing are worktable processes, and the default state of the worktable is flatness. So, the articulation of space is more quotation than formal assertion, more tableau (root: table) than narrative—and as it were, more Photoshop than Maya. Images that truly embrace the full spatial articulation in this period were located outside the mainstream art world, as in Bernie Wrightson's graphic fusion of perspective and light in his illustrations for *Frankenstein*, or Mark Ryden's application of nuanced chiaroscuro to banal cuteness, or Nicola Verlato's baroque space engineered in Maya. Much of this hails from the "lowbrow" movement Pop Surrealism, pioneered by Robert Williams.

Early Modernist approaches to space dismantled the Western spectatorial edifice while Postmodernist developments reconstruct and reinvent that structure. For the recent advances in the language of space in art, we can thank the current pluralism, which has invited traditions and idioms of spatial construction back into common practice. The latest generation of gallery artists, such as Paul Noble, Jonas Burgert, and Adrian Ghenie, exhibit abundant spatial cues, clarity of foreshortening, and causal sequencing. In Noble's *Nobson Newtown* project a fully dimensional world unfolds, rendered only in oblique projection (without vanishing points), a graphical perspective used normally for technical drawings. Like Hilary Harkness, he applies an engineer's drafting system to worlds with uncanny resemblance to virtual reality. Both Burgert and Ghenie embody Expressionism's legacy of gesture and emotional metaphor, but with a pictorial infrastructure based on premodern notions of a deep and contiguous space. With both old and new technologies, twenty-first-century artists are building out their respective "believable fictions" with the precision of surveyors, evidence of a new figuration that is uncompromisingly spatial. Their absorption of VR tools, not unlike Paolo Uccello's embrace of linear perspective, represents a further step toward the "artist as cyborg," composing at times in machinic language, and with that engendering new content.

JOHN WELLINGTON

For more than thirty years I have kept sketchbooks to draw, study, copy, journalize, philosophize, complain, and misspell. In them I explore visual and conceptual ideas that might turn into paintings; they accept the pure process of creating without judgment; the good, the bad, and the ugly. As an artist who spends a lot of time correcting my corrections, gouache and tempera paint are the perfect color sketch medium for studies, to record en plein air vistas, portraits, and moments or memories of my travels. In my more complex or larger paintings, I mix images from life, photographs, and imagination, but it's easy to take a photo of some scene or place and not really see it. When I am drawing, however, I am responsible for every line, masterful and not, in each moment. I see almost everything, even if it is omitted in the final drawing. And unlike the click of a shutter, the hatch of the pen takes time. Drawing and painting from life, translating the three-dimensional world to a flat page or panel, are still a great challenge for me. While working I often feel I am failing upward; but in not capturing exactly what I see, I leave a record of visual moments and concepts that keeps the making of art exciting and fresh.

In drawing and painting I work on toned ground to work darks and lights simultaneously. Oil paint is magical for me; I am awed by the multiple visions and techniques that have expressed artists' voices since its invention. I use both direct and indirect techniques. My indirect painting methods derive from a number of artists, including Vermeer, Velázquez, and Ingres. If I want the image to glow and feel otherworldly, I begin with an underpainting grisaille (a monochromatic painting). A great lead white is the most difficult color to find, but I am very happy with Rublev's, and I also use their bone black. Most of my other paints are from Vasari—stunning colors made only with pigment and oil, no fillers. I am also very fond of Robert Gamblin's materials. My medium is a combination of sun-thickened linseed oil, copal resin, and triple-rectified turpentine. I often underpaint flesh with either a combination of white with viridian, bone black, or burnt sienna. Then each layer is built up with glazes and veils of paint, pulling toward the impasto in the lightest areas and transparency in the shadows. I alternate warm and cool applications of color to give depth to the finished work. If I want an area to feel immediate and fresh then I will work more directly with *ébauche* (wash) and impasto brush strokes, leaving the initial applications in the final painting. My best moments are when the quality of the paint varies from area to area, surprising me as I work.

With the purchase of a Mac PowerBook in 2000, I began to use programs like Photoshop to play with composition, scale, and other visual choices. Like photography, Photoshop offers quick solutions, but lacks the depth of observational study. SketchUp is another program I use for creating complex architectural forms. It saves me the time of making countless perspective studies on vellum to place the viewer's eye. After using SketchUp I make a detailed vellum perspective drawing to adjust for the program's limitations. I enjoy the access, speed, and abundance of visual images that computers, iPhones, iPads, and the Internet give me. But the pixel world has also made me value the simple act of painting in a much different way than when I first started. I am more aware now when making an image that I am working with mud, burnt bone, crushed stone, and flaxseed (linseed) oil thickened on my window ledge, and that these pigments are applied with the hairs

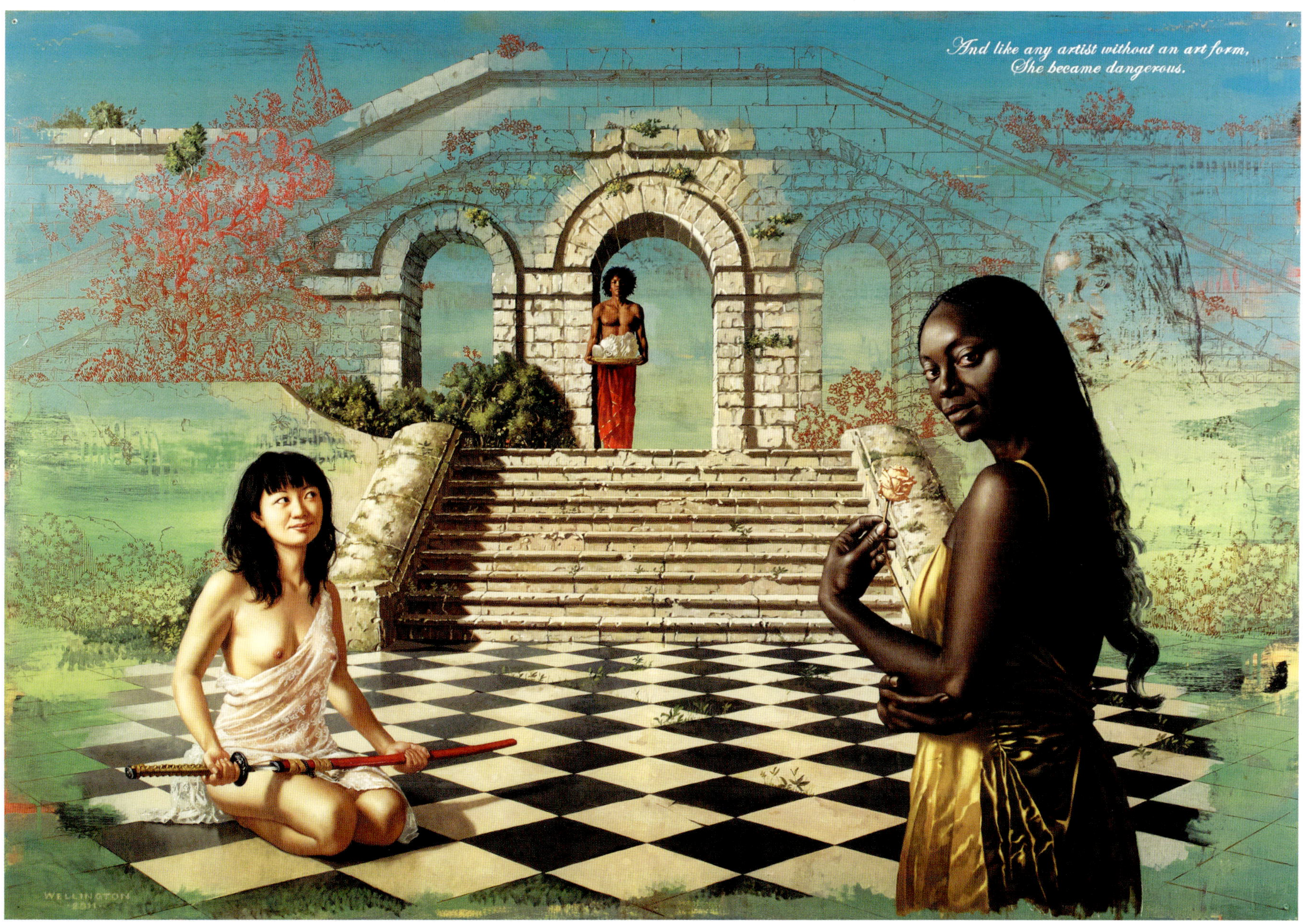

of badger, mongoose, and sable to wood, linen, or copper. In a world that needs electricity to work, I am comforted that the art I produce does not need to be plugged in. Although contemporary taste can favor art that has been manufactured by artisans directed by artists, I would not know how to instruct an assistant to paint, as I never know what will come next in the act of painting.

I admire artwork that is singular to the artist's inner spirit. If the conceptual idea is too clear and vivid while working, I alter it; I enjoy being at least one step behind completely understanding my creative choices. Sometimes I know why a work should be painted, but more often I am drawn to a mixture of visual imagery that just feels the need to be born. When I feel this I paint with devotion, and others will feel the energy put into the work, whether or not they relate to my subject matter.

John Wellington
Dangerous, 2011
Oil on aluminum panel
48 x 68 inches

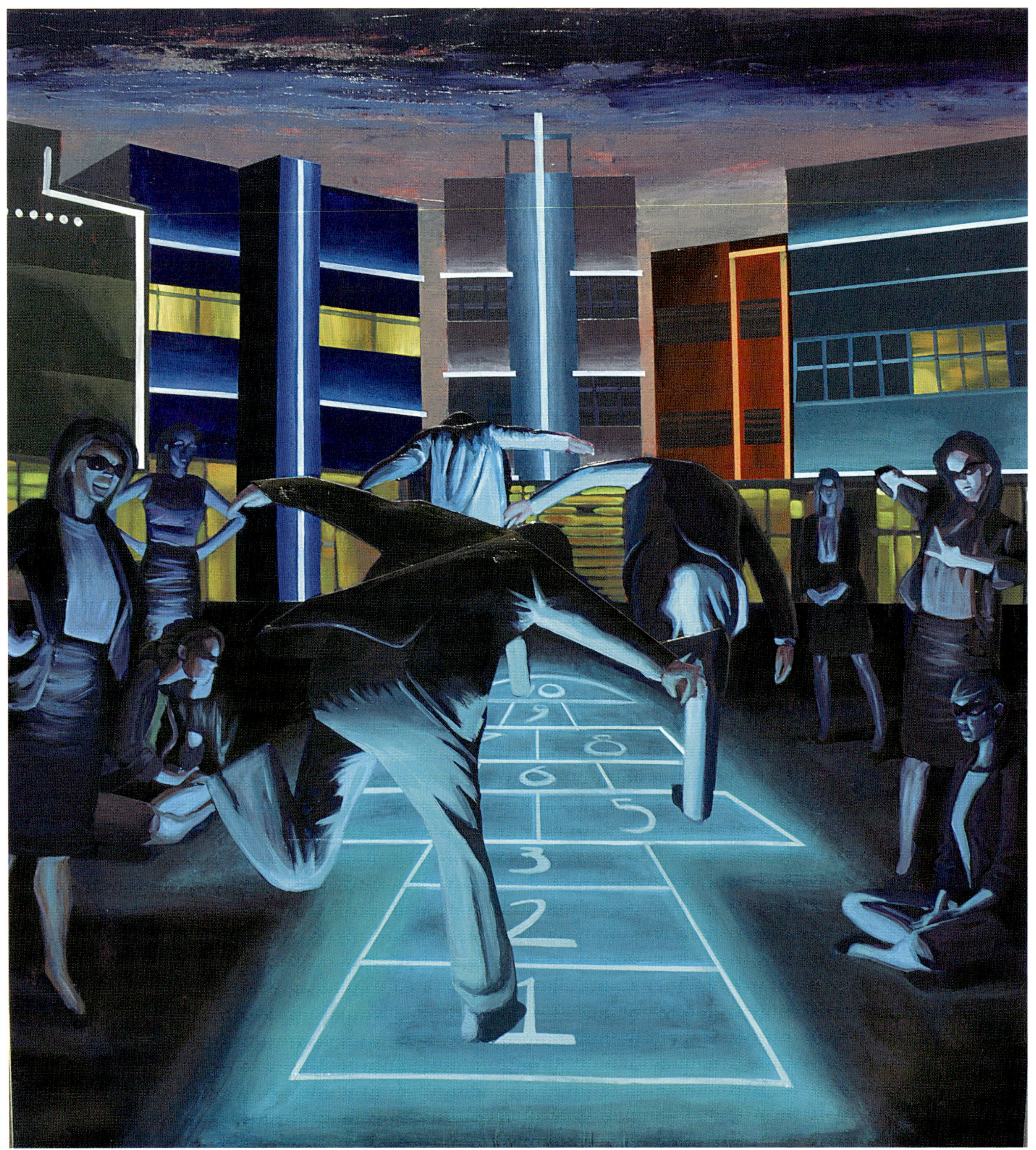

PERSPECTIVE, REPRESENTATION, AND DEMOCRACY

NICOLA VERLATO

VIDEO GAMES AND MAZZOCCHI

I became enraptured with computer-generated imagery (CGI) in the distant year 1982, when I saw *Tron*, the first film to use 3-D digital modeling with spectacular results. I was shocked by the process through which digital images were elaborated, through wire-frame graphics underlying the computer-rendered models. I had already been fascinated by similar forms in arcade games such as Tac/Scan, but it was only in that moment that the connection between those digital creations and the beautiful drawings by Paolo Uccello and the multifaceted geometric forms, *mazzocchi*, of Piero della Francesca's "chalice" became clear to me.

I immediately understood that in order to revitalize painted images (a problem that had been obsessing me), a computer would be necessary. Unfortunately, in those years in Italy it was impossible for a seventeen-year-old from the countryside around Vicenza to gain access to the necessary machines and computer programs to work off that intuition. I waited with anticipation, keeping up to date on innovations in the field. Finally in 1992 I was able to satisfy my curiosity. Using the software Strata Vision combined with AutoCAD, Giulio Bertoncello and I built the architectural model of a building for the background of an enormous painting. We worked together on another project, and then at long last, in 1998 I obtained the computer program Softimage, which allowed me to work independently. Since then, computers have become a fundamental part in my process, and I've introduced a good number of students to my methods at the New York Academy of Art.

ITALIAN AND GREEK GEOMETRIC PERSPECTIVE

The impact of 3-D graphics programs in painting may be as astronomical as the introduction of perspective to painting. The Renaissance's perspective technique is that used in classical Greek and Roman civilizations, according to ancient writers like Vitruvius, but it can be seen to be the same by analyzing the paintings. I suspect that the common misconception regarding the use of central perspective in classical art is due to scholars having applied rigid, linear historical models, which do not take repetitions of the same, or similar, phenomena into consideration. It can be difficult to find a single, unified point of view in ancient painting as opposed to a general central area. But it is also true that "even among fifteenth- and sixteenth-century Renaissance paintings we find few entirely consistent examples of truly unified single vanishing point perspective."[1] The paintings with a rigorous single vanishing point are especially small and only from the Renaissance, and Greek examples have not endured. Perspective in painting was abandoned in both medieval and modern art. In both circumstances, the deliberate decision to do so was based on cultural and ideological considerations.

PERSPECTIVE AND DEMOCRACY

Geometric perspective seems to have originated in ancient Greek theater with the work of Agatharcus and quickly moved to two-dimensional figurative art, as the images on many vases, Roman paintings, and literary sources testify. It is not by chance that perspective started in theater. The rational representation of space on a stage mirrors the political ideology underlying Greek theater. In order to represent objects in perspective, one must postulate models that can be placed in space. By analogy, ancient Greek theater boasted

(opposite)
Austin Park
After Hours, 2011
Acrylic on canvas
72 x 64 inches

stories that began to be analyzed according to points of view that were new and different, compared to the linear narrations from which they derived.

Agamemnon's return in the first of the three tragedies in Aeschylus's *Oresteia* is an example of how the playwright analyzed a story, one well known to audiences at the time, from a non-conventional view point. Similarly in *The Persians*, Aeschylus tells the story not from the point of view that was common in Athens of those days, but from the point of view of the people who lost the war. Apparently, this was the culmination of a long historical process in which epic narrations had become so relevant to Greek democratic societies that they required more complex transpositions into theater. Multiple, alternative points of view of the same story had to be considered by the army of playwrights competing against each other, all tackling basically the same stories. Each play was then compared to similar ones and judged by the audience, practically determining its survival throughout time. Because this process happened in a democratic society, it needed to be codified in a way that could always be rationally illustrated. If this had not been the case, writers would have created subjective deformations of the stories, rather than diverse perspectives on it.

Perspective and tragedy share the conceptual foundation of rational debate within democratic governing policies. Greek citizens in democratic assemblies compared and contrasted different points of view on all political decisions. Every citizen participating in the assembly had the right to express his individual point of view on a topic. It could be argued that the arts consolidated and propelled democracy, thanks to their creative methods. This is indicated by the fact that negative philosophical criticism toward the democratic system went hand in hand with comparable criticisms of perspectival painting, as in Plato's rejection of the misleading, partial views of the painter, "an imitator of that which the others make."[2]

SCULPTURE AND REPRESENTATION

Sculpture is central to this field of analysis. The people of Athens and Florence were thinking three-dimensionally in both art and reasoning. Vasari described how Leonardo, Michelangelo, and Jacopo da Pontormo, as well as artists outside Florence like Antonio da Correggio, had three-dimensional clay or wax models (*modelli*) in their ateliers, because studying them was considered fundamental to the beginning stages of artistic creation. As Pietro Marani describes, "For Leonardo drawing delimits the body's surface, which is the true object of sculpture . . . there's no doubt that whenever Leonardo discusses *surface*, he has sculpture in the back of his mind, even when he writes about painting . . .";[3] Leonardo's painting design (*disegno*) was the same Michelangelo used, and thus "sculpture . . . is used to illustrate the second principle of painting, where the effect of relief in painting is best exemplified by the process of modeling a surface."

A sculptural model implies the possibility that infinite points of view of it exist, but the painter is more limited. In a process that involves whoever commissioned the work, viewers, and intellectuals, the painter only chooses the point of view that best and most functionally captures the episode into a single, self-contained image.

Classical philosophers applied the practice of constructing a model and then observing it from multiple perspectives in language. Socrates himself worked as a youth in his father's stone cutting shop. He was thus used to constantly changing points of view on the object he was sculpting, possibly the origin of his thought process, which shifts between different points of view on the same subject matter. Plato, a great mudslinger toward Athenian classical art, used dialogue as a form to expose one or more positions on the same concept in order to get to its most definite meaning. Through Socrates's thoughts in his writings, Plato criticized the arts of his time basically because he considered written language the only valid instrument of producing knowledge, so he needed to philosophically slander competing mediums like painting and sculpture.

It's no coincidence that modern science was first practiced in Tuscany, where the arts were interrelated with science for decades, as Leonardo's example illustrates. The consolidation of Galileo's experimental method in the late sixteenth century could be described as an empirically observed simulation of natural phenomena, just as artists had long studied three-dimensional models prior to creating their works. It's well known that Galileo Galilei consulted the Florentine painter known as Cigoli regarding geometrical representations and projections. Nicolaus Copernicus trained as a painter for some time, producing a self-portrait. The artistic creation of a method of rationally representing reality may have preceded, and influenced, important philosophical and scientific revolutions. Thereafter, other culture-creating agents took over this task, and relegated art to a purely aesthetic/emotional role, nearly defining it as obsolete.

REBIRTH #1

The rebirth of perspective in the Western world in the Renaissance occurred in a political and social environment that closely resembled ancient Greece. After a long absence of images, linked with the sedimentation of universally known literary works such as the Gospels and the Bible that took the place of *The Iliad* and *The Odyssey*, process not unlike the earlier one of classical times started again. Late medieval Italian and ancient Greek city-states share many political aspects. Not only did they both function through more or less democratic institutions, but they also gave birth to very specific forms of theater. In the same way Greek cities had tragedies, Italian cities started to organize, with the encouragement of pivotal holy figures like St. Francis of Assisi, *sacre rappresentazioni* (holy plays) based on narrations inspired by sacred subject matter. From the first paintings of the late thirteenth century, it is evident how freely artists like Pietro Cavallini and Giotto, like the Greeks, used a spirit of observation, with consequently more realistic iconography. For example, in *St. Francis of Assisi Preparing the Christmas Crib at Grecchio* (1297), Giotto depicts the cross from the back, keenly and objectively showing all its carpentry. At this developmental point, rationalizing the representation of

(opposite)
Joseph Ventura
In-Phase Feedback Loop of Time, Space and the Probability Wavefunction of an apparently frustrated Human Subject, Part II, 2011
Oil on canvas
22 x 28 inches

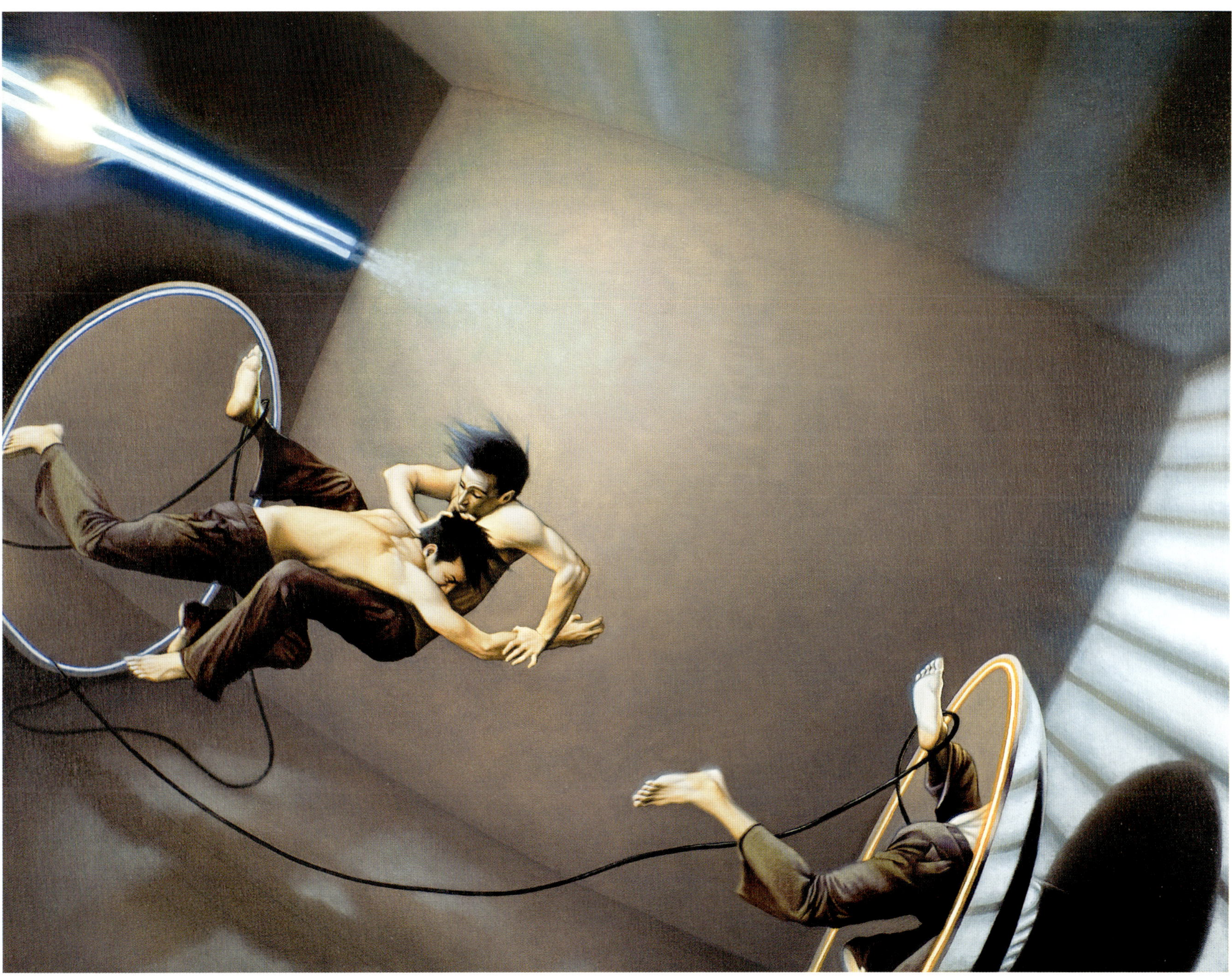

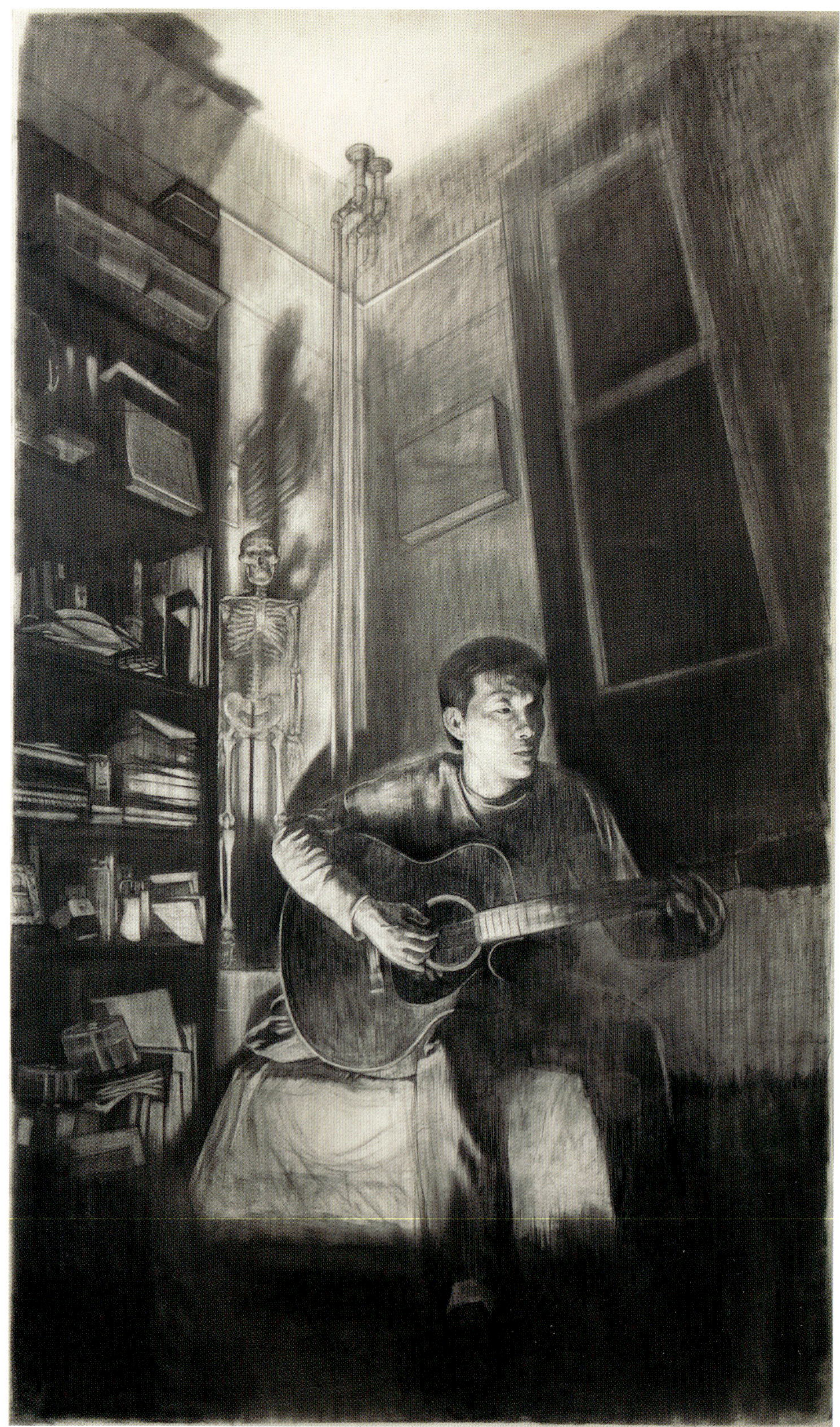

Guno Park
Self-Portrait, 2010
Charcoal on paper
108 x 60 inches

(opposite)
Leslie Adams
The Art of Life, 2012
Charcoal, white
chalk on paper
97 x 60 inches

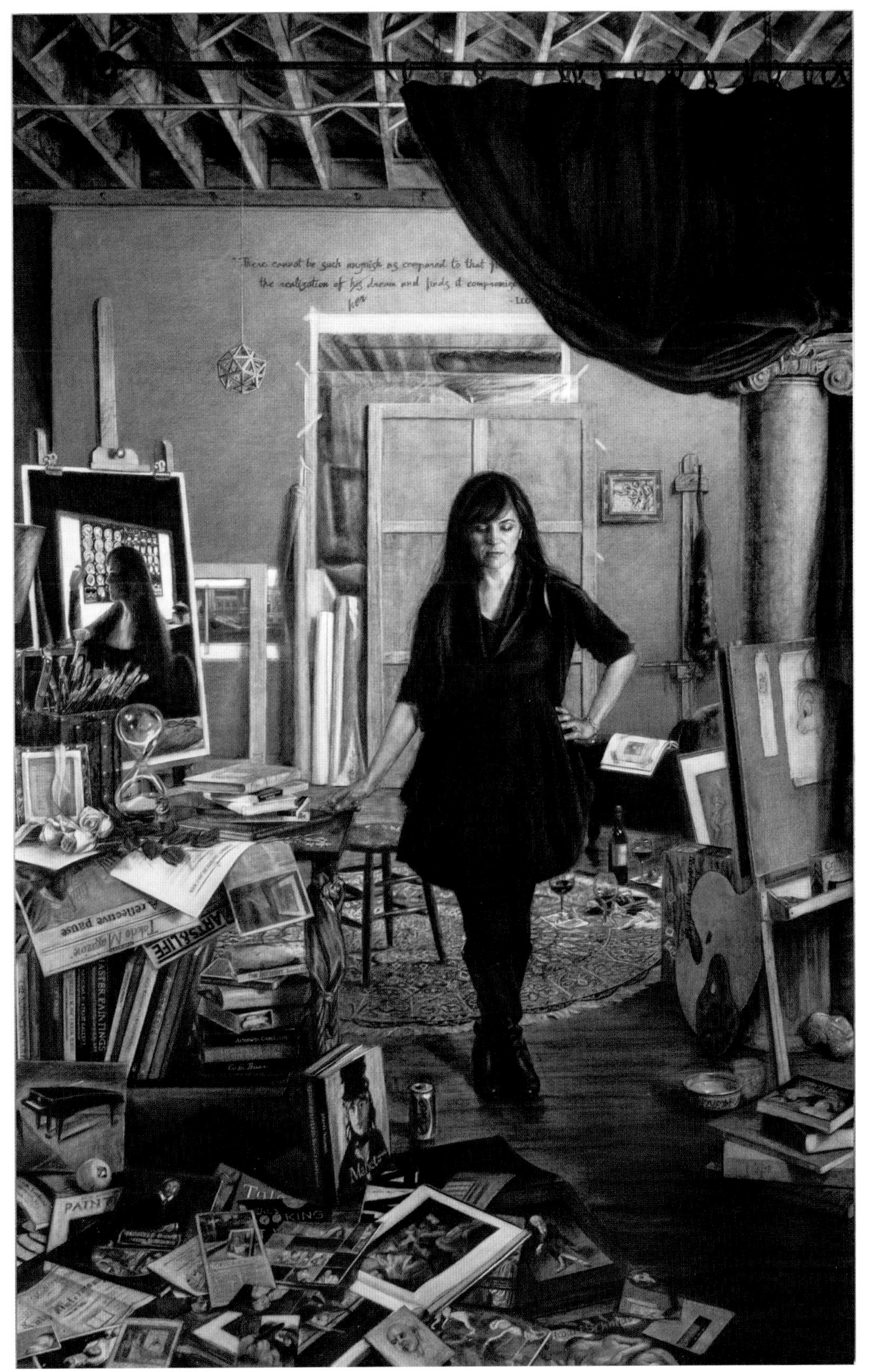
"There cannot be such anguish as compared to that
the realization of his dream and finds it
her
ARTS&LIFE
a reflective pause

space as well became necessary. Filippo Brunelleschi was the first to create a systematic approach to the matter (which Leon Battista Alberti described in his treatise). It seems that democratic forms of government and the geometric representation of reality are intrinsically connected; the latter is the only approach that allows one to constantly shift points of view around a single object.

VANISHING POINT AND POINT OF VIEW

In English, the technical term "vanishing point" indicates the point on a canvas where all the lines of perspective representation converge. The term *punto di vista* ("point of view") is used in Italian (the language spoken by Brunelleschi and Alberti) to define the same point. The two terms have diverse meanings, emphasizing two distinct ways of appreciating works of art that have different roles in Anglo-Saxon and Italian cultures. The Italian *punto di vista* indicates the specific standpoint from which a subject views an object. (In everyday Italian, as in English, it is also used to denote an individual's personal opinion.) However, the English "vanishing point" refers to the point itself, and substitutes that for the concept related to the specific position from which someone physically views the pictured perspective plane. The vanishing point also indicates where reality seems to disappear and become confused; a precise place, yet one that cannot be comprehended. Thus, the relation between the viewer and the image derived from this latter concept is a disconnected one. While the Italian concept *punto di vista* is objective, even democratic, made tangible by painters like Piero della Francesca, the English vanishing point is more mystical and subjective, as could be exemplified in J.M.W. Turner's paintings.

REBIRTH #2

The rebirth of geometric perspective this time around is happening in the digital realm, also following Alberti's codified rules of perspective. On the World Wide Web the incredible amount of accessible information regarding every topic imaginable has transformed the linear process of continuous consumption of knowledge into a nearly infinitely explorable realm, allowing the hypothesizing of the same number of restructurings of thought. Once again, sculpture is fundamental in the process. Armies of digital modelers are transcribing information into 3-D digital models, replicating the world as we know it into a collection of numerically derived sculptures.

The evolution of epic poetry into theater was an incredible paradigm shift. Linear narration became more complex and three-dimensional. Something very similar is happening now. How else to explain the automatic adaptation of all the greatest film box office hits—narratives with culturally wide appeal—such as *Star Wars* and *The Lord of the Rings* into video games? The market, an expression of consumer desires, along with the constant evolution of technology, has brought about a rapid development in perspective representation in video games. From the orthogonal projections of the early 1970s and the later parallel representations (leaving aside the very rare vectorial games, conceptualized in perspective terms beginning in the late 1970s), programmers began using ambiguous perspective in games in the 1980s and '90s. Today, perspective representation reign, and is sophisticated beyond all expectations. Video games have turned the impenetrable space behind the computer monitor into an accessible and ductile realm.

Why is it that in the digital field, where any form of representation is possible, the use of geometric perspective has become so dominant over axonometric projection, or over more modern, alternative representation systems such as Cubism? Perhaps it is because the way geometric perspective vision works is strongly connected to how our visual system works[4] and consistently offers rational proof. Erwin Panofsky and others who have undermined perspective's importance in the modern age correctly point out the differences between the retinal image and the perspectival representation. Yet more recent studies of the brain suggest that the path from the retina to human comprehension is complex, and involves complex processes, which correct optical deformations to produce a much more completely pictured result. Modern art history has discredited images produced through traditional perspective methods because they became incapable of portraying the complexity of a modern, industrialized world in a relevant and signifying way. The world disintegrates in the Impressionist works of Monet and Sisley, becoming blurry and unknowable, while coeval Academic painters sought answers in the exotic or in the past. Photography offered documentation more than vision, giving only the illusion of knowing reality by capturing its ghost. Photography cannot solve the problem of creating the "ultimate images" of the aforementioned long narrative-consolidation process. But the use of digital 3-D modeling in painting enables it to achieve multiple points of view like those of sculpture, reflecting the new infinity of the Internet. Going from video games to painting is not as tricky as it sounds; computer programs like Maya are relatively easy to learn to apply to painting.

If our societies wish to transform modern narratives into solid and stable presences in the real world, painting and sculpture have a part to play. Once precipitated into video games and the Internet, the linearly written accounts of newspapers, cinema, television, and comic books can be analyzed from multiple points of view. These can then translate into the material structures of art and architecture, just as ancient Greek mythology was manifest in the Parthenon and biblical stories in the Sistine Chapel. In today's outlying artistic environments, the transformation of contemporary narrations into painting and sculpture is an absolute norm. For too long this tendency, discredited as "illustration" and labeled with denominations like Pop Surrealism and Lowbrow, has been kept outside "fine arts." The challenge now is to invade not only the iconic sanctuaries of museums and galleries, the cathedrals of the secularized world, but also public spaces with new images relevant to our age.

NICOLA VERLATO

I'm interested in exploring and illuminating chaos; the rational formal process transforms even the grotesque into beauty. My work may be a reaction, even a radical one, to religious art, but I had an unusually secular upbringing for an Italian. My narratives are just visions—I try to create strong sensation of living form. My imagination leads to a stream-of-consciousness generation of imagery. I grew up in a very isolated place outside Vicenza—lots of animals, almost no people. My father came from wine makers, very cultivated people, and my mother was into high culture, so we had many art books. I remember being transfixed by the flesh in Caravaggio's *Flagellation* (1607), the one in Naples—something about its nervous tension. When I was five I started copying comic books, then Old Master paintings, and drew my hands over and over. Then I started clay modeling the *terra creta* surrounding our house and told my parents I wanted to be a sculptor. They inquired at a local workshop that made decorative sculpture, but it was far too dangerous for a child. Finally they found Fra Terenzio, and I studied with him every summer day for five years. His instruction was rigorous—measuring, chiaroscuro, perspective, drawing plaster casts. We took mathematical measurements of the objects we drew and compared them to perceptual distortions, so I learned a great deal about illusionism. He painted for his church but also sold paintings of nudes before Christmas each year to visitors to the monastery.

Later, while studying lute and composition at a conservatory I discovered Richard Corben's *Den*, which had a huge impact on me. I also studied architecture in Venice and wanted to use classical orders, but my teachers wanted me to use rationalist language I couldn't relate to. I also wrote commercial musical scores, but my strength was always visual art. I got commissions to paint mythological murals for wealthy families in the Veneto and Paris. I moved to Milan to focus on contemporary art, and when I saw a *Flash Art* with an image of *The Lion King* on it, I started to see a way to incorporate my interest in ambitious realism with pop culture and contemporary art. Nietzsche's *The Birth of Tragedy* had a big influence on me. He says art must be connected to the dynamics of society; American culture has vitality, so I moved here. In Italy so much has been done already.

I believe the final result in art depends greatly on the conceptual correctness of the process, with coherent steps toward the ultimate goal, the image. I constantly refine my painting process and am not fully satisfied yet. I use four sequential steps, whose order can be fluid: 1) a long phase of sketches from imagination; 2) the transposition of the secondary ideas generated into the previous phase into a three-dimensional model; 3) researching references and relevant information; and 4) execution of the actual painting. In the first step of sketching from imagination lies the essence of art, transforming imagination itself into an object inhabiting the real world. The rest of the process is basically about enriching the results of this phase, which opens up the mind to a sort of "image seeking," or visionary ritual. I look mostly for the composition of the image: an architecture made of figures, but also a narration which can spring from the act of drawing itself.

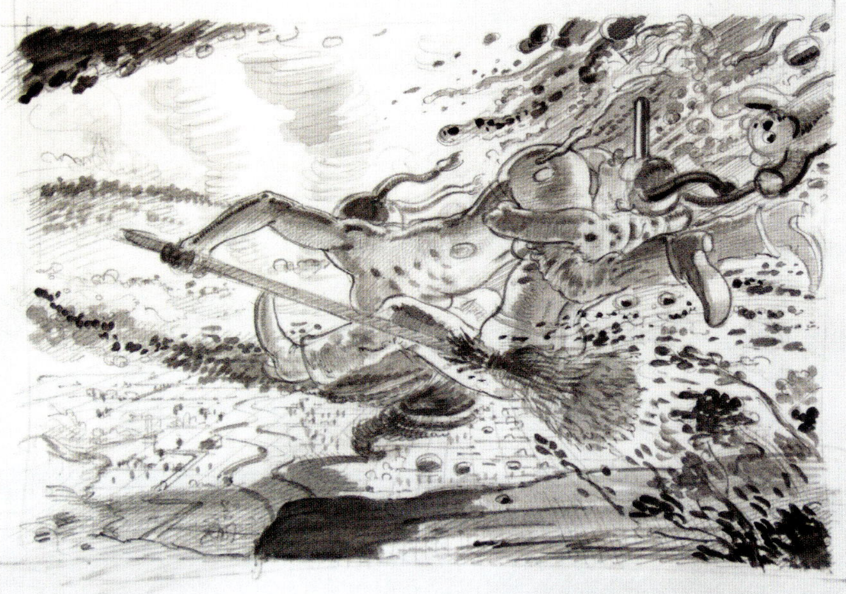

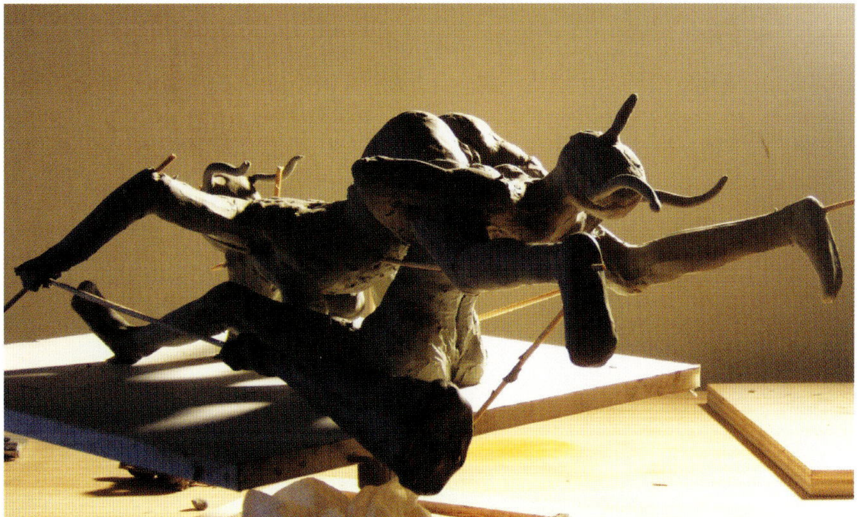

(top)
Nicola Verlato
37 (Study for Mothers), 2005
Pencil, ink on paper
9.5 x 12 inches

(bottom)
Nicola Verlato
Study for Mothers, 2005
Plasticine
20 x 67 x 25 inches

The second phase corresponds to an urge to verify in three dimensions what is imaged in two. I use two different tools in this second step, rough sculpture in Plasticine, and/or digital 3-D modeling programs such as Maya, Zbrush, and Poser. This passage may seem superfluous, but analyzing and structuring the composition in three dimensions gives me profound and otherwise inaccessible knowledge of the world I'm enacting. What I value most in this phase is reaching a unity of perspective and chiaroscuro. In this way I avoid "collage" effects that aren't processed through a three-dimensional environment. The other advantage is in exceeding the limitations of working only from models or photography, which documents a situation too dependent on specific circumstances. After the nineteenth century, this three-dimensional passage in the painting process has been completely removed from the painter studio; Zola condemned Gérôme's use of this practice, considering it contrary to the purity of the meaning of painting. Yet since the Renaissance, almost every painter made and used three-dimensional models as an essential aspect of the pictorial practice. The models of Michelangelo, Daniele da Volterra, or Pontormo were almost completely finished sculptures. I think a lot of the beauty of the works of the Renaissance comes from the use of very sophisticated 3-D models, which allow the artists to combine idealization and synthesis with great realism. Vasari talks about this precisely in his *Le Vite*, yet hardly any scholars or art historians mention it. The three-dimensional object makes the idea able to inhabit the real world. I can turn the model around, changing point of view on it infinitely, and can alter the relation of the model to the light source in turn until the right composition of light and shadow is found, and the composition adjusted accordingly. In 1993 I began incorporating 3-D programs into this process. Their great advantage is in introducing and controlling perspectival representation of complex objects of the industrial world, technological elements almost impossible to manage with traditional perspectival drawing.

Once the composition is settled I fill it with information coming from the real world, using the tool I long resisted, photography. I didn't want to get dependent on its aesthetic or means of composing an image—not that of painting. Copying a photograph would take away all the fun; I can't understand the hyper-realist people—even the simpler Richter's process would be suicidal for me. On the other hand, for the painter who paints only from life there's the risk of turning oneself into a camera, switching the brain off and just registering what's in front of his or her eyes. I use photography exclusively as a source of information. I take pictures of the models, adapting them to the positions previously determined in sculpture and/or 3-D modeling, and may need fifty images to get all different aspects of each body. I have used video cameras, too, to determine positions of the figures: I'll shoot a model doing an action like climbing a fence and jumping down, then analyze the sequence frame by frame to find the exact position that fits the composition. I then model each figure in Plasticine and incorporate it into a multifigure maquette.

If I need to describe a precise character in a narration, like Robert Johnson, James Dean, Brian Jones, or Madonna, I construct their faces in 3-D. One great advantage we have today is the incredible abundance of visual information on the Internet. Back in 1996, when I rebuilt Brian Jones's face, I had to buy books and go almost crazy finding videotapes of Rolling Stones concerts to extract sequences. Today it's possible to download and analyze frame by frame every video sequence with a video-editing program. One further step is modeling a character with Zbrush, Maya, or Mudbox, and animating it for every possible facial expression.

Finally, after this long preparation, I start to paint. Keeping the process open using 3-D models means painting is not just the execution of what has been decided before, and not just copying an image made with Photoshop. Although the composition is settled, it can always change if the act of painting suggests it. I transfer to the canvas just the general structure and all the geometric objects, and the figures very loosely. I never use a projector because I hate to work in the dark; it is not precise enough, and it distorts the image in a photographic way. In the past I would painstakingly draw with charcoal every single detail before starting to paint, but I'm finally getting to the same or better level only using brushes. My painting technique is very simply based, starting with a grisaille, then applying subsequent layers of half-transparent and transparent paint. The palette is of very few colors; I get all the different tonalities by the overlapping of different layers of colors. I consider a painting finished when the gallerist takes it from my hands or when it's sold. But in reality for me a painting is never finished. I have even continued working on a painting during a show, at night when the gallery was closed.

(opposite)
Nicola Verlato
Mothers, 2005
Oil on linen
42 x 64 inches

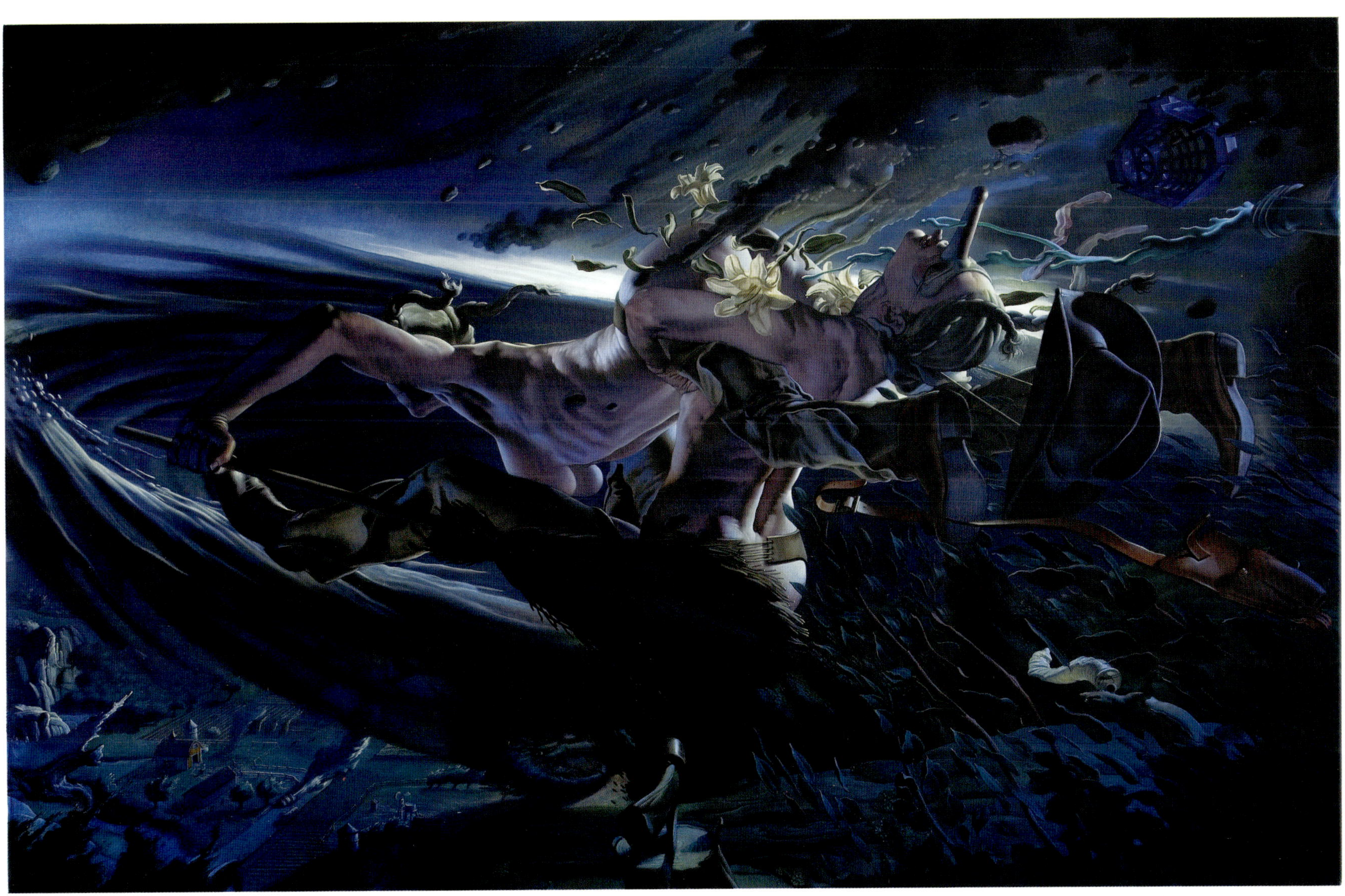

ENDNOTES

McCANN INTRODUCTION

1. Kenneth Clark, *The Nude: A Study in Ideal Form* (New York: Pantheon Books, 1956).
2. John Onian, *Neuroarthistory from Aristotle and Pliny to Baxandall and Zeki* (New Haven and London: Yale University Press, 2007), 44.

GERMANO

1. Carol Plazzotta, Hugo Chapman, Tom Henry, *Raphael: From Urbino to Rome* (New Haven: Yale University Press, 2004), 16.
2. Giorgio Vasari, *Lives of the Most Excellent Painters, Sculptors, and Architects* (New York and Oxford: Oxford University Press, 1987), 57.
3. Janet Backhouse, *Lindisfarne Gospels* (London: Phaidon, 1997), 55.
6. Michael Scholz-Hänsel, *Masters of Spanish Art: Jusepe de Ribera* (New York: Konemann, 2000), 6.
7. Albrecht Dürer, *Dürer's Record of Journeys to Venice and the Low Countries*, Roger Fry, ed. (New York: Dover, 1995).
8. Marcia Tucker and Nica Gutman, "Photographs and the Making of Paintings," *Thomas Eakins, American Realist* (Philadelphia Museum of Art, 2001).

BARTOLOZZI

1. Cennino d'Andrea Cennini, *The Craftsman's Handbook* (New Haven: Yale University Press, 1933).
2. Antonella Fuga, "Artist's Techniques and Materials," *A Guide to Imagery Series* (Los Angeles: Getty Publications, 2006), 99–111.
3. Rutherford J. Gettens and George L. Stout, *Painting Materials: A Short Encyclopaedia* (New York: Dover, 1966), 299–301.
4. Tiarna Doherty and Anne T. Woollett, *Looking at Paintings: A Guide to Technical Terms* (Los Angeles: Getty Publications, 2009), 2, 46.
5. Roberto Bellucci and Cecilia Frosinini, "Piero della Francesca's Process: Panel Painting Technique," *IIC Dublin Congress: Painting Techniques - History, Materials and Studio Practice*, Ashok Roy, Perry Smith, eds. (London: Archetype, 1998) 89–93.
6. Margaret Krug, *An Artist's Handbook: Materials and Techniques* (New York: Abrams, 2007), 223.
7. Gettens, Stout, 279–281.
8. Doherty, Woollett, 48–50.
9. Ibid., 2
10. Peter C. Sutton and Marjorie E. Wieseman, *Drawn by the Brush:Oil Sketches by Peter Paul Rubens* (New Haven: Yale University Press, 2004), 1–6.
11. Al Gury, *Alla Prima: A Contemporary Guide to Traditional Direct Painting* (New York: Watson-Guptill, 2008), 10–21.

SIMON

1. Rudolf Wittkower, *Sculpture, Processes and Principles* (New York: Harper and Row, 1977), passim.
2. Jeffrey Hurwit, *Polykleitos, the Doryphoros, and Tradition*, W. G. Moon, ed. (Madison: University of Wisconsin Press, 1995), 12.
3. James Hall, *The World as Sculpture* (New York: Random House), 13–29.
4. Ian Wardropper, et al., *From the Sculptor's Hand: Italian Baroque Terracottas from the State Hermitage Museum* (Chicago: Art Institute, 1998), 37.
5. H. W. Janson, *Nineteenth Century Sculpture* (New York: Abrams, 1985), 9–16.
6. Patrick Elliott, *Bronze*, David Ekserdjian, ed., (London: Royal Academy, 2012), 95.
7. Erwin Panofsky, *Studies in Iconology: Humanistic Themes in the Art of the Renaissance* (Oxford University Press, 1939);"The Neoplatonic Movement and Michelangelo," passim.
8. Kirk Varnedoe, *Rodin Redisovered*, Albert Elsen, ed., (Washington DC: National Gallery, 1981), 203–238.
9. James Lord, *A Giacometti Portrait* (New York: Farrar, Straus & Giroux, 1965), passim.
10. Michael Fried, *Art and Objecthood* (London, Chicago: University Of Chicago Press, 1998), 148–173.

DESIDERIO

1. Harold Bloom, *The Anxiety of Influence: A Theory of Poetry* (New York: Oxford University Press, 1997).
2. Leon Battista Alberti, *On Painting* (New Haven: Yale University Press, translated by John R. Spencer, 1966), 28.
3. Harries, Karsten, *Perspective and Infinity* (Cambridge, MA: MIT Press, 2001), 68.
4. Frederick Copleston, *A History of Medieval Philosophy* (University of Notre Dame Press, 1972), 284 (quoting Plotinus's *Enneads*).
5. Ibid.
6. Michael Fried, *Absorption and Theatricality, Painting and Beholder in the Age of Diderot* (Chicago: University of Chicago Press, 1980), quoting Diderot's *Discours*, 89.
7. Fried, *Absorption and Theatricality*, 95.
8. Alberti, 78.
9. Fried, 231.
10. Eugène Delacroix, *The Journal of Eugène Delacroix*, Herbert Wellington, ed. (Ithaca: Cornell University Press, 1980), 154–5.
11. Norman Bryson, *Vision and Painting, The Logic of the Gaze* (New Haven: Yale University Press, 1983), 133–162.
12. Michael Fried, *Manet's Modernism or The Face of Painting in the 1860s* (Chicago and London: University of Chicago Press, 1998), 360.
13. Juliet Wilson-Bareau, *Manet: The Execution of Maximilian: Painting, Politics and Censorship* (London: National Gallery, 1992).
14. Georges Bataille, *Manet: Biographical and Critical Study* (New York: Skira, 1955), 51.
15. Fried, *Manet's Modernism*, 358.

WORTH

1. Eugène Delacroix, *Journal* 1822–1863 (Paris: Plon, 1980), 350.
2. Ibid.
3. Ibid.
4. Aaron Scharf, *Art and Photography* (1968; London: Penguin, 1990), 144; Ernest Chesneau quoted; Baudelaire famously made similar accusations in his *Salon of 1859*.
5. Scharf, 146 (quoting Delacroix's essay, "Réalisme et Idéalisme," 1859).
6. "The strange thing," Jules-Antoine Castagnary wrote, "is that Manet is as soft as he is hard." Other critics shared this bafflement over Manet's "inequality of execution," the way he shifts from "slip-shod" to "well-handled" passages. These disparities may have been intended as a reversion to earlier art's hierarchical attentiveness. Castagnary, et al. quoted in George Heard Hamilton's *Manet and His Critics* (New Haven and London: Yale University Press, 1954), 45–47.
7. The clearest evidence that Manet staged photographs is his use of harsh, directed artificial lighting in *Olympia*, for instance, where the light source is at bed level. At the time, non-gas lighting was not durable enough to paint by. Nadar, however, had been operating his "electric portrait studio" since 1860. The similarities between Nadar's electric-lit portraits and Manet's are striking enough to suggest the possibility that Nadar was Manet's Durieu. See Alexi Worth, "The Lost Photographs of Édouard Manet," *Art in America*, February 2007.
8. Kirk Varnedoe, "The Artifice of Candor: Impressionism and Photography Reconsidered," *Art in America*, January 1980, 66–78.
9. Nadar, who had campaigned in favor of a photographic Salon, celebrated its arrival in an amiable cartoon, showing a palette and camera arm in arm like newlyweds. Baudelaire, however, responded with a passionate diatribe against photography. Delacroix followed with "Réalisme et Idéalisme," a judicious, pragmatic essay proposing that photography could be an aid to painters who used it wisely. Three years later, the divisive Mayer et Pierson trial established photography as an art under French copyright law, with ensuing petitions of protest signed by Neoclassical painters Jean-Auguste-Dominique Ingres, Jean-Hippolyte Flandrin, Pierre Puvis de Chavannes, and others.
10. See, for example, Anne Baldessari's *Picasso and Photography: The Dark Mirror* (1997), and Elizabeth Easton's *Snapshot: Painters and Photography, Bonnard to Vuillard* (2012).

McCANN

1. Sigmund Freud, *Leonardo da Vinci, A Psychosexual Study of an Infantile Reminiscence* (New York: Moffat and Yard, 1916), 14.
2. Francis Frascina, Nigel Blake, Briony Fer, Tamar Garb, and Charles Harrison, *Modernity and Modernism French Painting in the 19th Century* (New Haven and London: Yale University Press—Open University, 1993), 86.
3. Linda Nochlin, *Realism* (New York: Penguin Books, 1971), 60.
4. Linda Nochlin, *The Politics of Vision: Essays on Nineteenth-Century Art and Society* (New York: Harper and Row, 1989), 88.
5. Frascina et al., *Modernity and Modernism*, 97; passim 86–111.
6. Frascina et al., 87.
7. Nochlin, *Politics*, 13.
8. Karl Marx and Friedrich Engels, "The Communist Manifesto" (London, 1848).
9. Charles Baudelaire, *The Painter of Modern Life* (Paris: Le Figaro, 1863).
10. Nochlin, *Politics*, 62.
11. Philip Ball, *Bright Earth: Art and the Invention of Color* (Chicago: University of Chicago Press, 2003), 180.
12. John Rewald, *History of Impressionism* (New York: Museum of Modern Art, 1961), 458.
13. Michael Langford, *Story of Photography* (Oxford: Focal Pres, 1980), 6.
14. Charles Baudelaire, "Review of the Salon of 1859," (Paris: *Revue Française*, 1859).
15. Aaron Scharf, *Art and Photography* (1968; London: Penguin, 1990), 249.
16. Jonathan Crary, *Techniques of the Observer: On Vision and Modernity in the Nineteenth Century* (Cambridge, MA: MIT Press, 1990), 133; passim 118–146.
17. Jonathan Crary, *Suspensions of Perception: Attention, Spectacle, and Modern Culture* (Cambridge, MA: MIT Press, 1999), 344.
18. Linda Nochlin, *Politics*, 178; referencing the observations of Ernst Bloch and Roger Fry.
19. Clement Greenberg, "Avant-Garde and Kistch" *Art and Culture, Critical Essays* (first published *Partisan Review* 1939; Boston: Beacon Press, 1961), 5.
20. Ibid., 19.
21. Frances Saunders, "Modern art was CIA 'weapon'... how the spy agency used unwitting artists...in a cultural Cold War," *The Guardian*, Oct. 1995.
22. Lauren Ross, "When art fought the Cold War: A touring exhibition recreates the CIA's 1946 secret weapon..." *The Art Newspaper*, May 2013.
23. Saunders, "Modern art was CIA 'weapon' ".
24. See Daniele Ganser, "Terrorism in Western Europe: An Approach to NATO's Secret Stay-Behind Armies," *The Whitehead Journal of Diplomacy and International Relations*, winter/spring 2005.
25. PBS Newshour, "General Stanley McChrystal on 'Task' in Afghanistan..." January 2013.
26. Hu Bei, "The Man Who Painted Mao" (*Global Times*, July 2013).
27. Greenberg, "Avant Garde and Kitsch," 10.
28. Tony Monda, "Dumas Journey to the Top," *The Sunday Mail (Zimbabwe)* April 2011.

KUSPIT

1. Morse Peckham, "Reflections on Historical Modes in the Nineteenth Century," *Romanticism and Behavior, Collected Essays* (Columbia, SC: University of South Carolina Press, 1974), II, 44.
2. André Breton, *Surrealism and Painting* (New York and London: Harper & Row, 1965), 207, 211.
3. Quoted in Herschel B. Chipp, ed., *Theories of Modern Art* (Berkeley and London: University of California Press, 1968), 60.
4. Quoted in Lucy R. Lippard, ed., *Surrealists on Art* (Englewood Cliffs, NJ: Prentice-Hall, 1970), 20.
5. Chipp, 87.
6. Ibid., 73.
7. Chipp, 126.

8. Robert J. Campbell, *Psychiatric Dictionary* (New York and Oxford: Oxford University Press, 1981), 256.
9. Ibid., 256.
10. Breton, 74.
11. Campbell, 310.
12. Sigmund Freud, *The Interpretation of Dreams, Standard Edition* (London: Hogarth Press and the Institute of Psycho-Analysis, 1953), IV, 116–17.
13. Ibid.
14. E. H. Gombrich, *The Preference for the Primitive* (London and New York: Phaidon, 2002), 235.
15. Chipp, 86. 15. Dore Ashton, ed., *Picasso on Art: A Selection of Views* (New York: Viking, 1972).
16. Wolfgang Lederer, *The Fear of Woman* (New York and London: Harcourt Brace Jovanovich, 1968).
17. Gombrich, 235.
18. Lippard, 20.
19. Breton, 129.
20. Lippard, 73.
21. Chipp, 131.
22. Michael Balint, *Thrills and Regressions* (London: Maresfield Library, 1959), 115 writes that art is an "underhand way of getting back to real personal objects," a "roundabout way of conquering human objects—i.e., people—without admitting that this is [its] real aim." Nowhere is this more evident than in abstract art. Balint's "Notes on the Dissolution of Object Representation in Modern Art," *Problems of Human Pleasure and Behavior* (London: Maresfield Library, 1957), 117–24 is an extensive discussion of the destructive treatment of the figure—that is, its nihilistic reduction to absurdity—in modern art.

KAUPER

1. I realize that the phrase "Representational Art" is imprecise. In this essay, however, I'm using it to refer specifically to painting and sculpture that comes out of the Western mimetic tradition, which began during the Italian Renaissance with the development of linear perspective and other techniques for constructing illusionistic space. The range of artists included in that category is broad: Pre-twentieth-century artists as different as Jan van Eyck and Francisco de Goya would be included; and from the twentieth and twenty-first centuries, artists as different as Käthe Kollwitz, Christian Schad, Pietro Annigoni, Isabel Bishop, and Kerry James Marshall, just to randomly choose several to illustrate my point, would fall under its definition. The few times in the essay when, out of necessity, I use the term "representational" in order to refer to nontraditional art or artists, I make sure to clearly indicate the exception. I am intentionally excluding Photorealist painters and hyperrealist sculptors, because I consider their work to be closer to Pop art, Conceptual art, and the Pictures Generation than to traditional art. I know that some of my explicit or implied inclusions and exclusions might be arguable; that's a debate that I would be happy to participate in. And while I could have chosen a different phrase, all other options were either equally imprecise or, in the case of something like "traditional Western representation," too cumbersome.
2. Blazenka Perica, "Kitsch in the Age of Painterly Reproduction, or a Short History of Kitsch," in *Dear Painter, Paint Me…: Painting the Figure since late Picabia*, Alison M. Gingeras, ed. (Paris: Centre Pompidou, 2002), 19.
3. Matei Călinescu, *Faces of Modernity* (Bloomington: Indiana University Press, 1977), 234.
4. Roberta Smith, "Blazing a Trail for Hypnotic Hyper-Realism: 'Pre-Raphaelites at the National Gallery of Art'" (*New York Times*, March 29, 2013), C23.
5. Odd Nerdrum, "Kitsch Serves Life," *On Kitsch*, Odd Nerdrum, ed. (Oslo: Kagge Forlag As, 2001), 12.
6. Hermann Broch, "Evil in the Value System of Art," *Geist and Zeitgeist*, John Hargraves, ed. (New York: Counterpoint, 2002), 4.
7. Ibid., 31.
8. Theodor Adorno, "On Kitsch," *Essays on Music*, Richard Leppert, ed. (Berkeley: University of California Press, 2002), 502.
9. Clement Greenberg, "Avant-Garde and Kitsch," in *Art and Culture: Critical Essays*, by Clement Greenberg, 3-21.
10. Adorno, 504.
11. Ibid., 502.
12. Milan Kundera, *The Unbearable Lightness of Being* (New York: Harper, 1991), 244.
13. Gillo Dorfles, *Kitsch: The World of Bad Taste* (New York: Universe Books, 1969).
14. Ibid., 292.
15. Barbara Kirshenblatt-Gimblett, *Destination Culture: Tourism, Museums, and Heritage* (Berkeley: University of California Press, 1998), 278.
16. Daniel J. Boorstin, *The Image: A Guide to Pseudo Events in America* (New York: Vintage Books, 1961).
17. Guy Debord, *The Society of the Spectacle* (New York: Zone Books, 1994).
18. Greenberg, 9.
19. Anne McClintock, "Soft-Soaping Empire: Commodity Racism and Imperial Advertising," *The Visual Culture Reader*, Nicholas Mirzoeff, ed. (London: Routledge, 2002), 510.
20. Ellen Gruber Garvey, *The Adman in the Parlor: Magazines and the Gendering of Consumer Culture* (New York: Oxford University Press, 1996), 104.
21. Thorough discussions of Barratt's use of Millais's painting can be found in both McClintock's and Garvey's texts, cited in the two previous endnotes.
22. This argument is made by Benjamin Buchloh in "Figures of Authority, Ciphers of Aggression," *Art After Modernism*, Brian Wallis, ed. (New York: The New Museum of Contemporary Art, 1984), 104-135. While Benjamin doesn't actually use the word "kitsch," his description of the problem of art based on a return to classical representation amounts to an accusation of kitsch.
23. Sara Cochran, *Francis Picabia: The Late Works 1933-1953* (Ostfildern-Ruit: Verlag Gerd Hatje, 1998), 17.
24. Alison Gingeras, *Subversion du Kitsch: Conjectures on Conceptual Uses of Figurative Realism* (artpress 263, 2000), 28-36.
25. Mike Kelley, "Death and Transfiguration," *Foul Perfection: Essays and Criticism*, John Welchman, ed. (Cambridge, MA: MIT Press, 2003), 146.
26. Ibid., 146.
27. Ibid., 141.
28. Ibid.
29. Ibid., 146.
30. Adorno, 502.
31. Alix Rule and David Levine, "International Art English" (Triple Canopy 16, 2013).

TAPLIN

1. Jeff Wall, "An Outline of a Context for Stephan Balkenhol's Work" (1988), in *Selected Essays and Interviews* (New York: Museum of Modern Art, 2007), 107.
2. Ibid., 107.
3. An exhibition at the Solomon R. Guggenheim Museum, New York, "Chaos and Classicism: Art in France, Italy and Germany 1918–1936," October 2011, examined this era in depth.
4. Jeff Wall, "Representation, Suspicions and Critical Transparency: An Interview with Jeff Wall by T.J. Clark, Claude Gintz, Serge Guilbaut, and Anne Wagner," in *Selected Essays and Interviews*, p.215.
5. Ibid., 215.
6. Ibid., 107.

SANDLER

1. Clement Greenberg, "Abstract and Representational," *Art Digest* (November 1954), 7.
2. Fairfield Porter, "Jane Freilicher Paints a Picture," *Art News* (September 1956), 66.
3. Meyer Schapiro, "The Liberating Quality of Avant-Garde Art," *Art News* (Summer 1957), 38–40.
4. Thomas B. Hess, *Willem de Kooning* (New York: Braziller, 1959), 21.
5. Dorothy C. Miller, ed., *12 Americans* (New York: Museum of Modern Art, 1956), p. 53.
6. Leo Steinberg, "Month in Review," *Arts* (January 1956), 48.
7. Lawrence Campbell, "New Figures at the Uptown Whitney," *Art News* (February 1955), 24–35.
8. Irving Sandler, Interview with John Cage, May 6, 1966.
9. Philip Pearlstein, "Figure Paintings Today Are Not Made in Heaven," *Art News* (Summer 1962), 39.
10. Andy Warhol and Pat Hackett, *POPism: The Warhol Sixties* (New York: Harcourt Brace Jovanovich, 1980), 3.
11. Linda Chase and Ted McBurnett, "The Photo-Realists: 12 Interviews," *Art in America* (November-December 1972), 79.

EBONY

1. Robert Storr, *Disparities and Deformations: Our Grotesque* (Santa Fe: SITE, 2004), 12.
2. Alessandra Zamperini, *Ornament and the Grotesque: Fantastical Decoration from Antiquity to Art Nouveau* (London: Thames & Hudson, 2008), 121–122, 171.
3. Michael Bracewell, "Concerning the Art of Glenn Brown" (New York: Gagosian Gallery, 2007), 58.
4. Dan Cameron and Michael Duncan, *Peter Saul* (Ostifildern: Hatje Cantz Verlag, 2008), 50.
5. *Statuesque*, Public Art Fund, New York, 2011; Matthew Monahan quote excerpted from a talk at the New School, New York, March 17, 2010, 113.

HEFFERNAN

1. Laura Mulvey, *Feminism and Film History*, Vicki Callahan, ed. (Detroit: Wayne State University Press, 2010), 20.
2. Dave Hickey, *The Invisible Dragon* (Los Angeles: Art Issues Press, 1993), 49.

HOGIN

1. Hal Foster, *The Return of the Real: The Avant-Garde at the End of the Century* (Cambridge, MA: MIT Press, 1999).
2. Elizabeth Grosz *Chaos, Territory, Art: Deleuze and the Framing of the Earth*, (New York: Columbia University Press, 2008).
3. Victor Burgin, *The End of Art Theory* (Atlantic Heights, NJ; Humanities International Press, 1986).

JACOBSMEYER

1. Giorgio Vasari, *The Lives of the Most Eminent Painters, Sculptors, and Architects 1550 and 1568* (New York and Oxford: Oxford University Press, 1987).
2. Svetlana Alpers, *The Art of Describing: Dutch Art in the Seventeenth Century* (Chicago: University of Chicago Press, 1984), 52.
3. Ibid., 31.
4. Thomas Puttfarken, *The Discovery of Pictorial Composition: Theories of Visual Order in Painting, 1400–1800* (New Haven: Yale University Press, 2000), 279–299.
5. Michael Fried, *Manet's Modernism or The Face of Painting in the 1860s* (Chicago: University of Chicago Press, 1996), 151.
6. Herschel B. Chipp, *Theories in Modern Art: A Source Book by Artists and Critics* (Berkeley: University of California Press, 1968), 542.

VERLATO

1. Jesper Christensen,"Vindicating Vitruvius on the Subject of Perspective," *The Journal of Hellenic Studies*, Vol. 119 (The Society for the Promotion of Hellenic Studies 1999), 162.
2. Plato, *The Republic Book X*, 360 bce translated by Benjamin Jowett (classics.mit.edu).
3. Pietro Marani, paraphrasing Carlo Pedretti, "Leonardo, the Vitruvian Man, and the De Statua Treatise," *Leonardo da Vinci and the Art of Sculpture*, Gary Radke, ed. (New Haven: Yale University Press, 2009).
4. Donald D. Hoffman, *Visual Intelligence: How we Create What We See* (New York: Norton 1998).

INDEX

A

Abakanowicz, Magdalena, 144, 202
Abstract Expressionism, 47, 51, 96, 100, 116, 120, 134, 156, 169
abstraction, 12, 17, 18, 96, 99, 119, 138, 152, 155, 188, 192, 198, 221
academic painting, 80, 99
academies, 17, 27, 29–30, 100, 129–130
Adams, Jamie, *Niagaradown, 127*
Adams, Leslie, *The Art of Life, 229*
Adorno, Theodor, 126, 128–129, 136
advertising, 128, 129, 130, 133, 156, 158
Aeschylus, 226
Africa/African art, 17, 18
African Americans, 100, 170–171
Alberti, Leon Battista, 12, 27, 52, 54, 62–63, 64, 66, 219
Albers, Josef, 108
Albright, Ivan, 168
Alloway, Lawrence, 31
Allsbrook, Luke, *Edge of the Ocean, 220*
Altmejd, David, 169
Ananian, Michael, 106–108; *Presto!, 107*
anatomy, 17, 18, 22, 24, 27, 29, 72, 96, 122, 146, 168
Anderson, Lennart, 72
Anderson, Mamma, 100
Andre, Carl, 144
animation, 18, 140, 212
Appropriation, 11, 100
Armetta, Robert, Ted, 154
Armory Show, 166
Arte Povera, 202
Ashcan School, 30, 99
Assaell, Steven, *Bride I 46*
Atature, Buket Savci, *Untitled, 177*
atelier(s), 29, 72, 187, 226
AutoCAD, Autodesk (computer software) 212, 216, 225
avant garde, 69, 72, 100, 134, 136, 150–158, 187, 188, 194, 221
Avenarius, Ferdinand, 126

B

Bacon, Francis, 112, 116, 166
Bad Painting, 11
Baldaccini, Cesar, 203
Balint, Michael, 119
Balkenhol, Stephan, 143, 144
Ballets Russes, 198
Balthus (Balthasar Klossowski), 221
Banisadr, Ali, *The Devil, 193*
Barbizon School, 95
Baroque era, 30, 45, 200, 219
Barratt, Thomas J., 133
Bartlett, Bo, 187
Bartolozzi, Lisa, 36–45; *Caught, 37*
Barton, Alexander, *Trilateral, 189*
Baselitz, Georg, 119, 144
Bataille, Georges, 70, 72
Baudelaire, Charles, 82, 95, 96, 99, 100
Baxandall, Michael, 99
Bay Area artists, 203
Bayre, Antoine-Louis, 22
Beal, Jack, 221
Beckmann, Max, 99, 221
Bellini, Giovanni, 30, 219
Bellmer, Hans, 116, 143
Bellows, George, 99
Bennett, Amy, *Exposure, 81*
Benton, Thomas Hart, 221
Berlind, Robert, 152, 175
Bernini, Gian Lorenzo, 18, 22, 54, 55–56, 205
Berrios, Alexandro, *Boy in Round, 28*
Bertoncello, Giulio, 225
Bhabha, Huma, 144, 169
Bierstadt, Albert, 30, 212
Bilodeau, Daniel, *Pile 1, 125*
Blake, William, 30
Bloom, Harold, 60
Blume, Peter, 99
body casting/live casting, 55, 202, 205–206
Bonnard, Pierre, 69, 99, 173, 175
Boorstin, Daniel, 129
Borremans, Michaël, 100
Borges, Jorge Luis, 100
Botticelli, Sandro, 29, 30, 40
Boudin, Eugène, 95
Bouguereau, William, 7, 129
Bowland, Margaret, *White Fives, 179*
Bracco, Carrie-Ann, *Following Robyn, Perito Moreno Glacier, 94*
Brady, Julie Elizabeth, *Lily, 174*
Bramante, 27
Brancusi, Constantin, 55, 143, 205, 206
Brandão, João Henrique, *Occupy, 117*
Braque, Georges, 214, 221
Brauner, Victor, 120
Breton, André, 115, 116, 119, 120
Brewster, David, 99
Broch, Hermann, 126, 128–129
Brodsky, Dina, *Jersey City, 45*
Brodsky, Maya, *Natasha and Yotam, 64*
bronze(s), 27, 52, 54–55, 58, 146, 169, 200, 202
Bronzino (Agnolo di Cosimo di Mariano), 29
Brown, Cecily, 112, 176
Brown, Glenn, 166
Brueghel, Jan, 108, 171
Brunelleschi, Filippo, 27, 62, 219, 230
Bryson, Norman, 69
Buchanan, Noah, *Summer, 38*
Buckley, Tim, *Vacation 166*
Burgert, Jonas, 222
Butler, Reg, 143–144
Byzantine art, 29, 30, 146, 213

C

Cabanel, Alexandre, 79, 129
Cadmus, Paul, 168
Cage, John, 150
Călinescu, Matei, 126
camera lucida, 11, 219
camera obscura, 11, 99, 100, 219, 221
Campbell, Gretna, 108
Campbell, Lawrence, 150
Campion, Jane, 175
Canova, Antonio, 22, 54
capitalism, 95, 100, 187, 188
Caravaggio (Michelangelo Merisi), 11, 29, 30, 63–64, 108, 175, 219, 221, 231
Caro, Anthony, 144
Carlson, Thomas John, *Passed Out, 108*
Carnes, Adam, *M Train, 31*
cartoon imagery (comics, graphic novels), 106, 156, 169, 170–171, *171*, 214, 221, 230
carving *versus* modeling, 54–55
casein, 24, 106, 206
casting. *See* body casting
Carpeaux, Jean-Baptiste, 22
Cattelan, Maurizio, 144
Cavallini, Pietro, 226
Cerletty, Mathew, *David Brooks, 130*
Cézanne, Paul, 99, 144, 221
CGI (computer-generated imagery), 225
Cennini, Cennino, 36, 40
Chapin, Aleah, *Auntie, 10*
Chapman, Jake and Dinos, 143
Chéret, Jules, 130
Chevreul, Michel, 96
chiaroscuro, 30, 34, 63, 64, 216, 219, 221
Chillag, Colin, 100
China/Chinese art, 99, 100
Chirico, Giorgio de, 115, 119, 221
Christianity, 18, 29, 166, 170, 214
Church, Frederic Edwin, 80, 212
CIA, 100, 106
Cinema 4D (computer software), 216
Citron, Harvey, 22; *Sisyphus, 23*
Civil Rights Era, 99
Clark, Kenneth, 152
Claude glass, 92
Clemente, Francesco, 7
Clodion (Claude Michel), 22
Close, Chuck, 158, 169
CNC (computer numerical control), 203–204
Cockrill, Mike, 222
Colacello, Bob, 7
Cold War, 11, 100
collage, 108, 119, 140, 169, 198, 210, 214, 221
Color Field painting, 152, 155
color theory, 7, 96, 212
comics. *See* cartoon imagery (comics, graphic novels)
communism, 99, 100, 133
computer-generated imagery (CGI), 225
computers 17, 35, 100, 206, 222, 225. *See also* digital technology, cyberspace
computer software: *See* AutoCAD, AutoDesk, Cinema 4D, Maya, Mudbox, Photoshop, Poser, Sketchup, Soft Image, Strata Vision, ZBrush
Conceptualism, Conceptual art, 7, 9, 51, 136, 188
Condo, George, 7, 169
Constable, John, 30, 92, 96
Constructivism, 55, 143
consumer society, consumerism 129, 156, 194
Cook, Monica, *Sprouting Potatoes, 164*
Copernicus, Nicholas, 226
Copley, John S., 30
Corot, Jean-Baptiste-Camille, 92, 95
Correggio, Antonio da, 226
Cotton, Will, *Fairy Floss, 71*
Courbet, Gustave, 30, 92, 95, 99, 100, 152, 176
Couture, Thomas, 95
Craig, Brian Booth, *Suicide Machine, 8*
Crary, Jonathan, 99
Cross, Adam, *Healing of a Paralytic, 42*
Crumb, R., 136, 169
Cubism, 72, 99, 108, 119, 143, 146, 221, 230
Cultural Revolution. *See* communism
Currin, John, 11, 136, 169, 176
cyberspace 11, 100

D

Dada, Dadaism, 18, 134, 143, 221, 222
daguerreotypes, 79, 80, 82, 96
Dalí, Salvador, 115, 116, 120, 166, 168
Dalou, Jules, 51, 156, 204
David, Jacques-Louis, 30, 43, 66
Davies, Jonathan, *Death Following a Young Woman Home One Night, 53*
da Vinci, Leonardo, 27, 29–30, 36, 38, 54, 63, 72, 92, 115, 165, 170, 219, 221, 226
da Volterra, Daniele, 232
Dawn, Norman, 210
Day, Walter Percy, 212
De Andrea, John, 202
decalcomania, 221
Degas, Edgar, 72, 82, 96, 133, 146, 161, 198, 219–221
Delacroix, Eugène, 30, 64–66, 69–70, 71, 79–80, 82, 92, 96, 161
Delaroche, Paul, 96
Del Debbio, Enrico, 200
della Francesca, Piero, 30, 42, 62, 92, 225, 230
democracy, 226, 230
de Piles, Roger, 221
de Ribera, Jusepe, 30
Desiderio, Vincent, 60–72, 187; *Sleep, 62, 63; Redux, 61*
Dickinson, Edwin, 99, 140, 161
digital technology and computers, 12, 17, 35, 100, 122, 203, 206, 209–210, 212, 222, 225, 230. *See also* Internet
Dinnerstein, Harvey, 136
direct painting, 36, 43, 45, 46, 95–96, 161
Disney, Walt, 134, 136
di Suvero, Mark, 144
Dix, Otto, 99, 100
Doll, Michelle, *Mother Child EE1, 176*
Donatello, 22
Dorfles, Gillo, 128
Downes, Rackstraw, 152
Drake, Peter, 138–140; *Parade, 139*
dreams and dream figures, 115–116, 119–120, 122, 140
Drury, Bryan, *Jann, 83*
Duccio di Buoninsegna, 40
Duchamp, Marcel, 72, 120, 143, 150, 156, 166, 202, 222
Dürer, Albrecht, 30
Dusseault, Yannick, 212
Dutch Realism, 30, 122, 219

E

Eakins, Thomas, 30, 96, 221,
Eardley, Cynthia, *Witness (1), 206*
Earle, Ferdinand, 212
Ebony, David, 165–166, 168–171
Egyptian art, 18, 27, 92, 205, 206, 213
Essenhigh, Inka, 176
El Greco (Domenikos Theotokopoulos), 30, 63
Ellenshaw, Peter, 212
engraving (printmaking), 31–32, 34, 72, 79, 80, 96
Enlightenment, 30, 95
Ensor, James, 69, 96, 169, 198
Erlebacher, Martha Mayer, *The Cycle of Life, Fire: Youth, 68*
Erlebacher, Walter, 22
Ernst, Max, 115, 116, 119, 166, 221
Estes, Richard, 158
Etruscan art, 205
Evans, Alexandra, *John Jacobsmeyer as Master of His Piney New World, 80*
Eversen, Samuel, *Morning, 40*
Ewert, Megan, *Sweet/Tart, 88*
Expressionism, 96, 99, 111, 116, 119, 120, 144, 222

F

fabrication, fabricators (sculpture), 51–52, 54–56
Fabritius, Carel, 219
Fagerlund, Christian, *Untitled, 44*
fascism, 12, 133, 143
Faust, 115
Fauves, Fauvism, 96
Fazzini, Pericle, 22
Fechner, Gustav, 99
feminism. See women
Ferris Jr., Michael, 148; *Toufic, 149*
Ficino, Marsilio, 27, 62
Figurative Expressionism, 116
film, 55, 106, 133, 158, 173, 175, 182, 210, 212, 214, 225, 230
Finkelchtein, Alexandra, *Expulsion from Paradise, 98*
Fiorentino, Rosso, 29
Fischl, Eric, *The Bed, the Chair, Waiting, 6*

Fish, Janet, 152, 155, 221
Folk art, 143
Ford, Walton, 187
Forster, Steve, *New Republic, 29*
Foster, Hal, 188
Fox, Judy, 17–18, 20, 24, 144; *Mermaid, 25*
Fragonard, Jean-Honoré, 43, 166, 175
Frank, Natalie, 198; *Woman, 199*
French Academy, 30, 45, 92, 221
French Revolution, 30, 92
fresco, 27, 36, 38, 92, 138, 162
Freud, Lucian, 11, 108, 112, 166
Freud, Sigmund, Freudianism, 11, 92, 115–116, 119–120, 122, 173
Fried, Michael, 56, 66, 70, 144
Fritsch, Katharina, 144
frottage, 115, 116, 221
Fundis, Robert, *Presence, 2*
Futurism, Futurists, 143

G

Gagnier, Bruce, 146, 148; *Les, 147*
Galilei, Galileo, 226
Gauguin, Paul, 72, 100, 115, 116, 144
gaze, male/female, 120, 173, 175–176
Gentileschi, Artemisia, 173
Gericault, Théodore, 30, 72, 92
Germano, Thomas, 27, 29–30
Gérôme, Jean-Léon, 30, 79, 129, 232
Ghenie, Adrian, 222
Giacometti, Alberto, 17, 55, 56, 99, 143–144, 221
Giambologna, 54
Gingeras, Alison, 134
Giordano, Luca, 43
Giotto di Bondone, 29, 36, 219, 226, 230
Giorgione, 30, 219
Goertz, Debra, *Downdraft #2, 211*
Goethe, Johann Wolfgang von, 96, 99, 119
Gombrich, Ernst, 116
González, Julio, 144
Goodman, Sidney, 221
Gordon, Kristy, *Passing Through II, 13*
Gorky, Arshile, 74, 120
Gormley, Antony, 144
Gothic, 17, 18, 24, 30, 213, 214
gouache, 72, 88, 222
Goya, Francisco de, 86, 92, 198, 206
Graham, Robert, 17, 144
Gram, Angela, *Devolve, 49*
graphic novels. *See* cartoon imagery (comics, graphic novels)
Greek art/Ancient Greece, 18, 27, 52, 225–226
Green, Elliott, 169
Greenberg, Clement, 95, 96, 100, 126, 128–129, 130, 131, 150
Greenwold, Mark, 9, 169; *The Banker's Daughter, 168*
Grimaldi, Michael, *Windowsill Self-Portrait 2, 70*
Grosz, Elizabeth, 192
Grosz, George, 86, 168
Grünewald, Matthias, 100, 166, 170
guilds (artist), 27–29
Guston, Philip, 99
Guttuso, Renato, 99
Guyton, Wade, 136

H

Hale, Robert Beverly, 22, 72, 161
Hals, Frans, 43, 70, 161
Hancock, Trenton Doyle, 170–171, *The Former and the Ladder or Ascension and a Cinchin', 171*
Hanson, Duane, 55, 202
Harkness, Hilary, 176, 182, 222; *Flipwreck, 183*
Harris, Anne, 180–182; *Portrait (Pearls), 181*
Hartigan, Grace, 150
Hauer, Erwin, 24
Hawthorne, Charles, 161
Healy, Ian, *Pigs, 65*
Heffernan, Julie, 173, 187, 175–176; *Self-Portrait Dressing Wounds, 172*
Henri, Robert, 30
Hess, F. Scott, 122; *Self-Portrait with Upturned Collar, 123*
Hess, Thomas B., 150
Hesser, Jeff, *Baby Head II, 55*
Hickey, Dave, 175
Hicks, Jacob, *Venus and Time, 198*
Hi-Fructose, 187
High Renaissance, 30, 38, 42
Hirsch, Ann, *Watchers, 201*
history painting, 12, 92–100, 104
Hockney, David, 11, 100, 219
Hodler, Ferdinand, 34
Hofmann, Hans, 221
Hogarth, William, 106
Hogin, Laurie, 187–194; *Darwin's Dream (Habitat Diorama with Critical Threshold Survivor Species), 186*
Holiber, Nicolas, *Trophy, 145*
Homer, 226
Hooch, Pieter de, 219
Hoogstraten, Nicholas van, 219
Hopper, Edward, 30, 138, 144, 221
Houseago, Thomas, 144, 169
Howe, Catherine, *Proserpina (Winter), 191*
Hradecky, Elyse, *Leda and the Swan, 52*
Hudson River School, 30, 212
Hughes, Robert, 99
Hurd, Caitlin, *Somewhere Else, 138*
hydrocal (plaster), 22, 55, 58, 147, 200, 206
Hyland, Sean, *Chris Laughing, 197*
hyperrealism, 22, 144

I

illusion/illusionism, 55, 60, 62, 64, 70, 72, 99, 144, 194, 210, 212, 221
illustration, 130, 133, 221, 222, 230
Imagism, 144, 219
Impressionism, Neo-Impressionism, 45, 69, 95–96, 99, 122, 221, 230
imprimatura, 42, 47–48, 140
India/Indian art, 17
indirect painting, 36, 40, 42–45, 92, 96, 222
Industrial Revolution, 12, 95
Ingres, Jean-Auguste-Dominique, 11, 30, 112, 161, 219, 222
Internet, 11, 100, 230, 232
iPad, iPhone, 122, 222
Iraq War, 58, 104–106
Ito, Tat, *Toyotamahime 96*

J

Jackson, Peter, 212
Jacobsmeyer, John, 216, 217, 219, 221–222
Jang, Yunsung, *Portrait of Mother, 67*
Japan/Japanese art, 17
Jensen, Wilhelm, 119–120
Jerins, Edgar, 86–88; *Daina & Doyle at Home with Anita's Children, 86*
Jong, Folkert de, 143
Jongkind, Johan, 95
Johns, Jasper, 134, 150
Judd, Donald, 51, 56
Juxtapoz, 187

K

Kagan, Michael, *The Hold, 210*
Kandinsky, Wassily, 96, 116
Kanevsky, Alex, 111–113; *J.F.H., 110*
Katz, Alex, 150–152
Kauper, Kurt, 126–136; *Derek, 129*
Kearns, Jerry, 214; *One Trick Pony, 215*
Kelley, Mike, 134, 136
Kenney, Jeanne, *Bryant Park, 87*
Kent, Rockwell, 34
Kiefer, Anselm, 221
Kienholz, Ed, 144, 198
Kirchner, Ernst Ludwig, 116, 144
Kirshenblatt-Gimblett, Barbara, 128–129
kitsch, 95, 126–136, 156
Knoll, Thomas and John, 212
Kooning, Willem de, 120, 150, 168, 169
Koons, Jeff, 51, 55, 129, 144, 202
Kovacic, Daniela, *Black Virgin, 118*
Kratz, David, 9; *Evening, 84*
Kundera, Milan, 128, 129
Kurtz, Will, *Coming Together, 202*
Kuspit, Donald, 115–116, 119–120, 122

L

Lachaise, Gaston, 17, 143
Laderman, Gabriel, 22, 72, 106
LaPorte, Chris, *Funeral, 91*
LeBoeuf, Bryan, *Age of Man, 85*
Lebofsky, Lisa, *Threshold, 104*
Le Brun, Charles, 30
Lehmbruck, Wilhelm, 17
Lenaghan, Andrew, 158–161; *Self-Portrait in the Garret II, 159*
Lenin, Vladimir, 100, 210
Lerman, Leonid, *Drawing, Figure Study, 19*
Levine, David, 136
Levy, Nina, *Couple, 203*
Lewis, Stanley, 99
Lichtenstein, Roy, 156
Lieu, Clara, *Self-Portrait No. 5, 120*
light and shadow, 30, 43, 64, 66, 69, 96, 106, 216, 219. *See also* chiaroscuro
Lin, Maya, 204
Linkous, James, *Standing Male Nude, 50*
Lippi, Filippo, 29, 108
Liu, Dik, 140, *Woman Eating a Steak, 141*
López-García, Antonio, 11, 140, 144
Lord, James, 56
Lotto, Beau, 212
Lowbrow Art. *See* Pop Surrealism

M

Macdonald, Dwight, 128
Magic Realism, 99
Maillol, Aristide, 17, 55
Majoli, Monica, 136
Malekzadeh, Panni, *Tara Playing, 134*
Manet, Édouard, 30, 69–70, 72, 82, 95, 100, 111, 133, 221–222; *Le déjeuner sur l'herbe*, 82, 95, 221
Mannerism, 29, 63, 69, 70, 72
Manship, Paul, 143
Mantegna, Andrea, 219
Mariani, Carlo Maria, 165
Marini, Marino, 143
Marlatt, Megan, *LeRoi's Toys, 97*
Marshall, Kerry James, 136, 222
Marshall Plan, 100
Martini, Arturo, 143
Masaccio, 29, 63, 138, 219
Masereel, Frans, 106
Mason, Raymond, 143–144
Matisse, Henri, 55, 69, 82, 143, 166
Maya (computer software), 11, 216, 230, 232
Matte painting (film), 212
McCann, Margaret, 11–12, 92–100; *Believe It or Not!, 109*
McCarthy, Paul, 144
McGee, Barry, 187
McIver, Randolphlee, 58; *Slaughter of the Innocents, 58*
McQuarrie, Ralph, 212
Meadors, Michael, *Connected, 218*
Medieval art/Middle Ages, 18, 27, 29, 38, 52, 54, 226
Meissonier, Jean, 79
Mellan, Claude, 32
Mennin, Mark, 200–205; *Sleepy Hollow II, 204*
Mershimer, Frederick, 34–35; *Manhattan Bound, 34*
Meta-modernism, 11, 92
Mexican muralists, 99
mezzotint engraving, 34–35
Michelangelo, 18, 29, 30, 38,51, 54, 56, 92, 138, 226
Middle Ages. *See* Medieval art/Middle Ages
Millais, John Everett, 79, 133
Miller, Elisabeth, *Red Shoes, 43*
Miller, Matthew, *Untitled, 133*
Minimalism, 9, 56, 152, 155
Modernism, 17, 24, 51, 55–56, 69–72, 79–82, 92–100, 115–120, 126–136, 143–144, 176, 187, 200, 210, 221–222
Monahan, Matthew, 169
Monks, Alyssa, 88, 90; *Purple, 89*
Moore, Diana, 143
Morandi, Giorgio, 108
Morgan, Heather, *Sourpuss, 135*
Morley, Malcolm, 158
Morris, Robert, 56
Mount Rushmore, 12, 204
Mudbox (computer software), 232
Mueck, Ron, 55, 144, 166, 168
Mühlhäußer, Peter Simon, *Phoenix, 20*
Mullins, Craig, 212
Mulvey, Laura, 173, 175–176
Mumford, Steve, 104–106; *Empire, 105*
Munch, Edvard, 69
Muñoz, Juan, 144
Murphy, Gary, *Rêveur, 131*
Muybridge, Eadweard, 56, 212
Myaing, Tun, *Hallway Study 1, 41*

N

Nabis, 96
Nadar, 82
Nadelman, Elie, 34
Nazi(s), 99, 133, 143, 165–166
Neel, Alice, 22, 99
Neoclassicism, 66, 200, 221
Neo-Expressionism, 11, 119, 144, 202, 221
Neo-Impressionism, 99
Neoplatonism, 18, 27, 56, 62–66
Neo-Realism, 187
Nerdrum, Odd, 126, 136, 221
Neri, Manuel, 202
Neue Sachlichkeit (New Objectivity), 133
neuroscience, 190, 192, 194, 230
New Objectivity, 86, 133
New Perceptual Realism, 150, 152, 155
New/Neo Realism, 72, 187
Nick, George, 99, 140
Noble, Paul, 222
Nochlin, Linda, 95, 173
Noguchi, Isamu, 205
Noel, Scott, 161; *Eurydice, 160*
Nouveau Realism, 202
"The Nude" (as concept), 11–12, 17, 92, 99, 173, 175–176

O

Ofili, Chris, 166
Oldenburg, Claes, 108, 158
optics, optical devices and illusions, 11, 55, 60–70, 99–100, 210, 212, 219, 221

O'Reilly, John, *Bitch, 21*
Osti, Roberto, *Deconstruction of a Werewolf, 192*

P
Paczkowski, Mark, *Pardon, 128*
Painter (computer software), 209
painting techniques, 36–45, 40, 42–43, 45, 88, 92–100, 130, 133, 156, 158, 166, 168, 187, 221, 222
Pangrazio, Michael, 212
Panofsky, Erwin, 56, 230
Park, Austin, *After Hours, 224*
Park, David, 99
Park, Guno, *Self-Portrait, 228*
Parmagianino, 27
Peckham, Morse, 115
Penny, Evan, 144
Penone, Giuseppe, 202
perception, 56, 96, 99
Pearlstein, Philip, 22, 72, 152,
perspective, 27, 60–64, 216, 219, 221–222, 225–226
Pettibone, David, *Monoculture Pollination, 102*
Phillips, Richard, 161–162; *Large Nude, 163*
photography, 11–12, 22, 24, 30, 35, 47, 48–49, 56, 79–80, 82, 86, 88–89, 92–100,104, 108, 113, 122, 134, 140, 155–156, 161, 162, 165, 166, 182, 198, 200, 209–210, 214, 219, 221, 222, 230, 232
photorealism, 155, 158, 202
Photoshop (computer software), 11, 35, 74, 100, 104, 113, 205, 209–212, 214, 216, 222, 232
Picabia, Francis, 99, 133–134
Picasso, Pablo, 17, 72, 116, 166, 221
Pissarro, Camile, 95, 96
Pistoletto, Michelangelo, 202
Pivar, Stuart, 7
Plater, Robert, *Portrait of an Artist, 196*
Plato, 27, 62, 226
plein air painting, 95, 158
Plotinus, 62, 63, 64
Pollack, Jackson, 51
Polykleitos, 221
Pondick, Rona, 205–206; *Dog, 207*
Pontormo, Jacopo, 29, 63, 226, 232
Pop Art, 136, 150, 152, 155–158, 168, 202, 210, 212, 219
Pop Expressionism, 158
Pop Surrealism, 187, 222, 230
pornography, 136, 166, 176
Porter, Fairfield, 150
Poser (computer software), 216, 232
Post-colonialism, 143
Post-Impressionism, 99
Postmodernism, 18, 51, 100, 136, 144, 176, 188
Poussin, Nicolas, 30, 43, 66, 221
Praxiteles, 18
Pre-Raphaelites, 95, 126
Presant, Jennifer, *Blue Room, 101*
projection, projector (machine), 74, 100, 113, 122, 209, 210, 212, 219, 230
psychoanalysis, 115–116, 119–120, 122
psychology 22, 190
Puritanism, 188
Pylypchuk, John, 169
Pythagorus, 27, 52

Q
Quinn, Marc, 203

R
Raczkowski, James, *Still Life, 59*
Raftery, Andrew, 31–32; *Open House Model, 32; Scene One Study, 32; Open House: Scene One, 33*
Raimondi, Marcantonio, 79–80, 82
Raphael, 27, 165; *The School of Athens, 27, 30*
Rauch, Neo, 11, 222
Rauschenberg, Robert, 134
Ray, Charles, 144
Realism, 72, 90, 92, 95, 99, 150–158, 219, 221. *See also* Hyperrealism, New Perceptual Realism, Magic Realism, New/Neo Realism, Photorealism, Social Realism, Socialist Realism
Regionalism, 133
Rego, Paula, 106
Reinhardt, Ad, 128
relief sculpture, 34, 54, 58, 119
Rembrandt van Rijn, 30, 43, 112, 122, 140, 166, 169
Renaissance, 11, 18, 22, 27, 29–30, 36, 38–45, 52, 54, 58, 62, 79, 146, 165, 173, 200, 216, 225–226, 232
Renoir, Pierre-Auguste, 96, 116
Reynolds, Sir Joshua, 30
Richter, Gerhard, 72, 232
Rimbaud, 115
Ritacco, Roxanne, *Child on Bed, 73*
Rivera, Diego, 100, 221
Rivers, Larry, 150
Rockwell, Norman, 126
Rococo, 43, 175, 200
Rodin, Auguste, 17, 22, 51, 54, 56, 133, 146, 200, 202
Romanticism, 66, 69, 70, 92, 152
Rome/Roman art, 18, 22, 27, 30, 108, 165, 225
Romine, Patrick, *Willie Gets a Beatin', 195*
Ronk, Grayson, *Self, 156*
Rosenbluth, Alfred, *Mocking Bird, 146*
Rosenquist, James, 156
Rosso, Medardo, 133, 200
Roszak, Theodore, 202
Roy, Jean-Pierre, 209–210, 212; *To Break You Must Be Broken, 208*
Rozin, Daniel, 212
Rubens, Peter Paul, 30, 43, 45, 64, 173, 219, 221
Rude, François, 22
Rule, Alix, 136
Ruskin, John, 99
Russia/Russian art, 99–100, 143
Ryden, Mark, 187

S
Saenredam, Pieter, 219
Sailors, Holly Ann, *We Found Her Hidden, 124*
Salons, 30, 60, 80, 82, 202
Sanchez, Nicolas V., *Search: Top Ten Ways to Milk a Goat, 155*
Sandler, Irving, 150–158
Sassi, Raphael, Old Man Looking at Kate Middleton's Portrait, 111
Saul, Peter, 136, 169
Saville, Jenny, 112, 166; *Isis, 4*
Schactmann, Barry, 108
Schaechter, Judith, 213–214; *The Sin Eater, 213*
Schapiro, Meyer, 150
Scharf, Aaron, 12, 82, 99
Shimizu, Chie, *Untitled, 16*
Schmidt, Edward, 72, 74; *Danae, 74; Conversation (Diana and Callisto), 75;*
Schnell, David, 222
Schreuders, Claudette, 143
Schuman, Wade, 47–48; *Virtue: Sacrifice, 48*
Schutz, Dana, 169
Scuglia, Amanda, *Idle Hands, 121*
Segal, George, 55, 202, 203
Selwyn, Robert, *News, 103*
Sena, Amber, *Chosen, 112*
Serra, Richard, 51, 200, 205
Seurat, Georges, 99
Shea, Judith, 143
Siegel, Susan, *In Pink, 190*
Simon, Robert G., 51–52, 54–56; *Slump Head, 57*
Signorelli, Luca, 108
Sistine Chapel, ceiling, 22, 30, 38, 92
Situationist International, 134
SketchUp (computer software), 222
Sleigh, Sylvia, 120
Smith, David, 51, 143, 144, 202
Smith, Dennis, 7
Smith, Kiki, 18, 20, 143, 144, 202
Smith, Roberta, 9, 126
Socialist Realism, 11, 92, 99, 100, 111
Social Realism, 99, 221
Socrates, 226
Softimage (computer software), 225
Sontag, Susan, 100
Soviet Union, 99–100
Special Effects, FX, 22
stained glass, 213–214
Stalin, Joseph, 126, 210
Stapleton, Joe, 46
Stegner, Jansson, *The Foxhunter, 132*
Steinberg, Leo, 150
stereoscope, 99
Stern, Jesse, *Self-Portrait, 157*
Stoichita, Victor, 106
Storr, Robert, 165, 169
Strata Vision (computer software), 225
Stuart, Gilbert, 12
Surrealism, 24, 72, 106, 111, 115, 116, 119–120, 143, 156, 166, 176, 221. *See also* Pop Surrealism
Sutherland, Graham, 166
Surls, James, 143
Synthetic Cubism, 221

T
tableau(x), 66, 129, 216, 219, 221, 222
Takaezu, Toshiko, 205
Tansey, Mark, 100
Taplin, Robert, 143–144; *VII: One Nation Rules (Fortune), 142*
Tatlin, Vladimir, 143
Teicher, Maria, *Alexis and the Veil, 178*
television, 99, 100, 156, 158, 214, 230
Telfort, Eric, *Maya, 152*
Thek, Paul, 134
Thomas, Phillip, *Portrait #3, 137*
Three Dimensional, 3-D graphics, modeling and scanning, 203, 206, 212, 216–219, 221–222, 225–232
Tiepolo, Giovanni Battista, 175, 198
Tintoretto, 30, 63, 219
Titian, 42, 43, 161, 173, 219
Tooker, George, 40, 99
Tübke, Werner, 100
Turner, Joseph M. W., 30, 95, 99, 230
Turrell, James, 205, 210
Tuymans, Luc, 100

U
Uccello, Paolo, 219, 222, 225
Udovidchik-Sentypal, Olesya, *Lust, 180*
Uglow, Euan, 112
underpainting/underdrawing, 36, 40, 42, 43, 44, 92, 95, 222

V
Van Dyck, Anthony, 30, 92
Van Eyck, Jan, 42–43
Van Gogh, Vincent, 69, 96, 111
Van Heemskerck, Maarten, 40
vanishing point, 62, 63, 66, 88, 219, 222, 225, 230
Varnedoe, Kirk, 82
Vasari, Giorgio, 29, 36, 219, 232
Velázquez, Diego, 11, 30, 43, 64, 70, 112, 140, 161, 216, 219, 222
Ventura, Joseph, *In-Phase Feedback of Time, Space and the Probability Wavefunction of an apparently frustrated Human Subject, Part II, 227*
Verhoeven, Helen, *Event Two, 188*
Verlato, Nicola, 222, 225–226, 230–232; *Mothers, 231, 233*
Vermeer, Johannes, 140, 219, 222
Veronese, Paolo, 30, 92
Verrocchio, 29
video games, 216, 225, 230
VR/virtual reality, 216, 219
Vollo, Stephen, *Vanitas, 153*
Vote, Melanie, *In Tub, 39*
Vuillard, Éduard, 34, 82

W
Wacom tablet, 212
Wagner, Dave, *Noli Me Tangere, 114*
Wall, Jeff, 143, 144
Wang, Tun Ping, *Vague, 151*
war, 58, 86, 99, 104, 106, 182, 200. *See also* World War I, World War II
Warhol, Andy, 7, 134, 156, 158, 168–169, 210
Watwood, Patricia, *Pandora, 26*
Weiner, Lawrence, *Declaration of Intent, 51*
Weischer, Matthias, 100
welding, 202
Wellington, John, 222–223; *Dangerous, 223*
West, Benjamin, 30
West Coast Funk, 202
Western canon, 18, 144
Whistler, James M., 212
White, Eric, *Intermezzo, 90*
Wilkinson, Russell, 7
Williams, Robert, 169, 222
Wilson-Bareau, Juliet, 70
Witkin, Jerome, 100; *Taken, 93*
Wittkower, Rudolf, 51, 54
women
  female artists and "The Nude," 173, 175–176
  history painting and, 100
  symbolism of, 115–116, 119–120, 122
Wood, Jonas, 100
Woodruff, Thomas, 169
World War I, 99, 143, 166, 200
World War II, 86, 143, 165–166, 182, 198, 200
World Wide Web. *See* Internet
Worth, Alexi, 79–80, 82; *Square II, 78*
WPA (Works Progress Administration), 100
Wrightson, Bernie, 222
Wyeth, Andrew, 40
Wyeth, N.C., 221

X
Xiaodong, Liu, 100

Y
Yale University, School of Art, 24, 106, 108, 140, 205,
Yu, Shangkai Kevin, *Portrait Sketches, London, 113*
Yuskavage, Lisa, 136, 169, 187

Z
Zack, Kim, *Dream, 175*
Zamperini, Alessandra, 165
ZBrush, 232
Zeki, Semir, 190
Zola, 232

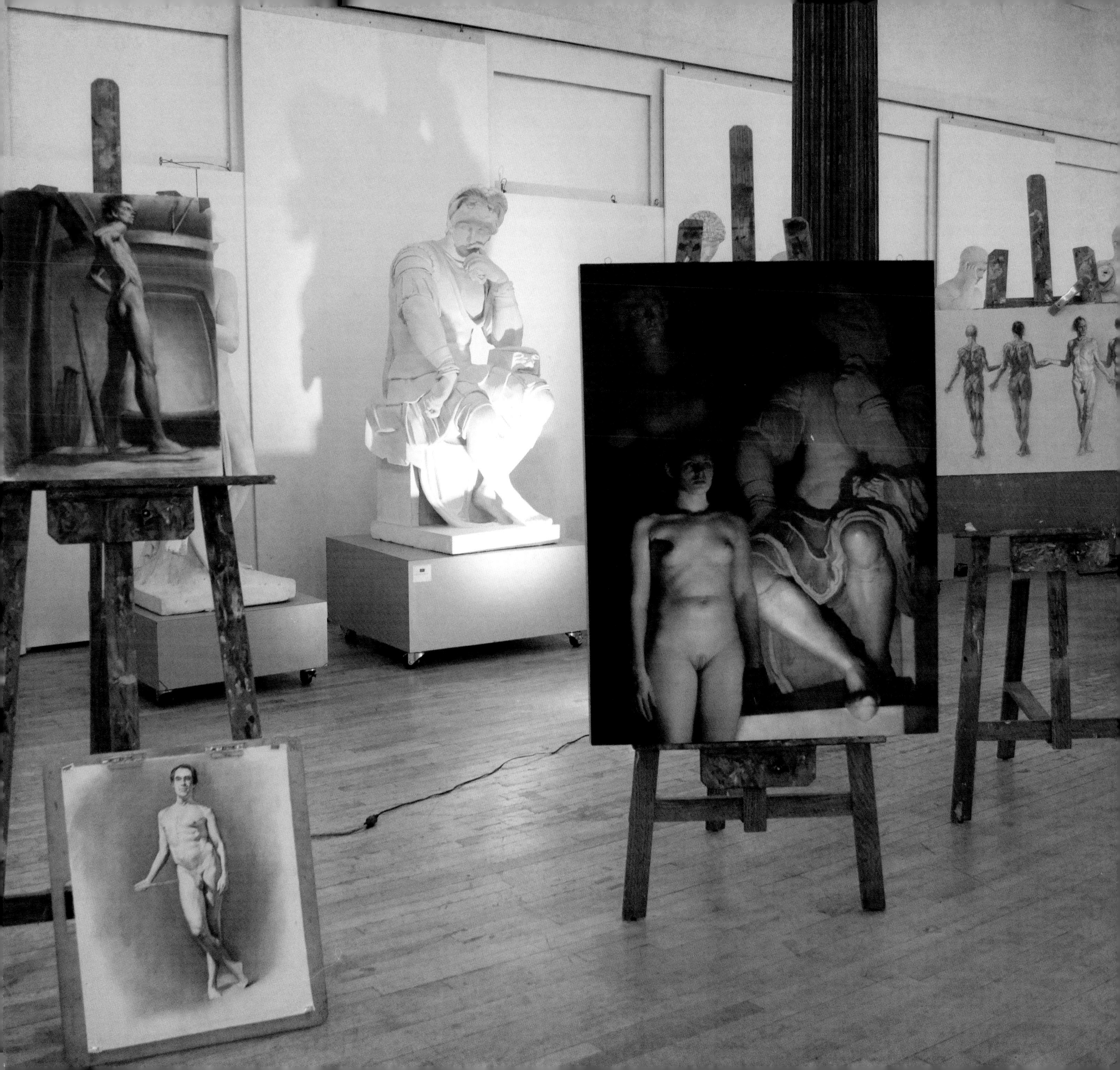

First published in the United States of America in 2014 by

SKIRA RIZZOLI PUBLICATIONS, INC.
300 Park Avenue South
New York, NY 10010
www.rizzoliusa.com

ISBN-13: 978-0-8478-4375-6
Library of Congress Control Number: 2014937508

For Skira Rizzoli Publications, Inc.:
Margaret Chace, Associate Publisher
Ellen Cohen and Philip Reeser, Project Editors

For New York Academy of Art:
Margaret McCann, Editor

Design: MGMT. design

Printed and bound in China

2014 2015 2016 2017 / 10 9 8 7 6 5 4 3 2 1

IMAGE CREDITS

Copyright to all works of art is held by the respective artists. All rights reserved. Reproductions of the works are courtesy of the artist unless noted below:

Page 25: Courtesy of the artist and P•P•O•W. Page 26: Photograph by Stefan Hagen. Page 37: Photograph by Carson Zullinger. Courtesy of Forum Gallery. Page 38: Photograph by R.R. Jones. Courtesy of Winfield Gallery. Pages 46, 48: Courtesy of Forum Gallery. Pages 61, 62, and 63: Courtesy of the artist and Marlborough Gallery. Page 68: Courtesy of Seraphin Gallery and the estate of Martha Mayer Erlebacher. Pages 71, 183: Courtesy of the artist and Mary Boone Gallery. Page 78: Courtesy of the artist and DC Moore Gallery. Page 81: Courtesy of the artist and Richard Heller Gallery. Page 83: Courtesy of Dean Project. Pages 84, 180, 198, 211: Photograph by Guno Park. Courtesy of the artist. Page 86: Courtesy of ACA Galleries. Page 87: Photograph by Donna Aristo. Courtesy of the artist. Page 93: Courtesy of the artist and Jack Rutberg Fine Arts, Inc. Page 96: Photograph by Matthew MacMullen Smith. Courtesy of the artist. Page 101: Courtesy of Linda Warren Projects. Page 105: Courtesy of Postmasters Gallery. Page 111: Courtesy of the artist and Carla Massoni Gallery. Page 112: Courtesy of the artist and Accesso Galleria. Page 117: Photograph by Yunsung Yang. Courtesy of the artist. Page 123: Courtesy of Koplin Del Rio Gallery. Page 125: Photograph by Maria Teicher. Courtesy of the artist. Page 127: Courtesy of the artist and David Klein Gallery. Page 129: Courtesy of Deitch Projects. Page 131: Photograph by Christopher Burke Studios. Courtesy of the artist. Page 133: Courtesy of Pocket Utopia. Page 139: Courtesy of the artist and Linda Warren Projects. Page 147: Courtesy of Lori Bookstein Fine Art. Page 154: Courtesy of Hersh Fine Art. Page 159: Courtesy of George Adams Gallery. Page 160: Courtesy of the artist and Gross McCleaf Gallery. Page 163: Courtesy of the artist and Gagosian Gallery. Page 167: Photograph by Arielle Morgan. Courtesy of the artist. Page 176: Photograph by Ka Huen Kwong. Courtesy of the artist. Page 179: Courtesy of the artist and Driscoll Babcock Galleries. Page 181: Courtesy of the artist and Alexandre Gallery. Page 186: Photograph by Greg Boozell. Courtesy of the artist. Page 188: Photograph by Mark Woods. Courtesy of Saatchi Gallery. Page 189: Courtesy of www.alexanderbarton.com. Page 190: Photograph by Jeanette May. Courtesy of the artist. Page 191: Courtesy of the artist and Von Lintel Gallery. Page 192: Photograph by Cathy Carver. Courtesy of the artist. Page 193: Courtesy of the artist and Sperone Westwater. Page 201: Photograph by Chris Yeager. Courtesy of the artist. Page 202: Courtesy of Mike Weiss Gallery. Page 207: Courtesy of Sonnabend Gallery and Galerie Thaddaeus Ropac. Page 213: Photograph by Dom Episcopo. Courtesy of Claire Oliver Gallery. Page 227: Photograph by Michael Kagan. Courtesy of the artist. Page 229: Photograph by Tim Thayer. Courtesy of the artist.

CAPTION ON PAGE 239

Wilkinson Hall at the New York Academy of Art. Works of art by (from left) Max Perkins (on easel), Chao Wang (on floor), Richard Morris, and Jacob Hayes. Photograph by Margaret McCann.